The Science of Facial Expression

OXFORD SERIES IN SOCIAL COGNITION AND SOCIAL NEUROSCIENCE

The New Unconscious
Edited by Ran R. Hassin, James S. Uleman, and John A. Bargh

Oxford Handbook of Human Action
Edited by Eziquiel Morsella, John A. Bargh, and Peter M. Gollwitzer

Social Neuroscience: Toward Understanding the Underpinnings of the Social Mind
Edited by Alexander Todorov, Susan T. Fiske, and Deborah Prentice

Self Control in Society, Mind, and Brain
Edited by Ran R. Hassin, Kevin N. Ochsner, and Yaacov Trope

Attention in a Social World
Michael I. Posner

Navigating the Social World: What Infants, Children, and Other Species Can Teach Us
Edited by Mahzarin R. Banaji and Susan A. Gelman

Beyond Pleasure and Pain
E. Tory Higgins

The Sense of Agency
Edited by Patrick Haggard and Baruch Eitam

The Science of Facial Expression
Edited by José-Miguel Fernández-Dols and James A. Russell

The Science of Facial Expression

Edited by

José-Miguel Fernández-Dols

and James A. Russell

OXFORD
UNIVERSITY PRESS

OXFORD
UNIVERSITY PRESS

Oxford University Press is a department of the University of Oxford. It furthers the University's objective of excellence in research, scholarship, and education by publishing worldwide. Oxford is a registered trade mark of Oxford University Press in the UK and certain other countries.

Published in the United States of America by Oxford University Press
198 Madison Avenue, New York, NY 10016, United States of America.

Library of Congress Cataloging-in-Publication Data
Names: Fernández-Dols, José-Miguel, editor. | Russell, James A.
(James Albert), 1947– editor.
Title: The science of facial expression / edited by José-Miguel
Fernández-Dols and James A. Russell.
Description: New York, NY : Oxford University Press, [2017] |
Series: Oxford series in social cognition and social neuroscience
Identifiers: LCCN 2017000953 (print) | LCCN 2017009572 (ebook) |
ISBN 9780190613501 (hardcover : alk. paper) | ISBN 9780190613518 (UPDF) |
ISBN 9780190669041 (EPUB)
Subjects: LCSH: Facial expression. | Body language.
Classification: LCC BF592.F33 S46 2017 (print) | LCC BF592.F33 (ebook) |
DDC 153.6/9—dc23
LC record available at https://lccn.loc.gov/2017000953

9 8 7 6 5 4 3 2 1

Printed by Sheridan Books, Inc., United States of America

In the cover photograph, Marta at age 1 year displayed the classic disgust face, caught on camera by her mother. Marta had just tasted lemon sorbet for the first time. Immediately after the "disgust face," she pointed to the lemon sorbet and asked for more.

CONTENTS

CONTRIBUTORS

Reginald B. Adams, Jr.
Department of Psychology
The Pennsylvania State University
University Park, Pennsylvania, USA

Daniel N. Albohn
Department of Psychology
The Pennsylvania State University
University Park, Pennsylvania, USA

Adam K. Anderson
Department of Human Development
Cornell University
Ithaca, New York, USA

Hillel Aviezer
Department of Psychology
The Hebrew University of Jerusalem, Mount Scopus
Jerusalem, Israel

Lisa Feldman Barrett
Department of Psychology
Northeastern University
Athinoula A. Martinos Center for Biomedical Imaging
Massachusetts General Hospital
Boston, Massachusetts, USA

Eliza Bliss-Moreau
Department of Psychology
California National Primate Research Center
University of California, Davis
Davis, California, USA

Lauren M. Bylsma
Department of Psychiatry
University of Pittsburgh
Pittsburgh, Pennsylvania, USA

Linda A. Camras
College of Science and Health
DePaul University
Chicago, Illinois, USA

Vanessa L. Castro
Department of Psychology
Northeastern University
Boston, Massachusetts, USA

Samantha Chavez
College of Public Health
The Ohio State University
Columbus, Ohio, USA

Daniel T. Cordaro
Yale Center for Emotional Intelligence
Yale University
New Haven, Connecticut, USA

Carlos Crivelli
Division of Psychology
School of Applied Social Sciences
De Montfort University
Leicester, England, UK

F. C. Davis
Cognitive Science Team
US Army Natick Soldier Research, Development & Engineering Center
Natick, Massachusetts, USA

Rui Diogo
Department of Anatomy
Howard University
Washington D.C., USA

Cameron M. Doyle
Department of Psychology and Neuroscience
University of North Carolina, Chapel Hill
Chapel Hill, North Carolina, USA

Juan I. Duran
School of Psychology
Universidad Autónoma de Madrid
Centro Universitario Cardenal Cisneros
Madrid, Spain

Paul Ekman
Department of Psychology
University of California, San Francisco
San Francisco, California, USA

Hillary Anger Elfenbein
Olin School of Business
Washington University
St. Louis, Missouri, USA

José-Miguel Fernández-Dols
School of Psychology
Universidad Autónoma de Madrid
Madrid, Spain

Alan J. Fridlund
Psychological & Brain Sciences
University of California, Santa Barbara
Santa Barbara, California, USA

Maria Gendron
Department of Psychology
Northeastern University
Boston, Massachusetts, USA

Asmir Gračanin
Department of Psychology
University of Rijeka
Rijeka, Croatia

Amy G. Halberstadt
Department of Psychology
North Carolina State University
Raleigh, North Carolina, USA

Shlomo Hareli
Department of Business Administration
University of Haifa
Haifa, Israel

Ahmad R. Hariri
Laboratory of NeuroGenetics
Department of Psychology & Neuroscience
Duke University
Durham, North Carolina, USA

Ran R. Hassin
Psychology Department
The Hebrew University of Jerusalem, Mount Scopus
Jerusalem, Israel

Ursula Hess
Department of Psychology
Humboldt Universität zu Berlin
Berlin, Germany

Dacher Keltner
Department of Psychology
University of California, Berkeley
Berkeley, California, USA

M. Justin Kim
Department of Psychological and Brain Sciences
Dartmouth College
Hanover, New Hampshire, USA

Sebastian Korb
Faculty of Psychology
University of Vienna
Vienna, Austria

Kestutis Kveraga
Athinoula A. Martinos Center for Biomedical Imaging
Department of Radiology
Massachusetts General Hospital and Harvard Medical School
Boston, Massachusetts, USA

Brenda Lee
Department of Psychology
Tufts University
Medford, Massachusetts, USA;
Department of Psychiatry
Massachusetts General Hospital
Charlestown, Massachusetts, USA

Daniel H. Lee
Department of Psychology & Neuroscience
Institute of Cognitive Science
University of Colorado
Boulder, Colorado, USA

Kristen A. Lindquist
Department of Psychology and Neuroscience
University of North Carolina, Chapel Hill
Chapel Hill, North Carolina, USA

Alison M. Mattek
Department of Psychological and Brain Sciences
Dartmouth College
Hanover, New Hampshire, USA

Marc Mehu
Department of Psychology
Webster Vienna Private University
Vienna, Austria

Gilda Moadab
Department of Psychology
California National Primate Research Center
University of California, Davis
Davis, California, USA

Marcello Mortillaro
Swiss Center for Affective Sciences
University of Geneva
Geneva, Switzerland

Maital Neta
Department of Psychology
University of Nebraska-Lincoln
Lincoln, Nebraska, USA

Paula M. Niedenthal
Department of Psychology
University of Wisconsin-Madison
Madison, Wisconsin, USA

Brian Parkinson
Department of Experimental Psychology
University of Oxford
Oxford, England, UK

Robert R. Provine
Department of Psychology
University of Maryland, Baltimore County
Baltimore, Maryland, USA

Rainer Reisenzein
Institute of Psychology
University of Greifswald
Greifswald, Germany

James A. Russell
Department of Psychology
Boston College
Chestnut Hill, Massachusetts, USA

Magdalena Rychlowska
School of Psychology
Cardiff University
Cardiff, Wales, UK

Sharlene E. Santana
Department of Biology and
Burke Museum
University of Washington
Seattle, Washington, USA

Klaus R. Scherer
Department of Psychology
University of Geneva
Geneva, Switzerland;
University of Munich
Munich, Germany

Lisa M. Shin
Department of Psychology
Tufts University
Medford, Massachusetts, USA;
Department of Psychiatry
Massachusetts General Hospital
Charlestown, Massachusetts, USA

Michael M. Shuster
Department of Psychology
DePaul University
Chicago, Illinois, USA

Johnna R. Swartz
Department of Human Ecology
University of California, Davis
Davis, California, USA

James M. Taylor
Department of Psychological and
Brain Sciences
Dartmouth College
Hanover, New Hampshire, USA

Ad J. J. M. Vingerhoets
Department of Medical and Clinical
Psychology
Tilburg University
Tilburg, the Netherlands

Paul J. Whalen
Department of Psychological and
Brain Sciences
Dartmouth College
Hanover, New Hampshire, USA

Sherri C. Widen
Center for Education Policy
Analysis (CEPA)
Graduate School of Education
Stanford University
Stanford, California, USA

Adrienne Wood
Department of Psychology
University of Wisconsin-Madison
Madison, Wisconsin, USA

PART I

Introduction

1

Introduction

JOSÉ-MIGUEL FERNÁNDEZ-DOLS AND
JAMES A. RUSSELL

In various practical enterprises such as border security, cosmetics, animation, robotics, dramatic art, computer software design, or the emotional-intelligence industry, facial expressions are a key part. Much like the man on the street, practitioners in these specialties evidence a monolithic simplicity in their assumptions about faces, as if questions and answers in this field were sealed by Darwin's time, almost 150 years ago. These specialties and folk understanding may seem to be grounded in scientific research, but the fact is that the relationship between scientific approaches and practical specialties is often problematic or, in a significant number of cases, nonexistent. Perhaps more surprising is that many scientific research projects and claims are based on the same set of folk ideas.

In *The Psychology of Facial Expression* (Russell & Fernández-Dols, 1997), we sought to survey the most telling psychological research on facial expressions, much of which was at odds with the assumptions of Darwin, the practical specialties, and folk beliefs. Since that publication, the field has continued to grow in quantity and quality. One of the purposes of the present book is to provide an updated review of the current psychology of facial expression. We expanded the scope and title to acknowledge the growing contribution of neuroscientists, biologists, anthropologists, linguists, and other scientists to this field. Our aim was to allow the readers—from lay to practitioners to research scientists—to discover the most recent scientific developments in the field and its associated questions and controversies. As will become obvious, the most fundamental questions, such as whether "facial expressions of emotion" in fact express emotions, remain subjects of great controversy. Just as important, readers will find that new research questions and proposals are animating this field.

A BRIEF HISTORICAL SKETCH

The classic, almost unavoidable, scientific reference in the history of the study of facial expression is Charles Darwin. Darwin instituted the term "expression of emotion" in a work that was one of the first popular books on science—indeed, probably the most important *popular* scientific book of all times in terms of its lasting influence.

Pointing out that *The Expression of the Emotions in Man and Animals* is a "popular book"—that is, a book aimed at a general, lay audience more than at the scientific community—is important because it partially exonerates Darwin of some of the conceptual and methodological problems created by his work since 1872. Darwin's book was basically aimed at defending the theory of evolution by questioning the creationist assumption that our facial expressions were God-given instruments solely for the purpose of expressing our emotions.

Darwin crafted a number of plausible alternative scientific explanations ("principles") of the existence of facial expressions, spiced with a collection of anecdotal but convincing examples that supported the continuity between animal and human expression and the existence of some innate, and consequently universal, expressions. Darwin's persuasiveness was, to a great extent, based on his pioneering use of images for backing his arguments.

THE FACIAL EXPRESSION PROGRAM

As Gendron and Barrett (this volume) describe in their chapter, acceptance of Darwin's hypotheses was not unanimous during the 19th and 20th centuries. Psychologists pursued a continuous debate on the precise role of facial expressions from an evolutionary and a psychological point of view. Since the 1970s, influential researchers assumed that emotion and facial expression are constitutive elements of an innate module that has been labeled in different ways. Classical labels for such modules are Tomkins' "affect programs" and Ekman's "basic emotions" (see Ekman's chapter, this volume). Affect programs or basic emotions would be ancestral human adaptations, and they would include a universal emotional conscious experience (the feeling of the emotion), an emotion-specific pattern of autonomic nervous system activation, a tendency to a specific overt behavior, and, in most cases, its corresponding universal facial expression. As a signal, the facial expression coevolved with the ability to read the signal.

Russell and Fernández-Dols (1997) labeled this view, which is extremely popular with scientific and lay audiences, as the Facial Expression Program (FEP). Figure 1.1 reproduces the 14 points that summarized this approach. These points revolve around a central assumption: a tight identity between facial expression and emotion.

FEP is, nevertheless, rarely endorsed in its entirety as stated in Figure 1.1. Different authors or the same author at different times endorsed different parts in different ways. Besides those who simply take for granted the

1. *There are a small number of basic emotions.*
2. *Each basic emotion is genetically determined, universal, and discrete. Each is a highly coherent pattern consisting of characteristic facial behavior, distinctive conscious experience (a feeling), physiological underpinnings, and other characteristic expressive and instrumental actions.*
3. *The production (encoding) and recognition (decoding) of distinct facial expressions constitute an evolutionary adaptation as a signaling system.*
4. *Any state lacking its own facial signal is not a basic emotion.*
5. *All emotions other than the basic ones are subcategories or mixtures (patterns, blends, combinations) of the basic emotions.*
6. *Voluntary facial expressions can simulate spontaneous ones. Voluntary expressions are deceptive in nature and culturally conditioned.*
7. *Any facial expression that deviates from the universal signals is a mixture of the basic signals or stems from the operations of culture-specific display rules.*
8. *Emotional state is revealed by facial measurement.*
9. *The subjective feelings associated with an emotion are due, at least in part, to proprioceptive feedback from facial movements.*
10. *Deliberately manipulating the face into the appropriate configuration creates the neurological pattern of the corresponding emotion.*
11. *The seven (plus or minus two) facial signals are easily recognized by all human beings regardless of their culture.*
12. *The ability to recognize the emotion in a facial expression is innate rather than culturally determined.*
13. *The mental categories by means of which recognition occurs (in the self as facial feedback or in others through facial signaling) are genetically rather than culturally determined.*
14. *Like encoding and decoding, the meaning ("signal value") of a facial expression is fixed by nature and invariant across changes in the context in which it occurs.*

Fig. 1.1 The Facial Expression Program
(Adapted from Russell & Fernández-Dols, 1997)

fundamental identity (that expression = emotion) in their experimental designs (e.g., assuming that if a brain region is involved in the processing of facial expressions, it is involved in the processing of emotion through terms such as "facial emotion"), FEP is also endorsed by scholars who have tried to overcome the potential limitations of this approach through different strategies. For example, some researchers have adopted a more open version of FEP in which facial expressions are sensitive to environmental inputs (e.g., see Elfenbein on expressive dialects, this volume). Others have opted for an extension of FEP through a larger and more flexible number of basic emotions or new multimodal expressions (e.g., see Keltner & Cordaro, this volume).

The Debate Around the Facial Expression Program

FEP also has its critics. Critics of FEP hold different theoretical and methodological positions, but they generally challenge the supposed close relation of emotion to expression. Theoretical challenges range from questioning one or both of the central terms in FEP (i.e., challenge the scientific feasibility of concepts such as "emotion" and "expression"; e.g., Russell, this volume) to a denial of any identity itself by emphasizing the role of mediating mechanisms such as conceptual knowledge (e.g., Doyle & Lindquist, this volume).

MINIMAL UNIVERSALITY

The contemporary science of facial expression is experiencing an occasionally intense debate between the followers of FEP and its critics. Is there a common ground on which all the experts, both supporters and critics of FEP, agree? Russell and Fernández-Dols (1997) described what they termed the "minimal universality hypothesis." Rather than just a synonym for universality as usually assumed, the minimal universality hypothesis tried to include all those assumptions that could be accepted by almost all facial expression researchers, independently of their theoretical views. These assumptions were as follows:

> (1) *Certain patterns of muscle movement occur in all human beings.*
> (2) *Facial movements are coordinated with psychological states.*
> (3) *Most people everywhere can infer something of another's psychological state from facial movement, just as they can from anything else that another person does.*
> (4) *People in Western cultures have a set of beliefs in which specific types of facial actions are expressions of specific types of emotion.*
>
> (Russell & Fernández-Dols, 1997, p. 17)

Today, even this minimalist approach is, or should be, a subject of scrutiny. For example, technical advances in the description and analysis of expressions through fine-grained video records are opening a way to a more careful consideration of the synchrony between facial patterns and psychological states; if facial patterns are dynamic events, rather than static objects, the fixation of the criterion of coordination becomes a serious methodological problem in itself: Which temporal range of the face and the psychological state should fit each other in order to claim the existence of such coordination? Assumption 2 is not yet a finding, but, well, an assumption.

A second example concerns the third assumption: Anthropological evidence suggests that cultural factors might inhibit (or exacerbate, as probably is the case in Western literate cultures) the practice of inferring psychological states from facial movements. Anthropologists have found that some Micronesian and Melanesian societies (Robins & Rumsey, 2008) as well as other societies such as the Maya (Danziger, 2006) held the assumption that others' minds are opaque to the receiver. A cultural belief in opacity would inhibit any conscious process of categorization of facial expressions in terms of mental states. If the mind-opacity assumption exists in a significant number of human cultures, its existence would require qualifying the minimalist assumption about a universal trend to infer mental states through expressions.

The reconsideration of any of these four minimalist assumptions might have important theoretical and methodological consequences on a long-term basis. Such uncertainty is a good illustration of the extent to which the study of facial expression is still a field that raises more questions than answers.

One of the aims of this volume is not just to provide information about some of the most important or promising approaches to facial expression, from either of the two camps, but also to make readers aware of this lack of consensus, which, in science, is a fertile ground for exciting new findings. Our bet is that these new findings will be related not just to conceptual but also to methodological future trends.

FUTURE TRENDS

In the introduction of the predecessor of this volume, Russell and Fernández-Dols (1997) suggested broad guidelines for future research: the idea that faces are associated with more than emotion, the suggestion that there are more to faces than seven prototypical configurations, the invitation to develop a more sophisticated approach to the distinction between spontaneous and posed expressions, and a plea for a careful consideration of ecological questions, for taking culture seriously, and for testing among rival hypotheses. We believe that, happily, these questions have begun to be seriously considered by the different writers of this volume, 20 years later. We hope that their readers will find many sources of inspiration to pursue in the scientific study of facial expression in new and exciting theoretical ways. That said, the present chapters indicate that these questions have yet to receive adequate attention.

Additionally, and on the methodological rather than on the theoretical side, this volume reflects, with independence of the authors' theoretical assumptions, that research on the "expression of emotion" is moving away from some of the technical and methodological limitations of empirical research in the 19th and 20th centuries (Fernández-Dols, 2013): the use of facial expressions as self-contained, static, bidimensional stimuli; the assumption that muscular tension is synonymous with emotion intensity (the sequence and timing of the unfolding of facial muscles being irrelevant); the use of simple multiple-choice questionnaires for which some small number of emotions is expressed by the face; and limited extension of our scientific knowledge to map human diversity beyond Western industrialized societies (Crivelli, Russell, Jarillo, & Fernández-Dols, 2016).

Current research is coming to assume that both the production and perception of facial expression are dynamic events. To study these events, researchers must take into account the relative position of the sender and receiver of expressions into a spatial, social, and cultural location. Facial expression may constitute an embodiment of different cognitive and affective processes. Taking this multiplicity into account will lead to more sophisticated views of facial behavior, in which context would be seen to play an important role in the production and interpretation of facial expression.

THE CONTRIBUTIONS

This book is organized into 11 parts. They try to help the reader to obtain a broad perspective on current scientific research on facial expression. The chapters relate to one another in complex and crisscrossing ways. Organizing them into parts was thus somewhat arbitrary, but we tried to convey a sense of the "geography" of the science of facial expression.

Part I: Introduction. A chapter by Gendron and Barrett complements our introduction by providing an historical background.

Part II: The Great Debate. As Gendron and Barrett indicated in their chapter, the dominant force in the study of facial expressions has been and remains the FEP (see Fig. 1.1) embedded in the theory of basic emotions. Criticisms of that program continue. The central question for the science of facial expression, therefore, is whether to build upon that program, modify the program, or abandon it. If the answer is to retain the program, then how might criticisms be answered? If the answer is to modify the program, then what needs to be changed? If the answer is to abandon the program, then what can replace it? We therefore offer a debate on these issues.

The first chapter of the part is a presentation by Paul Ekman of his current thinking. As with any scientific research program, the FEP is continually honed as new evidence accumulates. Both advocates and critics of the FEP need to be aware of its current state.

The other chapters in this part began as a discussion organized by Andrea Scarantino for the newsletter of the *International Society for Research on Emotion*. Scarantino invited advocates of the program (Keltner and Cordaro) and two critics (Fridlund and Russell) to summarize their current thinking on facial expressions. Scarantino then cross-examined each scientist with a series of clarifying questions. We, the editors of this volume, then invited each of the contributors to present their current thinking, especially as clarified and modified by the exchange in the newsletter. The result was three chapters, those by Keltner and Cordaro; Fridlund; and Russell. Additionally, we have also included a chapter that was not included in the newsletter, but that provides an empirical assessment of the key assumption at the heart of FEP. Duran, Reisenzein, and Fernández-Dols report a meta-analysis of the studies that tested whether the experience of those emotions typically characterized as basic (e.g., fear, anger, and so on) predicted the occurrence of their alleged corresponding facial expression.

The chapters in the remaining parts of the book resonate with the overall impression seen in the Great Debate. Some chapters build upon the FEP, some retain certain of its assumptions but propose major renovations, and some abandon FEP and offer alternatives instead.

Part III: Evolution. In this part we included three chapters that explore the evolutionary origins and functions of facial behavior. On the study of phylogeny, Diogo and Santana contribute a description of primates' faces and the ways in which this musculature has communicative functions. Bliss-Moreau and Moadab review research on how primates', specifically macaques', facial expressions have multiple functions depending on the context; their analysis of primate facial behavior abandons thinking of them as expressions of emotion, but it does maintain phylogenetic continuity between humans and other primates. Finally, Lee and Anderson echo Darwin by characterizing a facial expression as a frequently co-occurring cluster of muscular actions that originally served a nonemotional function (e.g., a sensory function such as increasing the visual field by eye opening) but were co-opted as signals of emotion in a later evolutionary stage.

Part IV: Less Explored Signals. Provine's chapter is an exploration of some facial behaviors (such as yawning, laughing, vocal crying, coughing, scratching, or vomiting) that have been largely ignored in mainstream research on facial behavior. Provine takes advantage of the description of these behaviors to explore one of the central questions of this volume: the conceptual obscurities around the distinction between voluntary and involuntary facial behavior. In the same vein, Gračanin, Bylsma, and Vingerhoets provide a review on the communicative and social functions of human crying, a facial behavior with obvious emotional connotations that—despite being one of Darwin's central examples of expression of emotion—has been surprisingly understudied by psychologists. Vingerhoets's chapter points out that we know practically nothing about why only humans weep and about the precise function of tears in human psychology.

Part V: Neural Processes. Whalen and his collaborators approach facial expressions as conditioned stimuli, and they describe some key neural and behavioral processes aimed at their interpretation. One of the main goals of their review is to report studies on the dimensional constructs that clarify the amygdala response to facial expressions of emotion.

Whalen et al. also point out that facial expressions offer a relatively innocuous strategy with which to investigate variations in affective processing, and the chapter by Swartz, Shin, Lee, and Hariri delves into this idea by using facial expressions to explore the neural bases of mood and anxiety disorders, with special attention to the amygdala and the prefrontal cortex.

Part VI: Individual Development. Two chapters address the development of facial expression. Camras, Castro, Halberstadt, and Shuster address the production of facial expressions in emotional situations, whereas Widen's chapter is mainly focused on the perception and understanding of emotions through expressions.

Camras et al. discuss empirical evidence on the production of facial expressions in children with a focus on three main questions: Do infants produce the expressions predicted for basic emotions on the basis of studies of adults? Do young children exclusively produce such expressions when experiencing strong emotions? And do older children produce the expressions of basic emotions during social interaction? They conclude that early emotion communication does not require the use of full expressions of basic emotions (the sort of stimuli studied in adult "recognition" studies).

Widen's chapter is also written from a developmental point of view, but this time on the side of the receiver rather than the producer of facial expressions; Widen describes her broad-to-differentiated hypothesis, which ties concept acquisition—rather than automatic recognition—with the categorization of emotions displayed in facial expressions. According to this hypothesis, children's understanding of emotions, and their categorization of facial expressions, over the course of childhood slowly evolves from broad, valence-based categorizations to discrete categories. The valence-based categorization is probably universal, but the final discrete categories show both similarity and differences in different languages and cultures.

Part VII: Social Perception. Adams et al. apply an ecological approach to the study of the perception of facial expressions. In their framework, such perception is the outcome of a combined set of factors that include not just the face but also other forms of nonverbal behavior and situational information. Hassin and Aviezer's straightforward take-home message is that all facial expressions are inherently ambiguous, and they conclude that the context plays a pivotal, almost exclusive role in the attribution of emotions to faces.

Part VIII: Appraisal. An already classical theoretical reference in the study of emotion is appraisal theory. In this part we include two chapters that approach facial expression from this theoretical perspective.

Scherer, Mortillaro, and Mehu review the empirical evidence that supports appraisal-drive view of vocal and facial expression in the framework of the component process model of emotion; facial expressions would be "push effects" of physiological and cognitive processes and "pull effects" of socially shared communication codes. Hess and Hareli discuss the role of contextual information in the appraisal of the emotional message of facial expressions.

Part IX: Concepts. Implicit in the theory that faces convey emotions are the concepts by which emotions are grouped and organized. Niedenthal et al.'s chapter applies embodied simulation theories of concepts to the study of the decoding of expressions of emotion. Their chapter reviews the empirical evidence on the role of mimicry in the recognition of facial expressions and provides theoretical insights about the particular motor, somatosensory, affective, and reward systems simulated by the perceiver in order to decode emotional information. Doyle and Lindquist discuss the role of language in the perception of emotion through facial expressions in the framework of a psychological constructionist approach. Their main hypotheses are that the production of facial expressions is not automatically communicating emotion and that the recognition of emotion from facial expressions is the outcome of conceptual processing supported by language. Their chapter resonates with that of Widen, which examined developmental changes in the use of language in understanding emotion from facial expressions.

Part X: Social Interaction. Two chapters emphasize the role of facial behavior in social interactions. For Parkinson, facial behavior's signaling of emotion is a side effect of its primary functions, which are the implementation of actions, the regulation of interaction, and the coordination with objects, events, and other people. Inspired by pragmatics, Fernández-Dols provides an alternative to the FEP. He concludes that facial expressions do not "mean" an emotion, but they direct the receiver's attention to the sender's affective state and trigger inferential processes about the context, the sender, or the future interaction between sender and receiver. For example, a wide-eyed stare directed at the bear does not mean "bear" or "danger" or "fear," but instead helps the receiver locate important information in the current situation.

Part XI: Culture. In this last part we include chapters focused on culture. Elfenbein reviews the dialect theory's assumptions and its supporting empirical evidence. According to the dialect theory, there are universals in emotion and facial expression, but with local dialects that have subtle differences from each other. Crivelli and Gendron focus on societies relatively isolated from the rest of the world. They review the most recent cross-cultural studies aimed at testing the universality of facial expressions in remote societies. They discuss limitations of this approach and offer guidelines for overcoming its challenges.

A SUGGESTED COMPANION LIST OF READINGS FOR THIS BOOK

Of course, our selection of authors and subjects tried to provide the reader with a representative sample of the latest theoretical frameworks and lines of research that constitute the current scientific approach to facial expression beyond the practical specialties around faces. The reader who approaches this field for the first time might also need to read less current background sources which are frequently cited in this field. We ran a perfunctory content analysis of the most cited references in this volume, excluding self-references and the references from the chapters on history (Barrett & Gendron) and meta-analysis (Duran, Reisenzein, & Fernandez-Dols).

Some sources were cited in more than six chapters, that is, by at least approximately 25% of the authors: Besides Darwin's (1872) *The Expression of the Emotions in Man and Animals*, the most cited reference is Ekman (1972), followed by Fridlund (1994), Izard (1971), Russell (1980), and Russell (1994). Interestingly, four of these six references are books or chapters in books. Additionally, other references are cited by approximately 20% of the chapters: Aviezer, Trope, and Todorov (2012) is one of the most recent references, followed—in alphabetical order—by Barrett (2006); Carroll and Russell (1996); Ekman and Friesen (1971); Ekman, Sorenson, and Friesen (1969); Fernández-Dols and Ruiz-Belda (1995); Gendron, Roberson, van der Vyver, and Barrett (2014); Jack, Garrod, Yu, Caldara, and Schyns (2012); Nelson and Russell (2013); Shariff and Tracy (2011); Tomkins (1962); and Vuilleumier, Armony, Driver, and Dolan (2003). Notice that these references are not necessarily representative of the importance of some authors in the field but of the authors' consensus about the relevance of some particular references. A number of senior authors in this volume are cited in a substantial number of chapters but the specific references varied, thus decreasing the chances of accumulating citations of the same reference across different chapters. In any case, this list can help readers and teachers to outline a companion list of background readings for the contributions of this volume.

REFERENCES

Aviezer, H., Trope, Y., & Todorov, A. (2012). Body cues, not facial expressions, discriminate between intense positive and negative emotions. *Science, 338*(6111), 1225–1229.

Barrett, L. F. (2006). Solving the emotion paradox: Categorization and the experience of emotion. *Personality and Social Psychology Review, 10*, 20–46.

Carroll, J. M., & Russell, J. A. (1996). Do facial expressions express specific emotions? Judging emotion from the face in context. *Journal of Personality and Social Psychology, 70*, 205–218.

Crivelli, C., Russell, J. A., Jarillo, S., & Fernández-Dols, J. M. (2016). The fear gasping face as a threat display in a Melanesian society. *Proceedings of the National Academy of Sciences of the United States of America, 113*(44), 12403–12407.

Danziger, E. (2006). The thought that counts: Understanding variation in cultural theories of interaction. In S. Levinson & N. Enfield (Eds.), *The roots of human sociality: Culture, cognition and human interaction* (pp. 259–278). Oxford, UK: Berg Press

Darwin, C. (1872/1965). *The expression of the emotions in man and animals*. Chicago, IL: University of Chicago Press.

Ekman, P. (1972). Universals and cultural differences in facial expressions of emotion. In J. Cole (Ed.), *Nebraska Symposium on Motivation* (Vol. 19, pp. 207–283). Lincoln, NE: University of Nebraska Press.

Ekman, P., & Friesen, W. V. (1971). Constants across cultures in the face and emotion. *Journal of Personality and Social Psychology, 17*, 124-129.

Ekman, P., Sorenson, E. R., & Friesen, W. V. (1969). Pan-cultural elements in the facial display of emotions. *Science, 164*, 86–88.

Fernández-Dols, J. M. (2013). Advances in the study of facial expression: An introduction to the special section. *Emotion Review, 5*, 3–7.

Fernández-Dols, J. M., & Ruiz-Belda, M A. (1995). Are smiles a sign of happiness? Gold medal winners at the Olympic Games. *Journal of Personality and Social Psychology, 69*, 1113–1119.

Fridlund, A. J. (1994). *Human facial expression: An evolutionary view*. San Diego, CA: Academic Press.

Gendron, M., Roberson, D., van der Vyver, J. M., & Barrett, L. F. (2014). Perceptions of emotion from facial expressions are not culturally universal: Evidence from a remote culture. *Emotion, 14*, 251–262.

Izard, C. (1971). *The face of emotion*. New York, NY: Appleton-CenturyCrofts.

Jack, R. E., Garrod, O. G. B., Yu, H., Caldara, R., & Schyns, P. G. (2012). Facial expressions of emotion are not culturally universal. *Proceedings of the National Academy of Sciences of the United States of America, 109*(19), 7241–7244.

Nelson, N., & Russell, J.A. (2013). Universality revisited. *Emotion Review, 5*, 8–15.

Robins, J., & Rumsey, A. (2008). Introduction: Cultural and linguistic anthropology and the opacity of other minds. *Anthropological Quarterly, 81*, 407–420.

Russell, J. A., & Fernández-Dols, J. M. (1997). What does a facial expression mean? In J. A. Russell & J. M. Fernández-Dols (Eds.), *The psychology of facial expression* (pp. 3–30). Cambridge, UK: Cambridge University Press.

Russell, J. A. (1980). A circumplex model of affect. *Journal of Personality and Social Psychology, 39*, 1161–1178.

Russell, J. A. (1994). Is there universal recognition of emotion from facial expression?: A review of the cross-cultural studies. *Psychological Bulletin, 115*, 102–141.

Shariff, A. F., & Tracy, J. L. (2011). What are emotion expressions for? *Current Directions in Psychological Science, 20*(6), 395–399.

Tomkins, S. S. (1962). *Affect, imagery, consciousness: Vol. I. The positive affects.* New York, NY: Springer.

Vuilleumier, P., Armony, J. L., Driver, J., & Dolan, R. J. (2003). Distinct spatial frequency sensitivities for processing faces and emotional expressions. *Nature Neuroscience, 6*, 624–631.

2

Facing the Past

A History of the Face in Psychological Research on Emotion Perception

MARIA GENDRON AND LISA FELDMAN BARRETT

Faces loom large in the science of emotion. Over the past century, countless experiments have been conducted to study how configurations of facial actions reflect (and potentially direct) emotions. Recent advances in sensing and computational modeling make it possible to measure even subtle changes in facial movements, promising the possibility of noninvasively characterizing the spontaneous facial movements of people with remarkable accuracy and sensitivity. To fully realize the potential and avoid the pitfalls of these new advances, it is necessary to appreciate the historical roots of the current research landscape on the role of the face in studies of emotion.

In the present chapter, we use a historical lens to examine how the face has been understood, and studied, in relation to emotion, with an emphasis on research within psychological science. We begin our historical account in the mid-1800s, just prior to the emergence of psychology as a discipline and continue through to modern psychological and neuroscience approaches to the face. This research on facial actions associated with emotional states can be loosely organized into two distinct viewpoints: (1) a classical view that assumes certain emotion categories have necessary and sufficient features, each with its own facial configuration that expresses said emotion, and (2) a constructionist (perceiver-dependent) view that assumes emotion categories are populations of highly variable instances, such that human perceivers construct experiences and perceptions of emotion, but individual instances emphasize various features across multiple sensory inputs, based on the situational affordances. These two theoretical perspectives have jockeyed with one another to become the guiding theoretical perspective in the science of emotion (Gendron & Barrett, 2009). In this historical account, we trace their dynamic across four epochs of time, outlining the emergence (and reemergence) of the classical and constructionist views.

We begin our review by outlining the critical assumptions of each theoretical approach, with an emphasis on how these assumptions pertain to facial actions associated with emotion. We then spend the bulk of this chapter demonstrating the recurring themes and tensions in the repeated emergence of these two perspectives over time, highlighting their impact on the questions asked, the research methods used, and the interpretation of previously published work. We close by suggesting that the science of emotion is, yet again, at a critical precipice with the emergence of computationally powerful computer-vision approaches to capturing facial movements. The current shift in research methods may finally provide an unprecedented opening for resolving these long-standing debates, by allowing for robust measurement of the face within the contexts of everyday life. Yet without careful consideration of the lineage of these two theoretical perspectives, it is possible that this opportunity for progress may be stalled for another generation.

TWO-FACED: COMPETING PERSPECTIVES ON THE FACE IN EMOTION

The Classical View of Emotion

As the name would suggest, the classical view assumes an emotion word, such as "angry," refers to a classical category: All instances within the category have a set of necessary and sufficient features—essences that make them what they are—and not instances of other emotion categories. In this approach, one configuration of facial actions is said to express one emotion in a consistent and specific fashion. That is, each biological category has its own specific set of facial muscle movements (termed a "facial expression") that are consistently triggered by the internal emotional state. In many accounts, these facial actions are considered the product of early evolution such that homologous facial actions are shared with nonhuman animals, in particular nonhuman primates (e.g., Waller & Micheletta, 2013). These configurations should be observable in all people (barring illness) across contexts (i.e., a 1:1 correspondence). Any deviation from this pattern of facial muscle movements within the episodes of a single emotion category are presumed to be caused by something epiphenomenal to the emotion itself, such as cultural learning in the form of display rules governing what is condoned to express (Ekman, 1972; Klineberg, 1938) or expressive dialects that subtly modify the form of the actions (Elfenbein, 2013; Elfenbein & Ambady, 2003), emotion regulation (e.g., Gross & Levenson, 1993), or simply measurement error. From this assumption, others emerge. It is assumed that people around the world will have the universal capacity to perceive (i.e., "recognize") these facial configurations as emotional expressions, without the benefit of learning or shared language (i.e., the universality assumption; Ekman, 1972; Ekman & Cordaro, 2011; Izard, 1994, 2011; Matsumoto, Keltner, Shiota, O'Sullivan, & Frank, 2008; Tomkins, 1962, 1963; Tracy, 2014; Tracy & Randles, 2011). Furthermore, it is assumed that this innate recognition capacity will be observable early on in infant development (Hoehl & Striano, 2010; Izard, Woodburn, & Finlon, 2010; Leppänen & Nelson, 2009).

The Constructionist View of Emotion

The alternative perspective, which can be understood as a constructionist approach to understanding the nature of emotion, assumes that emotions are not entities in the classical sense. Where the classical view is a perceiver-independent view of emotion (emotions exist whether there is anyone there to perceive them or not), the constructionist view is a perceiver-dependent view (emotional experiences and emotion perceptions are assembled by a perceiver as a way of making meaning) (Barrett, 2017; Barrett & Simmons, 2015; Clore & Ortony, 2013; for a review of older constructionist views, see Gendron & Barrett, 2009; Lindquist, 2013; Lindquist, MacCormack, & Shablack, 2015; Lindquist, Wager, Bliss-Moreau, Kober, & Barrett, 2012; Lindquist, Wager, Kober, Bliss-Moreau, & Barrett, 2012; Mandler, 1975; Russell, 2003, 2009).

In constructionist approaches, the face alone does not provide a clear, unambiguous cue to emotion, because one configuration of facial actions can be associated with many different emotion categories, and many configurations can be associated with one category (many:many correspondence).[1] Critically, the face is not assumed to be psychologically inert, but its emotional meaning in a given situation is thought to be constrained by context. In our own account, we view this as a joint function of the conceptual processes that guide facial action in the target (i.e., as prediction signals; Barrett, 2017; Barrett & Simmons, 2015; Chanes & Barrett, 2016; Gendron & Barrett, in press) and the conceptual processes of the person(s) perceiving the facial actions (i.e., also prediction signals; Gendron & Barrett, in press). When target and perceiver are relatively synchronized in their conceptualizations, the face can support correct inferences about the target's internal state (correct in the sense of self–other agreement); when there is conceptual asynchrony, then the perceiver's inferences will not match the target's intent, and misunderstandings will ensue (Gendron & Barrett, in press; Stolk, Verhagen, & Toni, 2016).

Unlike the classical view, where variation in facial movements that occur within an emotion category is considered epiphenomenal to emotion, the constructionist view considers variation to be a potential signal, not necessarily noise (i.e., not epiphenomenal to emotional episodes). Furthermore, there is no assumption that a face speaks for itself when it comes to emotion. As a result, much of the research inspired by the constructionist perspective has focused on the role that "context" plays in emotion perception (e.g., bodily posture, prosody, words, etc.); these influences are often referred to as a context for the face, but even this language is a holdover from the classical view, as we will see. In the constructionist approach to emotion, faces are not considered to be the dominant source of information upon which a mental state inference proceeds.

THE EARLY YEARS (1860–1930): DARWIN, HIS INFLUENCES, AND THE BIRTH OF FACIAL EXPRESSION RESEARCH

The clearest assumption that cross-cuts early classical accounts is that the face can serve as a direct indicator of an underlying emotional state. That is, specific facial muscle movements are caused by specific internal states (emotions), and thus they can be used by the perceiver to read the emotions of others. This viewpoint was not new to this time period; for example, it was Cicero (46 BCE) who wrote that the face is a picture of the mind. But this core assumption seeded a number of critical developments in these early years, ultimately forming into a standard research paradigm for studying facial expressions within the classical approach.

Building a Taxonomy of Facial Expressions

The first, and perhaps ultimately most influential, innovation of the early years was the concentrated effort to build a taxonomy for facial expressions of emotion. This taxonomic approach was inspired by, and built on, academic treatment of artistic depictions of emotion in the face as well as direct stimulation of facial muscles.

Perhaps the most notable taxonomic approach from this time period was that of Charles Darwin (1916/1872). Darwin's motivation was quite distinct from his predecessors—he wanted to make the case for continuity between humans and other species (i.e., an evolutionary perspective). As a result, Darwin also emphasized mechanisms that could account for the form of facial actions in humans, providing a novel contribution theoretically. Yet the specific forms for facial actions that Darwin described were heavily derived from prior authors—particularly that of Bell (1806) and Duchenne (1990/1862)—continuing a tradition of stipulation, rather than discovery.

Facial Expressions as Functional Forms

One of the key misunderstandings of Darwin's writing is with regard to the adaptive functions of facial actions. Darwin did not postulate there was functional value in the facial actions of humans. Instead, he argued for a vestigial association between actions of the face and body and categories of experience (acquired in a Lamarckian manner and *then* passed down through natural selection). Darwin used his ideas about "emotional expressions" to make his case for the evolutionary continuity between humans and other animals (Gendron & Barrett, 2009; Russell, 1994). Yet his view has been muddied in the years since, such that viewpoints that hypothesize human facial expressions are evolved functional forms (for review, see Shariff & Tracy, 2011) are described as Darwinian.

It was actually Floyd Allport (1924) who introduced the idea that facial actions are "functional," but in the context of communication and differentiation of emotions. Allport put forward the idea that facial expressions serve the function of differentiating emotions. Specifically, Allport argued that feedback from the face is necessary to differentiate a person's general physical changes (which is otherwise only characterized by general changes in peripheral physiology) into separate emotions. This idea can be thought of as a precursor to the "facial feedback hypothesis" and was even introduced in a rudimentary form by Duchenne (1990/1862), but Duchenne quickly dismissed it as implausible. Allport developed and endorsed this hypothesis, and gave the face a primary role in the differentiation of emotions (an idea that was echoed in the 1960s and 1970s in Tomkins's and Ekman's work).

Experimental Methods in the Classical Approach

Perhaps one of the more consequential yet overlooked aspects of these early years was the emergence of research methods for testing the link between facial actions and emotions. For example, Darwin (1916/1872) introduced the idea that cross-cultural data can be used to evaluate claims of innateness of facial expressions. He conducted his own (informal) survey about facial movements and emotion with collaborators around the world. In his survey, he sent verbal descriptions of specific expressive forms and the emotion they should express and asked his collaborators to verify that those forms appeared in other cultures. This particular cross-cultural work doesn't stand the test of time well, since it constituted an overly confirmatory approach. Not only did Darwin stipulate the forms of expressions to be verified through observation, but he asked cultural outsiders to make these assessments.

Darwin's confirmatory oriented approach continued in his second innovation: the emotion perception experiment. Darwin conducted perhaps the first study aimed at testing the 1:1 relationship between facial expressions and emotion perceptions. He presented 20 participants with preselected, static photographs from Duchenne's (1990/1862) stimulation studies to see the extent to which people perceived the "target" emotion in the faces. What is critical is that this initial experiment actually tested perception based on intuitive labels (i.e., the stipulated forms of prior generations), which were not themselves based on data.

Psychological research in the early 1900s replicated and extended Darwin's preliminary study. This led to the emergence of two additional methods: the portrayal paradigm and forced-choice responses. The portrayal paradigm involves the use of posed (typically static) expressions in research. The portrayals are stipulated (i.e., posers are directed to configure their face in a predetermined manner), or at a minimum, refined, by researchers. The origin of the particular poses used in research likely derives from multiple sources. In early investigations of emotion perception, the faces were often illustrations derived from artistic depictions of individuals experiencing emotion (for examples, see Darwin, 1872) and anatomical drawings of facial muscle movements thought to be associated with emotion (e.g., Bell, 1806). In later research, investigators employed face sets that involved posed faces in exaggerated configurations, likely inspired by earlier depictions (e.g., the Rudolph collection used by Allport [1924] and Langfeld [1918a]; or independent sets generated by Feleky [1914] or Ruckmick [1921]). These efforts served to craft a clear science of stereotypes in emotions research. Work during this time period even attempted to identify the specific actions in different regions of the face (e.g., brows, eyes, nose, mouth) that make these stereotypes most effective (Boring & Titchener, 1923; Buzby, 1924; Frois-Wittman, 1930; Ruckmick, 1921). For example, Frois-Wittman (1930) constructed a data-driven face set based on perceiver agreement by presenting subjects with illustrations of chimera of different posed expressions and examining which facial actions were consistently associated with a given emotion response. Not surprisingly, entire configurations, not single facial actions, were critical for the stereotypes to achieve perceiver agreement. This can be thought of as an early precursor to reverse-correlation approaches that reveal emotion stereotypes held by perceivers (Jack, Garrod, Yu, Caldara, & Schyns, 2012; Schyns, Bonnar, & Gosselin, 2002).

The second method to emerge in this time period was the use of label choices that perceivers were asked to apply to a given facial expression. This method has been referred to as "forced choice" or "multiple choice." Early use of this method was quite varied, however. For example, Feleky (1914) presented participants with 110 labels, including many that would not be considered mental state labels in modern psychological approaches (e.g., "sneering," "beauty," "physical suffering"). Whereas other researchers presented much more constrained sets of labels (e.g., 18 labels used by Fernberger, 1927). Critically, like the portrayal paradigm, this method was built on intuition such that emotion labels were preselected by researchers, rather than discovered in data.

Spontaneous Expressions and the Birth of Context

In contrast to the burgeoning literature using the standard paradigm, this time period yielded relatively little research that used unconstrained methods, such as measuring spontaneous facial muscle movements that occur in the context of emotion. That is, little research actually evaluated whether naturalistic expressions conform to the stereotypes. In one, now infamous, experiment, Carney Landis attempted to perturb his subjects' emotional states by placing them in a number of situations in the lab, one of which involved decapitation of a rat. In this experiment and others, Landis (1924a, 1924b, 1929) consistently observed that judgments of spontaneous expressions were at chance in their agreement with the eliciting situation. He interpreted his findings as evidence that posed facial expressions were providing a context that inflated agreement beyond what would be observed in naturalistic settings.

These findings were complimented by research examining how knowledge of the eliciting situation would shift attributions about spontaneous facial behaviors (Sherman, 1927). In Sherman's pioneering experiment, he found that knowledge of the eliciting situation constrained interpretations, such that face stimuli that produced a diversity of responses (>25 different emotion labels) produced near perfect agreement when accompanied by a situational description. Similar conclusions were reached by other research studies investigating the impact of context on emotion perception (Fernberger, 1930; Landis, 1929b; Sherman, 1927a, 1927b; Woodworth, 1928), setting the stage for concentrated efforts to understand emotion perceptions as perceiver-constructed phenomena.

THE FORGOTTEN YEARS (1930–1970): THE GROWTH OF CONSTRUCTIONISM AND THE REBIRTH OF THE CLASSICAL VIEW

Experimental Work From a Constructionist Approach

Following the evidence that spontaneous facial actions failed to provide the degree of interrater agreement seen for the stipulated posed stereotypes, the 1930s and beyond brought a flurry of research on emotion perception from a constructionist viewpoint. The perceiver dependence of emotion perception was examined in a handful of studies on individual factors such as age (Gates, 1923) and training (Guilford, 1929; for review, see Landis, 1929a) and the use of perceiver-based strategies such as imagery and mimicry (Langfeld, 1918b).

The main innovation of this time period, however, was to emphasize other "channels" of information that the perceiver could rely on to perceive emotion. For example, Kline and Johannsen (1935) studied how perceivers use both bodily and facial information from the target individual in order to arrive at an emotional percept. In a similar vein, Cline (1956) demonstrated that the meaning of schematic facial behaviors (line drawings) were impacted by other surrounding faces, such that the meaning of a given facial behavior changed depending on the other face it was paired with. Other research sought to replicate Sherman's finding that knowledge of the situation shifted perceptions of emotion (Goldberg, 1951; Goodenough & Tinker, 1931; Munn, 1940). Across these different lines of work, the data supported the constructionist assumption that perceptions of emotion routinely integrate multiple sources of information.

Experimental Critiques of Classical Methods

Researchers during this period also critiqued the classical approach by evaluating the impact of aspects of the standard paradigm. Specifically, researchers examined whether the label choices routinely used in experimental tasks impacted perceiver agreement. Emotion labels were either removed as choices in the response format, resulting in low agreement (e.g., Kanner, 1931), or the presence of labels was manipulated (Buzby, 1924; Fernberger, 1930; Kline & Johannsen, 1935; Langfeld, 1918b), resulting in shifting agreement (by 16% when directly compared; Kline & Johannsen, 1935). Furthermore, labels that were assumed by researchers to "mismatch" a set of facial actions were also applied by perceivers when they were provided by researchers as foils (Buzby, 1924; Langfeld, 1918b) or as direct suggestions (Fernberger, 1930). These findings served to challenge the utility of the forced-choice method in revealing the nature of spontaneous attributions that perceivers make about others' emotions.

Although these perceiver-dependent studies departed from the classical approach, the underlying assumptions and methods of this research often implicitly anchored on a classical approach. For example, many (but not all; e.g., Cline, 1956; Sherman, 1927a) perceiver-dependent studies maintained 1:1 assumptions, but the 1:1 correspondence was shifted to the situation rather than internal experience, implying that a specific emotional response is obligatory, based on the situation. Furthermore, context effects from this era were still framed as means of increasing or decreasing the "accuracy" of a response. Finally, a number of the experiments employed posed or preselected static faces, carrying over the experimental legacy from the classical view.

Constructionist Theory Builds on Perceiver-Dependence Research

While assumptions didn't always clearly shift for researchers conducting experimental work, there was a noticeable theoretical shift toward constructionist assumptions based on the research findings. Reviews of the literature concluded that facial actions do not serve as reliable information about emotion (Bruner & Tagiuri, 1954), and therefore any consistency in facial action must be due to culturally acquired forms (Hunt, 1941; Landis, 1929a). Schlosberg (1952) came to a similar conclusion regarding the classical approach, albeit via experimental means. He demonstrated that latent dimensions (discovered via factor analysis) of affect and attention, rather than discrete emotion dimensions, accounted for similarity judgments of facial expressions. Schlosberg suggested that discrete emotion judgments are probably driven by other contextual cues, not the face alone.

Other broader theoretical treatment of emotion mirrored this shift away from the classical view. Writers such as Dashiell (1928), Duffy (1941), Dunlap (1932), and Harlow and Stagner (1933) as well as those already mentioned (e.g., Hunt, 1941) articulated constructionist assumptions in their writing, such as (1) emphasizing considerable (often meaningful) variability in emotion, (2) positing that conceptualization (or meaning making) is a critical element in emotional events, (3) arguing for psychological mechanisms or features (e.g., affect) that underlie emotional events, and (4) suggesting that cultural learning is responsible for emotional forms. These viewpoints codified the mounting evidence for perceiver dependence into a set of clear theoretical assumptions about the nature of emotional events, including the role of facial actions.

A Classical Revival

Despite the budding empirical record and theoretical agreement surrounding constructionism, the classical approach had a strong revival starting in the 1960s. This reemergence involved both the methods (taxonomic treatment of the face, the portrayal paradigm, forced choice, and cross-cultural comparisons) and theoretical assumptions (1:1 link between face and emotion, facial actions as functional forms) of the earlier classical approach (Ekman, Friesen, & Ellsworth, 1972; Izard, 1971; Tomkins, 1962, 1963). Silvan Tomkins was instrumental in setting the revival in motion. He followed Allport in suggesting a functional role of the face in the differentiation of emotional states (Tomkins & McCarter, 1964). Although the face was critical in Tomkins's view of how emotions are conveyed and differentiated, he placed only a moderate emphasis on accuracy and consensus in emotion perception.

It was Ekman who made emotion perception of the face a true cornerstone of the classical revival. Ekman's "neurocultural" theory was timely and impactful due to its use of the language of modularity, which was gaining traction within cognitive sciences. He argued for encapsulated neural architecture responsible for the "triggering" of facial expressions and the perception of those expressions. Yet much of Ekman's contribution can be considered a throwback to the early years of the classical approach. He developed a system for coding for the presence of facial actions (i.e., the Facial Action Coding System [FACS]; Ekman & Friesen, 1978) building directly on the electrical stimulation work by Duchenne (1990/1862) as well as the work of anatomist Hjortsjö (1969). But this was also accompanied by Ekman's own taxonomy of stipulated emotional expressions, likely based on intuitive forms stipulated by Darwin and his predecessors. Whereas FACS itself held the promise of testing the 1:1 assumptions of the classical approach by quantifying spontaneous expressions (which has been done in the years since; for a review, see Matsumoto et al., 2008), it also served as a tool to standardize the facial actions that were configured in the portrayal paradigm (e.g., as in Ekman & Friesen, 1975), leading to increased conformity in the stereotypes used in emotions research.

Ekman also revived forced-choice methods, even implementing even more constrained methods (i.e., embedding words in scenarios) for some of his most impactful research.[2] For example, the portrayal paradigm and forced-choice methods were implemented in Ekman's high-profile cross-cultural experiments (Ekman & Friesen, 1971; Ekman, Sorenson, & Friesen, 1969), a choice that has come under scrutiny given the historical context (Nelson & Russell, 2013; Russell, 1994). It was these cross-cultural experiments, conducted with remote indigenous societies in Papau New Guinea, that solidified Ekman's legacy as a close follower of Darwin's work.

Ekman's work has clear discontinuity with the constructionist approach that had formed in the prior decades. Part of this discontinuity can be traced to a critical review of the perceiver-dependence literature, in which Ekman and coauthors cast doubt on the quality of prior research (Ekman et al., 1972). Ekman and coauthors expressed concern regarding the quality of the face stimuli used in prior work (e.g., the use of 1-week-old infant expressions in Sherman's experiments or the use of facial actions culled from media sources such that no "emotional" criterion existed). Yet some of the key observations of the previous decades (e.g., the influence of the forced-choice method, problems with the preselection of stimuli in the portrayal paradigm) were not addressed. Nor were these same critiques turned inward (e.g., stipulated expressions also lack an "emotional" criterion). Ekman and his coauthors also made many recommendations regarding what constitutes strong support for emotion perception, emphasizing the use of features of the classical approach (portrayal paradigm, forced choice) because they allow for "accuracy" to be computed. This review also served to change the terms of the debate, reframing the question of perceiver dependence as one of the *relative* contribution of the face and context.

Other contemporaries of Ekman, notably Carroll Izard as well as Rosenthal and colleagues (1979), also conducted large-scale cross-cultural research using standard paradigm (portrayals, forced choice), comparing emotion "recognition" of Western-style expressions across a variety of Western and non-Western cultural contexts (for reviews, see Ekman, 1998; Izard, 1977). Although emotion perception did vary by culture, the authors emphasized the amount of cross-cultural accuracy that was observed. Importantly, this research failed to introduce the methods caveats discovered in the prior era. As a result, this research was instrumental in solidifying the resurgence of the classical view and leaving the constructionist literature in the past.

THE MODERN ERA (1980S–TODAY): THE DOMINANCE OF THE CLASSICAL APPROACH AND REPEAT EMERGENCE OF CONSTRUCTIONISM

Ekman and his contemporaries provided a tipping point in the tension between classical and constructionist approaches and served to usher in the modern era of research on facial actions in emotion. Whereas the classical approach literature is too wide in scope to be covered in the present chapter, we will outline organizing themes that recapitulated the classical research agenda both in theoretical assumptions and methods. The reaction to this modern literature from the constructionist viewpoint equally mimicked the prior era, and will also highlight the ways in which it did so.

The Classical Research Agenda

The bulk of research in the modern era under the classical approach on emotion *perception* relies on the standard experimental features that have a long controversial history, as we have seen. The portrayal paradigm, in which static, posed facial actions that represent extreme, idealized configurations are used, is standard practice in most research studies on perception. And there is a striking amount of consistency in the face sets widely used in research today, which we likely owe to the stipulated and intuitive lineage of these particular poses. The use of the forced-choice method is also standard practice. That is, posed faces are typically presented to perceivers with a list of emotion words. Participants are asked to choose which word matches the face rather than generating their own attribution. Finally, the majority of the literature presents faces in a decontextualized manner. Critically for this historical account, these research methods persisted, despite earlier experiments operating from the constructionist viewpoint demonstrating the considerable impact of these methods.

This standard paradigm of the classical approach has been widely implemented in tests of cross-cultural consistency in emotion perception, as well as work on emotion perception as an automatic, innate, and perceptually basic phenomenon. For example, in the large research literature on cross-cultural "recognition" of emotion (for a meta-analysis, see Elfenbein & Ambady, 2002) an overwhelming majority (97%) of studies have used the forced-choice method. All three aspects of the standard paradigm outlined earlier (use of forced choice, the portrayal paradigm, and decontextualized stimuli) have also been critical to research aimed at establishing the automaticity of emotion perception (e.g., Tracy & Robins, 2008) and the perceptual "basicness" of certain emotional expressions (such as furrowed brows portraying anger) in categorical perception (e.g., Etcoff & Magee, 1992) and visual search paradigms (e.g., E. Fox et al., 2000). Furthermore, tests of innateness of perception in infants often follow an even more constrained format, with only a handful (sometimes as few as two) posed stereotypes presented repeatedly in habituation paradigms where looking behavior and/or brain activity is measured. Yet despite the artificially high perceptual regularity in these expressions, habituation or neural differentiation between posed configurations is taken as strong support for the innateness of emotion perception (Hoehl & Striano, 2010).

A second, but less prominent theme of the classical approach in the modern era is the limited attempts to validate the 1:1 assumption by examining the spontaneous production of facial actions in emotion. Although spontaneous expression research has been conducted in a number of Western samples, as well as across cultures (e.g., Ekman, 1973), and in congenitally blind individuals (e.g., Matsumoto & Willingham, 2009), most data used to support this assumption have simply coded for presence of stipulated expression forms that the science of emotion inherited (typically using FACS or the even more constrained EMFACS; see Table 13.2 in Matsumoto et al., 2008). Furthermore, these stipulated expressions are rarely compared to reports of emotional experience. In their review of the literature in 2008, Matsumoto and colleagues only reported one experiment that produced correlations testing 1:1 assumptions across discrete emotions (i.e., Ekman, Friesen & Ancoli, 1980).[3] This gap in the literature highlights the conformity of methods in the classical approach that have limited strict and necessary tests of the 1:1 assumption.

Constructionist Research in the Modern Era

Picking up on the short historical lens of many experiments within the classical view, several researchers in the modern era have revived perceiver-dependent methods. Similar to the research literature in the first wave, this second wave of perceiver-dependence research was also theoretically heterogeneous. Across perspectives, the methods were very homogenous, at least initially—borrowing heavily from the classical view. For example, posed expressions were generally used, largely to combat critiques of poor "source clarity" leveled against the stimuli used in earlier perceiver-dependence experiments (e.g., Ekman's critiques of Sherman's studies). Second, label choices were also common, despite the earlier findings that this is not a psychologically inert choice.

Despite the frequent adoption of classical methods, the findings from this era still replicated earlier findings supporting perceiver dependence. A number of studies (for a review, see Fernández-Dols & Carroll, 1997) demonstrated "context" effects on emotion perception (e.g., a situation description impacting the label assigned to a posed face). Yet Ekman's reframing of this literature also led to an agenda to demonstrate the "primacy" of the face over "context." As a result, this literature is often framed as demonstrating that the face is equivalent (e.g., Fernandez-Dols, Sierra, & Ruiz-Belda, 1993) or more potent (e.g., Nakamura, Buck, & Kenny, 1990) than context at determining attributions of emotion. Yet, given the gaps in the literature on prevalence of these expressions, pitting posed, stipulated faces against other sources of information may not have clear translational value for modeling real-world emotion perception. Only recently have researchers begun to dispense with posed faces in research, with encouraging results. Emotion attributions are even more robustly shaped by other sources of information than the previous literature suggested (Aviezer et al., 2015; Aviezer, Trope, & Todorov, 2012).

A few researchers have also aimed to (again) experimentally critique other aspects of the standard experimental paradigm itself. For example, Russell reillustrated the potency of emotion labels by manipulating which words were included as choices (Russell, 1993) and by removing them completely from cross-cultural comparisons (Russell, Suzuki, & Ishida, 1993). Work from our own lab and others has manipulated accessibility of emotion labels experimentally and demonstrated its impact on perceptions (Gendron, Lindquist, Barsalou, & Barrett, 2012; Lindquist, Barrett, Bliss-Moreau, & Russell, 2006), including in the context of cross-cultural experiments (Gendron, Roberson, van der Vyver, & Barrett, 2014). More recently, Nelson and Russell (2016) demonstrated that an artificially constructed facial expression (e.g., a blowfish expression for "pax") can produce results comparable to the stipulated classic ones (e.g., a wide-eyed "fear" face) when embedded in the standard paradigm.

Building on the insights that this literature has afforded, constructionist theoretical approaches have also reemerged in recent years (Barrett, 2013; Boiger & Mesquita, 2012; Clore & Ortony, 2013; Cunningham, Dunfield, & Stillman, 2013; Lindquist, 2013; Russell, 2009) united by an attempt to provide an explanatory framework that predicts perceiver-dependence findings like the ones demonstrated for facial emotion perception.

The Classical View Meets the Brain

Largely in parallel with the second wave of perceiver-dependent research in the behavioral literature, the advent of human neuroimaging technology ushered in new methods for testing the classical approach to emotion perception. The overwhelming majority of experiments in this literature have adhered to the standard paradigm by presenting posed expressions, devoid of context (95% of the published emotion perception papers between 1992 and 2003 in Lindquist, Wager, Kober, et al. (2012) meta-analytic database), with all experiments employing the forced-choice method (100% of experiments that assessed emotion perception from the face behaviorally between 1992 and 2003 in the Lindquist et al. meta-analytic database). Indeed, many early studies were entrenched in classical assumptions and hyperfocused on the locationist goals of early "brain mapping" research (i.e., identifying specific brain regions associated with specific functions). As a result, these experiments often failed to test alternative assumptions. For example, the assumption that the amygdala is a module for detecting fear dominated early studies (Whalen, 1998). It took a number of years for researchers to appreciate the broader role for the amygdala in tagging salient stimuli, after it was discovered that the amygdala is engaged by the sclera of the eyes in fear poses (Whalen et al., 2004), not *fear* per se, and that the amygdala is routinely engaged by positive stimuli (Mather et al., 2004) and novelty (Dubois et al., 1999).

Perceiver-Dependence Research Mirrors a Shift in Neuroscience

Shifts in neuroscience away from locationist views toward whole-brain, network-based approaches have led to a corresponding shift in the neuroimaging of emotion perception. Advancement in meta-analytic techniques have made it possible to carefully summarize the vast literature on emotion perception from the face that has accumulated over the last few decades. These meta-analytic data do not support the classical assumption that there is consistent and specific circuity for the perception of distinct emotions (Lindquist, Wager, Kober, et al., 2012). Instead, this research has revealed large-scale networks that support domain-general functions, a key constructionist assumption (Barrett & Satpute, 2013).

A second shift has been the move away from "feedforward," stimulus-driven, and locationist models of neural activity toward whole-brain dynamics that are context sensitive. A handful of experiments have demonstrated that emotion perception is a perceiver-dependent phenomenon at the neural level as well. Neural responses to emotional faces are shaped by contexts such as video clips (Mobbs et al., 2006), a sentence describing an eliciting circumstance (Kim et al., 2004), or even the emotion label applied by the perceiver (C. J. Fox, Moon, Iaria, & Barton, 2009; Lieberman et al., 2007). Research using electroencephalography (EEG) lends similar conclusions regarding the perceiver dependence of emotion perception (e.g., Van den Stock, Righart, & De Gelder, 2007).

Despite constructionist leanings, neuroscience research in the modern era has yet to grasp on to the full agenda of the constructionist approach. As a result, much of this work still makes 1:1 assumptions regarding linkage between other cues (e.g., bodily poses) and emotions (de Gelder et al., 2010), uses portrayed, rather than spontaneous facial actions, and forced-choice methods. It remains to be seen how profoundly constructionist approaches will impact the trajectory of research in this area going forward.

ON THE PRECIPICE?

Despite the compelling findings and movement toward perceiver dependence in the neuroscience literature, there is a robust trend that is emerging in both the scientific literature and industry that is shifting back toward the classical view on emotion perception. Specifically, the last few years have seen the emergence of automated "solutions" for the analysis and automated detection of facial expressions. Not only is there a robust literature in computer vision and machine learning communities, but this trend is being proliferated in the form of software available to researchers (e.g., Computer Expression Recognition Toolbox [CERT]), marketing firms/industry (Affectiva, Emotient), and even for the general public's amusement (e.g., IBM's API). The implicit assumption in these applications is that automated detection and coding of facial actions (using an action unit framework heavily influenced by FACS coding) can be used to automatically *infer* the internal mental state of the person being measured, based on the stipulated configurations. As a result, the lessons regarding perceiver dependence are once again being set aside in favor of a strong classical approach.

Yet the advent of automated detection programs is a technological feat that has the potential to produce progress in the long-standing debate between classical and constructionist approaches to the face. We are hopeful that in the years to come, another swell of perceiver-dependence research will become an important counterpoint to strong inferences made based on automated detection programs. The unparalleled computational power of computer-vision approaches will allow researchers to understand the literature we have built with more clarity. We can ask how well our science of stereotypes really captures real-world facial actions (e.g., what are the base rates of the stipulated expressions?). Perhaps even more exciting is the promise that automated detection tools hold for more completely mapping the grammar of facial actions, within different individuals, different situations, and different cultures, allowing researchers to build a science of facial expression directly on data, rather than stipulated stereotypes.

NOTES

1. A many:many correspondence between facial action and internal state is also hypothesized in other approaches that are not covered in detail here. For example, Fridlund's (1991) approach views some expressive forms as evolved signals that are for social communication and motive intention, rather than a readout of an emotional state. As a result, no tight linkage between experience and expressive facial actions would be expected.
2. Ekman used methods specifically designed by Dashiell (1927) to overcome issues with interrater agreement seen in developmental samples. In this method, participants from the most remote indigenous societies selected faces from an array of choices after hearing a situational description. Interestingly, this method seems to more closely follow the lineage of approaches for supporting perceiver-dependent perception, and indeed the researcher who developed this method published a constructionist account of the nature of emotion only a year later (Dashiell, 1928).

3. The remaining nine studies summarized by Matsumoto et al. (2008) had insufficient conditions or measurements to test for more specificity in facial action beyond valence congruence (e.g., smiling in positive but not negative emotions).

REFERENCES

Allport, F. H. (1924). *Social psychology*. New York, NY: Houghton Mifflin.

Aviezer, H., Messinger, D. S., Zangvil, S., Mattson, W. I., Gangi, D. N., & Todorov, A. (2015). Thrill of victory or agony of defeat? Perceivers fail to utilize information in facial movements. *Emotion, 15*(6), 791–797.

Aviezer, H., Trope, Y., & Todorov, A. (2012). Body cues, not facial expressions, discriminate between intense positive and negative emotions. *Science, 338*(6111), 1225–1229.

Barrett, L. F. (2013). Psychological construction: The Darwinian approach to the science of emotion. *Emotion Review, 5*(4), 379–389.

Barrett, L. F. (2017). *How emotions are made: The secret life of the brain*. xxx: Houghton Mifflin Harcourt.

Barrett, L. F., & Satpute, A. B. (2013). Large-scale brain networks in affective and social neuroscience: Towards an integrative functional architecture of the brain. *Current Opinion in Neurobiology, 23*(3), 361–372.

Barrett, L. F., & Simmons, W. K. (2015). Interoceptive predictions in the brain. *Nature Reviews Neuroscience, 16*(7), 419–429.

Bell, C. (1806). *Essays on the anatomy of expression in painting*. London: Longman, Hurst, Rees, and Orme.

Boiger, M., & Mesquita, B. (2012). The construction of emotion in interactions, relationships, and cultures. *Emotion Review, 4*(3), 221–229.

Boring, E. G., & Titchener, E. (1923). A model for the demonstration of facial expression. *The American Journal of Psychology, 34*(4), 471–485.

Bruner, J. S., & Tagiuri, R. (1954). The perception of people. In G. Lindzey (Ed.), *Handbook of social psychology* (Vol. 2, pp. 634–654). Reading, MA: Addison-Wesley.

Buzby, D. E. (1924). The interpretation of facial expression. *The American Journal of Psychology*, 35, 602–604.

Chanes, L., & Barrett, L. F. (2016). Redefining the role of limbic areas in cortical processing. *Trends in Cognitive Sciences, 20*(2), 96–106.

Cline, M. G. (1956). The influence of social context on the perception of faces. *Journal of Personality, 25*(2), 142–158.

Clore, G. L., & Ortony, A. (2013). Psychological construction in the OCC model of emotion. *Emotion Review, 5*(4), 335–343.

Cunningham, W. A., Dunfield, K. A., & Stillman, P. E. (2013). Emotional states from affective dynamics. *Emotion Review, 5*(4), 344–355.

Darwin, C. (1872). *The expression of the emotions in man and animals*. London: John Murray.

Dashiell, J. (1928). Are there any native emotions? *Psychological Review, 35*(4), 319.

de Gelder, B., Van den Stock, J., Meeren, H. K., Sinke, C. B., Kret, M. E., & Tamietto, M. (2010). Standing up for the body: Recent progress in uncovering the networks involved in the perception of bodies and bodily expressions. *Neuroscience & Biobehavioral Reviews, 34*(4), 513–527.

Dubois, S., Rossion, B., Schiltz, C., Bodart, J.-M., Michel, C., Bruyer, R., & Crommelinck, M. (1999). Effect of familiarity on the processing of human faces. *NeuroImage, 9*(3), 278–289.

Duchenne, G.-B. (1990/1862). *The mechanism of human facial expression*. New York, NY: Cambridge University Press.

Duffy, E. (1941). An explanation of "emotional" phenomena without the use of the concept "emotion." *The Journal of General Psychology, 25*(2), 283–293.

Dunlap, K. (1932). Are emotions teleological constructs? *The American Journal of Psychology, 44*(3), 572–576.

Ekman, P. (1972). *Universals and cultural differences in facial expressions of emotion*. Paper presented at the Nebraska symposium on motivation, 1971, Lincoln, Nebraska.

Ekman, P. (1973). Cross-cultural studies of facial expression. In P. Ekman (Eds.), *Darwin and facial expression: A century of research in review* (pp. 169–222). Cambridge, MA: Malor Books.

Ekman, P., & Cordaro, D. (2011). What is meant by calling emotions basic. *Emotion Review, 3*(4), 364–370.

Ekman, P., & Friesen, W. V. (1971). Constants across cultures in the face and emotion. *Journal of Personality and Social Psychology, 17*(2), 124–129.

Ekman, P., & Friesen, W. V. (1975). *Pictures of facial affect*. Palo Alto, CA: Consulting Psychologists Press.

Ekman, P., & Friesen, W. V. (1978). *Manual for the facial action coding system*. Palo Alto, CA: Consulting Psychologists Press.

Ekman, P., Friesen, W. V., & Ancoli, S. (1980). Facial signs of emotional experience. *Journal of Personality and Social Psychology, 39*(6), 1125-1134.

Ekman, P., Friesen, W. V., & Ellsworth, P. (1972). *Emotion in the human face: Guidelines for research and an integration of findings*. New York, NY: Pergamon Press.

Ekman, P., Sorenson, E. R., & Friesen, W. V. (1969). Pan-cultural elements in facial displays of emotion. *Science, 164*(3875), 86–88.

Elfenbein, H. A. (2013). Nonverbal dialects and accents in facial expressions of emotion. *Emotion Review, 5*(1), 90–96.

Elfenbein, H. A., & Ambady, N. (2002). On the universality and cultural specificity of emotion recognition: A meta-analysis. *Psychological Bulletin, 128*(2), 203–235.

Elfenbein, H. A., & Ambady, N. (2003). When familiarity breeds accuracy: cultural exposure and facial emotion recognition. *Journal of Personality and Social Psychology, 85*(2), 276–290.

Etcoff, N. L., & Magee, J. J. (1992). Categorical perception of facial expressions. *Cognition, 44*(3), 227–240.

Feleky, A. M. (1914). The expression of the emotions. *Psychological Review, 21*(1), 33–41.

Fernández-Dols, J. M., & Carroll, J. M. (1997). Is the meaning perceived in facial expression independent of its context? In J. A. Russell & J. M. Fernández-Dols (Eds.), *The psychology of facial expression*. (Vol. Studies in emotion and social interaction, pp. 275–294). New York, NY: Cambridge University Press.

Fernandez-Dols, J. M., Sierra, B., & Ruiz-Belda, M. (1993). On the clarity of expressive and contextual information in the recognition of emotions: A methodological critique. *European Journal of Social Psychology, 23*(2), 195–202.

Fernberger, S. W. (1927). Six more Piderit faces. *The American Journal of Psychology, 39*(1/4), 162–166.

Fernberger, S. W. (1930). Can an emotion be accurately judged by its facial expression alone? *Journal of Criminal Law & Criminology, 20*(4), 554–564.

Fox, C. J., Moon, S. Y., Iaria, G., & Barton, J. J. (2009). The correlates of subjective perception of identity and expression in the face network: An fMRI adaptation study. *NeuroImage, 44*(2), 569–580.

Fox, E., Lester, V., Russo, R., Bowles, R., Pichler, A., & Dutton, K. (2000). Facial expressions of emotion: Are angry faces detected more efficiently? *Cognition & Emotion, 14*(1), 61–92.

Frois-Wittman, J. (1930). The judgment of facial expression. *Journal of Experimental Psychology, 13*(2), 113–151.

Gates, G. S. (1923). An experimental study of the growth of social perception. *Journal of Educational Psychology, 14*(8), 449–461.

Gendron, M., & Barrett, L. F. (2009). Reconstructing the past: A century of ideas about emotion in psychology. *Emotion Review, 1*(4), 316–339.

Gendron, M., & Barrett, L. F. (in press). How and why are emotions communicated? In A. S. Fox, R. C. Lapate, A. J. Shackman & R. J. Davidson (Eds.), *The nature of emotion: Fundamental questions* (2nd ed.). New York, NY: Oxford University Press.

Gendron, M., Lindquist, K. A., Barsalou, L., & Barrett, L. F. (2012). Emotion words shape emotion percepts. *Emotion, 12*(2), 314–325.

Gendron, M., Roberson, D., van der Vyver, J. M., & Barrett, L. F. (2014). Perceptions of emotion from facial expressions are not culturally universal: Evidence from a remote culture. *Emotion, 14*(2), 251–262.

Goldberg, H. D. (1951). The role of" cutting" in the perception of the motion picture. *Journal of Applied Psychology, 35*(1), 70–71.

Goodenough, F. L., & Tinker, M. A. (1931). The relative potency of facial expression and verbal description of stimulus in the judgment of emotion. *Journal of Comparative Psychology, 12*(4), 365–370.

Gross, J. J., & Levenson, R. W. (1993). Emotional suppression: Physiology, self-report, and expressive behavior. *Journal of Personality and Social Psychology, 64*(6), 970–986.

Guilford, J. P. (1929). An experiment in learning to read facial expression. *The Journal of Abnormal and Social Psychology, 24*(2), 191–202.

Harlow, H. F., & Stagner, R. (1933). Psychology of feelings and emotions. II. Theory of emotions. *Psychological Review, 40*(2), 184–195.

Hjortsjö, C.-H. (1969). *Man's face and mimic language.* Lund, Sweeden: Student-Litteratur.

Hoehl, S., & Striano, T. (2010). Discrete emotions in infancy: Perception without production? *Emotion Review, 2*(2), 132–133.

Hunt, W. A. (1941). Recent developments in the field of emotion. *Psychological Bulletin, 38*(5), 249–276.

Izard, C. E. (1971). *The face of emotion.* New York, NY: Appleton-Century-Crofts.

Izard, C. E. (1994). Innate and universal facial expressions: Evidence from developmental and cross-cultural research. *Psychological bulletin, 115*(2), 288–299.

Izard, C. E. (2011). Forms and functions of emotions: Matters of emotion–cognition interactions. *Emotion Review, 3*(4), 371–378.

Izard, C. E., Woodburn, E. M., & Finlon, K. J. (2010). Extending emotion science to the study of discrete emotions in infants. *Emotion Review, 2*(2), 134–136.

Jack, R. E., Garrod, O. G., Yu, H., Caldara, R., & Schyns, P. G. (2012). Facial expressions of emotion are not culturally universal. *Proceedings of the National Academy of Sciences, 109*(19), 7241–7244.

Kanner, L. (1931). Judging emotions from facial expressions. *Psychological monographs, 41*(3), i–91.

Kim, H.-y., Somerville, L. H., Johnstone, T., Polis, S., Alexander, A., Shin, L. M., & Whalen, P. J. (2004). Contextual modulation of amygdala responsivity to surprised faces. *Cognitive Neuroscience, Journal of, 16*(10), 1730–1745.

Kline, L. W., & Johannsen, D. E. (1935). Comparative role of the face and of the face-body-hands as aids in identifying emotions. *The Journal of Abnormal and Social Psychology, 29*(4), 415–426.

Klineberg, O. (1938). Emotional expression in Chinese literature. *The Journal of Abnormal and Social Psychology, 33*(4), 517–520.

Landis, C. (1929a). Emotion: II. The expressions of emotion. In C. Murchison (Ed)., *The foundations of experimental psychology* (pp. 488–523). Worcester, MA: Clark University Press.

Landis, C. (1929b). The interpretation of facial expression in emotion. *The Journal of General Psychology, 2*(1), 59–72.

Langfeld, H. S. (1918a). The judgment of emotions from facial expressions. *The Journal of Abnormal Psychology, 13*(3), 172–184.

Langfeld, H. S. (1918b). Judgments of facial expression and suggestion. *Psychological Review, 25*(6), 488–494.

Leppänen, J. M., & Nelson, C. A. (2009). Tuning the developing brain to social signals of emotions. *Nature Reviews Neuroscience, 10*(1), 37–47.

Lieberman, M. D., Eisenberger, N. I., Crockett, M. J., Tom, S. M., Pfeifer, J. H., & Way, B. M. (2007). Putting feelings into words affect labeling disrupts amygdala activity in response to affective stimuli. *Psychological Science, 18*(5), 421–428.

Lindquist, K. A. (2013). Emotions emerge from more basic psychological ingredients: A modern psychological constructionist model. *Emotion Review, 5*(4), 356–368.

Lindquist, K. A., Barrett, L. F., Bliss-Moreau, E., & Russell, J. A. (2006). Language and the perception of emotion. *Emotion, 6*(1), 125–138.

Lindquist, K. A., MacCormack, J. K., & Shablack, H. (2015). The role of language in emotion: Predictions from psychological constructionism. *Frontiers in Psychology, 6*, 444.

Lindquist, K. A., Wager, T. D., Bliss-Moreau, E., Kober, H., & Barrett, L. F. (2012). What are emotions and how are they created in the brain? *Behavioral and Brain Sciences, 35*(03), 172–202.

Lindquist, K. A., Wager, T. D., Kober, H., Bliss-Moreau, E., & Barrett, L. F. (2012). The brain basis of emotion: A meta-analytic review. *Behavioral and Brain Sciences, 35*(03), 121–143.

Mandler, G. (1975). *Mind and emotion*. New York, NY: Wiley.

Mather, M., Canli, T., English, T., Whitfield, S., Wais, P., Ochsner, K., . . . Carstensen, L. L. (2004). Amygdala responses to emotionally valenced stimuli in older and younger adults. *Psychological Science, 15*(4), 259–263.

Matsumoto, D., Keltner, D., Shiota, M. N., O'Sullivan, M., & Frank, M. (2008). Facial expressions of emotion. *Handbook of Emotions, 3*, 211–234.

Matsumoto, D., & Willingham, B. (2009). Spontaneous facial expressions of emotion of congenitally and noncongenitally blind individuals. *Journal of Personality and Social Psychology, 96*(1), 1–10.

Mobbs, D., Weiskopf, N., Lau, H. C., Featherstone, E., Dolan, R. J., & Frith, C. D. (2006). The Kuleshov Effect: the influence of contextual framing on emotional attributions. *Social Cognitive and Affective Neuroscience, 1*(2), 95–106.

Munn, N. L. (1940). The effect of knowledge of the situation upon judgment of emotion from facial expressions. *The Journal of Abnormal and Social Psychology, 35*(3), 324–338.

Nakamura, M., Buck, R., & Kenny, D. A. (1990). Relative contributions of expressive behavior and contextual information to the judgment of the emotional state of another. *Journal of Personality and Social Psychology, 59*(5), 1032–1039.

Nelson, N. L., & Russell, J. A. (2013). Universality revisited. *Emotion Review, 5*(1), 8–15.

Nelson, N. L., & Russell, J. A. (2016). A facial expression of pax: Assessing children's "recognition" of emotion from faces. *Journal of Experimental Child Psychology, 141*, 49–64.

Ruckmick, C. (1921). A preliminary study of the emotions. *Psychological Monographs, 30*(3), 30–35.

Russell, J. A. (1993). Forced-choice response format in the study of facial expression. *Motivation and Emotion, 17*(1), 41–51.

Russell, J. A. (1994). Is there universal recognition of emotion from facial expressions? A review of the cross-cultural studies. *Psychological Bulletin, 115*(1), 102–141.

Russell, J. A. (2003). Core affect and the psychological construction of emotion. *Psychological Review, 110*(1), 145–172.

Russell, J. A. (2009). Emotion, core affect, and psychological construction. *Cognition and Emotion, 23*(7), 1259–1283.

Russell, J. A., Suzuki, N., & Ishida, N. (1993). Canadian, Greek, and Japanese freely produced emotion labels for facial expressions. *Motivation and Emotion, 17*(4), 337–351.

Schlosberg, H. (1952). The description of facial expressions in terms of two dimensions. *Journal of Experimental Social Psychology, 44*, 229–237.

Schyns, P. G., Bonnar, L., & Gosselin, F. (2002). Show me the features! Understanding recognition from the use of visual information. *Psychological Science, 13*(5), 402–409.

Shariff, A. F., & Tracy, J. L. (2011). What are emotion expressions for? *Current Directions in Psychological Science, 20*(6), 395–399.

Sherman, M. (1927a). The differentiation of emotional responses in infants. I. Judgments of emotional responses from motion picture views and from actual observation. *Journal of Comparative Psychology, 7*(3), 265–284.

Sherman, M. (1927b). The differentiation of emotional responses in infants. II. The ability of observers to judge the emotional characteristics of the crying of infants, and of the voice of an adult. *Journal of Comparative Psychology, 7*(5), 335–351.

Stolk, A., Verhagen, L., & Toni, I. (2016). Conceptual alignment: How brains achieve mutual understanding. *Trends in Cognitive Science, 20*(3), 180–191.

Tomkins, S. S. (1962). *Affect, imagery, consciousness: Vol. I. The positive affects.* New York, NY: Springer.

Tomkins, S. S. (1963). *Affect, imagery, consciousness: Vol. 2. The negative affects.* New York, NY: Springer.

Tomkins, S. S., & McCarter, R. (1964). What and where are the primary affects? Some evidence for a theory. *Perceptual and Motor Skills, 18*(1), 119–158.

Tracy, J. L. (2014). An evolutionary approach to understanding distinct emotions. *Emotion Review, 6*(4), 308–312.

Tracy, J. L., & Randles, D. (2011). Four models of basic emotions: A review of Ekman and Cordaro, Izard, Levenson, and Panksepp and Watt. *Emotion Review, 3*(4), 397–405.

Tracy, J. L., & Robins, R. W. (2008). The automaticity of emotion recognition. *Emotion, 8*(1), 81–95.

Van den Stock, J., Righart, R., & De Gelder, B. (2007). Body expressions influence recognition of emotions in the face and voice. *Emotion, 7*(3), 487–494.

Waller, B. M., & Micheletta, J. (2013). Facial expression in nonhuman animals. *Emotion Review, 5*(1), 54–59.

Whalen, P. J. (1998). Fear, vigilance, and ambiguity: Initial neuroimaging studies of the human amygdala. *Current Directions in Psychological Science, 7*(6), 177–188.

Whalen, P. J., Kagan, J., Cook, R. G., Davis, F. C., Kim, H., Polis, S., . . . Maxwell, J. S. (2004). Human amygdala responsivity to masked fearful eye whites. *Science, 306*(5704), 2061–2061.

Woodworth, R. (1928). *How emotions are identified and classified.* Paper presented at Feelings and Emotions: The Wittenberg Symposium.

PART II

The Great Debate: The Facial Expression Program

3

Facial Expressions

PAUL EKMAN

The argument about whether facial expressions of emotion are universal or culture-specific goes back more than 100 years. I will review the different kinds of evidence that support universals in expression and cultural differences. I will present eight challenges to that evidence, and how those challenges have been met by proponents of universality. I will try to present the evidence and counterarguments as fairly as I can, so that readers can make up their own minds.

THE EVIDENCE

Evidence From Darwin's Study

It begins with Charles Darwin's *The Expression of the Emotions in Man and Animals* (1872/1998). His evidence for universality was the answers to 16 questions he sent to Englishmen living or traveling in eight parts of the world: Africa, America, Australia, Borneo, China, India, Malaysia, and New Zealand. Even by today's standard, that is a very good, diverse, sample. They wrote that they saw the same expressions of emotion in these foreign lands as they had known in England, leading Darwin to say: "It follows, from the information thus acquired, that the same state of mind is expressed throughout the world with remarkable uniformity." (Darwin, 1998)

CHALLENGE 1: EXAMPLES OF CULTURAL DIFFERENCES

A very influential example of the challenge to Darwin's view that facial expressions are universal to the species was raised by the eminent social psychologist Otto Klineberg. While he acknowledged that a few patterns of behavior are universal, such as crying, laughing, and trembling, Klineberg (1940) said the expressions of anger, fear, disgust, sadness, and so on are not. Klineberg cited many observations of cultural differences in expressions noted by anthropologists, but the deciding evidence for Klineberg was a study which found that humans could not understand a chimpanzee's facial expressions.

The leading advocate of the view that expressions are specific to each culture in the 1960s and 1970s was anthropologist/linguist Ray Birdwhistell. Birdwhistell (1970) attempted to prove that body movement and facial expression, what he called kinesics, can be best viewed as another language, with the same type of units and organization as spoken language. Birdwhistell wrote as follows:

> I attempted to study the human smile.... Not only did I find that a number of my subjects "smiled" when they were subjected to what seemed to be a positive environment but some "smiled" in an aversive one. (pp. 29–30)

Birdwhistell failed to consider that there may be more than one form of smiling. The mistake may have been avoided if he had read the work of Duchenne de Boulogne, a 19th-century neurologist whom Darwin had quoted extensively. Duchenne (1862/1990) distinguished between the smile of actual enjoyment and other kinds of smiling. In the enjoyment smile, not only are the lip corners pulled up, but the muscles around the eyes are contracted, while nonenjoyment smiles involve just the smiling lips.

Up until 1982, no one else who studied the smile had made this distinction. Many social scientists were confused by the fact that people smiled when they were not happy. In the last 10 years, my own research group and many other research groups have found very strong evidence indicating that Duchenne was correct; there is not one smile, but different types of smiling, only one of which is associated with actual enjoyment (for a review, see Ekman, 1992).

Evidence in Which Multiple Observers in Different Literate Cultures Judge Expressions

Darwin's method of showing photographs and asking people to judge the emotion shown in the photograph has been the principal method. Because there have been so many studies using this research approach, critics have often ignored the other evidence relevant to universals which used very different methods of research (see later discussion) (see challenges 7–10 below). But first, let us consider what have often been called "judgment studies," because this method directs people in each culture to judge the emotion shown in each of a series of photographs.

Many countries were studied, in which only natives in each country were examined. They were shown photographs of facial expression and asked, not told, what emotion was shown. Apart from technical problems—a particular photograph not being a very good depiction of a real emotional expression, the words for emotion not being well translated in a particular language, or the task of judging what emotion is being shown being very unfamiliar—people from different countries should ascribe the same emotion to the expressions if there is universality.

Previous studies had uncritically accepted every one of the actor's attempts to pose an emotion as satisfactory, and they had shown them to people in each culture. It was obvious that some were better than others. However, rather than relying upon our intuitions, we scored the photographs with a new technique we had developed for measuring facial behavior (Ekman, Friesen, & Tomkins, 1971); we selected the ones which met a priori criteria for what configurations should be present in each picture. Izard also selected the photographs to show in his experiments, but by a different procedure. He first showed many photographs to American students and then chose only the ones that Americans agreed about to show people in other cultures.

I have chosen as the data set to discuss the findings listed and discussed by Russell (1994) in his attack on universality (a detailed account of how Russell misunderstood those data can be found in my reply; Ekman, 1994). There were data on 21 literate countries: Africa (this included subjects from more than one country in Africa, and it is the only group who were not tested in their own languages but in English), Argentina, Brazil, Chile, China, England, Estonia, Ethiopia, France, Germany, Greece, Italy, Japan, Kirghizistan, Malaysia, Scotland, Sweden, Indonesia (Sumatra), Switzerland, Turkey, and the United States. This includes two studies which I led (Ekman, Sorenson, & Friesen, 1969; Ekman et al., 1987) and separate independent studies by five other investigators or groups of investigators (Boucher & Carlson, 1980; Ducci, Arcuri, Georgis, & Sineshaw, 1982; Izard, 1971; McAndrew, 1986; Niit & Valsiner, 1977).

In all of these studies the observers from each culture who saw the picture selected one emotion term from a short list of six to ten emotion terms, translated, of course, into their own language. I will focus on just the results for the photographs the scientists intended to show: happiness, anger, fear, sadness, disgust, and surprise. These were included in all of the experiments.

There was an extraordinary amount of agreement about which emotion was shown in which photographs across the 21 countries. In every case, the majority of those in each of the 21 countries agreed about the pictures that showed happiness, those that showed sadness, and those that showed disgust. For surprise expressions there was agreement by the majority in 20 out of the 21 countries, for fear in 19 out of 21, and for anger in 18 out of 21. In those 6 cases in which the majority did not choose the same emotion as was chosen in every other country, the most frequent response (although it was not the majority) was the same as was given by the majority in the other countries. In my own studies, the only studies in which the expressions were selected on the basis of measuring the muscle movements shown in the photographs, all of the expressions were judged as showing the same emotion by the majority in every country we studied.

Contrary evidence, evidence against universality, would have found that the expressions that the majority of people in one country judged as showing one emotion (let us say anger) were judged as showing another emotion (fear) by the majority in another culture. This never happened.

CHALLENGE 2: NOT EVERY CULTURE WAS STUDIED

If the requirement is that every country must be studied, and every subculture in every country, then no one could ever establish that anything is universal. The anthropologist Brown (1991) wrote on just this point:

> The first and most obvious point about the demonstration of universals is that it is never done by exhaustive enumeration, showing that a phenomenon exists and existed in each known individual, society, culture or language. There are too many known peoples to make this feasible. (p. 51)

CHALLENGE 3: THE OBSERVERS COULDN'T CHOOSE THEIR OWN WORDS

A second challenge, which has been forcefully, but I believe fallaciously, made is that the appearance of universality was found only because the people were not allowed to say what emotion they really thought each expression showed. Recall that the people in every culture had to register their judgment about the emotion shown in an expression by choosing one emotion word from a list of emotion terms, such as anger, fear, sadness, disgust, and so on. What if they had been given other words? If only the scientists had allowed them to choose their own words, rather than forcing them to choose from the scientists' list of emotion words, then evidence for cultural differences in emotional expression may have emerged.

There are two answers to this challenge, one logical and the other experimental. If words like fear, anger, disgust, and happiness are truly unrelated to the expressions, if they are as meaningless when it comes to registering the emotion shown in an expression as a set of nonsense syllables (oto, nim, faz, etc.), then widespread disagreement would have been found when people were asked to use this list to choose a word which fit each expression. People within each culture would have disagreed with each other, and that is not what was found. And people across cultures would have disagreed with each other, and that also was not found. Just the opposite happened. In every culture the people agreed with each other in their choices of emotion words. And across cultures they agreed in their choice of emotion words. So it is unlikely that these emotion words are unrelated to the expressions they saw.

Evidence From Free-Choice Judgments of Facial Expressions

Of course, the best rebuttal is to allow people to choose their own words in judging the emotion they see in each expression and to determine whether the same results are obtained. Izard (1971) did just that in one of his studies. He allowed people in Britain, France, Greece, and America to give their own word for each photograph. Boucher and Carlson (1980) did the same in America and among the Temuans, an aboriginal group in Malaysia. Rosenberg and Ekman (1994) did the same thing in the United States, comparing agreement when people choose their own words, to the agreement that is found when people were restricted to choosing one word from a list of six or seven emotions.

In all of these studies in which people could choose their own words, the words they chose were quite similar, within and between cultures. Furthermore, the words they chose were quite similar to the emotion words that had been used in the 21 countries in which people were given a list of words to choose from. Russell (1995) dismissed this evidence, because Rosenberg and Ekman had only studied one culture, ignoring the Boucher and Carlson data and the Izard data on multiple cultures.

One of Russell's own studies (Russell, Suzuki, & Ishida, 1993), in which observers were allowed to choose their own word to describe the emotion shown in a photograph, strongly supports universality. English-speaking Canadians, Greeks, and Japanese were shown seven photographs from Ekman and Friesen's set (1976), and they were allowed to give their own response rather than choosing from a list (I will not report the findings on contempt, as I discuss that emotion later). There were 18 opportunities for disagreement (three cultures x six emotions); on 17 of those 18 opportunities the most frequent word the subjects gave was the emotion term that Ekman and Friesen had specified for the photographs.

CHALLENGE 4: SHARED VISUAL INPUT CREATED THE APPEARANCE OF UNIVERSALITY

A third and perhaps more serious challenge to the findings of universality was that all the people studied had the opportunity to learn these expressions from each other or from a common source. Perhaps everyone learned their "universal" expressions from watching Sesame Street on television! If people who were visually isolated were studied, this argument goes, if people who had seen no magazines, cinema, or television were studied, they might show completely different facial expressions. Birdwhistell made this argument when I first showed him my cross-cultural findings.

Evidence From Judgments by Observers in a Preliterate, Visually Isolated Culture

To answer this criticism, I went to Papua New Guinea in 1967 to study the South Fore culture. These people were visually isolated: Most had seen few or no outsiders, they were still using stone implements, and they had never seen a photograph, magazine, film, or television. I could not do what others and I had done in the 21 literate cultures.

The procedure I adopted had been used many years earlier (Dashiell, 1927) for studying young children who also cannot read. My translator read the person a brief story and asked the person to point to the picture, which fitted that story. Before using this procedure I had to have a story that clearly described a situation in which an emotion was likely to occur for these people. To discover the stories, I showed people one photograph at a time and asked them to make up a story which described what had happened to produce each expression. This was demanding on both the subject and the translator, and very time-consuming. Even if there is no language barrier, it is harder to make up a story than to hear a story and point to a picture. But I had to ask people to make up a story for each picture so that I could find out what themes are most common in this culture for each of the expressions, so I could use stories based on those themes in the main research study in which the stories were read and the people just had to point to the picture.

These preliterate people, who could not have learned expressions from the media, chose the same expressions for each emotion as had the people in the 21 literate cultures (Ekman & Friesen, 1971). The only exception was that they failed to distinguish the fear and surprise faces from each other, although both were distinguished from anger, happiness, sadness, and disgust expressions.

Evidence From Posing Facial Expressions by Members of a Visually Isolated Preliterate Culture

In another study I asked some of these people to show me what their face would look like if they were in one of the stories. I videotaped them as they enacted the emotions, and then showed these videotapes to Americans. If expressions are universal, then the Americans who have never seen any people from this New Guinea culture should have no trouble judging what emotion they are showing. That is just what happened except, once again, that fear and surprise were not distinguishable from one another (Ekman, 1972).

CHALLENGE 5: UNWITTINGLY BIASING THE NEW GUINEA SUBJECTS

Although our New Guinea study was considered crucial evidence for universality by many social scientists who commented on our work, Russell criticized this work. He (Russell, 1995, p. 381) tried to dilute the extent of agreement we found by combining our study with a study conducted by Sorenson (1975), who did not use our procedures and was a cinematographer when he did that work, not a trained social scientist. But Russell's major attack on our New Guinea study was his claim that we had influenced our subjects to give the responses we wanted. Although we described in our published reports the many steps we took to ensure that neither our translators nor we acted in a way which could have suggested to the New Guineans which photograph was the "correct" choice for each photograph, Russell credited reports by Sorenson, who was present only in our first-year study before we developed our procedures to guard against influencing our subjects. Sorenson was not present to see how we did the study reported earlier.

No matter how many precautions you take, it is impossible to prove that something might not have happened that you were unaware of and which could have biased your results. Fortunately, another study, conducted by a team which was trying to prove us wrong, provides the decisive answer to any such doubts about our work. For if an investigator's attitudes and expectations could influence the findings, then this team should have found results opposite to our own.

Evidence From a Second Preliterate, Visually Isolated Culture

Karl Heider, an anthropologist, and Eleanor Rosch, a psychologist, thought we were wrong about universals. The Dani people of West Irian, whom Heider had studied for many years, do not have words for all six emotions we had studied. When Heider heard about our findings in Papua New Guinea, he visited me to learn how to conduct our experiment so that he could go back to

West Irian, use our methods, and prove us wrong. Their results, with a people more isolated than those I had studied, were nearly identical to our findings (reported in Ekman, 1972).

CHALLENGE 6: ONLY POSED EXPRESSIONS ARE UNIVERSAL

Another challenge to the findings of universality came from the anthropologist Margaret Mead (1975). She pointed out that all of our evidence was on posed, not spontaneous, facial expression. Establishing that posed expressions are universal, she said, does not necessarily mean that spontaneous expressions are universal. I replied (Ekman, 1977) that it seemed illogical to presume that people can readily interpret posed facial expressions if they had not seen those facial expressions and experienced them in actual social life. Once again, the best answer to a challenge is not just logical argument, but to have findings that directly meet that challenge.

Evidence From Observers' Judgments of Spontaneous Facial Behavior

We studied the spontaneous facial expressions shown by Japanese and American college students. We selected Japan as the comparison culture because of the popular notion of their inscrutability. We hoped to show that this was due to display rules about masking negative affect in the presence of an authority. Students in Tokyo and in California watched a neutral travelogue and stress-inducing films (of surgery, accidents, etc.) while a hidden camera recorded their facial expressions. Two studies were done of these materials. In the first, the videotapes were shown to people in the United States and Japan who were asked to guess whether the people they saw had been watching the stressful or the neutral film. In the second study, the actual facial expressions shown by the Japanese and American students when they had been watching the stressful and travelogue films were measured.

The first study of spontaneous facial expressions strongly supported universals. The judgments made by the Japanese and Americans who saw the videotapes of the spontaneous facial expressions were highly correlated. It didn't matter whether a Japanese or an American was judging someone from their own or another culture; they made virtually the same judgments.

If the Japanese observers were correct in judging whether a Japanese student was watching a stressful or nonstressful film, so were the Americans. And so it was when Americans were judged by Americans and Japanese. We repeated this study a second time, with a new set of students in Japan and in California watching the stressful and nonstressful films, and a new group of observers in Japan and in California judging their spontaneous facial expressions. The results were the same. Neither the culture of the observer nor the culture of the person showing the facial expressions mattered in the accurate judgment of whether facial expressions had occurred during the stressful or neutral film. Facial expressions shown by Americans must have had the same meaning to Japanese observers as they had to American observers, and the same was true for the interpretation of the facial expressions of the Japanese subjects. This is very strong evidence, and it is evidence not on the judgment of still photographs of posed behavior, but on the judgment of videotapes showing spontaneous facial expressions.

CHALLENGE 7: AGREEMENT ABOUT JUDGMENTS DOES NOT PROVE IDENTICAL EXPRESSIONS

This criticism was not made by someone else, but it is a problem we recognized when we did the study. Our results do not rule out the possibility that all the Japanese showed disgust when they saw a surgical film, and all the Americans showed sadness. Remember that the observers were not asked what emotion they saw, but only when that expression was shown, during the stress or neutral film. Our results could have been found as long as both Japanese and American observers decided that the Americans' sadness occurred during the stressful, not the neutral, film and the Japanese disgust similarly occurred during the stressful, not the neutral, film. To rule this out—to show that the same facial expressions were shown—a very different type of study had to be done in which the actual facial expressions themselves were measured, not what observers judged them to be.

Evidence From Measuring the Spontaneous Facial Behavior of Subjects in Two Cultures

This is the first study that does not rely upon observers' judgments of emotions but instead measured the actual facial movements to see if they are the same or different in two cultures. The videotapes were measured by persons who did not know which film was being seen when the facial expressions occurred. A very high correlation was found in the particular facial movements shown by the American and Japanese students. Virtually the same repertoire of facial movements occurred at the same points in time. Later in the same experiment, a scientist dressed in a white coat entered the room and sat with the subject while he watched a stress film. We expected that now what we (Ekman & Friesen, 1969) had termed display rules for managing facial expressions in the presence of an authority figure would be operative, more so in Japan than in the United States. The Japanese did indeed show more positive emotions (masking the negative emotions) than the Americans, and fewer negative emotions.

Thus, this study showed that when spontaneous, not posed, facial expressions were studied, once again evidence of universals was obtained. Japanese and Americans interpreted the spontaneous behavior in the same way, regardless of whether they were judging the expressions of a Japanese or an American. When the students were alone, the facial expressions in response to the stress film were the same for the Japanese and the Americans. In the presence of another person, the Japanese subjects masked negative emotions with positive expressions more than did the Americans.

CHALLENGE 8: FLAWS IN THE DESIGN AND CONTRADICTIONS IN THE EVIDENCE

Fridlund (1994) has criticized just the study in which we measured the facial expressions the students had shown when alone and when with another person. He complained that it was not easy to compare the facial behavior in the alone condition and in the condition in which they watched stress films in the presence of an authority figure, because we used different measurements in each. He is incorrect; we used the same measurement technique in both. Fridlund also objected that we reported only partial face findings in the alone condition, but he must have missed our report, which did also provide findings on the whole face.

Fridlund noted correctly that 20% of our subjects showed no facial activity and wondered why that would be so. Not everybody is expressive, but the key issue is that the same percentage of Japanese and Americans showed no expressions. Fridlund also correctly noted that there was a third condition in which Japanese and Americans showed similar facial behavior. After watching the films alone, they were then interviewed by a graduate student (dressed in a white coat to enhance his authority), and then watched the stress films in the presence of that authority figure. The Japanese and Americans showed the same expressions when alone, and when being interviewed, but differed when watching the films in the presence of the authority, with the Japanese showing more positive and fewer negative expressions. Rather than regarding the similarity when being interviewed as further evidence of universality, Fridlund viewed it as a challenge to our findings of differences in the third condition, when watching the film with the authority figure present. Why did they not show differences in the second condition when being interviewed?, Fridlund asked. The answer is straightforward. The differences occur when negative emotions were being aroused by a film and masked by smiling. The interview did not elicit sufficiently strong negative emotion, and it was not intended to. It is only when they were viewing the very unpleasant films with the authority figure present that the differences emerged.

Fridlund asked why we did not report the data we collected on what the students said after the experiment about how they felt. But these reports should also be influenced by cultural differences. The same display rules which cause the Japanese to mask negative expressions in the presence of an authority figure would lead them not to report as much negative emotion in questionnaires given to them by that very same authority figure. For that reason we never analyzed those reports. Instead, we used a very different strategy. The films we showed to these subjects we already knew had the same emotional impact, from prior research by Richard Lazarus and his colleagues, which found the same physiological response to these films in Japanese and American subjects. We selected these films precisely because of that fact, because we could be certain that they would arouse the same emotions.

Evidence From Measuring Spontaneous Facial Behavior in Infants

Camras et al. (1992) measured Japanese and American infants' facial responses to arm restraints with an adaptation of the Facial Action Coding System (Oster & Rosenstein, 1991). Japanese and American infants displayed the same emotional expressions. There was a cultural difference in the latency of negative emotional expressions, with Americans responding more quickly than Japanese to the arm restraint procedure. This study has not yet been challenged by any of the critics of universality. It is an especially powerful study because it examined young infants and directly measured facial behavior rather than being a judgment study.

I believe this is the wrong way to think about the matter. I will suggest that the evidence strongly suggests universality on some aspects and cultural differences on other aspects of facial expressions of emotion. But first, more briefly, let me summarize other relevant evidence.

OTHER EVIDENCE

Continuity of the Species

If the particular configuration of facial muscle movements that we make for each emotion is the product of our evolution, as Darwin suggested, it is likely that we might find evidence of these expressions in other primates. Evidence that some of our expressions are shared with other primates would therefore be consistent with the proposal that these expressions are shared by all human beings.

Klineberg (1940, Challenge 1) also thought that commonality in expressions between humans and another primate, such as a chimpanzee, was crucial in deciding whether human expressions are universal: "If expression is largely biological and innately determined, we should expect considerable similarity between . . . two closely related species. If on the other hand culture is largely responsible for expression we should expect marked differences" (p. 179). Citing a doctoral dissertation by Foley (1938), which found that humans' judgments of a chimpanzee's expressions were not accurate, Klineberg concluded: "[This research] . . . strengthens the hypothesis of cultural or social determination of the expressions of emotions in man. Emotional expression is analogous to language in that it functions as a means of communication, and that it must be learned, at least in part."

Foley had said the students were inaccurate because they disagreed with what the photographer who took the pictures said the chimp had been feeling. I showed Foley's pictures to a modern primatologist, Chevalier-Skolnikoff, and asked her to interpret the expressions based on the decades of research on chimpanzee expression since Foley's time. When I compared what Foley's college students had said the chimp was feeling with Chevalier-Skolnikoff's interpretations, I found that the students had been right all along (this is reported more fully in Ekman, 1973).

Chevalier-Skolnikoff (1973) and another primatologist, Redican (1982), each reviewed the literature on facial expressions in New and Old World monkeys. Each came to the conclusion that the same facial configurations can be observed in humans and a number of other primates.

Expression and Physiology

If the association between facial expressions and emotions is in some part given, then it is logical to expect that facial expressions should be related to changes in the physiology of emotion. Ekman and Davidson found such evidence examining electroencephalography (EEG) measures of cerebral brain activity while subjects watched emotionally provocative films. Different patterns of brain activity occurred when disgust or a Duchenne smile (i.e., smiling lips plus the contraction of the muscle orbiting the eye) was spontaneously shown (Davidson, Ekman, Saron, Senulis, & Friesen. 1990; Ekman, Davidson, & Friesen, 1990). These differences were consistent with previous findings on asymmetries in cerebral activity for negative and positive emotions. In another study they had subjects voluntarily make both a Duchenne smile and a non-Duchenne smile. Only the Duchenne smile generated the pattern of EEG activity previously found in many other studies for positive emotion (Ekman & Davidson. 1993). Although Ekman and Davidson's findings are only for one culture, there is no reason to expect that these findings would be any different in any other culture.

In another set of studies, Ekman and Levenson found different patterns of autonomic nervous system (ANS) activity occurring with different facial expressions (Ekman, Levenson, & Friesen, 1983; Levenson, Ekman, & Friesen, 1990). They replicated their findings in a Moslem, matrilineal society in Western Sumatra (Levenson et al., 1992).

Subjective Experience

If facial expressions are universal signs of emotion, they should be related to the subjective experience of emotion. Until very recently it has been uncertain whether such a relationship was weak or strong. Two studies have found evidence of a very strong relationship. Ruch (1995), studying German subjects, showed that within subject designs, with aggregated data, yield quite high correlations between expression and self-report. Rosenberg and Ekman (1994) found that when subjects were provided with a means of retrieving memories for specific emotional experiences at specific points in time, there was a strong relationship between expression and self-report.

CONDITIONING

Further support for an evolutionary view of facial expressions of emotion comes from a series of studies by Dimberg and Ohman (1996). They did not find that different facial expressions are interchangeable, as one might expect if expressions are only arbitrarily linked to emotion. Instead, they found that an angry face is a more effective conditioned stimulus for an aversive unconditioned stimulus than a happy face. Conditioned responses could be established to masked angry, but not to masked happy, faces.

CONCLUSIONS

Taking account of the evidence, not just the judgment studies but the other evidence as well, I believe it is reasonable to propose that the universal in facial expressions of emotion is the connection between particular facial configurations and specific emotions. That does not mean that expressions will always occur when emotions are experienced, for we are capable of inhibiting our expressions. Nor does it mean that emotions will always occur when a facial expression is shown, for we are capable of fabricating an expression (but note that there is evidence to suggest that the fabrication differs from the spontaneous expression when emotion is occurring; Ekman, 1992). How did this universal connection between expression and emotion become established? In all likelihood it is by natural selection; however, we cannot rule out the possibility that some of these expressions are acquired through species-constant learning (Ekman, 1979).

It is not certain how many different expressions are universal for any one emotion. There is some evidence to suggest there is more than one universal expression: both closed- and open-mouth versions of anger and disgust, and variations in the intensity of muscular contractions for each emotion. It is also not certain exactly how many emotions have a universal facial expression, but it is more than simply the distinction between positive and negative emotional states. The evidence is strongest for happiness, anger, disgust, sadness, and fear/surprise.

I believe that fear and surprise do have separate distinct expressions, but the evidence for that comes only from literate cultures. In preliterate cultures fear and surprise were distinguished from other emotions but not from each other. There is (Ekman & Friesen, 1986; Ekman & Heider, 1988; Matsumoto, 1992) also evidence that contempt, the emotion in which one feels morally superior to another person, has a universal expression. But this evidence is also only from literate cultures, as this research was done in the 1980s and it was not possible to find any visually isolated preliterate cultures. Keltner (1995) has evidence that there is a universal expression for embarrassment.

To say that there is a universal connection between expression and emotion does not specify to what aspect of emotion the expression is connected. It may be the message that another person perceives when looking at the face (what has been studied in all the judgment studies), or it may be the feelings the person is experiencing, or the physiological changes that are occurring, or the memories and plans the person is formulating, or the particular social context in which the expression is shown.

Even if we limit ourselves just to the message that another person derives when looking at an expression, that itself is not a simple matter. Most of the judgment studies represented that message in a single word or two (e.g., angry, enraged), but such words are a shorthand, an abstraction that represents all of the other changes that occur during emotional experience. It is just as likely that the information typically derived from facial expressions is about the situational context: so that instead of thinking, "he is angry," the perceiver thinks, "he is about to fight," or "something provoked him." Elsewhere (Ekman, 1993, 1997) I have delineated seven classes of information that may be signaled by an expression.

Culture, social groupings within cultures, and individual differences all produce large differences in facial expressions of emotions. There are differences in the expression itself, and in what the expression signifies to the person showing the expression and to others. I expect the largest difference to be with regard to the words that represent emotions. I expect that languages differ not only in that they have a word which gives subtle nuances, or combines emotions, or tells us about what caused the emotion or what behavior is most likely to be shown. The Germans have the word *Schadenfreude* for that distinctive enjoyment that comes when one learns about a misfortune which has befallen one's enemy. English speakers have no single word for that feeling, although they feel the emotion. Not having a word for an emotional state, or as many words, may well influence emotional experience. Without being able to name feelings, it is harder to distinguish them, think about them, plan regarding them, and so on.

Given the likelihood that the words used to refer to emotions are so permeated by culture-specific differences, it is amazing that agreement has been so high in the judgment studies.

There are differences also in display rules, regarding the management of emotional expressions in specific social situations. Izard (1971) reported differences in attitudes about emotions, how positively or negatively the experience of one or another emotion was experienced. Gottman, Katz, and Hooven (1996) have defined "meta-emotion philosophy" as one's organized set of feelings and thoughts about one's own and others emotions. They have shown how individual differences in a parent's meta-emotion philosophy about their child's emotions related to how they parent, the child's regulatory abilities, and various child outcomes in middle childhood. However, the research has yet to be done.

I believe it is very likely that, in addition to the individual differences they have observed, there are also social class differences and cultural differences in meta-emotion philosophies.

Cultures differ also in some of the specific events that are likely to call forth an emotion. For example, some of the foods that are prized in one culture may be repulsive in another cultural setting. Of course, such differences in food preferences and aversions are also found within a culture. Notice that although the specific event varies (the type of food), the general theme (ingesting something repulsive as a cause for disgust or ingesting something attractive as a cause of enjoyment) is universal. I think this is a good model for all the emotions. The specific event that gets an American angry may be different from what gets a Samoan angry, but the theme will be the same. Anger can be brought forth by something that is provocative, insulting, or frustrating, to name just a few of the anger themes, although what each person finds provocative, insulting, or frustrating may not be the same across or within cultures.

There are, then, major differences in facial expressions of emotion between cultures, and differences within any culture: in the words for emotions, in what is learned about the events that call forth an emotion, in display rules, in attitudes about emotions, and, I expect, in meta-emotion philosophies. All these differences shape our emotional experience. Our evolution gives us universal expressions, which tell others some important information about us, but exactly what an expression tells us is not the same in every culture.

REFERENCES

Birdwhistiell, R. (1970). *Kinesics and context.* Philadelphia, PA: University of Pennsylvania Press.

Boucher, J. D., & Carlson, G. E. (1980). Recognition of facial expression in three cultures. *Journal of Cross-cultural Psychology, 11*, 263–280.

Brown, D. E. (1991). *Human universals.* Philadelphia, PA: Temple University Press.

Camras, L. A., Oster, H., Campos, J. J., Miyake, K., & Bradshaw, D. (1992). Japanese and American infants' response to arm restraint. *Developmental Psychology, 28*, 578–583.

Chevalier-Skolnikoff, S. (1973). Facial expression of emotion in non-human primates. In P. Ekman (Ed.), *Darwin and facial expression* (pp. 11–98). New York, NY: Academic Press.

Darwin, C. (1872). *The expression of the emotions in man and animals.* New York, NY: Philosophical Library.

Darwin, C. (1998). *The expression of the emotions in man and animals* (3rd ed.). With Introduction, Afterword, and Commentary by Paul Ekman. London, UK: Harper Collins.

Dashiell, J. F. (1927). A new method of measuring reactions to facial expression of emotion. *Psychological Bulletin, 24*, 174–175.

Davidson, R. J., Ekman, P., Saran, C., Senulis, J., & Friesen, W. V. (1990). Emotional expression and brain physiology. I: Approach/withdrawal and cerebral asymmetry. *Journal of Personality and Social Psychology, 58*, 330–341.

Dimberg, U., & Ohman, A. (1996). Behold the wrath: Psychophysiological responses to facial stimuli. *Motivation and Emotion, 20*, 149–182.

Ducci, L., Arcuri, L., Georgis, T., & Sineshaw, T. (1982). Emotion recognition in Ethiopia. *Journal of Cross-cultural Psychology, 13*, 340–351.

Duchenne, B. (1862). *Mechanisme de la physionomie humaine ou analyse electrophysiologique de le'expression des passions.* Paris, France: Bailliére.

Duchenne, B. (1990). *The mechanism of human facial expression or an electro-physiological analysis of the expression of emotions* (trans. A. Cuthbertson). New York, NY: Cambridge University Press.

Ekman, P. (1972). Universals and cultural differences in facial expressions of emotion. In J. Cole (Ed.), *Nebraska Symposium on Motivation,* 1971 (pp. 207–283). Lincoln, NE: University of Nebraska Press.

Ekman, P. (1973). Cross-cultural studies of facial expression. In P. Ekman (Ed.), *Darwin and facial expression: A century of research in review* (pp. 169–222). New York, NY: Academic Press.

Ekman, P. (1977). Biological and cultural contributions to body and facial movement. In J. Blacking (Ed.), *Anthropology of the body* (pp. 34–84). London, UK: Academic Press.

Ekman, P. (1979). About brows: Emotional and conversational signals. In M. von Cranach, K. Foppa, W. Lepenies, & D. Ploog (Eds.), *Human ethology* (pp. 169–248). Cambridge, UK: Cambridge University Press.

Ekman, P. (1992). Facial expression of emotion: New findings, new questions. *Psychological Science, 3*, 34–38.

Ekman, P. (1993). Facial expression of emotion. *American Psychologist, 48*, 384–392.

Ekman, P. (1994). Strong evidence for universals in facial expressions: A reply to Russell's mistaken critique. *Psychological Bulletin, 115*, 268–287.

Ekman, P. (1997). Expression or communication about emotion. In N. Segal. G. E. Weisfeld, & C. C. Weisfeld (Eds.), *Genetic, ethological and evolutionary perspectives on human development: Essays in honor of Dr. Daniel G. Freedman* (pp. 315–338). Washington, DC: American Psychiatric Association.

Ekman, P., & Davidson, R. J. (1993). Voluntary smiling changes regional brain activity. *Psychological Science, 4*, 342–345.

Ekman, P., Davidson, R. J., & Friesen, W. V. (1990). The Duchenne smile: Emotional expression and brain physiology II. *Journal of Personality and Social Psychology, 58*, 342–353.

Ekman, P., & Friesen, W. V. (1969). The repertoire of nonverbal behavior: Categories, origins, usage, and coding. *Semiotica, 1*, 49–98.

Ekman, P., & Friesen, W. V. (1986). A new pan-cultural expression of emotion. *Motivation and Emotion, 10*, 159–168.

Ekman, P., & Friesen, W. V. (1971). Constants across cultures in the face and emotion. *Journal of Personality and Social Psychology, 17*, 124–129.

Ekman, P., & Friesen, W. V. (1976). *Pictures of facial affect.* Palo Alto, CA: Consulting Psychologists Press.

Ekman, P., Friesen, W. V., & Tomkins, S. S. (1971). Facial affect scoring technique: A first validity study. *Semiotica, 3*, 37–58.

Ekman, P., Friesen, W. V., O'Sullivan, M., Chan, A., Diacovanni-Tarlatzis, I., Heider, K., . . . Tzavaras, A. (1987). Universals and cultural differences in the judgments of facial expressions of emotion. *Journal of Personality and Social Psychology, 53*, 712–717.

Ekman, P., & Heider, K. G. (1988). The universality of contempt expression: A replication. *Motivation and Emotion, 12*, 303–308.

Ekman, P., Levenson, R. W., & Friesen, W. V. (1983). Autonomic nervous system activity distinguishes between emotions. *Science, 221*, 1208–1210.

Ekman, P., Sorenson, E. R., & Friesen, W. V. (1969). Pan-cultural elements in facial displays of emotions. *Science, 164*(3875), 86–88.

Foley, J. P. Jr. (1938). Judgments of facial expression of emotion in the chimpanzee. *Journal of Social Psychology, 6*, 31–54.

Fridlund, A. (1994). *Human facial expression: An evolutionary view.* San Diego, CA: Academic Press. 203–237

Gottman, J.M., Katz, L.F., & Hooven, C. (1996). Parental meta-emotion philosophy and the emotional life of families: Theoretical models and preliminary data. *Journal of Family Psychology, 10*, 243–268.

Izard, C. (1971). *The face of emotion*. New York, NY: Appleton-Century-Crofts.

Keltner, D. (1995). Signs of appeasement: Evidence for the distinct displays of embarrassment, amusement, and shame. *Journal of Personality and Social Psychology, 68*, 441–454.

Klineberg, O. (1940). *Social psychology*. New York, NY: Holt.

Levenson, R. W., Ekman, P., & Friesen, W. V. (1990). Voluntary facial action generates emotion-specific autonomic nervous system activity. *Psychophysiology, 27*, 363–384.

Levenson, R. W., Ekman, P., Heider, K., & Friesen, W. V. (1992). Emotion and autonomic nervous system activity in the Minangkabau of West Sumatra. *Journal of Personality and Social Psychology, 62*, 972–988.

Matsumoto, D. R. (1992). More evidence for the universality of a contempt expression. *Motivation and Emotion, 16*, 363–368.

McAndrew, F. T. (1986). A cross-cultural study of recognition thresholds for facial expression of emotion. *Journal of Cross-cultural Psychology, 17*, 211–224.

Mead, M. (1975). Review of Darwin and facial expression. *Journal of Communication, 25*, 209–213.

Oster, H., & Rosenstein, D. (1991). Baby FACS: Analyzing facial movement in infants. Unpublished manuscript.

Rosenberg, E. L., & Ekman, P. (1994). Coherence between expressive and experiential systems in emotion. *Cognition and Emotion, 8*, 201–229.

Redican, W. K. (1982). An evolutionary perspective on human facial displays. In P. Ekman (Ed.), *Emotion in the human face* (2nd ed., pp. 212–280). Elmsford, NY: Pergamon.

Ruch, W. (1995). Will the real relationship between facial expression and affective experience please stand up: The case of exhilaration. *Cognition and Emotion, 9*, 33–58.

Russell, J. A. (1994). Is there universal recognition of emotion from facial expression? A review of cross-cultural studies. *Psychological Bulletin, 115*, 102–141.

Russell, J. A. (1995). Facial expressions of emotion: What lies beyond minimal universality? *Psychological Bulletin, 118*, 379–391.

Russell, J. A., Suzuki, N., & Ishida, N. (1993). Canadian, Greek, and Japanese freely produced emotion labels for facial expression. *Motivation and Emotion, 17*, 337–351.

Sorenson, E. R. (1975). Culture and the expression of emotion. In T. R. Williams (Ed.), *Psychological anthropology* (pp. 361–372). Chicago, IL: Aldine.

4

Understanding Multimodal Emotional Expressions

Recent Advances in Basic Emotion Theory

DACHER KELTNER AND DANIEL T. CORDARO

Basic emotion theory has proven to be a fruitful yet controversial set of ideas in the science of emotion, generating vigorous debate over the past 30 years (Barrett, Lindquist, & Gendron, 2007; Ekman, 1992; Ortony & Turner, 1990; Russell, 1994). At its core, basic emotion theory consists of specific theses concerning (1) what the emotions are—in general terms, they are brief, unbidden, pancultural functional states that enable humans to respond efficiently to evolutionarily significant problems; and (2) how scientific research is to differentiate distinct emotions from one another—in expression, peripheral physiology, appraisal, and neural process (Ekman, 1992; Ekman & Cordaro, 2011; Ekman & Davidson, 1994).

Here, we focus on an especially contentious subdomain of basic emotion theory, namely its specific claims regarding emotional expression. Within this tradition, it is more specifically assumed that expressions of emotion (1) are brief, coherent patterns of facial behavior that covary with distinct experiences; (2) signal the current emotional state, intentions, and assessment of the eliciting situation of the individual; (3) manifest some degree of cross-cultural universality in both production and recognition; (4) find evolutionary precursors in the signaling behaviors of other mammals in contexts similar to the social contexts humans encounter (e.g., when signaling adversarial intentions); and (5) covary with emotion-related physiological responses (for summaries, see

Ekman, 1994; Hess & Fischer, 2013; Keltner & Haidt, 2001; Keltner & Kring, 1998; Matsumoto et al., 2008).

Original support for basic emotion theory comes from the well-known studies of Ekman and Friesen in New Guinea (Ekman, Sorenson, & Friesen, 1969; for meta-analysis of these kinds of studies, see Elfenbein & Ambady, 2002). Using still photographs of prototypical emotional facial expressions, Ekman and Friesen were able to document universality in the production and recognition of a limited set of "basic" emotions, including anger, fear, happiness, sadness, disgust, and surprise (for review, see Matsumoto et al., 2008). Subsequent critiques have raised questions about the degree of universality in the recognition of these emotional facial expressions (Russell, 1994), about what such expressions signal (Fridlund, 1991), about the response formats in the studies (Russell, 1994), and about the ecological validity of such exaggerated, prototypical expressions.

These productive debates have inspired a next wave of research on emotional expression, which advances basic emotion theory in fundamental ways. In this essay we summarize—in broad strokes—what has been learned in the past 20 years of empirical study—highlighting for the first time how the evidence yields a new set of propositions concerning the nature and universality of emotional expression within the framework of basic emotion theory.

EMOTIONAL EXPRESSIONS ARE MULTIMODAL, DYNAMIC PATTERNS OF BEHAVIOR

Central to basic emotion theory is the assumption that emotions enable the individual to respond adaptively to evolutionarily significant threats and opportunities in the environment—the cry of offspring, a threat from an adversary, pursuing sexual opportunity in a social setting of rivals and potential mates (Ekman, 1992; Keltner & Haidt, 2001). Emotions enable such responses primarily through shifts in peripheral physiology (Levenson, Ekman, & Friesen, 1990), patterns of cognition (Oveis, Horberg, & Keltner, 2010), movements of the body (e.g., the proverbial fight-or-flight response), and expressive behavior that coordinates social interactions through the information it conveys and responses it evokes in others (e.g., Keltner & Kring, 1998; van Kleef, 2009).

Within this framework, emotions are fundamentally about action (Frijda, 1986). Emotions enable people to react to significant stimuli in the environment (or within themselves), in complex patterns of behavior involving multiple modalities—facial muscle movement, vocal cues, bodily movements, gesture, posture, and so on. For example, studies capturing experiences of sympathy find that this brief state involves bodily movements forward, soothing tactile behavior, oblique eyebrows, a fixed pattern of gaze, vocalizations, and skin-to-skin contact when sympathy leads to embrace (Goetz, Keltner, & Simon-Thomas, 2010).

Early studies of emotional expression, and the controversies they engendered, largely focused on the meaning of static portrayals of prototypical configurations of facial muscles of anger, disgust, fear, sadness, surprise, and happiness (Ekman, 1994; Russell, 1994). In the last 20 years, the scientific study of facial expressions has moved significantly beyond static portrayals of six emotions, revealing that emotional expressions are multimodal, dynamic patterns of behavior, involving facial action, vocalization, bodily movement, gaze, gesture, head movements, touch, autonomic response, and even scent (for a review of the signaling properties of these modalities, see Keltner et al., in press).

Notably, the notion that emotional expressions are *multimodal patterns of behavior* is evident in Charles Darwin's own rich descriptions of the expressions of over 40 emotional states (Keltner, 2009), a portion of which we summarize in Table 4.1 (with a focus on positive emotions).

We notice here that Darwin did not focus on what Ekman (1992) once called *momentary* facial expressions, the sorts of expressions that can be captured with a snapshot, but rather on *multimodal* dynamic patterns of behavior that unfold over time, in which the signal consists of a sequence of facial and nonfacial actions that only collectively and over time convey the relevant message.

Focusing on more modalities than facial expression alone has enabled the discovery of new emotional expressions. For example, gaze patterns and head movements covary with the experience and signaling of embarrassment (Keltner, 1995), pride (Tracy & Robins, 2004), and awe (Campos et al., 2013), as we detail herein. Thinking of emotional expressions as dynamic multimodal patterns of behavior also points to intriguing new questions (e.g., Aviezer, Trope, & Todorov, 2012). What is the relative contribution of different modalities to the perception and signal value of emotional expressions (e.g., Flack, 2006; Scherer & Ellgring, 2007)? Why is it that certain emotions are more reliably signaled in multiple modalities, whereas other emotions are only recognized in one modality? For example, sympathy is reliably signaled in touch and the voice, but less so in the face (Goetz et al., 2010). It is nearly impossible to communicate embarrassment through touch, but it is reliably communicated in patterns of gaze, head, and facial behavior.

THERE ARE MORE EMOTIONAL EXPRESSIONS THAN THE "BASIC" SIX

Critical to basic emotion theory is the question of which emotions have distinctive signals. Evidence germane to this question informs taxonomies of

Table 4.1 DARWIN'S DESCRIPTIONS OF THE EXPRESSIVE BEHAVIOR OF POSITIVE EMOTIONS

Emotion	Description
Astonishment	Eyes open, mouth open, eyebrows raised, hands placed over mouth
Contemplation	Frown, wrinkle skin under lower eyelids, eyes divergent, head droops, hands to forehead, mouth, or chin, thumb/index finger to lip
Determination	Firmly closed mouth, arms folded across breast, shoulders raised
Devotion	Face upward, eyelids upturned, fainting, pupils upward and inward, humbling kneeling posture, hands upturned
Happiness	Eyes sparkle, skin under eyes wrinkled, mouth drawn back at corners
High spirits, Cheerfulness	Smile, body erect, head upright, eyes open, eyebrows raised, eyelids raised, nostrils raised, eating gestures (rubbing belly), air suck, lip smacks
Joy	Muscle tremble, purposeless movements, laughter, clapping hands, jumping, dancing about, stamping, chuckle/giggle, smile, muscle around eyes contracted, upper lip raised
Laughter	Tears, deep inspiration, contraction of chest, shaking of body, head nods to and fro, lower jaw quivers up/down, lip corners drawn backward, head thrown backward, shakes, head/face red, muscle around eyes contracted, lip press/bite
Love	Beaming eyes, smiling cheeks (when seeing old friend), touch, gentle smile, protruding lips (in chimps), kissing, nose rubs
Maternal love	Touch, gentle smile, tender eyes
Pride	Head, body erect, look down on others
Tender (sympathy)	Tears

emotion (e.g., Keltner & Lerner, 2010) and the search for emotion-specific responses in other systems, such as neuroendocrine or autonomic response systems (see later discussion).

Past studies focused on figuring out momentary expressions captured by still photographs. As a result, only the "basic six" emotions—anger, disgust, fear, sadness, surprise, and happiness—emerged as having clear distinctive signals. But if emotional expressions are, as we claim and as suggested by Darwin, multimodal and dynamic, many more emotions may have distinctive signals, which could consist of facial changes over time in combination with other behaviors (e.g., vocal changes).

In recent years, dozens of studies have sought to differentiate the expressions of emotions other than the basic six, expanding the focus to modalities such as touch, voice, and artistic portrayal. In *emotion recognition* paradigms, participants attempted to choose the right label to designate an emotion-related facial expression, vocalization, or piece of music. In *emotion production* studies, participants attempted to communicate emotions to a naïve observer, who was tasked with guessing the emotion expressed. In *emotion encoding* studies, behavioral analyses ascertained whether the experience of an emotion was expressed in different behaviors than closely related states.

In Table 4.2, we summarize this new literature, indicating whether studies reveal that the facial, vocal, tactile, and music-related expressions of the

Table 4.2 EVIDENCE RELATED TO THE EXPRESSION OF EMOTION IN DIFFERENT MODALITIES

Emotion	Facial Action	Voice	Touch	Music
Amused	yes[a,b,d,i]	yes[y,z,bb]	n/a	n/a
Anger	yes[d,w,x]	yes[y,aa,bb]	yes[dd,ee]	yes[ff]
Awe	yes[a,c,d]	yes[y]	no	n/a
Boredom	yes[n]	yes[aa]	n/a	n/a
Confused	yes[n,u]	n/a	n/a	n/a
Contempt	yes[v,w]	yes[y,aa]	n/a	n/a
Content	yes[d]	yes[z]	n/a	n/a
Coy	yes[e,f,g]	n/a	n/a	n/a
Desire	yes[h,i]	no[y]	n/a	n/a
Disgust	yes[d,w,x]	yes[y,aa,bb]	yes[dd,ee]	n/a
Embarrassed	yes[d,i,j,k,l]	yes[y]	no[ee]	n/a
Fear	yes[d,w,x]	yes[y,aa,bb]	yes[dd,ee]	yes[ff]
Gratitude	n/a	no[y]	yes[dd,ee]	n/a
Happiness	yes[i,w,x]	yes[aa]	yes[dd]	yes[ff]
Interested	yes[i,m,n]	yes[y]	n/a	n/a
Love	yes[d,i]	no[y]	yes[dd,ee]	yes[ff]
Pain	yes[o,p,q,r]	yes[cc]	n/a	n/a
Pride	yes[a,i]	no[y]	no[ee]	n/a
Relief	n/a	yes[y,z,aa,bb]	n/a	n/a
Sadness	yes[d,w,x]	yes[y,bb]	yes[dd,ee]	yes[ff]
Shame	yes[d,i,t]	no[y]	n/a	n/a
Surprise	yes[w,x]	yes[y,bb,ee]	no[ee]	n/a
Sympathy	yes[i]	yes[y]	yes[dd,ee]	n/a
Triumph	n/a	yes[y]	n/a	n/a

[a]Shiota, Campos, & Keltner (2003). [b]Keltner & Bonanno (1997). [c]Shiota, Keltner, & Mossman (2007). [d]Hejmadi, Davidson, & Rozin (2000). [e]Reddy (2000). [f]Reddy (2005). [g]Bretherton & Ainsworth (1974). [h]Gonzaga et al. (2006). [i]Keltner & Shiota (2003). [j]Keltner & Buswell (1997). [k]Keltner (1996). [l]Ekman & Rosenberg (1997). [m]Silvia (2008). [n]Reeve (1993). [o]Prkachin (1992). [p]Williams (2002). [q]Grunau & Craig (1987). [r]Botvinick et al. (2005). [s]Tracy & Robins (2004). [t]Tracy & Matsumoto (2008). [u]Rozin & Cohen (2003). [v]Ekman & Friesen (1986). [w]Ekman (1992). [x]Levenson, Ekman, & Friesen (1990). [y]Simon-Thomas, et al. (2009). [z]Sauter & Scott (2007). [aa]Schroder (2003). [bb]Sauter, Eisner, Ekman, & Scott (2010). [cc]Dubois et al. (2008). [dd]Hertenstein et al. (2009). [ee]Hertenstein et al. (2006). [ff]Juslin & Laukka (2003). [gg]Hejmadi, Davidson, & Rozin (2000). [hh]Piff et al. (2012).

emotion can be differentiated from expressions of other emotions. We note the relative paucity of emotion encoding studies linking the experience of a distinct emotion with spontaneous expressive behavior: All of the studies of emotion-related voice and touch are recognition and production studies; select studies of the face have documented spontaneous behaviors that uniquely relate to the experience of distinct emotions (e.g., Gonzaga et al., 2001, on love and desire; Keltner, 1995, on embarrassment, amusement, and shame). Turning to the extant evidence, in the respective columns, "yes" indicates that the evidence suggests that the emotion is communicated in a modality at above chance levels; "no" indicates that the emotion cannot be reliably communicated in the modality. These data make the case for distinct expression of 24 emotional states when different modalities are considered, although we note that few if any studies have looked at multimodal expressions of emotion.

This new literature reveals that there are more emotions than the "basic six" and that emotions can be expressed in nonfacial modalities. These discoveries speak to the promise of a multimodal approach to emotional expression. Several critical questions await attention. Most notably, few if any production studies have examined how the different modalities of expression—face, voice, touch, body, and gaze activity—covary during emotional expressions. Few if any emotion recognition studies have addressed whether multimodal expressions are more reliably recognized than single modality expressions, for example in the face or voice—largely the focus of research to the present date.

PATTERNS OF EMOTIONAL EXPRESSION VARY WITHIN EMOTION AND ACROSS INDIVIDUALS AND CULTURES

Within traditional basic emotion theory, the focus has been on prototypical facial expressions, namely facial expressions that involve the fullest combination of actions that covary with a state and are "best examples" of the expressions associated with an emotion (Ekman, 1992). This has been a prerequisite of the still photograph method, so profoundly influential in the field, which demanded focusing on behaviors that characterize paradigmatic cases of the emotion and can be captured with a snapshot (e.g., the tightened lips, teeth bare, furrowed brow, and glare during prototypical episodes of anger).

As critics have pointed out, this focus has led to a neglect of less prototypical expressions of emotions, namely expressions of emotion that do not involve the full complement of signaling behaviors specific to the state or that involve other behaviors that vary more in whether or not they occur during an emotional experience (e.g., the face touch during embarrassment). These latter behaviors are more likely to vary across context, individuals, or cultures. Once we expand the focus from prototypical momentary expressions to *all* expressions of any given emotion, it becomes clear that there is no one-to-one correspondence between a specific set of facial muscle actions or vocal cues and any and every experience of an emotion; instead, this approach suggests probabilistic associations between the multimodal behaviors and the occurrence of the emotion.

One clear implication is that there will be significant variation within a category of emotion (e.g., embarrassment, awe) in the patterns of behavior that covary with the occurrence of the emotion, most typically ascertained with self-report measures. For example, in an early study of the expressive behavior of embarrassment, it was found that different patterns of behavior arose during the experience of embarrassment (Keltner, 1995; for similar evidence concerning pride, see Tracy & Robins, 2004). Most displays of embarrassment involved gaze down, head movements down, and awkward smiles, but some involved face touching, some involved shoulder shrugs, and some involved pained, self-conscious vocalizations. Additionally, the more expressions of embarrassment include the full complement of prototypical features—the gaze down, head movement down, awkward smile, face touch–the more naïve observers reliably recognize the emotion in the display. Studies of emotion-related tactile contact similarly find variation in the patterns of tactile behavior (location, pressure, configuration of hand) within the expression of one emotion, such as gratitude or sympathy (Hertenstein et al., 2006).

In moving away from the assumption that there is necessarily a one-to-one correspondence between emotional experience and specific expressive behaviors, empirical research can capture different sources of emotion-related variation in expressive behavior. A first is to study subtypes of an emotion, which vary according to specific appraisal themes. Emotion concepts such as "embarrassment" or "awe" or "anger" actually refer to a variety of states within that emotion family (Fehr & Russell, 1984). For example, people experience awe that varies in the sense of beauty, fear, and supernatural causation (Keltner & Haidt, 2003). The challenge for future research will be to map specific variations of an emotional state—such as awe involving threat versus no threat—to specific elements of the pattern of expressive behavior.

A second source of variation consists of cultural differences in the multimodal expression of emotions. As an illustration, in one recent study participants in five different cultures—China, India, Japan, Korea, and the United States—heard 22 emotion-specific situations in their native language and were asked to express the emotion in whatever fashion they desired, which could include facial, vocal, or bodily expressions (Cordaro, 2013). The only instruction was that the expressions were to be nonverbal. Over 5,500 facial expressions, bodily movements, gaze movements, hand gestures, and patterns of breathing were coded using an expanded Facial Action Coding System

(Ekman & Friesen, 1978), and a large subset of these was analyzed for patterns across and within cultures. For all emotions studied, certain collections of expressive behaviors were frequently observed across all five cultural groups, which were deemed *international core sequences*—the prototypical elements of the multimodal hyperspace of variation in emotional expression. Across cultures the expression of awe, for example, tended to involve the widening of the eyes and a smile as well as a head movement up. Across cultures, head nods expressed interest. Confusion was generally expressed with behaviors including furrowed brows, narrowed eyes, and a head tilt. At the same time, there were certain patterns of behavior that were observed within, but not between, cultures, and these were deemed *culturally varying sequences.* These patterns of expressive behavior were unique to the culture and have been called "emotion accents" in other studies (Elfenbein, 2013). We propose that these cultural accents are shaped by display rules that predicate the amplification or masking of emotional displays according to the value attached to the specific emotion.

SEARCH FOR NEUROPHYSIOLOGICAL CORRELATES OF EMOTIONAL EXPRESSION

Within basic emotion theory, it is assumed that emotions involve emotion-specific physiology, which enables specific behaviors in response to eliciting stimuli—flight, skin-to-skin contact, the widening of the eyes to take in more information, clasping, and striking. On this view, expressive behaviors are elements of more complex, emotion-specific patterns of action, useful in our evolutionary past (e.g., Darwin, 1872; Shariff & Tracy, 2011). This analysis suggests that patterns of expression should covary with activation in different neurophysiological systems that are conserved across mammals. Early studies of emotion-specific physiology focused on a limited set of emotions and select measures of peripheral physiology—heart rate, skin conductance, temperature of the skin (Levenson, Ekman, & Friesen, 1990).

New discoveries of multimodal patterns of expression of a far wider array of emotions than the basic six have enabled new areas of inquiry in the search for emotion-specific physiology. For example, brief nonverbal displays of love (Duchenne smile, head tilt, open-handed gestures) correlate with oxytocin release, whereas cues of sexual desire (lip licks, lip puckers) do not (Gonzaga et al., 2006), a finding that is in keeping with functional analyses of oxytocin as a motivator of commitment and the provision of care in mammalian species (Keltner et al., 2014). Sympathy-related oblique eyebrow movements relate to increased activation in the vagus nerve, a branch of the parasympathetic autonomic nervous system that supports caregiving in mammals (Eisenberg et al., 1989; Stellar, Cohen, Oveis, & Keltner, 2015). Again, this is in keeping with

Table 4.3 ASSOCIATIONS BETWEEN EMOTIONAL EXPRESSION AND NEUROPHYSIOLOGICAL RESPONSE

Emotion	Neurophysiological Response
Awe	Piloerection
Embarrassment	Blush response
Love	Oxytocin release
Pride	Testosterone release
Shame	Cytokine release
Sympathy	Vagus nerve elevation

functional analyses of sympathy as a caregiving emotion. Still other studies have documented that dominance-related postural expansion associated with pride elevates levels of testosterone, a hormone thought to be involved in the signaling of elevated status (Carney, Cuddy, & Yap, 2010).

In Table 4.3 we summarize these findings. For example, the cytokine system is part of an inflammation response and is associated with submissive responses in nonhuman species, and shame in humans (Dickerson & Kemeny, 2004), and we would suggest, shame-related displays. Recent self-report studies find unique associations between cold shivers and fear and disgust, and between goosebumps (piloerection) and awe (Campos et al., 2013; Maruskin et al., 2012). By integrating studies of multimodal expressions for a variety of emotions other than the basic six with advances in neurophysiology, new insights are gained into emotion-specific physiology. Critical questions await empirical attention. Most notably, it will be important to examine the temporal sequences in which experience, expression, and emotion-specific physiology unfold, and the degree of coherence between these systems.

MAMMALIAN PRECURSORS TO HUMAN EMOTIONAL EXPRESSION

Critical to basic emotion theory is the notion that human emotional expression arose during the process of mammalian evolution and, by implication, that there should be compelling homologies between human and nonhuman display behavior. Careful cross-species comparisons between human and nonhuman expressive behavior have revealed functional origins of laughter, smiling, embarrassment, affiliative cues involved in love, sexual signaling, threat displays, and dominance (for review, see Keltner et al., in press). Careful analyses of nonhuman vocal display find distinct displays for sex, food, affiliation, caregiving, and threat (Snowdon, 2003).

These cross-species comparisons are critical to functional claims so central to basic emotion theory: that emotional expressions serve specific functions within social contexts common to many mammals—for example, that human embarrassment resembles the behaviors of other species' appeasement displays, and triggers similar patterns of conflict de-escalating reconciliation (Keltner & Buswell, 1997). This search for mammalian precursors, an enduring theme in basic emotion theory, points to a means to understand the deeper origins of human emotion, providing suggestive evidence of what patterns of mammalian social behavior gave rise to human emotional expression. For example, it is interesting to speculate how human expressions of gratitude involved in touch (Hertenstein et al., 2006) trace back to the grooming exchanges and food sharing in primates that support reciprocal sharing and cooperation (de Waal, 1996). It is provocative but speculative to consider how the contexts in which nonhuman piloerection occur might inform the understanding of the evolution of awe. How do rodent displays of shuddering and shivering give rise to our own shudders of social disgust? Looking to nonhuman species is a critical means by which basic emotion theory reveals the origins of different emotions.

GRADIENTS OF RECOGNITION IN UNIVERSAL RECOGNITION OF EMOTIONAL EXPRESSION

Emotion recognition studies have sought to ascertain the extent to which emotional expressions—facial expressions and vocalizations in particular—are recognized in different cultures (Gendron et al., 2014; Haidt & Keltner, 1999; Sauter et al., 2014). Subsequent critiques of this literature have brought into focus the limitations of forced-choice paradigms, the need to study more ecologically valid displays, and the continuing need to study cultures who have not been influenced by media portrayals of emotional expression (Gendron et al., 2014; Haidt & Keltner, 1999; Russell, 1994; Sauter et al., 2014).

Yet another advance in this area of research is the notion that emotions vary in the degree to which they can be reliably signaled, in the sense that there are gradients of recognition (Haidt & Keltner, 1999; Russell, 1994). As one illustration, in a recent study, Cordaro (2013), guided by the emotion expression taxonomy represented in Table 4.4, produced static photos of 18 emotions expressed in the face and body, and presented these photos to naïve observers in 10 cultures: China, Japan, Korea, New Zealand, Germany, Poland, Pakistan, India, Turkey, and the United States. Those participants were required to choose the best label, from four emotion labels of the same valence as well as "none of the above," that matched the expression in the photo. The photos are portrayed in Table 4.4, and the data from this study, summed across cultures, are presented in Figure 4.1.

Table 4.4 FACIAL EXPRESSION EXAMPLES, FACS ACTION UNITS, AND PHYSICAL DESCRIPTIONS FOR EACH EXPRESSION

Emotion	Example photo	Action units	Physical description
Amusement	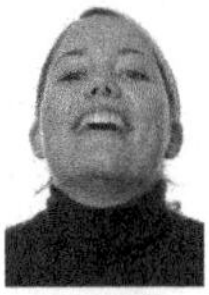	6+7+12+25+26+53	Head back, Duchenne smile, lips separated, jaw dropped
Anger		4+5+17+23+24	Brows furrowed, eyes wide, lips tightened and pressed together
Boredom		43+55	Eyelids drooping, head tilted, (not scored with FACS: slouched posture, head resting on hand)
Confusion		4+7+56	Brows furrowed, eyelids narrowed, head tilted
Contentment		12+43	Smile, eyelids drooping
Coyness		6+7+12+25+26+52+54+61	Duchenne smile, lips separated, head turned and down, eyes turned opposite to head turn
Desire		19+25+26+43	Tongue show, lips parted, jaw dropped, eyelids drooping
Disgust	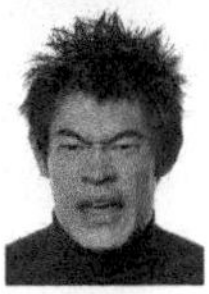	7+9+19+25+26	Eyes narrowed, nose wrinkled, lips parted, jaw dropped, tongue show
Embarrassment		7+12+15+52+54+64	Eyelids narrowed, controlled smile, head turned and down, (not scored with FACS: hand touches face)

(*continued*)

Table 4.4 CONTINUED

Emotion	Example photo	Action units	Physical description
Fear		1+2+4+5+7+20+25	Eyebrows raised and pulled together, upper eyelid raised, lower eyelid tense, lips parted and stretched
Happiness		6+7+12+25+26	Duchenne display
Interest		1+2+12	Eyebrows raised, slight smile
Pain		4+6+7+9+17+18+23+24	Eyes tightly closed, nose wrinkled, brows furrowed, lips tight, pressed together, and slightly puckered
Pride		53+64	Head up, eyes down
Sadness		1+4+6+15+17	Brows knitted, eyes slightly tightened, lip corners depressed, lower lip raised
Shame		54+64	Head down, eyes down
Surprise	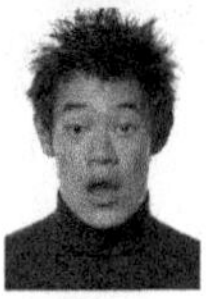	1+2+5+25+26	Eyebrows raised, upper eyelid raised, lips parted, jaw dropped
Sympathy		1+17+24+57	Inner eyebrow raised, lower lip raised, lips pressed together, head slightly forward

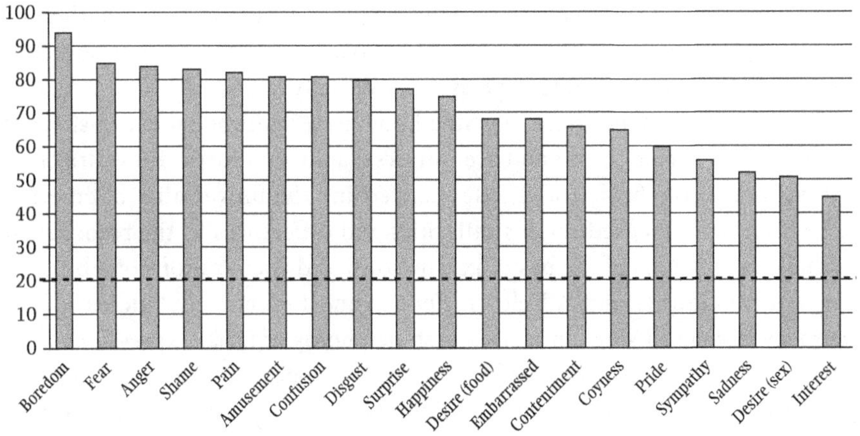

Figure 4.1 Recognition rates in identifying 19 emotional expressions in the face and body across 10 cultures. Dashed lines indicate chance levels of guessing (20%).

The dashed lines represent levels of recognition that would be observed by chance guessing alone, which would be 20% given that participants chose one label from five options in each judgment. What one can see in Figure 4.1 is clear evidence that when static photos capture head movements, gaze activity, and face touching, many more emotions than the basic six can be recognized, even in static photos, as we have been arguing. These data also illustrate something systematically observed in nearly every recognition study: Some emotions are more easily recognized than others (e.g., boredom is more easily recognized than interest). Framing the debate about the recognition of emotion across cultures in either/or terms does not represent what the evidence more typically reveals, that there are gradients of recognition, with some emotions more reliably recognized than others.

TOWARD THE FUTURE EMPIRICAL STUDY OF EMOTIONAL EXPRESSION

The study of emotional expression has changed dramatically in the past 20 years. The field is now investigating a much wider array of emotions and how they are expressed in dynamic, multimodal patterns of behavior. Significant advances have been made in understanding the neurophysiological correlates of these patterns of behavior, and their homologues in other mammals.

We end with several critical questions. First, it is striking how few emotion encoding studies there are wherein researchers study how expressive behavior correlates with emotional experience; instead, almost all studies we have considered have been emotion recognition studies, as illustrated earlier, or emotion production studies wherein participants are given an emotion concept ("disgust") and asked to express it nonverbally.

Similarly, few studies have examined how well multimodal expressions of emotion can be recognized and are universal across cultures. These are critical lacunae in the field. The debates concerning the universality of emotion have been more focused upon similarities and differences in the recognition of facial expressions of the basic six emotions, and vocalizations of a broader array of emotions (Haidt & Keltner, 1999). Almost exclusively, studies of universality have used single modalities: static photos of facial expressions (e.g., Matsumoto et al., 2008) or brief vocal bursts or epochs of emotional prosody (Juslin & Laukka, 2003) or videos of emotional tactile contact (Hertenstein et al., 2006). Across these kinds of studies emotion recognition across cultures tends to hover between 55% and 70%, where chance guessing would yield accuracy levels between 12.5% and 25%, depending on estimates of chance. We believe accuracy levels may typically be higher once multimodal expressions, which are much closer to the natural expressions we should ultimately be focusing on, are presented rather than unimodal expressions.

Finally, it will be important to move beyond emotion matching paradigms, where single emotion words are matched to stimuli, and to move to free response studies that investigate the communicative dimensions of multimodal emotional expressions. The problem with forced-choice studies is not only that they inflate consensus (Russell, 1994), but also that they wrongly suggest that what matters from a communicative point of view is only which discrete emotion the subject is experiencing. But it is clear that emotional expressions can signal multiple things besides interior experiences ("I feel grateful"): They can signal intentions ("I would like to kiss you"), relations with the perceiver ("you are more powerful than me"), assessments of the eliciting situation ("the actions of that officer are unjust"), and trait-like tendencies ("I am hostile").

We suggest that specific expressive modalities may communicate different kinds of information. For example, body movement—expanding versus concave chest—differentiates the displays of pride and shame and would seem to relate to the relational dimension of dominance and submissiveness. Eye contact versus gaze aversion may instead signal behavioral intentions, namely social approach versus withdrawal. Understanding the role of each expressive modality in the communication of distinct types of information will be crucial for understanding how emotions evolved.

Finally, debates over the universality of emotional expressions have too often been carried out in dichotomous terms, with the two sides debating whether expressions are universal. New developments in the study of emotional expression suggest that it is time to move away from such Manichean formulations. The extent to which a certain pattern of expressive behavior is universally produced and recognized in radically different cultures will vary according to the emotion (e.g., anger may be more recognizable than sadness), its modality of expression (e.g., relief may be recognizable in the voice but not in the face), its subtype (e.g., awe about beauty may be more recognizable than awe about supernatural causation), and the culture in which it is presented (e.g., Japanese facial expressions may be better recognized by Japanese people). We hope that the new perspective we have offered here concerning dynamic, multimodal expressions, grounded in basic emotion theory, sets the stage for studies seeking answers to these and other questions.

ACKNOWLEDGMENTS

This essay benefitted enormously from the thoughtful recommendations of Andrea Scarantino.

REFERENCES

Aviezer, H., Trope, Y., & Todorov, A. (2012). Body cues, not facial expressions, discriminate between intense positive and negative emotions. *Science, 338*(6111), 1225–1229.

Barrett, L. F., Lindquist, K. A., & Gendron, M. (2007). Language as context for the perception of emotion. *Trends in Cognitive Sciences, 11*(8), 327–332.

Botvinick, M., Jha, A. P., Bylsma, L. M., Fabian, S. A., Solomon, P. E., & Prkachin, K. M. (2005). Viewing facial expressions of pain engages cortical areas involved in the direct experience of pain. *Neuroimage, 25*(1), 312–319.

Bretherton, I., & Ainsworth, M. D. S. (1974). Responses of one-year-olds to a stranger in a strange situation. In M. Lewis & L. A. Rosenblum (Eds.), *The origin of fear* (pp. 131–164). New York, NY: Wiley.

Campos, B., Shiota, M., Keltner, D., Gonzaga, G., & Goetz, J. (2013). What is shared, what is different? Core relational themes and expressive displays of eight positive emotions. *Cognition & Emotion, 27*, 37–52.

Carney, D. R., Cuddy, A. J., & Yap, A. J. (2010). Power posing brief nonverbal displays affect neuroendocrine levels and risk tolerance. *Psychological Science, 21*(10), 1363–1368.

Cordaro, D. T. (2013). Universals and cultural variations in expression in five cultures. Unpublished doctoral dissertation, University of California, Berkeley.

Darwin, C. (1872/1998). *The expression of the emotions in man and animals* (3rd ed.). New York, NY: Oxford University Press.

De Waal, F. B. (1996). *Good natured* (No. 87). Cambridge, MA: Harvard University Press.

Dickerson, S. S., & Kemeny, M. E. (2004). Acute stressors and cortisol responses: A theoretical integration and synthesis of laboratory research. *Psychological Bulletin, 130*(3), 355.

Dubois, A., Bringuier, S., Capdevilla, X., & Pry, R. (2008). Vocal and verbal expression of postoperative pain in preschoolers. *Pain Management Nursing, 9*(4), 160–165.

Eisenberg, N., Fabes, R. A., Miller, P. A., Fultz, J., Shell, R., Mathy, R. M., & Reno, R. R. (1989). Relation of sympathy and personal distress to prosocial behavior: A multimethod study. *Journal of Personality and Social Psychology, 57*(1), 55.

Ekman, P. (1992). All emotions are basic. In P. Ekman & R. J. Davidson (Eds.), *The nature of emotion* (pp. 15–19). New York, NY: Oxford University Press.

Ekman, P., & Cordaro, D. (2011). What is meant by calling emotions basic. *Emotion Review, 3*(4), 364–370.

Ekman, P., & Friesen, W. V. (1978). *Facial Action Coding System: Investigator's Guide.* Palo Alto, CA: Consulting Psychologists Press.

Ekman, P., & Friesen, W. V. (1986). A new pan-cultural facial expression of emotion. *Motivation and Emotion, 10*(2), 159–168.

Ekman, P., & Rosenberg, E. L. (Eds.). (1997). *What the face reveals: Basic and applied studies of spontaneous expression using the Facial Action Coding System (FACS).* New York, NY: Oxford University Press.

Ekman, P., Sorenson, E. R., & Friesen, W. V. (1969). Pan-cultural elements in the facial display of emotions. *Science*, 164, 86–88.

Ekman, P. E., & Davidson, R. J. (1994). *The nature of emotion: Fundamental questions.* New York, NY: Oxford University Press.

Elfenbein, H. A. (2013). Nonverbal dialects and accents in facial expressions of emotion. *Emotion Review, 5*(1), 90–96.

Elfenbein, H. A., & Ambady, N. (2002). On the universality and cultural specificity of emotion regulation: A meta-analysis. *Psychological Bulletin, 128*(2), 203–235.

Fehr, B., & Russell, J. (1984). Concept of emotion viewed from a prototype perspective. *Journal of Experimental Psychology, General, 113*, 464–486.

Flack, W. (2006). Peripheral feedback effects of facial expressions, bodily postures, and vocal expressions on emotional feelings. *Cognition & Emotion, 20*(2), 177–195.

Fridlund, A. J. (1991). Evolution and facial action in reflex, social motive, and paralanguage. *Biological Psychology, 32*(1), 3–100.

Frijda, N. H. (1986). *The emotions*. New York, NY: Cambridge University Press.

Gendron, M., Roberson, D., van der Vyver, J. M., & Barrett, L. F. (2014). Cultural relativity in perceiving emotion from vocalizations. *Psychological Science, 25*(4), 911–920.

Goetz, J. L., Keltner, D., & Simon-Thomas, E. (2010). Compassion: An evolutionary analysis and empirical review. *Psychological Bulletin, 136*(3), 351–374.

Gonzaga, G. C., Turner, R. A., Keltner, D., Campos, B., & Altemus, M. (2006). Romantic love and sexual desire in close relationships. *Emotion, 6*(2), 163.

Grunau, R. V., & Craig, K. D. (1987). Pain expression in neonates: Facial action and cry. *Pain, 28*(3), 395–410.

Haidt, J., & Keltner, D. (1999). Culture and facial expression: Open-ended methods find more faces and a gradient of recognition. *Cognition & Emotion, 13*, 225–266.

Hejmadi, A., Davidson, R. J., & Rozin, P. (2000). Exploring Hindu Indian emotion expressions: Evidence for accurate recognition by Americans and Indians. *Psychological Science, 11*(3), 183–187.

Hertenstein, M. J., Holmes, R., McCullough, M., & Keltner, D. (2009). The communication of emotion via touch. *Emotion, 9*(4), 566.

Hertenstein, M. J., Keltner, D., App, B., Bulleit, B. A., & Jaskolka, A. R. (2006). Touch communicates distinct emotions. *Emotion, 6*(3), 528.

Hess, U., & Fischer, A. (2013). Emotional mimicry as social regulation. *Personality and Social Psychology Review*, 17(2), 142–157.

Juslin, P. N., & Laukka, P. (2003). Communication of emotions in vocal expression and music performance: Different channels, same code? *Psychological Bulletin, 129*(5), 770.

Keltner, D. (1995). Signs of appeasement: Evidence for the distinct displays of embarrassment, amusement, and shame. *Journal of Personality and Social Psychology, 68*(3), 441–454.

Keltner, D. (1996). Evidence for the distinctness of embarrassment, shame, and guilt: A study of recalled antecedents and facial expressions of emotion. *Cognition & Emotion, 10*(2), 155–172.

Keltner, D. (2009). *Born to be good: The science of a meaningful life.* New York, NY: WW Norton & Company.

Keltner, D., & Bonanno, G. A. (1997). A study of laughter and dissociation: Distinct correlates of laughter and smiling during bereavement. *Journal of Personality and Social Psychology, 73*(4), 687.

Keltner, D., & Buswell, B. N. (1997). Embarrassment: Its distinct form and appeasement functions. *Psychological Bulletin, 122*(3), 250.

Keltner, D., & Haidt, J. (2003). Approaching awe: A moral, spiritual, and aesthetic emotion. *Cognition & Emotion, 17*(2), 297–314.

Keltner, D., & Haidt, J. A. (2001). Social functions of emotions. In T. Mayne & G.A. Bonanno (Eds.), *Emotions: Current Issues and future directions.* New York, NY: Guilford Press.

Keltner, D., Kogan, A., Piff, P. K., & Saturn, S. R. (2014). The sociocultural appraisals, values, and emotions (SAVE) framework of prosociality: Core processes from gene to meme. *Annual Review of Psychology, 65*, 425–460.

Keltner, D., & Kring, A. M. (1998). Emotion, social function, and psychopathology. *Review of General Psychology, 2*(3), 320–342.

Keltner, D., & Lerner, J. (2010). Emotion. In S.T. Fiske, D.T. Giblert, and G. Lindzey (Eds.), *Handbook of social psychology*, Volume 1 (pp. 317–342). Hoboken, NJ: John Wiley & Sons, Inc.

Keltner, D., & Shiota, M. N. (2003). New displays and new emotions: A commentary on Rozin and Cohen (2003).

Keltner, D., Tracy, J., Sauter, D., Cordaro, D., & McNeil, G. (2016). Emotional expression. In L. F. Barrett, M. Lewis, & J.M. Haviland-Jones (Ed.), *Handbook of emotion* (pp. 467–482). New York, NY: Guilford Press.

Levenson, R. W., Ekman, P., & Friesen, W. V. (1990). Voluntary facial action generates emotion-specific autonomic nervous system activity. *Psychophysiology, 27*(4), 363–384.

Maruskin, L. A., Thrash, T. M., & Elliot, A. J. (2012). The chills as a psychological construct: Content universe, factor structure, affective composition, elicitors, trait antecedents, and consequences. *Journal of Personality and Social Psychology, 103*(1), 135.

Matsumoto, D., et al. (2008). Facial expressions of emotion. In M. Lewis, J.M. Haviland-Jones, & L. Feldman-Barrett (Eds.), *Handbook of emotions* (3rd ed., pp. 211–234). New York, NY: The Guilford Press.

Ortony, A., & Turner, T. J. (1990). What's basic about basic emotions? *Psychological Review, 97*(3), 315.

Oveis, C., Horberg, E. J., & Keltner, D. (2010). Compassion, pride, and social intuitions of self-other similarity. *Journal of Personality and Social Psychology, 98*(4), 618.

Piff, P. K., Purcell, A., Gruber, J., Hertenstein, M. J., & Keltner, D. (2012). Contact high: Mania proneness and positive perception of emotional touches. *Cognition & Emotion, 26*(6), 1116–1123.

Prkachin, K. M. (1992). The consistency of facial expressions of pain: A comparison across modalities. *Pain, 51*(3), 297–306.

Reddy, V. (2000). Coyness in early infancy. *Developmental Science, 3*(2), 186–192.

Reddy, V. (2005). Feeling shy and showing-off: Self-conscious emotions must regulate self-awareness. In J. Nadel & D. Muir *Emotional Development*, 183–204, Oxford: Oxford University Press.

Reeve, J. (1993). The face of interest. *Motivation and Emotion, 17*(4), 353–375.

Rozin, P., & Cohen, A. B. (2003). High frequency of facial expressions corresponding to confusion, concentration, and worry in an analysis of naturally occurring facial expressions of Americans. *Emotion, 3*(1), 68.

Russell, J. A. (1994). Is there universal recognition of emotion from facial expressions? A review of the cross-cultural studies. *Psychological Bulletin, 115*(1), 102–141.

Sauter, D. A., Eisner, F., Ekman, P., & Scott, S. K. (2010). Cross-cultural recognition of basic emotions through nonverbal emotional vocalizations. *Proceedings of the National Academy of Sciences, 107*(6), 2408–2412.

Sauter, D. A., Gangi, D., McDonald, N., & Messinger, D. S. (2014). Nonverbal expressions of positive emotions. In M. N. Shiota, M. M. Tugade, and L. D. Kirby (Eds.), *Handbook of positive emotion* (pp. 179–200). New York, NY: Guilford Press.

Sauter, D. A., & Scott, S. K. (2007). More than one kind of happiness: Can we recognize vocal expressions of different positive states? *Motivation and Emotion, 31*(3), 192–199.

Scherer, K. R., & Ellgring, H. (2007). Multimodal expression of emotion: Affect programs or componential appraisal patterns? *Emotion, 7*(1), 158.

Shariff, A. F., & Tracy, J. L. (2011). What are emotion expressions for? *Current Directions in Psychological Science, 20*(6), 395–399.

Shiota, M. N., Campos, B., & Keltner, D. (2003). The faces of positive emotion: Prototype displays of awe, amusement, and pride. *Annals of the New York Academy of Sciences, 1000*, 296.

Shiota, M. N., Keltner, D., & Mossman, A. (2007). The nature of awe: Elicitors, appraisals, and effects on self-concept. *Cognition & Emotion, 21*(5), 944–963.

Silvia, P. J. (2008). Interest—The curious emotion. *Current Directions in Psychological Science, 17*(1), 57–60.

Simon-Thomas, E. R., Keltner, D. J., Sauter, D., Sinicropi-Yao, L., & Abramson, A. (2009). The voice conveys specific emotions: Evidence from vocal burst displays. *Emotion, 9*(6), 838.

Snowdon, C. T. (2003). Expression of emotion in nonhuman animals. In R. J. Davidson, K. Scherer, & H. H. Goldsmith (Eds.), *Handbook of affective sciences* (pp. 457–534). New York, NY: Oxford University Press.

Stellar, J. E., Cohen, A., Oveis, C., & Keltner, D. (2015, January 26). Affective and physiological responses to the suffering of others: Compassion and vagal activity. *Journal of Personality and Social Psychology.* Advance online publication.

Tracy, J. L., & Matsumoto, D. (2008). The spontaneous expression of pride and shame: Evidence for biologically innate nonverbal displays. *Proceedings of the National Academy of Sciences, 105*(33), 11655–11660.

Tracy, J. L., & Robins, R. W. (2004). Show your pride evidence for a discrete emotion expression. *Psychological Science, 15*(3), 194–197.

Van Kleef, G. A. (2009). How emotions regulate social life: The emotions as social information (EASI) model. *Current Directions in Psychological Science, 18*, 184–188.

Williams, A. C. (2002). Facial expression of pain, empathy, evolution, and social learning. *Behavioral and Brain Sciences, 25*(04), 475–480.

5

The Behavioral Ecology View of Facial Displays, 25 Years Later

ALAN J. FRIDLUND

The behavioral ecology view (BECV) of facial expressions represents a wholly different way of understanding our facial behavior than the reigning basic emotions theory (BET). BECV contends that our facial expressions are fundamentally social, attuned to the context of social interactions, and serve to shape the trajectories of those interactions. BECV is functionalist, "externalist," and independent of essentialist theories of emotion such as BET. I review here the evolution of BECV from fringe theory to mainstream BET counterpoint.[1]

THE BEHAVIORAL ECOLOGY VIEW'S ORIGINS LIE IN THE BASIC EMOTIONS THEORY'S SHORTCOMINGS

I am, frankly, an apostate of BET, and only by being an insider did I come to realize its shortcomings. In most formulations, BET held that emotions, understood as internal states or discrete affect categories, were associated with specific patterned movements termed "facial expressions of emotion." The foundation for BET was research in which members of diverse cultures matched a small number of photos of posed facial expressions to a similarly small number of emotion terms, suitably translated or mapped onto stories (Ekman, 1972; Ekman & Friesen, 1971; Ekman, Sorenson, & Friesen, 1969; Izard, 1971). These matching-to-sample studies, jointly with other evidence, were declared to mean that (1) the emotions signified by the terms/stories were "biologically based," that is, they were phylogenetic; (2) the emotional facial expressions matched to the emotion terms were uniform in their production and universal in their recognition; and (3) there was an automatic, causal link between the prototypical emotional faces and the respective internal emotional mechanisms (collectively, the "Facial Affect Program") that produced them. In BET, any deviation from the predicted correspondence between a triggered emotion and the emission of its counterpart facial expression was due to the intervention of cultural "display rules" governing social behavior (Ekman & Friesen, 1969). Such culturally dependent control was imperfect, however, and so a muted, throttled, or distorted expression might "leak" traces of the suppressed, genuine emotion of the expressor onto the face.

At the start of my career, BET was the dominant framework for studying emotion and facial expression, and I had no reason to challenge it. I began by conducting electromyographic studies of the tiny facial movements people made during emotional imagery (Fridlund, Schwartz, & Fowler, 1984), work begun by Paul Fair and Gary Schwartz (Schwartz, Fair, Salt, Mandel, & Klerman, 1976). Gary invited me to his Yale lab to conduct my doctoral studies, and he introduced me to Silvan Tomkins. Later he arranged for me to meet Carroll Izard and Paul Ekman, the two leading BET theorists at the time. I came to know both men well, and I may be the only person to have written papers with each (Ekman & Fridlund, 1987; Fridlund, Ekman, & Oster, 1988; Fridlund & Izard, 1983; Matsumoto, Ekman, & Fridlund, 1990). Over time, however, I developed unresolvable disagreements with them over the tenets of BET.

My skepticism grew with several realizations: (1) the cross-cultural findings could never have been helpful in apportioning roles to "biology" versus "culture," because both diversity and uniformity can arise from natural selection (e.g., Darwin's Galapagos finches showed *adaptive radiation*, developing different beak shapes suited to the food available on each island, whereas creatures like bats and birds with different phyletic histories showed *convergent evolution*, evolving superficially similar structures for flight); (2) claiming cross-cultural uniformity for certain iconic facial expressions after obtaining matches to emotion categories, *and* universality of those "basic emotions" based on the same matches, was circular and tautological; (3) on closer inspection, the matching between facial displays and emotion terms/stories began to appear inflated to me and other researchers, due to technical deficiencies in the experimental protocols; and, most important, (4) regarding the face as an automatic but suppressible readout of internal, "authentic" emotional states conflicted with modern views of animal communication. This last point was most critical in convincing me that BET was fatally flawed.

HOW DARWIN'S REFLEXOLOGY OF EXPRESSION WAS SUPPLANTED AND LEFT BASIC EMOTIONS THEORY STRANDED

Darwin first attempted systematically to link animal signaling with our facial expressions, and BET theorists duly pay homage to him, but misread him when they cite him to support their claim that our facial expressions evolved "to express emotion" (see Fridlund, 1992a). In promulgating evolution by natural selection, Darwin had first to dispose of a contending position: the argument from design, made by Charles Bell, William Paley, and others, which held that creatures were well suited to their niches because *God made them so*. Thus, in *On the Origin of Species*, Darwin could not repeat identical evidence of goodness-of-fit and then argue a different conclusion. Instead, he used evidence of *imperfect* design—vestigial structures such as webbed feet on land birds, phalanges in a seal's flipper, and the human appendix—as proof of common origins and to vitiate notions of perfect design ex nihilo (Browne, 1985; Darwin, 1859; Fridlund, 1992a; Gruber, 1974).

In *The Expression of the Emotions in Man and Animals*, Darwin extended his assault on the design argument to Bell's view of facial expressions: "I want, anyhow, to upset Sir C. Bell's view . . . that certain muscles have been given to man solely that he may reveal to other men his feelings" (F. Darwin, 1887, Vol. 2, p. 78.). He proposed instead that, as with vestigial organs, most facial behaviors were likewise rudimentary *and* "of no service, often of much disservice," or "purposeless" (Darwin, 1872, pp. 67, 76). They were largely remnants of reflexes that had been useful ancestrally ("serviceable associated habits"), with any communicative value incidental. Although Darwin's account neutered Bell's creationism, it left him unequipped to argue that facial expressions evolved *for* anything (Fridlund, 1992a).

While honoring Darwin, BET actually co-opted the 1950s mechanistic ethology of Lorenz and Tinbergen (Lorenz, 1967, 1970; Tinbergen, 1952, 1953). These early ethologists' tripwire fixed-action patterns became the "Facial Affect Program" of the neurocultural version of BET (even the "FAP" acronyms were identical; Fridlund, 1992b). Instead of red spots on beaks that released appeasement displays and food calls, prototypical emotional events triggered the release ("expression") of emotion that spilled out on our faces and reflected our "true feelings" except if modified by tradition ("display rules"), training, or treachery.

If BET was drawing upon the Lorenz-Tinbergen formulations, modern ethology was abandoning them, leaving BET gutted of its claim to Darwin's imprimatur and severing BET from any continuity with developing models of animal communication. Animal behaviorists began to note that most nonhuman signals didn't look fixed or cartooney, but flexible, social, and contextual (Alcock, 1984; Hinde, 1985a, 1985b; Smith, 1977). Such *behavioral ecologists* (cf. Davies, Krebs, & West, 2012; Maynard Smith, 1982) saw animal signaling not as vestigial reflexes, or readouts of internal state, but as adaptations that served the interests of signalers within their social environments. Signaler and recipient—even when they were predator and prey (e.g., "pursuit deterrence" signals; see Caro, 2005)—were reconceived as coevolved dyads in which displays indicated the likely behavior of issuers, with recipients using such behavior as cues to the issuers' next moves (Krebs & Davies, 1987; Krebs & Dawkins, 1984).

Although Darwin's vestigial reflexology in *Expression* was outdated, modern behavioral ecology's view of expressive behavior as dynamic and contextual suggested a way to preserve Darwin's grander vision of continuity between human and nonhuman signaling. Thus, in the 1990s, my colleagues and I began writing position papers and conducting studies on what became the BECV. In this account, human facial displays, like animal signals, serve the momentary "intent" of the displayer toward others in social interaction (Fridlund, 1990, 1991a, 1991b, 1992a, 1992b, 1994, 1996, 1997, 2002, 2006; Fridlund et al., 1990, 1992; Fridlund & Russell, 1996; Gilbert, Fridlund, & Sabini, 1987). ("Intent" here is adduced from people's interactional trajectory; it does not presuppose that people know, can articulate, and/or will disclose what they intend).

REINTERPRETING HUMAN FACIAL EXPRESSIONS: FUNCTION TRUMPS FEELING

Many of the classic, iconic BET expressions can be recast in such intentional, functional terms, although in BECV it is an open question whether these time-worn, hand-picked, photographed expressions are in any way special. In suitable contexts, BET's so-called happy faces solicit affiliation or play, whereas "sad faces" recruit succor, "anger faces" threaten or deter, "fear faces" predict submission or withdrawal, "disgust faces" indicate rejection or intent to spew, and so on (see Table 5.1).

When participants are asked to match the set of iconic BET expressions to functional redescriptions (e.g., "back off or I'll attack"), such redescriptions achieve matching rates equal to emotion terms (e.g., "anger"; Yik, 1999). Unlike emotion terms, however, these functional descriptors imply neither any particular internal state (e.g., one can solicit affiliation or play when happy or unhappy), nor any moral assignations about which signals are "honest" or "genuine" (e.g., a face recruiting succor is not "honest" because one is sad and dishonest when one is not). Such functional descriptions are predicated merely on the view that facial displays are only probabilistic signals of social

Table 5.1 TWO VIEWS OF FACIAL EXPRESSIVE BEHAVIOR: BASIC EMOTIONS THEORY'S "FACIAL EXPRESSIONS OF EMOTIONS" VERSUS BEHAVIORAL ECOLOGY VIEW'S FUNCTIONAL SOCIAL TOOLS

Basic Emotions Theory [Facial "Expressions of Emotion"]	Behavioral Ecology View [Partial Sample of Possible Context-Dependent Functions]
"Felt" (happy, "Duchenne") smile	Intent to play or affiliate
"False" smile (feigned happiness)	Display of courtesy, appeasement
"Sad" face	Recruitment of succor; display of surrender, damage, or vulnerability to damage
"Anger" face	Readiness to attack or subdue
"Leaked" (inhibited) anger	Conflict between attacking and not attacking
"Fear" face	Readiness to submit or escape
"Contentment" face	Readiness to continue current situation/interaction
"Disgust" face	Intent to spew or analogously reject another
"Contempt" face	Display of superiority
"Poker" face (suppressed emotion)	Display of neutrality

intentions that would, in everyday life, be accompanied by the words, vocal prosodies, and gestures congruent with the intent.

According to BECV, facial displays serve as social tools. To wit, in accusing a relationship partner of committing an infidelity, one might exclaim, "You are a stinking, lying turd!" and supply the concordant tone of voice, an upturned nose, and the appropriate hand and finger gestures. All this sound and fury would force a nixing or resetting of the relationship. For BECV, understanding that the shock-and-awe display was a tool for relationship realignment is all it takes to explain why the signaling occurred. Any detour to *qualia* (or other internal proxy for emotion) as causal is extraneous because, in BECV, there is no necessary connection between those signals and any one emotion: The accuser/displayer may have been disgusted, contemptuous, devastated, livid—or relieved or thrilled, if the entire rejection drama was staged to divert the partner from discovering that he or she cheated first.

BET advocates objected to this interactional view of facial displays, noting that "Facial expressions do occur when people are alone . . . and contradict the theoretical proposals of those who view expressions solely as social signals" (Ekman, Davidson & Friesen, 1990, p. 351). To the contrary, being alone physically does not imply that we are alone *psychologically.*

In this social media age, when people have their faces glued to their smartphones and begin and end relationships with right and left swipes, this explanation now seems obvious, but it was originally contentious. Examples in which we are alone but implicitly social are easy to list (Fridlund, 1991a): imagining or misbelieving that others are present (daydreams, flashbacks, or talking to someone who's left the room), interacting with inanimate objects (computers, houseplants), grieving (when we crave reunion), sexual fantasy, soliciting an interaction (recruiting succor with a pained or crying face, as infants do), or preparing for one (rehearsing for a play or interview). In all these cases, individuals may subvocalize—they are "talking to people in their heads"—and any accompanying "solitary" faces would be equally social. It makes no difference if the interactant is *myself*: If I scowl and tell myself, "Now Fridlund, don't screw up!", both my words (*sotto voce*) and accompanying face (*sotto facie*?) serve to keep Fridlund focused and out of trouble.

We showed this experimentally, with human studies that extended novel avian research by the much-missed Peter Marler (Marler, Duffy, & Pickert, 1986a, 1986b). We demonstrated *audience effects* in solitary smiling (Fridlund, 1991b) with audiences that were both explicit (friends were present) and implicit (participants were alone but believed friends were co-participants elsewhere), and with social versus nonsocial imagery (Fridlund et al., 1990, 1992). Several investigators have replicated such *implicit audience effects*, expanding the findings to infants, beyond smiling, and to augmenting versus decrementing effects of friends versus strangers (Hesse, Banse, & Kappas, 1995; Jones, Collins, & Hong, 1991; Schützwohl & Reisenzein, 2012; Wagner & Smith, 1991).

BASIC EMOTIONS THEORY'S TREATMENT OF BEHAVIORAL ECOLOGY VIEW FINDINGS: REPUDIATE, THEN ACCOMMODATE

BET partisans dismissed these findings peremptorily: "No account should be taken of studies that do not distinguish between Duchenne and non-Duchenne smiles" (Ekman & Keltner, 1997, p. 41). "Duchenne smiles," according to BET, were genuine, emotional, "felt" smiles, unlike other, intrinsically social smiles, which might be "false," "phony," or "unfelt" (Ekman & Friesen, 1982; Frank & Ekman, 1993; Frank, Ekman & Friesen, 1993). The criticism was entirely misplaced, since in the implicit-audience studies, the smiles in question varied substantially with sociality but were all emitted in solitude—which, for BET, would make them emotional and genuine (again, Ekman et al., 1990, p. 351).

As Ruth Leys noted (personal communication, March 5, 2015), Ekman soon changed course from dismissing these implicit-sociality findings to accommodating them: "I expect that some display rules are so well established that some people may follow them even when they are alone. And some people when alone may imagine the reactions of others, and then follow the appropriate display rule, as if the others were present. And finally, there may be display rules that specify the management of expression not just with others but when alone" (Ekman, 1997, p. 328). Notably, Ekman did not specify how one might ascertain when such "solitary display rules" were in effect and when they were not.

If Ekman's turnabout solved one problem, it opened up a bigger one. Prior to this change, Ekman contended that solitary facial behavior was free of display rules. Of the paradigmatic Japanese-American study cited most as a demonstration of the display-rules concept (Ekman, 1972; Friesen, 1972), Ekman summarized the findings: "In private, when no display rules to mask expression were operative, we saw the biologically based, evolved, universal facial expressions of emotion. In a social situation, we had shown how rules for the management of expression led to culturally different facial expressions" (Ekman, 1984, p. 321). With Ekman's expansion of BET to include solitary display rules, can it now be certain that the solitary faces observed in the Japanese-American study were display-rule-free and thus "biologically based, evolved, universal facial expressions of emotion"? If so, how would that be verified?

There are wider repercussions. Ekman's concession that private behavior may be conventional like our public behavior reduces considerably the distance between the claims posed by his neurocultural version of BET and those struck earlier by the cultural relativists he so staunchly opposed, such as Margaret Mead and Ray Birdwhistell, who argued for the pervasiveness of cultural learning in all aspects of life.

If the notion of "private" display rules enlarged their role in BET, yet another development appeared to limit them. In the early 1990s, Ekman (1992) adopted Tooby and Cosmides's (1990) loose formulation of emotions as a set of instrumental adaptations, including expressions, that evolved to solve common life tasks such as mating and threat detection. In earlier versions of BET, cultures *had* to evolve display rules to manage our troublesome vestigial Darwinian expressions; in Ekman's post-1992 version of BET, the expressions are not *once*-serviceable but serviceable *now*. Extending display rules to private life while adopting a view of emotion that doesn't need them, or need them as much, is an issue of theoretical coherence that BET theorists have not resolved or even acknowledged.

Findings that solitary smiles could be "social" also seemed problematic for BET's felt/false, Duchenne/non-Duchenne smile dichotomy, because that dichotomy hinged on the social/nonsocial distinction. Smiles that were presumed "felt" or "emotional" because they were solitary could now also be "unfelt" or "false," even if they were Duchenne smiles. For BECV, the smile dichotomy is specious because "Duchenne" smiles are not one entity but two: a co-occurrence of smiling *plus* tonic elicitation of the blink reflex of Descartes ("wincing"), the latter of which could occur with any strong stimulus and not any specified emotional state (Fridlund, 1994). Studies now indicate that, contrary to BET, Duchenne smiles are at least as affected by sociality as non-Duchenne ones (Crivelli, Carrera, & Fernández-Dols, 2015; Fernández-Dols & Ruiz-Belda, 1995; Mehu, Grammer, & Dunbar, 2007; Ruiz-Belda, Fernández-Dols, & Barchard, 2003), that they can be produced deliberately (Gosselin, Perron, & Beaupré, 2010; Gunnery & Hall, 2014; Gunnery, Hall, & Ruben, 2013), and that their occurrence varies both with smile intensity (Krumhuber & Manstead, 2009) and stimulus intensity regardless of valence (Harris & Alvarado, 2005).

BECV rejects the idea that some display, or class of displays, can have intrinsic properties outside the context of its issuance. Smiles may be made by mothers toward children or assailants toward victims. Tears may flow in grief, retribution, reconciliation, or triumph. The meanings of these displays can be understood only by considering who makes them and when they occur.

In the neurocultural version of BET, however, morphology dictates not just emotionality but authenticity. Duchenne smiles are "genuine" because they are "felt," and non-Duchenne ones are disingenuous because they are "unfelt" or "false." This stark dichotomy turns everyday courtesy into mendacity. It also leads to futile diversions. A used-car salesman may be a consummate Duchenne smiler and scam nearly every customer who walks onto his lot. His winning Duchenne smiles sell cars. For BET, then, his smiles must be "felt." Is this what we care about, whether he's happy if he scams us?

For BECV, the "authenticity" of his smile lies not in what he feels, but in whether it predicts whether he will treat us fairly if we buy a car from him. More generally, we learn whose words and expressions are reliable indicators of their intent, and over time we bond with those individuals who prove reliable and avoid those who prove otherwise.

In deception, therefore, the "truth" of a display inheres neither in the display nor its displayer, but in the moving average by which a recipient continually calibrates and recalibrates the reliability of the signals issued in *that* context by *that* displayer. Greater predictability of displayers' signals and lower skepticism by recipients toward those signals naturally coevolve with repeated cooperation, else breaches occur that force recalibration, confrontation, or termination of interaction (Mitchell & Thompson, 1986). The "leakage" seen by BET theorists as the breakout of "genuine emotion" through an outer mask is simply a momentary conflict in intentions in social negotiation (Fridlund, 1991a). This interactional perspective is decidedly anti-Darwin qua *Expression* but resoundingly Darwinian (Fridlund, 1992a).

MISINTERPRETING THE BEHAVIORAL ECOLOGY VIEW: POINTS OF CONTENTION AND THE ISSUE OF "EMOTION"

Certain questions have been raised repeatedly about BECV. Does BECV deny "emotion"? Does BECV deny a privileged relationship between "emotion" and certain facial displays? Do "emotions" serve as "commitment devices" that reveal our authentic, internal states (Frank, 1988; and see crucial treatment of the emotion-as-commitment issue by Leys, 2013)? To BECV, all these questions mean little, because they rest entirely on how one defines emotion (cf., Schattschneider, 1960; to paraphrase: defining the terms determines the outcome). Over a century's theory and research have demonstrated that "emotion" has proven intractable to consensual, let alone operational, definition.

BET theorists often identify "emotion," at least implicitly, with *qualia* or "feelings." For example, an observer may claim that someone "felt sad" and his sadness produced his "sad expression." In the neurocultural version of BET, "felt" ("Duchenne") smiles are "all smiles in which the person actually experiences . . . a positive emotion" (Ekman & Friesen, 1982, p. 242). Both the "sadness" and "positive emotion" contentions make *qualia*—or their putative proximal generators—causal, and both are untenable when they make accountable something ineffable and unverifiable. But what if one *were* to localize the proximal generators for *qualia*, the "feeling centers," in the brain? Could we then say that changes in *qualia*, or those generators that produced the *qualia* changes, caused the associated events in the neuromuscular centers that produced the facial expressions? How does one ever determine that event A *causes* event B in the brain?

The complexities in determining neurocausality are labyrinthine, and I invite readers new to this question to Google "Libet's experiment," conducted to test the concept of free will. Benjamin Libet had participants wired up for EEG recording and seated in front of a CRT clock timer. He asked them to flex a finger or press a key while watching a timer, and then report when on the timer they were "first aware of the wish or urge to act." Libet's team (Libet, Gleason, Wright, & Pearl, 1983) discovered the escalation of EEG activity (a "readiness potential"), chiefly over secondary motor cortex, fully half a second before participants made their movement, with the reported awareness of the urge to act occurring up to 300 ms after the readiness potential. What caused the action, the urge to act, or the neural activity that proceeded the urge? Arguments that what-comes-first must be causal were countered by angels-on-pins speculations about whether there would be time for conscious vetos, whether the timer reports weren't also lagged or even backdated, and so on. Libet conducted his studies in the late 1970s, but researchers and philosophers still cannot agree upon what the studies show or mean (Block, Flanagan, & Güzeldere, 1997; and see Chalmers, 1995).

Qualia are on even thinner ice as causal agents. One common BET recourse to according *qualia* strict agency and keep "emotion" scientific is to make facial expressions just part of the package of changes (neurochemical, behavioral, cognitive) that constitutes an emotion or "affect program," *qualia* being among them. On this view, the presence or absence of emotion cannot be determined by the presence or absence of *qualia*, or of any other single component or subset of components (e.g., testimony about feelings, facial or bodily movements, autonomic adjustments, hormonal changes, fMRI voxel patterns). This view reduces to no more than hand-waving about the knottiness of the phenomena and ad hoc choices of stipulated "emotion measures," with the result that surveys of research and formal meta-analyses continually find disappointing links between "emotion" and "expression" (cf., Ortony & Turner, 1990). Newer backstops include (1) trying to reobjectify "emotion" as a neo-Kantian, categorical "conceptual act" that belongs more to the emoter-as-self-observer (Barrett, Wilson-Mendenhall, & Barsalou, 2015), and (2) paradoxically trying to nail down the "emotion" concept by declaring it intrinsically fuzzy (Scarantino & Griffiths, 2011).

For BECV, all this reasoning is tendentious and wasteful if the purpose is to understand our facial displays. The same holds for ecumenical BET formulations that begin with emotion, variously defined, and end with how "everyone knows" that the expressions have social functions, too (e.g., Hauser, 1996). For BECV, displays evolved as social tools *directly*, not as parts of underlying mechanisms for the production of displays. Natural and cultural selection do not "care about" (specifically select for) the inner workings of traits, only the traits themselves. Facial behaviors that aid individuals in navigating their social terrains (i.e., displays) will, via their displayers, tend to proliferate horizontally (i.e., culturally and geographically) and vertically (via genetic/epigenetic inheritance), regardless of what neural operations produce them; accompanying these displays is the coevolution of recipient behavior that is attentive yet skeptical (Krebs & Dawkins, 1984).

THE BEHAVIORAL ECOLOGY VIEW'S CURRENT STATUS

How has BECV fared against BET? James Russell's influential critique of the cross-cultural matching-to-sample studies (Russell, 1994), and his team's demonstration of powerful context effects in facial-expression perception (Carroll & Russell, 1996; Russell & Fehr, 1987), broke the paradigm lock BET had on facial-expression research. BECV's contribution has been to supply a new framework for understanding our facial displays, one that restores Darwin's vision of human-animal continuity and places it on a solid evolutionary footing. I believe it's what Darwin *would* have proposed had he been able.

I am pleased by how much serious scholarly attention BECV has received. I grounded it in behavioral ecology and evolutionary theory, but Brian Parkinson's generous review reminded me of its debt to Dewey (Parkinson, 2005). With penetrating depth, Ruth Leys has shown how BECV can clarify philosophical and technical problems in the objectification and neural localization of emotion (Leys, 2007, 2010, 2011, 2014). BECV has informed research on both public and implicit-audience accounts of responses to social media (Litt, 2012), smiling in pain (Kunz, Prkachin, & Lautenbacher, 2013), human–computer communication (Aharoni & Fridlund, 2007), persuasion (Cesario & Higgins, 2008), power and dominance (Burgoon & Dunbar, 2006), facial displays in rats (Nakashima, Ukezono, Nishida, Sudo, & Takano, 2015) and chimpanzees (Parr & Waller, 2006), *intra*personal communication in therapeutic narrative writing (Brody & Park, 2004), and the game-theoretic analysis of human deception (Andrews, 2002). Finally, José-Miguel Fernández-Dols and his colleagues have conducted a line of masterful studies showing how BECV can account for facial behavior in naturalistic settings (e.g., Crivelli et al., 2015; Fernández-Dols & Ruiz-Belda, 1995; Ruiz-Belda et al., 2003).

It also seems that the *battle royale* between BET and BECV has liberated inquiry on facial expressions: Investigators can now pursue hypotheses (e.g., genetic/epigenetic diversity in facial displays, facial dialects, infant deception) that, because they transgressed BET, were previously inconceivable or taboo.

BECV will always be a tough sell. It requires shaking off a romanticized view of human nature that makes the face a battleground between an "authentic self" and an impression-managed "social self" (Fridlund, 1994; Fridlund & Duchaine, 1996). The first concept we treasure; the second we concede reluctantly. To BECV, both are illusory. Like our words, voice, and gestures, our facial displays—even those we make as infants, and which will be deployed by our android companions (will they make felt or false Duchenne smiles?)—are part of our plans of action in social commerce.

ACKNOWLEDGMENTS

The current version benefitted from the editorial efforts of Andrea Scarantino.

NOTE

1. I am indebted to Ruth Leys for incisive comments and suggestions.

REFERENCES

Aharoni, E., & Fridlund, A. (2007). Social reactions toward people vs. computers: How mere labels shape interactions. *Computers in Human Behavior, 23*, 2175–2189.

Alcock, J. (1984). *Animal behavior: An evolutionary approach* (3rd. ed.). Sunderland, MA: Sinauer.

Andrews, P. W. (2002). The influence of postreliance detection on the deceptive efficacy of dishonest signals of intent: Understanding facial clues to deceit as the outcome of signaling tradeoffs. *Evolution and Human Behavior, 23*, 103–121.

Barrett, L. F., Wilson-Mendenhall, C. D., & Barsalou, L. W. (2015. The conceptual act theory: A road map. In L. F. Barrett and J. A. Russell (Eds.), *The psychological construction of emotion* (pp. 83–110). New York, NY: Guilford.

Block, N. J., Flanagan, O. J., & Güzeldere, G. (1997). *The nature of consciousness: Philosophical debates*. Cambridge, MA: MIT Press.

Brody, L. R., & Park, S. H. (2004). Narratives, mindfulness, and the implicit audience. *Clinical Psychology: Science and Practice, 11*, 147–154.

Browne, J. (1985). Darwin and the expression of the emotions. In D. Kohn (Ed.), *The Darwinian heritage* (pp. 307–326). Princeton, NJ: Princeton University Press.

Burgoon, J. K., & Dunbar, N. E. (2006). Nonverbal expressions of dominance and power in human relationships. In V. Manusov & M. L. Patterson (Eds.), *Sage handbook of nonverbal communication* (pp. 279–297). Thousand Oaks, CA: Sage.

Caro, T. M. (2005). *Antipredator defenses in birds and mammals*. Chicago, IL: University of Chicago Press.

Carroll, J. M., & Russell, J. A. (1996). Do facial expressions express specific emotions? Judging emotion from the face in context. *Journal of Personality and Social Psychology, 70*, 205–218.

Cesario, J., & Higgins, E. T. (2008). Making message recipients "feel right": How nonverbal cues can increase persuasion. *Psychological Science, 19*, 415–420.

Chalmers, D. (1995). Facing up to the problem of consciousness. *Journal of Consciousness Studies, 2*, 200–219.

Crivelli, C., Carrera, P., & Fernández-Dols, J. M. (2015). Are smiles a sign of happiness? Spontaneous expressions of judo winners. *Evolution and Human Behavior, 36*, 52–58.

Darwin, C. R. (1859). *On the origin of species, or the preservation of favoured races in the struggle for life*. London, UK: Murray.

Darwin, C. R. (1872). *The expression of the emotions in man and animals*. London, UK: Murray.

Darwin, F. (Ed.) (1887). *The life and letters of Charles Darwin, including an autobiographical chapter*. (Vols. 1 and 2). London, UK: Murray.

Davies, N. B., Krebs, J. R., & West, S. A. (2012). *An introduction to behavioral ecology* (4th ed.). Oxford, UK: Wiley-Blackwell.

Ekman, P. (1972). Universals and cultural differences in facial expressions of emotion. In J. Cole (Ed.), *Nebraska Symposium on Motivation, 1971* (Vol. 19, pp. 207–282). Lincoln, NE: University of Nebraska Press.

Ekman, P. (1992). An argument for basic emotions. *Cognition and Emotion, 6*, 169–200.

Ekman, P. (1997). Expression or communication about emotion. In N. L. Segal, G. E. Weisfeld, & C. C. Weisfeld (Eds.), *Uniting biology and psychology: Integrated perspectives on human development* (pp. 315–338). Washington, DC: APA Press.

Ekman, P., Davidson, R. J., & Friesen, W. V. (1990). The Duchenne smile: Emotional expression and brain physiology II. *Journal of Personality and Social Psychology, 58*, 342–353.

Ekman, P., & Fridlund, A. J. (1987). Assessment of facial behavior in affective disorders. In J. D. Maser (Ed.), *Depression and expressive behavior.* Hillsdale, NJ: Erlbaum.

Ekman, P., & Friesen, W. V. (1969). The repertoire of nonverbal behavior: Categories, origins, usage, and coding. *Semiotica, 1*, 49–98.

Ekman, P., & Friesen, W. V. (1971). Constants across cultures in the face and emotion. *Journal of Personality and Social Psychology, 17*, 124–129.

Ekman, P., & Friesen, W. V. (1982). Felt, false, and miserable smiles. *Journal of Nonverbal Behavior, 6*, 238–258.

Ekman, P., & Keltner, D. (1997). Universal facial expressions of emotion: An old controversy and new findings. In U. Segerstrâle & P. Molnár (Eds.), *Nonverbal communication: Where nature meets culture* (pp. 27–46). Mahway, NJ: Erlbaum.

Ekman, P., Sorenson, E. R., & Friesen, W. V. (1969). Pan-cultural elements in facial displays of emotions. *Science, 164*, 86–88.

Fernández-Dols, J. M., & Ruiz-Belda, M. A. (1995). Are smiles a sign of happiness? Gold medal winners at the Olympic Games. *Journal of Personality and Social Psychology, 69*, 1113–1119.

Frank, M. G., & Ekman, P. (1993). Not all smiles are created equal: The differences between enjoyment and nonenjoyment smiles. *Humor: International Journal of Humor Research, 6*, 9–26.

Frank, M. G., Ekman, P., & Friesen, W. V. (1993). Behavioral markers and recognizability of the smile of enjoyment. *Journal of Personality and Social Psychology, 64*, 83–93.

Frank, R. H. (1988). *Passions within reason: The strategic role of the emotions.* New York, NY: Norton.

Fridlund, A. J. (1991a). Evolution and facial action in reflex, social motive, and paralanguage. *Biological Psychology, 32*, 3–100.

Fridlund, A. J. (1991b). The sociality of solitary smiles: Effects of an implicit audience. *Journal of Personality and Social Psychology, 60*, 229–240.

Fridlund, A. J. (1992a). Darwin's anti-Darwinism in *The expression of the emotions in man and animals.* In K. Strongman (Ed.), *International review of emotion*, Vol. 2. New York: Wiley.

Fridlund, A. J. (1992b). The behavioral ecology and sociality of human faces. In M. S. Clark (Ed.), *Review of personality and social psychology, 13*, 90–121. Newbury Park, CA: Sage.

Fridlund, A. J. (1994). *Human facial expression: An evolutionary view.* San Diego, CA: Academic Press.

Fridlund, A. J. (1997). The new ethology of human facial expressions. In J. A. Russell & J.-M. Fernandez-Dols (Eds.), *The psychology of facial expression* (pp. 103–129). Cambridge, UK: Cambridge University Press.

Fridlund, A. J. (2002). The behavioral ecology view of smiling and other facial expressions. In M. Abel (Ed.), *An empirical reflection on the smile* (pp. 45–82). New York, NY: Edwin Mellen Press.

Fridlund, A. J., Ekman, P., & Oster, H. (1988). Emotions and facial expressions. In A. Kendon (Ed.), *International encyclopedia of communications*. Philadelphia, PA: Annenberg School of Communications/Oxford University Press.

Fridlund, A. J., & Duchaine, B. (1996). "Facial expressions of emotion" and the delusion of the hermetic self. In R. Harré & W. G. Parrott, *The emotions* (pp. 259–284). Cambridge, UK: Cambridge University Press.

Fridlund, A. J., & Izard, C. E. (1983). Electromyographic studies of facial expressions of emotions and patterns of emotions. In J. T. Cacioppo & R. E. Petty (Eds.), *Social psychophysiology: A sourcebook* (pp. 243–286). New York, NY: Guilford Press.

Fridlund, A. J., Kenworthy, K., & Jaffey, A. K. (1992). Audience effects in affective imagery: Replication and extension to dysphoric imagery. *Journal of Nonverbal Behavior, 16*, 191–212.

Fridlund, A. J., & Russell, J. A. (2006). The functions of facial expression: What's in a face? In V. Manusov and M. L. Patterson (Eds.), *Sage handbook of nonverbal communication* (pp. 299–319). Thousand Oaks, CA: Sage.

Fridlund, A. J., Sabini, J. P., Hedlund, L. E., Schaut, J. A., Shenker, J. I., & Knauer, M. J. (1990). Social determinants of facial expressions during affective imagery: Displaying to the people in your head. *Journal of Nonverbal Behavior, 14*, 113–137.

Fridlund, A. J., Schwartz, G. E., & Fowler, S. C. (1984). Pattern-recognition of self-reported emotional state from multiple-site facial EMG activity during affective imagery. *Psychophysiology, 21*, 622–636.

Gilbert, A. N., Fridlund, A. J., & Sabini, J. (1987). Hedonic and social determinants of facial displays to odor. *Chemical Senses, 12*, 355–363.

Gosselin, P., Perron, M., & Beaupré, M. (2010). The voluntary control of facial action units in adults. *Emotion, 10*, 266–271.

Gruber, H. E., with Barnett, H. P. (1974). *Darwin on man: A psychological study of scientific creativity*. New York, NY: Dutton.

Gunnery, S. D., & Hall, J. (2014). The Duchenne smile and persuasion. *Journal of Nonverbal Behavior*, 38, 181–194.

Gunnery, S. D., Hall, J. A., & Ruben, M. A. (2013). The deliberate Duchenne smile: Individual differences in expressive control. *Journal of Nonverbal Behavior, 37*, 29–41.

Harris, C. R., & Alvarado, N. (2005). Facial expressions, smile types, and self-report during humor, tickle, and pain. *Cognition and Emotion, 19*, 655–669.

Hauser, M. (1996). *The evolution of communication*. Cambridge, MA: MIT Press.

Hess, U., Banse, R., & Kappas, A. (1995). The intensity of facial expression is determined by underlying affective state and social situation. *Journal of Personality and Social Psychology, 69*, 280–288.

Hinde, R. A. (1985a). Expression and negotiation. In G. Zivin (Ed.), *The development of expressive behavior* (pp. 103–116). Orlando, FL: Academic Press.

Hinde, R. A. (1985b). Was "the expression of the emotions" a misleading phrase? *Animal Behaviour, 33*, 985–992.

Izard, C. E. (1971). *The face of emotion*. New York, NY: Appleton-Century-Crofts.

Jones, S. S., Collins, K., & Hong, H.-W. (1991). An audience effect on smile production in 10-month-old-infants. *Psychological Science, 2*, 45–49.

Krebs, J. R., & Davies, N. B. (1987). *An introduction to behavioral ecology* (2nd ed.). Sunderland, MA: Sinauer.

Krebs, J. R., & Dawkins, R. (1984). Animal signals: Mind-reading and manipulation. In J. R. Krebs & N. B. Davies (Eds.), *Behavioural ecology* (2nd ed.) (pp. 380–402). Oxford, UK: Blackwell.

Krumhuber, E. G., & Manstead, A. S. R. (2009). Can Duchenne smiles be feigned?: New evidence on felt and false smiles. *Emotion, 9*, 807–820.

Kunz, M., Prkachin, K., & Lautenbacher, S. (2013). Smiling in pain: Explorations of its social motives. *Pain Research and Treatment*, doi:10.1155/2013/128093.

Leys, R. (2007). *From guilt to shame: Auschwitz and after*. Princeton, NJ: Princeton University Press.

Leys, R. (2010). How did fear become a scientific object and what kind of object is it? *Representations, 110*, 66–104.

Leys, R. (2011). The turn to affect: A critique. *Critical Inquiry, 37*, 434–472.

Leys, R. (2014). "Both of us disgusted in my insula": Mirror neuron theory and emotional empathy. In F. Biess & D. M. Gross (Eds.), *Science and emotions after 1945: A transatlantic perspective* (pp. 67–95). Chicago, IL: University of Chicago Press.

Leys, R. (2013). A world without pretense? Honest and dishonest signaling in social life. In C. Mayo (Ed.), *Philosophy of education 2013* (pp. 25–42). Urbana, IL: Philosophy of Education Society.

Libet, B., Gleason, C. A., Wright, E. W., & Pearl, D. K. (1983). Time of conscious intention to act in relation to onset of cerebral activity (readiness-potential)—The unconscious initiation of a freely voluntary act. *Brain*, 106, 623–642. doi:10.1093/brain/106.3.623

Litt, E. (2012). Knock, knock. Who's there? The imagined audience. *Journal of Broadcasting & Electronic Media, 56*, 330–345.

Lorenz, K. Z. (1967). The biology of expression and impression. *Psychologische Forschung, 37*.

Lorenz, K. Z. (1970). *Studies on animal and human behavior* (Vols. 1 and 2). Cambridge, MA: Harvard University Press.

Marler, P. R., Duffy, A., & Pickert, R. (1986a). Vocal communication in the domestic chicken: I. Does a sender communicate information about the quality of a food referent to a receiver? *Animal Behaviour, 34*, 188–193.

Marler, P. R., Duffy, A., & Pickert, R. (1986b). Vocal communication in the domestic chicken: II. Is a sender sensitive to the presence and nature of a receiver? *Animal Behaviour, 34*, 194–198.

Matsumoto, D., Ekman, P., & Fridlund, A. J. (1990). Analyzing nonverbal behavior. In P. Dowrick (Ed.), *A practical guide to using video in the behavioral sciences*. New York, NY: Wiley.

Maynard Smith, J. (1982). *Evolution and the theory of games*. Cambridge, UK: Cambridge University Press.

Mehu, M., Grammer, K., & Dunbar, R. I. M. (2007). Smiles when sharing. *Evolution and Human Behavior, 28*, 415–422.

Mitchell, R. W., & Thompson, N. S. (Eds.) (1986). *Deception: Perspectives on human and nonhuman deceit*. Albany, NY: SUNY Press.

Nakashima, S. F., Ukezono, M., Nishida, H., Sudo, R., & Takado, Y. (2015). Receiving of emotional signal of pain from conspecifics in laboratory rats. *Royal Society Open Science*, doi: 10.1098/rsos.140381

Parkinson, B. (2005). Do facial movements express emotions or communicate motives? *Personality and Social Psychology Review, 9*, 278–311.

Parr, L. A., & Waller, B. M. (2006). Understanding chimpanzee facial expression: Insights into the evolution of communication. *Social Cognition and Affective Neuroscience, 1*, 221–228.

Ruiz-Belda, M. A., Fernández-Dols, J. M., Carrera, P., & Barchard, K. (2003). Spontaneous facial expressions of happy bowlers and soccer fans. *Cognition and Emotion, 17*, 315–326.

Russell, J. A. (1994). Is there universal recognition of emotion from facial expression? *Psychological Bulletin, 115*, 102–141.

Russell, J. A., & Fehr, B. (1987). Relativity in the perception of emotion in facial expressions. *Journal of Experimental Psychology: General, 116*, 223–237.

Scarantino, A., & Griffiths, P. (2011). Don't give up on basic emotions. *Emotion Review, 3*, 1–11.

Schattschneider, E. E. (1960). *The semisovereign people*. New York, NY: Holt, Rinehart, & Winston.

Schützwohl, A., & Reisenzein, R. (2012). Facial expressions in response to a highly surprising event exceeding the field of vision: A test of Darwin's theory of surprise. *Evolution and Human Behavior, 33*, 657–664.

Schwartz, G. E., Fair, P. L., Salt, P., Mandel, M. R., & Klerman, G. L. (1976). Facial muscle patterning to affective imagery in depressed and nondepressed subjects. *Science, 192*, 489–491.

Smith, W. J. (1977). *The behavior of communicating*. Cambridge, MA: Harvard University Press.

Tinbergen, N. (1952). "Derived" activities: their causation, biological significance, origin and emancipation during evolution, *Quarterly Review of Biology, 27*, 1–32.

Tinbergen, N. (1953). *Social behaviour in animals*. London, UK: Chapman and Hall.

Tooby, J., & Cosmides, L. (1990). The past explains the present: Emotional adaptations and the structure of ancestral environments. *Ethology and Sociobiology, 11*, 375–424.

Wagner, H. L., & Smith, J. (1991). Social influence and expressiveness. *Journal of Nonverbal Behavior, 15*, 201–214.

Yik, M. (1999). Interpretation of faces: A cross-cultural study of a prediction from Fridlund's theory. *Cognition and Emotion, 13*, 93–104.

6

Toward a Broader Perspective on Facial Expressions

Moving on From Basic Emotion Theory

JAMES A. RUSSELL

People frown, smile, laugh, grimace, wince, scowl, pout, sneer, and so on. In turn, observers interpret these facial muscle movements, inferring what the expresser is doing (thinking, feeling, perceiving, faking, and so on). Basic emotion theory (BET) offered an account of certain facial movements and their interpretation in terms of discrete emotions. Here I offer a skeptical view of BET's prospects and suggest some promising alternative approaches.

At the heart of BET is a seemingly obvious claim: Feeling happy makes you smile, feeling fear makes you gasp, feeling disgusted makes you wrinkle your nose, and so on. This idea is a folk theory that dates back at least to Aristotle. As such, it captures our commonsense, taken-for-granted presuppositions about facial expressions—presuppositions that underlie the way those of us in the Western tradition think about and perceive facial movements and that make certain claims seem obvious. Adding an evolutionary account, a neural mechanism, and a famous trek in the highlands of Papua New Guinea made BET a highly influential and plausible theory. BET became the dominant research program in the field of affective science and stimulated much valuable research.

A scientific theory often begins with a folk theory, but then changes as its conceptual problems become evident and as nature is probed for unpredicted facts and anomalies. A clear example of this development comes from physics.

Aristotle based his physics on the folk theory of the four elements, but observations and analyses led eventually to the qualitatively different physics of today. How far from obvious are nature's ways!

BET suffers from the problems that most early scientific theories encounter. It has unresolved conceptual issues. Observations and experiments have uncovered unpredicted facts and anomalies about faces. Much more than emotions are involved in facial expressions. Even with respect to the role of emotion, researchers must choose between revising BET or, as I suggest, take a different approach entirely. These considerations suggest a move beyond folk theory and BET.

I next separate issues of the sender's production of facial movements from the issues of an onlooker's interpretation of those movements. After all, we perceive melancholy in the baying of wolves and joy in birdsong; what we perceive is not always the true cause.

THE SENDER'S PRODUCTION OF FACIAL MOVEMENTS

Faces move, obviously. We need a descriptive system of facial movements. Ekman, Friesen, and Hager's (2002) elaboration of Hjortsjö's (1969) anatomically based catalog of facial movements was a major advance. Still, much (but not all) of the research inspired by BET has focused on a small number of exaggerated facial configurations. An example is Ekman and Friesen's (1975) *Pictures of Facial Affect*. How often the prototypical facial configurations seen in this set actually occur remains unknown, but they are likely rare. Gaspar and Esteves (2012) recorded the facial behavior of 3-year-olds during emotional episodes. They found much facial movement, but rarely the prototypical BET faces. Configurations "matching the prototypical expression of joy/happiness are the highest, reaching 27% . . . The surprise matching proportion is 5%, anger 0%, and fear 11%" (p. 353). Carroll and Russell (1997) found similar results with adults. We need to go beyond the facial configurations seen in *Pictures of Facial Affect*.

We also need an account of what produces facial movements. Ekman (1980) wrote, "When someone feels an emotion and is not trying to disguise it, his or her face appears the same no matter who that person is or where he or she comes from" (p. 7). Ekman allowed that there are other causes of any facial expression (such as a display rule requiring a smile when greeting a stranger or when having your photograph taken). All the same, he implied that feeling happy, unless disguised, is sufficient to produce smiling. Surprisingly little evidence supports the production side of BET's account.

Reporting the "first evidence" alleged to support the emotion-face link, Rosenberg and Ekman (1994) wrote, "Our results provide the first evidence that there is coherence between facial expression and self-report of emotion at specific moments" (p. 223). Viewers of one (of four) film clips of a disgusting event had a significantly higher probability (.50 vs .30) of showing a facial expression of a specific emotion at the moment in the film that they reported having felt that emotion than at other moments. Analysis of a second film clip failed to replicate this result, and no analysis of results from the remaining two film clips was reported. The study was correlational (thereby unable to test causality) and failed to specify precisely which facial expressions were scored as corresponding to which emotions.

Improved research on the emotion–face link followed, but continued to find evidence at odds with folk wisdom and BET. Reisenzein, Studtmann, and Horstmann (2013) reviewed the laboratory evidence; Fernández-Dols and Crivelli (2013) the field evidence. (For an update, see the chapter in the present volume by Duran, Reisenzein, and Fernández-Dols.) In brief, happy people do not always smile, and smiles occur without happiness. Smiles are easily posed, do not always correlate with the smiler's emotional state (Fridlund, 1991; Krumhuber & Manstead, 2009), and can be caused by negative experiences such as losing a game (Schneider & Josephs, 1991), being embarrassed (Keltner & Cordaro, this volume), or being in pain (Kunz, Prkachin, & Lautenbacher, 2009). Similar problems arise for other emotion–face associations.

Might BET be rescued with a simple acknowledgment: Smiling can be caused by events other than happiness? Ditto for other emotions and their corresponding facial expressions. And BET agrees; the sources of human facial movements are many. As we talk, eat, breathe, exert effort, smell, feel pain, or reach orgasm, our faces move. Our faces move as part of certain reflexes (gag, orienting, startle, and so on), as part of perception (looking, tasting, and so on), and as part of social interaction (social greeting, threatening, exerting dominance or submission). Our faces move as we unconsciously imitate others. Our faces move as part of information processing and of subsequent behavior. We therefore need to explore other possible sources of facial movement both for the complete story of how facial expressions are produced and as a way to test BET. All such sources of movement are potential confounds when testing BET's assumption that discrete emotions cause facial movements.

Besides BET, there are various possible accounts of the production of facial movement, including the following: (1) Perception involves bodily movements (reaching to feel, turning to look), and facial movements are part of this process. For example, BET's "fear expression" might enhance visual exposure (Susskind et al., 2008). (2) Cognitions (appraisals of current events) might produce facial movement (Scherer, 1992; Scherer, Mortillaro, & Mehu, this volume). Ortony and Turner (1990) noted that a frown (brow contraction) often occurs when one is uncertain or puzzled. (3) Fridja proposed that facial movements are part of the preparation for action. (4) As social animals, a large part of our behavior is negotiating social interaction. Fridlund (1994; this volume) suggested that facial movements signal to an audience projected plans and goals including contingencies. (5) Facial movements are part of paralanguage. Chovil (1991) offered a taxonomy for paralanguage in which facial movements are part of speech communication. An example is substituting a "disgust face" for the words "that stinks." (6) Core affect—a neurophysiological state consciously accessible as simply feeling good or bad, energized or quiescent—might produce facial movement.

Return now to the hypothesis that emotion, unless disguised, is sufficient to produce the corresponding facial expression. The hypothesis is difficult to test for various reasons, one of which is that emotion is typically confounded with other possible causes of the facial behavior. So, the scientific question is whether the emotion can be shown to cause the predicted facial expression when disentangled from other possible causes. Consider the research program of Jose-Miguel Fernández-Dols and his colleagues on happiness and smiling (e.g., Fernández-Dols & Ruiz-Belda, 1995; Ruiz-Belda, Fernández-Dols, Carrera, & Barchard, 2003; Crivelli, Carrera, & Fernández-Dols, 2015; Fernández-Dols, Carrera, & Crivelli, 2011; for general review, see Fernandez-Dols & Crivelli, 2013). In a series of field studies, they found instances of intense happiness (such as winning in sports or orgasm) that could be disentangled from other plausible sources of smiling and in which attempts at disguise were unlikely. Intensely happy people rarely smiled, except during a social exchange. So, evidence goes against the claim that happiness is sufficient for smiling. Put more generously, we have *no evidence* that feeling happy, unless disguised, is sufficient for smiling. Similar results are accumulating for other emotions (Reisenzein, Studtmann, & Horstmann, 2013; Duran, Reisenzein, & Fernandez-Dols, this volume).

In short, discrete emotions are sometimes correlated with the production of the corresponding facial expressions, although surprisingly weakly, but there are alternative explanations to the theory that the emotions are causal. When confounds are taken into account, we have no convincing evidence that emotions cause facial movements: The (weak) correlation between emotions and facial movements may have other underlying causes.

THE OBSERVER'S INTERPRETATION OF FACIAL MOVEMENTS

We open our eyes and see that this person is happy, that one angry, and so on. BET articulated the common belief that we "recognize" happiness, anger, disgust, and so on in the faces of others. Many studies purported to demonstrate consensual recognition by asking people to match a photo of a static facial expression to one of BET's predicted emotion terms. Such demonstrations, even if reliable, would not show that people spontaneously recognize the predicted emotion but that, once told that one of a number of emotions is expressed, they can select the predicted one.

Even more troubling, the high matching scores found may be partly due to design methods that favored finding them. No single design problem need be fatal, but cumulatively they combine to push scores in the predicted direction: within-subjects designs, posed exaggerated facial expressions (devoid of voice, motion, body, and information about the expresser's context), and the use of forced-choice response format (Russell, 1994). For example, when observers see spontaneous rather than posed faces, matching scores plummet (Kayyal & Russell, 2013). We recently found that people can achieve a high matching score between a label and a face, without recognizing any emotion. Instead, they used an elimination strategy: After matching several standard faces with standard labels, both children and adults chose a nonword, "pax," from the list as the emotion expressed by a novel face (DiGirolamo & Russell, 2014; Nelson & Russell, 2016). If so, then such an elimination strategy may account for high matching found for some (but not all) emotion labels.

Outside the laboratory, the observer does not use someone's facial expression alone. To infer that person's emotion, the observer interprets the facial expression in light of the expresser's situation and other aspects of the face's context, including the expresser's body (Fantoni & Gerbino, 2014). So, removing the context in a "recognition" experiment stands in the way of understanding how observers typically interpret facial expressions.

More important, specifying context as well as face in such experiments can provide a test of BET. BET implies that the facial expression is more powerful for "recognition" of emotion than is its context because, according to BET, the facial expression is an automatic signal of the specific emotion (or that the facial expression is part of that emotion), whereas context can provide only probabilistic information because different individuals respond differently to the same situation. To the contrary, when an observer judges the emotion of another, context is more powerful than the other's face (Carroll & Russell, 1996): A person in an anger-inducing situation who showed BET's "fear face" was interpreted as angry rather than as afraid. I also followed folk theory in predicting that, according to my valence-based theory of facial expressions, face trumps context on the judgment of valence (whether the expresser's emotion is seen as pleasant or unpleasant). Alas, I was wrong: Context trumps face even on judgments of valence (Aviezer et al., 2008; Kayyal, Widen, & Russell, 2015).

In the "universality thesis," BET emphasized the uniformity of recognition: Basic emotions were claimed to be easily recognized from the predicted facial expressions by all people whatever their culture, language, or education. Yet in-groups are better than out-groups in their matching scores (Elfenbein, this volume). Meta-analyses found that matching scores vary with culture, language, and education (Nelson & Russell, 2013; Trauffer, Widen, & Russell 2013). Jack et al. (2012) used a psychophysical technique and again found cultural differences in which facial configurations were matched to specific emotions. BET presupposed that the English words *fear, anger, disgust*, and so on express universal categories in terms of which recognition proceeds; evidence indicates that the way in which emotions are categorized is not universal: Emotion categories expressed in different languages are in some ways similar to but in some ways different from those in English (Russell, 1991; Wierzbicka, 1999).

As Ekman and Friesen (1971) emphasized, the most telling test of universality involves societies remote from Western culture and media. The few such studies carried out showed a large cultural difference in matching scores (Nelson & Russell, 2016; Russell, 1994). Several recent studies of remote indigenous societies found weak to nonexistent support for BET's prediction of uniformity of interpretation of facial expressions (Crivelli, Jarillo, Russell, & Fernandez-Dols, 2016a; 2016b; Crivelli, Russell, Jarillo, & Fernandez-Dols, 2016; Gendron, Roberson, van der Vyver, & Barrett, 2014). Diversity needs our attention as much does as uniformity (Crivelli & Gendron, this volume).

Some writers emphasize that BET's hypotheses are supported to a statistically significant degree: Observers often select BET's predicted emotion label more often than they would if they chose emotion labels randomly. But then no one predicts that humans are random in interpreting faces. Ruling *out* the null hypothesis of random responding does not rule *in* the experimenter's hypothesis. There are many ways to explain nonrandom responding; Russell (1994) offered eight alternative accounts, and surely there are more. All of them predict nonrandom responding. (Aristotle's physics based on the four elements makes some valid predictions: Put earth, water, and air in a beaker, shake, and watch the elements settle: earth at the bottom, water in the middle, and air at the top—just as his theory predicts.) Folk theories and the scientific theories inspired by them provide first approximations, which result in better-than-chance associations.

What the classic BET studies called "recognition" is interpretation. Observers may use facial information to make inferences not just about emotion but about any psychological state. The interpretation of the face is influenced by many factors, some rarely studied (color of the sclera), some more studied: by the observer's situation (state, interests, motives), by the face's context (the expresser's context, words, gaze, vocal prosody, body position and proxemics, motor behavior, underlying physiognomy), and by features of the experimental method. Furthermore, the observer does more than interpret. Rendall, Owren, and Ryan (2009) suggested that some facial movements influence the emotional state of the observer directly: Receiving a smile might simply make you feel better.

I suggested an alternative account—called minimal universality—of an onlooker's interpretation of facial expressions (Russell, 1995). Universally, humans perceive others in simple general terms (valence and arousal): Is the person feeling good or bad, energized or quiescent? This part of the proposal is consistent with above-chance matching of faces with emotion labels, because the meaning of an emotion label includes, among other elements, valence and arousal. (This part of the proposal is also consistent with Osgood's theory that all humans perceive everything in terms of simple affective dimensions of evaluation and activity. And Osgood may also be correct that we perceive facial movements in terms of potency as well.) Young children interpret faces in terms of valence (Widen & Russell, 2008, Widen, this volume). For example, the typical 3-year-old uses the same one label (typically *angry*) for four of BET's canonical faces: those for fear, anger, sadness, and disgust. As children develop, they add new emotion concepts by differentiating: Feeling bad is divided into feeling bad because of loss versus feeling bad because of receiving a hostile action. The end product is a set of adult emotion concepts, which are similar but not uniform across individuals, languages, and cultures (Russell, 1991). In interpreting facial expressions, older children and adults go beyond valence and arousal, including categorization by discrete emotions. On my initial proposal, the face is typically relied on to provide the values of valence and arousal, but context provides the specific emotion. The hypothesis that the face provides valence, however, was recently found wanting, as I reported earlier.

In short, sufficient evidence has now accumulated to conclude that BET's claims about universal recognition of a specific discrete emotion from its facial expression are unwarranted. Research should shift to the broader topic of how a person's facial movement influences an observer, including, but not limited to, the interpretation that the observer makes for the face and the many factors that influence that interpretation. We need to study not just English folk terms for emotion (*happiness, anger, disgust*, etc.) but many more psychological categories and how their accessibility or even existence varies with language and culture.

CAN BASIC EMOTION THEORY BE SALVAGED?

One response to the evidence mentioned here might be to revise BET. This tack appears less viable in light of evidence on other aspects of the theory. There is no consensually agreed-upon confirmatory evidence for emotion-specific signatures in the autonomic nervous system (Cacioppo et al., 2000) or specific behavioral responses (Baumeister, Vohs, DeWall, & Zhang, 2007). BET predicts tight coherence among each emotion's components, but such components turn out to be surprisingly weakly correlated (Reisenzein, 2000).

Caution is also warranted when revising BET because the revision may introduce problems as much as solutions. For example, evidence of cultural differences led Ekman (1972) to embrace Klineberg's (1938) hypothesis of cultural rules prescribing or proscribing facial expressions. On Ekman's treatment, these display rules render his theory immune to evidence: Happiness leads to smiles, except when it doesn't, in which case a display rule intervened. Without a prior specification of the display rules, no evidence could falsify the theory. Consider, for example, the highly cited Japanese-American study on display rules (Ekman, 1972). American and Japanese participants showed similar facial movements to a disgusting film during a private viewing, whereas they showed different facial movements to the film in a social situation. Ekman (1984) summarized: "In private, when no display rules to mask expression were operative, we saw the biologically based, evolved, universal facial expressions of emotion. In a social situation, we had shown how rules for the management of expression led to culturally different facial expressions." No particular display rule had been specified ahead of time, and thus no prediction as to what facial behavior the rule required. No evidence was offered that Japanese are subject to a display rule and Americans not. No evidence for the operation of a display rule was offered other than the lack of BET's predicted facial expression. No evidence was offered for the nonoperation of a display rule when the predicted facial expression occurred during the private viewing, other than the occurrence of the expression. A display rule was offered as the explanation of the observed cultural difference in the social situation, but alternative explanations, such as differences in emotion or in focus of attention, were not ruled out. (Incidentally, I followed Ekman in assuming that BET's predicted facial expressions occurred during the private viewing, but it is not clear that this assumption is correct.) See Fridlund (1994) for a revealing analysis of this study and the display rule concept more generally.

There are also deeper problems with BET. Modern understanding of evolution by natural selection raises doubts about BET and provides an alternative (Buss, 2014; Fridlund, 1994). Automatic signaling to an enemy of one's true emotion would incur heavy costs, and evolution likely produced deceptive as well as veridical signals because of conflict of interest between expresser and observer. Recurring problems such as danger, loss, disease-producing contacts, and frustration are not solved by fixed ready-made solutions. Faced with the danger of a train moving toward you, flight is the best solution. But faced with the danger of missing the train, running toward the train is a better solution. Faced with the danger of one's child being sick, phoning a doctor is a better solution. We have no evidence that fear produces a tendency to flee in such situations.

BET's problems are deeper still. I do not know exactly how BET defines "emotion." On one interpretation, emotion is a package of components. At least in the Western cultural tradition, we tend to "see" emotions by packaging together various components. Indeed, the key concepts in BET (anger, fear, etc.) originated in folk psychology, concepts that are vaguely defined, heterogeneous, culture-specific, and permeated with questionable assumptions. A similar tendency can be seen when ancient astronomers "saw" constellations made up of stars that were actually unrelated cosmologically. Packaging disparate phenomena into a discrete emotion may make the world seem simpler and serve cognitive economy, but the packages may be merely convenient fictions.

On another interpretation, an emotion is an entity that causes the components (e.g., Tomkins's 1962–63, affect program): Emotion makes us flee, makes our heart race, makes us feel a certain way, and moves our faces. The "affect program" is simply a metaphor from computers to the brain. If the affect program is a hypothesized brain circuit dedicated to a specific emotion and only that emotion, then it is relevant that neuroscientists are abandoning the notion of hardwired emotion-specific brain circuits (LeDoux, 2012, 2014; Lindquist et al. 2012). BET explains the occurrence of an observable emotional component by activation of the affect program. This explanation is reminiscent of faculty psychology in which an observable event is explained by an unseen faculty of the same name: Remembering is explained by the memory faculty, imagining by the imagination faculty, and moral behavior by the morality faculty.

In short, BET initially seemed plausible, even obvious, built as it was on our intuitive folk theory about emotions and faces, combined with an early understanding of brain mechanisms and of evolution by natural selection. Subsequent scientific scrutiny, however, has not supported its predictions. Its evolutionary presuppositions and neural basis lack support. Hypotheses about peripheral physiology and instrumental behavior lack support. Co-occurrence of emotional components has been found much less frequent than predicted.

ALTERNATIVE APPROACHES TO EMOTION

As often happens with scientific progress, conceptual alternatives to BET begin with different assumptions and tend to be more complex and less intuitive, because they part ways with folk theory. Examples are Fridlund's (1994) behavioral ecology view based on modern evolutionary theory and Scherer's

(1992) and Ortony and Turner's (1990) appraisal theories based on links between perception-cognition and specific muscle movements.

In psychological construction (Barrett & Russell, 2015; Russell, 2003), I offer an alternative account of emotion and other affective phenomena that explicitly abandons certain commonsense presuppositions, although it retains all the observable facts. People get angry or scared, obviously. Such folk terms as *emotion, anger,* and *fear* point to important phenomena, and the terms express folk concepts that can play a role in those phenomena. All the same, the question is how to develop a scientific account of those phenomena. On my proposal, the terms *emotion, anger,* and the rest are treated as a folk rather than as a scientific terms. Folk terms as such can play an actual role in the phenomena (much as the concept of "ghost" plays an actual role in some people's thoughts and actions), but the terms are not part of the theoretical mechanism used to explain the phenomena.

Episodes called "emotional" consist of changes in various component processes (peripheral physiological changes, appraisals and attributions, expressive and instrumental behavior, subjective experiences), no one of which is itself an emotion or necessary or sufficient for an emotion to be instantiated. Emotion is not invoked as the cause of the components nor as the mechanism that coordinates the components. Each component has its own semi-independent causal process.

This general approach implies that the production of facial expressions is accounted for by one or more of the six alternative sources discussed earlier, not by a discrete emotion or affect program dedicated exclusively to emotion or to a specific emotion. Facial "expression" is at most modestly correlated with other components of the emotional episode.

An emotional episode's components are coordinated, as are all human processes, but, again, not by an affect program. Although emotion is not an entity causing the components, still, a witness, scientist, or the person having the emotion might categorize the episode as a specific emotion: We see emotions in others and experience emotions in ourselves. That categorization too is a process to be studied. Once the categorization occurs (hey! I'm annoyed), then the categorization can influence other components, but the categorization is neither necessary nor sufficient for those processes.

Psychological construction abandons the assumption that emotional episodes are prefabricated; it proposes instead that they are assembled in the moment to suit current circumstances. The assembly is a rapidly changing, interactive process not well captured by an Event—Affect Program—Emotion framework. An emotional episode is not qualitatively different from any other behavioral episode, and it is assembled in the same way as is any other behavioral episode, although often with a more extreme dose of valence and arousal.

REFERENCES

Aviezer, H., Hassin, R. R., Ryan, J., Grady, C., Susskind, J., Anderson, A., Moscovitch, M., & Bentin, S. (2008). Angry, disgusted, or afraid? Studies on the malleability of emotion perception. *Psychological Science, 19*(7), 724–732.

Barrett, L. F., & Russell, J. A. (Eds.). (2015). *The psychological construction of emotion.* New York, NY: Guilford.

Baumeister, R. F., Vohs, K. D., DeWall, C. N., & Zhang, L. (2007). How emotion shapes behavior: Feedback, anticipation, and reflection, rather than direct causation. *Personality and Social Psychology Review, 11*(2), 167–203.

Buss, D. M. (2014). Comment: Evolutionary criteria for considering an emotion "basic": Jealousy as an illustration. *Emotion Review, 6*(4), 313–315.

Cacioppo, J. T., Berntson, G. G., Larsen, J. T., Poehlmann, K. M., & Ito, T. A. (2000). The psychophysiology of emotion. *Handbook of emotions* (2nd ed., pp. 173–191). New York, NY: Guilford.

Carroll, J. M., & Russell, J. A. (1996). Do facial expressions signal specific emotions? Judging emotion from the face in context. *Journal of Personality and Social Psychology, 70*(2), 205.

Carroll, J. M., & Russell, J. A. (1997). Facial expressions in Hollywood's portrayal of emotion. *Journal of Personality and Social Psychology, 72*, 164–176.

Chovil, N. (1991). Discourse-oriented facial displays in conversation. *Research on Language and Social Interaction, 25*, 163–194.

Crivelli, C., Jarillo, S., Russell, J. A., & Fernandez-Dols, J. M. (2016a). Reading emotions from faces in two indigenous societies. *Journal of Experimental Psychology: General, 145*, 830-843.

Crivelli, C., Jarillo, S., Russell, J. A., & Fernandez-Dols, J. M. (2016b). Recognizing spontaneous facial expressions of emotion in a small-scale society of Papua New Guinea. *Emotion.* Advance online publication. http://dx.doi.org/10.1037/emo0000236

Crivelli, C., Russell, J. A., Jarillo, S., & Fernandez-Dols, J. M. (2016). The fear gasping face as a threat display in a Melanesian society. *PNAS, 113 (44)*,12403-12407. doi:10.1073/pnas.1611622113

DiGirolamo, M. A., & Russell, J. A. (in press). The emotion seen in a face as a methodological artifact: The process of elimination hypothesis. *Emotion.*

Ekman, P. (1972). Universal and cultural differences in facial expressions of emotions. In J. K. Cole (Ed.), *Nebraska symposium on motivation, 1971* (pp. 207–283). Lincoln: University of Nebraska Press.

Ekman, P., & Friesen, W. V. (1971). Constants across cultures in the face and emotion. *Journal of Personality and Social Psychology, 17*(2), 124.

Ekman, P., & Friesen, W. V. (1975). *Pictures of facial affect.* Palo Alto, CA: Consulting Psychologists Press.

Ekman, P., Friesen, W. V., & Hager, J. C. (2002). *Facial action coding system* (2nd ed.). Salt Lake City, UT: Research Nexus eBook.

Fantoni, C., & Gerbino, W. (2014). Body actions change the appearance of facial expressions. *PLoS One, 9*(9): e108211

Fernández-Dols, J. M., & Crivelli, C. (2013). Emotion and expression: Naturalistic studies. *Emotion Review, 5*(1), 24–29.

Fernández-Dols, J. M., & Ruiz-Belda, M. A. (1995). Are smiles a sign of happiness? Gold medal winners at the Olympic Games. *Journal of Personality and Social Psychology*, *69*(6), 1113–1119.

Fridlund, A. J. (1991). Sociality of solitary smiling: Potentiation by an implicit audience. *Journal of Personality and Social Psychology*, *60*, 229–240.

Fridlund, A. J. (1994). *Human facial expression: An evolutionary view*. New York, NY: Academic Press.

Gaspar, A., & Esteves, F. G. (2012). Preschooler's faces in spontaneous emotional contexts—how well do they match adult facial expression prototypes? *International Journal of Behavioral Development, 36, 348–357.*

Gendron, M., Roberson, D., van der Vyver, J. M., & Barrett, L. F (2014). Perceptions of emotion from facial expressions are not culturally universal: Evidence from a remote culture. *Emotion*, *14*, 251–262.

Hjortsjö, C. H. (1969). *Man's face and mimic language*. Lund, Sweden: Studentlitteratur.

Jack, R. E., Garrod, O. G., Yu, H., Caldara, R., & Schyns, P. G. (2012). Facial expressions of emotion are not culturally universal. *Proceedings of the National Academy of Sciences*, *109*(19), 7241–7244.

Kayyal, M. H., & Russell, J. A. (2013). Palestinians and Americans judge spontaneous facial expressions of emotion. *Emotion*, *13*, 891–904.

Kayyal, M. H., Widen, S. C., & Russell, J. A. (2015). Context is more powerful than we think: Contextual cues override facial cues even on valence. *Emotion*. Advance online publication. http://dx.doi.org/10.1037/emo0000032.

Klineberg, O. (1938). Emotional expression in Chinese literature. *Journal of Abnormal and Social Psychology*, *33*, 517–520.

Kraut, R. E., & Johnston, R. E. (1979). Social and emotional messages of smiling: An ethological approach. *Journal of Personality and Social Psychology*, *37*(9), 1539–1553.

Krumhuber, E. G., & Manstead, A. S. (2009). Can Duchenne smiles be feigned? New evidence on felt and false smiles. *Emotion*, *9*(6), 807.

Kunz, M., Prkachin, K., & Lautenbacher, S. (2009). The smile of pain. *Pain*, *145*(3), 273–275.

LeDoux, J. E. (2012). Rethinking the emotional brain. *Neuron*, *73*, 653–676.

LeDoux, J. E. (2014). Afterword: Emotion construction in the brain. In L. F. Barrett & J. A. Russell (Eds.), *The psychological construction of emotion* (pp. 459–463). New York, NY: Guilford.

Lindquist, K. A., Wager, T. D., Kober, H., Bliss-Moreau, E., & Barrett, L. F. (2012). The brain locus of emotion: A meta-analytic review. *Behavioral and Brain Sciences*, *35*, 121–143.

Nelson, N. L., & Russell, J. A. (2013). Universality revisited. *Emotion Review*, *5*(1), 8–15.

Nelson, N. L., & Russell, J. A. (2016). A facial expression of pax: Assessing children's "recognition" of emotion from faces. *Journal of Experimental Child Psychology*, *141*, 49–64.

Ortony, A., & Turner, T. J. (1990). What's basic about basic emotions? *Psychological Review*, *97*(3), 315.

Reisenzein, R. (2000). Exploring the strength of association between the components of emotion syndromes: The case of surprise. *Cognition & Emotion*, *14*(1), 1–38.

Reisenzein, R., Studtmann, M., & Horstmann, G. (2013). Coherence between emotion and facial expression: Evidence from laboratory experiments. *Emotion Review, 5*(1), 16–23.

Rendall, D., Owren, M. J., & Ryan, M. J. (2009). What do animal signals mean? *Animal Behaviour, 78*(2), 233–240.

Rosenberg, E. L., & Ekman, P. (1994). Coherence between expressive and experiential systems in emotion. *Cognition & Emotion, 8*(3), 201–229.

Ruiz-Belda, M. A., Fernández-Dols, J. M., Carrera, P., & Barchard, K. (2003). Spontaneous facial expressions of happy bowlers and soccer fans. *Cognition & Emotion, 17*(2), 315–326.

Russell, J. A. (1991). Culture and the categorization of emotion. *Psychological Bulletin, 110*, 426–450.

Russell, J. A. (1994). Is there universal recognition of emotion from facial expressions? A review of the cross-cultural studies. *Psychological Bulletin, 115*(1), 102.

Russell, J. A. (1995). Facial expressions of emotion: What lies beyond minimal universality? *Psychological Bulletin, 118*(3), 379–391.

Russell, J. A. (2003). Core affect and the psychological construction of emotion. *Psychological Review, 110*(1), 145.

Scherer, K. R. (1992). What does facial expression express? In K. Strongman (Eds.), *International review of studies on emotion* (Vol. 2, pp. 139–165). Chichester, UK: Wiley.

Schneider, K., & Josephs, I. (1991). The expressive and communicative functions of preschool children's smiles in an achievement-situation. *Journal of Nonverbal Behavior, 15*(3), 185–198.

Susskind, J. M., Lee, D. H., Cusi, A., Feiman, R., Grabski, W., & Anderson, A. K. (2008). Expressing fear enhances sensory acquisition. *Nature Neuroscience, 11*(7), 843–850.

Tomkins, S. S. (1962–1963). *Affect, imagery, consciousness* (Vols. 1 and 2). New York, NY: Springer.

Trauffer, N. M., Widen, S. C., & Russell, J. A. (2013). Education and the attribution of emotion to facial expressions. *Psychological Topics, 22*, 237–248.

Widen, S. C., & Russell, J. A. (2008). Young children's understanding of other's emotions. In M. Lewis, J. M. Haviland-Jones, & L. F. Barrett (Eds.), *Handbook of emotions* (pp. 348–363). New York, NY: Guilford.

Wierzbicka, A. (1999). *Emotions across languages and cultures: Diversity and universals*. Cambridge, UK: Cambridge University Press.

7

Coherence Between Emotions and Facial Expressions

A Research Synthesis

JUAN I. DURÁN, RAINER REISENZEIN, AND JOSÉ-MIGUEL FERNÁNDEZ-DOLS

The phrase "facial expression of emotion" contains the implicit assumption that facial expressions co-occur with emotions. Is this assumption true, or more precisely, to what degree is it true? In other words, what is the degree of statistical covariation, or *coherence* (Rosenberg & Ekman, 1994), between emotions and facial expressions? In this chapter, we review empirical evidence from laboratory and field studies that speaks to this question. We summarize the studies using meta-analysis (Borenstein, Hedges, Higgins, & Rothstein, 2009) because we agree with Valentine, Pigott, and Rothstein (2010) that the quantitative integration of findings is preferable to a narrative review even if the sample of studies is small (as is the case for several of the emotions considered). We present the main findings using forest plots, boxplot-like graphical representations of the effect-size estimates and their confidence intervals (CIs) obtained in the different studies together with the overall effect-size estimate and its CI produced by the meta-analysis (see Borenstein et al., 2009; Lewis & Clarke, 2001).

The meta-analysis required several decisions. We had to decide on the emotions to be considered in the review, which assessments of emotions and facial expressions should be regarded as acceptable, the index of emotion-expression coherence, the statistical model to be used in the meta-analysis, the inclusion criteria for participants, and the question of how to deal with coherence estimates for complete versus incomplete facial expressions, with missing data, and with redundant data.

Emotions considered. We report coherence estimates for the six "basic emotions" proposed by Ekman (1972): happiness (including amusement), surprise, disgust, sadness, anger, and fear. These make up the core set of emotions for which universal facial expressions (UEs) have been claimed to exist by basic emotion theorists, and on which empirical research on coherence has accordingly focused.

Assessment of emotions. The most straightforward method to determine the degree of coherence between an emotion and the expression assumed to be associated with it consists of measuring both the emotion and the expression, and then computing a suitable index of the statistical association between them (e.g., the correlation). This procedure has been used in the majority of the reviewed studies. The emotion indicator most often used in these studies was the person's self-report of her emotional experience. Apart from their face validity, experience self-reports are the most discriminative currently available measures of emotion (Reisenzein, Junge, Studtmann, & Huber, 2014). Although other indicators of emotion, such as peripheral-physiological variables or reaction times, have also been assessed in some studies (e.g., Mauss, Levenson, McCarter, Wilhelm, & Gross, 2005; Reisenzein, 2000), they have typically not been used to estimate emotion-expression coherence because their emotion specificity is low and their correlation to facial expressions is typically lower than that to self-reports.

Even if self-reports or other independent indicators of the target emotion are not available, the presence of the emotion can often be inferred with high accuracy from information about the stimuli used to induce the emotion (Reisenzein et al., 2014). The reason is that certain stimuli or events are universal or near-universal elicitors of particular emotions. For example, unexpected events are universal elicitors of surprise, and certain objects are disgusting to nearly everybody. This fact allows for estimating coherence even in studies in which no independent indicator of the target emotion is assessed (see later discussion). Because of the relatively small number of existing studies on emotion-expression coherence, we also accepted this "cause-based" method of emotion assessment.

Assessment of facial expressions. In most studies, facial expressions were assessed using (a) an objective coding system, typically a subset of the codes of the facial action coding system (FACS; Ekman, Friesen, & Hager, 2002), or (b) observer judgments of facial expressions described in everyday terms (e.g., "smiling") (see also Reisenzein et al., 2014). However, in some studies, observers (c) coded or judged facial display in terms of expressed emotions (e.g., "sadness") and hence, in effect, inferred the emotion (presumably) underlying the expression (e.g., Lerner, Dahl, Hariri, & Taylor, 2007; Mauss et al., 2005). Finally, in some studies, (d) components of facial expressions were measured using facial electromyography (EMG). Again to be as inclusive as possible, we accepted all of these methods as valid measurements of facial expressions.

Indices of emotion-expression coherence. We conducted separate meta-analyses for the two most frequently used coherence indices (see Reisenzein, Studtmann, & Horstmann, 2013). The first is the correlation between an independent indicator of the target emotion (usually the self-report) and the UE presumably associated with this emotion. Because most studies used an interindividual design, most coherence correlations are between subjects; however, some studies used an intraindividual design, which allowed computing the theoretically more adequate (Reisenzein, 2000; Ruch, 1995) within-subjects correlation (cf. "Suboptimal Designs" in the final section of this chapter).

The second frequently used coherence index is the proportion of the participants (presumably) undergoing a target emotion who show the associated UE; we call this the proportion of (facially) reactive participants. In most cases, this index represents the proportion of participants who showed (components of) an UE *in response to face-valid emotional stimuli*, as it stems mostly from studies in which an independent indicator of the target emotion was not assessed. Note that, strictly speaking, the percentage of reactive participants is not an index of covariation or coherence, but an estimate of the conditional probability P(expression UE| emotion E). However, the *difference* P(UE | E)-P(UE | not E) is a bona fide index of covariation, which in fact is closely related to the binary correlation r(UE, E) (see, e.g., Jenkins & Ward, 1965; McKenzie, 1994); and this difference reduces to P(UE | E) if P(UE | not E) is 0. Hence, if one assumes that in the laboratory and field settings investigated in the reviewed studies, the target expression was not shown in the absence of the emotion (e.g., in a study on disgust, nose-wrinkling was not shown when no disgust stimuli were presented), the percentage index can be interpreted as a coherence index close to the binary correlation.

Statistical model. The meta-analyses were performed for the two described coherence indices using the random-effects model (see Borenstein et al., 2009), which is appropriate if the summarized studies differ on multiple dimensions (e.g., participant sample, induction and measurement methods, study design) and are therefore unlikely to estimate a common effect. Instead, the effect sizes estimated by the different studies are regarded as samples from a distribution of effect sizes. All calculations were performed in R (R Core Team, 2015) using the add-on package *metafor* (Viechtbauer, 2010).

Inclusion criteria for participants. We decided to include only studies with adults and nonclinical samples.

Missing information. We included all relevant studies that reported, or allowed to calculate, at least one of the two effect-size indices (correlation, proportion) and its confidence interval. If an author did not report an effect size but the article included sufficient data (e.g., in tables) to compute it, the effect size was computed from these data. Occasionally an author did not report an exact correlation but stated that it was below a cutoff value (e.g., $r < .20$); in this case, we estimated the correlation as being .05 below the cutoff (e.g., .20 .05 = .15).

Redundant information. (1) If an article reported coherence coefficients for both complete and partial versions of the predicted UE, we used the theoretically more relevant coefficient for the complete UE (e.g., Duchenne smiles instead of simple smiles); if only the coherence coefficient for a partial UE was reported, we used that (in the figures, the partial-expression coefficients are marked with "*"). (2) If an article reported both interindividual and intraindividual correlations, we used the theoretically more adequate intraindividual correlation. (3) If effect sizes were reported for subsamples as well as for the complete sample (e.g., for males, females, and both genders combined), we used the effect size for the complete sample. (4) All coefficients used in the meta-analyses of individual emotions (Figs. 7.1 to 7.6) had to be based on data from different samples. However, the same sample could contribute coherence coefficients to the meta-analyses of more than one emotion (although this was only rarely the case).

Finding relevant studies. We began by including the studies summarized in two recent narrative reviews of laboratory (Reisenzein et al., 2013) and naturalistic (Fernández-Dols & Crivelli, 2013) studies of emotion-expression coherence. These data were supplemented by several additional studies identified through a 2015 *PsychInfo* search, using as search terms "facial expression" and "spontaneous expression" combined with "coherence," "correlation," "production," or "display." Studies with children or with clinical samples were excluded. We also decided to exclude unpublished studies and studies published in languages other than English.

In all, we were able to locate 37 articles (several of which reported more than one study) on emotion-face coherence that fulfilled the described criteria. These articles provided 78 coherence estimates: 44 correlations and 34 percentages of facially reactive participants.

HAPPINESS/AMUSEMENT

The expression of happiness/amusement. According to basic emotion theorists, the smile and, more specifically, the Duchenne smile (Ekman,

Davidson, & Friesen, 1990) is the expression of the basic emotion of happiness or joy (Ekman, 1972; Izard, 1971). Whereas simple smiles consist of raising the corners of the mouth (AU12 in the FACS), Duchenne smiles in addition include cheek rising, which causes wrinkles around the corners of the eyes (AU6).

Most basic emotion researchers define the joy/happiness category broadly; that is, they assume that it includes, in addition to joy and happiness as understood in common sense, related positive emotions such as pride and contentment, sensory pleasantness (Ekman, 2003), and amusement (Ruch, 1995). Other researchers regard amusement as a distinct emotion that, however, shares the smile expression with happiness (e.g., Herring, Burleson, Roberts, & Devine, 2011). To take account of both views, we considered both happiness and related positive emotions, including amusement, in the meta-analysis, but we also conducted separate meta-analyses for happiness and related positive emotions, on the one hand, and amusement, on the other hand.

Elicitors of happiness and amusement. *Happiness and related positive emotions* were elicited in the reviewed studies by a variety of—naturally occurring or deliberately presented—stimuli, including film clips (e.g., Ekman, Friesen, & Ancoli, 1980), emotional imagery (e.g., Brown & Schwartz, 1980), positive social situations (e.g., Mehu, Grammer, & Dunbar, 2007), and positive pictures from the IAPS (International Affective Picture System) (e.g., Lang, Greenwald, Bradley, & Hamm, 1993). *Amusement* was induced using diverse humor stimuli, including funny cartoons, musical mood induction, jokes, film clips, tickling, and a clowning experimenter (see Reisenzein et al., 2013).

It should be noted that some of the happiness studies (e.g., Ekman, Davidson, & Friesen, 1990) report correlations between smiling and self-reports of happiness in situations that probably comprised several happy events, which makes these correlations problematic as estimates of coherence (see Reisenzein et al., 2013).

Number of effect-size estimates and participants. The studies on happiness and related positive emotions such as sensory pleasantness (marked with an "H" in Figs. 7.1a and 7.1b) provided 13 effect-size estimates: 12 correlations (based on a total sample of 732 participants), one of which is intraindividual (marked "ii" in Fig. 7.1a), and one proportion of reactive participants (based on 98 participants).

The amusement studies (marked with an "A" in Figs. 7.1a and 7.1b) provided 16 effect size estimates: 13 correlations (based on 666 participants), 5 of which are intraindividual (marked "ii" in Fig. 7.1a), and 5 proportions (based on 119 participants).

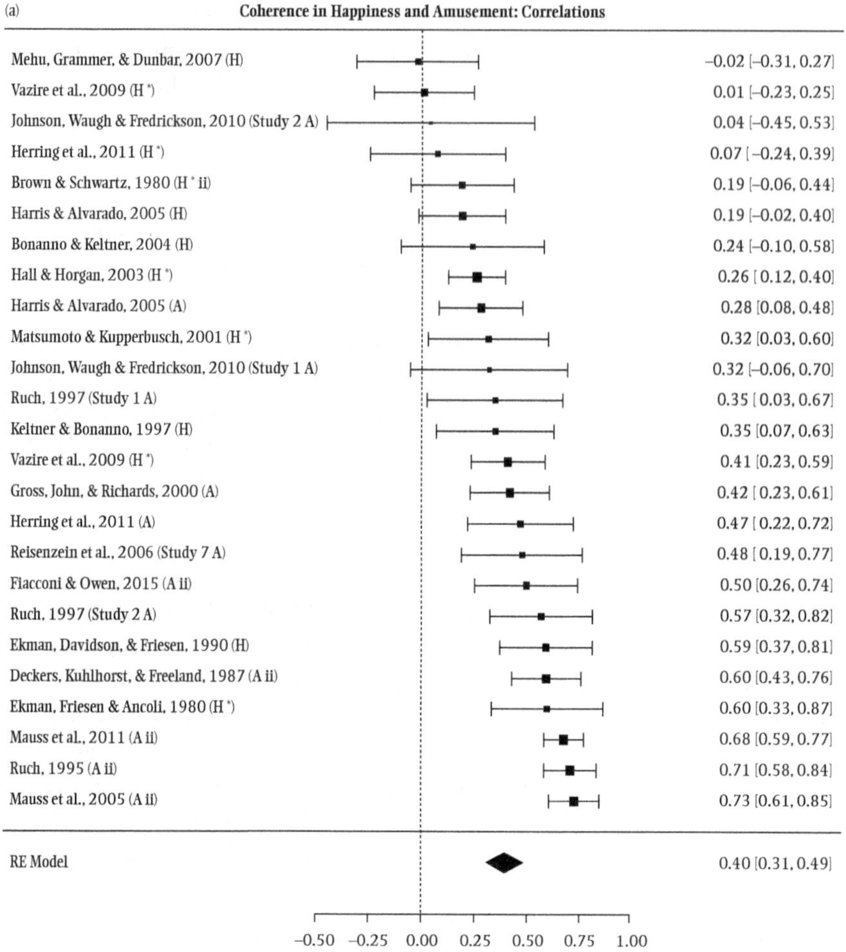

Figure 7.1a–b Forest plots of (a) the correlations and (b) the proportions of reactive participants for happiness and amusement. Studies reporting intra-individual correlations are marked with "ii" and those reporting coherence coefficients based on partial rather than complete UE's with "*".The X-axis represents either correlations (Figure a) or the proportion of participants showing the expression (Figure b). The horizontal lines represent the confidence intervals (CI's) of the point estimates of the correlations or proportions obtained in the different studies. The point estimates are represented by black squares whose area is proportional to the estimate's weight in the meta-analysis. The diamond shown at the bottom of the figures represents the overall point estimate obtained from the meta-analysis (center of the diamond) and its confidence interval (horizontal tips of the diamond).

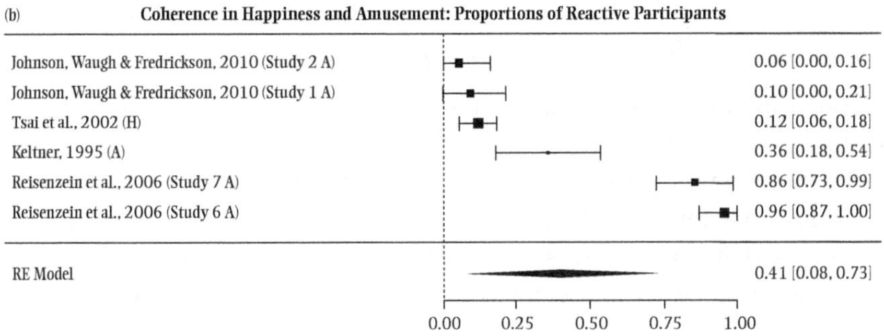

Figure 7.1a–b Continued.

Meta-analysis. Figure 7.1a shows the forest plot of the correlational coherence indices for happiness/amusement. The overall estimate of the correlation produced by the meta-analysis (which in the random-effects model is the mean of an estimated distribution of coherence effects) is .40, with a 95% confidence interval ranging from .31 to .49. If we take happiness and amusement to be separate emotions, the overall estimate of the correlation to smiling is .27 [.16, .39] for happiness and .52 [.43, .62] for amusement.

Six studies reported the proportions of participants who smiled while presumably happy (marked with an "H" in Fig. 7.1b) or amused (marked with an "A"). The forest plot is shown in Figure 7.1b. The overall estimate of the proportion of reactive participants is .41 [.08 .73]. If happiness and amusement are considered separately, the estimate is .12 [.06, .18] for happiness and .47 [.09, .84] for amusement.

SURPRISE

The expression of surprise. The UE of surprise comprises three components: eyebrow raising (AU1/AU2 in FACS), eye widening (AU5), and mouth opening/jaw drop (AU25/AU26).
Surprise elicitors. Surprise is generally thought to be elicited by events that disconfirm a person's explicit or implicit expectations (Reisenzein, Meyer, & Niepel, 2012). Accordingly, researchers interested in surprise expressions have studied facial reactions to diverse unexpected events. For example, participants were presented with a picture of their own face at the end of a face judgment task (Reisenzein, Bördgen, Holdtbernt, & Matz, 2006), were unexpectedly informed that a lottery prize had been raised (Vanhamme, 2000), were confronted with unexpected answers to quiz items (Reisenzein, 2000; Visser, Krahmer, & Swerts, 2014), or found themselves in a novel, strange

room after exiting the door of the laboratory room that had led to a corridor a few minutes earlier (Schützwohl & Reisenzein, 2012).

Number of effect-size estimates and participants. After happiness/amusement, surprise is the emotion for which the largest number of effect size estimates (19) was available (see Figs. 7.2a and 7.2b). Three of them are correlations (one intraindividual, marked "ii" in Fig. 7.2a) based on a total of 168 participants, whereas 16 are proportions of surprised participants who showed at least one component of the surprise face, based on 515 participants.

Meta-analysis. Figures 7.2a and 7.2b show the corresponding forest plots. The estimated coefficients for the combined samples were $r = .24$ [.04, .44] for the correlation and .09 [.05, .14] for the proportion of reactive participants.

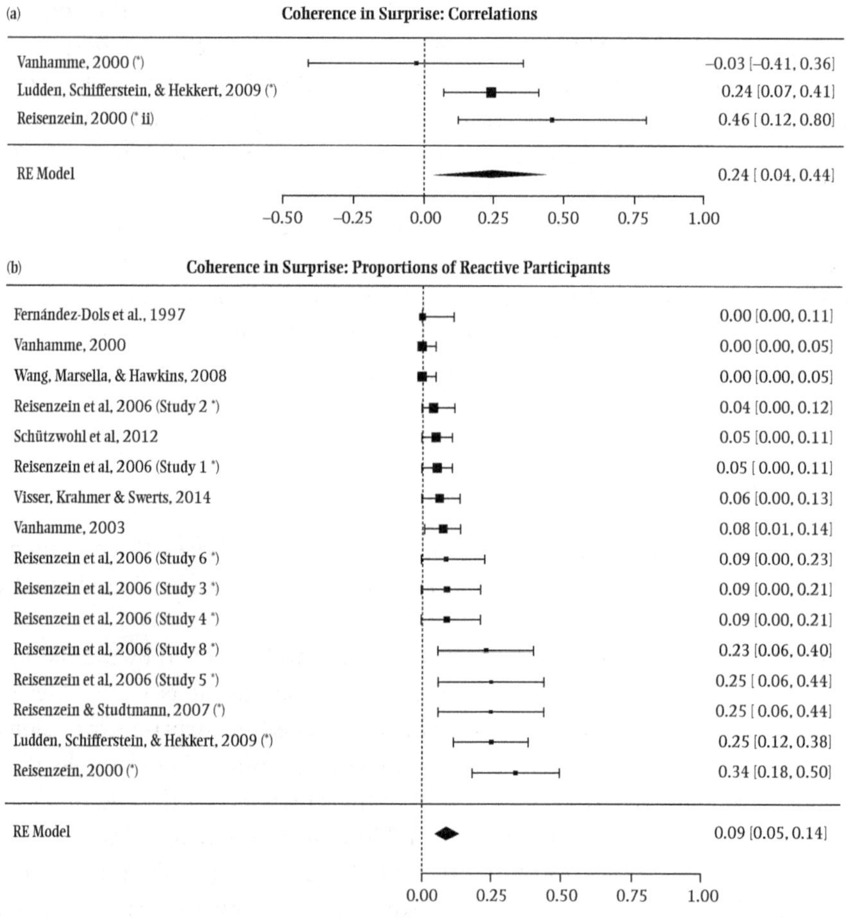

Figure 7.2a–b Forest plots of (a) correlations and (b) proportions of reactive participants for surprise (see Figure 1 caption).

DISGUST

The expression of disgust. The two central components of the disgust expression are raising of the upper lip (AU 10) and nose wrinkling (AU 9).

Disgust elicitors. Disgust was most often induced by presenting disgusting movies (e.g., Ekman, Friesen, & Ancoli, 1980; Fernández-Dols, Sánchez, Carrera, & Ruiz-Belda, 1997), but some authors used other procedures, including reliving past experiences of disgust (e.g., Tsai, Chentsova-Dutton, Freire-Bebeau, & Przymus, 2002), exposing snake- or spider-phobic subjects to live snakes and spiders (Vernon & Berenbaum, 2002), and the presentation of fecal or fishy odors (Jäncke & Kaufmann, 1994). It should be noted that some of the disgust studies (e.g., Ekman, Davidson, & Friesen, 1990; Vernon & Berenbaum, 2002) likely overestimated coherence because the participants were counted as having shown a disgust expression if they had reacted to at least one of several disgusting events (see Reisenzein et al., 2013).

Number of effect-size estimates and participants. Nine effect-size estimates for disgust were available, four correlations (all interindividual) based on 187 participants, and five proportions of participants who showed components of the disgust expression in response to disgusting stimuli, based on 279 participants.

Meta-analysis. The results of the meta-analyses for disgust are shown in Figures 7.3a and 7.3b. The overall correlation estimate was .24 [.10, .37],

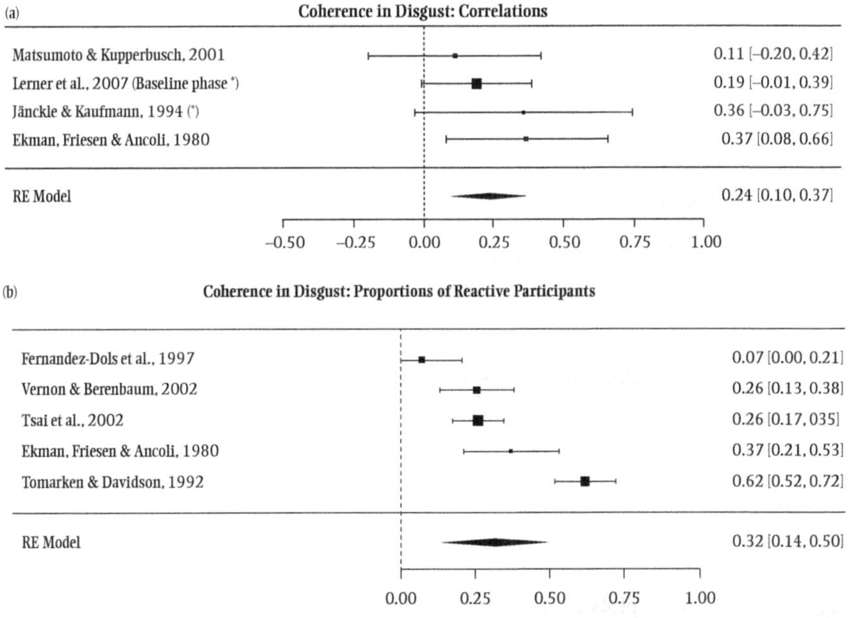

Figure 7.3a–b Forest plots of (a) correlations and (b) proportions of reactive participants for disgust (see Figure 1 caption).

and the overall estimate of the proportion of reactive participants was .32 [.14, .50].

SADNESS

The expression of sadness. The core components of the sadness expression are oblique eyebrows (a combination of AU1, inner brow raise, and AU4, brow lowering) and pulling down the lip corners (AU15).
Sadness elicitors. Sadness was elicited by films (Mauss et al., 2005), imagery (e.g., Brown & Schwartz, 1980), and clinical interviews (Bonnano & Keltner, 2004).

Number of effect-size estimates and participants. Seven effect-size estimates were available. With two exceptions (Johnson, Waugh, & Fredrickson, 2010; Tsai et al., 2002, 119 participants), they were correlations (two intraindividual, marked "ii" in Fig. 7.4a), based on 247 participants (see Figs. 7.4a and 7.4b).

Meta-analysis. Figure 7.4a shows the correlations between sadness and its full or partial predicted UE. The estimated population correlation of .41 [.20 .63] is higher than that for any other emotion with the exception of amusement. However, as can be seen from Figure 7.4a, this finding is mainly due to the presence of a positive outlier (Mauss et al. 2005; see Reisenzein et al., 2013, for a possible methodological explanation of this outlier). The two studies that reported the proportion of reactive participants (Fig. 7.4b) found that .21 [.14,

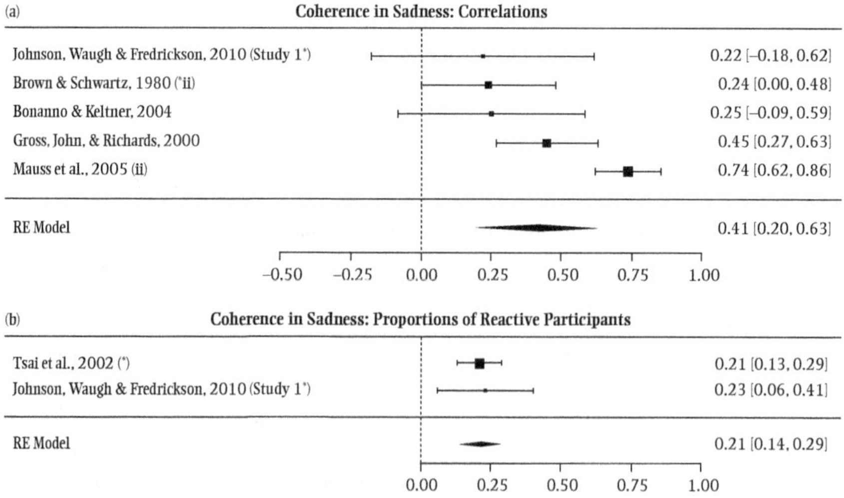

Figure 7.4a–b Forest plots of (a) correlations and (b) proportions of reactive participants for sadness (see Figure 1 caption).

.29] of the participants who relived a saddening experience showed a partial version of the sadness UE.

ANGER

The expression of anger. The prototypical facial expression of anger consists of frowning (AU4), lid tightening (AU7), and lip tightening/lip pressing (AUs 23/24), but there are several variations (Ekman et al., 2002).

Anger elicitors. Anger was elicited in the reviewed studies by, among others, insulting performance feedback (Jäncke, 1996), anger-inducing films (Johnson et al., 2010, Exp. 1), reliving experiences of anger (Tsai et al., 2002), a clinical interview (Bonanno & Keltner, 2004), and a variant of the Velten technique (Johnson et al., 2010, Exp. 2).

Number of effect-size estimates and participants. The meta-analyses included six estimates of correlations (one intraindividual) based on 281 participants and three estimates of the proportion of reactive participants, based on 133 participants (see Figs. 7.5a and 7.5b).

Meta-analysis. The overall estimated correlation for anger was .22 [.11, .33] (Fig. 7.5a). The three studies that reported the proportion of facially reactive

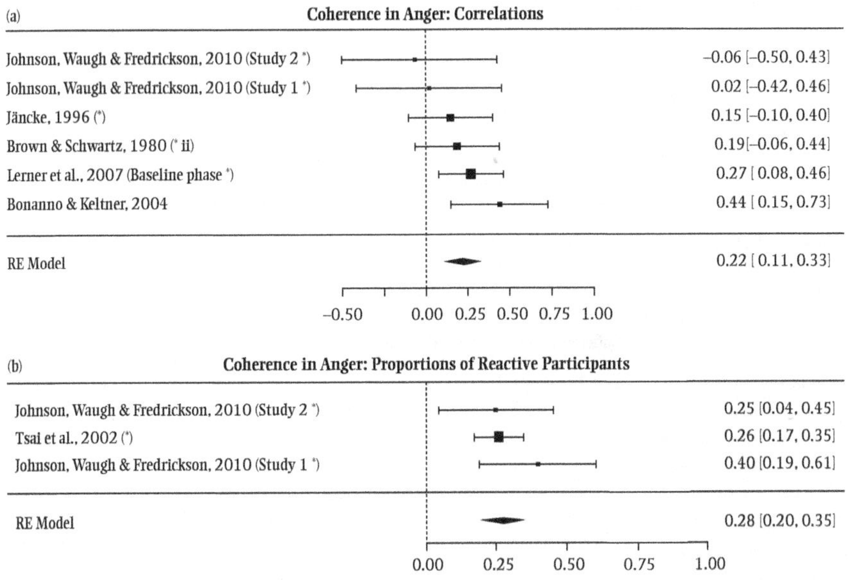

Figure 7.5a–b Forest plots of (a) correlations and (b) proportions of reactive participants for anger (see Figure 1 caption).

participants found that .28 [.20, .35] of the participants who reported anger showed a partial version of the anger UE (Fig. 7.5b).

FEAR

The expression of fear. Core components of the UE of fear are brow raising (AU1/2) and eye widening (AU5) combined with brow knitting (AU4) and retraction of the mouth (AU20); but there are several variations (Ekman et al., 2002).

Fear elicitors. Fear was elicited by imagery (Brown & Schwartz, 1980), the reliving of anxiety episodes (Harrigan & O'Connell, 1996), and exposing spider phobics to the feared animals (Vernon & Berenbaum, 2002).

Number of effect-size estimates and participants. Four effect-size estimates were available, one correlation (60 participants) and three proportions of reactive participants (170 participants).

Meta-analysis. In the single correlational study (Brown & Schwartz, 1980), a partial version of the UE of fear (AU4, frowning) was measured using EMG (corrugator activity) and correlated to self-reports of fear. This correlation was .11 and its CI includes zero [–.14, .36] (Fig. 7.6a). The meta-analytic estimate of the proportion of reactive participants, which is based on three studies, was .34 [.00, .74] (see Fig. 7.6b). Note that two proportions were obtained for a partial version of the fear expression.

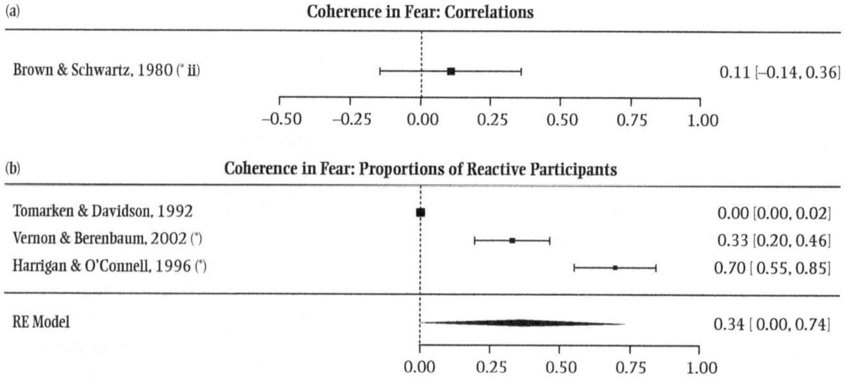

Figure 7.6a–b Forest plots of (a) correlations and (b) proportions of reactive participants for fear (see Figure 1 caption).

META-ANALYSIS FOR ALL EMOTIONS COMBINED

The reported meta-analyses for happiness/amusement (when combined), surprise, disgust, sadness, anger, and fear found that all six emotions were on average only weakly associated with the facial expressions that have been posited as their UEs. This conclusion is supported by the results of additional meta-analyses for all emotions combined (Figs. 7.7a and 7.7b). According to these analyses, the overall estimate of emotion-face coherence (which represents the average coherence effect across emotions and studies) is .35 [.28, .42] for correlations and .23 [.15, .31] for proportions of reactive participants. Note also that the majority of the estimates reported in the individual studies (those marked with "*" in the figures) refer to the coherence between emotions and partial UEs; the coherence for complete UEs is consistently lower (e.g., Reisenzein et al., 2006).

HETEROGENEITY AND MODERATORS

Beyond integrating the results of a set of studies, a second important goal of meta-analysis is to evaluate the homogeneity versus heterogeneity of the studies (Borenstein et al., 2009). The presence of heterogeneity is commonly decided using the Q-test, which is based on the squared deviations of the effect estimates obtained in the individual studies from the overall effect estimate (see also Huedo-Medina, Sanchez-Meca, Marin-Martinez, & Botella, 2006). A significant Q-value means that the variation in effect sizes across studies is too large to be due to sampling error, suggesting that a search for moderators is warranted. In the emotion-expression coherence studies, potential moderators include sample characteristics, the methods used to induce the emotions and to verify their presence, the facial measurement methods (e.g., FACS codings vs. observer judgments), and the study design (inter- versus intraindividual; Ruch, 1995):

We performed the Q-test separately for each emotion (see Table 7.1; NA entries mark cases for which the Q-test could not be computed because fewer than two coefficients were available). The main results can be summarized as follows: (1) For proportions of reactive participants, the Q-test was significant for all emotions for which it could be estimated but sadness and anger; for correlations, it was significant for happiness/amusement (both considered separately and combined) and sadness. (2) The highest Q-values were obtained for happiness/amusement (both correlations and proportions of reactive participants) and fear (proportions).

A main reason for the heterogeneity of the happiness/amusement category is that the two emotions subsumed in this category show very different degrees

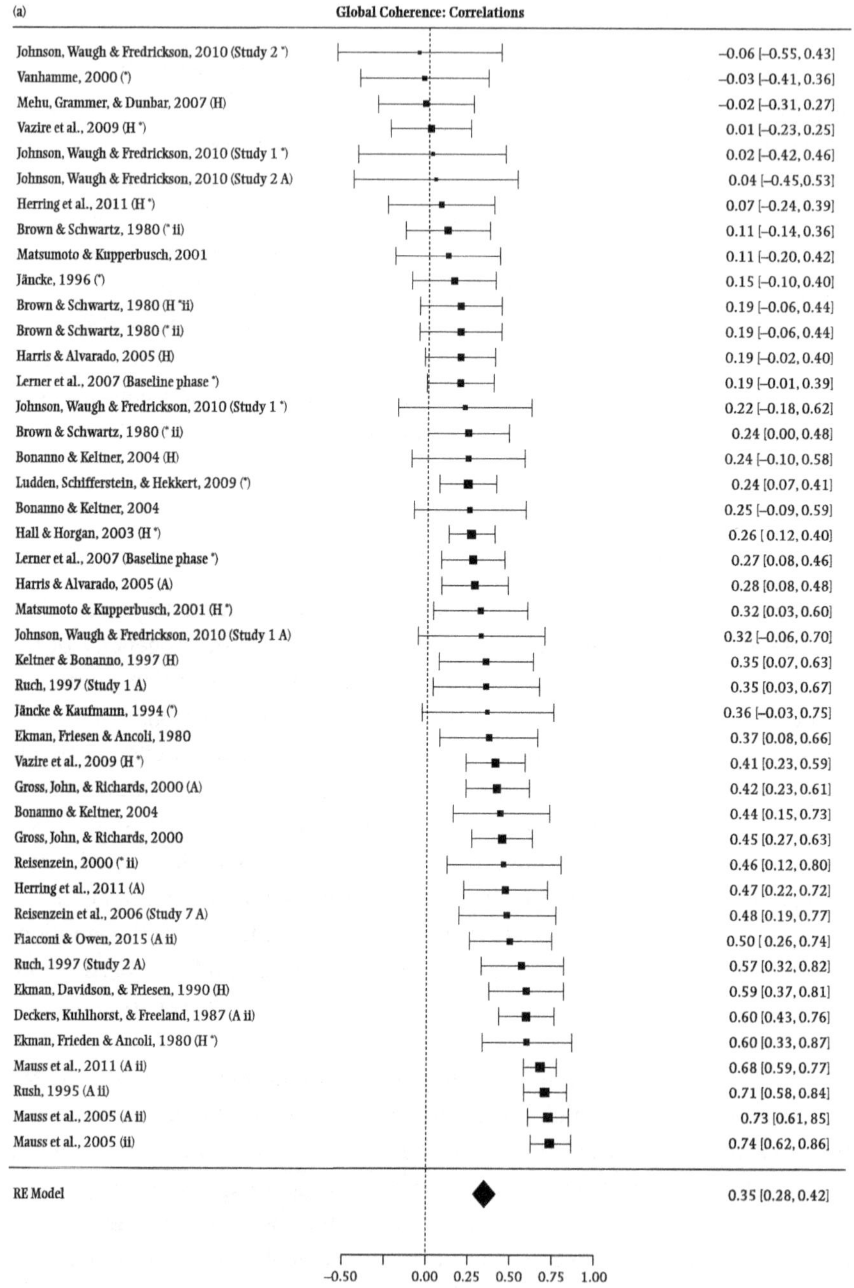

Figure 7.7a–b Forest plots of (a) correlations and (b) proportions of reactive participants for all emotions combined (see Figure 1 caption).

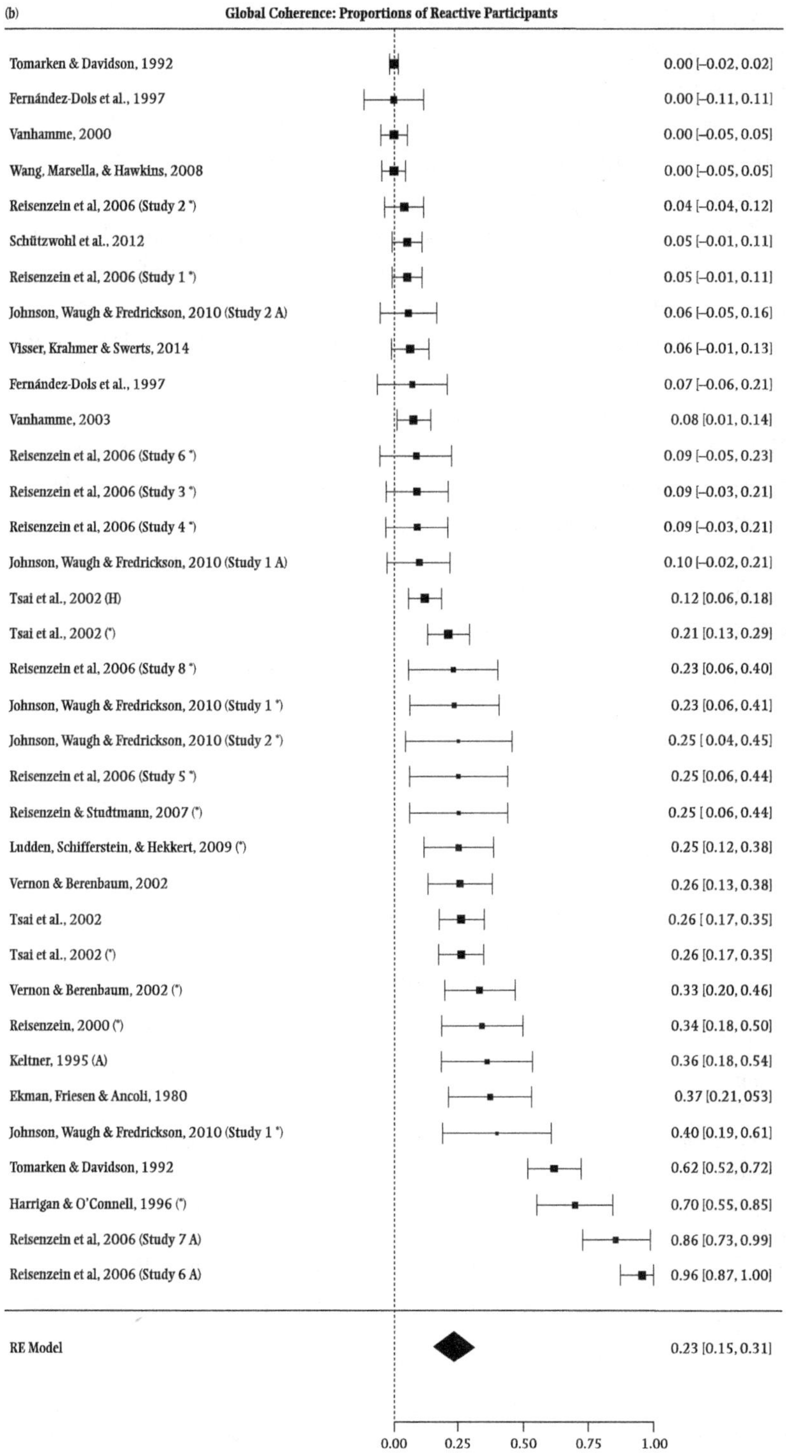

Figure 7.7a–b Continued.

of coherence to smiling. For amusement, coherence is fairly high for the correlation (.52 [.43, .62]) and for the proportion index (.47 [.09, .84]). In contrast, coherence is low for happiness and related emotions: 27 [.16, .39] for the correlation and .12 [.06, .18] for the proportion index. Nevertheless, it should be noted that the Q-values for happiness and amusement are also significant when considered separately.

The observed within-emotion heterogeneity, however, should not detract from the main finding: The coherence between emotion and facial expression is modest to low for all emotions with the exception of happiness/amusement, which as mentioned was mainly due to the amusement studies. If these studies are excluded, the coherence estimates for happiness are similarly low as the estimates for the remaining emotions.

The different degrees of coherence to smiling found for amusement and happiness speak against regarding amusement as a subtype of happiness and support the assumption (e.g., Herring et al., 2011) that amusement is distinct from happiness. Indeed, judged by the degree of emotion-expression coherence, amusement would have more right to be called a "basic emotion" than any of the five classical basic emotions (Ekman, 1972). Interestingly, amusement is also associated with laughter, the only human facial display clearly homologous to a facial behavior (the "play" face) observed in primates (e.g., Gervais & Wilson, 2005; Owren & Bachorowski, 2003).

Table 7.1 TEST FOR HETEROGENEITY (Q-TEST)

	Estimated Effect Size			
	Correlation		Proportion	
Emotion	Q (df)	p	Q (df)	p
Amusement + happiness	120.33 (24)	< .0001	357.11 (5)	< .0001
Amusement	36.60 (12)	0.0004	253.98 (4)	< .0001
Happiness	27.94 (11)	0.0033	NA	NA
Surprise	3.52 (2)	0.1721	45.59 (15)	< .0001
Disgust	2.02 (3)	0.5688	49.00 (4)	<.0001
Sadness	23.46 (4)	< .0001	0.06 (1)	0.8100
Anger	4.92 (5)	0.4257	1.50 (2)	0.4731
Fear	NA	NA	107.09 (2)	< .0001

Q is a measure of the heterogeneity of effect sizes. The higher the Q value, the higher the heterogeneity. Significant Q values ($p < .05$) indicate that random error is improbable as an explanation of the observed heterogeneity.

POSSIBLE REASONS FOR LOW COHERENCE

The results of our meta-analyses support the hypothesis that there is a statistically reliable association between emotions, on the one hand, and at least partial UEs, on the other hand (Figs. 7.1–7.7). However, with the noteworthy exception of amusement, this association was found to be low—much lower, we believe, than basic emotion theory predicts it to be. Basic emotion theory predicts that a (properly functioning) adult should show the UE associated with a basic emotion whenever (a) he or she experiences that emotion, at least beyond some threshold intensity, and (b) does not control the facial expression (see Reisenzein et al., 2006). To explain the obtained findings of low coherence, basic emotion theorists therefore need to assume either that these conditions were not met in most studies by the majority of the participants; or alternatively, that the findings are artifacts caused by suboptimal measurement or data analysis procedures. In line with this, adherents of basic emotion theory have advanced three main explanations for low emotion-UE coherence: (1) insufficient intensity of the emotions elicited by the stimuli used to evoke UEs; (2) deliberate or automatic inhibition or masking of the expressions; and (3) methodological problems, in particular suboptimal study designs and problems with the measurement of the emotions or facial expressions.

No intense emotions. Insufficient emotion intensity could explain the low incidence of UEs observed in some studies, but it is unlikely as a general explanation of low emotion-expression coherence. First, a large variety of emotion elicitors were considered in the reviewed studies, at least some of which seem to have induced strong emotions. Second, direct tests of the hypothesis that emotion-expression coherence increases with increasing emotion intensity found no support for surprise (Reisenzein, 2000; Reisenzein et al., 2006) and sadness (Mauss et al., 2005), although support was obtained for amusement (Mauss et al., 2005). Third, field studies of the expressions associated specifically with intense enjoyment (Fernández-Dols, Carrera, & Crivelli, 2011; García-Higuera, Crivelli, & Fernández-Dols, 2015) found that such experiences do not result in a higher frequency of the predicted UE (smiling); instead, they often lead to unpredicted expressions such as funnel lips or closed eyes (see also Hassin & Aviezer, this volume).

Control of expressions. The second explanation proposed by basic emotion theorists for low observed emotion-expression coherence is that people often try to hide or mask the UEs evoked by emotional stimuli to comply with social conventions about what expressions are appropriate or inappropriate in specific situations. To illustrate, one such display rule is presumably that when attending a (Western) funeral, one must not smile even if, for some reason, one experiences happiness or amusement.

The facial control hypothesis certainly has some prima facie plausibility and could explain some cases of low emotion-expression coherence. However, this hypothesis is again unlikely as a general explanation of low coherence. First, precisely to reduce the likelihood of facial control, in the majority of the reviewed studies researchers took care that the participants were not directly observed by others and therefore had (presumably) no reason to comply with social display rules. Second, even assuming that the effect of display rules is not completely eliminated in solitary situations, it should at least be reduced in these situations, and hence a higher frequency of UEs should be shown. However, studies in which the social context has been experimentally manipulated (typically "alone" versus "social") have obtained results that are inconsistent with a simple control hypothesis: The presence of others was found to have inconsistent (inhibition, enhancement, or null) effects on the facial expressions of happiness, disgust, and sadness, and enhancement effects on the expressions of amusement, as well as, in some situations, those of anger and fear (see Reisenzein et al., 2013). Third, studies in which the effects of display rules were investigated by comparing the emotional expressions of people from different cultures (Friesen, 1972) or age groups (Cole, 1986; Saarni, 1984) assumed to differ in the kind or strength of internalized display rules have yielded inconclusive results (see Fernández-Dols & Ruiz-Belda, 1997; Fernández-Dols, 1999; Fridlund, 1994).

Suboptimal designs. In most studies, the coherence between facial expression and emotion was estimated using a between-subjects rather than a within-subjects design. It has been argued that between-subject designs underestimate coherence due to theoretically irrelevant intraindividual differences (see Reisenzein, 2000; Ruch, 1995). In agreement with this proposal, intraindividual designs (marked "ii" in the forest plots) typically yielded higher coherence estimates than interindividual designs for the same emotions. Most of the intraindividual studies dealt with amusement. For this emotion, the weighted average intraindividual correlation was .68, whereas the weighted average interindividual correlation was only .40.

The three studies of other emotions that used an intraindividual designs found, respectively, low correlations for happiness and sadness (.07 and .24; Brown et al., 1990), a moderate correlation for surprise (.46; Reisenzein, 2000), and a high correlation for sadness (.74; Mauss et al., 2005; but see Reisenzein et al., 2013, for a possible methodological explanation of this finding).

In sum, although more intraindividual coherence studies for emotions other than amusement are desirable, the available data suggest that—in line with theoretical expectations—intraindividual designs increase coherence, but the achieved increase is limited (see also Reisenzein, 2000; Ruch, 1995).

Measurement issues: Have micro-expressions been overlooked? Partly to support the assumption that facial expressions in laboratory and natural settings are frequently inhibited in accordance with display rules, several proponents of basic emotion theory have referred to so-called micro-momentary expressions (Ekman & Friesen, 1969; Haggard & Isaacs, 1966). Micro-momentary expressions, also called micro-expressions, are defined as very brief (less than 500 ms and as short as 33 ms) facial expressions that occur rapidly after the onset of emotion-inducing stimuli. Ekman and Friesen (1969) argue that micro-expressions reflect stimulus-evoked emotions that "leak" to the face before the person is able to fully inhibit the expressions and /or (if the inhibition is at least partly successful) the person's attempt to control the expression. In addition, some micro-expressions might reflect uninhibited emotions that are simply very brief. Regardless of their cause, micro-expressions could provide yet another explanation for low observed coherence between emotions and facial expressions: It could be argued that many UEs were overlooked in the coherence studies because they were too brief or too weak to be detected by the observation methods used (which in most studies were observer based).

However, the few empirical studies on micro-expressions that exist to date (Porter, ten Brinke, & Wallace, 2012; Yan, Wu, Liang, Chen, & Fu, 2013) suggest that although micro-expressions do occur, they are too infrequent to explain low emotion coherence: Porter et al. found that only 18 of 1,711 expressions shown by subjects watching emotion-eliciting stimuli qualified as "micro-expressions" (expressions shorter than 500 ms), and Yan et al. (2013) classified only 109 of "more than 1,000 facial expressions recorded in camera" (Yan et al., 2013, p. 221) as micro-expressions. In addition, the micro-expressions observed in both studies were without exception only partial versions of the UEs of basic emotions (e.g., in the case of happiness, wrinkled eyes *or* raised lips, see also Yan et al., 2014). Taken together, these findings suggest that the observed micro-expressions were simply briefer (and perhaps also weaker) versions of the expressions found in the studies included in our meta-analysis: As reported, these studies also found that the emotional expressions elicited by emotional stimuli are, for most emotions, rare and incomplete. In fact, in several of the reviewed studies—those using frame-by-frame video coding, or facial EMG measurement—micro-expressions were most likely already taken into account (e.g., Reisenzein et al., 2006).

REFERENCES

Bonnano, G. A., & Keltner, D. (2004). The coherence of emotion systems: comparing "on line" measures of appraisal and facial expressions, and self-report. *Cognition and Emotion, 18*, 431–444.

Borenstein, M., Hedges, L. V., Higgins, J. P. T., & Rothstein, H. R. (2009). *Introduction to meta-analysis*. New York, NY: Wiley.

Brown, S.-L., & Schwartz, G. E. (1980). Relationships between facial electromyography and subjective experience during affective imagery. *Biological Psychology, 11*, 49–62.

Cole, P. M. (1986). Children's spontaneous control of facial expression. *Child Development, 57*, 1309–1321.

Cumming, G. (2012). *Understanding the new statistics: Effect sizes, confidence intervals, and meta-analysis*. New York, NY: Routledge.

Davidson, R. J. (1992). Prolegomena to the structure of emotion: Gleanings from neuropsychology. *Cognition and Emotion, 6*, 245–268.

Deckers, L., Kuhlhorst, L., & Freeland, L. (1987). The effects of spontaneous and voluntary facial reactions on surprise and humor. *Motivation and Emotion, 11*, 403–412.

Ekman, P. (1972). Universals and cultural differences in facial expressions of emotion. In J. Cole (Ed.), *Nebraska Symposium on Motivation* (Vol. 19, pp. 207–283). Lincoln: University of Nebraska Press.

Ekman, P. (2003). *Emotions revealed: Recognizing faces and feelings to improve communication and emotional life*. New York, NY: Times Books.

Ekman, P., Davidson, R. J., & Friesen, W. V. (1990). The Duchenne smile: Emotional expression and brain physiology: II. *Journal of Personality and Social Psychology, 58*, 342–353.

Ekman, P., & Friesen, W. V. (1969). Nonverbal leakage and clues to deception. *Psychiatry, 32*, 88–105.

Ekman, P., Friesen, W. V. (1978). *Facial action coding system: A technique for the measurement of facial movement*. Palo Alto, CA: Consulting Psychologists Press.

Ekman, P., Friesen, W. V., & Ancoli, S. (1980). Facial signs of emotional experience. *Journal of Personality and Social Psychology, 39*, 1125–1134.

Ekman, P., Friesen, W. V., & Hager, J. V. (2002). *Facial action coding system* (2nd ed.). Salt Lake City, UT: Research Nexus eBook.

Fernández-Dols, J-M. (1999). Facial expression and emotion: A situationist view. In P. Philippot, R. S. Feldman, & E. J. Coats (Eds.), *The social context of nonverbal behavior* (pp. 242–261). Cambridge, UK: Cambridge University Press.

Fernández-Dols, J. M., Carrera, P., & Crivelli, C. (2011). Facial behavior while experiencing sexual excitement. *Journal of Nonverbal Behavior, 35*, 63–71.

Fernández-Dols, J. M., & Crivelli, C. (2013). Emotion and expression: Naturalistic studies. *Emotion Review, 5*, 24–29.

Fernández-Dols, J. M., Sánchez, F., Carrera, P., & Ruiz-Belda, M.-A. (1997). Are spontaneous expressions and emotions linked? An experimental test of coherence. *Journal of Nonverbal Behavior, 21*, 163–177.

Fiacconi, C. M., & Owen, A. M. (2015). Using psychophysiological measures to examine the temporal profile of verbal humor elicitation. *PLoS ONE, 10*(9), e0135902. doi:10.1371/journal.pone.0135902.

Fridlund, A. (1994). *Human facial expression: An evolutionary view.* San Diego, CA: Academic Press.

Friesen, W. V. (1972). *Cultural differences in facial expression in a social situation: An experimental test of the concept of display rules.* Unpublished doctoral dissertation, University of California, San Francisco, CA.

Garcia Higuera, J. A., Crivelli, C., & Fernández-Dols, J. M. (2015). Facial expressions during an extremely intense emotional situation: Toreros' lip funnel. *Social Science Information, 54,* 439–454.

Gervais, M., & Wilson, D.S. (2005). The evolution and functions of laughter and humor: A synthetic approach. *The Quarterly Review of Biology, 80,* 395–430.

Gross, J. J., John, O. P., & Richards, J. M. (2000). The dissociation of emotion expression from emotion experience: A personality perspective. *Personality and Social Psychology Bulletin, 26,* 712–726.

Haggard, E. A., & Isaacs, K. S. (1966). Micro-momentary facial expressions as indicators of ego mechanisms in psychotherapy. In L. A. Gottschalk & A. H. Auerbach (Eds.), *Methods of research in psychotherapy* (pp. 154–165). New York, NY: Appleton Century Crofts.

Hall, J. A., & Horgan, T. G. (2003). Happy affect and smiling: Is their relation moderated by interpersonal power? *Emotion, 3,* 303–309.

Harrigan, J. A., & O'Connell, D. M. (1996). How do you look when feeling anxious? Facial displays of anxiety. *Personality and Individual Differences, 21,* 205–212.

Harris, C. R., & Alvarado, N. (2005). Facial expressions, smile types, and self-report during humour, tickle, and pain. *Cognition and Emotion, 19,* 655–669.

Herring, D. R., Burleson, M. H., Roberts, N. A., & Devine, M. J. (2011). Coherent with laughter: Subjective experience, behavior, and physiological responses during amusement and joy. *International Journal of Psychophysiology, 79,* 211–218.

Huedo-Medina, T. B., Sanchez-Meca, J., Martín-Sánchez, F., & Botella, J. (2006). Assessing heterogeneity in meta-analysis: Q statistic or I2 index? *Psychological Methods, 11,* 193–206.

Izard, C. E. (1971). *The face of emotion.* New York, NY: Appleton-Century-Crofts.

Jäncke, L., & Kaufmann, N. (1994). Facial EMG responses to odors in solitude and with an audience. *Chemical Senses, 19,* 99–111.

Jenkins, H. M., & Ward, W. C. (1965). Judgment of contingency between response and outcome. *Psychological Monographs, 79* (*1,* Whole No. 594).

Johnson, K. J., Waugh, C. E., & Fredrickson, B. L. (2010). Smile to see the forest: Facially expressed positive emotions broaden cognition. *Cognition and Emotion, 24,* 299–321.

Keltner, D. (1995). Signs of appeasement: Evidence for the distinct displays of embarrassment, amusement, and shame. *Journal of Personality and Social Psychology, 68,* 441–454.

Keltner, D., & Bonanno, G. A. (1997). A study of laughter and dissociation: Distinct correlates of laughter and smiling during bereavement. *Journal of Personality and Social Psychology, 73,* 687–702.

Lang, P. J., Greenwald, M. K., Bradley, M. M., & Hamm, A. O. (1993). Looking at pictures: Affective, facial, visceral, and behavioral reactions. *Psychophysiology, 30,* 261–273.

Lerner, J. S., Dahl, R., Hariri, A. R., & Taylor, S. E. (2007). Facial expressions of emotion reveal neuroendocrine and cardiovascular stress responses. *Biological Psychiatry, 61*, 253–260.

Lewis, S., & Clarke, M. (2001). Forest plots: Trying to see the wood and the trees. *British Medical Journal, 322*, 1479–1480.

Ludden, G. D. S., Schifferstein, H. N. J., & Hekkert, P. (2009). Visual-tactual incongruities in products as sources of surprise. *Empirical Studies of the Arts, 27*, 63–89.

Matsumoto, D., & Kupperbusch, C. (2001). Idiocentric and allocentric differences in emotional expression, experience, and the coherence between expression and experience. *Asian Journal of Social Psychology, 4*, 113–131.

Mauss, I. B., Levenson, R. W., McCarter, L., Wilhelm, F. H., & Gross, J. J. (2005). The tie that binds? Coherence among emotion experience, behavior, and physiology. *Emotion, 5*, 175–190.

McKenzie, C. R. M. (1994). The accuracy of intuitive judgment strategies: Covariation assessment and Bayesian inference. *Cognitive Psychology, 26*, 209–239.

Mehu, M., Grammer, K., & Dunbar, R. I. (2007). Smiles when sharing. *Evolution and Human Behavior, 28*, 415–422.

Ortony, A., & Turner, T. J. (1990). What's basic about basic emotions? *Psychological Review, 97*, 315–331.

Owren, M. J., & Bachorowski, J.A. (2003). Reconsidering the evolution of nonlinguistic communication: The case of laughter. *Journal of Nonverbal Behavior, 27*, 183–200.

Porter, S., ten Brinke, L., & Wallace, B. (2012). Secrets and lies: Involuntary leakage in deceptive facial expressions as a function of emotional intensity. *Journal of Nonverbal Behavior, 36*, 23–37.

R Core Team (2015). *R: A language and environment for statistical computing.* R Foundation for Statistical Computing, Vienna, Austria. http://www.R-project.org/

Reisenzein, R. (2000). Exploring the strength of association between the components of emotion syndromes: The case of surprise. *Cognition and Emotion, 14*, 1–38.

Reisenzein, R., Bördgen, S., Holtbernd, T., & Matz, D. (2006). Evidence for strong dissociation between emotion and facial displays: The case of surprise. *Journal of Personality and Social Psychology, 91*, 295–315.

Reisenzein, R., Junge, M., Studtmann, M., & Huber, O. (2014). Observational approaches to the measurement of emotions. In R. Pekrun & L. Linnenbrink-Garcia (Eds.), *International handbook of emotions in education* (pp. 580–606). Philadelphia, PA: Taylor & Francis/Routledge.

Reisenzein, R., Meyer, W.-U., & Niepel, M. (2012). Surprise. In V. S. Ramachandran (Ed.), *Encyclopedia of human behavior* (2nd ed., pp. 564–570). London, UK: Elsevier.

Reisenzein, R., & Studtmann, M. (2007). On the expression and experience of surprise: No evidence for facial feedback, but evidence for a reverse self-inference effect. *Emotion, 7*, 612–627.

Reisenzein, R., Studtmann, M., & Horstmann, G. (2013). Coherence between emotion and facial expression: Evidence from laboratory experiments. *Emotion Review, 5*, 16–23.

Rosenberg, E. L., & Ekman, P. (1994). Coherence between expressive and experiential systems in emotion. *Cognition and Emotion, 8*, 201–229.

Ruch, W. (1995). Will the real relationship between facial expression and affective experience please stand up: The case of exhilaration. *Cognition and Emotion*, *9*, 33–58.

Ruch, W. (1997). State and trait cheerfulness and the induction of exhilaration: A FACS study. *European Psychologist*, *2*, 328–341.

Ruiz-Belda, M. A., Fernández-Dols, J. M., Carrera, P., & Barchard, K. (2003). Spontaneous facial expressions of happy bowlers and soccer fans. *Cognition and Emotion*, *17*, 315–326.

Saarni, C. (1984). An observational study of children's attempts to monitor their expressive behavior. *Child Development*, *55*, 1504–1513.

Schützwohl, A., & Reisenzein, R. (2012). Facial expressions in response to a highly surprising event exceeding the field of vision: A test of Darwin's theory of surprise. *Evolution and Human Behavior*, *33*, 657–664.

Tsai, J. L., Chentsova-Dutton, Y., Freire-Bebeau, L., & Przymus, D. E. (2002). Emotional expression and physiology in European Americans and Hmong Americans. *Emotion*, *2*, 380–397.

Valentine, J. C., Pigott, T. D., & Rothstein, H. R. (2010). How many studies do you need? A primer on statistical power for meta-analysis. *Journal of Educational and Behavioral Statistics*, *35*, 215–247.

Vanhamme, J. (2000). The link between surprise and satisfaction: An exploratory research on how to best measure surprise. *Journal of Marketing Management*, *16*, 565–582.

Vanhamme, J. (2003). Surprise . . . surprise. An empirical investigation on how surprise is connected to consumer satisfaction. In *ERIM Report Series Research in Management ERS-2003-005-MKT*. Rotterdam: Erasmus Research Institute of Management.

Vazire, S., Naumann, L. P., Rentfrow, P. J., & Gosling, S. D. (2009). Smiling reflects different emotions in men and women. *Behavioral and Brain Sciences*, *32*, 403–405.

Vernon, L. L., & Berenbaum, H. (2002). Disgust and fear in response to spiders. *Cognition and Emotion*, *16*, 809–830.

Visser, M., Krahmer, E., & Swerts, M. (2014). Contextual effects on surprise expressions: A developmental study. *Journal of Nonverbal Behavior*, *38*, 523–547.

Viechtbauer, W. (2010). Conducting meta-analyses in R with the metafor package. *Journal of Statistical Software*, *36*, 1–48.

Wang, N., Marsella, S., & Hawkins, T. (2008). Individual differences in expressive response: A challenge for ECA design. *Proceedings of the 7th International Conference on Autonomous Agents and Multiagent Systems (AAMAS 2008)*, *3*, 1289–1292.

Yan, W., Wang, S., Liu, Y., Wu, Q., & Fu, X. (2014). For micro-expression recognition: Database and suggestions. *Neurocomputing: An International Journal*, *136*, 82–87.

Yan, W., Wu, Q., Liang, J., Chen, Y., & Fu, X. (2013). How fast are the leaked facial expressions: The duration of micro-expressions. *Journal of Nonverbal Behavior*, *37*, 217–230.

PART III

Evolution

8

Evolution of Facial Musculature

RUI DIOGO AND SHARLENE E. SANTANA

The face of humans and other mammals is a complex morphological structure (Figs. 8.1 and 8.2) in which both external and internal parts function in conveying information relevant for social interactions. Externally, facial features bear signals that allow recognition of conspecifics, individuals within the social group and potential mates. This information is encrypted in traits such as the shape of facial parts, and the complexity and hues of its color patterns (Fig. 8.1) (Setchell, 2005; Waitt et al., 2003). Internally, the facial musculature (Fig. 8.2) and neural centers control how the external morphology is showcased to other individuals through the production of facial expressions, which are important in communicating behavioral intentions within a social context (e.g., bared teeth communicate the intent to withdraw from an agonistic encounter; Preuschoft & Van Hooff, 1997). Therefore, internal and external anatomical features of the face are not only in close physical proximity but are also tightly connected in their function.

Facial coloration patterns evolved in tandem with sociality and sympatry (when two species or populations exist in the same geographic area) in primates (Santana, Alfaro, Noonan, & Alfaro, 2013; Santana, Lynch Alfaro, & Alfaro, 2012). In most primate radiations, highly social and sympatric species evolved multicolored faces, while less social species tend to have less colorful faces. Complex facial patterns potentially enable higher interindividual

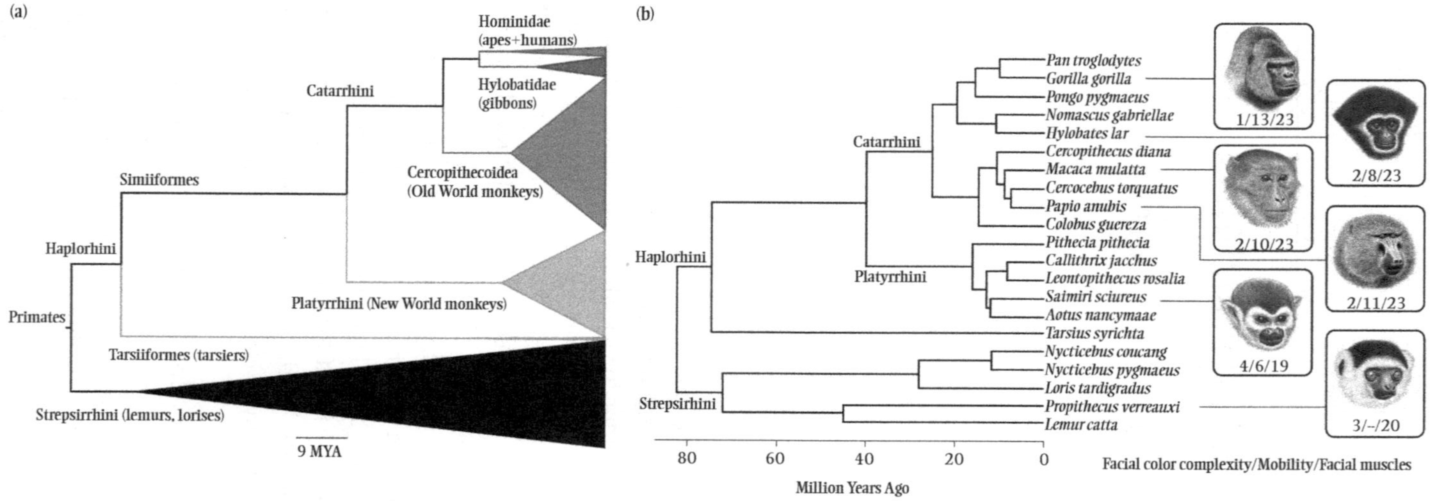

Figure 8.1 Phylogenies of (*a*) the Order Primates, showing the major lineages in proportion to their numbers of species, and (*b*) the primate species included in Santana et al.'s 2014 study, with examples illustrating major trends in facial color pattern complexity, mobility, and facial muscles. Species that are larger and have more plainly colored faces tend to have a larger repertoire of facial expressions. (©2012 Stephen D. Nash/IUCN/SSC Primate Specialist Group; modified with permission)

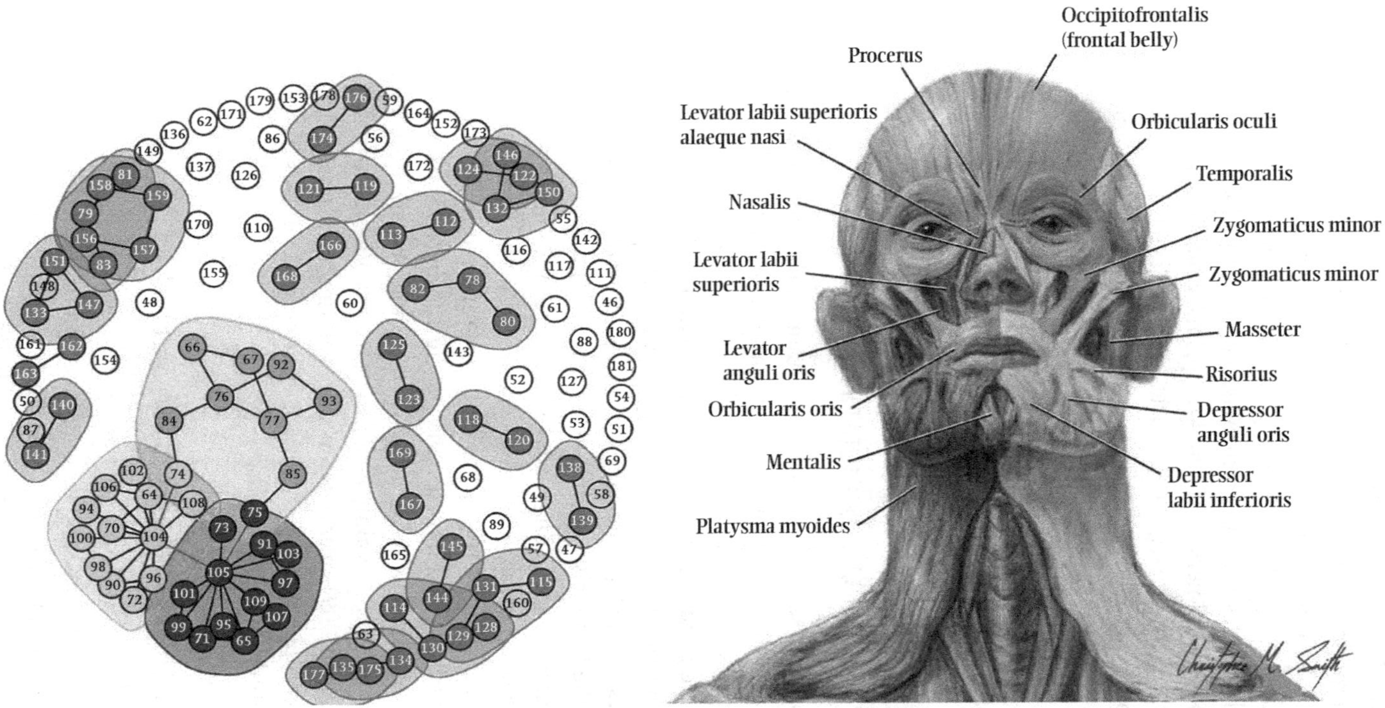

Figure 8.2 Muscle network modules of the normal adult head identified using anatomical networks: in yellow, the ocular/upper face module (66-67 Occipitalis left-right, 74-75 Zygomaticus minor left-right, 76-77 Frontalis left-right, 84-85 Orbicularis oculi left-right, 92-93 Procerus left-right); in light and dark blue, the left and right orofacial modules (64-65 Platsma myoides left-right, 70-71 Risorius left-right, 72-73 Zygomaticus major left-right, 90-91 Levator labii superioris alaeque nasi left-right, 94-95 Buccinatorius left-right, 96-97 Levator labii superioris left-right, 98-99 Nasalis left-right, 100-101 Depressor septi nasi left-right, 102-103 Levator anguli oris facialis left-right, 104-105 Orbicularis oris left-right, 106-107 Depressor labii inferioris left-right, 108-109 Depressor anguli oris left-right); and in gray/white, the smaller muscle modules, which, in the absence of bones, are mostly disconnected to the three major muscle modules (©2015 Christopher Smith/HU; modified from Esteve-Altava et al. 2015, with permission)

variation within social groups and among species, facilitating recognition at either of these levels. Facial expressions are also linked to sociality; highly gregarious species produce a wider variety of facial movements, which may function in group cohesion by enhancing communication during conflict management and bonding (Dobson, 2009ab). Facial expressions result from the action of facial muscles that are controlled by neural pathways (facial nucleus of the pons—cranial nerve VII—and the primary motor cortex), and primate species with relatively large facial nuclei tend to have highly dexterous faces (Sherwood et al., 2005). The primate facial musculature is among the most complex across mammals (although not as complex as that of, e.g., elephants; Boas & Paulli, 1908, 1925), but it is unclear if and how it has evolved in response to functional demands associated with ecology and sociality (Burrows, 2008; R. Diogo, Wood, Aziz, & Burrows, 2009; Rui Diogo & Wood, 2012).

EVOLUTION OF THE MUSCLES OF FACIAL EXPRESSION

The first (mandibular), second (hyoid), and more posterior branchial arches are formed from bilateral swellings on either side of the pharynx. The muscles of facial expression (Fig. 8.2)—usually designated simply as " facial muscles"—are a subgroup of the hyoid (second arch) muscles and are innervated by the facial nerve (cranial nerve VII). This means that all other hyoid muscles (e.g., stapedius, stylohyoideus) are not designated as facial muscles, despite being also innervated by the facial nerve. Except for the buccinatorius (and the mandibulo-auricularis present in many nonhuman mammals), the facial muscles are mainly attached to the dermis of the skin and the elastic cartilage of the pinna. They are involved in generating facial expressions during social interactions among conspecifics, as well as in feeding, chemosensation, whisker motility, hearing, vocalization, and human speech. This section is mainly based on, and provides a short summary of, Diogo et al.'s (2009) overview on the evolution of primate facial muscles, which is complemented by Table 8.1; interested readers should refer to this publication for more details.

Evolution of Mammalian Facial Muscles and the Ancestral Condition for Primates

The facial muscles are only present in mammals, probably deriving from the ventral hyoid muscle interhyoideus, and likely also from at least some dorso-medial hyoid muscles (e.g., cervicomandibularis) of other tetrapods. Monotremes such as the platypus only have 10 distinct facial muscles (not including the extrinsic muscles of the ear). Rodents, such as rats, have up to 24 facial muscles. The occipitalis + auricularis posterior, the procerus, and the dilatator nasi + levator labii superioris + levator anguli oris facialis of therian mammals (marsupials + placentals) probably correspond to part of the platysma cervicale (muscle connecting back of neck—nuchal region—to mouth, different from platysma myoides connecting front of neck and pectoral region to mouth: see also later discussion), of the levator labii superioris alaeque nasi, and of the orbicularis oris of monotremes, respectively. The sternofacialis, interscutularis, zygomaticus major, zygomaticus minor, and orbito-termporo-auricularis of therian mammals probably derive from the sphincter colli profundus, but it is possible that at least some of the former muscles derive from the platysma cervicale and/or platysma myoides. Colugos (Dermoptera or "flying lemurs") and tree-shrews (Scandentia), the closest living relatives of primates (Fig. 8.1), have a similar facial musculature, but the former lack two muscles that are usually present in the latter, the sphincter colli superficialis and the mandibulo-auricularis. As both these muscles are found in rodents, as well as in tree-shrews and at least some primates, they were likely present in the last common ancestor (LCA) of Primates + Dermaptera + Scandentia. The frontalis, auriculo-orbitalis, and auricularis superior of this LCA very likely derived from the orbito-temporo-auricularis of other mammals, while the zygomatico-orbicularis and corrugator supercilii most likely derived from the orbicularis oculi.

The facial musculature of the LCA of primates was probably very similar to that seen in the extant tree-shrew *Tupaia*. Muscles that have been described in the literature as peculiar to primates, for example, the zygomaticus major and zygomaticus minor, are now commonly accepted as homologues of muscles of other mammals (e.g., of the "auriculolabialis inferior" and "auriculolabialis superior"). The only muscle that is actually often present as a distinct structure in strepsirhines (primate group including extant members such as lemurs and lorises; Fig. 8.1), but not in tree-shrews or colugos, is the depressor supercilii, which derives from the orbicularis oris matrix. As the depressor supercilii is present in strepsirhine and nonstrepsirhine primates, it is likely that this muscle was present in the LCA of primates. In summary, the ancestral condition predicted for the LCA of primates is probably similar to that found in some extant strepsirhines (e.g., *Lepilemur*). Importantly, the number of facial muscles present in living strepsirhines is higher than that originally reported by authors in the 19th and first decades of the 20th century. For instance, Murie and Mivart (1869) reported only seven facial muscles in a lemur, grouping all the muscles associated with the nasal region into a single "nasolabial muscle mass." The supposed lack of complexity seen in strepsirhines was consistent with the anthropocentric, "scalae naturae," finalistic evolutionary paradigm subscribed to by

Table 8.1 SCHEME ILLUSTRATING THE AUTHORS' HYPOTHESES REGARDING THE HOMOLOGIES OF THE FACIAL MUSCLES OF ADULTS OF REPRESENTATIVE NONPRIMATE AND PRIMATE MAMMALIAN TAXA

Ornithorhynchus anatinus (10 mus. - not ex. ear)	*Rattus norvegicus* (24 mus. - not ex. ear)	*Tupaia* sp. (22 mus. - not ex. ear)	*Lepilemur ruficaudatus* (21 mus. - not ex. ear)	*Macaca mulatta* (23 mus.- not ex.ear)
Platysma cervicale	Platysma cervicale	Platysma cervicale	Platysma cervicale	Platysma cervicale
Platysma myoides	Platysma myoides	Platysma myoides	Platysma myoides	Platysma myoides
—	Occipitalis	Occipitalis	Occipitalis	Occipitalis
—	Aur. posterior	Aur. posterior	Aur. posterior	Aur. posterior
Ex. ear mus.	Ex. ear mus.	Ex. ear mus.	Ex. ear mus.	Ex. ear mus.
—	Mandibulo-aur.	Mandibulo-aur.	Mandibulo-aur.	—
—	—	—	—	—
Interhyoideus prof.	—	—	—	—
Sphincter colli supe.	Sphincter colli supe.	Sphincter colli supe.	—	—
—(colli prof. in Echidna)	Sphincter colli prof.	Sphincter colli prof.	Sphincter colli prof.	—
—	Sternofacialis	—	—	—
Cervicalis tra.	—	—	—	—
—	Interscutularis	—	—	—
—	Zygomaticus major	Zygomaticus maj.	Zygomaticus maj.	Zygomaticus maj.
—	Zygomaticus minor	Zygomaticus min.	Zygomaticus min.	Zygomaticus min.
—	Orbito-temporo-aur.	Frontalis	Frontalis	Frontalis
—	—	Auriculo-orbitalis	Auriculo-orbitalis	Auriculo-orbitalis
—	—	—	—	—
—	—	Aur. superior	Aur. superior	Aur. superior
Orbic. oculi	Orbic. oculi	Orbic. oculi	Orbic. oculi	Orbic. oculi
—	—	Zygomatico-orbic.	—	—
—	—	—	De. supercilii	De. supercilii
—	—	Corru. supercilii	Corru. supercilii	Corru. supercilii
Naso-labialis	Le. labii sup. al.nasi	Le. labii sup. al.nasi	Le. labii sup. al.nasi	Le. labii sup. al.nasi
—	Procerus	—	—	Procerus
Buccinatorius	Buccinatorius	Buccinatorius	Buccinatorius	Buccinatorius
—	Dilatator nasi	—	—	—
	Le. labii sup.	Le. labii sup.	Le. labii sup.	Le. labii sup.
—	Nasalis	Nasalis	Nasalis	Nasalis
—	De. septi nasi	—	—	De. septi nasi
—	De. rhinarii	—	—	—
—	Le. rhinari	—	—	—
—	Le. anguli oris fac.	Le. anguli oris fac.	Le. anguli oris fac.	Le. anguli oris fac.
Orbic. oris	Orbic. oris	Orbic. oris	Orbic. oris	Orbic. oris
—	—	—	—	De. labii inf.
—	—	—	—	De. anguli oris
Mentalis	—	Mentalis	Mentalis	Mentalis

Data from evidence provided by our own dissections and comparisons and by a review of the literature. The black arrows indicate the hypotheses that are most strongly supported by the evidence available; the grey arrows indicate alternative hypotheses that are supported by some of the data, but overall they are not as strongly supported by the evidence available as are the hypotheses indicated by black arrows. al. = alaeque; aur. = auricularis; corru. = corrugator; fac. = facialis; de. = depressor; ex. = extrinsic; inf. = inferioris; lab. = labialis; le. = levator; maj. = major; min. = minor; mus. = muscles; orbic. = orbicularis; prof. = profundus; sup. = superioris; supe. = superficialis; tra. = transversus.

Hylobates lar (23 mus.- not ex. ear)	*Pongo pygmaeus* (21 mus.- not ex. ear)	*Gorilla gorilla* (24 mus.- not ex. ear)	*Pan troglodytes* (22 mus.- not ex. ear)	*Homo sapiens* (24 mus.- not ex. ear)
Platysma cervicale	—	Platysma cervicale	—	—
Platysma myoides	Platysma myoides	Platysma myoides	Platysma myoides	Platysma myoides
Occipitalis	Occipitalis	Occipitalis	Occipitalis	Occipitalis
Aur. posterior	—	Aur. posterior	Aur. posterior	Aur. posterior
Ex. ear mus.	Ex. ear mus.	Ex. ear mus.	Ex. ear mus.	Ex. ear mus.
—	—	—	—	—
—	—	—	—	Risorius
—	—	—	—	—
—	—	—	—	—
—	—	—	—	—
—	—	—	—	—
—	—	—	—	—
—	—	—	—	—
Zygomaticus maj.	Zygomaticus maj.	Zygomaticus maj.	Zygomaticus maj.	Zygomaticus maj.
Zygomaticus min.	Zygomaticus min.	Zygomaticus min.	Zygomaticus min.	Zygomaticus min.
Frontalis	Frontalis	Frontalis	Frontalis	Frontalis
Auriculo-orbitalis	Auriculo-orbitalis	Temporoparietalis	Auriculo-orbitalis	Temporoparietalis
—	—	Aur. anterior	—	Aur. anterior
Aur. superior	Aur. superior	Aur. superior	Aur. superior	Aur. superior
Orbic. oculi	Orbic. oculi	Orbic. oculi	Orbic. oculi	Orbic. oculi
—	—	—	—	—
De. supercilii	De. supercilii	De. supercilii	De. supercilii	De. supercilii
Corru. supercilii	Corru. supercilii	Corru. supercilii	Corru. supercilii	Corru. supercilii
Le. labii sup. al. nasi	Le. labii sup. al. nasi	Le. labii sup. al. nasi	Le. labii sup. al. nasi	Le. labii sup. al. nasi
Procerus	Procerus	Procerus	Procerus	Procerus
Buccinatorius	Buccinatorius	Buccinatorius	Buccinatorius	Buccinatorius
—	—	—	—	—
Le. labii sup.	Le. labii sup.	Le. labii sup.	Le. labii sup.	Le. labii sup.
Nasalis	Nasalis	Nasalis	Nasalis	Nasalis
De. septi nasi	De. septi nasi	De. septi nasi	De. septi nasi	De. septi nasi
—	—	—	—	—
—	—	—	—	—
Le. anguli oris fac.	Le. anguli oris fac.	Le. anguli oris fac.	Le. anguli oris fac.	Le. anguli oris fac.
Orbic. oris	Orbic. oris	Orbic. oris	Orbic. oris	Orbic. oris
De. labii inf.	De. labii inf.	De. labii inf.	De. labii inf.	De. labii inf.
De. anguli oris	De. anguli oris	De. anguli oris	De. anguli oris	De. anguli oris
Mentalis	Mentalis	Mentalis	Mentalis	Mentalis

many anatomists at that time. However, it is now accepted that strepsirhines often have more than 20 facial muscles, and that although humans have more facial muscles than most primates, the difference is minimal in general. In fact, the total number of facial muscles found in humans is similar to that found in rats, as shown in Table 8.1, contradicting one of the major myths of human complexity and exceptionalism (see Diogo & Wood, 2012, 2013, and Diogo et al., 2015, for more details on this subject).

To give a functional context for these descriptions of the evolution and comparative anatomy of the primate facial muscles, here we provide a brief account of the general function of the facial muscles that are present in strepsirhines. Then, when we refer in the next section to a certain muscle that is not differentiated in strepsirhines but that is present in anthropoids (monkeys and apes, including humans), we will also briefly describe the general function of that muscle. The platysma myoides most likely draws the oral commissure posteroinferiorly, an action that may be used in social interactions as well as feeding, while the platysma cervicale most likely elevates the skin of the neck. The occipitalis draws the scalp posteriorly toward the nuchal region while the frontalis elevates the skin/brow over the superciliary region. The auriculo-orbitalis may be used to draw the lateral corner of the eyelid posteroinferiorly or the external ear anterosuperiorly. The corrugator supercilii and the depressor supercilii are used to draw the medial edge of the superciliary region inferomedially and inferiorly, respectively. The mandibulo-auricularis may be used to approximate the superior and inferior edges of the external ear, as well as the external ear and the mandible. The muscles clustered around the upper lip, including the zygomaticus major and zygomaticus minor muscles, may be used to draw the upper lip and the posterior region of the mouth posterosuperiorly, functions which may be used in both social interactions and in use of the vomeronasal organ. As their names indicate, the extrinsic muscles of the ear, as well as the auricularis posterior and auricularis superior, are mostly related to movement of the external ear, while the orbicularis oculi and orbicularis oris are primarily associated with movement of the eyes and of the lips, respectively. The buccinatorius mainly pulls the corner of the mouth laterally and presses the cheek against the teeth. The levator labii superioris alaeque nasi, levator labii superioris, and levator anguli oris facialis are most likely used together in drawing the upper lip and the posterior region of the mouth superiorly and medially, which most likely is used in social interactions and in feeding. The mentalis mainly elevates the skin ventral to the lower lip, while the sphincter colli profundus most likely draws the skin of the neck posterosuperiorly.

Evolution of the Facial Muscles Within Anthropoids

There are some notable differences between the ancestral condition described earlier for nonanthropoid primates such as *Lepilemur* and the condition found in New World and Old World monkeys. For example, the mandibulo-auricularis is usually not present as an independent, fleshy muscle in most anthropoids, although some of these primates have fleshy vestiges of this muscle as a rare variant. It likely corresponds to the stylo-mandibular ligament seen in hominoids (apes, including humans) and in some monkeys. The sphincter colli profundus is also normally absent in anthropoids, but fleshy vestiges of this muscle have been described in a few macaques as well. Anthropoids often have a depressor anguli oris and a depressor labii inferioris. These muscles are probably derived from the orbicularis oris matrix; some authors suggested that the depressor anguli oris might be the result of a ventral extension of the levator anguli oris. Generally, the depressor anguli oris and depressor labii inferioris function in anthropoids to draw the corner of the mouth posteroinferiorly and to draw the lower lip inferiorly, respectively. These movements are seen in some displays of facial expression and in some feeding contexts.

Within hominoids the platysma cervicale is usually present in hylobatids (lesser apes: gibbons and siamangs) and gorillas, but it is often highly reduced or absent in adult orangutans, chimpanzees, and humans. The transversus nuchae, found as a variant in the three latter taxa, is often considered to be a vestigial remain/bundle of the platysma cervicale. Interestingly, the platysma cervicale is present early in the development of humans, but it normally disappears as an independent structure in later stages of development. Contrary to the platysma cervicale, the platysma myoides is usually present as a separate structure in adult members of all the major five extant hominoid taxa. The occipitalis is also usually present in these five, but the auricularis posterior is normally not differentiated in orangutans, although it has been described in a few species.

In humans the risorius is usually—but not always—present, pulling the lip corners backward, stretching the lips—a function that is, interestingly, usually associated with the display of fear, being likely derived from the platysma myoides, although it cannot be discarded that it is partly, or even wholly, derived from the zygomaticus major. Among A "risorius" is sometimes found in some other hominoids (e.g., chimps), but it does not seem to be present in the fixed phenotype (i.e., > 50% of the cases) of any of the four major nonhuman hominoid taxa. Moreover, some structures that are often named "risorius" in these hominoids are probably not homologous to the human risorius, and even to each other, because some apparently derive from the platysma myoides, others from the depressor anguli oris, and others from muscles such as the zygomaticus major. All the other facial muscles that are present in macaques are normally present in extant hominoids, but contrary to monkeys and to other hominoids, humans—and possibly also gorillas—usually also have an auricularis anterior and a temporoparietalis. Both of these muscles are derived from the auriculo-orbitalis, which, in other hominoids such as chimpanzees, has often been given the name "auricularis anterior," although it actually corresponds to the auricularis anterior plus the temporoparietalis of humans and gorillas. When present, the temporoparietalis stabilizes the epicranial aponeurosis (a tough layer of dense fibrous tissue covering the upper part of the cranium), whereas the auricularis anterior draws the external ear superoanteriorly, closer to the orbit.

Before ending this section, it is interesting to note that each of the three nonprimate taxa listed in Table 8.1 has at least one derived, peculiar muscle that is not differentiated in any other taxa listed in this table. So, for instance, *Ornithorhynchus* has a cervicalis transversus, *Rattus* has a sternofacialis and an interscutularis, and *Tupaia* has a zygomatico-orbicularis. This is an excellent example illustrating that evolution is not directed "toward" a goal, and surely not "toward" primates and humans; each taxon has its own particular mix of conserved and derived anatomical structures, which is the result of its unique evolutionary history (Diogo & Wood, 2013). This is why we encourage the use of the term *correspond* to describe evolutionary relationships among facial muscles, because muscles such as the zygomatico-orbicularis are not "*ancestral*" to the muscles of primates. The zygomatico-orbicularis simply corresponds to a part of the orbicularis oculi that, in taxa such as *Tupaia*, became sufficiently differentiated to deserve being recognized as a separate muscle. Also, strepsirhines and monkeys have muscles that are usually not differentiated in some hominoid taxa, for example, the platysma cervicale (usually not differentiated in orangutans, chimps and humans) and the auricularis posterior (usually not differentiated in orangutans).

Humans, together with gorillas, have the greatest number of facial muscles within primates, and this is consistent with the important role played by facial expression in anthropoids in general, and in humans in particular, for communication. Nevertheless, the evidence presented in this chapter, as well as in recent works by Burrows and colleagues (e.g., Burrows, 2008; Burrows et al., 2014), shows that the difference between the number of facial muscles present in humans and in hominoids such as hylobatids, chimpanzees, and orangutans, and between the number of muscles seen in these latter hominoids and in strepsirhines, is not as marked as previously thought. In fact, as will be shown next, the display of complex facial expressions in a certain taxon is not only related with the number of facial muscles but also with their subdivisions, arrangements of fibers, topology, biochemistry, and microanatomical mechanical properties, as well as with the peculiar osteological and external features (e.g., color) and specific social group and ecological features of the members of that taxon.

FACIAL PELAGE AND COLOR

From bright red to yellow, black, brown, and even blue, the faces of primates exhibit almost every possible hue in the spectrum of mammalian coloration. In many species, such as mandrills and guenons, facial skin and hair colors are combined to create remarkably complex patterns that are unique to the species. Is there a functional significance to these colors and their patterns? Recently, researchers have harnessed the tools of modern comparative methods and computer simulation to answer this question and investigate the factors underlying the evolution of facial color diversity across primate radiations.

Several lines of evidence suggest that facial colors are crucial to the ecology and social communication of primates. Variation in coloration within a species, such as the differences in brightness of red facial patches among male mandrills, appear to be used for assessment of overall health condition and potential mate quality (Setchell, Wickings, Knapp, & Jean Wickings, 2006; Setchell, 2005). At a broader scale, differences across species in facial color patterns are hypothesized to enable individuals of sympatric and closely related species to identify one another and avoid interbreeding. Phylogenetic comparative studies have demonstrated that social recognition explains trends in the evolution of primate facial color patterns. In the New World primate radiation (Platyrrhini), species that live in small social groups or are solitary (e.g., Owl monkeys, *Aotus*) have evolved more complexly patterned faces (Santana et al., 2012). In sharp contrast, diversity trends in Old World groups (Catarrhini) are the opposite, with highly gregarious species having more complexly patterned faces (Santana et al., 2013). These divergent trends may be explained by habitat differences and a higher reliance on facial expressions and displays for intraspecific communication in catarrhines (Dobson, 2009b; Mancini, Ferrari, & Palagi, 2013), in which facial colors may be further advertised through stereotyped head movements during courtship or appeasement behaviors (Kingdon, 1992, 2007).

Across all primates studied to date, the evolution of complexly patterned faces is also tightly linked to high levels of sympatry with closely related species (Santana et al., 2012, 2013). A face that is colorful may present features that are unique and more easily recognizable in the context of multiple sympatric species. Allen, Stevens, and Higham (2014) used computational face recognition algorithms to model primate face processing. Their results demonstrated that the evolution of facial color patterns in guenons fits models of selection to become more visually distinctive from other sympatric guenon species. This indicates that facial color patterns function as signals for species recognition in primates, and they may promote and maintain reproductive isolation among species.

The degree of facial skin and hair pigmentation is also highly variable across primates, and comparative studies suggest that this diversity may illustrate adaptations to habitat. Darker, melanin-based colors in the face and body are characteristic of primate species that inhabit tropical, more densely forested regions (Kamilar & Bradley, 2011). It is hypothesized that these darker colors may reduce predation pressure by making individuals more cryptic to visually oriented predators (Stevens & Merilaita, 2009; Zinck, Duffield, & Ormsbee, 2004) and increase resistance against pathogens (Burtt Jr & Ichida, 2004). Darker facial colors may also offer protection against high levels of UV radiation and solar glare (Caro, 2005) and aid in thermoregulation (Burtt, 1986). However, the role of facial pigmentation in these functions remains unclear because primates may use behaviors to regulate their physiology (e.g., arboreal species can move from the upper canopy, which has the highest UV levels, to the middle and lower canopy, which are highly shaded). In catarrhines, ecological trends in facial pigmentation are only significant in African species (Santana et al., 2013), presumably because the African continent presents more distinct habitat gradients than South East Asia. In platyrrhines, darker faces are found in species that live in warmer and more humid areas, such as the Amazon, and darker eye masks are predominant in species that live closer to the equator. Eye masks likely function in glare reduction in habitats with high ultraviolet incidence, and similar trends in this facial feature have also been observed in carnivorans and birds (Burtt, 1986; Ortolani, 1999).

The presence and length of facial hair are highly variable across primate species, but the role of facial hair in social communication, besides acting as a vehicle to display color, has not been broadly investigated. In platyrrhines, species that live in temperate regions have longer and denser facial hair (Santana et al., 2012), which could aid in thermoregulation (Rensch, 1938). Similar trends would be expected in other primate radiations.

COEVOLUTIONARY RELATIONSHIPS

To date, the evolutionary connections between external (coloration, facial shape) and internal (musculature) facial traits are poorly known. In a recent study (Santana et al., 2014), we contrasted two major hypotheses that could explain the evolution of primate facial diversity when these traits are integrated. First, if the evolution of facial displays has been primarily driven by social factors, highly gregarious primates would possess both complexly colored and highly expressive faces as two concurrent means for social communication. Alternatively, if external facial features influence the ability of primates to perceive and identify facial expressions (Vick, Waller, Parr, Smith Pasqualini, & Bard, 2007), there would be a tradeoff in the evolution of facial mobility and facial color patterning, such that highly expressive faces would have simpler color patterns. We used phylogenetic comparative analyses integrating data on facial mobility, facial musculature, facial color pattern complexity, body size, and orofacial motor nuclei across 21 primate species to test these hypotheses.

The results from our study indicated a significant association between the evolution of facial color patterns and facial mobility in primates. Supporting the second hypothesis, primates evolved plainly colored faces in tandem with an enhanced ability for facial expressions. Thus, while complex facial color patterns may be beneficial for advertising identity (Allen et al., 2014; Santana et al., 2013), a highly "cluttered" face may mask the visibility of facial expressions used to convey behavioral intention. Why a species may rely more on facial color patterns versus facial expressions for communication is still unclear, but it is possible that these different modalities may be differentially selected across primate lineages based on the species' habitat, social systems, or body size. Larger primates (e.g., apes), which have a larger facial nucleus, have more expressive faces than smaller species (e.g., marmosets; Dobson, 2009b), which in turn seem to use colorful facial patterns and head movements for communication. The evolution of larger bodies, potentially coupled with increased reliance on vision for other ecological tasks (e.g., finding food and avoiding predators) may have allowed a higher reliance on facial expressions, which was not possible at smaller body sizes due to physical constraints on the perception of facial movements. Smaller species are expected to have more difficulty discerning facial expressions because smaller mammalian eyes have lower visual acuity (Moynihan, 1967; Veilleux & Kirk, 2014).

Although the evolution of facial mobility is linked to facial coloration and body mass, we found that it is not directly related to the number of muscles that produce facial movements. The number of facial muscles is a slowly evolving trait that has strong phylogenetic inertia (Table 8.1; see Section 2 and also Diogo & Wood, 2012, 2013). Conversely, the size of the facial nucleus has evolved rapidly in the sample of primates studied. These results indicate that changes in facial mobility are likely to evolve first via changes in neurophysiology and body mass, instead of muscle morphology; that is, through motor control of muscles instead of the creation of new divisions of preexisting musculature. These patterns of evolution and potential tradeoffs give important insight into the simple organismal features, such as body mass, that have a strong relevance for which and how different types of facial cues evolve for social communication.

ADULT MODULARITY AND ASYMMETRICAL USE OF FACIAL EXPRESSIONS

Recent studies using a new quantitative and objective approach—anatomical networks—have revealed novel, and in some cases surprising, aspects about the modularity of the facial expression muscles of human adults and the developmental and evolutionary implications (Esteve-Altava, Diogo, Smith, Boughner, & Rasskin-Gutman, 2015). This method treats the skeletal, cartilaginous, and muscular units of the human head as the elements of a network (nodes), whose interactions at their physical contacts (links) determine the boundaries of the phenotypic modules of the head (Fig. 8.2). The use of this methodology revealed that the *muscular network* of the adult human head comprises 136 muscles sparsely connected at 78 contact points (fiber fusions and well-defined tendons), and it divides into three major modules (a single *ocular/upper face complex*, and *left and right orofacial complexes*) and 21 smaller blocks of 2–4 muscles each (Fig. 8.2). Remarkably, the three main muscular modules exclusively include muscles of facial expression. These results support the idea that the evolution of facial muscles has been crucial to human evolution and particularly for our unique abilities for verbal and visual communication.

Furthermore, these network analyses bring a new light to the debate on the symmetry/asymmetry of facial expression muscles in humans and primates. Recent developmental studies suggest that the left and right facial muscles separate from each other early in ontogeny; in fact, surprisingly, the left muscles are actually ontogenetically more closely related to the base of the pulmonary trunk, and the right ones to the base of the aorta, than they are to each other (R. Diogo et al., 2015; Lescroart et al., 2010). Also, functional studies in humans show that asymmetrical use of facial muscles is crucial to make complex facial expressions (Ahn, Gobron, Thalmann, & Boulic, 2013). Furthermore, functional and anatomical studies of human facial expressions have shown that asymmetrical use of facial muscles is less prominent, and that innervations patterns of muscles are more symmetric, in the upper face (muscles located above the upper brow) than in the mid-face and lower face (Rinn, 1984; Schmidt, Liu, & Cohn, 2006). Since human speech tends to involve symmetrical muscle contraction, asymmetrical use of facial muscles is likely related to nonverbal communication in our own species. The phenotypic modules identified in Figure 8.2 placed these developmental, functional, and anatomical observations in a completely new and quantitative context. That is, the existence of left and right orofacial muscle modules in the adult human head supports the ontogenetic separation of left and right facial muscles and the ability to asymmetrically contract or relax facial muscles, and thus strike more complex facial expressions in humans. In contrast, the single module including both the left and right ocular/upper face facial muscles is in line with previous studies showing that innervations patterns and use of muscles are more symmetric in the upper face. As emphasized by Esteve-Altava et al. (2015), future anatomical network studies specifically about the muscles of facial expression among other primate and mammal species are needed to investigate which modules may be unique to humans and which others have deeper evolutionary origins.

DEVELOPMENT, BIRTH DEFECTS, MODULARITY, AND EVOLVABILITY

A further study also using anatomical networks, but to investigate the modularity of the head of human infants as well as of a trisomy-18 cyclopic human fetus (Fig. 8.3), supports the idea that facial expression had a crucial importance in primate/human evolution (Esteve-Altava et al., 2015). This is because, apart from being the three major muscle modules in the adult, the facial expression ocular/upper face and left and right orofacial modules are also already present in the newborn head, with exactly the same components. Facial expressions play a particularly important role in the first years of life: While vocalizations (e.g., crying) lack enough nuance to keep parents guessing at their meanings, already-complex (nonverbal) facial expressions help infants to mimic, read, and make facial expressions learned from and to communicate with their parents and other individuals, immediately from birth toward becoming socialized. This might explain why muscles of facial expression are already differentiated, functional, and competent to display recognizable facial expressions much before birth. For instance, a recent study using 4D ultrasound scans has suggested that some facial expressions, related to pain and distress, are recognizable as early as the second trimester of pregnancy (Reissland, Francis, & Mason, 2013). In other words, the developmental phenomena of differentiation, modularity, and integration assure that the form and function of the facial expression muscle complexes are "ready" well before the moment of delivery, due to the importance of facial expressions immediately after birth.

The facial expression muscles are also a good example of the increasing integration that occurs in human postnatal development between soft and hard tissues, leading to fewer musculoskeletal modules that also seem to be more coherent functionally later in life. This is because in the adult, the muscles of the three major functional facial expression muscle modules (ocular/upper face and left and right orofacial: Fig. 8.2) are essentially included in the corresponding mid/upper face and left and right oral/ocular musculoskeletal modules (Esteve-Altava et al., 2015). However, in the newborn there is a functionally less integrated, and more asymmetrical, configuration: The facial expression muscles are distributed into four musculoskeletal modules, the orbicularis

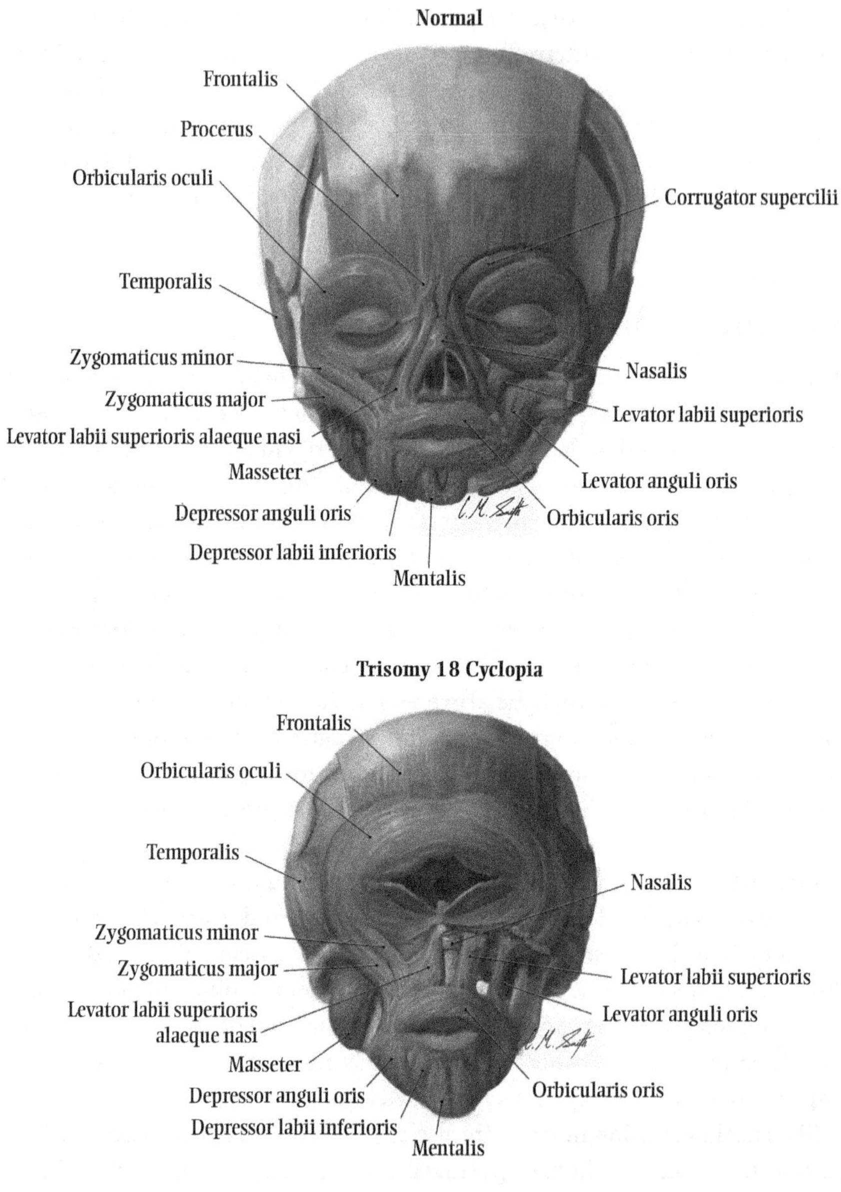

Figure 8.3 Comparison of anterior head musculature usually present in karyotypically normal infants and in a trisomy 18 cyclopic fetus. The platysma myoides, risorius, and buccal fat pad were removed; left side shows deep dissection (©2015 Christopher Smith/ HU; modified from Esteve-Altava et al. 2015, with permission)

oculi forming a module with most orofacial muscles on the left side and with only a few facial muscles and some branchial and masticatory muscles on the right side (Diogo et al., in press). This does not seem so much the product of direct adaptive pressure on the newborn, but instead part of a process in which the already well-defined muscle models are being properly integrated into the whole musculoskeletal modules.

It is particularly interesting to see that the independence of muscular and skeletal morphogenesis in early development still leads, later in development—and even in severe congenital malformations such as those seen in the trisomy 18 cyclopic fetus—to a recognizable general pattern of topological associations between the muscles of facial expression and the surrounding skeletal elements, despite the pronounced deformation of these elements (Diogo et al,. in press; Smith et al., 2015). The findings of Smith et al. (2015) thus support the idea that the muscles of facial expression probably display a "nearest neighbor" pattern of muscle-skeletal associations (Diogo et al., in press): When subjected to developmental/evolutionary changes, facial muscles tend to insert onto bones that lie closer to their normal insertions, mostly ignoring the embryonic origin of these bones. Also interestingly, such a "nearest neighbor" model of muscle-skeleton connections is similar to that proposed for the limbs, but markedly different from models normally proposed for non-facial-expression head muscles, which seem to follow instead a "seek and find" model in which they usually attach in a very precise way to skeletal structures derived from their own arches. Developmental studies have shown that in some aspects the facial muscles do behave as limb and hypobranchial migratory muscles (i.e., tongue and infrahyoid muscles, which derive from somites and thus are not true head muscles), migrating far away from their primary origin, contrary to other head muscles (Prunotto et al., 2004). The developmental differences between the facial muscles and the other muscles of the head might help to explain why the attachments, overall configuration, and number of the muscles of facial expressions are particularly variable in mammals, including in primates and in our own species (Diogo et al., 2009; Diogo & Wood, 2012). In fact, these muscles are not only associated with the remarkably diverse facial expressions of mammals and particularly humans, but also with completely different functions, such as suckling or mastication in most mammals (e.g., buccinator muscle) and flying in mammals such as bats (e.g., occipito-pollicalis muscle: Tokita, Abe, & Suzuki, 2012).

CONCLUSIONS

We hope that this chapter emphasizes the remarkable diversity of primate facial structures and the fact that the number of facial muscles present in our species is actually not as high when compared to many other mammals as previously thought. A multitude of factors, from ecological traits to external features, such as facial pelage and color, also play a crucial role in the display—and perception by others—of facial expressions. Future studies should thus make an effort to combine as much data as possible—including information not included in this chapter but included in this book as a whole, such as those from psychological studies—to have a better, more holistic understanding of the evolution and functional peculiarities of facial expressions. Importantly, the use of new tools, such as anatomical networks and phylogenetic analyses, should be further explored to compare the musculoskeletal and other features of humans across stages of development and with other animals. Such analyses will enable a better understanding of the links between the evolution of facial expressions, of their assymetric use, and the evolvability of the face in general.

REFERENCES

Ahn, J., Gobron, S., Thalmann, D., & Boulic, R. (2013). Asymmetric facial expressions: Revealing richer emotions for embodied conversational agents. *Computer Animation and Virtual Worlds, 24*, 539–551. doi:10.1002/cav.1539

Allen, W. L., Stevens, M., & Higham, J. P. (2014). Character displacement of Cercopithecini primate visual signals. *Nature Communications, 5*(May 2014), 4266. doi:10.1038/ncomms5266

Boas, J. E. V., & Paulli, S. (1908). *The elephant's head: Studies in the comparative anatomy of the organs of the head of the Indian elephant and other mammals. Part I.* Copenhagen: Folio, Gustav Fisher.

Boas, J. E. V., & Paulli, S. (1925). *The elephant's head: Studies in the comparative anatomy of the organs of the head of the Indian elephant and other mammals. Part II.* Copenhagen: Folio, Gustav Fisher.

Burrows, A. M. (2008). The facial expression musculature in primates and its evolutionary significance. *BioEssays, 30*(3), 212–225.

Burtt, E. H. (1986). An analysis of physical, physiological, and optical aspects of avian coloration with emphasis on wood-warblers. *Ornithological Monographs, 38*, 1–136.

Burtt Jr, E. H., & Ichida, J. M. (2004). Gloger's rule, feather-degrading bacteria, and color variation among song sparrows. *The Condor, 106*(3), 681–686.

Caro, T. (2005). The adaptive significance of coloration in mammals. *Bioscience, 55*(2), 125–136.

Diogo, R., Kelly, R., Christian, L., Levine, M., Ziermann, J., Molnar, J., . . . Tzahor, E. (2015). The cardiopharyngeal field and vertebrate evolution: A new heart for a new head. *Nature, 520*, 466–473.

Diogo, R., & Wood, B. (2013). The broader evolutionary lessons to be learned from a comparative and phylogenetic analysis of primate muscle morphology. *Biological Reviews, 88*, 988–1001. doi:10.1111/brv.12039

Diogo, R., & Wood, B. A. (2012). *Comparative anatomy and phylogeny of primate muscles and human evolution*. Oxford (UK): CRC Press.

Diogo, R., Wood, B. A., Aziz, M. A., & Burrows, A. (2009). On the origin, homologies and evolution of primate facial muscles, with a particular focus on hominoids and a suggested unifying nomenclature for the facial muscles of the Mammalia. *Journal of Anatomy, 215*(3), 300–319. doi:10.1111/j.1469-7580.2009.01111.x

Diogo, R., Smith, C., & Ziermann, J. M. (2015). Evolutionary developmental pathology and anthropology: A new area linking development, comparative anatomy, human evolution, morphological variations and defects, and medicine. *Developmental Dynamics*, 244(11), 13570–1374.

Dobson, S. D. (2009a). Allometry of facial mobility in anthropoid primates: Implications for the evolution of facial expression. *American Journal of Physical Anthropology*, *138*(1), 70–81.

Dobson, S. D. (2009b). Socioecological correlates of facial mobility in nonhuman anthropoids. *American Journal of Physical Anthropology*, *139*(3), 413–420.

Esteve-Altava, B., Diogo, R., Smith, C., Boughner, J. C., & Rasskin-Gutman, D. (2015). Anatomical networks reveal the musculoskeletal modularity of the human head. *Scientific Reports*, *5*, 8298. doi:10.1038/srep08298

Kamilar, J. M., & Bradley, B. J. (2011). Interspecific variation in primate coat colour supports Gloger's rule. *Journal of Biogeography*, *38*(12), 2270–2277. doi:10.1111/j.1365-2699.2011.02587.x

Kingdon, J. (1992). Facial patterns as signals and masks. In S. Jones et al. (Eds.), *The Cambridge encyclopedia of human evolution* (pp. 161–165). Cambridge University Press: Cambridge.

Kingdon, J. (2007). Primate visual signals in noisy environments. *Folia Primatologica*, *78*(5-6), 389–404.

Lescroart, F., Kelly, R. G., Le Garrec, J.-F., Nicolas, J.-F., Meilhac, S. M., & Buckingham, M. (2010). Clonal analysis reveals common lineage relationships between head muscles and second heart field derivatives in the mouse embryo. *Development*, *137*(2010), 3269–3279. doi:10.1242/dev.050674

Mancini, G., Ferrari, P. F., & Palagi, E. (2013). Rapid facial mimicry in Geladas. *Nature Scientific Reports*, *3*(1527).

Moynihan, M. (1967). *Comparative aspects of communication in New World primates* (D. Morris, Ed.). *Primate ethology*. Chicago, IL: Aldine.

Murie, J., & Mivart, S. T. (1869). On the anatomy of the Lemuroidea. *The Transactions of the Zoological Society of London*, *7*(1), 1–113.

Ortolani, A. (1999). Spots, stripes, tail tips and dark eyes: Predicting the function of carnivore colour patterns using the comparative method. *Biological Journal of the Linnean Society*, *67*(4), 433–476.

Preuschoft, S., & Van Hooff, J. (1997). The social function of "smile" and "laughter": Variations across primate species and societies. In U. Segerstrale & P. Molnar (Eds.), *Nonverbal communication: Where nature meets culture* (pp. 171–190). Hillsdale, NJ: Erlbaum.

Prunotto, C., Crepaldi, T., Forni, P. E., Ieraci, A., Kelly, R. G., Tajbakhsh, S., . . . Ponzetto, C. (2004). Analysis of Mlc-lacZ Met mutants highlights the essential function of Met for migratory precursors of hypaxial muscles and reveals a role for Met in the development of hyoid arch-derived facial muscles. *Developmental Dynamics*, *231*(3), 582–591.

Reissland, N., Francis, B., & Mason, J. (2013). Can healthy fetuses show facial expressions of "pain" or "distress"? *PLoS ONE*, *8*(June), 1–7. doi:10.1371/journal.pone.0065530

Rensch, B. (1938). Some problems of geographical variation and species-formation. *Proceedings of the Linnean Society of London*, *150*, 275–285.

Rinn, W. E. (1984). The neuropsychology of facial expression: A review of the neurological and psychological mechanisms for producing facial expressions. *Psychological Bulletin*, *95*(1), 52.

Santana, S. E., Alfaro, J. L., Noonan, A., & Alfaro, M. E. (2013). Adaptive response to sociality and ecology drives the diversification of facial colour patterns in catarrhines. *Nature Communications, 4*(2765), 2765. doi:10.1038/ncomms3765

Santana, S. E., Dobson, S. D., & Diogo, R. (2014). Plain faces are more expressive: Comparative study of facial colour, mobility and musculature in primates. *Biology Letters, 10*(May 2014). doi:10.1098/rsbl.2014.0275

Santana, S. E., Lynch Alfaro, J., & Alfaro, M. E. (2012). Adaptive evolution of facial colour patterns in Neotropical primates. *Proceedings of the Royal Society B: Biological Sciences, 279*(1736), 2204–2211. doi:10.1098/rspb.2011.2326

Schmidt, K. L., Liu, Y., & Cohn, J. F. (2006). The role of structural facial asymmetry in asymmetry of peak facial expressions. *Laterality, 11*(6), 540–561. doi:10.1080/13576500600832758

Setchell, J. M. (2005). Do female mandrills prefer brightly colored males? *International Journal of Primatology, 26*(4), 715–735. doi:10.1007/s10764-005-5305-7

Setchell, J. M., Wickings, E. J., Knapp, L. a, & Jean Wickings, E. (2006). Signal content of red facial coloration in female mandrills (*Mandrillus sphinx*). *Proceedings of the Royal Society B: Biological Sciences, 273*(1599), 2395–2400. doi:10.1098/rspb.2006.3573

Sherwood, C. C., Hof, P. R., Holloway, R. L., Semendeferi, K., Gannon, P. J., Frahm, H. D., & Zilles, K. (2005). Evolution of the brainstem orofacial motor system in primates: A comparative study of trigeminal, facial, and hypoglossal nuclei. *Journal of Human Evolution, 48*(1), 45–84.

Smith, C. M., Ziermann, J. M., Molnar, J. A., Gondre-Lewis, M. C., Sandone, C., Bersu, E. T., Aziz, M. A., & Diogo, R. (2015). *Muscular and skeletal anomalies in human trisomy in an evo-devo context: Description of a T18 cyclopic newborn and comparison between Edwards (T18), Patau (T13) and Down (T21) syndromes using 3-D imaging and anatomical illustrations*. Oxford, UK: Taylor & Francis.

Stevens, M., & Merilaita, S. (2009). Animal camouflage: Current issues and new perspectives. *Philosophical Transactions of the Royal Society B: Biological Sciences, 364*(1516), 423–427. doi:10.1098/rstb.2008.0217

Tokita, M., Abe, T., & Suzuki, K. (2012). The developmental basis of bat wing muscle. *Nature Communications, 3*, 1302.

Veilleux, C. C., & Kirk, E. C. (2014). Visual acuity in mammals: Effects of eye size and ecology. *Brain, Behavior and Evolution, 83*(1), 43–53. doi:10.1159/000357830

Vick, S.-J. J., Waller, B. M., Parr, L. a, Smith Pasqualini, M. C., & Bard, K. A. (2007). A cross-species comparison of facial morphology and movement in humans and chimpanzees using the facial action coding system (FACS). *Journal of Nonverbal Behavior, 31*(1), 1–20. doi:10.1007/s10919-006-0017-z

Waitt, C., Little, A. C., Wolfensohn, S., Honess, P., Brown, A. P., Buchanan-Smith, H. M., & Perrett, D. I. (2003). Evidence from rhesus macaques suggests that male coloration plays a role in female primate mate choice. *Proceedings of the Royal Society of London. Series B: Biological Sciences, 270*(Suppl 2), S144–S146. doi:10.1098/rsbl.2003.0065

Zinck, J. M., Duffield, D. A., & Ormsbee, P. C. (2004). Primers for identification and polymorphism assessment of Vespertilionid bats in the Pacific Northwest. *Molecular Ecology Notes, 4*(2), 239–242. doi:10.1111/j.1471-8286.2004.00629.x

9

The Faces Monkeys Make

ELIZA BLISS-MOREAU AND GILDA MOADAB

In 1872, Charles Darwin observed that humans and nonhuman animals generated stereotyped facial muscle movements, and he pondered that they might be related to emotions (Darwin, 1872/2009). His anecdotal observations have been used as justification for assuming that patterns of facial behaviors give vertical evidence of emotions in both humans and nonhuman animals alike (e.g., Ekman, 1972; Keltner & Ekman, 2000; Shariff & Tracy, 2011; but see Barrett, 2011; Fridlund, 2015). These facial behaviors are often called "facial expressions" based on the idea that faces serve to "express" an individual's internal state. To distance from this assumption, we use the term "facial behaviors" to describe these stereotyped facial movements so as not to imply that they express or signal emotion. Despite the fact that evaluating the structure, meaning, and function of human facial behaviors has long been an important domain of research, less attention has been paid to evaluating such claims in nonhuman animals in the psychological literature. This gap in the literature is problematic for a number of reasons, not the least of which is that descriptive evidence from the nonhuman animal (herein, simply "animal") literature is often taken at face value to justify claims about the evolution of human emotions (e.g., Chavalier-Skolnikov, 1973; Izard, 1992; Maestripieri, 1997; Ortony & Turner, 1990; Preuschoft, 1992). The goal of this chapter is to provide a brief psychological primer on the faces of one genus of nonhuman primates—those of macaque monkeys, arguably one of the most widely studied nonhuman primate genesis.

WHY MACAQUES?

Many nonhuman primates have faces that are similar to humans in terms of their appearance and musculature (Parr, Waller, Burrows, Gothard, & Vick, 2010; Parr, Waller, Vick, & Bard, 2007; Waller, Parr, Gothard, Burrows, & Fuglevand, 2008), but macaques are most commonly used in research (Carlsson, Schapiro, Farah, & Hau, 2004). Macaques and humans diverged on the evolutionary tree approximately 25 million years ago (Locke et al., 2011), with subsequent divisions of the macaque genus occurring over between 2 million and 250 thousand years ago, (Prueschoft & van Hooff, 1995; see Fig. 9.1). The 23 macaque species vary a great deal in terms of the environments in which they live, the breadth of their behavioral repertoires, the extent to which they are adaptable (Thierry, Singh, & Kaumanns, 2004), and the degree to which they are formally studied (Carlsson, Schaprio, Farah, & Hau, 2004). Approximately half of the macaques used in research are rhesus macaques (*Macaca mulatta*) (Carlsson et al., 2004). Rhesus macaques were historically available from India

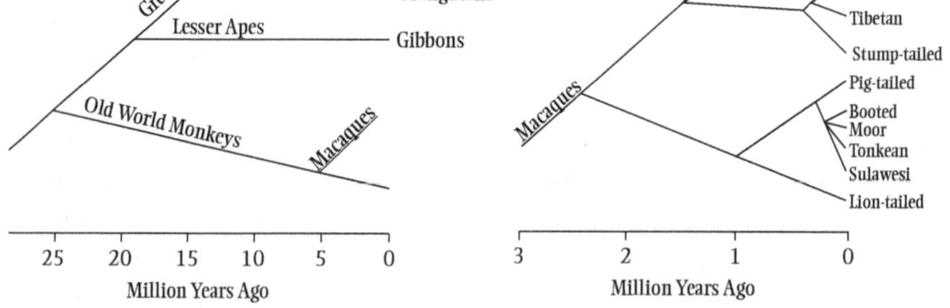

Figure 9.1 The primate phylogenetic tree. (*A*) Old world monkeys (e.g., macaques) and apes (e.g., humans) diverged on the evolutionary tree approximately 25 million years ago (Locke et al., 2011). (*B*) Subsequent divisions of the macaque genus occur beginning approximately 2.25 million years ago. (Diagram is based on that presented in Preuschoft & van Hooff, 1995.)

and brought in great numbers into the laboratory with the goal of vaccine development (namely polio; Ahuja, 2013; Rudacille, 2000).

Humans and rhesus macaques, in particular, share a number of important adaptations, making rhesus a particularly good model for human biology and behavior (Capitanio & Embourg, 2008; Phillips et al., 2014). Like humans, rhesus monkeys are highly adaptable to their environments. While all species of great apes and many other species of monkeys are threatened or endangered (IUCN, 2012), rhesus monkeys, like humans, are exceptionally resilient (Suomi, 2007). Humans and rhesus monkeys are both opportunistic omnivores, are not apex predators, and live and thrive in large social groups bound by sociopolitical rules and subserved by broad social behavior repertoires. That is, humans and rhesus monkeys share a similar ecological niche.

MACAQUE FACES

Like the human face, the macaque face is composed of a complex organization of muscles that allow for many unique configurations of muscle movements (Parr et al., 2010). Facial musculature in rhesus macaques is nearly identical to that of humans, with the only noticeable differences being in the musculature around the ear (Waller et al., 2008). Characterization of macaque facial muscle movements allows for facial behavior observations to record what individual or sets of muscles are moving (Parr et al., 2010), and the most common approach to the study of macaque faces has been ethnographic. Ethnographic approaches describe facial muscle movements linguistically (e.g., "lips pulled back into a grin exposing teeth with no accompanying vocalization") and conglomerate behaviors are given a symbolic label (e.g., "silent bared-teeth" or "fear grimace"). Observers are trained to recognize the occurrence of the behavior(s) and apply the associated label reliably. In service of this goal, ethograms (descriptions of behaviors with linguistic labels) specifying facial behaviors even provide contexts in which one might expect to see particular facial behaviors (Andrew, 1963; Chavalier-Skolnikoff, 1973; Hinde & Rowell, 1962; Maestripieri, 1997; Redican, 1975; van Hooff, 1967).

Early ethnographic descriptions of facial behaviors focused on the shape and movement of the face. The contexts in which facial behaviors occurred were discussed in probabilistic ways (face A is likely to occur in context B) without implying an inexorable or causal link between A and B (Hinde & Rowell, 1962; Redican, 1975; van Hooff, 1967). In fact, early reports from scientists studying nonhuman primates were especially careful to not imply causal links in the way that would support the hypothesis that faces veridically express emotions (or are signals of discrete emotions; see Andrew, 1963). Furthermore, these scientists recognized that a single face might be associated with different motivational states (e.g., a given face might occur with approach or avoidance; van Hooff, 1967) and in all likelihood be a response to changes in the environment driven by attention and affect (positivity, negativity, and some degree of arousal) but not emotion (Andrew, 1963).

Classic studies of the macaque face typically identified specific facial movements (e.g., open mouth, wide eyes, etc.) and then discussed the integration of those distinct movements into more complex facial behaviors or "expressions" (Andrew, 1963; Chavalier-Skolnikoff, 1973; Redican, 1975; van Hooff, 1967). These classic analyses all identified different numbers of facial behaviors and employed different numbers of linguistic labels based on who the observers and authors were. That is, there is heterogeneity in the descriptions of facial behaviors from their earliest documentation. It is also sometimes the case that a number of facial behaviors could be organized into broader, superordinate classes. For example, Chavalier-Skolnikoff (1973) identified four faces in which a wide-eyed stare is a key component but varied in terms of their mouth shape, the context in which they occur, and their function. Despite this variance, they were all considered "threats." Four facial behaviors are consistently discussed across disciplines and macaque species: threat, silent bared-teeth, lipsmack, and relaxed open-mouth. Of note, reports on the morphology and function of these faces sometimes generalized across macaque species (Andrew, 1963; van Hooff, 1967) and other times focused on a specific species (e.g., rhesus only, Hinde & Rowell, 1962; multiple species with differences and similarities between species indicated, Maestripieri, 1997; Prueschoft, 1995; Redican, 1975).

Threat

Although there are minor variations in specific configurations of the facial behavior across species and across contexts within species, certain elements of the threat facial behavior remain invariant. The most marked component of the threat facial behavior is eyes that are wide open, accompanied by an intense attentive stare (Andrew, 1963; Chavalier-Skolnikoff, 1973; Maestripieri, 1997; Redican, 1975; van Hooff, 1967). Corners of the mouth are typically pulled forward (Chavalier-Skolnikoff, 1973; Redican, 1975; van Hooff, 1967). The mouth may be opened or closed and the teeth are typically covered by the lips. Ears are typically forward (Chavalier-Skolnikoff, 1973; Redican, 1975), rather than pulled back against the head. The facial behavior may be accompanied by swift movement of the head up and down or jerked toward the object being threatened (Hinde & Rowell, 1962; see Fig. 9.2a). The threat behavior is nearly ubiquitous, although has been formally documented in about half of the macaque species, including those most likely to be used in laboratory research.

Silent Bared-Teeth

The silent bared-teeth behavior is characterized by the retraction of the mouth corners as well as the vertical retraction of the lips, displaying the animal's teeth and gums (Chavalier-Skolnikoff, 1973; Maestripieri, 1997; Preuschoft, 1992; Redican, 1975; van Hooff, 1967). Ears are typically pulled back against the head. The behavior is sometimes referred to as the "fear grimace" or "fear grin" (Maestripieri, 1997). Critically, this behavior often occurs in contexts that have nothing to do with fear (see later discussion), suggesting that its secondary moniker is inaccurate. It is sometimes the case that the bared-teeth behavior (i.e., the facial configuration) is accompanied by sound (e.g., a scream or teeth chattering). In those cases the face is referred to simply as the bared-teeth, rather than silent bared-teeth. For example, teeth chattering often accompanies the bared-teeth display in both Barbary macaques (Preuschoft, 1992) and stumptail macaques (de Waal & Luttrel, 1989). Like the threat facial behavior, the silent bared-teeth behavior occurs in many, if not most, of the macaque species (see Fig. 9.2b).

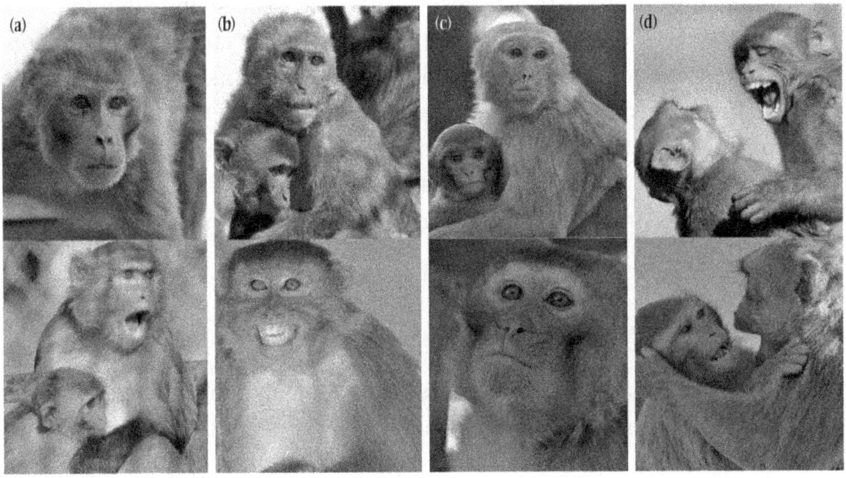

Figure 9.2 Examples of the four prototypical facial behaviors in rhesus macaques (*Macaca mulatta*). (*A*) Threat. Male (above) and female with infant (below) displaying a threat face. (*B*) Silent bared-teeth. Female with infant (above) and female (below) displaying the silent bared-teeth display. (*C*) Lipsmack. Female with infant (above) and male (below) displaying the lipsmack. (*D*) Relaxed open-mouth. Two juveniles (above) and a juvenile (below on left) and young adult (below on right) displaying the relaxed open-mouth face during a bout of play.

Lipsmack

The lipsmack facial behavior consists of the mouth and lips rapidly opening and closing, with mouth corners brought forward. There is often periodic tongue protrusion between the lips and a smacking sound generated by the tongue (Andrew, 1963; Chavalier-Skolnikoff, 1973; Maestripieri, 1997; van Hooff, 1967). It is a dynamic facial behavior, although the protrusion of the lips during smacking can be visualized in static images (see Fig. 9.2c). Like the threat and the silent bared-teeth facial behavior, the lipsmack behavior has been formally documented in many of the macaque species.

Relaxed Open-Mouth

The relaxed open-mouth behavior is sometimes referred to as a "play face" because it is likely to occur in play-related contexts. Van Hooff (1967) and Chevalier-Skolnikoff (1973) both describe the relaxed open-mouth behavior as physically similar to the threat. The relaxed open-mouth behavior differs from the threat behavior insofar as the eyes are less fixed, wide-eyed, and intense (i.e., more relaxed) and corners of the mouth are not pulled forward (van Hooff, 1967) or are retracted only slightly (Preuschoft, 1992; Redican, 1975; see Fig. 9.2d). Perhaps the most important difference between relaxed open-mouth and threat is that former occurs in prosocial and affiliative contexts and the latter does not. That is, the distinction is largely based on context. The relaxed open-mouth behavior has been formally documented in fewer macaque species than the other facial behaviors. Despite being classically compared to the threat face, socially tolerant (less despotic) species like liontail macaques and Tonkean macaques have relaxed open-mouth facial behaviors that are morphologically and functionally very similar to the silent bared-teeth face (Preuchoft, 2004).

DO MONKEY FACIAL BEHAVIORS SIGNAL EMOTIONS?

The fact that macaques generate stereotyped facial movements that are readily observed does not provide evidence about what those faces actually mean. On the basis of structural homologies, stereotyped facial behaviors are often associated with specific emotions (e.g., Ekman & Friesen, 1971; Izard, 1971) based on theory stipulating that emotions produce behaviors in a specific and discrete way (e.g., Ekman & Cordaro, 2011; Levenson, 2003; Shariff & Tracy, 2011). Approaches like these hinge on two assumptions. First, overt behaviors can be mapped to specific emotions and therefore behaviors can be "read" to understand emotion (or "emotion state" in the case of theories that beg the question of consciousness; Anderson & Adolphs, 2014). Second, overt behaviors generated by both humans and animals that appear to be the same are associated with the same internal state. That is, structural homologies are thought to confer functional homologies. It is on the basis of comparisons like this that most of nonhuman animal emotion science has been conducted. These linkages are tenuous for at least two reasons. First, animals cannot report on their experience, eliminating the possibility of confirming the specific experience occurring when particular behaviors occur. Second, the relationship between particular facial behaviors and emotions in humans is not clear (Russell, 2015; for meta-analytic reviews: Cacioppo et al., 2000; Nelson & Russell, 2013; Russell, 1994).

If specific behaviors map in a specific, one-to-one way with emotion—that is, behaviors "express" emotions—then it is possible that different facial behaviors are signals of specific emotions. If this is the case, that facial behaviors are really facial expressions, then a number of patterns should be evident in the nonhuman animal data. If macaque faces "express" emotion, the emotional context and the faces that are generated in that context should map to each other in specific and meaningful ways. Similarly, a single context (e.g., a context that provokes fear) should specifically produce behaviors that are associated with a single emotion (e.g., fear behaviors). Second, if macaque faces "express" emotion, and therefore represent meaningful information about an individual's internal state (e.g., fear vs. anger), then macaques themselves should be able to discriminate between different facial behaviors even without contextual information. In this view, the face is a direct readout of the animal's emotional state and as such no additional information should be required to differentiate between facial behaviors.

HOW IS CONTEXT RELATED TO MACAQUE FACIAL BEHAVIORS?

If it is the case that macaque facial behaviors are really facial "expressions" of emotion, then there should be clear mappings between emotional context and facial behaviors. Fearful contexts should produce faces that depict fear and not faces that depict other emotions. Similarly, a face that depicts fear should depict fear regardless of context. Since the face would be a signal of fear, representing a meaningful category of information, individuals should be able to distinguish it from faces that represent other categories of information. Extant data do not support this claim. Early descriptions of facial behaviors document the behaviors in a wide variety of contexts that, while sometimes potentially associated with emotions, are largely related to variation in social context and experience. Detailing the contextual variation in which each macaque facial behavior occurs provides insight to the meaning of these signals.

Threat

Early ethnographic descriptions of the threat facial behavior document its generation by a variety of different types of animals and its occurrence in a variety of settings. For example, van Hooff (1967) details animals who display the threat are just as likely to attack as they are to flee, although the behavior is most often performed by a dominant animal in an interaction. Maestripieri (1997) reports a specific type of threat facial behavior which he calls a "defensive threat" emitted by subordinate animals used when recruiting others animals to support them in threatening a dominant individual. As compared to other threats, the defensive threat includes the withdrawal of mouth corner, much like the bared-teeth display (Andrew, 1963). Hinde and Rowell (1962) describe yet another variation of the threat face. The "backing threat" is described by all the components of the threat face with the addition of a backward locomotion—moving away from the recipient of the behavior. While many reports detail the threat as occurring in social contexts, the "backing threat" is typically made by an "aggressive individual toward an object of which it is afraid" (Hinde & Rowell, 1962, p. 7). That is, threats are not only about aggression (or from an emotion perspective might be labeled anger) but may also occur in contexts related to fear.

Silent Bared-Teeth

The face that is most commonly linked to a discrete emotion is the silent bared-teeth behavior—so much so that claims such as "in species with a strict dominance style, bared-teeth behavior indicates submission and fear" (Visalberghi, Valenzano, & Preuschoft, 2006, p. 1691) are not uncommon. Like the threat behavior, the classic literature documents the silent bared-teeth behavior in many contexts and generalizes its functionality across species.

Recent studies support the claim that macaques appear to use the bared-teeth behavior to communicate in contexts unrelated to fear, and further that the meaning of the signal is modulated by the context in which it occurs. For example, while some pigtail macaques emit the behavior in conflict-related contexts (in response to aggression or threat by the receiver; consistent with the hypothesis that the behavior communicates fear), the behavior is also observed in peaceful contexts (no threat or aggressive behavior by the receiver; inconsistent with the hypothesis that the face communicates fear) (Flack & de Waal, 2007). Those animals who display the silent bared-teeth face in peaceful contexts engage in fighting less often and grooming more often than those who generate the face during conflict (Flack & de Waal, 2007). Rhesus monkeys generated the silent bared-teeth behavior in both peaceful and conflict/aggressive contexts (Beisner & McCowan, 2014), as well as during sexual consortships (i.e., "flirting"), mounting (Finn, Beisner, Bliss-Moreau, & McCowan, 2014), and orgasm (Allen & Lemmon, 1981). The meaning of the behavior has different social consequences, and therefore presumably different meanings, based on whether it occurs during the presence or absence of conflict. Furthermore, whether the signaler stays physically present or leaves the social interaction after generating the face alters the meaning of the face. Pairs of animals that use the silent bared-teeth face during peaceful contexts (in the absence of context) instigate less aggression than those that use it during conflict contexts; pairs that use the silent bared-teeth face during peaceful contexts without withdrawing after signaling groom more than those that use the same face and immediately withdraw and those that use the face during conflict (Beisner & McCowan, 2014). Directional use of the bared-teeth face in peaceful contexts is thought to confer social power on the receiver of the signal (Beisner, Hannibal, Finn, & McCowan, 2015).

In addition to having its function vary across contexts, the use of the silent bared-teeth facial behavior varies across species. Although it occurs in mostly subordinate/dominant interactions in most macaque species (including the rhesus macaque), the facial behavior is often given mutually between animals in prosocial positive contexts (i.e., when the animals are grooming) in the black Sulawesi macaque (de Waal, 2003) and the Tonkean macaque (Preuschoft & van Hooff, 1995). While highly despotic species (e.g., rhesus macaques, Japanese macaques, and pigtail macaques) use the face to communicate subordination, submission, and appeasement, it is used to communicate submission/appeasement, affiliation, reassurance, and in some cases even the willingness to play in the less despotic species (lion-tailed macaques and Tonkean macaques) (Preuschoft, 2004). The silent bared-teeth display therefore may communicate a negative affective state for some species and a positive affective state for others.

Lipsmack

Although the contexts in which the lipsmack facial behavior occurs vary, this facial behavior is most often displayed in nonhostile, affiliative settings (Andrew, 1963; Chavalier-Skolnikoff, 1973; van Hooff, 1967). The lipsmack may occur between novel conspecifics or between animals with previously established relationships (van Hooff, 1967). It may precede greeting or copulation (Andrew, 1963; Chavalier-Skolnikoff, 1973; van Hooff, 1967). Lipsmacking also often occurs prior to and during grooming bouts (Hinde & Rowell, 1962; Maestripieri, 1997; Redican, 1975; van Hooff, 1967). Hinde and Rowell (1962) describe the context in which the lipsmack occurs to involve "positive social advances to another individual . . . often combined with slight fear" (p. 15). An individual may lipsmack in the presence of a frightening object, directing the lipsmack not to that object, but to a different, desirable object (Hinde & Rowell, 1962). Evidence from our own laboratory supports that observation that lipsmacking occurs in the presence of objects thought to engender threat (e.g., toy snakes; Bliss-Moreau, unpublished data). The behavior can serve an appeasing and reassuring function (Altmann, 1962; van Hooff, 1967), decreasing the likelihood of others to attack or flee, as well as an attracting function, increasing the likelihood for others to approach (van Hooff, 1967). It may be this appeasement function that leads mothers to lipsmack to their infants while in ventral contact with one another (Ferrari et al., 2009).

Relaxed Open-Mouth

The "relaxed open-mouth" behavior occurs in the context of play in many species of macaque (Chevalier-Skolnikoff, 1973; van Hooff, 1967) and as a result is often referred to as the "play face." It is most likely to be displayed by juvenile or young adult macaques (Maestripieri, 1997). When generated by adult macaques, it occurs most often when they are engaged in play with younger animals (Redican, 1975). In socially tolerant species, the function of the relaxed open-mouth facial behavior is similar to that of the bared-teeth display (Preuschoft, 2004). As species range from socially intolerant to tolerant, the function of the two facial behaviors becomes more similar such that in the most socially tolerant species both facial behaviors communicate reconciliation, affiliation, reassurance, and playfulness (Preuschoft, 2004).

Macaques' stereotyped facial behaviors occur in a variety of contexts to serve a variety of functions. This variation calls into question the idea that facial behaviors map to emotions in a specific way, suggesting that they are not outward veridical representations of internal emotive states. That being said, some of the facial behaviors do appear to consistently map to affective states—the relaxed open-mouth face only occurs in positive, prosocial contexts, while the threat face never occurs in positive, prosocial contexts. Regardless of emotive or affective meaning, facial behaviors seem to communicate important information about social relationships that is context dependent. These findings also suggest that both senders and receivers of facial behavior signals are making complex computations that draw upon contextual information to determine the meaning of the signal. These findings therefore call into question whether monkeys can extract meaning from the faces in the absence of context.

CAN MONKEYS DISCRIMINATE BETWEEN FACES?

Animals should be able to discriminate between facial behaviors if those facial behaviors represent meaningful categories of information (e.g., emotions). Evidence to support claims about the emotive nature of macaque facial behaviors is typically drawn from experiments that utilize two types of laboratory tasks. In the first type of task, monkeys actively interact with stimuli (by touching them, for example) of faces from which their ability to discriminate can be discerned (e.g., a match-to-sample task; Parr & Heintz, 2009). In the second type of task, monkeys passively view faces in order to determine if perception differs between face types (e.g., using eye tracking; Gothard, Erickson, & Amaral, 2004; or neural recordings; Hasselmo, Rolls, & Baylis, 1989).

Active Discrimination Between Faces

Match-to-sample tasks used with monkeys mirror human category knowledge tasks (e.g., "X-AB" tasks; Calder, Young, Perrett, Etcoff, & Rowland, 1996) in design. In such tasks, monkeys are presented with one "sample" stimulus followed by two "comparison" stimuli. One of the comparison stimuli matches the sample (e.g., the "match") and the other one does not (e.g., the "foil"). Subjects are tasked with selecting the comparison stimulus that matches the sample. If an individual selects the match stimulus on greater than 50% of the trials, then he or she is said to be able to correctly discriminate the categories of information represented by the stimuli (significance levels are typically set to 67%, which is equivalent to $p < 0.05$). Critically, animals must be trained to perform these tasks, which usually involves rewarding correct responses with desired food or drinks.

Three published reports utilize a match-to-sample task to evaluate the extent to which three species of macaques can discriminate between facial behaviors. The take-home message is consistent across studies—discrimination between facial behaviors is challenging for macaques. When tested with five different facial muscle configurations (bared-teeth, threat, "tense mouth," "ambiguous," and neutral), Japanese macaques (*Macaca fuscata*) did remarkably poorly (Kanazawa, 1996). After each monkey completed 11,400 trials, only one of four monkeys performed above chance. The ability of crested macaques (or Sulawesi macaques, *Macaca nigra*) to discriminate facial behaviors was evaluated using match-to-sample testing in a recent report (Micheletta, Whitehouse, Parr, & Waller, 2015). Subjects were asked to discriminate the silent bared-teeth face, a mild threat, an intense threat, and the relaxed open-mouth face. The three test subjects performed above chance overall, although there was variation in the extent to which their discrimination of particular faces was accurate. While accuracy rates were 50% or greater for all face combinations, test subjects were only significantly above chance (greater than 67%) at matching a few select pairings (i.e., bared-teeth samples when foils were mild threats; relaxed open-mouth when the foils were intense threats; and intense threat samples when the foils were bared-teeth). Mild threat samples were never matched accurately at rates that were significantly above chance.

The challenge of discriminating facial behaviors is underscored by an evaluation of rhesus macaques (*Macaca mulatta*) (Parr & Heintz, 2009). Subjects were tested with five facial behaviors (bared-teeth, threat, scream, relaxed open-mouth, and neutral) and were, in general, accurate when tested with a neutral foil. Note that scream face looks similar to the bared-teeth face but is always accompanied by a shrill, sharp "scream-like" vocalization. Subjects matched relaxed open-mouth, bared-teeth, and threat at accuracy rates that were greater than chance (relaxed-open-mouth = 97.45%, bared-teeth = 97.45%, and threat = 87.50%), although scream face was only accurately matched on 66.07% of trials. That is, subjects accurately matched facial behaviors when the discrimination was between a face that included a behavior and one that did not (the neutral face). A different picture emerged when monkeys were tested with comparison stimuli (i.e., a match stimulus and a foil stimulus) that were both facial behaviors (i.e., a neutral face foil was not used; Parr & Heintz, 2009, Experiment 2). When the match and foil were selected from different affective valence categories (i.e., one face was a relaxed open-mouth face — the only stimulus thought to connote a positive experience), monkeys continued to do well, selecting the correct match significantly more frequently than chance (80.36%) across all trials (with all possible foils). In contrast, monkeys were not proficient at matching the bared-teeth, threat, and scream faces when they were presented with each other—accuracy rates were not significantly greater than chance. In other words, discrimination was possible when the affect of the comparison stimuli differed but more challenging when they belonged to the same affect category.

Taken together, the results of these three macaque category perception studies suggest that discrimination between facial behaviors in laboratory tasks is neither spontaneous nor highly accurate. Monkeys appear to be able to discriminate between facial behaviors when the behaviors represent affective information of different categories (i.e., positive: relaxed open-mouth versus negative: all others; or any facial behavior versus neutral). It does not appear, however, that macaques are readily able to discriminate between facial behaviors that are typically associated with negative emotions (e.g., threats of various intensities, bared-teeth). Importantly, when tested in this context (still faces presented on a computer screen), these sorts of discriminations must occur in the absence of contextual information. Contextual information that accompanies their generation likely allows animals to make meaning of facial behaviors and the presence of contextual information might improve discrimination.

Passive Viewing of Facial Behaviors

The ways that monkeys naturally look at faces, in the absence of a task requiring them to explicitly judge the faces, might also provide clues about whether they distinguish between facial behaviors. According to this logic, if visual scan patterns or neural activity differs significantly for different types of facial behaviors, then monkeys may be processing the information represented by those faces differently and therefore the information may be different. If variation in looking behaviors or neural activity is observed for different facial behaviors, then it is important to evaluate whether that variation is being driven by the meaning of the facial behaviors or whether a simpler explanation (e.g., variance in perceptual features such as exposed teeth) might suit the data.

Passive viewing experiments typically employ eye-tracking to evaluate how monkeys look at faces. When presented with threat, bared-teeth, and lipsmack behaviors, plus a neutral face and a yawning face to serve as nonaffective control stimuli, looking behavior in two studies did differ subtly across facial behaviors when faces were presented both as still pictures (Gothard et al., 2004) and as short dynamic videos (Nahm, Perret, Amaral, & Albright, 1997). Subject monkeys looked at the mouth and eyes for comparable durations of time when viewing the still threat and yawn (Gothard et al., 2004). Monkeys were biased, however, to look at the eyes for longer during lipsmack and neutral faces and at the mouths for longer in bared-teeth faces (Gothard et al., 2004). Although these data point to perceptual differences across facial behaviors, the variation in looking behavior across the stimuli was not reliable enough to predict the facial behavior (Gibboni, Zimmerman, & Gothard, 2009). That is, it would not have been possible to determine what facial behavior an animal was viewing based on the eye-tracking data alone. Furthermore, looking data were highly variable across individuals (Gibboni et al, 2009).

Studies of brain activity while viewing facial behaviors provide another potential source of information about whether macaques distinguish between facial behaviors. Neural recording studies that evaluate neural activity in single neurons or multiple neurons support the idea that cells in the amygdala (Gothard, Battaglia, Erickson, Spitler, & Amaral, 2007; Kuraoka, Konoike, & Nakamura, 2015) and superior temporal sulcus (Hasselmo et al., 1989) are differentially responsive to different facial behaviors. For example, the neural firing in the basolateral complex of amygdala in rhesus monkeys varied based on whether animals are viewing threat, lipsmack, or neutral faces, and distinct populations of cells were more responsive to one versus the other facial behaviors (Gothard et al., 2007). Some amygdala neurons also preferentially activated to faces made during the "scream" vocalization as compared to threat and "coo" (i.e., face accompanying an appeasement/prosocial vocalization;

Kuraoka et al., 2015). Despite variation in areas that activate to particular faces, recorded cells do not exclusively process one face instead of others. Furthermore, of the 119 neurons in the amygdala that responded to any face presentation, more than half of those (73) also evidenced significant responses to geometric shapes (Kuraoka et al., 2015).

Findings from facial behavior viewing experiments, regardless of task type, suggest that macaques do not spontaneously discriminate between different facial behaviors in a way that would be expected if those facial behaviors signaled a specific emotion. Match-to-sample tasks demonstrate that macaques have difficulty explicitly distinguishing between classes of facial behavior and are only consistently successful when asked to distinguish between a facial behavior when compared to a face without muscle movement (a neutral face)—a distinction that could be made on affective information alone (e.g., positivity-negativity + arousal; Barrett & Bliss-Moreau, 2009). Furthermore, neuroimaging and neural recording studies suggest that while particular areas of the brain are responsive to facial behaviors, there are not unique and specific signatures of particular facial behaviors in the brain. In the absence of explicit or neural distinction between facial behaviors in the available evidence, it is unlikely that they represent discrete categories of information.

CONCLUSIONS

The evidence reviewed in this chapter demonstrates that macaque facial behaviors occur in a wide variety of contexts and subserve a variety of social functions. A single facial display may have multiple functions depending on the context in which it is generated or the particular species that generated it. In the absence of this contextual information, macaques can distinguish between facial behaviors that vary in their affective meaning (e.g., positive or negative versus neutral, or negative versus positive) but struggle to distinguish between facial behaviors that represent the same category of affective information. Based on these findings, it seems unlikely that facial behaviors represent emotions in a one-to-one way; as such, macaque facial behaviors are not invariant outward expressions or signals of discrete internal states. Importantly, this view is consistent with evidence on human facial behaviors which demonstrates that contextual information shapes their meaning—that is, the information extracted from faces (e.g., Aviezer et al., 2008; Aviezer, Trope, & Todorov, 2012; Carroll & Russell, 1996; for reviews: Barrett, Mesquita, & Gendron, 2011; de Gelder et al., 2006). Instead, facial behaviors appear to be complex signals whose meaning emerges as a result of the context in which they are generated. Therefore, it is possible, even probable, that stereotyped facial behaviors evolved to serve flexible social communication functions rather than the expression of emotion per se.

What we also hope is clear from this review is that further research is needed to understand the communicative function of macaque facial behaviors. Classic and contemporary observational studies have illuminated many of the contexts in which facial behaviors occur. Detailed analyses of some of those contexts, such as the contexts in which the silent bared-teeth face occurs, that evaluate behaviors which immediately precede and follow the signals as well as long-term social implications of generating the signals suggest the functions of facial behaviors (e.g., as in Beisner & McCowan, 2014; Preuschoft & van Hooff, 1995). Insights on the importance of context gleaned from observational studies can inform laboratory-based studies that allow for greater experimental control and the measurement of outcome measures that may not have easily observable (from a field observation perspective) behavioral correlates (e.g., attention: Deaner & Platt, 2003; Machado, Bliss-Moreau, Platt, & Amaral, 2011; Shepherd, Deaner, & Platt, 2006; autonomic physiology: Bliss-Moreau, Machado, & Amaral, 2013; decision making: Hayden, Heilbronner, Nair, & Platt, 2008; Xu & Kralik, 2014). Facial behaviors and the contexts in which they occur can be systematically varied in the laboratory in the service of understanding the mechanism by which context shapes signal meaning. Adopting an interdisciplinary approach to investigate the meaning and function of macaque facial behaviors will ultimately help us not only to understand how they communicate but also, in concert with evidence from humans, shed light on how and why stereotyped facial behaviors evolved.

ACKNOWLEDGMENTS

EBM was supported by K99MH10138 during the preparation of this manuscript. The authors wish to thank Dr. Brianne Beisner for comments on a draft of the manuscript.

REFERENCES

Ahuja, N. (2013). Notes on medicine, culture, and the history of imported monkeys in Puerto Rico. In M. Few (Ed.), *Centering animals in Latin American history* (pp. 180–205). Durham, NC: Duke University Press.

Allen, M. L., & Lemmon, W. B. (1981). Orgasm in female primates. *American Journal of Primatology, 1*, 15–34.

Altmann, S. A. (1962). A field study of the sociobiology of rhesus monkeys, *Macaca mulatta. Evolution, 102*, 338–435.

Anderson, D. J., & Adolphs, R. (2014). A framework for studying emotions across species. *Cell, 157*, 187–200.

Andrew, R. J. (1963). The origin and evolution of the calls and facial expressions of the primate. *Behaviour, 20*(1/2), 1–109.

Aviezer, H., Hassin, R. R., Ryan, J., Grady, C., Susskind, J., Anderson, A., Moscovitch, M., & Bentin, S. (2008). Angry, disgusted, or afraid? Studies on the malleability of emotion perception. *Psychological Science, 19*(7), 724–732.

Aviezer, H., Trope, Y., & Todorov, A. (2012). Body cues, not facial expressions, discriminate between intense positive and negative emotions. *Science, 338*(6111), 1225–1229.

Barrett, L. F. (2011). Was Darwin wrong about emotional expressions? *Current Directions in Psychological Science, 20*(6), 400–406.

Barrett, L. F., & Bliss-Moreau, E. (2009). Affect as a psychological primitive. In M. P. Zanna (Ed.), *Advances in experimental social psychology* (pp. 167–218). Burlington, MA: Academic Press.

Barrett, L. F., Mesquita, B., & Gendron, M. (2011). Context in emotion perception. *Current Directions in Psychological Science, 20*(5), 286–290.

Beisner, B. A., & McCowan, B. (2014). Signaling context modulates social function of silent bared-teeth displays in rhesus macaques (*Macaca mulatta*). *American Journal of Primatology, 76*(2), 111–121.

Beisner, B., Hannibal, D., Finn, K., & McCowan, B. (2016). Social power, conflict policing, and the role of the subordination signals in rhesus macaque society. *Physical Anthropology 160*(1), 102–112.

Bliss-Moreau, E., Machado, C. J., & Amaral, D. G. (2013). Macaque cardiac physiology is sensitive to the valence of passively viewed sensory stimuli. *PLoS One, 8*(8), e71170.

Cacioppo, J. T., Berntson, G. G., Larsen, J. T., Poehlmann, K. M., & Ito, T. A. (2000). The psychophysiology of emotion. In *Handbook of emotions* (2nd ed., pp. 173–191). New York, NY: Guilford.

Calder, A. J., Young, A. W., Perrett, D. I., Etcoff, N. L., & Rowland, D. (1996). Categorical perception of morphed facial expressions. *Visual Cognition, 3*(2), 81–117.

Capitanio, J. P., & Emborg, M. E. (2008). Contributions of non-human primates to neuroscience research. *Lancet, 371*, 1126–1135.

Carlsson, H. E., Schapiro, S. J., Farah, I., & Hau, J. (2004). Use of primates in research: A global overview. *American Journal of Primatology, 63*(4), 225–237.

Carroll, J. M., & Russell, J. A. (1996). Do facial expressions signal specific emotions? Judging emotion from the face in context. *Journal of Personality and Social Psychology, 70*, 205–218.

Chevalier-Skolnikoff, S. (1973). Facial expression of emotion in nonhuman primates. In P. Eckman (Ed.), *Darwin and facial expression: A century of research and review* (pp. 11–89). New York, NY: Academic Press.

Darwin, C. (2009). *The expression of the emotions in man and animals.* J. Cain & S. Messenger (Eds.) London, UK: Penguin Classics. Original work published (1872).

de Gelder, B., Meeren, H. K. M., Righart, R., Van den Stock, J., van de Riet, W. A. C., & Tamietto, M. (2006). Beyond the face: Exploring rapid influences of context on face processing. *Progress in Brain Research*, *155*, 37–48.

de Waal, F. B. M. (2003). Darwin's legacy and the study of primate visual communication. *Annals of the New York Academy of Sciences*, *1000*, 7–31.

de Waal, F. B. M., & Luttrell, L. M. (1989). Toward a comparative socioecology of the genus *Macaca*: Different dominance styles in rhesus and stumptail monkeys. *American Journal of Primatology*, *19*, 83–109.

Deaner, R. O., & Platt, M. L. (2003). Reflexive social attention in monkeys and humans. *Current Biology*, *13*(18), 1609–1613.

Ekman, P. (1972). Universals and cultural differences in facial expressions of emotions. In J. Cole (Ed.), *Nebraska Symposium on Motivation* (pp. 207–282). Lincoln: University of Nebraska Press.

Ekman, P., & Friesen, W. V. (1971). Constants across cultures in the face and emotion. *Journal of Personality and Social Psychology*, *17*, 124–129.

Ekman P., & Cordaro D. (2011). What is meant by calling emotions basic. *Emotion Review*, *3*, 364–370.

Ferrari, P. F., Paukner, A., Ionica, C., & Suomi, S. J. (2009). Reciprocal face-to-face communication between rhesus macaque mothers and their newborn infants. *Current Biology*, *19*(20), 1768–1772.

Finn, K. R., Beisner, B. A., Bliss-Moreau, E., & McCowan, B. (September, 2014) Affiliative use of the bared teeth display in outdoor captive Rhesus macaques. Poster presented at the annual meeting of the American Society of Primatologists, Decatur, GA.

Flack, J. C., & de Waal, F. (2007). Context modulates signal meaning in primate communication. *Proceedings of the National Academy of Sciences*, *104*(5), 1581–1586.

Fridlund, A. J. (2015). The behavioral ecology view of facial displays, 25 years later. *Emotion Research*. Retrieved from http://emotionresearcher.com/the-behavioral-ecology-view-of-facial-displays-25-years-later/

Gibboni, R. R., Zimmerman, P. E., & Gothard, K. M. (2009). Individual differences in scanpaths correspond with serotonin transporter genotype and behavioral phenotype in rhesus monkeys (*Macaca mulatta*). *Behavioral Neuroscience*, *50*(3), 1–11.

Gothard, K. M., Battaglia, F. P., Erickson, C. A., Spitler, K. M., & Amaral, D. G. (2007). Neural responses to facial expression and face identity in the monkey amygdala. *Journal of Neurophysiology*, *97*(2), 1671–1683.

Gothard, K. M., Erickson, C. A., & Amaral, D. G. (2004). How do rhesus monkeys (*Macaca mulatta*) scan faces in a visual paired comparison task? *Animal Cognition*, *7*(1), 25–36.

Hasselmo, M. E., Rolls, E. T., & Baylis, G. C. (1989). The role of expression and identity in the face-selective responses of neurons in the temporal visual cortex of the monkey. *Behavioural Brain Research*, *32*, 203–218.

Hayden, B. Y., Heilbronner, S. R., Nair, A. C., & Platt, M. L. (2008). Cognitive influences on risk-seeking by rhesus macaques. *Judgment and Decision Making*, *3*(5), 389–395.

Hinde, R. A., & Rowell, T. E. (1962). Communication by postures and facial expressions in the rhesus monkey (*Macaca mulatta*). *Proceedings of the Zoological Society of London, 138*(1), 1–21.

IUCN. (2012). IUCN Red List Categories and Criteria: Version 3.1 (2nd ed.). Gland, Switzerland and Cambridge, UK: IUCN.

Izard, C. E. (1971). *The face of emotion*. New York, NY: Appleton-Century Crofts.

Izard, C. E. (1992). Basic emotions, relations among emotions, and emotion-cognition relations. *Psychological Review, 99*(3), 561–565.

Kanazawa, S. (1996). Recognition of facial expressions in a Japanese monkey. *Primates, 37*, 25–38.

Keltner, D., & Ekman, P. (2000). Facial expression of emotion. In M. Lewis & J. Haviland-Jones (Eds.), *Handbook of emotions* (2nd ed., pp. 236–249). New York, NY: Guilford.

Kuraoka, K., Konoike, N., & Nakamura, K. (2015). Functional differences in face processing between the amygdala and ventrolateral prefrontal cortex in monkeys. *Neuroscience, 304*, 71–80.

Levenson, R. W. (2003). *Autonomic specifity and emotion*. In R. J. Davidson, K. R. Scherer, & H. H. Goldsmith (Eds.), *Handbook of affective sciences* (pp. 212–224). New York, NY: Oxford University Press.

Locke, D. P., Hillier, L. W., Warren, W. C., Worley, K. C., Nazareth, L. V., Muzny, D. M., . . . Wilson, R. K. (2011). Comparative and demographic analysis of orang-utan genomes. *Nature, 469*, 529–533.

Machado, C. J., Bliss-Moreau, E., Platt, M., & Amaral D. G. (2011). Social and non-social content differentially modulates visual attention and autonomic arousal in rhesus macaques, *PLoS One, 6*(10), e26598.

Micheletta, J., Whitehouse, J., Parr, L. A., & Waller, B. M. (2015). Facial expression recognition in crested macaques (*Macaca nigra*). *Animal Cognition, 18*(4), 985–990.

Maestripieri, D. (1997). Gestural communicationin macaques: Usage and meaning of nonvocal signals. *Evolution of Communication, 1*(2), 193–222.

Nahm, F. K. D., Perret, A., Amaral, D. G., & Albright, T. D. (1997). How do monkeys look at faces? *Journal of Cognitive Neuroscience, 9*(5), 611–623.

Nelson, N. L., & Russell, J. A. (2013). Universality revisited. *Emotion Review, 5*(1), 8–15.

Ortony, A., & Turner, T. J. (1990). What's basic about basic emotion? *Psychological Review, 97*(3), 315–331.

Parr, L. A., & Heintz, M. (2009). Facial expression recognition in rhesus monkeys, *Macaca mulatta. Animal Behavior, 77*(6), 1507–1513.

Parr, L. A., Waller, B., Vick, S. J., & Bard, K. A. (2007). Classifying chimpanzee facial displays by muscle action. *Emotion, 7*, 172–181.

Parr, L., Waller, B. M., Burrows, A. M., Gothard, K. M., & Vick, S. J. (2010). Brief communication: MacFACS: A muscle-based facial movement coding system for the rhesus macaque. *American Journal of Physical Anthropology, 143*(4), 625–630.

Phillips, K. A., Bales, K. L., Capitanio, J. P., Conley, A., Czoty, P. W., 't Hart, B. A., . . . Voytko, M. L. (2014). Why primate models matter. *American Journal of Primatology, 76*(9), 801–827.

Preuschoft, S. (1992). "Laughter" and "smile" in Barbary macaques (*Macaca sylvanus*). *Ethology, 91*(3), 220–236.

Preuschoft, S. (2004). Power and communication. In B. Thierry, M. Singh, & W. Kaumanns (Eds.), *Macaque societies* (pp. 56–60). Cambridge, UK: Cambridge University Press.

Preuschoft, S., & van Hooff, J. A. R. A. M. (1995) Homologizing primate facial displays: A critical review of methods. *Folia Primotologica, 65*, 121–137.

Redican, W. K. (1975). Facial expressions in nonhuman primates. In L. A. Rosenblum (Ed.), *Primate behavior: Developments in field and laboratory research* (pp. 103–194). New York, NY: Academic Press.

Rudacille, D. (2000). *The scalpel and the butterfly: The war between animal research and animal protection*. New York, NY: Farrar, Straus, and Giroux.

Russell, J. A. (1994). Is there universal recognition of emotion from facial expressions? A review of the cross-cultural studies. *Psychological Bulletin, 115*(1), 102

Russell, J. A. (2015). Moving on from basic emotion theory of facial expressions. *Emotion Researcher*. http://emotionresearcher.com/moving-on-from-the-basic-emotion-theory-of-facial-expressions/

Shariff, A. F., & Tracy, J. L. (2011). What are emotion expressions for? *Current Directions in Psychological Science, 20*(6), 395–399.

Shepherd, S. V., Deaner, R. O., & Platt, M. L. (2006). Social status gates social attention in monkeys. *Current Biology, 16*(4), R119–120.

Suomi, S. J. (2007). Risk, resilience, and gene × environment interactions in rhesus monkeys. *Annals of the New York Academy of Sciences, 1094*(1), 52–62.

Thierry, B., Singh, M., & Kaumanns, W. (2004). Why macaque societies? In B. Thierry, M. Singh, & W. Kaumanns (Eds.), *Macaque societies: A model for the study of social organization* (pp. 3–10). Cambridge, UK: Cambridge University Press.

van Hooff, J. A. R. A. M. (1967). The facial displays of the catarrhine monkeys and apes. In D. Morris (Ed.), *Primate ethology* (pp. 7–68). London: Weidenfeld & Nicolson.

Visalberghi, E., Valenzano, D. R., & S. Preuschoft. (2006). Facial displays in Cebus apella. *International Journal of Pirmatology, 27*(6), 1689–1707.

Waller, B. M., Parr, L. A., Gothard, K. M., Burrows, A. M., & Fuglevand, A. J. (2008). Mapping the contribution of single muscles to facial movements in the rhesus macaque. *Physiology and Behavior*, 95, 93–100.

Xu, E. R., & Kralik, J. D. (2014). Risky business: Rhesus monkeys exhibit persistent preferences for risky options. *Frontiers in Psychology, 5*, 258.

10

Form and Function of Facial Expressive Origins

DANIEL H. LEE AND ADAM K. ANDERSON

Facial expression research has come a long way, accruing much evidence and theory in accounting *what* are our culturally invariant and variant forms of expressions. The early discovery of six basic expressions (Ekman, Sorenson, & Friesen, 1969) has been shown to communicate distinct mental states reliably across cultures (e.g., Elfenbein & Ambady, 2002; Etcoff & Magee, 1992; Scherer & Wallbott, 1994; Young et al., 1997), with the pattern of their forms being recognized similarly in machines as in humans (Susskind, Littlewort, Bartlett, Movellan, & Anderson, 2007). The cultural and contextual variations in how these expressions are perceived have also been shown (Aviezer et al., 2008; Aviezer, Trope, & Todorov, 2012; Jack, Garrod, Yu, Caldara, & Schyns, 2012), and that our faces are able to communicate more than just six mental state categories (Baron-Cohen, Wheelwright, & Jollife, 1997; Baron-Cohen, Wheelwright, Hill, Raste, & Plumb, 2001; Du, Tao, & Martinez, 2014).

However, a notably neglected line of research in our understanding of expressions forms is the question of *why*. Why do our expressions look the way they do? This investigation of the origins of facial expressive forms is worthwhile, akin to etymology, when we consider the scope of influence our nonverbal expressions encompass across cultures and time. In this chapter, we discuss research that asks *why* of our common expression forms, examining evidence for their origins in Darwin's (1872) theories of egocentric function.

Then, grounded in an evolutionary perspective, we take a preliminary look at how some of these egocentric functional forms may have been co-opted for allocentric function.

Although our facials expressions are now used primarily for communicative purposes, Darwin (1872) theorized that their forms originated for sensory function for the expresser, which were then co-opted for social function. Specifically, he proposed three principles by which emotional expressions may be understood: the principle of serviceable associated habits, the principle of antithesis, and the principle of direct action (or expressive discharge) of the nervous system. The first two of these principles addressed how nature shaped and organized our expressions and are relevant here. The first principle argues that expressions originated for some immediate egocentric functional benefit, rather than their modern, allocentric communicative purpose. Thus, an emotional expression's appearance is not arbitrary but was selected for its congruent adaptive function with its emotion. The second principle of antithetical form argues that expressions can be understood as originating from opposing actions. Thus, an expression may have another that is opposite in appearance for an opposing function. And because the face contains many of our key sensory apertures (e.g., eyes, nose, mouth, ears), Darwin theorized that the function of emotional expressivity was to adaptively modulate sensory intake, such as lowering of the brows to reduce the eyes' exposure to sunlight (Darwin, 1872).

Darwin's principles are less concerned with expressions' explicit categories and their higher order social associations. Instead, he placed emphasis on the bottom-up expressive features that once served the animal for some sensory function (i.e., *why* they appear the way they do). From this perspective, a basic "fear" expression represents not a universal ideal but rather a probable grouping of facial action tendencies that cohere toward some sensory function (e.g., vigilance toward threat in fear; Whalen, 1998). Then, the basis of these expressions, predicated on utility for the expresser, would have been co-opted as communicative signals for utility for the expressions' receiver (Andrew, 1963; Shariff & Tracy, 2011). In the following, we discuss a series of studies that examined Darwin's principles, toward understanding facial expressions' form and egocentric function, and how they may have undergone social exaptation for allocentric function. We begin with basic expressions' form.

FORM

A useful starting point in understanding expression form is to be impressed upon by the sheer physical breadth of the facial musculature that supports it—our potential expression space. Based on the taxonomy of our facial muscle units, the Facial Action Coding System (Ekman, Friesen, & Hager, 1978), we computed that a conservative estimate of our possible expression space amounts to 3.7×10^{16} possibilities (meaning that correctly identifying an expression in this space is the probabilistic equivalent of a person winning two Powerball jackpots). This combinatorial complexity affirms the multidimensional nature of our expression space, which cannot be fully captured by six distinct categories, and provide ample variance and possibility for higher order expressive associations for social utility, whether as in-group dialects (Elfenbein, 2013) or complex mental states (Baron-Cohen et al., 2001; Baron-Cohen, Wheelwright, & Jollife, 1997; Du, Tao, & Martinez, 2014). At the same time, it provides a statistically appropriate context for affirming the cross-cultural consistency of basic expressions. If our expressions were purely higher order associations, each shaped arbitrarily for social communication, there could not be any recognition of expressions across cultures. We would instead be left with sets of arbitrary expressions that would have to be translated across cultures, akin to the symbolic associations of verbal languages. Thus, within this expressive framework, basic expressions need not be universal in the strong sense but in having maintained statistical stability across the myriad influences of culture and context, they would indicate a common ancestry.

It is daunting to try to understand the raw complexity of this expressive space and how our basic expressions fit in it. A dimensional perspective (Oosterhof & Todorov, 2008; Plutchik, 1980; Rolls, 1990; Russell, 1980; Russell & Barrett, 1999; Watson & Tellegen, 1985) is helpful in keeping some of this variance tractable, but we still require a theory to organize and interpret those dimensions. Moreover, familiar dimensions of psychological experience (Rolls, 1990; Russell, 1980; Russell & Barrett, 1999; Watson & Tellegen, 1985) or physiological changes (Bradley, Codispoti, Cuthbert, & Lang, 2001; Caccioppo & Berntson, 1994), such as valence and arousal, may not be the most applicable way to frame dimensions of physical form, in particular if the physical forms have been evolutionarily selected for survival. A more suitable organizing principle may be that when it comes to evolutionary selection, especially when it comes to features that interface with the physical world, form follows function. We thus applied Darwin's (1872) principles as a framework for understanding basic expression form.

Framed by Darwinian principles, the cross-cultural consistency of basic expressions (Ekman, Sorenson, & Friesen, 1969) may be important as reference points that reveal how natural selection organized those expressive features as probable action tendencies rather than categorical ideals. Then, toward uncovering these natural origins, basic expressions' features may be useful to consider as anchors, without which we would find ourselves adrift in facial expressions' combinatorial complexity. Then, Darwin's second principle of antithesis provides an organizing influence of these anchors, aligning opposing basic expressions and the dimensional continua of their feature variance based on appearance and function. Applying these ideas may reveal a more predictable pattern for understanding our basic expressions and a way to navigate our vast expressive space.

Whereas facial action units may be taxonomized independently, our basic expressions appear to have systematic relationships in activation and thus expressive appearance (Dailey et al., 2002; Susskind et al., 2007). To examine these facial action tendencies, we applied a computer graphics model of facial appearance (Cootes, Edwards, & Taylor, 2001) to the six basic expressions from a standard cross-cultural dataset (Matsumoto & Ekman, 1988). The appearance model allowed us to create a prototype for each basic expression as vector representations that coded its expressive shape. This revealed an important dimension of expressive action of widening versus narrowing of the sensory apertures across a number of basic expressions. For example, fear and surprise demonstrated expressive widening, while disgust and anger opposingly demonstrated expressive narrowing (Susskind & Anderson, 2008). These similarities in expression form were corroborated by similarities in expression perception, where fear and surprise were perceived alike, disgust and anger were perceived alike, and each pair was perceived highly unlike the other pair (Susskind et al., 2007). Next, we focused our examination on the two expressions that occupied the extremes of expressive widening versus narrowing dimension: fear and disgust (Susskind et al., 2008).

Using the vectorized models of fear and disgust, we first tested a prediction of this widening versus narrowing expressive dimension. We generated computerized fear and disgust "antiprototypes" by reversing the direction of the facial action vectors of the fear and disgust prototypes, predicting that each antiprototype would most likely be perceived as its dimensional opposite. Indeed, participants perceived antifear most strongly as disgust and antidisgust most strongly as fear (Susskind et al., 2008). To visualize the facial action directions represented in these vectorized models, we generated vector flow diagrams of these expression prototypes relative to their antiprototypes (Fig. 10.1). They demonstrated expanding versus compressing longitudinal actions of the muscular frames around the mouth, nose, and eyes (Susskind et al., 2008; Susskind & Anderson, 2008), suggestive of Darwin's theories of expressive form and opposition.

Beyond demonstrating an opposition in form, if these actions that widen versus narrow the sensory apertures were indeed selected for function (Darwin, 1872), they should cohere with theorized functions of the emotions associated with the expressions. Next, we examine Darwin's principles on whether these forms confer sensory benefits to the expresser.

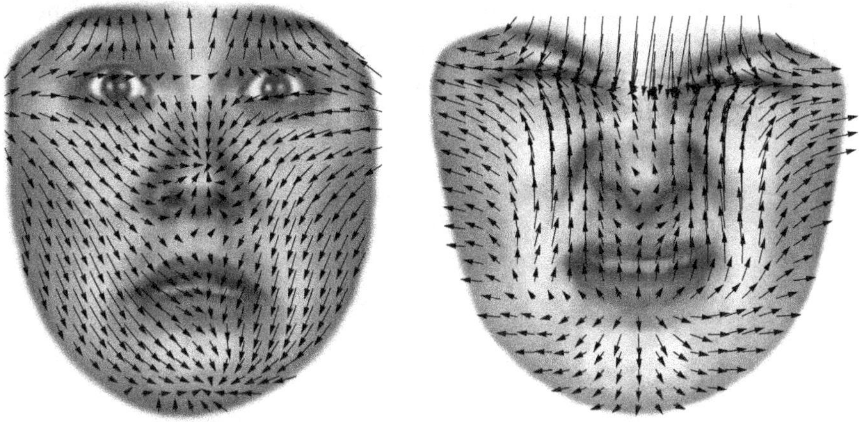

Figure 10.1 Opposition in facial actions of fear and disgust expressions. Arrows depict vector flow fields of skin surface deformations of an expression prototype from its corresponding antiprototype. Visualizing these underlying facial-action patterns indicates the opposing expansion in fear (left) versus compression in disgust (right) along the longitudinal axis emanating from the bridge of the nose, resulting in raised versus lowered brows, increased versus decreased eye aperture, and vertical elongation versus compression of the nose associated with raised versus lowered lips.

EGOCENTRIC FUNCTION

A prominent theory of the function of fear is vigilance toward threats (Öhman & Mineka, 2001; Whalen, 1998). For an animal confronted with immediate potential threats in its environment, survival would be enhanced by increasing its sensitivity toward detecting and locating those threats, even if they turned out to be benign, false positives. Thus, congruent with fear's theorized function, we predicted that widening of sensory apertures, such as the eyes and nasal passages, would promote the gathering of sensory information. Conversely, disgust is theorized to be an emotion of rejection toward threats of a different kind (Chapman & Anderson, 2012; Rozin & Fallon, 1987; Rozin, Haidt, & McCauley, 2000). Potentially originating in older principles of distaste and rejection of chemosensory stimuli (Chapman, Kim, Susskind, & Anderson, 2009), expressions of disgust may reflect a different response, such as protection from, or a more deliberate discrimination of (Anderson, Christoff, Panitz, De Rosa, & Gabrieli, 2003; Sherman, Haidt, & Clore, 2012), threats of a more proximal, stationary kind. Thus, in addition to fear and disgust expressions serving as anchoring ends of a widening versus narrowing facial expressive dimension (Susskind et al., 2008), these independently theorized functions of fear and disgust emotions provided specific hypotheses about the sensory consequences of their expressive forms.

We tested this thesis of facial form's function using a variety of experiments on how expressive actions influence two sensory apertures—the nose and the eyes. Participants posed expressions in a directed facial-action paradigm while we measured various sensory functions and perceptual consequences. The use of directed facial actions to pose fear and disgust (Ekman, Friesen, & Hager, 1978; Susskind et al., 2008) rather than inducing the emotions was important in being able to isolate the sensory effects of facial expression form, independent from the cognitive influences emotions can have at the level of the central nervous system (e.g., enhancing attention; Vuilleumier et al., 2001).

Nose

Beginning with nasal effects of expressive action, we acquired nasal respirometry, nasal temperature, and abdominal-thoracic respiratory measures during a controlled instructed breathing cycle. Given equal duration of inspiration (2.2 s in/out per breath), fear was associated with an increase in air velocity and volume relative to neutral and disgust expressions, even when corrected for respiratory effort (Fig. 10.2a; Susskind et al., 2008).

Altered air intake may reflect a variety of factors rather than genuine structural changes in sensory capacity afforded by expressions. We thus directly examined whether fear and disgust altered the underlying structure of the nasal passages in opposing manners. High-resolution magnetic resonance images of the nasal passages were acquired during the directed facial-action task, which resulted in nasal passage volume significantly modified by expression (Fig. 10.2b; Susskind et al., 2008). More specifically, these structural images revealed that fear expressions resulted in a dilation of the entry to the inferior nasal turbinates of the respiratory mucosa, consistent with horizontal mouth stretching and lowering facilitating nasal passage dilation; in contrast, disgust resulted in a sealing off of this normally open passage, consistent with upper lip raising and nose wrinkling (Fig. 10.2c).

Eyes

For visual function, we examined how expressions influence the visual field. First, testing subjective measures of visual field change, participants reported seeing farther out into the periphery of a visual grid space while posing fear relative to neutral as well as disgust (Fig. 10.3a; Susskind et al., 2008). Next, testing objective measures of visual field change, we used two kinds of stimuli in separate experiments. In a simple dot target detection task, fear widened the peripheral visual field relative to neutral and disgust (Susskind et al., 2008). This visual field expansion of fear was similarly found in a rigorous

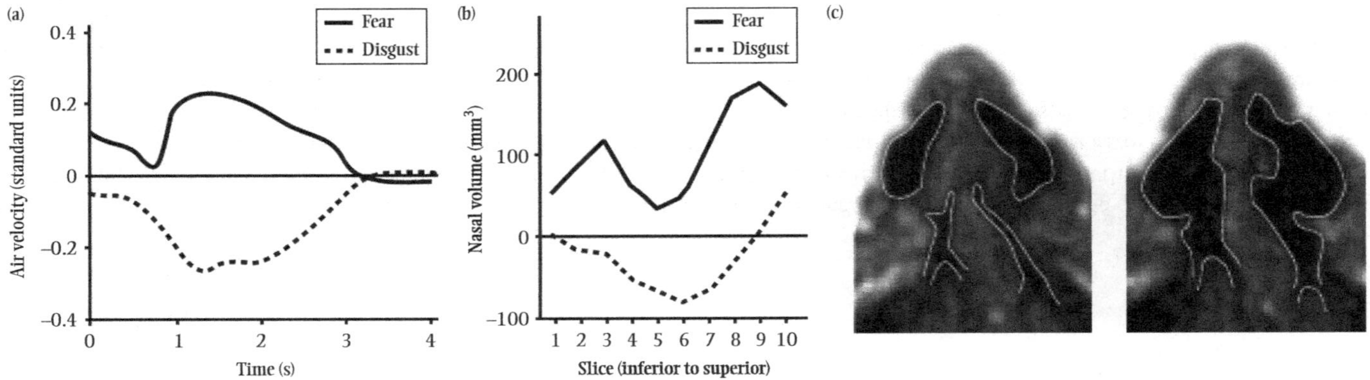

Figure 10.2 Nasal effects of fear and disgust expressions. (*a*) Mean air-flow velocity (in standardized units) for fear and disgust expressions relative to neutral during inhalation over time (2.2 s inhalation). (*b*) Volume of air cavity of the ventral portion (12 mm) of the nasal passages for fear and disgust expressions relative to neutral. Each slice was 1.2 mm thick with an in-plane resolution of 0.86 × 0.86 mm. (*c*) Passageways to the inferior turbinate of the respiratory mucosa from magnetic resonance imaging. Expressions of disgust (left) and fear (right) resulted in closure and dilation, respectively.

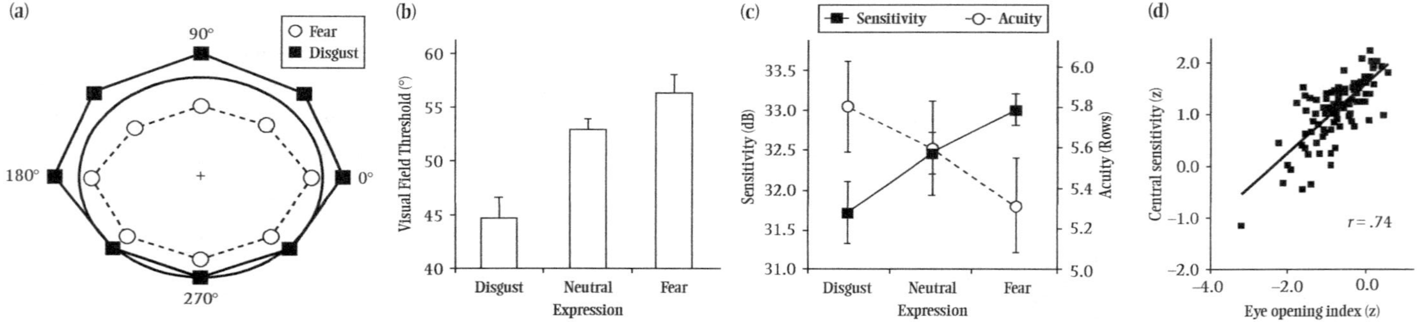

Figure 10.3 Visual effects of eye widening and narrowing in fear and disgust expressions. (*a*) Subjective visual-field changes in visual field estimation along horizontal, vertical, and oblique axes. Central ellipse is neutral baseline. (*b*) Objective visual field thresholds for identifying Gabor orientations for each expression. Fear expanded the visual field relative to neutral and disgust expressions. Error bars represent SEM. (*c*) Visual sensitivity (left y-axis) and visual acuity (right y-axis) effects of expression. Sensitivity scores are restricted to the central visual field (4.2° visual angle from fovea). Acuity scores are the number of correctly read rows of eye-chart letters. Higher scores indicate greater sensitivity or acuity. Error bars represent SEM. (*d*) Relationship of central visual field sensitivity to degree of eye opening, indexed by visual sensitivity measured at the peripheral visual field (mean visual angle from fovea = 20.6°, SD = 2.1°). Expression effects on visual sensitivity in the periphery are due to light occlusion by eyebrow and eyelids, whereas central visual field is due to light refraction.

psychophysical task where participants identified orientations of Gabor gratings that were controlled for visual angle size (Fig. 10.3b; Lee, Susskind, & Anderson, 2013). In the latter psychophysical study, eye widening of fear expressions enhanced the effective visual field of the expresser 9.4% farther out in the available periphery compared to neutral (Lee et al., 2013). These visual field changes were direct physical effects of opening versus occluding of the upper visual periphery by eye opening, as corroborated by the larger effect in the vertical rather than oblique meridians (due to the morphology of our vertically opening eyes) and an opposing visual periphery reduction for eye-narrowing disgust expressions.

Although we found visual field enhancements along the vertical and oblique meridians and not the horizontal, participants maintained central fixation in order to test their peripheral, not foveal vision. However, in the real world, eye movements are critical for gathering information about one's visual surroundings. In another experiment we examined whether fear expressions facilitate muscle units that facilitate eye scanning. Here, we found that horizontal saccades to peripheral targets (27° apart) were faster relative to neutral and disgust both in average and peak speeds (Susskind et al., 2008).

These visual field effects were due to a basic sensory gating mechanism, involving simple retraction of eye features that occlude the visual periphery. But beyond peripheral occlusion effects, we theorized that expressive eye opening may fundamentally influence how light is gathered, along a functional dimension seen throughout the visual system. Although facial muscles that reconfigure superficial eye features should have no direct influence on the pupil or the accommodative lens behind it, approximately two thirds of the eye's full refractive power comes from the cornea (Duke-Elder & Abrams, 1970). We thus predicted facial expressive behaviors that expose or conceal the cornea to have adaptive consequences on the eye's optics. Specifically, an optical model predicted eye widening to increase light gathering and enhance sensitivity over acuity, prioritizing fear's function for vigilance of threat detection and localization (Öhman & Mineka, 2001; Whalen, 1998). Conversely, eye narrowing would focus light more sharply to enhance acuity over sensitivity, prioritizing visual discrimination of different kinds of threat, such as contaminated foods or disease vectors (Chapman & Anderson, 2012; Rozin, Haidt, & McCauley, 2000; Sherman et al., 2012).

This functional trade-off between sensitivity and acuity is a familiar division in the visual system, from retinal rods and cones, to the crude but fast magnocellular and slow but sharp parvocellular systems (Livingstone & Hubel, 1987), which are carried on to the dorsal and ventral streams for processing "where" and "what" information, respectively (Ungerleider & Mishkin, 1982). The optical trade-off suggested by our model predicted that expressive actions that alter the eyes' capacity to gather and focus light may have arisen from a differential need to filter light information toward the "where" (magnocellular) versus "what" (parvocellular) channels, in a situation-appropriate manner.

We tested this optical trade-off hypothesis in experiments that used standard optometric measures of visual sensitivity and visual acuity. In a psychophysical contrast sensitivity task, eye-widening fear expressions enhanced visual sensitivity whereas disgust reduced it. Conversely, in a visual acuity task using standardized eye charts (Bailey & Lovie, 1976), eye-narrowing disgust expressions enhanced acuity while fear reduced it (Fig. 10.3c; Lee, Mirza, Flanagan, & Anderson, 2014).

CONTINUOUS PHYSICAL DIMENSION

Across the nasal and visual experiments, we also found reliable, linearly increasing effects from disgust to fear (Lee et al., 2013, 2014; Susskind et al., 2008). The clearest demonstration of this was in the sensitivity measures eye aperture, where degree of eye opening across participants and conditions was directly related to central sensitivity effects (Fig. 10.3d). This suggests that these sensory effects are tied to a continuum of expressive action tendencies rather than discrete facial configurations, emphasizing the underpinning of a physical nature, rather than psychological categories. The physical underpinning of these sensory effects, which can occur in the absence of their discrete emotions such as fear and disgust and their associated autonomic expression, suggest that the egocentric functional dimension of eye opening may extend to other expressions (e.g., raising eyebrows in surprise or lowering them in anger; Susskind & Anderson, 2008). This availability of continuous physical form and the degrees of influence on egocentric changes also leave open a potentially wider and more complex window into the intentions of the expresser (Baron-Cohen et al., 2001; Baron-Cohen, Wheelwright, & Jollife, 1997; Du, Tao, & Martinez, 2014) and cultural variance in their interpretation and emergence (Aviezer, Trope, & Todorov, 2012; Elfenbein & Ambady, 2003; Fridlund, 1997; Jack et al., 2012; Marsh, Elfenbein, & Ambady, 2003; Russell & Barrett, 1999).

Increasing evidence suggests that emotions influence the central nervous system at multiple levels to alter perception (e.g., Krusemark & Li, 2011; Li, Howard, Parrish, & Gottfried, 2008; Sherman et al., 2012; Todd, Talmi, Schmitz, Susskind, & Anderson, 2012). The collective evidence here shows that emotional expressions can exert potent effects at the earliest stage of sensory encoding. These effects are consistent with the theorized functions of fear and disgust (Chapman & Anderson, 2012; Öhman & Mineka, 2001; Rozin, Haidt, & McCauley, 2000; Sherman et al., 2012; Whalen, 1998) and the distinct processing dynamics proposed for them (Anderson et al., 2003), as the opposing sensory and perceptual effects discussed in this chapter shed light on why these two negatively valenced and avoidance-action-related emotions are associated with opposing facial actions (Susskind et al., 2008) and opposing effects on the autonomic nervous system (de Jong, van Overveld, & Peters, 2011; Levenson, 1992). For example, specific to the eyes, the functions of their expressive widening and narrowing may converge with the sympathetic dilation and parasympathetic constriction of the pupil (Beatty & Lucero-Wagoner, 2000), potentially acting as the initial filters toward the magnocellular (dorsal) and parvocellular (ventral) visual streams (Ungerleider & Mishkin, 1982). Thus, this functional view of expressions aligns with appraisal theories (Scherer, 2009) as early sensory filtering toward one of two channels implies downstream cognitive effects of information bias. And on the causal side of widening versus narrowing expressions, this functional view assumes that certain opposing appraisal demands would elicit opposing expressive patterns. The expressive effects here are attributable to direct sensory differences rather than indirect effects of facial feedback (e.g., Strack, Martin, & Stepper, 1988) or emotional embodiment (Niedenthal, 2007). In the sensitivity experiment, measurement of pupil size found no differences during posing expressions (indicating a lack of autonomic feedback) and no differences in behavioral tendency, measured by fixations away from center to peripheral targets (Lee et al., 2014). However, in full-fledged emotional expressions, we would expect these egocentric sensory functions to be further augmented—for instance, in fear, its eye-widening light sensitivity may be amplified by an increase in sympathetic autonomic tone (Levenson, 1992) that dilates the pupils, and the further conjunctive retracting of the eyelids through the involuntary, sympathetically innervated Müller's muscle (Brunton, 1938).

Although expressive forms may have been functionally shaped to modulate the expresser's sensory intake, the modern utility of our expressions extends beyond the self to serve as social signals. We next examine evidence on how such allocentric function may have been co-opted from egocentric functional forms.

ALLOCENTRIC FUNCTION

To examine how expressions' interpersonal function may have been co-opted from personal function, we focused on the eyes. The eyes are an important source of social information (e.g., Marsh, Adams, & Kleck, 2005; Smith, Cottrell, Gosselin, & Schyns, 2005) with the capacity to communicate a wide variety of complex mental states (Baron-Cohen, Wheelwright, Hill, Raste, & Plumb, 2001; Baron-Cohen, Wheelwright, & Jollife, 1997). Indeed, circumscribed brain regions in the superior temporal sulcus and gyrus, which are responsive to eye information (Allison, Puce, & McCarthy, 2000; Calder et al.,

2007), neighbor regions supporting how we read the mental states of others (in the temporoparietal junction; Saxe & Powell, 2006). Convergently, increasing failure to use the information conveyed by the eyes has been positively related with degrees of autism, a disorder tied to failures in the ability to understand the expresser's mental states (Baron-Cohen, 1995).

Prior work has also examined how emotional expressions influence processing of eye gazes. For instance, fear expressions facilitate faster judgments of averted gaze compared to direct gaze (Adams & Franklin, 2009) and, inversely, that averted gaze enhances the perceived intensity of fear (Adams & Kleck, 2005). Fear expressions' directional eye gazes have also been shown to deploy additional attention in the context of an attentional cueing paradigm (Putman, Hermans, & van Honk, 2006; Tipples, 2006). These eye gaze effects are hinged to the communicated emotion and illustrate a congruent social utility of eye gazes with fear expressions in facilitating a state of vigilance in the observer as well as fear's expresser—the state of alarm whose reverberation in the observer acts as the catalyst (e.g., Harrison, Singer, Rotshtein, Dolan, & Critchley, 2006).

We examined the egocentric-to-allocentric function co-option of our expressive eyes at two levels. First, at a basic level of physical signals transmitted by eye gazes, and second, at a more complex level of the variety of mental states conveyed by our expressive eyes.

Physical Signal

First, we tested the benefits of fear expressions on the eye gaze signal at a basic, physical signal level. We predicted that wider fear eyes would capitalize on the morphology of our eyes, such as the additional contrast provided by our white sclera thought to have coevolved with our social nature (Kobayashi & Kohshima, 1997). The enhancement of this physical signal in expressive eye widening would serve as the most expedient social signal of a significant event's location by way of a clearer "look here" gaze signal. Thus, the potential personal sensory benefit of eye widening would be directly conferred interpersonally prior to, or independent from, the need for the communicated emotion of the expresser.

We created schematic eye stimuli using modeled (Cootes, Edwards, & Taylor, 2001) expressions of fear and disgust, and removed the rest of the face, in order to impoverish any emotional influence of the full expressions while retaining the basic physical features (Lee et al., 2013). We then created four different eye sizes, from narrowest disgust to widest fear (Fig. 10.4a), of which participants judged the gaze directions. We found accuracy of gaze direction judgment linearly increased with increased eye widening (Fig. 10.4b).

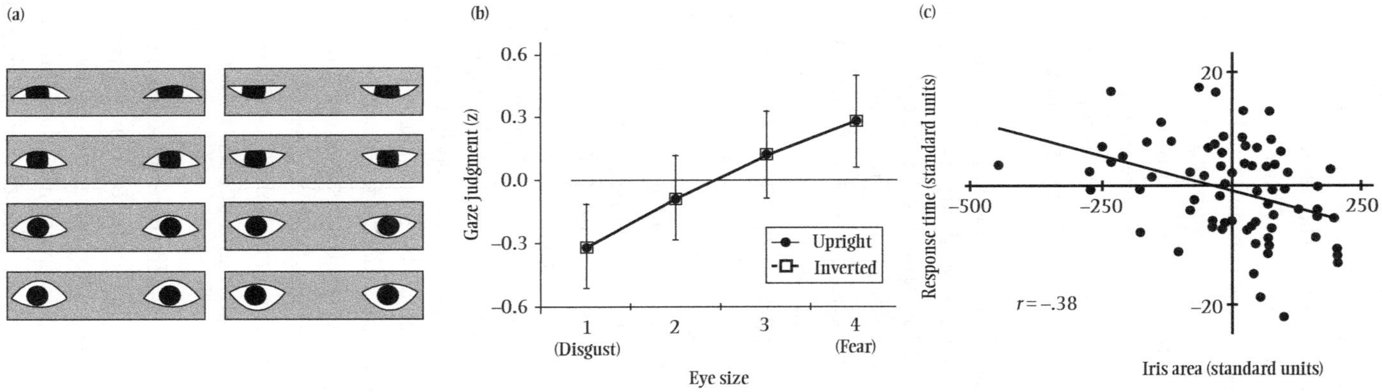

Figure 10.4 Allocentric physical signaling effects of eye widening. (*a*) Schematic eyes were modeled from participants who posed disgust expressions (top images; Size 1) and fear expressions (bottom images; Size 4). Intermediate Sizes 2 and 3 were interpolated linearly from Size 1 to Size 4 in equal steps of vertical aperture. Eyes in the right column are inverted versions of eyes in the left column. All eyes are gazing the same degree, slightly left of center. (*b*) Plot shows standardized scores of logistic regression slopes for each eye size for upright and inverted eyes. Accuracy of gaze direction judgments increased with eye widening, but not eye inversion. Error bars represent SEM. (*c*) Plot shows response time negatively correlated to visible iris information. Participants responded faster to peripheral targets cued by eye gaze as eyes got wider and revealed more iris.

Given that mere greater exposure of eye whites can activate the amygdala (Whalen et al., 2004) and widened eyes are sufficient to recognize fear (Smith, Cottrell, Gosselin, & Schyns, 2005), the recruitment of emotional circuitry as well as some degree of emotion contagion (Harrison et al., 2006) in modulating these effects was possible. To control for this, we used the same eyes inverted, as inverted fear expressions have demonstrated reduced fear perceptions (McKelvie, 1995), reductions in amygdalar activity (Sato, Kochiyama, & Yoshikawa, 2011), and attentional orienting (Bocanegra & Zeelenberg, 2009; Phelps, Ling, & Carrasco, 2006). Indeed, the inverted schematic eyes reduced the perception of fear but provided the identical physical gaze signal and retained the same enhancement in gaze judgment accuracy for wider eyes (Fig. 10.4b; Lee et al., 2013).

Separately, we examined whether fear eye widening would directly facilitate observer responsiveness in locating peripheral targets (i.e., to "look here"). In a gaze cueing experiment, we used the same schematic eyes and found that participants responded faster to cued peripheral targets, with response speed related to key physical features of the eyes, contrast and amount of visible iris (Fig. 10.4c; Lee et al., 2013). Furthermore, we found no attentional biasing effect of wider eyes, which further suggested that the effects of the emotionally impoverished gaze stimuli were not due to the communicated emotion, as full fear expressions and their gazes have been shown to bias attention (Putman et al., 2006; Tipples, 2006; Vuilleumier et al., 2001).

The importance of the physical signal of our eye gazes is highlighted in the features that are enhanced in fear's eye widening, which provide no direct function for the expresser. For example, the additional exposure of our physically salient white sclera, unique among primates (Kobayashi & Kohshima, 1997), suggests an additional social function supported by expressive eye widening. Thus, the egocentric sensory benefits of fear may have had a direct influence in shaping their allocentric benefits—by the single expressive action of eye widening that augments its physical saliency, fear's sensory function may be directly linked with that of the observer. In this way, the functional benefit of expressive fear at its basic sensory level in locating potential threat is passed on to the observer through transmission of a clearer "look here" gaze signal, highlighting the coevolution of egocentric and allocentric sensory functions of expressions.

Retracting the eyelids and eyebrows has likely resulted from multiple selective pressures. One such pressure may be the coevolution of an enhanced processing of events in the visual fields of the expresser passed onto the observer. Convergent evidence also suggests the interaction of these pressures toward a congruent social function, such as the emotionality of full fear expressions enhancing averted gaze direction processing (Adams & Franklin, 2009).

Further linking allocentric to egocentric function, fear expressions have also shown to improve early vision for observers (Phelps, Ling, & Carrasco, 2006), specifically along lower spatial frequency channels (Bocanegra & Zeelenberg, 2009), which is aligned with fear expressions' prioritized perception and action via the low-spatial-frequency tuned magnocellular pathway, projecting to the dorsal stream (Vuilleumier, Armony, Driver, & Dolan, 2003; West, Anderson, Bedwell, & Pratt, 2010). The basic, physical utility of these convergent functions may suggest their co-opted selection prior to expression's modern utility of communicating a particular emotion or mental state (Shariff & Tracy, 2011), which we examine next.

Mental State Signal

We know that our eyes convey a variety of complex mental states (Baron-Cohen et al., 2001; Baron-Cohen, Wheelwright, & Jollife, 1997), but we do not know what specific eye features convey mental states and how that came about. We hypothesized that the eye-widening versus eye-narrowing dimension that alters optical function for the expresser may explain how we have come to read basic and complex mental states from the eyes. Specifically, we predicted eye-widening versus eye-narrowing features that opposingly tune the expresser's visual perception for sensitivity versus discrimination (Lee et al., 2014) to denote basic and complex mental states of sensitivity versus discrimination (e.g., fear vs. disgust and awe vs. suspicion).

Anchoring our examination to basic expressions, we modeled (Cootes, Edwards, & Taylor, 2001) the eyes of basic expressions from facial expression databases (Ekman & Friesen, 1976; Matsumoto & Ekman, 1988), which participants rated on 50 different mental states (6 basic and 44 complex). We then analyzed the multidimensional relationship between mental state perception and a unique set of physical eye features extracted from the stimuli (i.e., eye aperture, eyebrow distance, eyebrow slope, eyebrow curvature, nasal wrinkles, temporal wrinkles, and lower wrinkles below the eyes). The similarity relationship of mental state perception from eye features was plotted in a mental states map (Fig. 10.5).

Confirming the importance of the eye-opening dimension for mental state content, the primary dimension showed that structural features were judged highly similar for eye-widening fear and surprise, which opposed eye-narrowing disgust and anger (Susskind et al., 2008; Susskind & Anderson, 2008), and these pairings opposed one another as highly dissimilar (Fig. 10.5). Largely orthogonal to this opposition, eye features of joy and sadness were also judged to represent highly dissimilar states. A principal components analysis showed that these two dimensions captured 88.8% of the total variance of

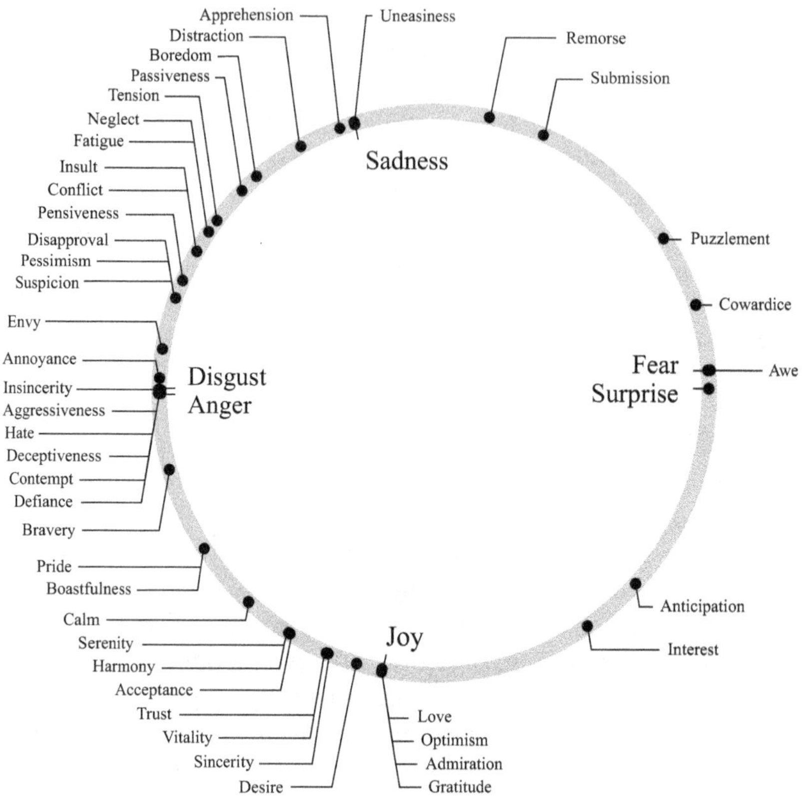

Figure 10.5 Relationship between 50 mental states based on features of and around the eyes. Mental states similar across features appear closer together. Basic emotion states matching the eye stimuli are highlighted for reference. The opposition of disgust and anger (eye narrowing enhancing discrimination) to fear and surprise (eye widening enhancing sensitivity) is illustrated in their maximal distance around the circle.

mental states, with the widening-narrowing dimension capturing the majority variance (61.7%). Examining the mental states map in detail, eye-widening features of fear and surprise aligned with mental states of information sensitivity, such as awe, anticipation, cowardice, and interest. Opposing these mental state attributions, eye-narrowing features of disgust and anger aligned mental states that convey social discrimination, such as hate, suspicion, aggressiveness, and contempt. In a follow-up experiment we found that these perceptions of sensitivity versus discrimination mental states were maintained in the context of full expressions of incongruent expressive information. For example, narrow eyes of disgust and anger, combined with lower nose and mouths of other basic expressions were still perceived as hate and suspicion, while wide eyes of fear and surprise in mixed facial contexts were perceived as awe and cowardice.

Illustrated in the mental states map, there was also an asymmetry in a smaller, more isolated cluster of sensitivity mental states compared to a larger cluster of discrimination mental states. This may reflect a signaling bias similar to wider eye gaze signals (Lee et al. 2013) that capitalizes on our unique eye whites (Kobayashi & Kohshima, 1997), where wide eyes represent a relatively unambiguous signal and associated mental state attributions. Thus, the opposing eye actions of widening and narrowing that enhance visual sensitivity versus discrimination in the sender (Lee et al., 2014) may resonate in how the receiver decodes them (Lee et al., 2013). Wide eyes are strong signals (Adolphs et al., 2005; Whalen et al., 2004) and more diagnostic, lessening the need for discrimination, while narrow eyes are weaker signals and much less diagnostic, requiring greater scrutiny to discriminate among underlying mental states.

The dimension of sensitivity-discrimination perception underscores the link to the sensory origins of our eyes' expressiveness (Darwin, 1872; Susskind et al., 2008). That this sensory antagonism may be engaged in contexts far removed from their sensory origins in complex states such as suspicion toward potentially unfair social transaction (Chapman, Kim, Susskind & Anderson, 2009) highlights how they have been socially exapted for purposes beyond their role in biasing visual encoding.

CONCLUSIONS

In this chapter, we attempted to bridge a gap in our understanding of facial expressions: why they look the way do and how they were shaped to be the varied social communicative signals of today. Our thesis taken from Darwin (1872) posited that our facial expressions originated for sensory function to provide egocentric benefits to the expresser, which were then socially co-opted for allocentric function to the expressions' observers.

This egocentric-to-allocentric functional perspective supports an integration of categorical and dimensional views in that basic expressions (Ekman, 1999; Izard, 1994) represent higher order probabilities organized by lower, adaptive actions as opposites along a dimension of an expressive continuum (Oosterhof & Todorov, 2008; Russell & Barrett, 1999; Susskind et al., 2008). The evidence for the functional basis of basic expressions provides a parsimonious, empirical account of their cultural consistency (Ekman, Sorenson, & Friesen, 1969), which were likely socially co-opted for communication (Andrew, 1963; Shariff & Tracy, 2011), serving as anchoring sources of invariance in expression perception across cultures and contexts.

The facial actions fell on a sensory regulatory dimension of widening versus narrowing expressive form. This continuous dimension makes available a variety of facial expressions that can be interpretable as signals of different mental states (Baron-Cohen, Wheelwright, & Jollife, 1997; Baron-Cohen et al., 2001; Du, Tao, & Martinez, 2014) and cultural dialects of expressive communications (Elfenbein, 2013). This perspective accommodates the constructivist view in that the labels that define specific facial actions and their degrees of expressivity (i.e., what the expressions are) is left up to social interpretation and context (e.g., Aviezer, Trope, & Todorov, 2012; Fridlund, 1997; Jack et al., 2012; Russell & Barrett, 1999). However, this functional perspective may provide guiding constraints for understanding why our expressions as social signals look the way they do. Although features could be arbitrarily mapped for communication, they cannot be arbitrarily mapped for function (Darwin, 1872; Susskind et al., 2008). For example, from a strictly constructivist perspective (Barrett, 2006a, 2006b), widening and narrowing of the eyes may not universally characterize fear and disgust expressions, especially given the powerful influences of culture (Jack et al., 2012) and social context (Aviezer et al., 2008; Aviezer, Trope, & Todorov, 2012) on perception of facial expressions. So if fear and disgust expressive forms were swapped, they would serve equally well as social signals of mental states but have misaligned functional consequences (e.g., reducing acuity in disgust or making it harder to tell where someone is gazing during fear). Indeed, a mental-states map of eye features (Fig. 10.5) reflected a nonarbitrary, basic structural logic of sensitivity versus discrimination along the widening versus narrowing dimension.

Taken together, the evidence connects the appearance of our expressions from their egocentric origins to their modern-day allocentric functions. Thus, our expressions not only socially connect us in the present, through the communication of mental states, but also to a coevolved history of how our individual survival was leveraged into a flourishing cooperative one.

REFERENCES

Adams, R. B., Jr., & Franklin, R. G., Jr. (2009). Influence of emotional expression on the processing of gaze direction. *Motivation and Emotion*, *33*, 106–112.

Adams, R. B., Jr., & Kleck, R. E. (2005). Effects of direct and averted gaze on the perception of facially communicated emotion. *Emotion*, *5*, 3–11.

Adolphs, R, Gosselin, F., Buchanan, T. W., Tranel, D., Schyns, P., & Damasio, A. R. (2005). A mechanism for impaired fear recognition after amygdala damage. *Nature*, *433*, 68–72.

Allison, T., Puce, A., & McCarthy, G. (2000). Social perception from visual cues: Role of the STS region. *Trends in Cognitive Sciences*, *4*, 267–278.

Anderson, A. K., Christoff, K., Panitz, D. A., De Rosa, E., & Gabrieli, J. D. E. (2003). Neural correlates of the automatic processing of threat facial signals. *Journal of Neuroscience*, *23*, 5627–5633.

Andrew, R. J. (1963). Evolution of facial expression. *Science, 142*, 1034–1041.

Aviezer, H., Hassin, R. R., Ryan, J., Grady, C., Susskind, J. M., Anderson, A. K., ... Bentin, S. (2008). Angry, disgusted, or afraid? Studies on the malleability of emotion perception. *Psychological Science, 19*, 724–732.

Aviezer, H., Trope, Y., & Todorov, A. (2012). Body cues, not facial expressions, discriminate between intense positive and negative emotions. *Science, 338*, 1225–1229.

Bailey, I. L., & Lovie, J. E. (1976). New design principles for visual acuity letter charts. *American Journal of Optometry and Physiological Optics, 53*, 740–745.

Baron-Cohen, S. (1995). *Mindblindness: An essay on autism and theory of mind.* Cambridge, MA: MIT Press/Bradford Books.

Baron-Cohen, S., Wheelwright, S., Hill, J., Raste, Y., & Plumb, I. (2001). The "reading the mind in the eyes" test revised version: A study with normal adults, and adults with Asperger syndrome or high-functioning autism. *Journal of Child Psychology and Psychiatry, 42*, 241–251.

Baron-Cohen, S., Wheelwright, S., & Jollifee, T. (1997). Is there a "language of the eyes"? Evidence from normal adults, and adults with autism or Asperger syndrome. *Visual Cognition, 4*, 311–331.

Barrett, L. F. (2006a). Are emotions natural kinds? *Perspectives on Psychological Science, 1*, 28–58.

Barrett, L. F. (2006b). Solving the emotion paradox: Categorization and the experience of emotion. *Personality and Social Psychology Review, 10*, 20–46.

Beatty, J., & Lucero-Wagoner, B. (2000). The pupillary system. In J. T. Cacioppo, G. Berntson, & L. G. Tassinary (Eds.), *Handbook of psychophysiology* (pp. 142–162). Cambridge, UK: Cambridge University Press.

Bocanegra, B. R., & Zeelenberg, R. (2009). Emotion improves and impairs early vision. *Psychological Science, 20*, 707–713.

Bradley, M. M., Codispoti, M., Cuthbert, B. N., & Lang, P. J. (2001). Emotion and motivation I: Defensive and appetitive reactions in picture processing. *Emotion, 1*, 276–298.

Brunton, C. E. (1938). Smooth muscle of the periorbita and the mechanism of exophthalmos. *British Journal of Ophthalmology, 22*, 257–268.

Caccioppo, J. T., & Berntson, G. G. (1994). Relationship between attitudes and evaluative space: a critical review, with emphasis on the separability of positive and negative substrates. *Psychological Bulletin, 115*, 401–423.

Calder, A. J., Beaver, J. D., Winston, J. S., Dolan, R. J., Jenkins, R., Eger, E., & Henson, R. N. A. (2007). Separate coding of different gaze directions in the superior temporal sulcus and inferior parietal lobule. *Current Biology, 17*, 20–25.

Chapman, H. A., & Anderson, A. K. (2012). Understanding disgust. *Annals of the New York Academy of Sciences: The Year in Cognitive Neuroscience, 1251*, 62–76.

Chapman, H. A., Kim, D. A., Susskind, J. M., & Anderson, A. K. (2009). In bad taste: Evidence for the oral origins of moral disgust. *Science, 323*, 1222–1226.

Cootes, T., Edwards, G., & Taylor, C. (2001). Active appearance models. *IEEE Transactions on Pattern Analysis and Machine Intelligence, 23*, 681–685.

Dailey, M. N., Cottrell, G. W., Padgett, C., & Adolphs, R. (2002). EMPATH: a neural network that categorizes facial expressions. *Journal of Cognitive Neuroscience, 14*, 1158–1173.

Darwin, C. (1872/1998). *The expression of the emotions in man and animals*. New York, NY: Oxford University Press.

de Jong, P. J., van Overveld, M., & Peters, M. L. (2011). Sympathetic and parasympathetic responses to a core disgust video clip as a function of disgust propensity and disgust sensitivity. *Biological Psychology, 88*, 174–179.

Du, S., Tao, Y., & Martinez, A. M. (2014). Compound facial expressions of emotion. *Proceedings of the National Academy of Sciences, USA, 111*, E1454-E1462.

Duke-Elder, S., & Abrams, D. (1970). Ophthalmic optics and refraction. In S. Duke-Elder (Ed.), *System of ophthalmology* (Vol. 5). London, UK: Henry Kimpton.

Ekman, P. (1999). Basic emotions. In T. Dalgleish & T. Power (Eds.), *The handbook of cognition and emotion* (pp. 45–60). Sussex, UK: John Wiley & Sons.

Ekman, P., Friesen, W. V., & Hager, J. C. (1978). *Facial action coding system*. Salt Lake City, UT: Research Nexus.

Ekman, P., Sorenson, E. R., & Friesen, W. V. (1969). Pan-cultural elements in facial displays of emotion. *Science, 164*, 86–88.

Elfenbein, H. A., & Ambady, N. (2003). When familiarity breeds accuracy: Cultural exposure and facial emotion recognition. *Journal of Personality and Social Psychology, 85*, 276–290.

Elfenbein, H. A., & Ambady, N. (2002). On the universality and cultural specificity of emotion recognition: A meta-analysis. *Psychological Bulletin, 128*, 203–235.

Etcoff, N. L., & Magee, J. J. (1992). Categorical perception of facial expressions. *Cognition, 44*, 227–240.

Fridlund, A. J. (1997). The new ethology of human facial expressions. In J. A. Russell & J. Fernandez-Dols (Eds.), *The psychology of facial expression* (pp. 103–129). Cambridge, UK: Cambridge University Press.

Harrison, N., Singer, T., Rotshtein, P., Dolan, R. J., & Critchley, H. D. (2006). Pupillary contagion: central mechanisms engaged in sadness processing. *Social Cognitive & Affective Neuroscience, 1*, 5–17.

Izard, C. E. (1994). Innate and universal facial expressions: Evidence from developmental and cross-cultural research. *Psychological Bulletin, 115*, 288–299.

Jack, R. E., Garrod, O. G. B., Yu, H., Caldara, R., & Schyns, P. (2012). Facial expressions of emotion are not culturally universal. *Proceedings of the National Academy of Sciences USA, 109*, 7241–7244.

Kobayashi, H., & Kohshima, S. (1997). Unique morphology of the human eye. *Nature, 387*, 767–768.

Krusemark, E., & Li, W. (2011). Do all threats work the same way? Divergent effects of fear and disgust on sensory perception and attention. *Journal of Neuroscience, 31*, 3429–3434.

Lee, D. H., Mirza, R., Flanagan, J. G., & Anderson, A. K. (2014). Optical origins of opposing facial expression actions. *Psychological Science, 25*, 745–752.

Lee, D. H., Susskind, J. M., & Anderson, A. K. (2013). Social transmission of the sensory benefits of fear eye-widening. *Psychological Science, 24*, 957–965.

Levenson, R. W. (1992). Autonomic nervous system differences among emotions. *Psychological Science, 3*, 23–27.

Li, W., Howard, J. D., Parrish, T. B., & Gottfried, J. A. (2008). Aversive learning enhances perceptual and cortical discrimination of indiscriminable odor cues. *Science, 319*, 1842–1845.

Livingstone, M. S., & Hubel, D. H. (1987). Psychophysical evidence for separate channels for the perception of form, color, movement, and depth. *Journal of Neuroscience, 7*, 3416–3468.

Marsh, A. A., Adams, R. B., Jr., & Kleck, R. E. (2005). Why do fear and anger look the way they do? Form and social function in facial expressions. *Personality and Social Psychology Bulletin, 31*, 73–86.

Marsh, A. A., Ambady, N., & Kleck, R. E. (2005). The effects of fear and anger facial expressions on approach- and avoidance-related behaviors. *Emotion, 5*, 118–124.

Marsh, A. A., Elfenbein, H. A., & Ambady, N. (2003). Nonverbal "accents": Cultural differences in facial expressions of emotion. *Current Directions in Psychological Science, 12*, 159–164.

Matsumoto, D., & Ekman, P. (1988). *Japanese and Caucasian facial expressions of emotion (JACFEE) [Slides]*. San Francisco, CA: San Francisco State University, Department of Psychology, Intercultural and Emotion Research Laboratory.

McKelvie, S. J. (1995). Emotional expression in upside-down faces: Evidence for configurational and componential processing. *British Journal of Social Psychology, 34*, 325–334.

Niedenthal, P. M. (2007). Embodying emotion. *Science, 316*, 1002–1005.

Öhman, A., & Mineka, S. (2001). Fears, phobias, and preparedness: toward an evolved module of fear and fear learning. *Psychological Review, 3*, 483–522.

Oosterhof, N. N., & Todorov, A. (2008). The functional basis of face evaluation. *Proceedings of the National Academy of Sciences, USA, 105*, 11087–11092.

Phelps, E. A., Ling, S., & Carrasco, M. (2006). Emotion facilitates perception and potentiates the perceptual benefits of attention. *Psychological Science, 17*, 292–299.

Plutchik, R. (1980). *Emotion: Theory, research, and experience: Vol. 1. Theories of emotion*. New York, NY: Academic Press.

Putman, P., Hermans, E., & van Honk, J. (2006). Anxiety meets fear in perception of dynamic expressive gaze. *Emotion, 6*, 94–102.

Rolls, E. T. (1990). A theory of emotion, and its application to understanding the neural basis of emotion. *Cognition & Emotion, 4*, 161–190.

Rozin, P., & Fallon, A. E. (1987). A perspective on disgust. *Psychological Review, 94*, 23–41.

Rozin, P., Haidt, J., & McCauley, C. (2000). Disgust. In M. Lewis & J. M. Haviland-Jones (Eds.), *Handbook of emotions* (pp. 637–653). New York, NY: Guilford.

Russell, J. A. (1980). A circumplex model of affect. *Journal of Personality and Social Psychology, 39*, 1161–1178.

Russell, J. A., & Barrett, L. F. (1999). Core affect, prototypical emotional episodes, and other things called emotion: Dissecting the elephant. *Journal of Personality and Social Psychology, 76*, 805–819.

Sato, W., Kochiyama, T., & Yoshikawa, S. (2011). The inversion effect for neutral and emotional facial expressions on amygdala activity. *Brain Research,1378*, 84–90.

Saxe, R., & Powell, L. J. (2006). It's the thought that counts: specific brain regions for one component of theory of mind. *Psychological Science, 17*, 692–699.

Scherer, K. R. (2009). Emotions are emergent processes: They require a dynamic computational architecture. *Philosophical Transactions of the Royal Society: B, 364*, 3459–3474.

Scherer, K. R., & Wallbott, H. G. (1994). Evidence for universality and cultural variation of differential emotion response patterning. *Journal of Personality and Social Psychology, 66*, 310–328.

Shariff, A., & Tracy, J. (2011). What are emotion expressions for? *Current Directions in Psychological Science, 20*, 395–399.

Sherman, G. D., Haidt, J., & Clore, G. L. (2012). The faintest speck of dirt: Disgust enhances the detection of impurity. *Psychological Science, 23*, 1506–1514.

Smith, M. L., Cottrell, G. W., Gosselin, F., & Schyns, P. G. (2005). Transmitting and decoding facial expressions. *Psychological Science, 16*, 184–189.

Strack, F., Martin, L., & Stepper, S. (1988). Inhibiting and facilitating conditions of the human smile: A nonobtrusive test of the facial feedback hypothesis. *Journal of Personality and Social Psychology, 54*, 768–777

Susskind, J. M., & Anderson, A. K. (2008). Facial expression form and function. *Communicative and Integrative Biology, 1*, 148–149.

Susskind, J. M., Lee, D. H., Cusi, A., Feiman, R., Grabski, W., & Anderson, A. K. (2008). Expressing fear enhances sensory acquisition. *Nature Neuroscience, 11*, 843–850.

Susskind, J. M., Littlewort, G., Bartlett, M. S., Movellan, J., & Anderson, A. K. (2007). Human and computer recognition of facial expressions of emotion. *Neuropsychologia, 45*, 152–162.

Tipples, J. (2006). Fear and fearfulness potentiate automatic orienting to eye gaze. *Cognition & Emotion, 20*, 309–320.

Todd, R. M., Talmi, D., Schmitz, T. W., Susskind, J. M., & Anderson, A. K. (2012). Psychophysical and neural evidence for emotion-enhanced perceptual vividness. *Journal of Neuroscience, 32*, 11201–11212.

Ungerleider, L. G., & Mishkin, M. (1982). Two cortical visual systems. In D. J. Ingle, M. A. Goodale, & R. J. Mansfield (Eds.), *Analysis of visual behavior* (pp. 549–586). Cambridge, MA: MIT Press.

Vuilleumier, P., Armony, J. L., Driver, J., & Dolan, R. J. (2001). Effects of attention and emotion on face processing in the human brain: An event-related fMRI study. *Neuron, 30*, 829–841.

Vuilleumier, P., Armony, J. L., Driver, J., & Dolan, R. J. (2003). Distinct spatial frequency sensitivities for processing faces and emotional expressions. *Nature Neuroscience, 6*, 624–631.

Watson, D., & Tellegen. A. (1985). Toward a consensual structure of mood. *Psychological Bulletin, 98*, 219–235.

West, G. L., Anderson, A. K., Bedwell, J. S., & Pratt, J. (2010). Red diffuse light suppresses the accelerated perception of fear. *Psychological Science, 21*, 992–999.

Whalen, P. J. (1998). Fear, vigilance, and ambiguity: Initial neuroimaging studies of the human amygdala. *Current Directions in Psychological Science, 7*, 177–188.

Whalen, P. J., Kagan, J., Cook. R. G., Davis, F. C., Kim, H., Polis, S., . . . Johnstone, T. (2004). Human amygdala responsivity to masked feaful eye whites. *Science, 306*, 2061.

Young, A. W., Rowland, D., Calder, A. J., Etcoff, N. L., Seth, A., & Perrett, D. I. (1997). Facial expression megamix: Tests of dimensional and category accounts of emotion recognition. *Cognition, 63*, 271–313.

PART IV

Unexplored Signals

11

Beyond the Smile

Nontraditional Facial, Emotional, and Social Behaviors

ROBERT R. PROVINE

Life is full of the important and unexpected if you know where to look and how to see. For decades, I have been seeking the scattered and often obscure behavioral pieces of a scientific puzzle with the expectation that, once assembled, they will provide a novel perspective of human nature (Provine, 1997, 2012). This ongoing project has provided false leads, entertaining diversions, and occasional serendipitous discoveries that suggest the value of the enterprise. Believing that scientific advances often come from the elemental, this *simple system* approach targets human instincts, including yawning, laughing, vocal crying, emotional tearing, coughing, nausea and vomiting, itching and scratching, belching, farting, and changes in scleral color. Most analyses are behavioral accounts of acts under low levels of voluntary control. Particular attention is paid to behaviors that are contagious, with the anticipation that they may reveal the roots of sociality and empathy. Another priority is uniquely human behaviors that may reveal the specific mechanisms and consequences of neurobehavioral evolution. Few of these curious behaviors are traditionally considered in the context of facial expression or emotion, but they deserve recognition for what they can contribute to behavioral neuroscience and social biology. A wide range of topics is presented, with the anticipation that the vigor of the approach is better realized with a broad than narrow focus, even if an occasional behavior seems out of place or a problem left unresolved.

A theme of this chapter is that many aspects of human behavior are better understood in terms of descriptions of overt behavior than guesses by individuals or researchers about the causes of their actions. This perspective is introduced via the technique of reaction times. Differences between the reaction times necessary to perform acts provide a means of defining levels of voluntary control and distinguishing between the neurological mechanisms producing behavior.

THE BEHAVIORAL KEYBOARD AND ERROR OF INTENTIONALITY

People generate a running, autobiographical narrative of events and decisions that is presumed to account for their actions, including facial behavior and emotional expression. However, this narrative is often fictive and the basis for what I term *philosopher's disease*, the erroneous tendency to rationalize irrational behavior, and the associated *error of intentionality*, the false presumption that we are conscious beings in full voluntary control of our actions (Provine, 2012). Symptoms of such misattribution of control are common and the basis of the distinction between voluntary ("false"/non-Duchenne) and involuntary ("felt"/Duchenne) smiles (Ekman & Friesen, 1982) and laughs (Gervais & Wilson, 2005). My concern with what people do and minimizing references to conscious, voluntary control, is a conservative, not a radical tact, because it makes the fewest assumptions about the causes of behavior. (This is the converse of the trend to assume that other animals possess what are presumed to be human-like consciousness and level of behavioral control. Although other animals may deserve more than their credited share, humans may deserve less.)

One means of escaping the semantic swamp of defining what is voluntary and what is involuntary is to finesse the problem by defining voluntary control in terms of relative reaction times, the rationale being that individuals are presumed to have the most voluntary control of behaviors that, upon verbal command, can be performed most quickly. Differences in reaction times also reflect differences in underlying neurological processing. The behavioral keyboard (Fig. 11.1) displays the relative reaction times and ease of voluntarily performing 10 common behaviors (Provine, 2012). Unlike an actual piano keyboard where all keys are easy to play, some keys on the behavioral keyboard—those toward the left—can hardly be played at all.

The average reaction times of the 103 participants range from the slow, hard-to-play vocal cry (9.8 seconds) on the far left, to the quick, easy-to-play eye-blink (0.5 seconds) on the far right. Some behaviors were so difficult to perform on command that only a few individuals attempted them during the

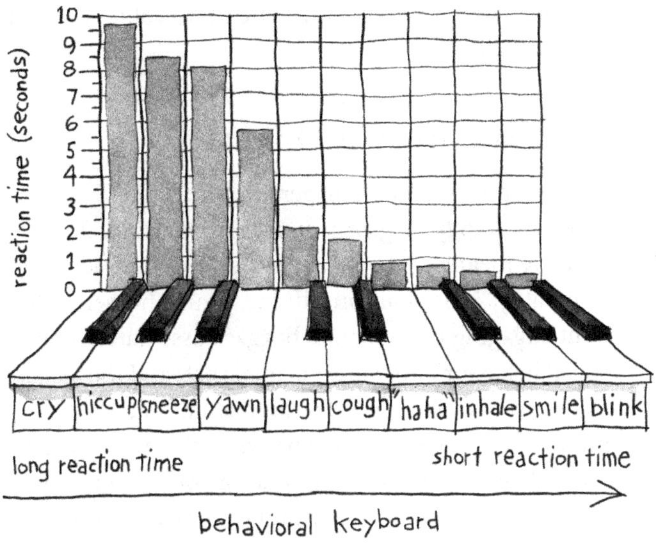

Figure 11.1 The behavioral keyboard summarizes the relative reaction times and associated levels of voluntary control of 10 common behaviors. Response latency is inversely related to voluntary control, ranging from the sluggish, hard-to-play vocal cry (left) to the quick, easy-to-play blink (right). (From Provine, 2012)

maximum 10-second interval, such as crying (3%), hiccups (18%), sneezes (22%), and yawns 58%). These low completion rates are probably inflated and the associated reaction times shortened by efforts of some participants to comply to the request by the experimenter. In contrast to these challenging acts, all participants were able to say "ha-ha," smile, blink, and inhale in less than 1 second. These reaction times differentiate between both neurological mechanism and social role. For example, both smiles and laughs are signals of positive affect, but based on reaction times, smiling (0.6 seconds) is under much more voluntary control than the vocal bludgeon of laughing (2.1 seconds). Furthermore, the much greater reaction time for laughing than saying "ha-ha" (2.1 seconds versus 0.9 seconds) indicates that laughing is not a matter of speaking "ha-ha." These and other data indicate that laughter is not a choice, but a behavior emitted in the proper social circumstance. The reaction times (and levels of voluntary control) of the eight airway maneuvers range from short to long: inhaling (0.8 seconds), saying "ha-ha" (0.9 seconds), coughing (1.7 seconds), laughing (2.1 seconds), yawning (5.7 seconds), sneezing (8.1 seconds), and vocal crying (9.8 seconds).

This demonstration justifies skepticism of efforts to micro-analyze ongoing behavior and consider the body to be a precise, finely tuned instrument played with great skill by its owner. We often presume more voluntary control of our behavior than is necessary or justified.

CONTAGIOUS BEHAVIOR: ROOTS OF SOCIALITY

Contagious behavior propagates from person to person, synchronizing the behavior and the physiology of group members (Provine, 2012). Contagion provides an objective means of studying problems associated with emotional and cognitive empathy, imitation, mindfulness, and higher order cognitive processes without engaging the semantic baggage associated with such terms. Contagion is social behavior of the most primal sort, and the austere, descriptive approach of its study facilitates developmental, pathological, and comparative analyses, and provides a bridge between the often estranged realms of social and neurological sciences. This analysis of contagion will focus on defining specific motor acts and the stimulus vectors responsible for their contagiousness.

Yawning

Yawning is famously contagious, but the nature of the process is full of surprises (Provine, 2005, 2012). We are all familiar with the motor act of yawning, a long inspiration followed by a shorter expiration, gaping of the mouth, squinting of eyes, and so on (Provine, 1986; Walusinski, 2010). Yawns are highly stereotyped in form, having durations between 3 1/2 to 6 seconds. Yawns have what ethologists term *typical intensity.* Once initiated, yawns go to completion; there are no partial yawns. The stereotypy of yawns is essential for the natural selection of a neurological process (feature detector) dedicated to their detection. There are at least superficial similarities between the facial components of yawns, sneezes (resembles a fast yawn), and orgasms, but only yawns are contagious. (Ads for nasal spray, allergy medicine, and facial tissue often provide entertaining images of pending, orgiastic-looking sneezes.) Some, but not all, folk wisdom about yawning is true; we do yawn when bored (Provine & Hamernik, 1986) and sleepy (Provine, Hamernik, & Curchack 1987), but not in response to high levels of carbon dioxide or a shortage of oxygen (Provine, Tate, & Geldmacher, 1987). We definitely yawn contagiously when we observe others yawning; 55% of observers of a series of video images of a yawning face yawned within 5 minutes, and almost everyone reported being at least tempted to yawn (Provine, 1986).

Unlike the stereotypy of the motor act, the stimulus triggers of contagious yawning are varied. For example, the obvious stimulus, the gaping mouth, is not involved (Provine, 1989). If the mouth of a video image of a yawning person is masked, the yawning face maintains its potency. The overall configuration of the yawning face, especially the squinting of the eyes, may serve as a stimulus vector. These results complement the discovery that the isolated image of the gaping mouth triggers no more yawns than a smile. A disembodied yawning mouth is an ambiguous stimulus; it could be engaged in stretching, singing, or yelling, as well as yawning. Remarkably, yawns are so contagious that anything related to a yawn will trigger a contagious response, even hearing a yawn, thinking about yawning, or reading about yawning, as you are now doing (Provine, 1986). In contagious yawning, we have a stereotyped motor pattern that is triggered by diverse, multimodal stimuli that are directly or indirectly related to the motor act of yawning.

Developmental milestones provide evidence about evolution. The phylogenetically ancient act of yawning, a behavior performed by most vertebrates, develops very early, toward the end of the first trimester of human prenatal development (de Vries, Visser, & Prechtl, 1982, 1985). In contrast, more recently evolved contagious yawning develops much later, between 4 and 5 years after birth (Anderson & Meno, 2003; Helt, Eigsti, Snyder, & Fein, 2010). Yawn contagion is diminished in autistic individuals (Giganti & Esposito Ziello, 2009; Senju et al., 2007), providing a nontraditional index of empathy and theory of mind that are presumed deficient in this population. Contagious yawning has been detected among baboons (Palagi, Leone, Mancini, & Ferrari, 2009) and chimpanzees (Anderson, Myowa-Yamakoshi, & Matsuzawa, 2004; Campbell & de Waal, 2011), with the effect being strongest among familiar chimpanzees. Contagious yawning has also been reported among dogs, pack animals that are highly attentive to their human companions (Joly-Mascherini, Senju, & Shepard, 2008). Yawning illustrates the power of analyses of contagion, providing an opportunity to trace development, compare species, and determine processes lost in pathology.

Laughing

Laughter is composed of short vocal bursts of around 1/15 second (ha) that recur at intervals of around 1/5 second (ha-ha) (Provine, 1996, 2016a; Provine & Yong, 1991). Although not invariant (Bachorowski & Owren, 2001), the motor program of laughter is stereotyped. Think of its range as variations on a theme. Without such underlying structure, we could not identify the utterance as laughter. There are also neuromuscular constraints on performing the motor act; it is difficult to laugh in other than the usual way, and if you can do so, it may sound odd (Bryant & Aktipis, 2014; Provine, 2012).

Laughter is an incredibly social vocalization—we laugh *30 times* more often in social than solitary situations (Provine & Fischer, 1989), with speakers laughing more than their audience, males being better laugh getters than females, and most laughter not following jokes or other formal attempts at humor (Provine, 1993; Scott, 2013). Contagion contributes to the sociality of laughter—the mere sound of laughter is sufficient to trigger laughter in those who hear it (Provine, 1992; Smoski & Bachorowski, 2003). Contagious laughter is present in conversation and is the basis for the "laugh tracks" of television situation comedies and the claques that have existed since the ancient Greek theatre (Provine, 2000). Laughter, like yawning, has the stereotypy necessary for the evolution of a feature detector that responds to and replicates the stimulus event. Unlike the broad range of multimodal stimuli of contagious yawning, the stimulus for contagious laughter is the sound of laughter itself; visually observing a laughing person or thinking or reading about laughter are not compelling triggers of contagious laughs.

Vocal Crying

Crying evolved to be a sound so annoying that it motivates us to stop it—now! It is a solicitation of caregiving; crying individuals really are needy. Crying is present at birth and its mere sound can increase breast temperature of lactating women (Vuorenkowski, Wasz-Hockert, Koivisto, & Lind, 1969) and trigger the milk letdown reflex (Mead & Newton, 1967). Crying ("waaa") is a voiced utterance that is sustained for about 1 second, the duration of an outward breath (Provine, 2012).

If hearing one cry is stressful, imagine a nursery full of bawling babies—vocal crying is contagious. Newborns cry or produce a stress reaction (vocal, facial, or physiological) when exposed to another crying infant (Provine, 2012; Simner, 1971). Newborns can discriminate between recordings of their own cries and those of other infants, showing more distress when hearing cries not their own (Martin & Clark, 1982). This pattern of contagious behavior extends into later childhood. Much more is known about crying in infancy than in later childhood and adulthood (Barr, Hopkins, & Green, 2000), a consequence of researchers specializing both in the vocalization and developmental stage. On several levels, vocal crying offers informative contrasts with laughter, another emotional utterance: Phylogenetically ancient crying is present at birth, whereas more recently evolved laughter does not appear until 3–4 months later (Sroufe & Waters, 1976; Sroufe & Wunch, 1972); crying is a relatively sustained utterance ("waaa"), whereas laughter is a parsed exhalation ("ha-ha"); and contagious crying is present at birth, whereas contagious laughter does not develop until a later, undetermined age.

Coughing

Cough is clinically important, joining headache as a leading medical complaint, and has interesting social dimensions, including contagiousness (Provine, 2012). A cough is a pneumatic blast that clears the throat and lungs of irritants and debris. The cough lasts about a half-second and involves an initial deep breath, followed by an exhalation driven by contraction of the abdominal muscles and diaphragm. Thoracic pressure rises because the exhaled air is dammed against the closed glottis. Sudden opening of the glottis produces an explosive release of the trapped, pressurized air. Coughs can be reflexive or produced voluntarily, in contrast to sneezes, a somewhat similar airway maneuver, but not under voluntary control. Coughs produce a massive surge in cerebrospinal fluid pressure that creates a hydraulic massage to the central nervous system that has significant but poorly understood neurobehavioral consequences (Provine, 2012; Walusinski, 2014). Strong coughs can produce a concussion and loss of consciousness (cough syncope) (Kerr & Eich, 1961).

James Pennebaker (1980) is a pioneer in the study of social coughing. He observed that college students in large classes cough more than those in small ones because there are more coughs to hear, and there is less social inhibition associated with the anonymity of a larger crowd. Coughs of different students tend to cluster, evidence of a social coupling process. Proximity is also a factor; the closer a student sits to a cougher, the more likely that she too will cough. A low-level of voluntary control seems to be involved because, when questioned, students have little awareness of coughing, whether their own or that of others. Coughing mindlessly triggers coughing in those who hear it, perhaps during sleep.

It is unclear if coughs are contagious in the manner of laughing and yawning; they may be a consequence of self-monitoring, with perceived coughs focusing the audience's attention on tickling in their own throats that must be relieved by coughing (Provine, 2012). Anecdotal observations indicate that we don't immediately cough in response to coughs of others, in the manner of contagious laughs, nor do we feel the building, inevitable urge to cough, in the manner of a contagious yawn.

Itching and Scratching

Itching is the sensation that causes the stereotyped act of scratching (Provine, 2012). The rapid, rhythmic, stereotyped scratching by dogs and other animals is ideal for rigorous quantitative descriptions of behavior and, in the hands of Sherrington, played a significant role in discovering the neurophysiological basis of movement production and control.

Itch and associated scratching are highly infectious, and the stimulus vector for their contagion is broadly tuned and multimodal. Although eczema, contact dermatitis, and other skin irritation can trigger itch, so can such abstract stimuli as hearing a lecture about itch, viewing itch causing parasites, or seeing someone else scratching, especially among individuals with preexisting dermatological conditions (Holle, Warne, Seth, Critchley, & Ward, 2012). The multimodal stimulus triggers for contagiousness are reminiscent of those for yawning, but such parallels do not extend to the motor act. All cases of contagious yawning, whatever the stimulus, yield nearly identical yawns. In contrast, contagious scratching is much more variable. Ward, Burckhardt, and Holle (2013) investigated how the behavior of a model influences the specific site of itchiness and scratching of an observer. When participants in their study viewed a movie depicting scratching, they were more likely to scratch themselves, but the hand that they used to scratch (left or right) and the site of scratching did not necessarily match the model. Although the model scratched only the arms and chest, the majority of participants viewing the video directed their scratching upward toward their face and hair. Thus, contagious itchiness may be more driven by vicarious perception of the feeling state (itchiness/unpleasantness) than contagion of the motor act or bodily target. A similar mechanism (self-monitoring) is suggested here for the stimulus of contagious coughing and nausea/vomiting.

Nausea and Vomiting

Vomiting (the reflexive, forceful ejection of stomach contents through the mouth) and nausea (the sensation that one is about to vomit) are of more interest to medical researchers and clinicians than behavioral scientists, but everyone, regardless of profession, understands the potency of these behaviors, including their appearance, sounds, and smells (Provine, 2012). Our universe shrinks when kneeling before a toilet waiting to vomit. Vomiting begins with a violent inspiration against a closed glottis (the retch), which increases abdominal pressure, which, upon relaxation of the esophageal sphincter, explosively discharges stomach contents. (Vomiting does not involve contraction of the stomach or reverse peristalsis of the esophagus.) The building and sudden release of pressure is also a characteristic mechanism of coughing and sneezing.

Nausea and vomiting are contagious, although literature about it is typically listed as hysteria, not contagion. When one person vomits or reports nausea, the sensation and behavior spread to others, especially female teens and below (Provine, 2012). School janitors quickly clean up vomitus in classrooms and hallways in an effort to stem a deluge. The next time you read about mass illness, you will probably learn that some exciting or anxiety-producing event is involved, perhaps a school trip, sporting event, or music competition, large groups were involved, most victims were female, and that the sickness was preceded by headaches, dizziness, and "strange smells," perhaps sewer gas, or exhaust fumes from waiting busses. Follow-up reports typically discover no obvious cause but are reluctant to label the sickness as psychogenic. (Psychogenic symptoms are compelling to those experiencing them.)

It makes evolutionary sense that we have a hair trigger for vomiting, a behavior critical to survival. Sickness, whatever its cause, triggers the cautionary defense of vomiting. When potentially tainted food is swallowed after passing the sniff and taste tests, it is better to be safe than sorry, and puke. The stimulus vectors for contagious nausea and vomiting are varied, acquired, and fine-tuned through learning. The sight and sound of a vomiting person are unsettling, and the smell of vomit can be disgusting, but there seems to be no innate, nonirritating gustatory or olfactory stimuli for nausea/vomiting (Rozin, Haidt, & McCauley, 2000). Many of us even enjoy eating soft, aged cheeses that smell like vomit. Other societies have their own nauseating culinary concoctions. Feces are one of the most reviled substances, but we may learn to avoid them. Young children do not reject feces and associated odors of decay until between 3 and 7 years of age, after the age of toilet training that starts around age 2. Food aversions can also be learned and are long lasting—we may avoid foods that made us sick for years.

Contagious nausea and vomiting are powerful defense mechanisms (Provine, 2012). The first person affected may experience actual physiological illness and, by default, becomes a group's communal taster. Others may experience a sympathetic response, especially in the presence of facilitating factors of stress, fatigue, or not feeling quite right, as our brain scrambles to find a cause. We are reluctant beneficiaries of this quirk in our sociobiological programming.

MIRROR NEURONS AND BEHAVIORAL CONTAGION

Contagious behavior may prompt questions about the involvement of *mirror neurons*, neurons implicated in a variety of behavioral, cognitive, and social processes, from imitation and theory of mind, to empathy. (Mirror neurons are brain neurons that respond both when an individual performs a motor act and when witnessing that act being performed by someone else.) This well-deserved attention should be tempered by the appreciation that, thus far, the most obvious output of mirror neurons has been essay writing by enthusiasts. At present, mirror neurons seem lost in thought, like disembodied computers not hooked up to printers, full of potential, but short on demonstrated function. Although the lay public immediately grasps the similarity between contagion and mirror processes, the association has been neglected by many mirror neuron pioneers (Iacobini, 2009; Rizzolatti & Fabbri-Destro, 2010).

Noninvasive imaging (functional magnetic resonance imaging, or fMRI) has detected mirror neuron activity in several regions of the human brain (premotor cortex, supplementary motor area, primary somatosensory cortex, and inferior parietal cortex) (Iacobini, 2009; Rizzolatti & Fabbri-Destro, 2010). Preliminary fMRI data indicate that the brain areas that respond uniquely to observed yawns, the most researched contagious behavior, are the same association areas linked to mirror activity and directly or indirectly to theory of mind and self-processing (Arnott, Singal, & Goodale, 2009; Nahab, Hattori, Saad, & Hallett, 2009; Platek, Mohammad, & Gallup, 2005; Schurmann et al., 2005).

I have a long-term interest in mirror processes because, in many respects, they were motives for the start of my contagious behavior research in the mid-1980s. However, the study of contagious behavior has two significant advantages over mirror neurons. Most notable is that contagious behavior has known, easily measured stimulus triggers and motor outputs that can be studied more rigorously than the higher order phenomena examined by most cognitive neuroscientists. A less obvious but practical consideration is that contagion is cheap and easy to study, requiring no pricey neurophysiology lab or fMRI machine.

HUMAN UNIQUENESS: INSIGHTS INTO EVOLUTIONARY CHANGE

Targeting behaviors that are unique to humans is not a celebration of the specialness of our species, but a tactic for detecting the specific changes responsible for neurobehavioral evolution (Provine, 2012). This *critical change* approach (Provine, 2016b) moves beyond the typical focus of evolutionary psychologists on the selection for or against abstract, disembodied traits and attends to specific changes at the organismic level. The contrast between a unique characteristic and its ancestral form reveals the nature of the transformation. Three examples of this approach are considered: laughter/speech, emotional tearing, and scleral cues.

Laughter and Speech

Contrary to Aristotle's report that laughter is uniquely human, play vocalizations resembling laughter have been identified in other great apes (Davila-Ross,

Owren, & Zimmermann, 2009; Provine, 2000) and mammalian species (Panksepp, 2007). Laughter is mammalian onomatopoeia, the ritualized sound of the labored breathing of rough-and-tumble play. Laughter is "ritualized" in that it represents the context in which the sound is made (rough-and-tumble) and signals "this is play, I'm not attacking you" (Provine, 2000). The link of laughter to breathing is obvious in chimpanzees whose laughter sounds like a dog panting, with one noisy vocalization made per inward and outward breathe—"pant-pant." Although Darwin, Fossey, Goodall, and others referred to such ape vocalization as laughing or chuckling, naïve human observers lacking context cues (e.g., tickling an animal) do not identify it as laughing, saying it sounds like a dog panting, people having sex, or even nonbiological sawing or sanding (Provine, 2000). This vocal pattern contrasts with the voiced (having a tonal property) human "ha-ha," which, like speech, is produced by parsing an exhalation. The bottom line is that humans and other apes and mammals produce homologous play vocalizations, but the sound and means of production are unique. The most significant result of this analysis is the discovery of the neurobehavioral changes responsible for the evolution of human-type laughter and, surprisingly, speech (Provine, 2000, 2004, 2016b).

The emergence of human ha-ha laughter from the ancestral pant-pant is the result of increased breath control conferred by the uncoupling of respiration and locomotion, a consequence of bipedal locomotion. During running, nonhuman primates and other quadrupeds have a one-to-one (1:1) link between stride and breathing, such that the lungs are filled during forelimb impacts (Bramble & Currier, 1983). Without full lungs, the thorax is a floppy, air-filled bag that does not provide adequate support. With the emergence of bipedal locomotion in humans, the rigid link between stride and breath is weakened, with humans being capable of a variety of ratios (4:1, 3:1, 5:2, 2:1, 3:2, or 1:1), with 2:1 being most common. This uncoupling of running and breathing made possible the natural selection both for the unique sound of human laughter and human speech, the basis for the *bipedal theory* of speech evolution (Provine, 2000, 2012, 2016b). Human speech did not evolve from laughter, but both speech and human-type laughter (ha-ha) are results of the improved breath control conferred by bipedality.

It is understandable why quadrupeds did not evolve similar vocal capacity—the selection for getting the hell out of here is more adaptive than making complex sounds. Other mammals with vocal virtuosity such as whales and harbor seals have solved the thoracic support problem through flotation in an aqueous medium, not bipedality. Some birds are bipedal vocal virtuosos but are a special case because of their unique vocal apparatus.

Emotional Tearing

Emotional tearing (Vingerhoets, 2013; Vingerhoets & Cornelius, 2001) is a potent, uniquely human visual cue that amplifies and may determine the character of facial expression, the *tear effect* (Provine, Krosnowski, & Brocato, 2009). Many animals secrete nonemotional tears that prevent ocular drying, provide ocular lubrication, antibiotic lysozyme, and Nerve Growth Factor (NGF) which heals and might offer antidepressant properties (Provine, 2011, 2012), but only humans secrete tears in response to emotional stimuli (Frey, 1985). The emotional impact of tears as a visual signal was tested by contrasting the perceived sadness of human facial images with tears against copies of those images that had the tears digitally removed. (The effect of tear removal can be approximated by using your finger to block-out tears in a photograph.) Tear removal produced faces rated as less sad, the experimental confirmation of folk wisdom relating tears to perceived sadness. More surprising was the finding that tear removal often produced faces of ambiguous emotional valence, perhaps awe, concern, contemplation, or puzzlement, not simply of less sadness. In other words, faces with tears removed may not appear sad. Tears resolve ambiguity, amplify emotional intensity, and determine the emotional character of the face. Tears may also provide a chemical signal that can act in darkness and does not require line of sight (Gelstein et al., 2011). Given the power of tears, it would be desirable to replicate much of the literature about facial expression of emotions adding tears as a variable, a daunting prospect. A similar argument can be made for scleral color, which is considered later.

The position of tears on the face, not simply their presence or absence, is necessary for the tear effect (Provine, 2012). Whether using a cartoon (Fig. 11.2) or a real face with cosmetic tears, tears located above instead of below the eye do not look like tears and lose their emotional impact. The relative effect of tears on the forehead versus the cheek on inverted faces has not been examined.

Emotional tearing may have originated with the nonemotional tears produced by disease or trauma to the eyes that elicited caregiving and inhibited aggression. This primal cue may have evolved through ritualization to become a sign of emotional as well as physical distress (Murube, Murube, & Murube, 1999; Provine, 2012). Phylogenetically ancient basal tears that moisten and lubricate the eye are present at birth, in contrast to recently evolved, uniquely human tears of emotion that do not develop until 3–4 months after birth (Darwin, 1872; Provine, 2012). The fact that crying newborns lack the important signaling channel of emotional tearing has been neglected by legions of investigators of child development. Emotional tearing provides an exciting opportunity to observe an evolutionary process still underway, when the intermediate steps are still visible, and tuning is a bit sloppy, an explanation why there is tearing during such diverse acts as vocal crying, laughing, yawning,

Figure 11.2 Tears make a face appear sad, the tear effect (top). When tears are removed, the resulting tearless face appears both less sad and emotionally ambivalent (center). The mere presence of tears does not have an emotional impact, as when they appear on the forehead above instead of below the eye (bottom). (From Provine, 2012)

coughing, sneezing and vomiting. If we check back in 100,000 years, the physiological profile of our emotional tearing may be tidied up, and the footprints of the evolutionary process will be lost.

Scleral Color

The sclera, the eye's tough white outer layer, provides the ground necessary for the display of its own color and that of the overlying transparent conjunctiva that vary in health, disease, and emotion (Provine, 2012). Scleral color cues, primarily the red of conjunctival blood vessel dilation and the yellow of aging (lipids) and jaundice (bilirubin), are unique to humans, being invisible in non-human primates because of their dark sclera (Kobayashi & Kohshima, 2001). The evolution of white sclera and the associated color cues contribute to the emergence of humans as a social species.

Research with digitally colored eye images suggests that the white sclera and transparent conjunctiva of humans are adaptations for the display of socially significant scleral coloration (Provine, 2012; Provine, Cabrera, Brocato, & Krosnowski, 2011). For example, individuals with digitally reddened or yellowed sclera are rated as less healthy, less attractive, and older than those with untinted, control sclera (Provine, Cabrera, & Nave-Blodgett, 2013a). The perceptual impact is greater for images with two than one red eye (only red was examined), indicating that the effect of scleral color was incremental, not all-or-none (Provine, Cabrera, & Nave-Blodgett, 2013b). White sclera joins such traits as smooth skin and long, lustrous hair as signs of health, beauty, and reproductive fitness. Given these results, eye drops that "get the red out" are beauty aids.

In the emotional domain, images of individuals with reddened sclera are rated as having more sadness, anger, fear, and disgust, and less happiness than those with normal, untinted sclera. Surprise was the only one of six basic emotions unaffected by scleral redness (Provine, Nave-Blodgett, & Cabrera, 2013). Images with two red eyes are perceived as sadder (only sadness was examined) than those with only one red eye (Provine, Cabrera, & Nave-Blodgett, 2013b).

The impact of white sclera on eye-related visual cues is demonstrated by digital manipulation of a human eye image (Fig. 11.3). Normal eyes are shown with three variants: dark, primate-like sclera that would be deficient in

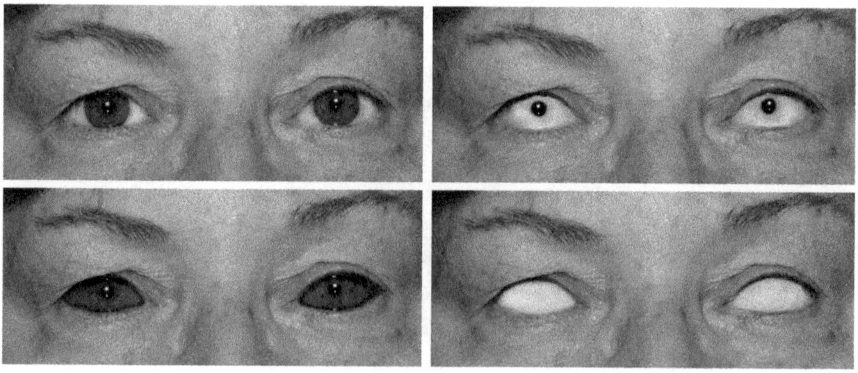

Figure 11.3 Digitally edited eye images demonstrate the visual impact of the white human sclera. Contrast normal eyes (upper left) with those having dark, ape-like sclera (lower left), sclera extending to the pupil (upper right), and sclera completely covering the iris and pupil. (From Provine, 2012)

signaling gaze direction and redness; the white sclera extended to the edge of the pupils; and completely whited-out sclera that obscures the iris and pupil. Some people find these variants startling and disturbing, strong evidence that they tap a socially significant stimulus dimension.

The analysis of scleral color will be rewarding at many levels. The conjunctiva provides a unique and easy means of directly and noninvasively visualizing the impact of emotion and physiological state on individual blood vessels in real time. Best of all, no special equipment is required to pursue this research—a still or video camera with a macro lens is sufficient. Few research problems offer such an attractive combination of low threshold for entry and potential for discovery.

SOCIAL AND LINGUISTIC INHIBITION: THE NEW SUPPRESSES THE OLD

When the ancient and the new, the unconscious and the conscious, compete for the brain's channel of expression, the more modern, conscious mechanism often prevails, suppressing its older unconscious rival (Provine, 2012). This effect is striking in the case of yawning and hiccupping, where anecdotal evidence indicates that vigorous ongoing bouts of these behaviors can be inhibited by the knowledge that they are being observed or recorded, instances of the inhibition of phylogenetically ancient behaviors by more recently evolved, consciously controlled ones (Provine, 2012)

The *punctuation effect*, the tendency of a speaker's laughter to appear at phrase breaks, the places in conversation where you would put punctuation in a transcript, indicates that speech is dominant over more ancient laughter (Provine, 1993). Thus, a speaker may say, "Where have you been?—ha-ha," but rarely, "Where have—ha-ha—you been?" Phrase structure is respected by both speaker and audience in a conversational dyad. The dominance of speech over laughter is not absolute because speakers do not completely cease laughing and they sometimes produce the hybrid vocalization of laughing speech. (My studies of punctuation exclusively examined the placement of classical ha-ha laughs.)

The punctuation phenomenon has significant neurological implications. Because laughter does not disrupt phrase structure, speech is dominant over laughter and has priority access to the common vocal apparatus. Vocal laughter also punctuates the American Sign Language (ASL) of deaf individuals, a form of manual linguistic expression that, unlike speech, does not compete with laughter for the vocal tract (Provine & Emmorey, 2006). Neither do emoticons (visual symbols of emotion such as LOL, "Laughing Out Loud," etc.) disrupt phrases in online text messages, a nonvocal linguistic medium (Provine, Spencer, & Mandell, 2007). Thus, laughter is regulated by a higher level linguistic process, not a lower level process governing access to the vocal tract by competing motor acts.

Punctuation effects are not unique to laughter in speech, signing, and texting. Other airway maneuvers show punctuation effects and the priority of linguistic expression. Speech involves breath-holding and redirecting the respiratory apparatus to vocalizing. People either speak or breathe during conversation, with breaths coming at linguistically significant punctuation points similar to those described for laughter (McFarland, 2001). Remarkably, the breathing and speaking of both speaker *and* audience are synchronized. This complex respiratory, vocal, and linguistic choreography occurs automatically; we do not consciously plan when to breathe, talk, or laugh.

CONCLUSIONS

Readers have probably concluded that this chapter will not end with an intellectual flourish and grand unified theory that ties everything together, and I will not disappoint. Instead, it has the more modest goal of expanding the range of inquiry, leaving it to readers to sort through the odds and ends and find what is useful. More questions are introduced than answered and a lot of empirical and theoretical heavy lifting remains. Is a yawn the facial expression of the emotion of boredom or sleepiness? Are boredom and sleepiness even emotions? If not, why not? Does itchiness qualify as an emotion associated with the nonfacial behavior of scratching? Is vomiting an expression of the emotion of nausea, an extreme case of disgust? Change of scleral color (redness) is a cue for several emotions, but it involves no movement, only cardiovascular dynamics of the conjunctiva. Although the secretory act of emotional tearing is associated with sadness and vocal crying, tears are also shed during laughing, yawning, coughing, and sneezing. A case can be made for the emotionality of laughing and yawning, but probably not for coughing and sneezing, however teary. Belching, farting, and hiccupping, other behaviors that I have studied (Provine, 2012), are blissfully unemotional and tear-free.

REFERENCES

Anderson, J. R., & Meno, P. (2003). Psychological influences on yawning in children. *Current Psychological Letters, 11*. http://cpl.revues.org/index390.html.

Anderson, J. R., Myowa-Yamakoshi, M., & Matsuzawa, T. (2004). Contagious yawning in chimpanzees. *Proceedings of the Royal Society B, 271*, S468–S470.

Arnott, S. R., Singhal, A., & Goodale, A. (2009). An investigation of auditory contagious yawning. *Cognitive, Affective, and Behavioral Neuroscience, 9*, 335–342.

Bachorowski, J.-A., & Owren, M. J. (2001). Not al laughs are alike: Voiced but not unvoiced laughter readily elicits positive affect. *Psychological Science, 12*, 252–257.

Barr, R. G., Hopkins, B., & Green, J. A. (Eds.) (2000). *Crying as a sign, a symptom, and a signal: Clinical, emotional and developmental aspects of infant and toddler crying.* London, England: MacKeith Press.

Bramble, D. M., & D. R. Currier (1983). Running and breathing in mammals. *Science, 219,* 251–256.

Bryant, G. A, & Aktipis, C. A. (2014). The animal nature of spontaneous human laughter. *Evolution and Human Behavior, 35,* 327–335.

Campbell, M. W., & de Waal, F. B. M. (2011). Ingroup-outgroup bias in contagious yawning by chimpanzees supports link to empathy. *PLoS One, 6,* e18283.

Davila-Ross, M., Owren, M. J., & Zimmermann, E. (2009). Reconstructing the evolution of laughter in great apes and humans. *Current Biology, 19,* 1106–1111.

de Vries, J. I. P., Visser, G. H., & Prechtl, H. F. (1982). The emergence of fetal behaviour. I. Qualitative aspects. *Early Human Development, 7,* 301–322.

de Vries, J. I. P., Visser, G. H., & Prechtl, H. F. (1985). The emergence of fetal behaviour. II. Quantitative aspects. *Early Human Development, 12,* 99–120.

Ekman, P., & Friesen, W. V. (1982). False, felt, and miserable smiles. *Journal of Nonverbal Behavior, 6,* 238–252.

Frey, W. H. (1985). *Crying: The mystery of tears.* Minneapolis, MN: Winston Press.

Gelstein, S., Yeshurum, Y., Rosenkrantz, L., Shushan, S., Frumin, I., Roth, Y., & Sobel, N. (2011). Human tears contain a chemosignal. *Science, 331,* 226–230.

Gervais, M., & Wilson, D. S. (2005). The evolution and function of laughter and humor: A synthetic approach. *Quarterly Review of Biology, 80,* 395–430.

Giganti, F., & Esposito Ziello, M. (2009). Contagious and spontaneous yawning in autistic and typically developing children. *Current Psychology Letters, 25,* 1-11.

Helt, M. S., Eigsti, I.-M., Snyder, P. J., & Fein, D. A. (2010). Contagious yawning in autistic and typical development. *Child Development, 81,* 1620–1631.

Holle, H., Warne, K., Seth, A. K., Critchley, H. D., & Ward, J. (2012). Neural basis of contagious itch and why some people are more prone to it. *Proceedings of the National Academy of Sciences (USA), 109,* 19816–19821.

Iacobini, M. (2009). Imitation, empathy, and mirror neurons. *Annual Review of Psychology, 60,* 653–670.

Joly-Mascheroni, R. M., Senju, A., & Shepherd, A. J. (2008). Dogs catch human yawns. *Biology Letters, 4,* 446–448.

Kerr, A., & Eich, R. H. (1961). Cerebral concussion as a cause of cough syncope. *Archives of Internal Medicine, 108,* 248–252.

Kobayashi, H., & Kohshima, S. (2001). Unique morphology of the human eye and its adaptive meaning: Comparative studies on external morphology of the primate eye. *Journal of Human Evolution, 40,* 419–435.

Martin, G., & Clark, R. (1982). Distress crying in neonates: Species and peer specificity. *Developmental Psychology, 18,* 3-9.

McFarland, D. H. (2001). Respiratory markers of conversational interaction. *Journal of Speech, Language, and Hearing, 44,* 128–143.

Mead, M., & Newton, N. (1967). Cultural patterning in perinatal behavior. In S. A. Richardson, & A. F. Guttmacher (Eds.), *Childbearing: Its social and psychological aspects.* (pp. 142–244). Baltimore, MD: Williams & Wilkins.

Murube, J., Murube, L., & Murube, A. (1999). Origin and types of emotional tearing. *European Jpurnal of Ophthalmology, 9*, 77–84.

Nahab, F. B., Hattori, N., Saad, Z. S., & Hallett, M. (2009). Contagious yawning and the frontal lobe: An fMRI study. *Human Brain Mapping, 30*, 1744–1751.

Palagi, E., Leone, A., Mancini, G., & Ferrari, P. F. (2009). Contagious yawning in gelada baboons as a possible expression of empathy. *Proceedings of the National Academy of Sciences, 106*, 19262–19267.

Panksepp, J. (2007). Neuroevolutionary sources of laughter and social joy: Modeling primal human laughter in laboratory rats. *Behavioral Brain Research, 182*, 231–244.

Pennebaker, J. W. (1980). Perceptual and environmental determinants of coughing. *Basic and Applied Social Psychology, 1*, 83–91.

Platek, S. M., Mohamed, F. B., & Gallup, G. G. (2005). Contagious yawning and the brain. *Brain Research. Cognitive Brain Research, 23*, 448–452.

Provine, R. R. (1986). Yawning as a stereotyped action pattern and releasing stimulus. *Ethology, 72*, 109–122.

Provine, R. R. (1989). Faces as releasers of contagious yawning: An approach to face detection using normal human subjects. *Bulletin of the Psychonomic Society, 27*, 211–214.

Provine, R. R. (1992). Contagious laughter: Laughter is a sufficient stimulus for laughs and smiles. *Bulletin of the Psychonomic Society, 30*, 1–4.

Provine, R. R. (1993). Laughter punctuates speech: Linguistic, social and gender contexts of laughter. *Ethology, 95*, 291–298.

Provine, R. R. (1996). Laughter. *American Scientist, 84*, 38–45.

Provine, R. R. (1997). Yawns, laughs, smiles, tickles, and talking: Naturalistic and laboratory studies of facial action and communication. In J. A. Russell & J. M. Fernandex-Dols (Eds.), *New directions in the study of facial expression* (pp. 158–175). Cambridge, England: Cambridge University Press.

Provine, R. R. (2000). *Laughter: A scientific investigation*. New York, NY: Viking.

Provine, R. R. (2004). Laughing, tickling, and the evolution of speech and self. *Current Directions in Psychological Science, 13*, 25–218.

Provine, R. R. (2005). Yawning. *American Scientist, 93*, 532–539.

Provine, R. R. (2011). Emotional tears and NGF: A biographical appreciation and research beginning. *Archives Italiennes de Biologie, 149*, 271–276.

Provine, R. R. (2012). *Curious behavior: Yawning, laughing, hiccupping, and beyond.* Cambridge, MA: Belknap/Harvard University Press.

Provine, R. R. (2016a). Laughter as a scientific problem: An adventure in sidewalk neuroscience. *Journal of Comparative Neurology, 524*, 1532-1539.

Provine, R. R. (2016b). Laughter as an approach to vocal evolution: The bipedal theory. *Psychonomic Bulletin and Review*. DOI 10.3758/s13423-016-1089-3.

Provine, R. R., Cabrera, M. O., & Nave-Blodgett, J. (2013a). Red, yellow, and super-white sclera: Uniquely human cues for healthiness, attractiveness, and age. *Human Nature, 24*, 126–136.

Provine, R. R., Cabrera, M. O., & Nave-Blodgett, J. (2013b). Binocular symmetry/asymmetry of scleral redness as a cue for sadness, healthiness, attractiveness and age. *Evolutionary Psychology, 11*, 873–884.

Provine, R. R., & Emmorey, K. (2006). Laughter among deaf signers. *Journal of Deaf Studies and Deaf Education, 11,* 403–409.

Provine, R. R., & Fischer, K. R. (1989). Laughing, smiling and talking: Relation to sleeping and social context in humans. *Ethology, 83,* 295–305.

Provine, R. R., & Hamernik, H. B. (1986). Yawning: Effects of stimulus interest. *Bulletin of the Psychonomic Society, 24,* 437–438.

Provine, R. R., Hamernik, H. B., & Curchack, B. C. (1987). Yawning: Relation to sleeping and stretching in humans. *Ethology, 76,* 152–160.

Provine, R. R., Krosnowski, K. A, & Brocato, N. W. (2009). Tearing: Breakthrough in human emotional signaling. *Evolutionary Psychology, 7,* 52-56.

Provine, R. R., Nave-Blodgett, J, & Cabrera, M. O. (2013). The emotional eye: Red sclera as a uniquely human cue of emotion. *Ethology, 119,* 993–998.

Provine, R. R., Tate, B. C., & Geldmacher, L. L. (1987). Yawning: No effect of 3-5% CO2, 100% O2, an exercise. *Behavioral and Neural Biology, 48,* 382–393.

Provine, R. R., & Yong, Y. L. (1991). Laughter: A stereotyped human vocalization. *Ethology, 89,* 115–124.

Rizzolatti, G., & Fabbri-Destro, M. (2010). Mirror neurons: From discovery to autism. *Experimental Brain Research, 200,* 223–237.

Rozin, P., Haidt, J., & McCauley, C. R. (2000). Disgust. In M. Lewis & M. J. Haviland, (Eds.), *Handbook of emotions* (2nd ed., pp. 637–653). New York, NY: Guilford.

Schurmann, M., Hesse, M. D., Stephan, K. E., Saarela, M., Zilles, K., Hari, R., & Fink, G. R. (2005). Yearning to yawn: The neural basis of contagious yawning. *Neuroimage, 24,* 1260–1264.

Senju, A., Maeda, M., Kikuchi, Y., Hasegawa, T., Tojo, Y., & Osanai, H. (2007). Absence of contagious yawning in children with autism spectrum disorder. *Biology Letters, 3,* 706–708.

Simner, M. L. (1971). Newborn's response to the cry of another infant. *Developmental Psychology, 5,* 136–150.

Smoski, M. J., & Bachorowski, J.-A. (2003). Antiphonal laughter between friends and strangers. *Cognition and Emotion, 17,* 327–340.

Sroufe, L. A., & Waters, E. (1976). The ontogenesis of smiling and laughter: A perspective on the organization of development in infancy. *Psychological Review, 83,* 173-189.

Sroufe, L. A., & Wunsch, J. P. (1972). The development of laughter in the first year of life. *Child Development, 43,* 1326-1344.

Vingerhoets, A. (2013). *Why only humans weep.* Oxford, England: Oxford University Press.

Vingerhoets, A. J. J. M., & Cornelius, R. R. (Eds.). (2001). *Adult crying: A biopsychosocial approach.* Philadelphia, PA: Brunner-Routledge.

Vuorenkowski, V., Wasz-Hockert, O., Koivisto, E., & Lind, J. (1969). The effect of cry stimulus on the lactating breast of primipara: A thermographic study. *Experienta, 25,* 1286–1287.

Walusinski, O. ed. (2010). *The mystery of yawning in physiology and disease.* Basel, Switzerland: Kaeger.

Walusinski, O. (2014). How yawning switches the default-mode network to the attentional network by activating the cerebrospinal flow. *Clinical Anatomy, 27*, 201–209.

Ward, J., Burckhardt, V., & Holle, H. (2013). Contagious scratching: Shared feelings but not shared body locations. *Frontiers in Human Neuroscience, 7*(122), 1–2.

12

The Communicative and Social Functions of Human Crying

ASMIR GRAČANIN, LAUREN M. BYLSMA, AND AD J. J. M. VINGERHOETS

Although emotional crying has received significant attention in the general literature and popular media (Cornelius, 1986; Vingerhoets, 2013), only recently has it been approached in a more thorough and systematic manner (e.g., Hasson, 2009; Trimble, 2012; Vingerhoets & Bylsma, 2016). Most scholars will agree that crying can be defined descriptively as a complex secretomotor phenomenon characterized by the shedding of tears from the lacrimal apparatus. It occurs without any irritation of the ocular structures, and it is often accompanied by alterations in the muscles of facial expressions, vocalizations, and (in some cases) sobbing, which is the convulsive inhaling and exhaling of air with spasms of the respiratory and truncal muscle groups (Patel, 1993). This might be an adequate description of the *phenomenology* of crying behavior, but it fails to refer to its *functions*, and as such, it fails to capture fully its complexity. In this chapter, we address this gap by focusing on the functions of crying and, in particular, on the communicative messages that are conveyed by shedding emotional tears.

Phylogenetically, human emotional crying originates from distress or separation calls, which are displayed by other animals as well, particularly birds and mammals, when separated from their parents. However, while in other animals these behaviors limit themselves to vocal expressions during their infancy, only humans shed emotional tears, which continues throughout their entire life span. Emotional crying is a universal reaction that exists in all human cultures. Across the world, adult women on average cry between 2–5 times a month, and men about once every 2 months (Vingerhoets, 2013), although there is a considerable interindividual and intercultural variation in crying frequency (Rottenberg, Bylsma, Wolvin, & Vingerhoets, 2008; Van Hemert, Van de Vijver, & Vingerhoets, 2011).

A long-awaited answer to the question of why emotional tears are unique to humans certainly will include functional explanations, particularly those pertaining to its role in communication and interpersonal interactions. We start with the description of the proposed general functions of crying, which is followed by a brief overview of the ontogenetic development of the various components of crying, as well as evolutionary accounts that might explain its emergence. This is followed by a discussion of the signal value of tears, the events and the emotional states that precede or accompany crying, the contexts in which crying typically occurs, as well as the benefits that crying may have for the crying individual. Finally, we draw general conclusions about the communicative and interpersonal functions of crying and suggest directions for further research.

FUNCTIONS OF HUMAN CRYING

From an evolutionary point of view, emotional expressions evolved because they solved certain adaptive problems during our evolutionary past, resulting in increased survival and reproductive success (Fridlund, 1991). There are both theoretical and empirical accounts suggesting that social effects of tears might improve one's mental and physical well-being (Vingerhoets & Bylsma, 2016), which should also be manifested in increases in survival and reproductive success. Surprisingly, although Darwin (1872) paid considerable attention to crying in his work *The Expression of the Emotion in Man and Animals*, he concluded that "We must look at weeping as an incidental result, as purposeless as the secretion of tears from a blow outside the eye, or as a sneeze from the retina being affected by a bright light" (Darwin, 1872, p. 175). On the other hand, he offered clear functional accounts of care-eliciting vocal crying of infants (see also Provine, this volume) and of nonemotional tears, which serve important functions like lubrication, nourishment, and protection of the eye. However, since Darwin, several hypotheses about the evolution of tearful crying and the further role of tears in human evolution have been elaborated (e.g., Hasson, 2009; Murube, 2009; Provine, 2012; Trimble, 2012; Vingerhoets, 2013; Walter, 2006). Before we turn to these hypotheses and related empirical data, we will first set forth a more general framework for the understanding of the functions of human crying.

In the scientific literature, human crying is proposed to serve two general domains of function: intraindividual and interindividual (Gračanin, Bylsma, & Vingerhoets, 2014; Vingerhoets & Bylsma, 2016). *Intraindividual functions* refer to beneficial changes for the crier following crying, in terms of improved mood and well-being (Cornelius, 2001). These effects of crying were initially emphasized in the psychodynamic literature (e.g., Breuer & Freud, 1895/1955), and later in relation to the notion that tears would remove toxins from the body (Frey, 1985). In contrast, *interindividual functions* of crying refer to the effects that tears have on observers, and these are related to the role of crying for attachment, social bonding, collaboration, and aggression reduction (e.g., Bowlby, 1980; Hasson, 2009; Nelson, 2008; Vingerhoets, 2013; Walter, 2006). The implicit assumption is that tears have a signal value, meaning that they transmit information from the crying person to observers, consequently changing their behavior in such a way that it, if the function is to be fulfilled, benefits the crier. These claims are supported by recent empirical data (Balsters, Krahmer, Swerts, & Vingerhoets, 2013; Hendriks & Vingerhoets, 2006; Provine, Krosnowski, & Brocato, 2009; see also Hasson, 2009). However, the mechanisms through which crying may affect perception and behavior of others are still largely unknown. The current chapter focuses on the communicative aspect of crying and, thus, will predominantly address its interindividual functions. However, since the two main functions of crying are not mutually independent and likely overlap and interact (Gračanin et al., 2014), we will also briefly discuss its intraindividual functions.

ONTOGENETIC DEVELOPMENT AND THE PHYLOGENETIC RIDDLE OF TEARFUL CRYING

The function of distress or separation calls in both humans and other animals is to promote the proximity of caregivers and to elicit caregiving. The main advantage of these vocalizations is that they provide a strong signal that is transmitted in all directions, making it also effective in the darkness and in the presence of visual barriers such as dense vegetation (Provine, 2012; Vingerhoets & Bylsma, 2016). Of all animals, human newborns are by far the most helpless (Kipp, 1991, 2008; Vingerhoets, 2013), making it plausible that distress signals might have been promoted by natural selection in humans even more so than in other animals. However, there is also an immense disadvantage of such vocal signaling: It may not only attract the attention of caregivers but also of potential predators or other assaulters (Vingerhoets, 2013; Walter, 2006). Thus, it can be expected that natural selection would promote the replacement of this vocal signal with a less costly one.

When an infant has developed the motoric capacity to move toward others, an acoustical signal is less essential. It is thus not surprising that the ontogenetic development of crying, as originally observed by Darwin (1872), runs from purely acoustical crying (birth through the first few weeks), to predominantly producing tears, where the acoustic component is much less prominently present. Vocal crying seems to be designed primarily to draw attention and promote approach toward the infant, whereas visual tears may transfer a message when the individual who has been attracted by the acoustical signal attends directly to the infant. In this *two-step model*, the vocal and tearful crying complement each other during infancy and early childhood, whereas this mutual function gradually disappears as we age. Recent research indeed shows that adult tears have a much larger impact on observers than tears of infants (Zeifman & Brown, 2011), which supports the idea that visual tears replace the acoustical crying of infants (Vingerhoets & Bylsma, 2016). The fact that tears can be targeted very specifically to a certain individual, such as one's mother, romantic partner, or other intimates, without notifying other conspecifics of one's helplessness, distress, and vulnerability (Vingerhoets & Bylsma, 2016), also can have a great advantage in terms of preservation of one's social status. Therefore, by removing such costs through the transition from a loud to a silent signal, together with the diminished costs related to risks of predation, tearful crying might have met the preconditions to evolve into a help-seeking behavior that extends throughout the life span. Finally, although adults occasionally also engage in sobbing, which includes both vocal crying and tears, the specific functions of this specific aspect of crying are still poorly understood (see Gračanin et al., 2014).

Due to its complex properties, crying can be considered a multimodal signal. However, in most studies it has been considered as an integrated behavior, with no attention paid to the possible specific functions of its vocal and visual components. There are only some preliminary indications that tears also might transmit specific information through pheromones (Gelstein et al., 2011; Oh, Kim, Park, & Cho, 2012). More specifically, Gelstein and colleagues concluded that tears contain a chemosignal whose function is to convey female sexual disinterest. The effects of smelling female tears on male testosterone levels have also been replicated (Oh et al., 2012). However, in a recent set of experiments with more than 250 participants, we were not able to replicate the effect of sniffing female tears on males' sexual and aggressive behavioral (Gračanin, van Assen, Vingerhoets, Omrčen, & Koraj, 2017).

Advantages of tears over vocal crying still do not satisfactorily answer the question of *how* tearful eyes might have evolved as a signal, including the prerequisites for and the advantages of placing this signal into the eyes. Hasson (2009) stresses that tears de facto emphasize one's helplessness and need for support. Blurred vision makes an individual more vulnerable and less capable of effective aggressive behavior, which in turn results in a decrease in aggression in potential assaulters and in increased willingness of others to provide support and caregiving. Although this *handicap* hypothesis may be debated, Hasson's (2009) suggestion that tears may function as reliable signals of readiness for reconciliation, need for help, or for social bonding seems to represent a set of more plausible and testable explanations (see also Vingerhoets, 2013; Vingerhoets, van de Ven, & van der Velden, 2016). Alternatively, but clearly related, Murube (2009) pointed out that eye infections might have been among the very first conditions that resulted in visible tears. Since eye infections, and the associated compromised vision, might have been a serious, even life-threatening problem for our ancestors, this might have been the very first unambiguous signal that the individual was in need of help. A similar proposal was advanced independently by Provine (2012), who stressed the presence of nerve-growth factor in tears, which helps to heal infected eyes. Provine further suggested that tears produced by physical distress gradually became a signal of emotional distress through the ethological process of ritualization, which assumes evolutionary transformation of functional nondisplay behavior into display behavior. We further propose that, in such a scenario, the first targets of the "infection" or "physical distress" tears might have been those individuals whose genes (i.e., relatives of the crier) or future cooperation prospects could, in their turn, also themselves benefit from helping the tearful person.

Simler (2014) hypothesized that crying evolved as a response to aggression, having an advantage over other emotional displays because of its genuine properties (i.e., hard to fake) and a relatively long duration of the signal (e.g., wet skin, puffy eyes) that allowed both the aggressor (immediately) and a possible helper (later) to receive the information. Simler further views crying as a submissive behavior by which individuals signal giving up their dominance and social status in exchange for possible formation or strengthening of alliances. Indeed, since crying individuals are generally perceived as weaker and less competent (Fischer, Eagly, & Oosterwijk, 2013), shedding of tears undoubtedly influences their dominance status. However, the response from others in terms of changes in their attributions and prosocial behaviors and, on a longer time scale, increased social bonding that may emerge (see Vingerhoets et al., 2016), can be a very important substitute for status-related resources that were lost.

But why did emotional tears only evolve in humans? Why wouldn't other primates also benefit from such a quiet, visual signal? First, there is simply a possibility that certain anatomical and/or physiological features prevented tears from becoming a signal that is reliably recognized. For example, chimps—our closest relatives—do not have whites of the eyes as we do, which could reduce the perception of teary eyes. Another, more scientifically supported answer comes from the fact that humans are also unique in their extended childhood, during which their flexible brain can freely develop in relation to the specific environment (Kipp, 1991/2008). Whereas other animals are both in terms of physical appearance and behavior, perfectly, but also rigidly, adapted to a specific environment, with the well-known disadvantages if their natural habitat would change, humans are not specialized for a certain environment, but are rather most flexible to adjust to a wide variety of surroundings and changes in their living conditions. It is precisely this prolonged childhood that allows humans to develop autonomy, flexibility, and independence from a specific environment, resulting from the fact that human children are real learning machines. At the same time, this makes them very vulnerable, which is why they badly need care, love, and protection from others (see Kipp 1991/2008). And tears are instrumental to elicit these important assets, while at the same time reducing the risk of being assaulted by others. Furthermore, Walter (2006) proposed that tears might have evolved because selection pressures for social bonding and connectedness became greater in humans relative to other primates once our ancestors left the secure shelter of trees and moved to savannah, facing there a much greater risk of predators. As will be clear from this contribution, there are several good reasons to believe that tearful crying facilitates these socially cohesive processes and, as such, may have been promoted by natural selection. Visible tears might have further fostered the empathetic skills of our species (Vingerhoets, 2013).

Finally, while MacLean's (1990) hypothesis that links the evolution of tearful crying to the emergence of the usage of fire during rituals via the reflexive reactions to smoke seems less plausible, the use of fire might have had other major influences on the emergence of tearful crying. Specifically, the frequency of social situations in which teary eyes might be visible substantially increased when humans began using fire, as it provided them with a valuable source of light after sunset. The reflective properties of tearful eyes might have also given them signaling advantage over other signaling systems in environments with artificial light, providing a strong evolutionary pressure for tears to evolve. Further signaling advantages of tears over muscular facial expressions might have also depended on the uniquely human abilities of empathy and theory of mind, which presumably increased attention to the eye region during social interactions.

WHAT DOES TEARFUL CRYING COMMUNICATE?

In explaining the social function of tears, we adhere to the *readout perspective* of emotion (Buck, 1985), which does not conceptualize facial expression as the major indicant of emotion (cf. Ekman & Friesen, 1975), but rather postulates the existence of three different readout systems—physiological, experiential, and expressive, which all may act as readouts of core emotional-motivational processes (Buck, 1985). In addition to muscular facial displays, the expressive system also includes expressions such as posture, vocalizations, and eye movements. Emphasizing the importance of learning processes and contextual influences, Buck (1985) postulates that facial displays do not necessarily reflect specific emotional states. Rather, this author assumes the existence of hard-wired *tendencies* of certain primary emotion systems (which he refers to as *primes*) to motivate specific expressive behaviors (e.g., angry motivation and possible facial expression of anger). We further elaborate this position by allowing for the possibility that certain expressive behaviors, such as tearful crying, have been designed to act as possible outputs of more than one specific prime.

Concerning the phylogenetic development of crying as a communication behavior, we assume that the sender and the receiver in the process of communication constitute a biological unit that itself participates in the process of evolution (Buck & Ginsburg, 1991). In order for that to happen, evolution must also favor the individuals who respond appropriately to the displays of others, meaning that crying must have benefited not just the crying individual but also those individuals who perceived the signal and reacted adequately to it. More precisely, these benefits of tears as signals for the observers include being reliably informed about the need for help and about the nonaggressive intentions. Especially when it concerns relatives, intimates, and social-exchange partners, but also others in general, knowing their need for help and prosocial intentions certainly allows for more adaptive responses.

The next question is then: To what extent is tearful crying informative and what kind of message does it convey? To answer that question, a comparison of shedding tears with other emotional expressions, such as blushing, might be useful. We can display a wide variety of emotional states with our highly developed facial musculature, but we nevertheless occasionally use additional means, such as producing tears or blushing. One of the possible obvious benefits of such additions is the increased capability to signal important states or emotional-motivational processes in an unambiguous way. Tears are suggested to act as an exclamation mark, meaning that the information about the importance of a situation for the crier is conveyed by the act of crying, not only to others but also to the crier him/herself (Vingerhoets, 2013). Furthermore, in contrast to the expressions of sadness, anger, or even happiness, which to a great extent may be produced voluntarily, both crying and blushing are expressions that are hard to fake and, interestingly, they are both considered to be highly prosocial (Provine, 2012; Vingerhoets, 2013). Indeed, there are numerous lay and prescientific accounts of tears as a genuine display of emotion (see Vingerhoets, 2013). However, while there are some indications that tearful individuals are perceived as more sincere in their emotional expression (Zeifman & Brown, 2011), more definitive empirical data are currently lacking.

If tears would have the effect of creating a more reliable display and, as a consequence, enhance the desirable impact on the receiver of the signal, this might add something functionally very important. Along these lines, research by Provine et al. (2009) demonstrated that tearful faces were much more easily identified as sad compared to the same faces with the tears being digitally removed. These results were also replicated in subsequent work (e.g., Zeifman & Brown, 2011), and it has been demonstrated that tears facilitate the perception of sadness and need for support even at the automatic, preattentive level (Balsters et al., 2013). However, it remains unclear whether tears also facilitate the recognition of other emotions besides sadness. Certain insights into states and intentions that are signaled by tears are offered by the existing research on self-reported emotions, individual needs, and contexts in which crying appears and, less directly, by the research on the reactions of others that observe crying individuals.

WHAT MAKES US CRY TEARFULLY?

Both negative and positive major life events, such as the death of a loved one, but also the birth of a child or a wedding, are among the most reliable triggers of tears. However, such events are rather rare, and thus they are not the most frequent antecedents of crying. People most often cry when encountering seemingly less important, rather mundane events that include arguments, minor failures, or watching movies or TV or listening to music (Vingerhoets, 2013). Human preference for fiction that evokes strong emotions, such as stories represented in books or movies and TV programs, might be functionally important in terms of preparation for dealing with real-life emotional situations (see Buck, 1985). In addition, this fiction also provides us with valuable information about the antecedents of crying in real life (see Denckla, Fiori, & Vingerhoets, 2014).

In experimental research (e.g., Provine et al., 2009) it is often implicitly assumed that tears are strongly associated with sadness. However, there are strong reasons for challenging this assumption. Darwin (1872) discussed emotional tears not only in his chapter on suffering (he did not even use the term *sadness*!), but also when addressing tender feelings. Recent research that focuses on the antecedents of crying (see Vingerhoets, 2013, Vingerhoets, Boelhouwer, van Tilburg, & van Heck, 2001; Vingerhoets, van Geleuken, van Tilburg, & van Heck, 1997) consistently reveals the broad range of emotions that accompany this behavior, including relief, grief, raptness, joy, self-pity, hopelessness, anger, frustration, and so on. It also has to be noted that infant crying, which is proposed to be a basis of the adult crying (Vingerhoets, 2013), does certainly not seem to be specifically tied to sadness, but rather with general discomfort and distress, including hunger, pain, cold, and separation from caregivers. Indeed, infant crying has been referred to as the "acoustical umbilical cord" (Ostwald, 1972) to emphasize that its origin is in the separation or distress call observed when a mammal offspring is separated from its mother. Relatedly, attachment theory (Bowlby, 1980) considers crying as an attachment behavior (similar to gazing, smiling, and grasping) that is predominantly a reaction to separation and loss. Accordingly, social rejection and homesickness are reported as important triggers of tears (Vingerhoets et al., 1997). Furthermore, recent research shows that tearful crying may also function as an adult type of distress call, as it promotes helping behavior in observers (Hendriks & Vingerhoets, 2006; Vingerhoets et al., 2016).

There is some evidence that, as we age, the reasons to shed tears become more diverse and that these changes are at least partially linked with other aspects of emotional development. For example, physical pain is an important trigger until late adolescence, whereas adults hardly cry for that reason. What seems to become increasingly important as a crying trigger, at a more advanced age, is the suffering of others, which is closely related to the development of our empathic skills (e.g., Murube, Murube, & Murube, 1999). Still another remarkable development is that we shed tears not only to negative situations but also to (witnessing) positive actions such as altruism and self-sacrifice (see Rottenberg & Vingerhoets 2012; Vingerhoets, 2013). The recently proposed concept of *Kama muta* or "being moved by love" (Fiske, Schubert, & Seibt, in press; see also Cova & Deona, 2014) refers to an emotion experienced when a communal sharing relationship suddenly intensifies, which is prototypically accompanied by shedding of tears, in addition to goose bumps and warm chest. Communal sharing denotes a relationship in which motives, actions, and thoughts of involved individuals are oriented toward something they have in common, leading to feelings of love, solidarity, identity, compassion, kindness, and devotion to each other (Fiske, 1991). Situations evoking *Kama muta* (and consequently tears) include reunions but also acts of extraordinary generosity or self-sacrifice (Fiske et al., in press). In addition, beautiful music or a sunset can move us to tears. Taken together, these observations challenge the view that emotional tears are specifically connected with a specific negative emotional state such as sadness.

Vingerhoets (2013) presented a summary of negative situations and their positive counterparts as possible triggers of crying (Box 12.1). It is evident that tears are elicited by a plethora of both negative and positive events and appraisals. But what do these factors have in common? Denckla

Box 12.1 NEGATIVE SITUATIONS AND THEIR POSITIVE COUNTERPARTS

Death/loss	Childbirth
Divorce, breakup	Wedding
Separation	Reunion
Conflict	Harmony, comradeship
Loneliness, solitude	Social bonding, union
Defeat	Victory
Powerlessness/failure	Extraordinary performance
Emotional suffering	Ultimate happiness, rapture
Old, discarded, worn-out	Young, vulnerable, with potential
Sin, egoism, the world is bad	Justice, altruism, the world is good
Tiny, vulnerable, helpless	Overwhelming, (all)mighty, awesome
Physical pain	Orgasm

et al. (2014) developed the *Crying Proneness Scale* aiming to tap individual differences in the probability that someone will cry when encountering different contents of books, movies, or documentaries. A factor analysis identified four major factors: (1) attachment tears (i.e., crying related to separations or reunions); (2) compassionate tears (i.e., crying because of the suffering of others); (3) sentimental/ moral tears (i.e., crying related to prosocial, positive emotions); and (4) societal tears (i.e., crying provoked by group conflict and harmony). Although this scale resolved the problem of assessing the crying threshold for rare events by including nonreal situations, it is important to keep in mind that many of these crying reactions are mediated by empathic processes. The mere fact that a substantial amount of crying episodes in adults is based on empathic responses to other people's experiences also contributes to our understanding of the major functions of tears, where they not only function to signal distress and elicit help but also to signal empathic responses and willingness to cooperate, and consequently enhance social bonding.

IS THERE A SINGLE, UNIFYING TEAR-ELICITING FACTOR?

The 17th-century British philosopher Thomas Hobbes (see Lutz, 1999) was among the first scholars to emphasize the relationship between tears and helplessness or powerlessness. Similar conclusions were reached later by Crile (1915), Frijda (1986), Miceli and Castelfranchi (2003), and Hasson (2009) in their examinations of the elicitors of emotional tears. They all considered perceived helplessness as the key underlying factor that most, if not all, situations that stimulate tears have in common. In a pilot study on specific attributed reasons for emotional tears, Vingerhoets et al. (1997) also observed that the self-reported accompanying feelings often included a blend of emotions, with helplessness or powerlessness being a key feature. It has even been suggested that the seeming "positive" tears may actually be due to the overwhelming power of joy, elation, awe, or tender feelings. An alternative formulation is that emotions that cannot be expressed in (other) behaviors or words find an outlet in tears (Vingerhoets & Bylsma, 2016).

The hypothesis that helplessness and powerlessness and the closely related need for succor are the core elicitors of crying is also supported by data showing group differences in crying proneness and frequency in relation to various triggers. Generally, it can be said that those who are weak and vulnerable (who tend to be in more powerless conditions) cry more easily and more often: Children cry more often than adults and women more frequently than men. Similarly, people tend to cry more when they are tired, depressed, or when lacking adequate coping skills to deal with environmental demands (Vingerhoets, 2013). However, this is not the whole story. To understand the meaning and functions of tears, we must consider not only specific triggers but also the context and broader psychosocial settings of the tears.

THE PSYCHOSOCIAL CONTEXT OF TEARS

In addition to questions about the antecedents of tears (i.e., what happened and what kind of emotion was experienced), the *International Study on Adult Crying* (ISAC; Bylsma, Vingerhoets, & Rottenberg, 2008) also collected detailed information about the context of the most recent crying episode. The answers to these questions revealed some remarkable facts. For example, people apparently prefer to shed tears between 7 and 10 p.m. Why might this be? First, given the gradual linear increase from 4 a.m. onward, one may wonder if crying follows a certain circadian rhythm (as it does among infants who also seem to prefer to cry in the evening) or that the threshold to shed tears may become gradually lower because we become more tired (cf. Young, 1937). But other factors may play a role as well, such as the fact that this is most likely the time that we are at home, in a safe environment with no strangers present, where we are much more likely to interact with our intimates (including arguments and conflicts), and where we expose ourselves more to our favorite music and to emotional films, literature, or television programs. It is possible that in that context, we feel less pressure to control our tears. Indeed, we seem to have a clear preference for who is with us when we cry. We feel most comfortable when crying in the company of our mother or romantic partner, as important attachment figures, but also in the presence of other attachment figures like pets, or symbolic objects such as pictures and letters from significant others (Fox, 2004; Vingerhoets, 2013). Interestingly, in the past, saints and clergymen often cried when praying to God, who also may be considered as a symbolic attachment figure. Also, an interesting phenomenon of ritual weeping during ritual greetings, weddings, conclusions of peace treaties between former enemies, and at initiation rites, in which people cry together, is observed in many cultures, which may stimulate social bonding and coherence (Vingerhoets, 2013).

The role of the presence of attachment figures is once more illustrated by a phenomenon referred to as delayed crying. For example, during a conflict or other stressful situation in the work setting, the tears might be inhibited, but when discussing what happened, later at home with one's partner, mother, or another close individual, the tears start flowing. Two more examples demonstrating that crying fulfils its communicative function primarily in the context of attachment relationships include the observation that students with romantic partners tend to cry more often than their single counterparts (e.g., Sung et al., 2009; Vingerhoets & Van Assen, 2009), and that people who feel lonely, although they report a relatively low well-being, tend to cry less than their nonlonely counterparts (Vingerhoets, 2013).

We may thus conclude that the emergence of tears depends on the exposure to specific events and the specific social context. In addition, the specific physical and psychological state before the exposure may play a role. When we are in the company of just strangers, we are more reluctant to cry and do our best to suppress our tears. This makes sense because the *ISAC* study also demonstrated that we should not expect as much support from strangers compared to intimates (Bylsma et al., 2008). However, in several self-report studies (e.g., Hendriks, Croon, & Vingerhoets, 2008) participants reported a greater willingness to provide comfort and assistance to crying individuals relative to noncrying individuals whom they were not familiar with, which seems to extend beneficial functions of crying outside of the attachment relationships.

BENEFICIAL EFFECTS OF CRYING

To understand the beneficial effects of crying, the distinction between a signal and a cue is important. *Cues* provide observers with useful and reliable information, but this does not normatively benefit the one who is the source of a particular cue (Hasson, 2009). For example, certain behavior might represent a cue for a predator that an animal is wounded, and thus, the predator can take advantage of this information by attacking the animal. Conversely, characteristic for signals, in addition to their reliability, is that both the sender and the receiver benefit from changes in the receiver's behavior. Accordingly, Hasson

(2009) concluded that one cannot regard crying as a signal only on the basis of the findings that it alters the recognition of specific emotion. So, to what extent is crying capable of altering the behavior of others in such a way that it benefits both the observer, as we already discussed, and the crying individual?

People generally believe that crying is beneficial and facilitates emotional recovery (e.g., Bylsma et al., 2008), which is proposed to result either from the neurophysiologically mediated effects of crying on mood and well-being of the crier, or indirectly from the reactions that crying elicits in other people. In other words, the intra-individual functions of crying may depend on both *self-soothing* and *social-soothing* effects of crying (Gračanin et al., 2014; Vingerhoets, 2013). In the latter case, tears affect a crying person (intraindividual effects) by their impact on perception, appraisal, emotions, and consequently, by the behavior of others (interindividual effects) in a way that can be beneficial to the crying individual (see Vingerhoets, 2013; Vingerhoets, Bylsma, & Rottenberg, 2009). This also fits with the attachment perspective, according to which crying improves the psychological and physiological well-being of a crying person by eliciting care from other people (Hendriks, Nelson, Cornelius, & Vingerhoets, 2008b; Nelson, 2008). The greater willingness of people to provide social support to crying than to noncrying individuals (Hendriks et al., 2008a, Vingerhoets et al., 2016) is further evidence in support of this notion.

Several studies demonstrated that criers who received social support while crying were more likely to report mood benefits relative to the criers without support (Bylsma et al., 2008; Cornelius, 1997), partially corroborating the hypothesis of the mediating role of the interindividual effects of crying on subsequent mood. The *crying-elicits-help* hypothesis is further substantiated by the results of a study in which participants were asked about their motivations to up-regulate crying. A considerable number of participants reported that they sometimes enhance their crying so that others know how they feel, or because they need support from others and feel that others' reactions will decrease their distress (Simons, Bruder, van der Lowe, & Parkinson, 2013). Altogether, these results suggest that tears fulfill their signaling function by affecting attributions in observers and eliciting their prosocial behavior.

CONCLUSIONS

In this contribution, we evaluated the evidence for the communication or signaling function of human tearful crying. Although there are reasons to believe that tearful crying evolved from signals known as distress or separation calls that are displayed in other animals as well, human adult emotional crying is unique by the shedding of tears, which has certain adaptive advantages over vocal crying. Adult crying is certainly not specifically associated with sadness or any other specific emotion, but rather with both positive and negative emotional situations, particularly those in which prosocial behavior is desired from others. Tears appear to be responses to predominantly interpersonal events that elicit strong emotional-motivational states marked by helplessness or being overwhelmed with emotion but also by prosocial tendencies. Tears also may act as a modulator of other facial expressions of emotions (e.g., sadness, Kama Muta), having the role of the exclamation mark that emphasizes the importance of the situation to both the crier and the observer. They certainly have attachment functions, but also other social functions outside the domain of attachment. The signal value of tears is reflected in their capability to promote help and nurturance, attenuate possible aggression in others, and facilitate social bonding. It can be further concluded that, in all these cases, tears signal prosocial intentions, since both asking for help (distress signal) and for reduction of aggression (submission signal) imply a willingness to cooperate.

While the research on crying currently might have reached a solid basis, still many questions remain. We still do not yet fully understand why only humans weep and what precisely makes weeping such an important social signal. We also still know very little about the possible role of specific crying components (e.g., vocal crying, sobbing, tears) for the intraindividual and interindividual effects of crying. The evident complexity of crying behavior clearly points to the need for a multidisciplinary approach to this phenomenon. We hope that in the near future more researchers, with different backgrounds, will be inspired to fathom this uniquely human behavior.

ACKNOWLEDGMENTS

This work was supported by the NEWFELPRO project of the Government of the Republic of Croatia and the MSES.

REFERENCES

Balsters, M. J. H., Krahmer, E. J., Swerts, M. G. J., & Vingerhoets, A. J. J. M. (2013). Emotional tears facilitate the recognition of sadness and the perceived need for social support. *Evolutionary Psychology, 11*(1), 148–158.

Bowlby, J. (1980). *Attachment and loss (Vol. 3): Loss, sadness and depression*. New York, NY: Basic Books.

Breuer, J., & Freud, S. (1895/1955). *Studies on hysteria* (trans. J. Strachey). London, UK: Hogarth Press (1955 edition). London, UK: Hogarth Press.

Buck, R. (1985). Prime theory: An integrated view of motivation and emotion. *Psychological Review, 92*, 389–413.

Buck, R., & Ginsburg, B. (1991). Emotional communication and altruism: The communicative gene hypothesis. In M. Clark (Ed.), *Altruism. Review of personality and social psychology, Vol. 11* (pp. 149–175). Newbury Park, CA: Sage.

Bylsma, L. M., Vingerhoets, A. J. J. M., & Rottenberg, J. (2008). When crying is cathartic? An international study. *Journal of Social and Clinical Psychology, 27*, 1165–1187.

Cornelius, R. R. (1986). *Prescience in the pre-scientific study of weeping? A history of weeping in the popular press from the mid-1800s to the present.* Paper presented at the 57th annual meeting of the Eastern Psychological Association. New York, NY.

Cornelius, R. R. (1997). Toward a new understanding of weeping and catharsis? In A. J. J. M. Vingerhoets, F. J. Van Bussel, & A. J. W. Boelhouwer (Eds.), *The (Non)expression of emotions in health and disease* (pp. 303–322). Tilburg, the Netherlands: Tilburg University Press.

Cornelius, R. R. (2001). Crying and catharsis. In A. J. J. M. Vingerhoets & R. R. Cornelius (Eds.), *Adult crying: A biopsychosocial approach* (199–212). Hove, UK: Routledge.

Cova, F., & Deonna, J. A. (2014). Being moved. *Philosophical Studies, 169*, 447–466.

Crile, G. W. (1915). *The origin and nature of the emotions*. Philadelphia, PA: Saunders.

Darwin, C. (1872). *The expression of the emotions in man and animals*. New York, NY: Oxford University Press (1998 edition, with an introduction, afterword, and commentaries by P. Ekman).

Denckla, C. A., Fiori, K. L., Vingerhoets, A. J. J. M. (2014). Development of the Crying proneness scale: Associations among crying proneness, empathy, attachment, and age. *Journal of Personality Assessment, 96*, 619–631.

Ekman, P., & Friesen, W. V. (1975). *Unmasking the face*. Englewood Cliffs, NJ: Prentice-Hall.

Fischer, A. Eagly, A. H., & Oosterwijk, S. (2013). The meaning of tears: Which sex seems emotional depends on the social context. *European Journal of Social Psychology, 43*, 505–515.

Fiske, A. P. (1991). *Structures of social life: The four elementary forms of human relations*. New York, NY: Free Press.

Fiske, A. P., Schubert, T., & Seibt, B. (in press). "Kama muta" or 'Being moved by love': A bootstrapping approach to the ontology and epistemology of an emotion. In J. Cassaniti & U. Menon (Eds.), *Universalism without uniformity: Explorations in mind and culture*. Chicago, IL: University of Chicago Press.

Fox, K. (2004). *The Kleenex © for Men Crying Game Report: A study of men and crying.* Oxford, UK: Social Issues Research Center.

Frey, W.H. (1985). *Crying: The mystery of tears*. Minneapolis, MN: Winston Press.

Fridlund, A. J. (1991). Evolution and facial action in reflex, social motive, and paralanguage. *Biological Psychology, 32*, 3–100.

Frijda, N. H. (1986). *The emotions*. Cambridge, UK: Cambridge University Press.

Gelstein, S., Yeshurun, Y., Rozenkrantz, L., Shushan, S., Frumin, I., Roth, Y., & Sobel, N. (2011). Human tears contain a chemosignal. *Science, 331*, 226–230.

Gračanin, A., Bylsma, L., & Vingerhoets, A. J. J. M. (2014). Is crying a self-soothing behaviour? *Frontiers in Psychology, 5*, 1–15.

Gračanin, A., van Assen, M. A. L. M., Vingerhoets, A. J. J. M., Omrčen, V., & Koraj, I. (2017). Chemo-signaling effects of human tears revisited: Does exposure to female tears decrease males' perception of female sexual attractiveness? *Cognition and Emotion, 31*, 139-150.

Hasson, O. (2009). Emotional tears as biological signals. *Evolutionary Psychology, 7*, 363–370.

Hendriks, M. C. P., Croon, M. A., & Vingerhoets, A. J. J. M. (2008a). Social reactions to adult crying: The help-soliciting function of tears. *Journal of Social Psychology, 148*, 22–41.

Hendriks, M. C. P., Nelson, J. K., Cornelius, R. R., & Vingerhoets, A. J. J. M (2008b). Why crying improves our well-being: An attachment-theory perspective on the functions of adult crying. In A. J. J. M. Vingerhoets, I. Nyklicek, & J. Denollet (Eds). *Emotion regulation: Conceptual and clinical issues* (pp. 87–96). New York, NY: Springer.

Hendriks, M. C. P., & Vingerhoets, A. J. J. M. (2006). Social messages of crying faces: Their influence on anticipated person perception, emotional and behavioral responses. *Cognition and Emotion, 20*, 878–886.

Kipp, F. (1991; 2008). *Die Evolution des Menschen im Hinblick auf seine lange Jugendzeit*. Translated by J. M. Barnes: Childhood and human evolution. Hillsdale, NY: Adonis Press.

Lutz, T. (1999). *Crying: The natural and cultural history of tears*. New York, NY: Norton.

MacLean, P.D. (1990). *The triune brain in evolution: Role in paleocerebral functions*. New York, NY: Plenum.

Miceli, M., & Castelfranchi, C. (2003). Crying: Discussing its basic reasons and uses. *New Ideas in Psychology, 21*, 247–273.

Murube, J. (2009). Hypotheses on the development of psychoemotional tearing. *The Ocular Surface, 7*, 171–175.

Murube, J., Murube, L., & Murube, A. (1999). Origin and types of emotional tearing. *European Journal of Ophthalmology, 9*, 77–84.

Nelson, J. K. (2008). Crying in psychotherapy: Its meaning, assessment and management based on attachment theory. In A. J. J. M. Vingerhoets, I. Nyklicek, & J. Denollet (Eds.), *Emotion regulation: Conceptual and clinical issues* (pp. 202–214). New York, NY: Springer.

Oh, T. J., Kim, M. Y., Park, K. S., & Cho, Y. M. (2012). Effects of chemosignals from sad tears and postprandial plasma on appetite and food intake in humans. *PLoS ONE, 7*(8), e42352.

Ostwald, P. (1972). The sounds of infancy. *Developmental Medicine and Child Neurology, 14*, 350–361.

Patel, V. (1993). Crying behavior and psychiatric disorder in adults: A review. *Comprehensive Psychiatry, 34*, 206–211.

Provine, R. R. (2012). *Curious behavior. Yawning, laughing, hiccupping, and beyond*. Cambridge, MA: The Belknap Press.

Provine, R. R., Krosnowski, K. A., & Brocato, N. W. (2009). Tearing: Breakthrough in human emotional signaling. *Evolutionary Psychology, 7*, 52–56.

Rottenberg, J. Bylsma, L. M., Wolvin, V, & Vingerhoets, A. J. J. M. (2008). Tears of sorrow, tears of joy: An individual differences approach to crying in Dutch females. *Personality and Individual Differences, 45*, 367–372.

Rottenberg, J., & Vingerhoets, A. J. J. M. (2012). Crying: Call for a developmental lifespan approach. *Personality and Social Psychology Compass, 6*, 217–227.

Simler, K. (2014). *Tears*. Retrieved from http://www.meltingasphalt.com/tears/

Simons, G., Bruder, M., van der Lowe, I., & Parkinson, B. (2013). Why try (not) to cry: Intra- and inter-personal motives for crying regulation. *Frontiers in Psychology, 3*, 1–9.

Sung, A. D., Collins, M. E., Smith, A. K., Sanders, A. M., Quinn, M. A., Block, S. D., & Arnold, R. M. (2009). Crying: experiences and attitudes of third-year medical students and interns. *Teaching and Learning in Medicine, 21*, 180–187.

Trimble, M. (2012). *Why humans like to cry. Tragedy, evolution, and the brain*. Oxford, UK: Oxford University Press.

Van Hemert, D. A., Van de Vijver, F. J. R., & Vingerhoets, A. J. J. M. (2011). Culture and crying: Prevalences and gender differences. *Cross-Cultural Research, 45*, 399–431.

Vingerhoets, A. J. J. M. (2013). *Why only humans weep: Unraveling the mysteries of tears*. Oxford, UK: Oxford University Press.

Vingerhoets, A. J. J. M., & Bylsma, L. (2016). The riddle of human emotional crying: A challenge for emotion researchers. *Emotion Review, 8*, 207–217.

Vingerhoets, A. J. J. M., Bylsma, L., & Rottenberg, J. (2009). Crying: A biopsychosocial phenomenon. In T. Fögen (Ed.), *Tears in the Graeco-Roman world* (pp. 439–475). Berlin, Germany: de Gruyter.

Vingerhoets, A. J. J. M., Boelhouwer, A. J. V., van Tilburg, M. A. L., & van Heck, G. L. (2001). The situational and emotional context of adult crying. In A. J. J. M. Vingerhoets & R. R. Cornelius (Eds.), *Adult crying: A biopsychosocial approach* (pp. 71–90). Hove, UK: Brunner-Routledge.

Vingerhoets, A. J. J. M., van de Ven, N., & van der Velden, Y. (2016). What crying does convey: The social messages of emotional tears. *Motivation and Emotion, 40*, 455–463.

Vingerhoets, A. J. J. M., van Geleuken, A. J. M. L., van Tilburg, M. A. L., & van Heck, G. L. (1997). The psychological context of crying episodes: Towards a model of adult crying. In A. J. J. M. Vingerhoets, F. van Bussel, & A. Boelhouwer (Eds.), The *(non)expression of emotions in health and disease* (pp. 323–336). Tilburg, the Netherlands: Tilburg University Press.

Vingerhoets, A. J. J. M., & van Assen, M. A. L. M. (2009). Love and tears. Poster presented at the *Biannual Meeting of the International Society for Research on Emotion (ISRE)*. Leuven, Belgium.

Walter, C. (2006). *Thumbs, toes, and tears: And other traits that make us human*. New York, NY: Walker & Co.

Young, P. T. (1937). Laughing and weeping, cheerfulness and depression: A study of moods among college students. *Journal of Social Psychology, 8*, 311–334.

Zeifman, D. M., & Brown, S. A. (2011). Age-related changes in the signal value of tears. *Evolutionary Psychology, 9*, 313–324.

PART V

Neural Processes

13

Neural and Behavioral Responses to Ambiguous Facial Expressions of Emotion

PAUL J. WHALEN, MAITAL NETA, M. JUSTIN KIM, ALISON M. MATTEK, F. C. DAVIS, JAMES M. TAYLOR, AND SAMANTHA CHAVEZ

Affective neuroscience has utilized a number of promising methods to investigate the neural bases of emotion. These have included methods that seek to provoke emotional responses in the participants of study (symptom provocation [e.g., Shin et al., 2005] and viewing photos from the International Affective Picture System [IAPS, e.g., Junghöfer et al., 2006]) as well as the training of strategies aimed at controlling these emotional responses (e.g., regulation strategies [e.g., Jackson, Malmstadt, Larson, & Davidson, 2000], behavioral therapy [e.g., Kennedy et al., 2007], and meditation [e.g., Slagter, Davidson, & Lutz, 2011]). Often these tasks involve viewing images of other people while they display emotion. Interestingly, while some of these images can evoke a strong emotional response in the viewer (e.g., a gruesome car accident scene from the IAPS), other images are more emotionally subtle. Photographs of facial expressions of emotion fit into this latter category, allowing affective neuroscientists to examine the neural substrates of detecting, perceiving, and/or identifying an emotional response in a conspecific without engaging additional neural circuitry that would underlie strong bodily reactions in the perceiver.

In this review we will focus on affective neuroscience studies that have deliberately set out to use facial expressions of emotion as stimuli to assess a fraction of the processes and neural substrates that comprise emotion. Indeed, standardized facial expression stimulus sets have been used for decades to assess bodily (e.g., skin conductance [e.g., Öhman & Dimberg, 1978], startle response [e.g., Balaban, 1995], and electromyography [e.g., Dimberg, 1982]) and neural responses (e.g., evoked response potentials, ERPs [e.g., Vanderploeg, Brown, & Marsh, 1987]; electroencephalograohy [EEG; e.g., Ekman, Davidson & Friesen, 1990]). The advent of neuroimaging techniques such as functional magnetic resonance imaging (fMRI) has led to an exponential increase in the use of facial expressions as stimuli. These studies have allowed affective neuroimaging researchers to visualize neural responses that correlate with diverse behavioral outcomes such as (a) the effects of early deprivation on development (Tottenham et al., 2009; 2011; see Gee & Whalen, 2014), (b) cognitive control in adolescence (Hare et al., 2008), (c) emotional regulation ability (Hariri, Bookheimer, & Mazziotta, 2000), (d) one's positivity-negativity bias (Kim, Somerville, Johnstone, Alexander, & Whalen, 2003), (e) the effect of facial muscle feedback on the perception of others' facial expressions (Kim et al., 2014), (f) the symptom severity of a participant with posttraumatic stress disorder (Shin et al., 2005), and (g) the prediction of whether a particular medication will work for a participant with generalized anxiety disorder (Whalen et al., 2008). For the present review, we focus on behavioral and neuroimaging studies that have assessed the role of the amygdala and prefrontal cortex in discerning the significance that the facial expressions of others have for predicting biologically relevant outcomes.

FACIAL EXPRESSIONS ARE USEFULLY THOUGHT OF AS NATURALLY CONDITIONED STIMULI

From the expressions of others we can glean information about their internal emotional state, their intentions, and/or their reaction to contextual events in our immediate environment. Facial expressions of emotion have predicted important events for us in the past, and we can use this information about previous associated outcomes to respond appropriately to expressions we encounter subsequently. Considered in this light, facial expressions constitute conditioned stimuli (CSs). Likening facial expressions of emotion to CSs allows us to draw parallels between two seemingly distinct avenues of research: that which characterizes the neural processes associated with learning about environmental cues that predict biologically relevant outcomes (i.e., Pavlovian conditioning), and that which characterizes reactions to environmental cues that have acquired similar predictive value through experiences in our social world (i.e., facial expressions of emotion; see Davis, Johnstone, Mazzulla, Oler, & Whalen, 2010).

FEAR, FEARFUL FACIAL EXPRESSIONS, AND THE HUMAN AMYGDALA

Numerous nonhuman animal and human studies of aversive Pavlovian conditioning have documented that the amygdala is critical to the acquisition and expression of conditioned behaviors (e.g., freezing) that have been interpreted as indicative of a learned state of fear (LeDoux, 1996). When it was documented that patients with bilateral lesions of the amygdala showed greater deficits in processing fearful facial expression (Adolphs, Tranel, Damasio, & Damasio, 1994; Broks et al., 1998; Hamann & Adolphs, 1999), these data were largely interpreted as consistent with the role of the amygdala in fear conditioning. Furthermore, subsequent demonstrations that presentation of static photographs of fearful expressions produced reliable activation of the human amygdala were also interpreted as consistent with the fear model (Breiter et al., 1996; Hariri et al., 2002; Morris et al., 1996; Phillips et al., 1997).

However, lesions of the amygdala also block associative orienting responses (Gallagher & Holland, 1994; Kapp, Whalen, Supple, & Pascoe, 1992; see Whalen, 1998). Associative orienting responses are defined as any autonomic or somatic responses that reflect increased vigilance or attention and which can serve to facilitate the animal's rate of learning during acquisition (see Kapp et al., 1992; Weisz, Harden, & Xiang, 1992)—for example, the potentiation of reflexes (e.g., nictitating membrane) observed in rats during early acquisition of conditioned responses. Critically, these responses are observed during the early stages of acquisition during Pavlovian conditioning, as well as any time during learning where the outcome predicted by a particular cue suddenly changes (see Whalen, 1998). In this way, amygdala lesions can ultimately attenuate learned conditioned responses, because animals with such lesions do not attentively engage the environment—they are poor consumers of potentially predictive information.

Indeed, evidence suggests that bilateral lesions of the human amygdala do not prevent individuals from learning about fear faces; rather, these lesions make them inefficient in orienting to the most informative feature of the face. Operationally, this manifests in these participants not looking to the eye region of the face (Adolphs et al., 2005). Thus, amygdala lesions affect orienting to the place on the face where the best potentially predictive information can be found—suggesting the amygdala is critical to normal face processing and may play a role in the aberration in eye region processing observed in disorders such as autism (Baron-Cohen et al., 1999; Klin, 2000; Osterling & Dawson, 1994; Pelphrey et al., 2002; Schultz, 2005).

Subsequent neuroimaging studies have demonstrated the sensitivity of amygdala responses to fearful expressions by observing activation though fearful expressions were presented using techniques that mitigated subjective awareness (e.g., backward masking, binocular suppression; Armony, Corbo, Clement, & Brunet, 2005; Etkin et al., 2004; Kim et al., 2010; 2016; Morris, Öhman, & Dolan, 1998, 1999; Rauch et al., 2000; Sheline et al., 2001; Whalen et al., 1998; Williams, Morris, McClone, Abbott, & Mattingly, 2004). Because a fearful face contains an immense amount of configural information (e.g., raised brows, wide eyes, slightly open mouth, etc.), it is likely that the amygdala does not compute all this information in such a short time frame. Indeed, the presentation of fearful eye whites using backward masking has been shown to be sufficient to produce amygdala activation (Whalen et al., 2004). These data suggest that the amygdala may use widened eyes as a crude proxy for the presence of fearful faces and offer a mechanism for this more automatic response to these complex social stimuli (see Whalen et al., 2009). Widened eyes are perhaps usefully thought of as a special "shape" that the amygdala has learned often predicts critical social/biological outcomes.

AMYGDALA RESPONSES TO OTHER PRIMARY FACIAL EXPRESSIONS

Further research has shown that in addition to fearful expressions, the human amygdala is responsive to all primary facial expressions, including anger (Fitzgerald, Angstadt, Jelsone, Nathan, & Phan, 2006; Whalen et al., 2001; Yang et al., 2002), surprise (Kim et al., 2003, 2004), disgust (Fitzgerald et al., 2006; Phillips et al., 1997), sadness (Fitzgerald et al., 2006; Harrison et al., 2006; Yang et al., 2002), and happy expressions (Fitzgerald et al., 2006; Yang et al., 2002). Taken together, we can conclude from these studies that the human amygdala is responsive to the potentially predictive value of all facial expressions in general, consistent with data showing that increased amygdala activation is not restricted to threat-related information (e.g., Gallagher & Holland, 1994; Paton, Belova, Morrison, & Salzman, 2006).

That said, one caveat when considering such data is whether amygdala activations observed in response to a particular expression are in any way causal to a behavioral outcome. For example, patients with bilateral lesions of the amygdala are more greatly impaired in their processing of fearful expressions but show no behavioral deficit to happy expressions (Adolphs et al., 1994). Amygdala activation in response to happy expressions may be a case of the amygdala monitoring the presence of some expressions in the environment without having a causal impact on behavioral responses observed in response to these expressions. Alternatively, it is possible that we simply have not yet figured out the behaviors that should be measured to document such a causal link. That said, we note that amygdala responses to happy faces show a distinctly different temporal time course—where many studies have observed high-magnitude amygdala responses to initial presentations of fearful expressions that strongly habituate over time (Kim et al., 2003; see Whalen et al., 2009), amygdala responses to happy facial expressions are notably lower in magnitude compared to fear, but this response magnitude does not change over time (i.e., the response magnitude is sustained; Somerville et al., 2004). Thus, though an averaged amygdala response observed to numerous facial expressions might look somewhat similar, there could be a critical difference in temporal response and thus function over time.

In the interim, a number of investigators have adopted the strategy of using fearful expressions as their starting point—given the reproducible nature of the human neuroimaging effect—and then directly pitting fearful faces against other primary expressions such as angry (Whalen et al., 2001), happy (Morris et al., 1996), disgusted (Phillips et al., 1997), or surprised (Kim et al., 2003) faces. Indeed, we believe direct comparison of fear with other expressions is a useful way to isolate the meaning of amygdala responses to fearful expressions, and more generally the fundamental role of the human amygdala in processing biologically relevant predictive stimuli.

USING FEARFUL AND ANGRY FACIAL EXPRESSIONS TO DEMONSTRATE THE AMYGDALA'S ROLE IN RESOLVING PREDICTIVE AMBUGUITY

Responses observed to the facial expressions of others are ultimately based on their predictive value. By predictive value, we mean—since we want to know what will happen next when encountering the information communicated by the face of another person, facial expressions evoke responses (involuntary or voluntary) that help us learn and better prepare us for the differential of outcomes that these expressions have predicted in the past. To this end, the facial expressions of others guide what we do next. Predictive ambiguity then, as it relates to facial expressions of emotion, refers to facial expressions that are context dependent—they do not embody predictive information (e.g., anger); they point us in the direction that we might look to in order to learn that information (e.g., fear, surprise).

Two negatively valenced facial expressions are usefully contrasted in this respect. Angry and fearful expressions both signal the presence of threat based upon past learning, and activity within the amygdala will increase in response to this negative value. But angry expressions also provide information about the source of threat, and decisions can more immediately be made about how to handle that threat (e.g., fight, flee, cry like a baby, etc). Fearful expressions predict that the probability of threat has increased, but they do not embody the source of threat. Instead, fearful facial expressions are more context dependent, suggesting that the viewer needs to extract additional information from the context to resolve this predictive ambiguity—namely what is the other person afraid of, and should the viewer be afraid too? In response to this predictive ambiguity, in order to call upon other brain regions to become more vigilant to assist in this learning, greater amygdala activation will be observed in response to fearful expressions when directly contrasted with anger (Whalen et al., 2001).

Two recent behavioral demonstrations supported this hypothesis (Davis et al., 2011; Taylor & Whalen, 2014). In one study, participants were presented with pictures of individuals with either fearful or angry expressions in presentation blocks that included alternating neutral words. After passively viewing the fearful face/neutral word blocks and angry face/neutral word blocks, participants were given recognition tests to assess their memory for the words and faces. Participants recognized more words that alternated with fearful face presentations compared to angry faces—consistent with the notion that the predictive ambiguity of fearful expressions diffuses attention, thereby increasing memory for the surrounding context. When tested for their recognition of the presented faces, participants recognized more angry than fearful faces—consistent with the notion that angry faces capture attention since they embody a direct source of threat (Davis et al., 2011). Note that these are memory effects, but based upon an attentional hypothesis. Thus, in a second study, Taylor and Whalen (2014) used the same logic to directly measure differential attentional effects in response to fearful and angry facial expressions, using the "attentional blink" paradigm. In this task, participants viewed "rapid serial visual presentation" of faces in the center of the screen, consistently surrounded by four hashtags in the periphery (see Fig. 13.1). Participants were told that the repeating neutral faces would be of one sex, but were told to then watch for a change to the other sex—an event referred to as Target 1 (T1) in the present paradigm. In response to the T1 event, participants were told to look for a change in the color of one of four gray hashtags in the periphery (color changed from white to green). Participants had to then report by button press (1) when they observed the change and (2) which of the hashtags had changed color. The key to the experiment was as follows: When the sex of the presented face changed at T1, it also displayed a fearful, angry, or neutral expression. All participants showed a typical attentional blink effect regardless of facial expression—that is, it was more difficult to detect the subsequent hashtag color change immediately following the Target 1 event (i.e., within ~500 ms), but participants could reliably report the Target 2 hashtag event if it occurred greater than 500 ms after the Target 1 event. Critically, fearful facial expressions caused participants to more accurately detect the T2 event, compared to neutral faces. Angry facial

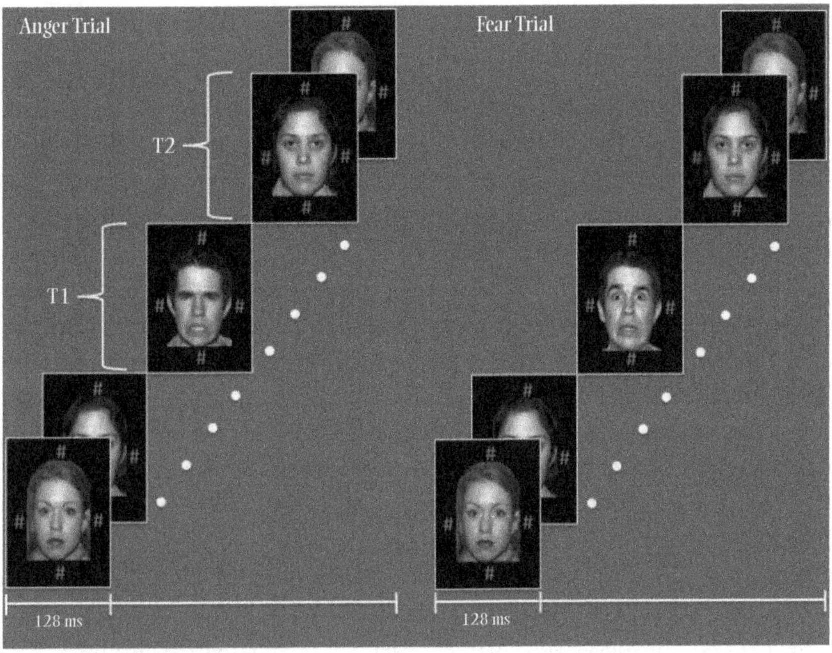

Figure 13.1 Depiction of experimental paradigm from Taylor and Whalen (2014).

expressions showed no such effect. The fact that the to-be-detected targets were in the periphery (i.e., the context) is consistent with the notion that fearful expressions diffuse attention to the context compared to angry expressions.

The fact that these fearful and angry facial expressions can be equated for their intensity of valence and arousal value subjectively (Davis et al., 2011) and arousal objectively (heart rate [Ekman, Levenson, & Friesen, 1983] and skin conductance [Johnsen, Thayer, & Hugdahl, 1995]) suggests that these effects are not related to the dimensions of valence or arousal, but another dimension related to information value—or, in this example, predictive ambiguity (Whalen, 1998).

In using these two expressions to study the amygdala, we have asserted that the predictive ambiguity associated with fearful facial expressions will produce amygdala activation above and beyond that observed to the detection of negativity per se. This amygdala activation serves to facilitate processing in other brain systems that might disambiguate the environmental source of this expressive change in the facial features of a conspecific (see Whalen, 1998). If this assertion has merit, then a compelling demonstration would involve showing a similar amygdala signal increase to another facial expression that has a similar predictive ambiguity, but is not necessarily negatively valenced.

USING SURPRISED EXPRESSIONS TO SEPARATE VALENCE FROM AROUSAL VALUE

One such expression is that of surprise, which provides a critical comparison expression for fear. Though neither expression indicates the exact nature of its eliciting event, fearful expressions do provide additional information concerning predicted negative valence. Surprise, on the other hand, can be interpreted either positively or negatively (Tomkins & McCarter, 1964). For example, a surprised expression might be observed in response to an oncoming car (negative) or an unexpected birthday party (positive). Thus, we can take advantage of the inherent valence ambiguity associated with surprised facial expressions. Measuring the valence direction that individuals tend to lean in when encountering surprised facial expressions can be used to reveal important individual differences in both (a) the propensity to subjectively ascribe positive or negative valence to an ambiguous predictor and (b) the relationship between these subjective ratings and fMRI signal changes.

While viewing surprised faces during neuroimaging, high signal change magnitudes were observed in the amygdala in participants who interpreted these expressions negatively, while lower signal change magnitudes were observed in participants who interpreted these expressions positively (Kim et al., 2003). Critically, these valence-related activations were observed in one portion of the amygdala (i.e., ventral) while another region (i.e., dorsal amygdala/substantia innominata [SI]) showed comparable signal increases in all participants to surprised faces despite their differing valence interpretations. Thus, within a single group of participants the amygdala tracked both valence (i.e., positive or negative) and arousal (i.e., predictive ambiguity—what is she reacting to?).

That some individuals would show such a positivity bias associated with lower amygdala activity might seem a bit surprising for a brain region that functions to implicitly monitor the environment for potential threat (e.g., Whalen, 1998). That is, one might have thought that the amygdala would have responded to the *potential* negativity of surprised faces similarly in all participants. Individual differences of this type suggested to us that another region of the brain might be exerting a regulatory influence over the amygdala while viewing surprised expressions. Accordingly, we observed two regions of the medial prefrontal cortex (mPFC) that were correlated with participants' valence interpretations of surprised faces. Like the amygdala, a dorsal region of the mPFC (specifically the rostral, dorsal anterior cingulate cortex [ACC; see Kim et al., 2003]) displayed a positive relationship with negative valence ratings (i.e., higher activity with more negative ratings). A ventral region of the mPFC (perhaps ventral ACC or BA 10; see Kim et al., 2003) showed an

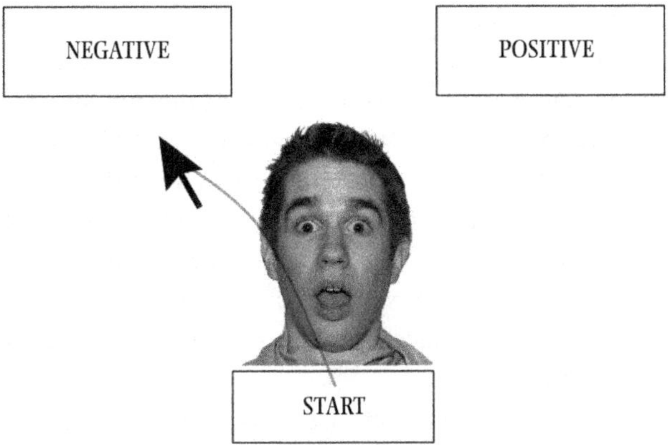

Figure 13.2 Depiction of experimental paradigm from Mattek et al. (in press).

opposite relationship with valence ratings of surprised faces compared to the amygdala and dorsal mPFC (i.e., higher activity with more positive ratings). Thus, activity in the ventral mPFC was inversely related to activity in the amygdala and dorsal mPFC. Note that this inversely correlated ventral mPFC-amygdala fMRI activity was observed during passive viewing of these expressions, predicting the ratings that participants would offer after the scanning session. Thus, these amygdala-prefrontal activations that matched subsequent valence interpretations were not task driven and thereby appear to be relatively automatic/implicit (Kim et al., 2003). Furthermore, the bias represented by these judgments appears to be more trait- than state-like as participants who were tested a year later gave similar ratings (Neta, Norris, & Whalen, 2009).

One interpretation of these data is that, in response to ambiguous surprised expressions, a regulatory override message from the ventral region of the mPFC is required to interpret these faces as positively valenced. Inherent in this assertion is the presumption that initial amygdala activation is part of an early default negative interpretation of surprised faces in all participants, after which some participants are able to regulate the initial amygdala response and respond more positively. Such a hypothesis is consistent with data showing that participants take longer to ascribe a positive rating to these faces compared to a negative rating (Neta et al., 2009), in that the prefrontal response would require additional time to reverse the initial amygdala reaction. A subsequent study showing that low spatial frequency (LSF) versions of surprised faces are rated as more negative compared to high spatial frequency (HSF) versions (Neta & Whalen, 2010) is potentially consistent with the hypothesized default negativity of surprise in that LSF versions of fearful expressions have been shown to more readily engage the amygdala (Vuilleumier, Armony, Driver, &

Dolan, 2001; 2003). In addition, surprised facial expressions presented in an unpredictable fashion (compared to consistent predictable presentations) produce greater amygdala and corrugator responses, presumably related to more negative interpretations of these faces (Davis et al., 2016). Finally, when surprised faces serve as the infrequent stimulus in an oddball paradigm, they are detected more readily when the more frequent expression presented is a happy expression (i.e., positive context) compared to an angry expression (i.e., negative context)—presumably because the default negativity of surprise makes them more of an "oddball" adjacent to happy versus angry expressions (Neta, Davis, & Whalen, 2011).

The aforementioned four data sets are consistent with the notion that initial amygdala responses to surprised expressions are part of a default negativity response (see Kim et al., 2003). Interestingly, a more recent study has used computer mouse tracking as a dependent measure to assess valence interpretations of surprised facial expressions as either positive or negative in nature—rather than simple button presses (See Fig. 13.2; Mattek et al., 2016). This technique offers an alternative dependent measure that can provide reaction time information as well as the tendency to deviate toward the "alternative" choice while making an "ultimate" choice. So, for example, for participants selecting the negative option, mouse movements would also assess the degree to which their hand deviated toward the positive option while they ultimately selected a negative interpretation, and vice versa. As a group, more participants showed higher mean negative ratings, and deviations toward the negative option were greatest when participants were selecting the positive option, consistent with the data presented earlier. That said, when participants' overall bias was taken into account (i.e., selected the negative or positive option most often), those who were more likely to interpret surprised faces as positive still gravitated to the positive option even when ultimately selecting the negative option—suggesting that even if a default bias to assume potential negativity when encountering a surprised conspecific exists, individual differences in interpretative bias exert a strong influence on response choice behavior during the decision phase. One possibility is that an individual who operates with a more positive bias is not regulating per se but requires less regulatory control and, thus, less prefrontal input to interpret ambiguous affective events in a more positive light.

It is critical to note that skin conductance responses in participants rating surprise as negative or positive do not differ (Neta et al., 2009). Thus, surprised facial expressions uniquely offer the field the opportunity to study an emotional stimulus where arousal could be held constant and valence could be studied, or vice versa. To the extent that one was interested in behavioral and/or physiological/neural responses to the dimensions of arousal and valence, surprised expressions can do this in a way where these dimensions will not be confounded. Recently, we have devised a mathematical model that captures the relationship between subjective ratings of valence and arousal and demonstrate the utility of using surprised facial expressions to explore the critical role of valence ambiguity to this relationship (Mattek, Wolford & Whalen, In Press).

Pragmatically, these data suggest that future studies could utilize surprised faces as presented stimuli as part of a simple, innocuous strategy to measure individual differences in valence bias and the engagement of prefrontal-amygdala circuitry. Failure of such regulation is thought to be at the heart of some anxiety disorders (e.g., Shin et al., 2005, 2009; Whalen et al., 2008) and the negativity bias that accompanies major depression (e.g., Alloy & Abramson, 1979; Bouhuys, Geerts, & Gordijn, 1999; Fales et al., 2008; Johnstone, van Reekum, Urry, Kalin, & Davidson, 2007; Ramel et al., 2007).

USING FACIAL EXPRESSIONS TO ASSESS AMYGDALA–PREFRONTAL INTERACTIONS

Clearly, we view positive valence interpetations of surprised facial expressions as an example of a behavioral outcome that results from prefrontal cortical regulation of amygdala activity (see Whalen, 2007). The amygdala and medial prefrontal cortex (mPFC), among other brain regions, play a central role in behavioral phenomena that are highlighted by the competition between bottom-up and top-down processes, such as emotion regulation, fear conditioning, and extinction (Bishop, 2007; Ochsner & Gross, 2005; Quirk & Beer, 2006). Importantly, the amygdala is known to be heavily interconnected with multiple regions within the mPFC, including the orbital cortex and anterior cingulate cortex (see Freese & Amaral, 2009; Ghashghaei, Hilgetag, & Barbas, 2007). It is hypothesized that the mPFC regulates and controls amygdala output as part of the top-down control mechanism that keeps bottom-up signals in check (Bishop, 2007; Morgan, Romanski, & Ledoux, 1993; Ochsner & Gross, 2005; Quirk & Beer, 2006). Although numerous studies have assessed the separate contributions the amygdala and mPFC make to bottom-up and top-down interactions in emotion, respectively (Bishop, Duncan, Brett, & Lawrence, 2004; Bishop, Duncan, & Lawrence, 2004; Simmons et al., 2008; Simpson, Drevets, Snyder, Gusnard, & Raichle, 2001; Straube, Schmidt, Weiss, Mentzel, & Miltner, 2009), more recent studies suggest that the structural and functional connectivity between these two regions is a better predictor of these outcomes than the activity of either region alone (Kim & Whalen, 2009; Kim et al., 2011; Pezawas et al., 2005).

AMYGDALA-PREFRONTAL CIRCUITRY, FACES, AND ANXIETY

Anxiety is characterized by chronic, nonspecific apprehension and arousal related to the potential occurrence of future threat (Eysenck, 1992; Rosen & Schulkin, 1998). Based on the findings highlighting the importance of both the amygdala and mPFC regions in anxiety, a number of facial expression studies have investigated amygdala-mPFC circuitry in conjunction with assessing anxiety using functional and structural connectivity measures (Kim et al., 2011; 2016; Kim & Whalen, 2009; Pezawas et al., 2005). For example, individuals with anxious temperaments had weaker functional coupling between the amygdala and the vmPFC during a task that involved matching fearful and angry faces (Pezawas et al., 2005). Using diffusion tensor imaging (DTI), we demonstrated that individual differences in functional amygdala responses to presentations of fearful facial expressions correlated with the strength of a structural white matter connection between the amygdala and the mPFC (Kim & Whalen, 2009). Furthermore, the greater strength of this pathway predicted lower levels of anxiety in this group of healthy participants. Critically, we have recently replicated this effect in a large sample and show that this effect is strongest in female participants (Kim, et al., 2016). Notably, in our original study (Kim & Whalen, 2009), we also demonstrated that amygdala reactions to fearful faces did not show a significant relationship with reported anxiety, suggesting that amygdala–prefrontal connectivity may be a better predictor of this behavioral outcome rather than amygdala responses to overt fearful faces themselves. Interestingly, amygdala responses to masked fearful faces do correlate with reported anxiety (Etkin et al., 2004) as do amygdala responses to neutral faces (Somerville et al., 2004), suggesting that the activity of the amygdala may be more related to anxiety when the potential threat posed by presented faces is evaluated more implicitly, rather than explicitly.

As noted earlier, using facial expressions as presented stimuli represents a convenient strategy to recruit amygdala and prefrontal regions engaged during emotional regulation. This point is even more germane to the study of psychopathology. As we have argued, images of facial expressions as experimental stimuli are innocuous. They do not produce a strong emotional response in the moment and thus are a useful experimental choice for the study of patient groups where high arousal responses are a key part of the symptomatology (e.g., posttraumatic stress disorder [PTSD]; panic disorder). Indeed, Shin and colleagues (2005) have demonstrated that the presentation of fearful expressions produces exaggerated amygdala and attenuated mPFC fMRI responses in participants with PTSD. Moreover, within the PTSD group, the degree of mPFC recruitment exquisitely predicted symptom severity where participants who showed greater mPFC activation in response to fearful expressions showed fewer symptoms (Shin et al., 2005).

Amygdala-mPFC responses to fearful facial expressions have been used in a study of individuals with generalized anxiety disorder (GAD) to determine if we could use these data to predict treatment response (Whalen et al., 2008). Participants with GAD who were about to start SNRI treatment for 8 weeks first underwent fMRI where they viewed fearful and neutral facial expressions. Eight weeks later their anxiety levels were measured in comparison to their pretreatment anxiety levels. Pretreatment amygdala-prefrontal cortex responses were shown to predict beneficial decreases in anxiety with treatment—participants who showed lower amygdala and higher mPFC responses showed a greater decrease in anxiety over the 8 weeks, while participants who showed high amygdala–low prefrontal activity, showed modest decreases in anxiety (Whalen et al., 2008). While this was a preliminary study in one disorder (GAD) with only one dose of one drug (venlafaxine), it offers the promise that if enough treatment types (e.g., drugs, therapy) across enough disorders are studied, we may one day be able to use neuroimaging to make treatment recommendations for individuals with anxiety disorders.

CONCLUSIONS

Studies reviewed here sought to define dimensional constructs (e.g., valence, arousal, ambiguity) that might explain human amygdala responses to specific facial expressions of emotion (i.e., fearful, angry, and surprised). Existing data show that the amygdala can solely track arousal in some instances (Anderson, Christoff, Panitz, De Rosa, & Gabrieli, 2003; Canli, Zhao, Brewer, Gabrieli, & Cahill, 2000; Demos, Kelley, Ryan, Davis, & Whalen, 2008; Garavan, Pendergrass, Ross, Stein, & Risinger, 2001; Kensinger & Schacter, 2006; Lewis, Critchley, Rothstein, & Dolan, 2007; Somerville, Wig, Whalen, & Kelley, 2006; Williams et al., 2004) and valence in others (Anders, Lotze, Erb, Grodd, & Birbaumer, 2004; Kim et al., 2003, 2004; Pessoa, Padmala, & Morlan, 2005; Straube, Pohlack, Mentzel, & Miltner, 2008). With specific reference to facial expressions, surprised expressions were utilized to demonstrate that the amygdala can simultaneously track both arousal and valence (Kim et al., 2003; see also Whalen et al., 1998, and Winston, Gottfried, Kilner, & Dolan, 2005) and offer a strategy to explore the relationship between subjective ratings of valence and arousal in terms of the valence ambiguity of a given presented stimulus item (Mattek, Wolford & Whalen, In Press). One study even set arousal and valence aside for a moment, by equating presented fearful and angry faces on these dimensions, to show that predictive ambiguity per se can also modulate amygdala responsivity (Davis et al., 2016; Herry et al., 2007; Whalen et al., 2001).

The main aim of this review was to show the fruitfulness of using facial expressions as experimental stimuli in order to study how neural systems support biologically relevant learning as it relates to social interactions. Though use of these stimuli means we will lack the ability to control for reinforcement history, it is this history that will give rise to individual differences in neural responsivity and subsequent behavior. Finally, facial expressions offer a relatively innocuous strategy with which to investigate normal variations in affective processing, as well as the promise of elucidating what role the aberrance of such processing might play in emotional disorders (Armony et al., 2005; Bouhuys et al., 1999; Fales et al., 2008; Rauch et al., 2000; Sheline et al., 2001; Shin et al., 2005).

ACKNOWLEDGMENTS

Preparation of this manuscript was supported by funding from the National Institute of Mental Health of the National Institutes of Health, grant number 2R01MH087016.

REFERENCES

Adolphs, R., Gosselin, F., Buchanan, T. W., Tranel, D., Schyns, P., & Damasio, A. R. (2005). A mechanism for impaired fear recognition after amygdala damage. *Nature, 433*(7021), 68–72.

Adolphs, R., Tranel, D., Damasio, A. R., & Damasio, H. (1994). Impaired recognition of emotion in facial expressions following bilateral damage to the human amygdala. *Nature, 372*, 669–672.

Alloy, L. B., & Abramson, L. Y. (1979). Judgment of contingency in depressed and non-depressed students: Sadder but wiser? *Journal of Experimental Psychology General, 108*, 441–485.

Anders, S., Lotze, M., Erb, M., Grodd, W., & Birbaumer, N. (2004). Brain activity underlying emotional valence and arousal: A response-related fMRI study. *Human Brain Mapping, 23*, 200–209.

Anderson, A. K., Christoff, K., Panitz, D., De Rosa, E., & Gabrieli, J. D. (2003). Neural correlates of the automatic processing of threat facial signals. *Journal of Neuroscience, 23*(13), 5627–5633.

Armony, J. L., Corbo, V., Clement, M. H., & Brunet, A. (2005). Amygdala response in patients with acute PTSD to masked and unmasked emotional facial expressions. *American Journal of Psychiatry, 162*(10), 1961–1963.

Balaban, M. T. (1995). Affective influences on startle in five month old infants: Reactions to facial expressions of emotion. *Child Development, 66*, 28–36.

Baron-Cohen, S., Ring, H. A., Wheelwright, S., Bullmore, E. T., Brammer, M. J., Simmons, A., & Williams, S. C. R. (1999). Social intelligence in the normal and autistic brain: An fMRI study. *European Journal of Neuroscience, 11*, 1891–1898.

Bishop, S. J. (2007). Neurocognitive mechanisms of anxiety: An integrative account. *Trends in Cognitive Science, 11*, 307–316.

Bishop, S. J., Duncan, J., Brett, M., & Lawrence, A. D. (2004). Prefrontal cortical function and anxiety: Controlling attention to threat-related stimuli. *Nature Neuroscience, 7*, 184–188.

Bishop, S. J., Duncan, J., & Lawrence, A. D. (2004). State anxiety modulation of the amygdala response to unattended threat-related stimuli. *Journal of Neuroscience, 24*, 10364–10368.

Bouhuys, A. L., Geerts, E., & Gordijn, M. C. M. (1999). Depressed patients' perceptions of facial emotions in depressed and remitted states are associated with relapse. *Journal of Nervous Mental Disorders, 187*, 595–602.

Breiter, H. C., Etcoff, N. L., Whalen, P. J., Kennedy, W. A., Rauch, S. L., Buckner, R. L., . . . Rosen, B. R. (1996). Response and habituation of the human amygdala during visual processing of facial expression. *Neuron, 17*(5), 875–887.

Broks, P., Young, A. W., Maratos, E. J., Coffey, P. J., Calder, A. J., Isaac, C. L., . . . Hadley, D. (1998). Face processing impairments after encephalitis: Amygdala damage and recognition of fear. *Neuropsychologia, 36*(1), 59–70.

Canli, T., Zhao, Z., Brewer, J., Gabrieli, J. D. E., & Cahill, L. (2000). Event-related activation in the human amygdala associates with later memory for individual emotional experience. *Journal of Neuroscience, 20*(19): RC99.

Davis, F. C., Johnstone, T., Mazzulla, E. C., Oler, J. A., & Whalen, P. J. (2010). Regional response differences across the human amygdaloid complex during social conditioning. *Cerebral Cortex, 20*, 612–621.

Davis, F. C., Neta, M., Kim, M. J., Moran, J., & Whalen, P. J. (2016). Interpreting ambiguous social cues in unpredictable contexts. *Social, Cognitive and Affective Neuroscience, 11*, 775–782

Davis, F. C., Somerville, L. H., Ruberry, E. J., Berry, A., Shin, L. M., & Whalen, P. J. (2011). A tale of two negatives: Differential memory effects associated with fearful and angry facial expressions. *Emotion, 11*, 647–655.

Demos, K. E., Kelley, W. M., Ryan, S. L., Davis, F. C., & Whalen, P. J. (2008). Human Amygdala Sensitivity to the Pupil Size of Others. *Cerebral Cortex, 18*(12), 2729–2734.

Dimberg, U. (1982). Facial reactions to facial expressions. *Psychophysiology, 19*(6), 643–647.

Ekman, P., Davidson, R. J., & Friesen, W. V. (1990). The Duchenne smile: Emotional expression and brain physiology: II. *Journal of Personality and Social Psychology, 58*(2), 342–353.

Ekman, P., Levenson, R. W., & Friesen, W. V. (1983). Autonomic nervous system activity distinguishes among emotions. *Science, 221*(4616), 1208–1210.

Etkin, A., Klemenhagen, K. C., Dudman, J. T., Rogan, M. T., Hen, R., Kandel, E. R., & Hirsh, J. (2004). Individual differences in trait anxiety predict the response of the basolateral amygdala to unconsciously processed fearful faces. *Neuron, 44*(6), 1043–1055.

Eysenck, M. (1992). *Anxiety: The cognitive perspective*. Hillsdale, NJ: Erlbaum.

Fales, C. L., Barch, D. M., Rundle, M. M., Mintun, M. A., Snyder, A. Z., Cohen, J. D., . . . Sheline, Y. L. (2008). Altered emotional processing in affective and cognitive-control brain circuitry in major depression. *Biological Psychiatry, 63*, 377–384.

Fitzgerald, D. A., Angstadt, M., Jelsone, L. M., Nathan, P. J., & Phan, K. L. (2006). Beyond threat: Amygdala reactivity across multiple expressions of facial affect. *Neuroimage, 30*(4), 1441–1448.

Freese, J., & Amaral, D. (2009). Neuroanatomy of the primate amygdala. In P. J. Whalen & E. A. Phelps (Eds.), *The human amygdala*. New York, NY: Guilford.

Gallagher, M., & Holland, P. C. (1994). The amygdala complex: Multiple roles in associative learning and attention. *Proceedings of the National Academy of Sciences, 91*, 11771–11776.

Garavan, H., Pendergrass, J. C., Ross, T. J., Stein, E. A., & Risinger, R. C. (2001). Amygdala response to both positively and negatively valenced stimuli. *Neuroreport, 12*, 2779–2783.

Gee, D. G. & Whalen, P. J. (2014). The amygdala: relations to biologically relevant learning and development. In: M. Gazzaniga (Ed.). *The New Cognitive Neurosciences, Fifth Edition (pp. 741-750)*. Cambridge, MA: MIT Press.

Ghashghaei, H. T., Hilgetag, C. C., & Barbas, H. (2007). Sequence of information processing for emotions based on the anatomic dialogue between prefrontal cortex and amygdala. *Neuroimage, 34*(3), 905–923.

Hamann, S. B., & Adolphs, R. (1999). Normal recognition of emotional similarity between facial expressions following bilateral amygdala damage. *Neuropsychologia, 37*(10), 1135–1141.

Hare, T. A., Tottenham, N., Galvan, A., Voss, H. U., Glover, G. H., & Casey, B. J. (2008). Biological substrates of emotional reactivity and regulation in adolescence during an emotional go-nogo task. *Biological Psychiatry, 14*(2), 190–204.

Hariri, A. R., Bookheimer, S. Y., & Mazziotta, J. C. (2000). Modulating emotional responses: Effects of a neocortical network on the limbic system. *Neuroreport, 11*(1), 43–48.

Hariri, A. R., Mattay, V. S., Tessitore, A., Kolachana, B., Fera, F., Goldman, D., . . .Weinberger, D. R. (2002). Serotonin transporter genetic variation and the response of the human amygdala. *Science, 297*, 400–403.

Harrison, N. A., Singer, T., Rotshtein, P. Dolan, R. J., & Critchley, H. D. (2006) Pupillary contagion: Central mechanisms engaged in sadness processing. *Soc Cognitive Affect Neuroscience, 1*, 5–17.

Herry, C., Bach, D. R., Esposito, F., Di Salle, F., Perrig, W. J., Scheffler, K., . . . Seifritz, E. (2007). Processing of temporal unpredictability in human and animal amygdala. *Journal of Neuroscience*, 27(22), 5958–5966.

Jackson, D. C., Malmstadt, J. R., Larson, C. L., & Davidson, R. J. (2000). Suppression and enhancement of emotion responses to unpleasant pictures. *Psychophysiology, 37*(4), 515–522.

Johnsen, B. H., Thayer, J. F., & Hugdahl, K. (1995). Affective judgment of the Ekman faces: A dimensional approach. *Journal of Psychophysiology, 9*, 193–202.

Johnstone, T., van Reekum, C. M., Urry, H. L., Kalin, N. H., & Davidson, R. J. (2007). Failure to regulate: Counterproductive recruitment of top-down prefrontal-subcortical circuitry in major depression. *Journal of Neuroscience, 27*, 8877–8884.

Junghöfer, M., Sabatinelli, D., Bradley, M. M., Schupp, H. T., Elbert, T. R., & Lang, P. J. (2006). Fleeting images: Rapid affect discrimination in the visual cortex. *Neuroreport, 17*(2), 225–229.

Kapp, B. S., Whalen, P. J., Supple, W. F., & Pascoe, J. P. (1992). Amygdaloid contributions to conditioned arousal and sensory information processing. In J. P. Aggelton (Ed.), *The amygdala: Neurobiological aspects of emotion, memory, and mental dysfunction* (pp. 229–254). New York, NY: Wiley-Liss.

Kensinger, E. A., & Schacter, D. L. (2006). Processing emotional pictures and words: Effects of valence and arousal. *Cognitive, Affective, and Behavioral Neuroscience, 6*, 110–126.

Kennedy, S. H., Konarski, J. Z., Segal, Z. V., Lau, M. A., Bieling, P. J., McIntyre, R. S., & Mayberg, H. S. (2007). Differences in brain glucose metabolism between responders to CBT and venlafaxine in a 16-week randomized controlled trial. *American Journal of Psychiatry, 164*(5), 778–788.

Kim, H., Somerville, L. H., Johnstone, T., Alexander, A. L., & Whalen, P. J. (2003). Inverse amygdala and medial prefrontal cortex responses to surprised faces. *Neuroreport, 14*(18), 2317–2322.

Kim, H., Somerville, L. H., Johnstone, T., Polis, S., Alexander, A. L., Shin, L. M. & Whalen, P.J. (2004). Contextual modulation of amygdala responsivity to surprised faces. *Journal of Cognitive Neuroscience, 16*, 1730–1745.

Kim, M. J., Brown, A. C., Mattek, A. M., Chavez, S. J., Taylor, J. M., Palmer, A. L., . . . Whalen, P. J. (2016). The inverse relationship between the microstructural variability of amygdala-prefrontal pathways and trait anxiety is moderated by sex. *Frontiers in Systems Neuroscience, 10*, 93. dx.doi.org/10.3389/fnsys.2016.00093.

Kim, M. J., Gee, D. G., Loucks, R. A., Davis, F. C., & Whalen, P. J. (2011). Anxiety dissociates dorsal and ventral medial prefrontal cortex functional connectivity with the amygdala at rest. *Cerebral Cortex, 21*, 1667–1673.

Kim, M. J., Loucks, R. A., Neta, M., Davis, F. C., Oler, J. A., Mazzulla, E. C., & Whalen, P. J. (2010). Behind the mask: The influence of mask-type on amygdala response to fearful faces. *Social Cognitive and Affective Neuroscience, 5*, 363–368.

Kim, M. J., Neta, M., Davis, F. C., Ruberry, E. J., Dinescu, D., Heatherton, T. F., . . . Whalen, P. J. (2014). Botulinum toxin-induced facial muscle paralysis affects amygdala responses to the perception of emotional expressions: Preliminary findings from an A-B-A design. *Biology of Mood and Anxiety Disorders, 4*, 11. doi:10.1186/2045-5380-4-11.

Kim, M. J., Solomon, K. M., Neta, M., Davis, F. C., Oler, J. A., Mazzulla, E. C. & Whalen, P. J. (2016). A face versus non-face context influences amygdala responses to masked fearful eye whites. *Social Cognitive and Affective Neuroscience, 11*, 1933-1941.

Kim, M. J., & Whalen, P. J. (2009). The structural integrity of an amygdala-prefrontal pathway predicts trait anxiety. *Journal of Neuroscience, 29*, 11614–11618.

Klin, A. (2000). Attributing social meaning to ambiguous visual stimuli in higher functioning autism and Asperger syndrome: The social attribution task. *Journal of Child Psychology and Psychiatry, 41*(7), 831–846.

LeDoux, J. E. (1996). *The emotional brain: The mysterious underpinnings of emotional life*. New York, NY: Simon & Schuster.

Lewis, P. A., Critchley, H. D., Rotshtein, P., & Dolan, R. J. (2007). Neural correlates of processing valence and arousal in affective words. *Cerebral Cortex, 17*, 742–748.

Mattek, A. M., Whalen, P. J., Berkowitz, J. L., & Freeman, J. M. (2016). Differential effects of cognitive load on subjective versus motor responses to ambiguously valenced facial expressions. *Emotion, 16*, 929-936.

Mattek, A. M., Wolford, G. & Whalen, P. J. (In Press). A mathematical model captures the structure of subjective affect. *Perspectives in Psychological Science.*

Morgan, M. A., Romanski, L. M., & LeDoux, J. E. (1993). Extinction of emotional learning: contribution of medial prefrontal cortex. *Neuroscience Letters, 163*, 109–113.

Morris, J. S., Frith, C. D., Perrett, D. I., Rowland, D., Young, A. W., Calder, A. J., & Dolan, R. J. (1996). A differential neural response in the human amygdala to fearful and happy facial expressions. *Nature, 383*, 812–814.

Morris, J. S., Öhman, A., & Dolan, R. J. (1998). Conscious and unconscious emotional learning in the human amygdala. *Nature, 393*(6684), 467–470.

Morris, J. S., Öhman, A., & Dolan, R. J. (1999). A subcorticol pathway to the right amygdala mediating "unseen" fear. *Proceedings of the National Academy of Sciences, 96*(4), 1680–1685.

Neta, M., Davis, F. C., & Whalen, P.J. (2011). Valence resolution of ambiguous facial expressions using an emotional odd-ball task. *Emotion, 11*(6), 1425–1433.

Neta, M., Norris, C. J., & Whalen, P. J. (2009). Corrugator muscle responses are associated with individual differences in positivity-negativity bias. *Emotion, 9*, 640–648.

Neta, M., & Whalen, P. J. (2010). The primacy of negative interpretations when resolving the valence of ambiguous facial expressions. *Psychology Science, 21*, 901–907.

Ochsner, K. N., & Gross, J. J. (2005). The cognitive control of emotion. *Trends in Cognitive Science, 9*, 242–249.

Öhman, A., & Dimberg, U. (1978). Facial expressions as conditioned stimuli for electrodermal responses: A case of "preparedness"? *Journal of Personality and Social Psychology, 36*(11), 1251–1258.

Osterling, J., & Dawson, G. (1994). Early recognition of children with autism: A study of first birthday home video tapes. *Journal of Autism and Developmental Disorders, 24*, 247–257.

Paton, J. J., Belova, M. A., Morrison, S. E., & Salzman, C. D. (2006). The primate amygdala represents the positive and negative value of visual stimuli during learning. *Nature, 439*, 865–870.

Pelphrey, K. A., Sasson, N. J., Reznick, J. S., Paul, G., Goldman, B., & Piven, J. (2002). Visual scanning of faces in autism. *Journal of Autism and Developmental Disorders, 32*(4), 249–261.

Pessoa, L., Padmala, S., & Morlan, T. (2005). Fate of unattended fearful faces in the amygdala is determined by both attentional resources and cognitive modulation. *Neuroimage, 28*, 249–255.

Pezawas, L., Meyer-Lindenberg, A., Drabant, E. M., Verchinski, B. A., Munoz, K. E., Kolachana, B. S., . . . Weinberger, D. R. (2005). 5-HTTLPR polymorphism impacts human cingulate-amygdala interactions: A genetic susceptibility mechanism for depression. *Nature Neuroscience, 8*, 828–34.

Phillips, M. L., Young, A. W., Senior, C., Brammer, M., Andrew, C., Calder, A.J., et al. (1997). A specific neural substrate for perceiving facial expressions of disgust. *Nature, 389*(6650), 495–498.

Quirk, G. J., & Beer, J. S. (2006). Prefrontal involvement in the regulation of emotion: convergence of rat and human studies. *Current Opinion Neurobiology, 16*, 723–727.

Ramel, W., Goldin, P. R., Eyler, L. T., Brown, G. G, Gotlib, I. H., & McQuaid, J. R. (2007). Amygdala reactivity and mood-congruent memory in individuals at risk for depressive relapse. *Biological Psychiatry, 61*, 231–239.

Rauch, S. L., Shin, L. M., & Phelps, E. A. (2006). Neurocircuitry models of posttraumatic stress disorder and extinction: Human neuroimaging research—past, present, and future. *Biological Psychiatry, 60*, 376–382.

Rauch, S. L., Whalen, P. J., Shin, L. M., McInerney, S. C., Macklin, M. L., Lasko, N. B., . . . Pitman, R. K. (2000). Exaggerated amygdala response to masked facial stimuli in posttraumatic stress disorder: A functional MRI study. *Biological Psychiatry, 47*, 769–776.

Rosen, J. B., & Schulkin, J. (1998). From normal fear to pathological anxiety. *Psychology Review, 105*, 325–350.

Schultz, R. T. (2005). Developmental deficits in social perception in autism: The role of the amygdala and fusiform face area. *International Journal of Developmental Neuroscience, 23*, 125–141.

Sheline, Y. I., Barch, D. M., Donnelly, J. M., Ollinger, J. M., Snyder, A. Z., & Mintun, M. A. (2001). Increased amygdala response to masked emotional faces in depressed subjects resolves with antidepressant treatment: An fMRI study. *Biological Psychiatry, 50*(9), 651–658.

Shin, L. M., & Handwerger, K. (2009). Is posttraumatic stress disorder a stress-induced fear circuitry disorder? *Journal of Trauma Stress, 22*, 409–415.

Shin, L. M., Wright, C. I., Cannistraro, P., Wedig, M., McMullin, K., Martis, B., . . . Rauch, S. L. (2005). A functional magnetic resonance imaging study of amygdala and medial prefrontal cortex responses to overtly presented fearful faces in posttraumatic stress disorder. *Archives in General Psychiatry, 62*(3), 273–281.

Simmons, A., Matthews, S. C., Feinstein, J. S., Hitchcock, C., Paulus, M. P., & Stein, M.B. (2008). Anxiety vulnerability is associated with altered anterior cingulate response to an affective appraisal task. *Neuroreport, 19*, 1033–1037.

Simpson, J. R., Jr., Drevets, W. C., Snyder, A. Z., Gusnard, D. A., & Raichle, M. E. (2001). Emotion-induced changes in human medial prefrontal cortex: II. During anticipatory anxiety. *Proceedings of the National Academy of Sciences USA, 98*, 688–693.

Slagter, H. A., Davidson, R. J., & Lutz, A. (2011). Mental training as a tool in the neuroscientific study of brain and cognitive plasticity. *Frontiers in Human Neuroscience, 5*(17), 1–12.

Somerville, L. H., Kim, H., Johnstone, T., Alexander, A. L., & Whalen, P. J. (2004). Human amygdala responses during presentation of happy and neutral faces: Correlations with state anxiety. *Biological Psychiatry, 55*(9), 897–903.

Somerville, L. H., Wig, G. S., Whalen, P. J., & Kelley, W. M. (2006). Dissociable medial temporal lobe contributions to social memory. *Journal of Cognitive Neuroscience, 18*, 1253–1265.

Straube, T., Pohlack, S., Mentzel, H. J., & Miltner, W. H. (2008). Differential amygdala activation to negative and positive emotional pictures during an indirect task. *Behavioral Brain Research, 191*, 285–288.

Straube, T., Schmidt, S., Weiss, T., Mentzel, H. J., & Miltner, W. H. (2009). Dynamic activation of the anterior cingulate cortex during anticipatory anxiety. *Neuroimage, 44*, 975–981.

Taylor, J.M. & Whalen, P.J. (2014). Fearful, but not angry, facial expressions diffuse attention to peripheral targets in the attentional blink paradigm. *Emotion*, 14, 462-468.

Tomkins, S. S., & McCarter, R. (1964). What and where are the primary affects? Some evidence for a theory. *Perceptual and Motor Skills, 18*, 119–158.

Tottenham, N., Hare, T. A., & Casey, B. J. (2009). A developmental perspective on human amygdala function. In P. J. Whalen and E. A. Phelps (Eds.), *The human amygdala* (pp. 107–117). New York, NY: The Guilford Press.

Tottenham, N., Hare, T. A., Millner, A., Gilhooly, T., Zevin, J. D., & Casey, B. J. (2011). Elevated amygdala response to faces following early deprivation. *Developmental Science, 14*(2), 190–204.

Vanderploeg, R. D., Brown, W. S., & Marsh, J. T. (1987). Judgments of emotion in words and face: ERP correlates. *International Journal of Psychophysiology, 5(3), 193–205.*

Vuilleumier, P., Armony, J. L., Driver, J., & Dolan, R. J. (2001). Effects of attention and emotion on face processing in the human brain: An event-related fMRI study. *Neuron, 30*(3), 829–841.

Vuilleumier, P., Armony, J. L., Driver, J., & Dolan, R.J. (2003). Distinct spatial frequency sensitivities for processing faces and emotion expressions. *Nature Neuroscience, 6*, 624–631.

Weisz, D. J., Harden, D. G., & Xiang, Z. (1992). Effects of amygdala lesions on reflex facilitation and conditioned response acquisition during nictitating membrane response conditioning in rabbit. *Behavioral Neuroscience, 106*(2), 262–273.

Whalen, P. J. (1998). Fear, vigilance, and ambiguity: Initial neuroimaging studies of the human amygdala. *Current Directions in Psychological Science, 7*(6), 177–188.

Whalen, P. J. (2007). The uncertainty of it all. *Trends in Cognitive Science*, 11, 499-500.

Whalen, P. J., Davis, F. C., Oler, J. A., Kim, H., Justin, M. J., & Neta, M. (2009). Human amygdala responses to facial expressions of emotion (pp. 265–288). In P. J. Whalen and E. A. Phelps (Eds.), *The human amygdala* (pp. 265–288). New York, NY: The Guilford Press.

Whalen, P. J., Johnstone, T., Somerville, L. H., Nitschke, J. B., Polis, S., Alexander, A. L., . . . Kalin, N. H. (2008). A functional magnetic resonance imaging predictor of treatment response to venlafaxine in generalized anxiety disorder. *Biological Psychiatry, 63*(9), 858–863.

Whalen, P. J., Kagan, J., Cook, R. G., Davis, F. C., Kim, H., Polis, S., . . . Johnstone, T. (2004). Human amygdala responsivity to masked fearful eye-whites. *Science, 306*(5704), 2061.

Whalen, P. J., Rauch, S. L., Etcoff, N. L., McInerney, S. C., Lee, M. B., & Jenike, M. A. (1998). Masked presentations of emotional facial expressions modulate amygdala activity without explicit knowledge. *Journal of Neuroscience, 18*(1), 411–418.

Whalen, P. J., Shin, L. M., McInerney, S. C., & Fischer, H. (2001). A functional MRI study of human amygdala responses to facial expressions of fear versus anger. *Emotion, 1*(1), 70–83.

Williams, M. A., Morris A. P., McGlone, F., Abbott, D. F., & Mattingly, J. B. (2004). Amygdala responses to fearful and happy expressions under conditions of binocular suppression. *Journal of Neuroscience, 24*, 2898–2904.

Winston, J. S., Gottfried, J. A., Kilner, J. M, & Dolan, R. J. (2005). Integrated neural representations of odor intensity and affective valence in human amygdala. *Journal of Neuroscience, 25*, 8903–8907.

Yang, T. T., Menon, V., Eliez, S., Blasey, C., White, C. D., Reid, A. J., . . . Reiss, A. L. (2002). Amygdalar activation associated with positive and negative facial expressions. *Neuroreport, 13*(14), 1737–1741.

14

Using Facial Expressions to Probe Brain Circuitry Associated With Anxiety and Depression

JOHNNA R. SWARTZ, LISA M. SHIN, BRENDA LEE, AND AHMAD R. HARIRI

Every day, we encounter an array of human faces that convey information regarding the relative safety of our environments. Smiling, happy faces tell us that we are likely safe from immediate threats. Angry and fearful expressions, on the other hand, are unique in that they often convey information critical for our survival. Angry facial expressions are clear indicators of threat and its source, and fearful facial expressions are indicators of threat, but without a clear source, thus prompting a search for additional information to inform an appropriate response. Our interpretation of and responses to threat cues, like angry and fearful facial expressions, usually help us to navigate the social and physical world; however, for some people, such as those with anxiety or mood disorders, these interpretations and/or responses become exaggerated and impairing.

When presented during functional magnetic resonance imaging (fMRI), facial expressions elicit activation within a distributed neural circuitry, including regions associated with visual processing (the occipital cortex and the fusiform gyrus), emotion processing (the amygdala and the insula), evaluating the significance of emotional stimuli (the orbitofrontal cortex [OFC]), mentalizing or self-referential processing (the dorsomedial prefrontal cortex [dmPFC] and ventromedial prefrontal cortex [vmPFC]), and integrating and regulating responses to emotional stimuli (the dorsolateral prefrontal cortex [dlPFC], ventrolateral prefrontal cortex [vlPFC], and anterior cingulate cortex [ACC]) (Fusar-Poli et al., 2009). Tasks used to examine the functioning of this circuitry can include explicit emotion processing tasks, such as labeling the expression of emotional faces, as well as implicit tasks, such as passive viewing, gender identification, or perceptual matching. Of prime interest in studies of mood and anxiety disorder patients are the amygdala and the prefrontal cortex, given their roles in threat detection and higher order cognitive processing, respectively. We begin by reviewing evidence for altered brain circuit function in response to facial expressions within specific categorical disorders.

ANXIETY DISORDERS

Social Anxiety Disorder

Given that social anxiety disorder (SAD) is marked by a fear of negative evaluation and criticism from others, one might predict that individuals with this disorder would be more responsive to facial expressions signaling negative evaluation (e.g., anger, contempt). Indeed, this appears to be the case at the level of both behavior and the brain (e.g., Arrais et al., 2010).

Several studies have reported exaggerated amygdala activation in response to facial expressions of anger, contempt, or fear in individuals with SAD relative to comparison subjects (e.g., Blair et al., 2008; Phan, Fitzgerald, Nathan, & Tancer, 2006; Stein, Goldin, Sareen, Zorrilla, & Brown, 2002; Straube, Kolassa, Glauer, Mentzel, & Miltner, 2004). Furthermore, amygdala activation to these faces was positively correlated with severity of SAD symptoms (Goldin, Manber, Hakimi, Canli, & Gross, 2009; Phan et al., 2006) and severity of anxiety (Blair et al., 2008). In the context of an aversive conditioning study in which neutral faces predicted an aversive unconditioned stimulus, patients with SAD displayed greater amygdala, insula, anterior cingulate, and orbitofrontal activation to these conditioned face stimuli compared to healthy controls (Veit et al., 2002). Some studies have reported exaggerated amygdala activation in response to neutral faces in social anxiety disorder (Cooney, Atlas, Joormann, Eugene, & Gotlib, 2006), as well as a positive correlation between this amygdala activation and anxiety severity (Cooney et al., 2006; but see also Stein et al., 2002; Straube, Mentzel, & Miltner, 2005), suggesting that even relatively less expressive faces can be interpreted as threatening in SAD (Winton, Clark, & Edelmann, 1995). This finding is important from a methodological standpoint because neutral faces are often used in baseline conditions. Thus, a failure to find amygdala activation in response to angry versus neutral faces in SAD could be due to elevated activation in the neutral face condition.

Several studies have reported greater insular cortex responses to angry versus neutral or happy faces in SAD (e.g., Klumpp, Angstadt, & Phan, 2012; Straube et al., 2004). Even schematic line drawings of angry facial expressions are sufficient to elicit exaggerated insula activation in this disorder (Straube et al., 2004). Insula activation to angry/emotional faces appears to be positively correlated with SAD symptom severity (Carre et al., 2014; Klumpp, Post, Angstadt, Fitzgerald, & Phan, 2013).

Consistent with the role of the medial prefrontal cortex in self-referential processing (Kelley et al., 2002), individuals with SAD exhibit exaggerated medial prefrontal cortex responses to angry, contemptuous, fearful, or sad faces (Blair et al., 2008; Goldin et al., 2009; Stein et al., 2002; but see also Phan et al., 2013), and rostral ACC activation is positively correlated with SAD symptom severity (Blair et al., 2011). However, when required to ignore emotional faces, individuals with SAD have shown relatively diminished rostral ACC activation (Klumpp, Post et al., 2013). In a different paradigm involving explicit emotion regulation in response to angry and contemptuous faces, patients with SAD showed less activation in dorsal ACC, dorsolateral prefrontal cortex, and inferior frontal and orbitofrontal cortex than controls (Goldin et al., 2009; Ziv, Goldin, Jazaieri, Hahn, & Gross, 2013). Thus, in SAD, relatively diminished prefrontal activation may be apparent in conditions involving disengaging attention from emotional stimuli or purposefully regulating emotional responses.

If the amygdala, insula, and medial prefrontal cortex responses to threatening facial expressions are elevated in SAD, are positively correlated with symptom severity, and are state markers of illness, then successful treatment ought to be related to decreased activation in these brain regions. Indeed, amygdala and insula activation to fearful/angry facial expressions has been shown to decrease following treatment (Klumpp, Fitzgerald, & Phan, 2013; Phan et al., 2013; Schneier, Pomplun, Sy, & Hirsch, 2011; but see also Gimenez et al., 2014). The findings in medial prefrontal cortex have been more mixed (Klumpp, Fitzgerald et al., 2013; Phan et al., 2013).

Because not all patients with SAD respond to treatment, identifying pretreatment functional neuroimaging (or other objective) measures that predict treatment response would be clinically helpful (Shin, Davis, Vanelzakker, Dahlgren, & Dubois, 2013). Recent studies have found that lower pretreatment amygdala activation to emotional facial expressions predicted better response to cognitive-behavioral therapy (Klumpp, Fitzgerald, Angstadt, Post, & Phan, 2014). In addition, greater pretreatment medial prefrontal cortex activation to fearful versus happy faces or in the presence of emotional face distractors predicted greater improvement with cognitive-behavioral therapy (Klumpp et al., 2014; Klumpp, Fitzgerald et al., 2013).

Posttraumatic Stress Disorder

Several studies have reported greater amygdala responses to backwardly masked fearful facial expressions in posttraumatic stress disorder (PTSD) relative to comparison groups (e.g., Bryant, Kemp et al., 2008; Killgore et al., 2014; Rauch et al., 2000). This finding suggests that the amygdala is hyperresponsive to indicators of potential threat even when they are presented below conscious awareness. In addition, several studies found a positive correlation between PTSD symptom severity and amygdala activation in response to masked fearful or other emotional facial expressions (Armony, Corbo, Clement, & Brunet, 2005; Rauch et al., 2000; but see also Bryant, Kemp et al., 2008).

As with masked faces, several studies have reported exaggerated amygdala and/or insular cortex activation in response to consciously perceived fearful versus happy or neutral faces in PTSD compared to control groups (e.g., Garrett et al., 2012; Shin et al., 2005; Stevens et al., 2013). Amygdala activation to fearful versus neutral faces is positively correlated with hyperarousal symptom severity (Stevens et al., 2013). Furthermore, amygdala activation declines less over repeated presentations of fearful or angry facial expressions in PTSD, relative to comparison participants (Garrett et al., 2012; Shin et al., 2005).

In PTSD, the direction of medial prefrontal cortex responses to emotional facial expressions may depend on whether those expressions are presented below or above the threshold of awareness. Medial prefrontal cortex activations appear to be (1) exaggerated when facial expressions are presented below the threshold of awareness (Bryant, Kemp et al., 2008) and (2) diminished when facial expressions are presented above the threshold of awareness (Offringa et al., 2013; Shin et al., 2005; but see also Garrett et al., 2012). In the latter type of study, medial prefrontal cortex responses are negatively correlated with PTSD symptom severity (Offringa et al., 2013; Shin et al., 2005; but see also Garrett et al., 2012).

Although most studies have examined brain responses to fearful facial expressions in PTSD, one recent study used happy and neutral expressions to assess the brain basis of emotional numbing in this disorder. In this study, the authors found reduced activation in ventral striatum and amygdala (trend) to happy versus neutral facial expressions in PTSD, relative to trauma-exposed comparison participants. Furthermore, they found that degree of activation in the ventral striatum was negatively correlated with severity of emotional numbing (Felmingham et al., 2014). Thus, different facial expressions (e.g., fearful, happy) can be used to assess different symptom types in PTSD (hyperarousal, numbing symptoms, respectively).

Importantly, some of these brain activation abnormalities in response to emotional facial expressions can occur with exposure to trauma alone, even in the absence of a PTSD diagnosis (e.g., Dannlowski et al., 2012). This underscores the importance of including a trauma-exposed comparison group in imaging studies of PTSD.

According to the findings of one study, rostral ACC activation to unmasked fearful versus neutral facial expressions increased following successful cognitive-behavioral treatment in PTSD (Felmingham et al., 2007). Furthermore, correlational analyses demonstrated that greater increases in rostral ACC activation and greater decreases in amygdala activation with treatment were related to greater symptomatic improvement. In a prediction-of-treatment-response design, Bryant et al. (2008) found that lower pretreatment amygdala and rostral ACC activation to masked fearful versus neutral facial expressions predicted better response to cognitive-behavioral treatment in PTSD.

Generalized Anxiety Disorder

Several studies have found exaggerated amygdala activation in response to masked and unmasked fearful or angry (e.g., Fonzo et al., 2015; McClure, Monk et al., 2007; Monk et al., 2008) and even neutral facial expressions (Holzel et al., 2013) in generalized anxiety disorder (GAD); however, several other studies have not (e.g., Blair et al., 2008; Whalen et al., 2008).

Much less is known about ACC responses to emotional facial expressions in GAD. One study found greater ACC responses to fearful versus happy faces in pediatric GAD (McClure, Monk et al., 2007), and another found attenuated ACC response to happy faces in GAD (Palm, Elliott, McKie, Deakin, & Anderson, 2011). One study reported attenuated vlPFC response to fearful and happy faces in GAD (Palm et al., 2011), but another reported *greater* vlPFC response to angry faces in a dot probe task (Monk et al., 2006). In this latter study, as the vlPFC activation increased, symptom severity decreased, suggesting that vlPFC response could be compensatory.

Cognitive-behavioral therapy, mindfulness-based stress reduction, and stress management education have been associated with decreased amygdala activation to fearful, angry, or neutral faces in GAD (Fonzo et al., 2014; Holzel et al., 2013). Although ACC responses appear to decrease with treatment (Fonzo et al., 2014; Schneier et al., 2011), vlPFC responses appear to increase with treatment (Holzel et al., 2013), perhaps indicative of increased emotion regulation. In a predictors-of-treatment-response design, lower pretreatment amygdala responses and greater rostral ACC responses to fearful (versus neutral or happy) facial expressions were associated with relatively greater improvement (Whalen et al., 2008; but see also McClure, Adler et al., 2007).

Panic Disorder

In contrast to SAD and PTSD, panic disorder does not seem to be marked by exaggerated amygdala responses to emotional facial expressions (Pillay, Gruber, Rogowska, Simpson, & Yurgelun-Todd, 2006; but see also Fonzo et al., 2015). One study did find greater amygdala responses to angry and neutral faces in women versus men with panic disorder (Ohrmann et al., 2010). Given this sex difference, studies that include mostly men may be less likely to find amygdala hyperresponsivity. Another factor that might have led to relatively reduced amygdala activation in the aforementioned studies was the participants' use of antidepressants and/or benzodiazepines (Harmer, Mackay, Reid, Cowen, & Goodwin, 2006).

Given the heightened sensitivity to bodily sensations in panic disorder (Domschke, Stevens, Pfleiderer, & Gerlach, 2010) and the insula's involvement in the representation of internal bodily states (Paulus & Stein, 2006), one might expect to find exaggerated insula responses in panic disorder. Indeed, Fonzo et al. (2015) found greater posterior insula activation to emotional faces in individuals with panic disorder relative to control subjects and individuals with generalized anxiety disorder and social anxiety disorder (Fonzo et al., 2015), suggesting that the extent of insular cortex hyperresponsivity could be a "disorder distinguishing neural phenotype." One study reported greater insular cortex responses to angry and neutral faces in women versus men with panic disorder (Ohrmann et al., 2010).

Studies have also reported diminished ACC activation to fearful faces in panic disorder (e.g., Pillay et al., 2006), and one study found greater ACC activation to happy and neutral faces in individuals with panic disorder versus controls (Pillay, Rogowska, Gruber, Simpson, & Yurgelun-Todd, 2007).

Specific Phobia

Only two studies have used emotional facial expressions and fMRI to study brain function in specific phobia (Killgore et al., 2011; Wright, Martis, McMullin, Shin, & Rauch, 2003), and neither study reported greater amygdala activation. However, this may not be surprising, given that the participants included in these studies had very focal fears of small animals and that amygdala hyperactivation in phobias is much more consistently found in studies involving the presentation of phobic-relevant stimuli (e.g., spiders or snakes; Ipser, Singh, & Stein, 2013).

Summary

The studies reviewed herein suggest that amygdala responses to negative facial expressions are exaggerated in SAD and PTSD. The findings were more mixed for panic disorder, GAD, and phobias. Studies that directly compare amygdala activation to facial expressions across the anxiety disorders are needed to provide better evidence to evaluate the hypothesis of a shared amygdala pathology. Two studies that examined different anxiety disorder groups found similar amygdala activation across them (Fonzo et al., 2015; Killgore et al., 2014), although one study provided evidence for greater activation in SAD than in GAD (Blair et al., 2008). ACC responses to facial expressions tend to be increased in SAD and decreased in PTSD, particularly in response to consciously perceived fearful facial expressions. The evidence for abnormal ACC responses to emotional facial expressions is not especially strong or consistent in GAD, panic disorder, or phobias. Insular cortex responses appear to be exaggerated in all of the aforementioned anxiety disorders, especially in panic disorder (Fonzo et al., 2015).

MAJOR DEPRESSIVE DISORDER

Consistent with the phenomenology of major depressive disorder (MDD), sad facial expressions have been used in several studies to assess its pathophysiology. Amygdala activation appears to be exaggerated in response to sad facial expressions presented either above or below awareness in MDD relative to healthy control participants (e.g., Victor et al., 2012; Victor, Furey, Fromm, Ohman, & Drevets, 2010) and diminished in response to happy facial expressions (Victor et al., 2010). In addition, amygdala responses to sad faces are positively correlated with depression symptom severity (Henderson et al., 2014).

Even though fearful facial expressions may have less direct relevance to MDD as compared to sad facial expressions, several studies have shown that the former evoke exaggerated amygdala responses (Beesdo et al., 2009; Tao et al., 2012; Yang et al., 2010; but see also Demenescu et al., 2011). Furthermore, amygdala responses to negative (angry, fear) facial expressions are positively correlated with MDD symptom severity (Yang et al., 2010).

The findings regarding ACC responses to emotional facial expressions in MDD are somewhat mixed, with some studies reporting less ACC activation to emotional facial expressions in medial frontal gyrus or rostral ACC relative to nondepressed controls (Lai, 2014), and others reporting greater activation (Gotlib et al., 2005; Tao et al., 2012; Victor et al., 2012; Yang et al., 2010).

Dorsolateral prefrontal cortex responses to emotional (angry, sad, happy) facial expressions appear to be diminished in MDD (Fales et al., 2008; but see also Demenescu et al., 2011), consistent with neurocircuitry models of this disorder (e.g., Mayberg, 1997). In addition, reduced DLPFC activation to emotional facial expressions could be trait-like: Individuals with remitted depression showed relatively reduced activation in the DLPFC and OFC in response to fearful versus neutral facial expressions; furthermore, lower activation was associated with a shorter duration of euthymia (Kerestes et al., 2012).

With regard to the insular cortex in MDD, some studies have reported diminished insula activation to fearful facial expressions (Hall et al., 2014) or during facial expression matching tasks (Townsend et al., 2010). In contrast, greater insular cortex activation has been shown in response to masked happy facial expressions (Victor et al., 2012) and disgusted facial expressions in MDD (Surguladze et al., 2010). Finally, insula responses to fearful and sad facial expressions have been positively correlated with depression symptom severity and anhedonia severity, respectively (Henderson et al., 2014).

Although anhedonia is a major component of depression, few studies implementing facial expressions have examined activation abnormalities in brain regions that underlie reward processing, such as the ventral striatum. For example, compared to children of nondepressed parents, children of depressed parents had smaller responses in the nucleus accumbens to passively viewed happy faces (Monk et al., 2008). This finding is consistent with a larger imaging literature examining anhedonia using other tasks in MDD (Pizzagalli, 2014).

According to a recent meta-analysis, antidepressant treatment for MDD has generally been associated with (1) decreased activation of the amygdala, hippocampus, parahippocampal gyrus, ventral ACC, orbitofrontal cortex, and insula, and (2) increased activation of the dorsolateral, dorsomedial, and ventrolateral prefrontal cortices (Delaveau et al., 2011). Although this meta-analysis included studies that employed many different types of emotional stimuli, studies that used emotional facial expression stimuli generally yielded similar findings. Specifically, antidepressant treatment has been associated with reduced amygdala responses to masked and unmasked sad (Fu et al., 2004; Victor et al., 2010) and fearful faces (Tao et al., 2012; but see also Chen, Huang, Hung, Lane, & Hou, 2014). Interestingly, one study found that antidepressant treatment increased amygdala responses to happy faces (Victor et al., 2010), suggesting that the treatment may not simply dampen amygdala responses to all stimuli. Importantly, decreases in amygdala responses to sad faces have also been demonstrated following cognitive-behavioral therapy (Fu et al., 2008). Other antidepressant-related activation decreases have been reported in orbitofrontal cortex (Frodl et al., 2011; Tao et al., 2012) and insular cortex (Victor, Furey, Fromm, Ohman, & Drevets, 2013). Antidepressants and cognitive-behavioral therapy both appear to increase dorsolateral prefrontal cortex and ACC responses to negative facial expressions (Frodl et al., 2011; Fu et al., 2008; but see also Victor et al., 2013).

According to a recent meta-analysis, increased pretreatment activity in the pregenual and subgenual ACC predicts a higher likelihood of improvement, whereas increased baseline activation in the insula and striatum predicts a poorer clinical response (Fu, Steiner, & Costafreda, 2013; but see also Fu et al., 2008). Studies that used only emotional facial expression tasks appear to yield similar results. Specifically, pretreatment pregenual ACC responses to sad faces are positively associated with symptomatic improvement with serotonin reuptake inhibitors (Victor et al., 2013). In addition, greater responses to sad facial expressions in the subgenual ACC and visual cortex in the first 2 weeks of antidepressant treatment were associated with better clinical response (Keedwell et al., 2010).

Summary

Emotional facial expressions appear to elicit exaggerated amygdala responses and attenuated dorsolateral prefrontal cortex responses in MDD. In addition, these abnormalities are correlated with symptom severity and appear to improve with treatment. Furthermore, pretreatment ACC activation appears to predict treatment response. Because MDD can be assessed along several different dimensions (e.g., anhedonia, depressed mood; Henderson et al., 2014), it will be critical to examine the relationship between each of these dimensions and brain activation. Indeed, this emphasis on examining the neural substrates of dimensional constructs is consistent with the Research Domain Criteria approach of the National Institutes of Mental Health (Dillon et al., 2014).

Our qualitative review of the literatures suggests that anxiety disorders and depression are both marked by exaggerated amygdala activation in response to emotional facial expressions. This similarity could suggest that anxiety disorders and depression may have partially overlapping pathophysiology. Alternatively, exaggerated amygdala activation could be a premorbid, trait-like individual difference that increases the risk of developing either anxiety disorders or depression or both (see next section). However, it should be noted that very few studies have directly compared these two broad patient groups within the same study (Beesdo et al., 2009). Such comparisons would be needed to definitively test the idea of shared pathology or risk.

Our review also suggests that anxiety disorders and depression may differ in terms of frontal cortex responses to emotional facial expressions. Specifically, MDD is associated with relatively decreased *dorsolateral* prefrontal cortex responses, but anxiety disorders are associated with abnormal *medial* prefrontal cortex responses.

RISK FOR PSYCHOPATHOLOGY

The majority of fMRI studies to date have examined the neural correlates of emotional face processing in patients who have developed a clinical anxiety or mood disorder. Although this approach has greatly enhanced our understanding of the neural circuitry associated with anxiety and depression, a disadvantage of studying patient populations is that it is generally impossible to disentangle whether differences in brain function represent a premorbid risk factor or a pathophysiological consequence of psychiatric illness. To address this limitation, several different approaches have been taken to identify patterns of neural function that indicate risk for the future development of psychopathology.

Prospective Prediction of Symptoms

One of the most direct approaches for identifying premorbid risk factors for mood and anxiety disorders is to examine whether brain function prospectively predicts which individuals will develop higher levels of symptoms after exposure to a stressor. The only study of this kind to use emotional face expressions was conducted in a large sample of young adult university students (Swartz, Knodt, Radtke, & Hariri, 2015). Results of this prospective study indicated that individuals who had relatively increased amygdala reactivity to angry and fearful faces at baseline reported increased anxiety and depression symptoms in response to stress 1 to 4 years later. Although they did not employ emotional face stimuli, two additional studies have also provided support for heightened threat-related amygdala reactivity as a premorbid risk factor for posttraumatic stress symptoms in response to combat trauma (Admon et al., 2009) or a terrorist attack (McLaughlin et al., 2014).

High-Risk Family Designs

The second line of research has examined neural function in adolescents at familial risk for disorder before the emergence of psychiatric illness. Children and adolescents at familial risk for depression evidence heightened amygdala activation to fearful faces during passive viewing (Monk et al., 2008) and a face matching task (Chai et al., 2015). This premorbid risk factor appears to emerge over the course of adolescence, as a longitudinal study found that adolescents with a family history of depression did not differ from their low-risk peers in amygdala reactivity to fearful faces at the first wave of the study (during early adolescence), but they did exhibit increased amygdala reactivity to fearful faces 2 years later (Swartz, Williamson, & Hariri, 2015). In addition to heightened amygdala reactivity to fearful faces, diminished prefrontal cortex activation during fearful face matching has been identified in youth at familial risk for depression (Mannie, Taylor, Harmer, Cowen, & Norbury, 2011).

Traits Predicting Risk for Disorder

A third line of research has examined how neural function relates to variation in traits associated with risk for depression and anxiety, including trait anxiety, neuroticism, and behavioral inhibition, in the general population. Again, heightened amygdala reactivity to threatening emotional faces has emerged as a common correlate of these traits (Stein, Simmons, Feinstein, & Paulus, 2007; Etkin et al., 2004; Schwartz, Wright, Shin, Kagan, & Rauch, 2003). Additionally, euthymic participants identified as cognitively vulnerable to depression (by virtue of their causal attributions for negative events) had exaggerated amygdala activation to emotional facial expressions (Zhong et al., 2011).

Altered activation and connectivity of the prefrontal cortex has also been identified in individuals with risk-associated personality traits. For instance, during a gender discrimination task, higher neuroticism was associated with greater dmPFC activation to fearful faces, decreased amygdala-ACC connectivity to angry and fearful faces, and greater amygdala-dmPFC connectivity to angry and fearful faces (Cremers et al., 2010). Moreover, during a probe detection task, adolescents high in trait anxiety evidenced heightened dlPFC activation when a target probe was incongruent with the location of angry faces (and thus when attention needed to be shifted away from angry faces) and heightened vlPFC activation to all emotional face trials (Telzer et al., 2008).

Summary

Heightened baseline amygdala reactivity prospectively predicts greater anxiety and depression symptoms in response to trauma or stress. In addition, exaggerated amygdala reactivity to fearful or angry facial expressions has been found in individuals with familial or personality trait risk for anxiety or depression. Although a less consistent pattern of effects has emerged for prefrontal cortex activation and connectivity, initial results indicate that atypical prefrontal cortex activity is also associated with risk for anxiety or depression. This line of work may have important clinical utility in identifying individuals at highest risk for psychopathology before symptoms emerge.

CONCLUSIONS

Emotional facial expressions communicate critical information regarding the relative threat or safety of one's current circumstances, as well as the emotional state of other individuals within the environment. When neural circuitry becomes oversensitized to threat cues and underresponsive to safety cues, this may color one's perceptions of the world and predispose individuals to the development of mood and anxiety disorders. One direction for future research is to identify novel ways to retune this circuitry, which holds promise for improving the treatment and prevention of mood and anxiety disorders.

REFERENCES

Admon, R., Lubin, G., Stern, O., Rosenberg, K., Sela, L., Ben-Ami, H., . . . Hendler, T. (2009). Human vulnerability to stress depends on amygdala's predisposition and hippocampal plasticity. *Proceedings of the National Academy of Sciences of the United States of America, 106*(33), 14120–14125.

Armony, J. L., Corbo, V., Clement, M. H., & Brunet, A. (2005). Amygdala response in patients with acute PTSD to masked and unmasked emotional facial expressions. *The American Journal of Psychiatry, 162*(10), 1961–1963.

Arrais, K. C., Machado-de-Sousa, J. P., Trzesniak, C., Santos Filho, A., Ferrari, M. C., Osorio, F. L., . . . Crippa, J. A. (2010). Social anxiety disorder women easily recognize fearfull, sad and happy faces: The influence of gender. *Journal of Psychiatric Research, 44*(8), 535–540.

Beesdo, K., Lau, J. Y., Guyer, A. E., McClure-Tone, E. B., Monk, C. S., Nelson, E. E., . . . Pine, D. S. (2009). Common and distinct amygdala-function perturbations in depressed vs. anxious adolescents. *Archives of General Psychiatry, 66*(3), 275–285.

Blair, K., Shaywitz, J., Smith, B. W., Rhodes, R., Geraci, M., Jones, M., . . . Pine, D. S. (2008). Response to emotional expressions in generalized social phobia and generalized anxiety disorder: Evidence for separate disorders. *The American Journal of Psychiatry, 165*(9), 1193–1202.

Blair, K. S., Geraci, M., Korelitz, K., Otero, M., Towbin, K., Ernst, M., . . . Pine, D. S. (2011). The pathology of social phobia is independent of developmental changes in face processing. *The American Journal of Psychiatry, 168*(11), 1202–1209.

Bryant, R. A., Felmingham, K., Kemp, A., Das, P., Hughes, G., Peduto, A., . . . Williams, L. (2008). Amygdala and ventral anterior cingulate activation predicts treatment response to cognitive behaviour therapy for post-traumatic stress disorder. *Psychological Medicine, 38*, 555–561.

Bryant, R. A., Kemp, A. H., Felmingham, K. L., Liddell, B., Olivieri, G., Peduto, A., . . . Williams, L. M. (2008). Enhanced amygdala and medial prefrontal activation during nonconscious processing of fear in posttraumatic stress disorder: An fMRI study. *Human Brain Mapping, 29*, 517–523.

Carre, A., Gierski, F., Lemogne, C., Tran, E., Raucher-Chene, D., Bera-Potelle, C., . . . Limosin, F. (2014). Linear association between social anxiety symptoms and neural activations to angry faces: From subclinical to clinical levels. *Social Cognitive and Affective Neuroscience, 9*(6), 880–886.

Chai, X. J., Hirshfeld-Becker, D., Biederman, J., Uchida, M., Doehrmann, O., Leonard, J. A., . . . Gabrieli, J. D. E. (2015). Functional and structural brain correlates of risk for major depression in children with familial depression. *NeuroImage: Clinical, 8*, 398–407.

Chen, Y. T., Huang, M. W., Hung, I. C., Lane, H. Y., & Hou, C. J. (2014). Right and left amygdalae activation in patients with major depression receiving antidepressant treatment, as revealed by fMRI. *Behavioral and Brain Functions, 10*(1), 36.

Cooney, R. E., Atlas, L. Y., Joormann, J., Eugene, F., & Gotlib, I. H. (2006). Amygdala activation in the processing of neutral faces in social anxiety disorder: Is neutral really neutral? *Psychiatry Research, 148*(1), 55–59.

Cremers, H. R., Demenescu, L. R., Aleman, A., Renken, R., van Tol, M., van der Wee, N. J. A., . . . Roelofs, K. (2010). Neuroticism modulates amygdala-prefrontal connectivity in response to negative emotional facial expressions. *NeuroImage, 49*, 963–970.

Dannlowski, U., Stuhrmann, A., Beutelmann, V., Zwanzger, P., Lenzen, T., Grotegerd, D., . . . Kugel, H. (2012). Limbic scars: Long-term consequences of childhood maltreatment revealed by functional and structural magnetic resonance imaging. *Biological Psychiatry, 71*(4), 286–293.

Delaveau, P., Jabourian, M., Lemogne, C., Guionnet, S., Bergouignan, L., & Fossati, P. (2011). Brain effects of antidepressants in major depression: A meta-analysis of emotional processing studies. *Journal of Affective Disorders, 130*(1-2), 66–74.

Demenescu, L. R., Renken, R., Kortekaas, R., van Tol, M. J., Marsman, J. B., van Buchem, M. A., . . . Aleman, A. (2011). Neural correlates of perception of emotional facial expressions in out-patients with mild-to-moderate depression and anxiety. A multicenter fMRI study. *Psychological Medicine, 41*(11), 2253–2264.

Dillon, D. G., Rosso, I. M., Pechtel, P., Killgore, W. D., Rauch, S. L., & Pizzagalli, D. A. (2014). Peril and pleasure: An Rdoc-inspired examination of threat responses and reward processing in anxiety and depression. *Depression and Anxiety, 31*(3), 233–249.

Domschke, K., Stevens, S., Pfleiderer, B., & Gerlach, A. L. (2010). Interoceptive sensitivity in anxiety and anxiety disorders: An overview and integration of neurobiological findings. *Clinical Psychology Review, 30*(1), 1–11.

Etkin, A., Klemenhagen, K. C., Dudman, J. T., Rogan, M. T., Hen, R., Kandel, E. R., . . . Hirsch, J. (2004). Individual differences in trait anxiety predict the response of the basolateral amygdala to unconsciously processed fearful faces. *Neuron, 44*, 1043–1055.

Fales, C. L., Barch, D. M., Rundle, M. M., Mintun, M. A., Snyder, A. Z., Cohen, J. D., . . . Sheline, Y. I. (2008). Altered emotional interference processing in affective and cognitive-control brain circuitry in major depression. *Biological Psychiatry, 63*(4), 377–384.

Felmingham, K., Kemp, A., Williams, L., Das, P., Hughes, G., Peduto, A., . . . Bryant, R. (2007). Changes in anterior cingulate and amygdala after cognitive behavior therapy of posttraumatic stress disorder. *Psychological Science, 18*(2), 127–129.

Felmingham, K. L., Falconer, E. M., Williams, L., Kemp, A. H., Allen, A., Peduto, A., . . . Bryant, R. A. (2014). Reduced amygdala and ventral striatal activity to happy faces in PTSD is associated with emotional numbing. *PLoS One, 9*(9), e103653.

Fonzo, G. A., Ramsawh, H. J., Flagan, T. M., Sullivan, S. G., Letamendi, A., Simmons, A. N., . . . Stein, M. B. (2015). Common and disorder-specific neural responses to emotional faces in generalised anxiety, social anxiety and panic disorders. *British Journal of Psychiatry, 206*(3), 206–215.

Fonzo, G. A., Ramsawh, H. J., Flagan, T. M., Sullivan, S. G., Simmons, A. N., Paulus, M. P., & Stein, M. B. (2014). Cognitive-behavioral therapy for generalized anxiety disorder is associated with attenuation of limbic activation to threat-related facial emotions. *Journal of Affective Disorders, 169*, 76–85.

Frodl, T., Scheuerecker, J., Schoepf, V., Linn, J., Koutsouleris, N., Bokde, A. L., . . . Meisenzahl, E. (2011). Different effects of mirtazapine and venlafaxine on brain activation: An open randomized controlled fMRI study. *Journal of Clinical Psychiatry, 72*(4), 448–457.

Fu, C. H., Steiner, H., & Costafreda, S. G. (2013). Predictive neural biomarkers of clinical response in depression: A meta-analysis of functional and structural neuroimaging studies of pharmacological and psychological therapies. *Neurobiology of Disease, 52*, 75–83.

Fu, C. H., Williams, S. C., Cleare, A. J., Brammer, M. J., Walsh, N. D., Kim, J., . . . Bullmore, E. T. (2004). Attenuation of the neural response to sad faces in major depression by antidepressant treatment: A prospective, event-related functional magnetic resonance imaging study. *Archives of General Psychiatry, 61*(9), 877–889.

Fu, C. H., Williams, S. C., Cleare, A. J., Scott, J., Mitterschiffthaler, M. T., Walsh, N. D., . . . Murray, R. M. (2008). Neural responses to sad facial expressions in major depression following cognitive behavioral therapy. *Biological Psychiatry, 64*(6), 505–512.

Fusar-Poli, P., Placentino, A., Carletti, F., Landi, P., Allen, P., Surguladze, S., . . . Politi, P. (2009). Functional atlas of emotional faces processing: A voxel-based meta-analysis of 105 functional magnetic resonance imaging studies. *Journal of Psychiatry & Neuroscience, 34*(6), 418–432.

Garrett, A. S., Carrion, V., Kletter, H., Karchemskiy, A., Weems, C. F., & Reiss, A. (2012). Brain activation to facial expressions in youth with PTSD symptoms. *Depression and Anxiety, 29*(5), 449–459.

Gimenez, M., Ortiz, H., Soriano-Mas, C., Lopez-Sola, M., Farre, M., Deus, J., . . . Merlo-Pich, E. (2014). Functional effects of chronic paroxetine versus placebo on the fear, stress and anxiety brain circuit in Social Anxiety Disorder: Initial validation of an imaging protocol for drug discovery. *European Neuropsychopharmacology, 24*(1), 105–116.

Goldin, P. R., Manber, T., Hakimi, S., Canli, T., & Gross, J. J. (2009). Neural bases of social anxiety disorder: Emotional reactivity and cognitive regulation during social and physical threat. *Archives of General Psychiatry, 66*(2), 170–180.

Gotlib, I. H., Sivers, H., Gabrieli, J. D., Whitfield-Gabrieli, S., Goldin, P., Minor, K. L., & Canli, T. (2005). Subgenual anterior cingulate activation to valenced emotional stimuli in major depression. *Neuroreport, 16*(16), 1731–1734.

Hall, L. M., Klimes-Dougan, B., Hunt, R. H., Thomas, K. M., Houri, A., Noack, E., . . . Cullen, K. R. (2014). An fMRI study of emotional face processing in adolescent major depression. *Journal of Affective Disorders, 168*, 44–50.

Harmer, C. J., Mackay, C. E., Reid, C. B., Cowen, P. J., & Goodwin, G. M. (2006). Antidepressant drug treatment modifies the neural processing of nonconscious threat cues. *Biological Psychiatry, 59*(9), 816–820.

Henderson, S. E., Vallejo, A. I., Ely, B. A., Kang, G., Krain Roy, A., Pine, D. S., . . . Gabbay, V. (2014). The neural correlates of emotional face-processing in adolescent depression: A dimensional approach focusing on anhedonia and illness severity. *Psychiatry Research, 224*(3), 234–241.

Holzel, B. K., Hoge, E. A., Greve, D. N., Gard, T., Creswell, J. D., Brown, K. W., . . . Lazar, S. W. (2013). Neural mechanisms of symptom improvements in generalized anxiety disorder following mindfulness training. *Neuroimage Clinical, 2*, 448–458.

Ipser, J. C., Singh, L., & Stein, D. J. (2013). Meta-analysis of functional brain imaging in specific phobia. *Psychiatry and Clinical Neurosciences, 67*(5), 311–322.

Keedwell, P. A., Drapier, D., Surguladze, S., Giampietro, V., Brammer, M., & Phillips, M. (2010). Subgenual cingulate and visual cortex responses to sad faces predict clinical outcome during antidepressant treatment for depression. *Journal of Affective Disorders, 120*(1-3), 120–125.

Kelley, W. M., Macrae, C. N., Wyland, C. L., Caglar, S., Inati, S., & Heatherton, T. F. (2002). Finding the self? An event-related fMRI study. *Journal of Cognitive Neuroscience, 14*(5), 785–794.

Kerestes, R., Bhagwagar, Z., Nathan, P. J., Meda, S. A., Ladouceur, C. D., Maloney, K., . . . Blumberg, H. P. (2012). Prefrontal cortical response to emotional faces in individuals with major depressive disorder in remission. *Psychiatry Research, 202*(1), 30–37.

Killgore, W. D., Britton, J. C., Price, L. M., Gold, A. L., Deckersbach, T., & Rauch, S. L. (2011). Neural correlates of anxiety sensitivity during masked presentation of affective faces. *Depression and Anxiety, 28*(3), 243–249.

Killgore, W. D., Britton, J. C., Schwab, Z. J., Price, L. M., Weiner, M. R., Gold, A. L., . . . Rauch, S. L. (2014). Cortico-limbic responses to masked affective faces across PTSD, panic disorder, and specific phobia. *Depression and Anxiety, 31*(2), 150–159.

Klumpp, H., Angstadt, M., & Phan, K. L. (2012). Insula reactivity and connectivity to anterior cingulate cortex when processing threat in generalized social anxiety disorder. *Biological Psychology, 89*(1), 273–276.

Klumpp, H., Fitzgerald, D. A., Angstadt, M., Post, D., & Phan, K. L. (2014). Neural response during attentional control and emotion processing predicts improvement after cognitive behavioral therapy in generalized social anxiety disorder. *Psychological Medicine, 44*(14), 3109–3121.

Klumpp, H., Fitzgerald, D. A., & Phan, K. L. (2013). Neural predictors and mechanisms of cognitive behavioral therapy on threat processing in social anxiety disorder. *Progress in Neuropsychopharmacology and Biological Psychiatry, 45*, 83–91.

Klumpp, H., Post, D., Angstadt, M., Fitzgerald, D. A., & Phan, K. L. (2013). Anterior cingulate cortex and insula response during indirect and direct processing of emotional faces in generalized social anxiety disorder. *Biology of Mood and Anxiety Disorders, 3*, 7.

Lai, C. H. (2014). Patterns of cortico-limbic activations during visual processing of sad faces in depression patients: A coordinate-based meta-analysis. *The Journal of Neuropsychiatry and Clinical Neurosciences, 26*(1), 34–43.

Mannie, Z. N., Taylor, M. J., Harmer, C. J., Cowen, P. J., & Norbury, R. (2011). Frontolimbic responses to emotional faces in young people at familial risk of depression. *Journal of Affective Disorders, 130*, 127–132.

Mayberg, H. S. (1997). Limbic-cortical dysregulation: A proposed model of depression. *The Journal of Neuropsychiatry and Clinical Neurosciences, 9*(3), 471–481.

McClure, E. B., Adler, A., Monk, C. S., Cameron, J., Smith, S., Nelson, E. E., . . . Pine, D. S. (2007). fMRI predictors of treatment outcome in pediatric anxiety disorders. *Psychopharmacology, 191*(1), 97–105.

McClure, E. B., Monk, C. S., Nelson, E. E., Parrish, J. M., Adler, A., Blair, R. J., . . . Pine, D. S. (2007). Abnormal attention modulation of fear circuit function in pediatric generalized anxiety disorder. *Archives of General Psychiatry, 64*(1), 97–106.

McLaughlin, K. A., Busso, D. S., Duys, A., Green, J. G., Alves, S., Way, M., & Sheridan, M. A. (2014). Amygdala response to negative stimuli predicts PTSD symptom onset following a terrorist attack. *Depression and Anxiety, 31*(10), 834–842.

Monk, C. S., Klein, R. G., Telzer, E. H., Schroth, E. A., Mannuzza, S., Moulton, J. L., 3rd, . . . Ernst, M. (2008). Amygdala and nucleus accumbens activation to emotional facial expressions in children and adolescents at risk for major depression. *The American Journal of Psychiatry, 165*(1), 90–98.

Monk, C. S., Nelson, E. E., McClure, E. B., Mogg, K., Bradley, B. P., Leibenluft, E., . . . Pine, D. S. (2006). Ventrolateral prefrontal cortex activation and attentional bias in response to angry faces in adolescents with generalized anxiety disorder. *The American Journal of Psychiatry, 163*(6), 1091–1097.

Offringa, R., Handwerger Brohawn, K., Staples, L. K., Dubois, S. J., Hughes, K. C., Pfaff, D. L., . . . Shin, L. M. (2013). Diminished rostral anterior cingulate cortex activation during trauma-unrelated emotional interference in PTSD. *Biology of Mood and Anxiety Disorders, 3*(1), 10.

Ohrmann, P., Pedersen, A., Braun, M., Bauer, J., Kugel, H., Kersting, A., . . . Suslow, T. (2010). Effect of gender on processing threat-related stimuli in patients with panic disorder: Sex does matter. *Depression and Anxiety, 27*(11), 1034–1043.

Palm, M. E., Elliott, R., McKie, S., Deakin, J. F., & Anderson, I. M. (2011). Attenuated responses to emotional expressions in women with generalized anxiety disorder. *Psychological Medicine, 41*(5), 1009–1018.

Paulus, M. P., & Stein, M. B. (2006). An insular view of anxiety. *Biological Psychiatry, 60*(4), 383–387.

Phan, K. L., Coccaro, E. F., Angstadt, M., Kreger, K. J., Mayberg, H. S., Liberzon, I., & Stein, M. B. (2013). Corticolimbic brain reactivity to social signals of threat before and after sertraline treatment in generalized social phobia. *Biological Psychiatry, 73*(4), 329–336.

Phan, K. L., Fitzgerald, D. A., Nathan, P. J., & Tancer, M. E. (2006). Association between amygdala hyperactivity to harsh faces and severity of social anxiety in generalized social phobia. *Biological Psychiatry, 59*(5), 424–429.

Pillay, S. S., Gruber, S. A., Rogowska, J., Simpson, N., & Yurgelun-Todd, D. A. (2006). fMRI of fearful facial affect recognition in panic disorder: The cingulate gyrus-amygdala connection. *Journal of Affective Disorders, 94*(1-3), 173–181.

Pillay, S. S., Rogowska, J., Gruber, S. A., Simpson, N., & Yurgelun-Todd, D. A. (2007). Recognition of happy facial affect in panic disorder: An fMRI study. *Journal of Anxiety Disorders, 21*(3), 381–393.

Pizzagalli, D. A. (2014). Depression, stress, and anhedonia: Toward a synthesis and integrated model. *Annual Review of Clinical Psychology, 10*, 393–423.

Rauch, S. L., Whalen, P. J., Shin, L. M., McInerney, S. C., Macklin, M. L., Lasko, N. B., . . . Pitman, R. K. (2000). Exaggerated amygdala response to masked facial stimuli in posttraumatic stress disorder: A functional MRI study. *Biological Psychiatry, 47*(9), 769–776.

Schneier, F. R., Pomplun, M., Sy, M., & Hirsch, J. (2011). Neural response to eye contact and paroxetine treatment in generalized social anxiety disorder. *Psychiatry Research, 194*(3), 271–278.

Schwartz, C. E., Wright, C. I., Shin, L. M., Kagan, J., & Rauch, S. L. (2003). Inhibited and uninhibited infants "grown up": Adult amygdalar response to novelty. *Science, 300*(5627), 1952–1953.

Shin, L. M., Davis, F. C., Vanelzakker, M. B., Dahlgren, M. K., & Dubois, S. J. (2013). Neuroimaging predictors of treatment response in anxiety disorders. *Biology of Mood and Anxiety Disorders, 3*(1), 15.

Shin, L. M., Wright, C. I., Cannistraro, P. A., Wedig, M. M., McMullin, K., Martis, B., . . . Rauch, S. L. (2005). A functional magnetic resonance imaging study of amygdala and medial prefrontal cortex responses to overtly presented fearful faces in posttraumatic stress disorder. *Archives of General Psychiatry, 62*(3), 273–281.

Stein, M. B., Goldin, P. R., Sareen, J., Zorrilla, L. T., & Brown, G. G. (2002). Increased amygdala activation to angry and contemptuous faces in generalized social phobia. *Archives of General Psychiatry, 59*(11), 1027–1034.

Stein, M. B., Simmons, A. N., Feinstein, J. S., & Paulus, M. P. (2007). Increased amygdala and insula activation during emotion processing in anxiety-prone subjects. *The American Journal of Psychiatry, 164*(2), 318–327.

Stevens, J. S., Jovanovic, T., Fani, N., Ely, T. D., Glover, E. M., Bradley, B., & Ressler, K. J. (2013). Disrupted amygdala-prefrontal functional connectivity in civilian women with posttraumatic stress disorder. *Journal of Psychiatric Research, 47*(10), 1469–1478.

Straube, T., Kolassa, I. T., Glauer, M., Mentzel, H. J., & Miltner, W. H. (2004). Effect of task conditions on brain responses to threatening faces in social phobics: An event-related functional magnetic resonance imaging study. *Biological Psychiatry, 56*(12), 921–930.

Straube, T., Mentzel, H. J., & Miltner, W. H. (2005). Common and distinct brain activation to threat and safety signals in social phobia. *Neuropsychobiology, 52*(3), 163–168.

Surguladze, S. A., El-Hage, W., Dalgleish, T., Radua, J., Gohier, B., & Phillips, M. L. (2010). Depression is associated with increased sensitivity to signals of disgust: A functional magnetic resonance imaging study. *Journal of Psychiatr Research, 44*(14), 894–902.

Swartz, J. R., Knodt, A. R., Radtke, S. R., & Hariri, A. R. (2015). A neural biomarker of psychological vulnerability to future life stress. *Neuron, 85*(3), 505–511.

Swartz, J. R., Williamson, D. E., & Hariri, A. R. (2015). Developmental change in amygdala reactivity during adolescence: Effects of family history of depression and stressful life events. *The American Journal of Psychiatry, 172*(3), 276–283.

Tao, R., Calley, C. S., Hart, J., Mayes, T. L., Nakonezny, P. A., Lu, H., . . . Emslie, G. J. (2012). Brain activity in adolescent major depressive disorder before and after fluoxetine treatment. *The American Journal of Psychiatry, 169*(4), 381–388.

Telzer, E. H., Mogg, K., Bradley, B. P., Mai, X., Ernst, M., Pine, D. S., & Monk, C. S. (2008). Relationship between trait anxiety, prefrontal cortex, and attention bias to angry faces in children and adolescents. *Biological Psychology, 79*, 216–222.

Townsend, J. D., Eberhart, N. K., Bookheimer, S. Y., Eisenberger, N. I., Foland-Ross, L. C., Cook, I. A., . . . Altshuler, L. L. (2010). fMRI activation in the amygdala and the orbitofrontal cortex in unmedicated subjects with major depressive disorder. *Psychiatry Research, 183*(3), 209–217.

Veit, R., Flor, H., Erb, M., Hermann, C., Lotze, M., Grodd, W., & Birbaumer, N. (2002). Brain circuits involved in emotional learning in antisocial behavior and social phobia in humans. *Neuroscience Letters, 328*(3), 233–236.

Victor, T. A., Furey, M. L., Fromm, S. J., Bellgowan, P. S., Ohman, A., & Drevets, W. C. (2012). The extended functional neuroanatomy of emotional processing biases for masked faces in major depressive disorder. *PLoS One, 7*(10), e46439.

Victor, T. A., Furey, M. L., Fromm, S. J., Ohman, A., & Drevets, W. C. (2010). Relationship between amygdala responses to masked faces and mood state and treatment in major depressive disorder. *Archives of General Psychiatry, 67*(11), 1128–1138.

Victor, T. A., Furey, M. L., Fromm, S. J., Ohman, A., & Drevets, W. C. (2013). Changes in the neural correlates of implicit emotional face processing during antidepressant treatment in major depressive disorder. *International Journal of Neuropsychopharmacology, 16*(10), 2195–2208.

Whalen, P. J., Johnstone, T., Somerville, L. H., Nitschke, J. B., Polis, S., Alexander, A. L., . . . Kalin, N. H. (2008). A functional magnetic resonance imaging predictor of treatment response to venlafaxine in generalized anxiety disorder. *Biological Psychiatry, 63*(9), 858–863.

Winton, E. C., Clark, D. M., & Edelmann, R. J. (1995). Social anxiety, fear of negative evaluation and the detection of negative emotion in others. *Behaviour Research and Therapy, 33*(2), 193–196.

Wright, C. I., Martis, B., McMullin, K., Shin, L. M., & Rauch, S. L. (2003). Amygdala and insular responses to emotionally valenced human faces in small animal specific phobia. *Biological Psychiatry, 54*(10), 1067–1076.

Yang, T. T., Simmons, A. N., Matthews, S. C., Tapert, S. F., Frank, G. K., Max, J. E., . . . Paulus, M. P. (2010). Adolescents with major depression demonstrate increased amygdala activation. *Journal of the American Academy of Child and Adolescent Psychiatry, 49*(1), 42–51.

Zhong, M., Wang, X., Xiao, J., Yi, J., Zhu, X., Liao, J., . . . Yao, S. (2011). Amygdala hyperactivation and prefrontal hypoactivation in subjects with cognitive vulnerability to depression. *Biological Psychology, 88*(2-3), 233–242.

Ziv, M., Goldin, P. R., Jazaieri, H., Hahn, K. S., & Gross, J. J. (2013). Emotion regulation in social anxiety disorder: Behavioral and neural responses to three socio-emotional tasks. *Biology of Mood and Anxiety Disorders, 3*(1), 20.

PART VI

Individual Development

15

Spontaneously Produced Facial Expressions in Infants and Children

LINDA A. CAMRAS, VANESSA L. CASTRO,
AMY G. HALBERSTADT, AND MICHAEL M. SHUSTER

Developmental studies of emotional facial expressions can make a unique contribution to our understanding of emotion and emotion communication. Several important contemporary theories of emotion have proposed that expressive behaviors are automatic "readouts" of emotion and serve to communicate emotion in everyday life. Yet at the same time, it is also widely recognized that adults often regulate their expressive behavior in accordance with culturally, socially, or personally derived "display rules." Thus, it is not clear whether facial expressions really are spontaneously produced when emotion is experienced or to what extent they are the means through which emotion communication takes place. As illustrated in several contributions to this volume, one valuable approach to addressing these issues has been to study situations in which display rules are assumed to be irrelevant or inoperative (e.g., nonsocial situations or situations in which emotions are very strong). However, an alternative approach—recognized by developmentalists but often overlooked by investigators focusing on adults—is to study individuals who may be too young to have absorbed the socially based display rules of their culture or who are not yet capable of exerting a sufficient degree of control over their emotional expression.

In this chapter we will review developmental research relevant to several specific questions implied by this discussion: (1) Do infants—who are presumably too young to mask their emotions—produce the different theoretically predicted emotional expressions in different emotion situations? (2) Do young children produce such expressions in a unique natural situation during which they are judged to be experiencing a strong emotion? and (3) Do older children produce such expressions when they are judged to be effectively communicating emotion in the context of mother–child interactions? Regarding infants, the studies we review have previously been described in considerable detail (Camras, 2011; Camras & Shutter, 2010) and will be described relatively briefly. Regarding children, much less relevant research has been previously conducted. Therefore, we will present preliminary results from two new studies we have conducted with children.

Among contemporary emotion theories that emphasize the role of facial expressions, Izard's differential emotions theory (DET) includes the most explicit developmental component (Izard & Malatesta, 1987). In its original formulation, DET proposed that discrete emotions emerge during the course of development according to a maturational timetable. The marker for the emergence of an emotion is the appearance of its corresponding prototypic facial expression. Izard conducted a number of early studies in which he observed infant expressive behaviors in several presumptively emotion eliciting situations (e.g., inoculations administered during routine physician visits). Based on these observations along with his own expression recognition studies conducted with adults, Izard described a set of infant-oriented prototypic facial expressions that resembled—but were not always identical to—the expressions described by Darwin and studied by Tomkins, Ekman, and other researchers of adult expressive behavior. These expressions are the focal points of his MAX (Izard, 1995) and AFFEX (Izard, Dougherty, & Hembree, 1983) scoring systems for coding and interpreting infant facial expressions. One important corollary of his original developmental theory was the proposal that these expressions bear an invariant one-to-one relationship with infant emotion such that they were always produced when emotion was experienced and were never produced in other circumstances. Thus, they could serve as reliable indicators of infant emotion—at least during the first year of life when infants were presumed to be too young to inhibit or mask their spontaneous expressive behavior.

Izard's initial studies seemed to provide reasonable support for his proposals regarding the morphology of infant emotional expressions and their role in the development and communication of emotion. However, further investigation by other researchers led to questions regarding both the meaning of these expressions and their invariant and exclusive links to particular internal states (see Camras & Shutter, 2010, for a detailed review of this research). For example, Oster, Hegley, and Nagel (1992) pointed out that in recognition studies of infant expressions, participants were given a limited set of response options that typically did not include "distress" in addition to more discrete emotion labels such as "anger," "sadness," and "fear." Consistent with earlier work by Bridges (1932), Oster (2005) argued that several infant negative facial expressions may reflect different forms of distress rather than different adult-like negative emotions such as anger, sadness, and so on. Oster emphasized that the adaptive communicative functions of expressive behavior may be very different for infants and adults and thus the meaning of their facial expressions may not be the same.

One limitation of Izard's initial studies was that his observations of infants took place in a very restricted range of situations. Camras (1992) sought to expand this range through natural observation (and videotaping) of her own infant during the first weeks of life. These observations took place in the home setting and encompassed a variety of situations and interactions during the normal course of the day. Camras's initial goal was to identify the emergence of the AFFEX-specified emotional expressions (and thus their corresponding emotions) at earlier ages than had been specified by Izard based on his own studies. However, shortly after initiating her study, Camras began to observe a number of phenomena that were inconsistent with her initial expectations. First, she observed that some of the AFFEX-specified facial expressions were being produced in situations during which the corresponding emotions did not appear to be present. For example, her daughter often produced the prototypic "surprise" expression when presented with an attractive but very familiar stimulus (e.g., when looking up at an attractive lamp suspended from the ceiling above the kitchen table). Second, there appeared to be considerable overlap in the situations that elicited expressions identified as corresponding to very different sorts of negative emotions. For example, the AFFEX-specified expressions for physical pain/discomfort, anger, and sad were all produced when mother gave the baby to another person to hold, when she woke up from a nap, or during bathing. Of note, some of the situations in which the physical pain/discomfort expression occurred did not appear to involve any physical pain. Third, during episodes of crying, Camras's daughter often cycled systematically through the pain, anger, and sadness expressions as she exhaled with a loud cry (producing either pain or anger expressions) and then paused to take another breath (producing a sadness expression). Beyond these observations, Camras also reviewed the extant literature on infants' expression production and noted that several researchers had found infants did not produce the AFFEX-predicted facial expression in situations when they appeared to be experiencing an emotion (e.g., as they exhibited fear-related avoidance of the visual cliff; Hiatt, Campos, & Emde, 1979). Lastly, as noted by Oster et al. (1992), there existed morphological differences between the adult versions and infant versions of some emotional expressions. For example, the AFFEX-specified anger expression included a cheek-raising facial action (involving contraction of the outer portions of m. obicularis oculi) while this was not a component of the adult expression of anger as described by other researchers (e.g., Ekman, Friesen, & Hager, 2002). Furthermore, variable forms were described for some emotional expressions (i.e., the AFFEX-specified interest expression), but no theoretical explanation for these differences could be provided.

As a follow-up to these observations, Camras joined with several colleagues (see Camras et al., 2007) in a larger study designed to more systematically investigate infants' productions of facial expressions. Eleven-month-old infants from three cultures (China, Japan, and the United States) were videotaped during an anger/frustration-eliciting and fear-eliciting situation (arm restraint and growling gorilla toy). Naïve observers viewed the videotapes (edited to obscure the infants' facial expressions) and indicated (on a 7-point scale) how much the baby experienced each of nine different emotions. Data analyses confirmed that the arm restraint and growling gorilla situations each elicited its target emotion. Subsequently, facial behavior was coded using Oster's (2006) anatomically based scoring system (BabyFACS). Results were analyzed in light of two criteria for empirically distinguishing among emotional expressions that had been proposed by Campos. The first of these was intersituational specificity, that is, determining if a presumptive emotional expression was produced more often in situations eliciting the target emotion than in situations that elicited another emotion. For example, was the AFFEX-specified anger expression produced in the anger situation more often than in the fear situation? The second criterion was intrasituational specificity, that is, determining if a presumptive emotional expression was produced more often in an emotion situation than were expressions for other emotions. For example, in an anger-eliciting situation, was the AFFEX-specified anger expression produced more often than the AFFEX-expressions for other emotions such as fear, sadness, and so on.

Results showed that infants indeed produced the anger expression more often than other AFFEX-specified negative affect expressions (particularly the fear expression) in the anger situation. However, they also produced the anger expression more often than fear expressions in the fear-eliciting situation. Furthermore, a more comprehensive analysis of all of the infants' facial behaviors showed that the behaviors produced in the two situations were highly correlated. The investigators concluded that 11-month-old infants in all three cultures did indeed experience different emotions in the two eliciting situations but these were not accompanied by facial expressive behavior that was differentiated across the two situations.

In support of this conclusion, Bennett, Bendarsky, and Lewis (2002) conducted a similarly structured study of 4-month-old infants that included an even wider range of emotion-eliciting situations (e.g., sadness, disgust, as well as fear and anger). Their results were largely consistent with those obtained by Camras and her colleagues. However, interestingly, when these investigators conducted a similar study in which they compared the facial expressions of 4-month-olds with the expressions of older infants (12-month-old; Bennett, Bendarsky & Lewis, 2005), they did obtain evidence that some differentiation was beginning to take place. "That is, expressions of happiness, anger, and disgust were produced more often in the appropriate eliciting situations while this did not occur for fear expressions". Other recent studies also have suggested that some differentiation also occurs for toddlers (Buss & Kiel, 2004). However, there is clearly a dearth of research on older babies and young children that incorporates the "gold standard" criteria of intersituational and intrasituational specificity.

FEAR EXPRESSIONS IN YOUNG CHILDREN

One striking feature of both the adult and the developmental literature is the fact that prototypic fear expressions (as described by both Izard and Ekman and as identified in the emotion recognition literature) have rarely been observed. In part, this may be due to the fact is would be unethical to produce intense states of fear in research participants. However, recent trends in social media and self-publishing Web sites have resulted in the posting of hundreds of videos of children responding to the same fearful stimulus in a naturalistic setting. Herein, we describe preliminary analyses from an investigation designed to capitalize on the existence of publicly available videos.

The Scary Maze presents itself as an Internet puzzle game that requires the player to increase her focus as she advances to new levels of more difficult mazes. When the player finishes the last maze, a picture of the demon-possessed girl from the 1973 film *The Exorcist* suddenly appears on the screen accompanied by a loud scream. As the popularity of the Scary Maze increased, people eventually started recording videos of their friends, parents, siblings, or children reacting to the unexpected outcome of the game. Countless numbers of such "reaction videos" were uploaded on YouTube and are publicly accessible. These videos capture people's natural reactions to a consistent stimulus that was intended to be both fear inducing and unexpected. To our knowledge, no previous study utilizing naturalistic data has been able to sample from so many observations of individuals experiencing the same emotion-eliciting stimulus.

These videos provide a novel opportunity to examine the potentially uncontrolled facial responses of children in situations that would be impossible to re-create in a laboratory due to ethical standards guiding research with children. We used these videos in order to investigate the "intrasituational specificity" of the theoretically proposed prototypic expression of fear. As mentioned in previous sections, establishing this specificity requires demonstrating that individuals in an emotion situation create the predicted corresponding emotion expression more often than other expressions. A two-step process was used to assess the intrasituational specificity of the prototypic fear expression. In the first step, another emotion-related component of the children's behavior (i.e., body movements) was assessed by untrained observers in order to establish whether or not the situation was fear inducing. Next, the children's facial expressions were coded using FACS in order to determine if the elicitor (i.e., the scary face accompanied by a shrill scream) evoked more prototypical configurations of fear (or components thereof as described by leading researchers; i.e., Ekman, Friesen, & Hager, 2002; Izard et al., 1983) in comparison to other types of negative facial expressions.

The data for this examination were collected using a sample of 60 publicly accessible videos from YouTube. An undergraduate research assistant, blind to the goals of the study, randomly selected the videos in order to prevent the potentially biased selection of videos that display prototypic fear facial responses. Children in the videos appeared to be between 4 and 7 years of age and their faces were clearly visible. However, the actual stimulus (i.e., the Scary Maze game) was not seen.

Prior to examining the facial expressions that children made in response to the stimulus, the Scary Maze had to be validated as a situation that appeared to induce more fear than other negative emotions. Because we could not obtain self-report measures of the children's emotional experience or feelings, we adapted a method used in infant research (e.g., Camras et al., 2007) in order to overcome the problem that infants are unable to report their own emotions. For our study, 16 untrained undergraduate observers (with no prior knowledge of the Scary Maze) provided subjective ratings of the children's experience of seven different emotions (joy, anger, sadness, surprise, fear, disgust, and distress) on a scale of 1 (not at all) to 5 (very much). To focus the ratings on body movements, the videos were digitally edited so that the children's faces were blurred. Thus, the observer's ratings were based on the children's nonfacial physical actions (e.g., turning away, fleeing, or withdrawing from the computer screen). Such avoidant behaviors are considered to be fear-appropriate according to functionally oriented theories of emotion (Barrett & Campos, 1987; Frijda, 1986).

Children's facial expressions were then coded using FACS, a comprehensive anatomically based facial coding system that uses coding units (termed action units or AUs) to represent facial muscle contractions (Ekman et. al.,

2002). FACS requires coders to objectively determine which facial muscles are activated regardless of whether or not the configuration of muscle movements is considered to be an expression of emotion. Coders for the present study were FACS certified and established conventional levels of reliability on the Scary Maze videos. However, they were aware of the nature of the stimulus videos, and we therefore consider these analyses to be exploratory rather than definitive.

To generate emotional expression scores, the FACS coding was examined and emotion scores were assigned based on whether the configurations of facial muscle movements are considered to be expressions of emotion within either of two commonly used emotion interpretation systems: AFFEX (Izard et. al., 1983) and FACS (Ekman et al., 2002). Both these systems detail a set of prototypic facial expressions (as well as common variations of those expressions) that are said to correspond to discrete emotion categories. For each episode, the action units produced in the upper face (brows/eyes) and lower face (nose/mouth) were examined for the presence or absence of configurations hypothesized to express each of seven emotion categories: happy, surprise, anger, fear, disgust, sad, and physical pain/distress (as designated within FACS and/or MAX/AFFEX). Each episode was assigned a facial expression score of 0–2 for each emotion. Scores indicated whether an emotion-relevant configuration was produced in both areas of the face (upper and lower), only one part of the face (either upper or lower), or was not produced at all. Thus, a score of 2 for an emotion indicated the presence of *both* brow/eye (upper face) and mouth (lower face) configurations corresponding to that emotion. A score of 1 indicated the presence of *either* a brow/eye or a mouth configuration corresponding to the emotion. A score of 0 indicated the *absence* of any brow/eye or a nose/mouth configuration corresponding to the emotion.

Data analyses indicated that the 16 observers rated children's nonfacial responses as significantly higher in surprise than all other emotions. Presumably this was because of the unexpected and sudden appearance of the fear stimulus. Importantly, ratings also were significantly higher for fear than for the other *negative* emotions. Therefore, we attained evidence that the children in the videos were indeed exposed to a stimulus that induced more fear than other forms of negative affect.

Data analyses of the facial expression scoring indicated that children scored significantly higher for fearful expressions than for any other facial expressions, including surprise (see Table 15.1). Across all videos, 38.33% of the children displayed both upper and lower components of fear expressions, whereas 43.33% produced only one component of prototypic fear expressions (i.e., in either the upper or the lower area of the face). This was in contrast to the number of surprise components; across all videos-10% of the children displayed

Table 15.1 MEAN FACIAL EXPRESSION SCORES

Emotion	Mean (SD)
Joy	0.43 (.70)
Anger	0.23 (.50)
Sadness	0.35 (.48)
Surprise	0.70 (.65)
Fear	1.20 (.73)
Distress	0.43 (.78)

both upper and lower components of surprise expressions, whereas 50% of the children produced only one facial component of surprise.

In conclusion, the results tentatively demonstrate that components of the prototypic fear expressions are produced with some frequency in at least one fear-inducing situation occurring outside of the lab environment. This finding is in contrast to prior research, which found that prototypic fear expressions were produced very infrequently even when some degree of fear was experienced. For instance, in the previously most successful attempt, only 33% of spider-phobic adults exposed to spiders produced at least one component of fearful expressions (Vernon & Barenbaum, 2002). In comparison, 82% of children in the present study produced at least one component (upper and/or lower) of prototypic fear. Thus, the results of the present study provide somewhat more support for the validity of prototypic fearful facial expressions that are often used as experimental stimuli throughout emotion research. Still, full-face expressions (involving both components) were produced less than 40% of the time. Furthermore, it can be assumed that parents were most likely to have uploaded videos depicting intense reactions (high levels of fear or surprise). Thus, the rates of fearful and surprised expressions found in this sample of videos may actually be an overrepresentation of normative responses to the Scary Maze stimulus.

Although this study is among the first to examine the validity of prototypic fear expressions in a naturalistic setting, more studies are needed in order to identify the contextual factors that determine whether such expressions will (or will not) be produced. For instance, given that observers rated the children's nonfacial behavior highly on surprise requires one to consider that an unexpected situational element may be required to produce or at least facilitate the production of prototypic fear expressions. Moreover, it should be noted that prototypic surprise expressions were not often observed in the present study, although observers rated the children significantly higher on surprise than on fear. Surprise facial expressions also have not often been observed in previous laboratory-based studies of surprising situations (Schützwohl & Reisenzein, 2012). Thus, more research is needed to determine when surprise expressions are produced as well as when fear expressions are produced. Our third study (described later) provided some preliminary data related to this question.

Regarding the observer ratings of the children's emotional experience, the presence of surprise as well as fear does not invalidate our use of the Scary Maze videos to examine children's production of fear expressions. Previous controversy regarding the validity of prototypic emotional expressions has focused on differentiation among expressions of negative emotions (see Camras et al., 2007; Camras & Shutter, 2010). In the present study, observers rated the children as experiencing fear more highly than any other negative emotion. Thus, we were justified in examining our data to determine if fear-related expressions were correspondingly produced more often than expressions for other negative emotions. Given the relative success of this study, future researchers should consider utilizing video data from publically available sources to study emotions and emotional expressions other than fear. Further efforts in this area of research will help illuminate the association between facial expressions and other aspects of emotion.

CHILDREN'S EMOTIONAL EXPRESSIONS IN THE CONTEXT OF MOTHER–CHILD INTERACTIONS

Developmental studies with older children are also important in advancing the understanding of emotional expression. By the elementary school years, children have accumulated substantial experience in expressing emotion but are increasingly situated within social and interpersonal contexts that might constrain their expression. Because elementary-school-aged children also experience marked improvements in their capacity to manage emotional expressions (Eisenberg & Morris, 2002; Pons, Harris, & de Rosnay, 2004), such expressions may not always represent experienced emotion. Thus, as children get older, they are faced with new social challenges that likely require and utilize different skills in communicating emotion, such as navigating conflict with peers, or attempting to assert emotional and behavioral independence from parents.

As in the Scary Maze study earlier, it is useful to study socially and interpersonally relevant contexts with older children. We chose a parent–child interaction, as the family continues to be an important context in which children learn about emotions (Dunsmore & Halberstadt, 1997; Eisenberg, Cumberland, & Spinrad, 1998; Morris, Silk, Steinberg, Myers, & Robinson, 2007). By studying older children in a familial context, we can determine not only whether children's facial displays are characterized by inter- and intrasituational specificity but also whether children's emotional expressions are more or less prototypical in contexts that approximate the challenges of everyday life.

Specifically, we examined the inter- and intrasituational specificity of facial expressions within a parent–child conflict. The children we studied were drawn from a sample of 203 children who ranged in age from 7 to 9 years, were approximately evenly distributed by gender, and were racially diverse, including both African American and European American children. Third grade was selected as a specific criterion for participation given the dearth of research on the development of older children's emotion understanding, and to hold constant any effects related to the school context (e.g., children of the same age who are in different grade levels).

Children and their mothers were asked to discuss a conflict in a laboratory setting. Topics for discussion were proposed by each dyad member, and they included common sources of conflict for third-grade children and their parents (e.g., homework, chores, fighting with siblings, and bedtime). Three minutes from the beginning of these conflict discussions were then shown as 10-second episodes to nine undergraduate students who independently judged the emotion being expressed by the child in each episode. (Only the children were viewed.) The coders selected their responses from a list of six emotion categories (i.e., joy, anger, sadness, curious/interested/surprised, fear, and disgust) or no emotion. Following past research with this paradigm (Castro, Halberstadt, Lozada, & Craig, 2015), judgments of the nine naïve coders were combined to create an expressive clarity score for each episode. Specifically, expressive clarity was calculated as a ratio of the highest number of coders who agreed that a given episode displayed a given emotion out of the total number of coders. To illustrate, if 8 out of 9 coders rated episode 1 for child A as "joy," the expressive clarity for the episode was calculated as 0.89. Higher values of expressive clarity indicate that a greater number of coders agreed that the child was expressing a specific emotion.

From these data, a subsample of episodes were identified for FACS coding using the criterion of expressive clarity for which at least 7 out of 9 naïve coders agreed upon the emotion expressed by the child. The specific emotion category was not relevant to the identification of episodes, as we were most interested in episodes where emotion communication (or lack thereof in the case of "neutral/no emotion") was very clear. This criterion also resulted in a diverse subsample of emotional states. A total of 510 episodes across 134 children were identified using this process. Next, we present preliminary data from our FACS coding of 441 episodes contributed by 120 children.

Following the protocol used with younger children described earlier, we coded each episode for both the upper and lower facial action units associated with the following six emotion categories: joy, anger, sadness, surprise, fear, and disgust. These codes provided an overall FACS-specified expression score for each of the six emotional expressions. Six expression scores (one for each emotion) were calculated for each episode.

Data were analyzed using multilevel modeling that addressed the two criteria (inter- and intrasituational specificity) proposed by Campos and colleagues (Hiatt, Campos, & Emde, 1979). For the first criterion of intersituational specificity, we found that the FACS-specified joy expression scores were significantly higher in the episodes identified as joy by the naïve coders than in episodes identified for other emotions (see Table 15.2). Similar findings also occurred for FACS-specified expressions of anger and fear, supporting intersituational specificity for these emotional expressions. However, intersituational specificity was not observed for expressions of sadness or surprise. That is, the expression score for surprise was higher in the anger episodes than in the surprise/curious/interested episodes, and the expression score for sadness was virtually the same in the anger and sadness episodes.

With regard to the criterion of intrasituational specificity, we found that for the episodes identified as joy by naïve coders, the FACS expression score for joy was significantly higher than the expression scores for other emotions. Similarly, in the episodes identified as surprise/curious/interested by naïve coders, the FACS expression score for surprise was higher than the expression

Table 15.2 MEAN EMOTION FACIAL EXPRESSION SCORE WITHIN EACH CATEGORY OF EMOTION EPISODE

	Episode Categorization Based on Naive Coder Emotion Ratings				
	Joy	Anger	Sadness	Surprise/ Curious/ Interested	Fear
Facial Expression Emotion Category					
Joy	**1.96**	0.38	0.26	0.61	0.30
Anger	0.21	**0.79**	0.22	0.44	0.40
Sadness	0.09	0.46	**0.48**	0.13	0.30
Surprise	0.79	0.97	0.65	**0.89**	0.80
Fear	0.37	0.51	0.22	0.34	**0.80**
Disgust	0.32	0.43	0.26	0.31	0.30

Note: Values on the diagonal represent mean values of the FACS-specified facial emotion expression scores for the target emotion category averaged across episodes (value range: 0 to 2). All other values represent emotion expression scores for nontarget emotion expressions. No episodes were rated as displaying disgust by the naïve coders; thus, that column is omitted.

scores for the other emotions. However, the same degree of intrasituational specificity was not found in the negative emotion episodes. That is, for the emotion episode categories of anger and sadness, the FACS expression score for surprise was higher than the expression score for any of the other emotions. Moreover, in episodes identified as fear by the naïve coders, FACS expression scores were equally high for surprise and fear emotion categories. However, if only the negative emotional expressions were considered, greater intrasituational specificity was found. That is, the highest negative emotion expression FACS score corresponded to the episode's emotion category (i.e., the emotion category receiving an expressive clarity score of 0.78 or greater for the episode).

The data thus demonstrate considerable variability across emotions in the intersituational and intrasituational specificity of their theoretically predicted emotional expressions. Both criteria were met only for joy expressions. Intersituational specificity was lowest for surprise expressions. In fact, only 27% of the full-face surprise expressions occurred in episodes identified as surprise by naïve coders. Instead, the FACS-specified surprise expression was frequently produced in episodes identified as primarily involving other emotions according to naïve coders, most notably anger. The predominance of surprise-related expressions in the anger episodes contributed to the particularly low level of intrasituational specificity observed for anger episodes.

Interestingly, 106 of the 120 children in the final data set expressed two or more emotions within a single episode, with one child actually demonstrating components of all six FACS-specified expressions within one 10-second episode. This finding may reflect the fact that the same situation (i.e., episode) may elicit a range of emotional experiences (and consequently a range of emotional expressions) within the same episode and highlights the complexity and rapidity of emotion experience that may be available to 7- to 9-year-old children. Still it is noteworthy that in these presumably multiemotion episodes, components of the surprise expression typically occurred more often than components of the emotion rated highest by the naïve coders (i.e., for the anger, sadness, and fear episodes).

One possible explanation for this may be related to the multifunctionality of human facial expressions. In particular, it has long been recognized that facial movements may serve communicative functions other than the expression of emotions (Ekman, 1972; Ekman & Friesen, 1969). For example, brow raises may act as "conversational markers" conveying emphasis rather than surprise. This would not be unexpected in the type of mother–child conversations investigated herein. The fact that naïve coders often judged an episode to primarily involve a nonsurprise emotion (e.g., anger) despite the predominance of surprise expression components testifies to the complex multifaceted nature of interpersonal communication. That is, observers do not automatically read facial expressions as indicators of emotion, but instead they infer emotion based on an entire pattern of behavior interpreted within a particular situational context. Alternative nonemotion interpretations of facial expressions may be particularly likely when only components of such expressions (e.g., only the brow raise component of surprise) rather than full-face prototypical expressions are produced.

In the present study, third-grade children did not typically produce full-face prototypical expressions corresponding to the primary emotion they were judged to express. Consistent with findings presented earlier in the chapter with younger children. full-face fear expressions were produced in only 30% of the fear episodes. For the other negative emotions, the percentages were even lower: Only 14% of the anger episodes included a full-face anger expression, and only 17% of the sadness episodes included a full-face sadness expression. Full-face surprise expressions were produced in only 26% of the surprise episodes. In fact, only for the joy episodes were emotion-consistent full-face expressions produced most of the time (i.e., in 96% of the joy episodes). These findings are particularly striking, given that 7 out of 9 naïve judges had agreed about the primary emotion being expressed in the episode. Clearly, the emotions other than joy were often being expressed solely by means other than full-face prototypic facial expressions. It is thus important that we adapt our developmental and theoretical perspectives regarding normative emotion experience and expression to account for the nature of real emotions as communicated by real children in real contexts.

SUMMARY AND CONCLUDING REMARKS

This chapter addressed the issue of whether the "prototypic" facial expressions so often used in emotion recognition research are spontaneously produced in real-life situations. Taking a developmental perspective, we studied three age groups. We observed infants who are presumably too young to be regulating their spontaneous expressive behavior (e.g., inhibiting their expressions in accordance with social or personal "display rules"). We also looked at older children who would be capable of such regulation but were confronted with a sudden intense emotion stimulus (during the Scary Maze stimulus event) that may preclude the possibility of immediate expressive management. Lastly, we examined third-grade children's behavior in the context of mother–child conversations about areas of interpersonal conflict, and during which expressive regulation might indeed be expected to take place. Including this latter type of study is important in order to ascertain the extent to which prototypic emotional facial expressions are the means through which emotion is communicated in day-to-day life. Also of importance, participants in all of our studies were judged by observers to be experiencing or expressing emotion irrespective of whether they produced the predicted emotional facial expression. Thus, our studies did not simply "stack the deck" with regard to prototypic facial expressions, but rather drew on a broad representative sampling of spontaneous emotional communications.

Our data show that facial expressions which include the prototypes are indeed involved in emotion communication, but not to the extent originally predicted by expression-oriented emotion theories (e.g., Izard, Ekman). Full-face prototypic expressions of joy were often observed when the participant was judged by naïve observers to be experiencing joy (i.e., during the mother–child interactions). However, full-face prototypic expressions of discrete negative emotions were not typically seen in any of the research investigations presented in this chapter. This is in contrast to the "automatic readout" hypothesis, which suggests the communicative importance of automatically expressed emotion. In all three age groups, production of the full-face prototypes was infrequent—even when it could be assumed that expressers were not attempting to inhibit or regulate their expressivity (i.e., as would be true for infants) or when expressers appeared to be experiencing strong emotion (i.e., during the Scary Maze).

Although full-face prototypic expressions were infrequent, we did observe some differential use of emotion-related expression components. That is, our analyses examining intersituational specificity and intrasituational specificity indicated that for several emotions (particularly joy, anger, and fear), children selectively produced components of expressions associated with the emotion they were judged to experience or express. However, even for these emotions, some qualifications applied. In particular, selectivity for anger and fear expression components produced during the mother–child interactions was found only when comparisons were made among the negative emotions (i.e., not including the surprise expression). In addition, this differential use of anger-related versus fear-related expression components was seen in younger and older children—but not in infants less than 1 year of age. Furthermore, no differential use of sadness-related expression components was found in our research. Lastly, as indicated earlier, the relation between observers' judgments of surprise and participants' production of surprise-related expression components was particularly complex and differed markedly from that which might be predicted by any simple version of discrete emotion theory.

Our findings suggest several interesting (albeit tentative) conclusions, with implications for future research. Most notably, clear emotion communication does not seem to require the use of full-face prototypic emotional expressions, as suggested by theory. This point is especially salient in the findings from the study of mother–child interactions. Here, we examined episodes in which there was high agreement among naïve observers regarding the presence or absence of a primary emotion being expressed by the child. Yet, as emphasized earlier, full-face prototypic negative emotional expressions were infrequent. Thus, not only were they relatively rare in everyday life, but they appear to be unnecessary. Of course, our mother–child interactions did not include the very highest intensity events, and it may be in these cases that full-face prototypical expressions provide the most benefit.

If full-face prototypical expressions are relatively infrequent and possibly not necessary, then studies of emotional expression recognition might benefit from including "partial prototype" facial stimuli (i.e., expressions that include only some components of the full-face prototypes) in addition to full-face prototypic expressions. Our results indicate that children frequently produced some component of the prototype, highlighting the need to include such expressions in research. Partial-prototype expressions have indeed been employed in adult studies that focus on the issue of holistic versus featural expression processing (e.g., Bombari et. al., 2013). However, the ecological validity of these expressions (i.e., whether they reflect natural expressive behavior) has not been considered. One possibility would be to inspect facial coding datasets (such as ours) to identify the specific morphology of commonly used expressions that contain components of the prototypic expressions. Including such partial-prototype expressions might also prove useful in developmental studies that examine associations between emotion recognition and children's social competence.

With respect to development, the research described in this chapter also suggests that the association between emotion and emotional facial expression undergoes important changes between infancy and childhood. Together with additional work by other investigators (reviewed in Camras, Fatani, Fraumeni, & Shuster, 2016; Camras & Shutter, 2010), the findings are consistent with a number of related theories that posit that expressive differentiation and integration take place during the course of development. For example, in her highly influential theory, Bridges (1932) proposed that discrete negative emotions (and their accompanying facial expressions) emerge during infancy and childhood from an earlier state of relatively undifferentiated distress. Subsequently, Sroufe (1996) also presented a theory of emotional and expressive development in which discrete adult-like emotions are derived from earlier less differentiated emotion states. Drawing upon a dynamical systems theory, Camras (2011) has proposed that components of emotion systems (e.g., expressions, appraisals, instrumental actions) emerge heterochronically (i.e., at different times during the course of development) and are integrated into discrete emotion systems. However, the inclusion of any particular component in any particular emotion episode is dependent on the context in which the episode takes place. Importantly, all of these developmental theories differ markedly from nondevelopmental theories that posit the automatic production of prototypic emotional facial expressions during unregulated emotion episodes. These theories also raise questions about assumptions implicit in some emotion research, that is, that full-face prototypic expressions have overwhelming importance in day-to-day emotion communication.

Despite the noted strengths, particularly in advancing an understanding of spontaneous emotion communication, the research described in this chapter also has significant limitations. First, self-report measures of emotion experience were not included herein. Such measures cannot be collected from preverbal infants and would be difficult to obtain from children appearing in posted YouTube videos. Self-report measures were collected from children in the mother–child interaction study, but these data have not yet been examined. Thus, our studies are most accurately described as addressing questions regarding the association between the production of emotional facial expressions and the communication of emotion to observers (who hopefully do—but possibly do not—accurately perceive the expresser's experienced emotion). Clearly, future research should more directly examine the coherence between participants' facial behaviors and their self-reported affective experiences.

Second, our ability to accurately discern the frequency with which prototypic or partial-prototypic emotional expressions are produced in nature was hampered by our inability to eliminate a potential source of selection bias in one of our studies. Specifically, the Scary Maze videos posted on YouTube may not be a representative sample of all children's responses. Rather, it may be that parents posted their videos only when an intense emotional reaction was obtained. However, if we did assume that the posted videos displayed reactions at the higher end of the intensity range, we would be more likely to expect that the children appearing in them would show full-face prototypic fear expressions. Nonetheless, such expressions were still infrequent. This observation would seem to bolster our claim that full-face prototypic expressions are not the common currency of emotion communication.

In conclusion, the research we present in this chapter suggests that the association between facial expression and emotion is more complex than had been originally envisioned within expression-oriented emotion theories. Over the course of development, this association appears to change such that more specific links between discrete emotions and emotional facial expressions emerge. At the same time, a one-to-one invariant *relationship* between prototypic facial expressions and other components of discrete emotions may never arise. Beyond the several directions for future research indicated earlier, we believe that further work that documents circumstances under which prototypic emotional expressions and/or their components are produced is needed in order to enable a more confident assessment of the intrapersonal, interpersonal, and additional contextual factors that determine when and how emotion is communicated by means of facial expression.

REFERENCES

Barrett, K. C., & Campos, J. J. (1987). Perspectives on emotional development: II. A functionalist approach to emotions. In J. Osofsky (Ed.), *Handbook of infant development* (2nd ed., pp. 555–578). New York, NY: Wiley.

Bennett, D., Bendersky, M., & Lewis, M. (2002). Facial expressivity at 4 months: A context by expression analysis. *Infancy, 3*(1), 97–113.

Bennett, D., Bendersky, M., & Lewis, M. (2005). Does the organization of emotional expression change over time? Facial expressivity from 4 to 12 months. *Infancy, 8*, 167–187.

Bridges, K. M. B. (1932). Emotional development in early infancy. *Child Development, 3*, 324–341.

Bombari, D., Schmid, P., Schmid Mast, M., Birri, S., Mast, F., & Lobmaier, J. (2013). Emotion recognition: The role of featural and configural face information. *The Quarterly Journal of Experimental Psychology, 66*, 2426–2442. doi: 10.1080/17470218.2013.789065

Buss, K., & Kiel, E. (2004). Comparison of sadness, anger, and fear facial expressions when toddlers look at their mothers. *Child Development, 76*(6), 1761–1773.

Camras, L. A. (1992). Expressive development and basic emotion. *Cognition and Emotion, 6*(3/4), 269–283.

Camras, L. A. (2011). Differentiation, dynamical integration, and functional emotional development. *Emotion Review, 3*(2), 138–146.

Camras, L. A., Fatani, S., Fraumeni, B., & Shuster, M. (2016). The development of facial expressions: Current perspectives on infant emotions. In M. Lewis, J. Haviland-Jones, & L. Feldman Barrett (Eds.) *Handbook of emotions* (4rd ed., pp 255 - 271). New York, NY: Guilford.

Camras, L. A., Oster, H., Bakeman, R., Meng, Z., Ujiie, T., & Campos, J. J. (2007). Do infants show distinct negative facial expressions for different negative emotions? Emotional expression in European-American, Chinese, and Japanese infants. *Infancy, 11*(2), 131–155.

Camras, L. A., & Shutter, J. M. (2010). Emotional facial expressions in infancy. *Emotion Review, 2*(2), 120–129.

Castro, V. L., Halberstadt, A. G., Lozada, F. T., & Craig, A. B. (2015). Parents' emotion-related beliefs, behaviors, and skills predict children's recognition of emotion. *Infant and Child Development, 24*, 1–22. doi: 10.1002/icd.1868

Dunsmore, J. C., & Halberstadt, A. G. (1997). How does family emotional expressiveness affect children's schemas? *New Directions for Child and Adolescent Development, 77*, 45–68. doi:10.1002/cd.23219977704

Ekman, P. (1972). Universals and cultural differences in facial expressions of emotion. In J. Cole (Ed.), *Nebraska Symposium on Motivation, 1971* (Vol. 19, pp. 207–282). Lincoln: University of Nebraska Press.

Ekman, P., & Friesen, W. (1969). The repertoire of nonverbal behavior: Categories, origins, usage, and coding. *Semiotica, 1*(1), 49-98.

Ekman, P., Friesen, W. V., & Hager, J. (2002). Facial action coding system. Salt Lake City, UT: Research Nexus.

Eisenberg, N., & Morris, A. S. (2002). Children's emotion-related regulation. In R. V. Kail (Ed.), *Advances in child development and behavior* (Vol. 30) (pp. 189–229). San Diego, CA: Academic Press.

Eisenberg, N., Cumberland, A., & Spinrad, T. L. (1998). Parental socialization of emotion. *Psychological Inquiry, 9*, 241–273. doi:10.1207/s15327965pli0904_1

Frijda, N. (1986). *The emotions*. Cambridge, England: Cambridge University Press.

Hiatt, S. W., Campos, J. J., & Emde, R. N. (1979). Facial patterning and infant emotional expression: Happiness, surprise, and fear. *Child Development, 50*, 1020–1035. doi:10.2307/1129328

Izard, C. E. (1995). The maximally discriminative facial movement coding system. Unpublished manuscript.

Izard, C. E., Dougherty, L., & Hembree, E. (1983). A system for identifying affect expressions by holistic judgments (AFFEX). Newark: Instructional Resources Center, University of Delaware.

Izard, C. E., & Malatesta, C. (1987). Perspectives on emotional development I: Differential emotions theory of early emotional development. In J. Osofsky (Ed.), *Handbook of infant development* (2nd ed., pp. 494–554). New York, NY: Wiley.

Morris, A. S., Silk, J. S., Steinberg, L., Myers, S. S., & Robinson, L. R. (2007). The role of the family context in the development of emotion regulation. *Social Development, 16*, 361–388. doi:10.1111/j.1467-9507.2007.00389.x

Oster, H. (2005). The repertoire of infant facial expressions: An ontogenetic perspective. In J. Nadel & D. Muir (Eds.), *Emotional development* (pp. 261–292). Oxford, England: Oxford University Press.

Oster, H. (2006). Baby FACS: Facial Action Coding System for Infants and Young Children. Unpublished monograph and coding manual. New York University.

Oster, H., Hegley, D., & Nagel, L. (1992). Adult judgments and fine-grained analysis of infant facial expressions: Testing the validity of a priori coding formulas. *Developmental Psychology, 28*, 1115–1131.

Pons, F., Harris, P. L., & de Rosnay, M. (2004). Emotion comprehension between 3 and 11 years: Developmental periods and hierarchical organization. *European Journal of Developmental Psychology, 1*, 127–152. doi:10.1080/17405620344000022

Schützwohl, A., & Reisenzein, R. (2012). Facial expressions in response to a highly surprising event exceeding the field of vision: A test of Darwin's theory of surprise. *Evolution and Human Behavior*, 33, 657 – 664.

Sroufe, L. A. (1996). Emotional development. New York, NY: Cambridge University Press.

Vernon, L. L., & Berenbaum, H. (2002). Disgust and fear in response to spiders. *Cognition and Emotion, 16*, 809–830. doi:10.1080/02699930143000464

16

The Development of Emotion Recognition

The Broad-to-Differentiated Hypothesis

SHERRI C. WIDEN

Imagine a woman who encounters a bear on a forest path. She gasps then screams. Her eyes are open wide and she stands stock still (because to run would be folly). Likely you have already concluded that she is scared. How would a young child interpret this same scene? If the child concluded that the woman was angry, should we say that the child is incorrect or that this response is a reflection of his or her current emotion concepts? And what would the child focus on: the cause or some aspect of the person's reaction? The broad-to-differentiated hypothesis evolved from efforts to answer these types of questions and to describe the development of children's emotion concepts. It specifies the nature of children's emotion concepts at different ages and how these concepts are acquired and change with age.

EMOTION CONCEPTS ARE THE FOUNDATION FOR OTHER SKILLS AND ABILITIES

A clear description of the acquisition of emotion concepts is important in its own right. In addition, children's level of emotion concept acquisition predicts academic and social outcomes. For example, preschoolers with higher levels of emotion concept acquisition (labeling facial expressions and emotional situations) were more likely to have better school adjustment, higher academic performance, and more positive peer relationships (Denham et al., 2003; Garner & Waajid, 2012; Izard et al., 2001; O'Neil, Welsh, Parke, Wang, & Strand, 1997; Shields et al., 2001). Kindergarteners who selected the "correct" (i.e., made the expected or predicted response) facial expressions for brief emotion stories had stronger social skills and higher academic performance in subsequent grades (Farmer, Bierman, & Conduct Problems Prevention Research, 2002) and as much as 4 years later (Izard et al., 2001).

Emotion concept acquisition is an important part of emotional intelligence. Emotional intelligence skills enable the use of emotions for thinking and of thinking for emotion management in both the self and others (Salovey & Mayer, 1989). According to the ability model of emotional intelligence, there are four distinct but related branches of emotional intelligence: (1) perceiving, appraising, and expressing emotion; (2) using and generating emotions to facilitate performance on tasks; (3) understanding emotions in the self and others; and (4) regulating emotion to attain goals (Mayer & Salovey, 1997). Tasks in which children label or otherwise categorize emotions displayed in facial expressions measure *perceiving emotions*, which entails discriminating emotions in facial expressions, body postures, voices, and so on. Tasks in which children label or describe emotional situations measure *understanding emotions*, which entails knowing the causes and consequences of emotions. These tasks have been widely used in studies of children's acquisition of emotion concepts (Balconi & Carrera, 2007; Barbosa-Leiker, Strand, Mamey, & Downs, 2014; Russell & Widen, 2002b; Widen, Christy, Hewett, & Russell, 2011; Widen, Pochedly, & Russell, 2015; Widen & Russell, 2004, 2011). In addition, performance on these tasks is correlated with other assessments of children's emotional intelligence (Garner & Waajid, 2012; Parker, Mathis, & Kupersmidt, 2013).

Children's association of emotions with facial expressions and stories lays the foundation for more advanced emotion skills. In children between 3 and 11 years, emotion concept acquisition progressed in three steps (Pons, Harris, & de Rosnay, 2004). First, 3-year-olds "correctly" labeled facial expressions of emotions and emotional situations. Second, 5-year-olds also understood how beliefs and desires influenced others' emotional responses. Third, 7-year-olds also understood emotion regulation. In addition to being able to label some facial expressions by the end of preschool, children are acquiring other skills such as affective perspective-taking (recognizing that another person has feelings that may differ from their own), managing negative emotions more effectively, and using language to discuss and regulate their feelings (Carroll & Steward, 1984; Fischer, Shaver, & Carnochan, 1990; Greenberg, Kusche, Cook, & Quamma, 1995). Between 7 and 9 years, children's vocabulary of emotion words increases, and they are better able to discuss their own emotions, recognize others' emotions, and understand simultaneous emotions (Greenberg et al., 1995).

THE BROAD-TO-DIFFERENTIATED HYPOTHESIS

There is an abundant literature on the development of children's emotion concepts. A search on PsycInfo (April 13, 2015) found 57,600 publications (all fields search: child* AND emotion OR facial expression AND recognition OR understanding OR knowledge). Many of these publications share an underlying assumption that children understand facial expressions earliest and interpret them as specific emotions (e.g., a smile means happiness, wide eyes and wide-stretched lips means fear, lowered brows and compressed lips means anger, etc.) and that children can use that understanding to learn about other components of emotion, such as causes and consequences (e.g., Denham, 1998).

This assumption is based on basic emotions theory (Izard, 1971, 1994), which proposes that we evolved to both produce and recognize facial expressions. The subsequent acquisition of other components of emotion concepts has not been clearly described by this view. On this account, facial expressions are evolved signals of specific emotions which are also universally, automatically (and perhaps innately) recognized (Izard, 1994; Shariff & Tracy, 2011). It follows that if facial expressions are evolved signals, then recognition and production had to coevolve. Even infants in the first 6 months of life are thought to recognize emotion from facial expressions (e.g., D'Entremont & Muir, 1999; Haviland & Lelwica, 1987; Izard, 1971; Walker-Andrews, 2005). Indeed, recognition of facial expressions has been proposed as the primary mode of communication between infants and caregivers (Leppänen & Nelson, 2006). Some evidence is consistent with this assumption, but the majority is not. It is not even clear that infants and children produce the expected facial expressions in response to emotional situations (though they may produce individual components of the expected expression; see Camras, Castro, & Halberstadt, this volume). As described by the broad-to-differentiated hypothesis, facial expressions are neither the earliest nor the strongest components of most emotion concepts.

The broad-to-differentiated hypothesis describes children's acquisition of emotion concepts. According to this hypothesis, children's earliest emotion concepts are broad and valence-based (feels good vs. feels bad rather than more discrete adult-like concepts such as anger, fear, etc.) and gradually narrow as more discrete concepts are acquired. Children's acquisition of emotion concepts and labels is systematic. This order of acquisition was identified by analyzing children's "correct" and "incorrect" free labeling responses (rather

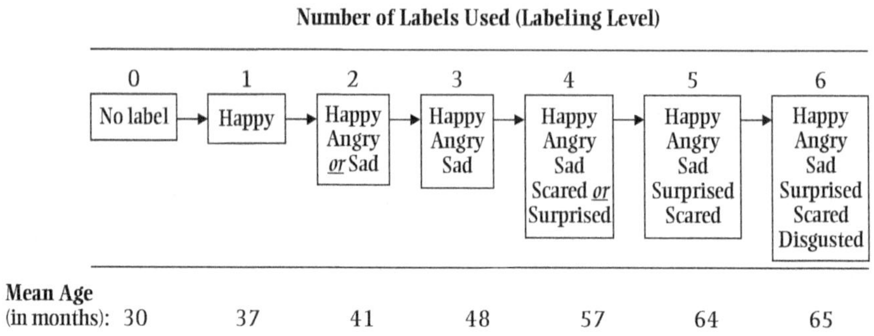

Figure 16.1 Labeling levels children (2–9 years) who labeled facial expressions of basic emotions. (Adapted from Widen, 2013)

than focusing on only the "correct" responses) to facial expressions of (so-called) basic emotions (happiness, sadness, anger, fear, surprise, disgust). To be counted as using a particular label (e.g., *angry*), children could use any of a family of close synonyms (e.g., for anger, *angry, mad, frustrated*, and so on, were all coded as *angry*). Based on the number of different emotion category labels used, children were grouped into different labeling levels (Widen & Russell, 2003, 2008b). Figure 16.1 illustrates the labels used by children in an aggregated sample (N = 1,050, ages 2–9 years; see Widen, 2013): At Labeling Level 0, children offer no labels. At Labeling Level 1, children use only *happy*. At Labeling Level 2, they add *sad* or *angry* and then, at Labeling Level 3, they add the other (*angry* or *sad*, respectively). At Labeling Level 4, children add *scared* or *surprised* and, then, at Labeling Level 5, they add the other (*surprised* or *scared*, respectively). At Labeling Level 6, children add *disgusted*, the last of the basic emotions. Of the 1,050 children, 971 (92.5%) fit this model. In addition, age increased with labeling level from 2 years; 6 months at Labeling Level 0 to 6 years; 5 months at Labeling Level 6.

Figure 16.2 further illustrates the differentiation of the broad negative emotion concept that young children in this aggregated sample called *angry* (Widen, 2013). At Labeling Level 2, *angry* was children's modal label for the anger, disgust, and sadness facial expressions. At Labeling Level 3, children differentiated the broad negative concept and used two labels modally: They used *angry* for the anger and disgust faces and *sad* for the sadness and fear faces. At Labeling Levels 4 and 5 (which did not differ from each other for this example), children used three labels modally: They again used *angry* for the anger and disgust faces. They differentiated the *sad* concept and now used *sad* for the sadness face and *scared* for the fear face. At Labeling Level 6, children's modal response for each of the facial expressions was the "correct" label.

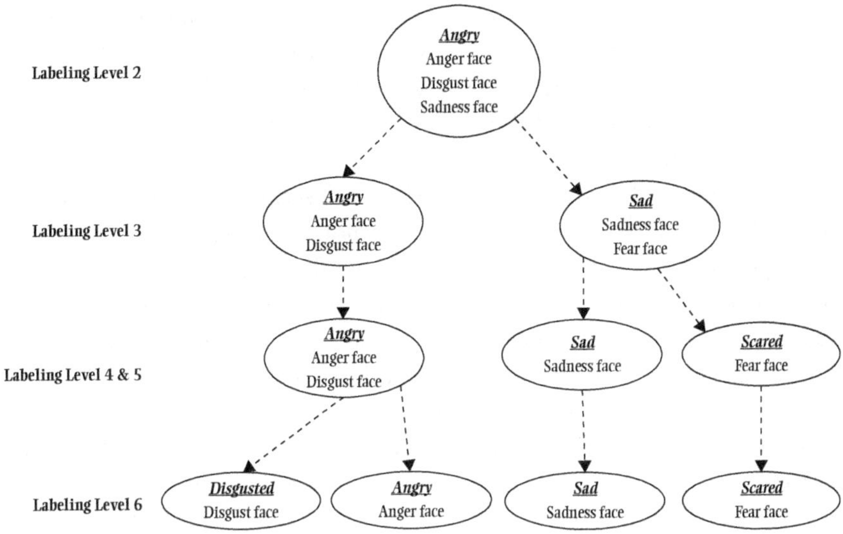

Figure 16.2 Modal emotion labels (in bold and underlined) that children at each labeling level used for facial expressions of basic emotions. (Adapted from Widen, 2013)

Children seem to label some facial expressions—happiness, anger, and sadness—"correctly" from an early age, but what does *correct* mean in this context? On all labeling tasks, participants are more likely to use some emotion labels more frequently than others (Wagner, 1993). For example, when children (2–10 years) were asked to freely label facial expressions or emotion stories, they used *happy, sad*, and *angry* most frequently, both "correctly" and "incorrectly" (Maassarani, Gosselin, Montembeault, & Gagnon, 2014; Widen & Russell, 2003, 2008a, 2010a). In contrast, children used *scared, surprised*, or *disgusted* less frequently, both "correctly" and "incorrectly." Thus, children's high percentage of "correct" responses for happiness, anger, and sadness may be in part a happy accident of their frequent use of these labels and reflects the broad nature of these early emotion concepts.

Although children use *happy, sad*, and *angry* "incorrectly" more often than other "incorrect" emotion labels, their use of these labels is systematic. When children make an "incorrect" response on a labeling task, their responses are of the same valence and similar levels of arousal as the "correct" label (e.g., labeling the disgust face as *angry* or the surprise face as *scared*) than from a dissimilar one (*happy* or *sad*, respectively). The unbiased hit rate (which takes into account both hit rate and overall use of that emotion label; Wagner, 1993) is one method to address both the frequency of label use as described earlier and the "incorrect" labels that children apply to different facial expressions. For example, 2-year-olds aggregated from five studies (N = 94, see Widen, 2013) used *angry* at above-chance levels for the anger, sadness, and disgust facial expressions—the two expressions with the most similar levels of displeasure and arousal to anger (Russell, 1980; Russell & Bullock, 1985), but not for the fear, surprise, or happiness faces.

The broad-to-differentiated hypothesis also describes how the narrowing of the initial valence-based concepts occurs. Emotion concepts can be described as scripts composed of causally and temporally related components (e.g., the cause occurs before the emotional behavior or the consequences; Fehr & Russell, 1984). Children's developmental task is to differentiate the valence-based concepts into more discrete emotion concepts—but how do they begin to do so? From among all the causes, consequences, behaviors, facial expressions, and so on that young children include in "feels bad", they might notice that certain causes (e.g., danger) are related to certain behaviors (e.g., running away).

The component that provides the initial toehold on an emotion concept is not the same for each emotion. Rather, children may initially understand some concepts via the emotion's cause (e.g., the threat of danger for fear), for others via the associated behaviors (e.g., aggressive behaviors for anger), and so on. Differentiation within the two initial valence-based concepts is a gradual process that occurs over the course of childhood—and even into adolescence (Widen et al., 2015)—as children connect the various components of a specific emotion concept (Widen, 2013, 2016; Widen & Russell, 2008b), until they have acquired the adult taxonomy of emotion concepts.

Facial expressions are components of basic emotion concepts (happiness, sadness, anger, fear, surprise, disgust) but are not the starting point of differentiation for most emotion concepts (Widen, 2013; Widen & Russell, 2008b, 2013). Indeed, although the pattern of differentiation is the same for both facial expressions and emotion stories, children differentiate stories faster than facial expressions (Widen & Russell, 2010a, 2010b). Disgust provides a particularly strong example of the difference in the acquisition of stories versus facial expressions: Preschoolers can both label disgust stories and describe the causes of disgust (presented as a label or a behavioral consequence; Widen & Russell, 2002, 2004), but it is not until 9 years or older that the majority of children label the disgust facial expressions as *disgusted* (Widen et al., 2015; Widen & Russell, 2013). Thus, like other components, facial expressions must be differentiated from the broad, valence-based concepts and connected to the other components in that emotion's concept.

The broad-to-differentiated hypothesis was based on English-speaking children's free labeling responses to facial expressions. It has now been extended to other languages and tasks. French Canadian children show the same pattern of differentiation (Maassarani et al., 2014). Palestinian children show the same narrowing of emotion concepts with age (Kayyal, Widen, & Russell, 2015). The model has also been found when children freely label body postures or emotion stories (Nelson, Hudspeth, & Russell, 2013; Nelson & Russell, 2011; Widen & Russell, 2008a, 2010a, 2010b) and on other categorization tasks (Kayyal et al., 2015; Widen & Russell, 2008a).

Although the pattern of differentiation is similar across languages and culture, there is also evidence that emotion concepts and the interpretation of facial expressions vary with both language and culture. For example, when people from illiterate, non-Westernized cultures have been asked to label the emotion in disgust facial expressions, they used words that translated as *contempt* and *happiness* or they had no consistent interpretation at all (Sorenson, 1976). Compared to American children, Palestinian children of the same age included a wider variety of negative facial expressions in categories such as anger, fear, and sadness (Kayyal et al., 2015).

The language participants are tested in can also impact their interpretation of facial expressions. The standard, prototypical facial expressions were developed by English-speaking researchers (Ekman & Friesen, 1971; Izard, 1971). But there is clear evidence that emotion words and concepts are not equivalent in different languages (Russell & Sato, 1995; Wierzbicka, 2009). Indeed, some languages have emotion words that do not directly translatable. Two common examples are the Japanese *amae* (the need to be in good favor with and able to depend upon an authority figure; Doi, 1981) and the German *schadenfreude* (pleasure at another's misfortune). A less common example is the Czech *litost* (which has no direct translation in any language and in has been equated to a synthesis of many emotions—in English, grief, sympathy, remorse, longing; Kundera, 1980). And the Spanish *verguenza* (which is commonly translated as the English *shame* but has a few overlapping features; Hurtado de Mendoza, Fernández-Dols, Parrott, & Carrera, 2010). Conversely, there is no word in Arabic for the English *frustration* (Russell, 1991).

A clear example of the impact of language on the interpretation of facial expressions comes from a study that had three samples of adults: English-speaking Americans, Arabic-speaking Palestinians, and English-speaking Palestinians (Kayyal & Russell, 2013). Americans and Palestinians differed in the emotion labels they associated with some facial expressions. And, more surprisingly, so did Arabic- and English-speaking Palestinians. The influence of language on perception and other psychological processes, including emotion attribution, has been investigated by others (Gelman, 2003; Gentner & Goldin-Meadow, 2003; Lindquist, Barrett, Bliss-Moreau, & Russell, 2006; Linquist & Gendron, 2013).

DEVELOPMENT OF EMOTION CONCEPTS FROM VALENCE BASED TO DISCRETE

Research on a wide variety of tasks and ages has shown that infants and young children understand emotions in terms of valence and that older children have an increasing command of more specific emotion concepts. In social referencing, infants (10 months) use another's expressions of emotion (e.g., facial expressions and vocalizations) to guide their own behavior in ambiguous situations. For example, based on the expression a parent makes when an infant is in an ambiguous situation (such as a visual cliff or a novel toy), the infant will approach the cause of the parent's emotion (given a positive parental expression) or avoid it (given a negative parental expression; Klinnert, Emde, Butterfield, & Campos, 1986; Moses, Baldwin, Rosicky, & Tidball, 2001; Walden & Kim, 2005). By 18 months, based on the positive or negative expression a person makes in response to different foods, toddlers can determine which food that person wants (Repacholi & Gopnik, 1997). These findings support the broad-to-differentiated hypothesis: Infants and toddlers can discriminate between emotions of opposite valence (such as joy and anger; Widen, 2013; Widen et al., 2015; Widen & Russell, 2008b)—but there is little evidence that infants and toddlers discriminate specific emotions of the same valence (e.g., anger vs. fear).

By 2 years of age, children can respond to emotional stimuli in more explicit and abstract ways than infants can. At this age, they categorize emotions in both nonverbal and verbal tasks (Russell & Widen, 2002a; Widen & Russell, 2008a). Nonetheless, 2-year-olds' emotion concepts are valence based rather than discrete. When 2-year-olds were asked to identify angry facial expressions by including them in an "angry box" and excluding others, they included all of the negative expressions (anger, disgust, fear, sadness) and excluded the positive ones (happiness, excitement, contentment; Widen & Russell, 2008a). Three-year-olds excluded more of the "incorrect" negative facial expressions from the angry box than the 2-year-olds, indicating that their anger concept was narrowing. The narrowing of the anger concept continues through preschool and into middle childhood until the adult concept is acquired (Gao & Maurer, 2009, 2010; Roberson, Kikutani, Döge, Whitaker, & Majid, 2011; Widen & Russell, 2008a). This pattern of narrowing from valence-based concepts in young children to more discrete concepts in older children also occurs when children freely label facial expressions or stories (Maassarani et al., 2014; Nelson & Russell, 2012; Widen & Russell, 2003, 2008a, 2010a).

To identify the components of emotion scripts that children acquire earlier and understand better, the components must be presented in isolation—for example, asking children to label faces and, separately, emotion stories. Studies that have done so have found a face inferiority effect (Balconi & Carrera,

2007; Reichenbach & Masters, 1983; Russell & Widen, 2002a, 2002b; Widen & Russell, 2002, 2004, 2010a, 2010b): Children are less likely to label facial expressions "correctly" than the corresponding stories. This effect holds overall and is especially strong for fear and disgust and for embarrassment, shame, compassion, and contempt (each of which has a proposed facial expression; Ekman & Heider, 1988; Haidt & Keltner, 1999; van der Schalk, Hawk, Fischer, & Doosje, 2011). It also holds whether children (from 3 to 18 years) free label, categorize, or describe the causes of emotions.

Similarly, when children's interpretation of emotion labels versus facial expressions is compared, a label superiority effect has been found. This effect is especially strong for disgust (Camras & Allison, 1985; Russell & Widen, 2002a, 2002b; Widen & Russell, 2004). In story-telling tasks, children described a cause for the label (*disgusted*) or for the disgust facial expression. Children's responses to the label were recognized (by adult judges) as disgust. Their responses to the facial expression were recognized as anger (Russell & Widen, 2002b; Widen & Russell, 2004, 2010c). The label superiority effect denotes the power of labels more generally as shown in research on the role of labels in concept acquisition (Gelman, 2003; Gentner & Goldin-Meadow, 2003), in the role of emotion labels in emotion concepts in particular (Lindquist, Barrett, Bliss-Moreau, & Russell, 2006; Lindquist & Gendron, 2013), and in research showing that the emotion domain is partitioned differently in different languages and cultures (de Mendoza, Fernández-Dols, Parrott, & Carrera, 2010; Russell & Sato, 1995; Wierzbicka, 2009).

Based on the available data, it is possible to identify the components that best tap children's emotion concepts. Facial expressions may be the strongest components for infants' and toddlers' early valence-based concepts—which are formed before language is acquired. Behavioral consequences are strongest for anger, labels for fear, and both labels and situations (as described in stories) for disgust. For other emotions such as embarrassment, shame, and so on, the strongest component is understudied, but so far situations are strongest. An open question is whether these are the components that provide the initial toehold children need to differentiate these emotions from the broad negative valence concept.

CONCLUSIONS

This chapter describes children's interpretation of emotional facial expressions and stories describing emotional situations and how emotion concepts are acquired. As described by the broad-to-differentiated hypothesis, children's initial emotion concepts are broad and valence based. Gradually, children differentiate within these initial concepts by linking the different components of an emotion together (e.g., the cause to the consequence, etc.) until their concepts resemble adults' emotion concepts. Contrary to traditional assumptions, facial expressions are neither the starting point for most emotion concepts nor are they the strongest cue to emotions. Instead, just like any other component of an emotion concept, facial expressions must be differentiated from the valence-based concepts and linked to the other components of the specific emotion concept.

To fully describe and understand the nature of emotion concepts, all of children's responses on an emotion task must be considered. While "correct" responses may indicate how adult-like children's emotion concepts are, their "incorrect" responses indicate how those same categories differ from adults'. Young children's emotion concepts are initially broader than are adults' and narrow gradually over a period of years. Failure to assess children's "incorrect" responses not only misses an important part of the development of emotion concepts, it also assumes that the stimuli presented to children communicate only the emotion that the researcher intends.

The literature on children's acquisition of emotion concepts has a strong bias toward basic emotions and facial expressions. As a result, we know much about the development of children's acquisition of happiness, sadness, anger, fear, surprise, and disgust—especially for the corresponding facial expressions. Children do not initially understand facial expressions in terms of specific discrete emotions. Instead, children gradually acquire the adult-like interpretation of facial expressions. This evidence recommends against the common practice of using facial expressions as the measure of children's emotion concepts—especially when those measures focus "correct" responses. Instead, children's emotion concepts might be better measured using stories about emotional situations, labels, other components of emotion concepts, or a combination of components to better triangulate on children's current level of emotion concept acquisition.

We know little about children's acquisition of concepts for other (nonbasic) emotions—especially those that have no corresponding facial expressions. Even preschoolers' emotion vocabularies are broader than basic emotions (Ridgeway, Waters, & Kuczaj, 1985; Wellman, Harris, Banerjee, & Sinclair, 1995), indicating that they know more about emotion than is currently being investigated. And children's emotion vocabularies continue to increase through middle childhood (Beck, Kumschick, Eid, & Klann-Delius, 2012) and beyond. The narrow focus on basic emotions and facial expressions limits our ability to describe the development of emotion concepts. Do children acquire concepts of basic emotions earlier than they do other emotion concepts? Or are some other emotion concepts acquired earlier than those for some basic emotions? What components (e.g., causes, consequences, behaviors, labels, and so on) of these emotion concepts are acquired earlier versus later?

ACKNOWLEDGMENTS

Thank you to Abigail Cobb and Erin Cofrancesco for their feedback on a prior draft of this manuscript.

REFERENCES

Balconi, M., & Carrera, A. (2007). Emotional representation in facial expression and script: A comparison between normal and autistic children. *Research in Developmental Disabilities, 28*, 409–422. doi: 10.1016/j.ridd.2006.05.001

Barbosa-Leiker, C., Strand, P. S., Mamey, M. R., & Downs, A. (2014). Psychometric properties of the emotion understanding assessment with Spanish- and English-speaking preschoolers attending head start. *Assessment, 21*(5), 628–636. doi: 10.1177/1073191114524017

Beck, L., Kumschick, I. R., Eid, M., & Klann-Delius, G. (2012). Relationship between language competence and emotional competence in middle childhood. *Emotion, 12*(3), 503. doi: 10.1037/a0026320

Camras, L. A., & Allison, K. (1985). Children's understanding of emotional facial expressions and verbal labels. *Journal of Nonverbal Behavior, 9*, 84–94. doi: 10.1007/BF00987140

Carroll, J. J., & Steward, M. S. (1984). The role of cognitive development in children's understandings of their own feelings. *Child Development, 55*(4), 1486–1492. doi: 10.2307/1130018

de Mendoza, A. H., Fernández-Dols, J. M., Parrott, W. G., & Carrera, P. (2010). Emotion terms, category structure, and the problem of translation: The case of shame and vergüenza. *Cognition & Emotion, 24*, 661–680. doi: 10.1080/02699930902958255

Denham, S. A. (1998). *Emotional development in young children*. New York, NY: Guilford Press.

Denham, S. A., Blair, K. A., DeMulder, E., Levitas, J., Sawyer, K., Auerbach-Major, S., & Queenan, P. (2003). Preschool emotional competence: Pathway to social competence? *Child Development, 74*(1), 238–256. doi: 10.1111/1467-8624.00533

D'Entremont, B., & Muir, D. (1999). Infant responses to adult happy and sad vocal and facial expressions during face-to-face interactions. *Infant Behavior & Development, 22*, 527–539. doi: 10.1016/S0163-6383(00)00021-7

Doi, T. (1981). *The anatomy of dependence: The key analysis of Japanese behavior.* English trans. John Bester (2nd ed.). Tokyo, Japan: Kodansha International.

Ekman, P., & Friesen, W. V. (1971). Constants across cultures in the face and emotion. *Journal of Personality & Social Psychology, 17*, 124–129. doi: 10.1037/h0030377

Ekman, P., & Heider, K. G. (1988). The universality of a contempt expression: A replication. *Motivation and Emotion, 12*(3), 303–308. doi: 10.1007/Bf00993116

Farmer, A. D., Jr., Bierman, K. L., & Conduct Problems Prevention Research, G. (2002). Predictors and consequences of aggressive-withdrawn problem profiles in early grade school. *Journal of Clinical Child and Adolesccent Psychology, 31*(3), 299–311. doi: 10.1207/S15374424JCCP3103_02

Fehr, B., & Russell, J. A. (1984). Concept of emotion viewed from a prototype perspective. *Journal of Experimental Psychology: General, 113*, 464–486. doi: 10.1037/0096-3445.113.3.464

Fischer, K. W., Shaver, P. R., & Carnochan, P. (1990). How emotions develop and how they organize development. *Cognition & Emotion*, *4*(2), 81–127. doi: 10.1080/02699939008407142

Gao, X., & Maurer, D. (2009). Influence of intensity on children's sensitivity to happy, sad, and fearful facial expressions. *Journal of Experimental Child Psychology*, *102*(4), 503–521. doi: 10.1016/j.jecp.2008.11.002

Gao, X., & Maurer, D. (2010). A happy story: Developmental changes in children's sensitivity to facial expressions of varying intensities. *Journal of Experimental Child Psychology*, *107*(2), 67–86. doi: 10.1016/j.jecp.2010.05.003

Garner, P. W., & Waajid, B. (2012). Emotion knowledge and self-regulation as predictors of preschoolers' cognitive ability, classroom behavior, and social competence. *Journal of Psychoeducational Assessment*, *30*(4), 330–343. doi: 10.1177/0734282912449441

Gelman, S. A. (2003). *The essential child: Origins of essentialism in everyday thought.* New York, NY: Oxford University Press.

Gentner, D., & Goldin-Meadow, S. (Eds.). (2003). *Language in mind.* Cambridge, MA: MIT Press.

Greenberg, M. T., Kusche, C. A., Cook, E. T., & Quamma, J. P. (1995). Promoting emotional competence in school-aged children: The effects of the PATHS curriculum. *Development and Psychopathology*, *7*, 117–136. doi: 10.1017/S0954579400006374

Haidt, J., & Keltner, D. (1999). Culture and facial expression: Open-ended methods find more expressions and a gradient of recognition. *Cognition & Emotion*, *13*, 225–266. doi: 10.1080/026999399379168

Haviland, J. M., & Lelwica, M. (1987). The induced affect response: 10-week-old infants' responses to three emotion expressions. *Developmental Psychology*, *23*, 97–104. doi: 10.1037/0012-1649.23.1.97

Hurtado de Mendoza, A., Fernández-Dols, J. M., Parrott, W. G., & Carrera, P. (2010). Emotion terms, category structure, and the problem of translation: The case of shame and vergüenza. *Cognition & Emotion*, *24*(4), 661–680. doi: 10.1080/02699930902958255

Izard, C. E. (1971). *The face of emotion.* New York, NY: Appleton Century Crofts.

Izard, C. E. (1994). Innate and universal facial expressions: Evidence from developmental and cross-cultural research. *Psychological Bulletin*, *2*, 288–299. doi: 10.1037/0033-2909.115.2.288

Izard, C. E., Fine, S., Schultz, D., Mostow, A., Ackerman, B., & Youngstrom, E. (2001). Emotion knowledge as a predictor of social behavior and academic competence in children at risk. *Psychological Science*, *12*, 18–23. doi: 10.1111/1467-9280.00304

Kayyal, M. H., Widen, S. C., & Russell, J. A. (2015). Palestinian and American children's understanding of facial expressions of emotion. [Manuscript in preparation.].

Kayyal, M. H., & Russell, J. A. (2013). Americans and Palestinians judge spontaneous facial expressions of emotion. *Emotion*, *13*(5), 891. doi: 10.1037/a0033244

Klinnert, M. D., Emde, R. N., Butterfield, P., & Campos, J. J. (1986). Social referencing: The infant's use of emotional signals from a friendly adult with mother present. *Developmental Psychology*, *22*(4), 427–432. doi: 10.1037/0012-1649.22.4.427

Kundera, M. (1980). *The book of laughter and forgetting.* New York, NY: Harper Perennial Modern Classics. (Original work published in 1979)

Leppänen, J. M., & Nelson, C. A. (2006). The development and neural bases of facial emotion recognition. In R. J. Kail (Ed.), *Advances in child development and behavior* (pp. 207–245). San Diego, CA: Academic Press.

Lindquist, K. A., Barrett, L. F., Bliss-Moreau, E., & Russell, J. A. (2006). Language and the perception of emotion. *Emotion Review, 6*, 125–138. doi: 10.1037/1528-3542.6.1.125

Lindquist, K. A., & Gendron, M. (2013). What's in a word? Language constructs emotion perception. *Emotion Review, 5*, 66–71. doi: 10.1177/1754073912451351

Maassarani, R., Gosselin, P., Montembeault, P., & Gagnon, M. (2014). French-speaking children's freely produced labels for facial expressions. *Frontiers in Psychology, 5*. doi: 10.3389/Fpsyg.2014.00555

Mayer, J. D., & Salovey, P. (1997). What is emotional intelligence? In P. Salovey & D. J. Sluyter (Eds.), *Emotional development and emotional intelligence: Educational implications* (pp. 3–34, 288, xvi). New York, NY: Basic Books.

Moses, L. J., Baldwin, D. A., Rosicky, J. G., & Tidball, G. (2001). Evidence for referential understanding in the emotions domain at twelve and eighteen months. *Child Development, 72*(3), 718–735. doi: 10.1111/1467-8624.00311

Nelson, N. L., Hudspeth, K., & Russell, J. A. (2013). A story superiority effect for disgust, fear, embarrassment, and pride. *British Journal of Developmental Psychology, 31*(Pt 3), 334–348. doi: 10.1111/bjdp.12011

Nelson, N. L., & Russell, J. A. (2011). Putting motion in emotion: Do dynamic presentations increase preschooler's recognition of emotion? *Cognitive Development, 26*, 248–259. doi: 10.1016/j.cogdev.2011.06.001

Nelson, N. L., & Russell, J. A. (2012). Children's understanding of nonverbal expressions of pride. *Journal of Experimental Child Psychology, 111*(3), 379–385. doi: 10.1016/j.jecp.2011.09.004

O'Neil, R., Welsh, M., Parke, R. D., Wang, S., & Strand, C. (1997). A longitudinal assessment of the academic correlates of early peer acceptance and rejection. *Journal of Clinical Child Psychology, 26*(3), 290–303. doi: 10.1207/s15374424jccp2603_8

Parker, A. E., Mathis, E. T., & Kupersmidt, J. B. (2013). How is this child feeling? Preschool-aged children's ability to recognize emotion in faces and body poses. *Early Education & Development, 24*(2), 188–211. doi: 10.1080/10409289.2012.657536

Pons, F., Harris, P. L., & de Rosnay, M. (2004). Emotion comprehension between 3 and 11 years: Developmental periods and hierarchical organization. *European Journal of Developmental Psychology, 1*(2), 127–152. doi: 10.1080/17405620344000022

Reichenbach, L., & Masters, J. C. (1983). Children's use of expressive and contextual cues in judgements of emotion. *Child Development, 53*, 993–1004. doi: 10.2307/1129903

Repacholi, B. M., & Gopnik, A. (1997). Early reasoning about desires: Evidence from 14- and 18-month-olds. *Developmental Psychology, 33*, 12–21. doi: 10.1037/0012-1649.33.1.12

Ridgeway, D., Waters, E., & Kuczaj II, S. A. (1985). Acquisition of emotion-descriptive language: Receptive and productive vocabulary norms for ages 18 months to 6 years. *Developmental Psychology, 21*, 901–908. doi: 10.1037/0012-1649.21.5.901

Roberson, D., Kikutani, M., Döge, P., Whitaker, L., & Majid, A. (2011). Shades of emotion: What the addition of sunglasses or masks to faces reveals about the development of facial expression processing. *Cognition, 125*(2), 11. doi: 10.1016/j.cognition.2012.06.018

Russell, J. A. (1980). A circumplex model of affect. *Journal of Personality and Social Psychology, 39*(6), 1161–1178. doi: 10.1037/H0077714

Russell, J. A. (1991). Culture and the categorization of emotions. *Psychological Bulletin, 110*(3), 426–450. doi: 10.1037/0033-2909.110.3.426

Russell, J. A., & Bullock, M. (1985). Multidimensional-scaling of emotional facial expressions—Similarity from preschoolers to adults. *Journal of Personality and Social Psychology, 48*(5), 1290–1298. doi: 10.1037/0022-3514.48.5.1290

Russell, J. A., & Sato, K. (1995). Comparing emotion words between languages. *Journal of Cross-Cultural Psychology, 26*, 384–391. doi: 10.1177/0022022195264004

Russell, J. A., & Widen, S. C. (2002a). A label superiority effect in children's categorization of facial expressions. *Social Development, 11*(1), 30–52. doi: 10.1111/1467-9507.00185

Russell, J. A., & Widen, S. C. (2002b). Words versus faces in evoking preschool children's knowledge of the causes of emotions. *International Journal of Behavioral Development, 26*(2), 97–103. doi: 10.1080/01650250042000582

Salovey, P., & Mayer, J. D. (1989). Emotional intelligence. *Imagination, Cognition and Personality, 9*(3), 185–211.

Shariff, A. F., & Tracy, J. L. (2011). What are emotion expressions for? *Current Directions in Psychological Science, 20*(6), 395–399. doi: 10.1177/0963721411424739

Shields, A., Dickstein, S., Seifer, R., Giusti, L., Dodge Magee, K., & Spritz, B. (2001). Emotional competence and early school adjustment: A study of preschoolers at risk. *Early Education and Development, 12*(1), 73–96. doi: 10.1207/s15566935eed1201_5

Sorenson, R. E. (1976). *The edge of the forest: Land, childhood and change in a New Guinea protoagricultural society.* Washington, DC: Smithsonian Institution Press.

van der Schalk, J., Hawk, S. T., Fischer, A. H., & Doosje, B. (2011). Moving faces, looking places: Validation of the Amsterdam Dynamic Facial Expression Set (ADFES). *Emotion, 11*(4), 907. doi: 10.1037/a0023853

Walden, T. A., & Kim, G. (2005). Infants' social looking toward mothers and strangers. *International Journal of Behavioral Development, 29*(5), 356–360. doi: 10.1080/01650250500166824

Walker-Andrews, A. (2005). Perceiving social affordances: The development of emotional understanding. In B. D. Homer & C. S. Tamis-LeMonda (Eds.), *The development of social cognition and communication* (pp. 93–116). Mahwah, NJ: Lawrence Erlbaum.

Wellman, H. M., Harris, P. L., Banerjee, M., & Sinclair, A. (1995). Early understanding of emotion: Evidence from natural language. *Cognition and Emotion, 9*, 117–149. doi: 10.1080/02699939508409005

Widen, S. C. (2013). Children's interpretation of facial expressions: The long path from valence-based to specific discrete categories. *Emotion Review, 5*(1), 72–77. doi: 10.1177/1754073912451492

Widen, S. C. (2016). The development of children's concepts of emotion. In L. F. Barrett, M. Lewis, J. M., & Haviland-Jones (Eds.), *Handbook of emotions* (4th ed., pp. 307–318). New York, NY: Guilford Press.

Widen, S. C., Christy, A. M., Hewett, K., & Russell, J. A. (2011). Do proposed facial expressions of contempt, shame, embarrassment, and compassion communicate the predicted emotion? *Cognition and Emotion, 25*(5), 898–906. doi: 10.1080/02699931.2010.508270

Widen, S. C., Pochedly, J. T., & Russell, J. A. (2015). The development of emotion concepts: a story superiority effect in older children and adolescents. *Journal of Experimental Child Psychology, 131*, 186–192. doi: 10.1016/j.jecp.2014.10.009

Widen, S. C., & Russell, J. A. (2002). Gender and preschoolers' perception of emotion. *Merrill-Palmer Quarterly, 48*(3), 248–262. doi: 10.1353/mpq.2002.0013

Widen, S. C., & Russell, J. A. (2003). A closer look at preschoolers' freely produced labels for facial expressions. *Developmental Psychology, 39*(1), 114–128. doi: 10.1037/0012-1649.39.1.114

Widen, S. C., & Russell, J. A. (2004). The relative power of an emotion's facial expression, label, and behavioral consequence to evoke preschoolers' knowledge of its cause. *Cognitive Development, 19*(1), 111–125. doi: 10.1016/j.cogdev.2003.11.004

Widen, S. C., & Russell, J. A. (2008a). Children acquire emotion categories gradually. *Cognitive Development, 23*(2), 291–312. doi: 10.1016/j.cogdev.2008.01.002

Widen, S. C., & Russell, J. A. (2008b). Young children's understanding of others' emotions. In M. Lewis, J. M. Haviland-Jones, & L. F. Barrett (Eds.), *Handbook of emotions* (3rd ed., pp. 348–363). New York, NY: Guilford Press.

Widen, S. C., & Russell, J. A. (2010a). Children's scripts for social emotions: Causes and consequences are more central than are facial expressions. *British Journal of Developmental Psychology, 28*(3), 565–581. doi: 10.1348/026151009X457550d

Widen, S. C., & Russell, J. A. (2010b). Differentiation in preschooler's categories of emotion. *Emotion, 10*(5), 651–661. doi: 10.1037/a0019005

Widen, S. C., & Russell, J. A. (2010c). The "disgust face" conveys anger to children. *Emotion, 10*(4), 455–466. doi: 10.1037/a0019151

Widen, S. C., & Russell, J. A. (2011). In building a script for an emotion, do preschoolers add its cause before its behavior consequence? *Social Development, 20*(3), 471–485. doi: 10.1111/j.1467-9507.2010.00594.x

Widen, S. C., & Russell, J. A. (2013). Children's recognition of disgust in others. *Psycholoigcal Bulletin, 139*(2), 271–299. doi: 10.1037/a0031640

Wierzbicka, A. (2009). Language and metalanguage: Key issues in emotion research. *Emotion Review, 1*, 3–14. doi: 10.1177/1754073908097175

PART VII

Social Perception

17

A Social Vision Account of Facial Expression Perception

REGINALD B. ADAMS, JR., DANIEL N. ALBOHN,
AND KESTUTIS KVERAGA

Despite varying perspectives on the nature of emotion and emotional expression, most existing theories agree that facial expressions reveal basic behavioral tendencies of the expresser (e.g., Ekman, 1973; Fridlund, 1994; Frijda & Tcherkassof, 1997; Izard, 1971; Lazarus, 1991; Russell, 1997). A few theories place behavioral forecasting at the center of facial expression perception (Fridlund, 1994, this volume), with some suggesting that feelings associated with emotion are essentially the conscious experience of underlying behavioral intentions, or "action tendencies" (Fridja, 1995; Fridja & Tcherkassof, 1997). These theories align fundamentally with assumptions of the ecological approach to visual perception (Gibson, 1979/2015), which contends that inherent to visual perception are behavioral affordances, defined as opportunities to act on or be acted upon by a visual stimulus.

At its most fundamental level, facial expression perception begins as a visual process. Thus, we argue that applying an ecological approach of vision to emotional expression perception helps elucidate the expression/action link as it unfolds, beginning at the level of the stimulus and progressing through the earliest stages of visual processing. Critically, this approach lends itself to understanding expression perception as a combinatorial process, integrating multiple social cues conveyed by the face, body, voice, scene, and situational context.

Early face processing theories have argued that functionally distinct sources of facial information (e.g., expression versus identity) engage distinct, doubly dissociable, and presumably noninteracting processing routes (e.g., Bruce & Young, 1986; Le Gal & Bruce, 2002; cf. Haxby, Hoffman, & Gobbini, 2000). Because the face supplies an abundance of visual information, a perceptual system that can parse all this information and process it in parallel should be able to increase processing efficiency and minimize the likelihood of perceptual interference. From a vision processing perspective, it could be argued that if all these cues were to interact in perceptual processing, it might interfere with the fundamental information needed to produce an adaptive response.

Likewise, within the domain of emotion perception, some early theories have articulated additional encapsulated processing of individual emotion expressions. Based on these theories, humans have arguably evolved distinct and universal affect programs (i.e., discrete emotions such as anger, fear, happiness) that enable us to experience, express, and perceive emotions (Keltner, Ekman, Gonzaga, & Beer, 2003). Each discrete emotion is thought to have evolved independently in response to different reoccurring environmental contingencies and afford us an adaptively tuned response to such contingencies. Neural and cross-cultural evidence has been used to support the notion that facial expressions are part of a set of motor commands directly associated with felt emotion (Ekman, 1997, 1972). Similarly, it has been assumed that we possess evolved modules for the adaptive responding and perceptual recognition of the emotional behavior of others (Matsumoto, 1992). The obligatory nature assumed to be part of these processes, however, downplays the power of contextual influences, personal learned knowledge, and individual traits and states that may impact emotion perception. From a neurological perspective, these approaches presume a "hardwired" and highly modularized aspect of our biological make-up, which governs fixed perceptual functions. Recent evidence in the visual neurosciences, however, has begun to challenge such assumptions (reviewed in Clark, 2013; Adams & Kveraga, 2015), calling instead for a more flexible understanding of visual perception in general, with important implications for social visual perception specifically.

SOCIAL VISION

In the 1950–1960s, two scientists offered theories suggesting that the visual system is principally functional in nature, positing that its primary purpose is to relay functionally relevant information. Horace Barlow (1961), trained as a visual neuroscientist, suggested that neurons "reduce" information by dispelling redundant information. Thus, what is left is a binary "yes" or "no" signal to the question "is the information being received new and important?" Another influential theorist of the time, J. J. Gibson (1950), trained as a psychologist, put forth an ecological approach to vision. Gibson posited that the function of the visual system was information gathering, but stressed optic coding of real-world functional properties (e.g., "fruit says 'eat me'," Koffka, 1935, quoted in Gibson, 1979/2015, p. 129).

While Barlow focused on the neural mechanisms and Gibson on the functional value within the visual system, both theories run in parallel, suggesting that the visual system evolved to collect information that is adaptive to the organism's survival. Many have built upon these ideas; one of particular interest to this chapter is the social brain hypothesis. Dunbar (1998) showed that neocortex size in primates correlates with social group size, suggesting that primate brains (including our own) evolved for social processing, and *not* simply for the integration and analysis of factual information such as color, shape, and pattern recognition (cf. Humphrey, 1976). In a related investigation, Redican (1982) showed that within primates, the ability to produce facial expressions is dependent on the social environment in which the primate lives. Specifically, arboreal New World monkeys exhibit less facial expressiveness than Old World monkeys, who live terrestrially. This difference is presumably related to an adaptive function for ground-dwelling primates to produce and visually recognize a variety of expressions where faces are less obscured by foliage, and thus more important for communication.

Gibson's (1979/2015) ecological model of visual perception fits well with these findings as it emphasizes that vision is shaped by the interaction between the perceiver and the perceived, examining what in the environment is meaningful to an individual through *affordances* and *attunements*. The ecological approach suggests that the brain evolved to perceive stimuli as conveying action affordances that are adaptive to the individual's survival. As noted earlier, Gibson defined functional affordances as opportunities inherent in a stimulus to act on or be acted upon. Gibson states that "the meaning or value of a thing consists of what it affords" and that "the affordances of the environment are what it offers the animal, what it provides or furnishes, either for good or for ill" (1979, p. 127). Thus, when one sees a plate of food or glass of water, part of that perceptual experience is linked to the functional behavior associated with it. In this case the food says "eat me" and the water says "drink me" (Gibson, 1979, p. 138). Because such action-based affordances are contextually bound, it should not be surprising that associative influences are evident in the recognition of even common objects (i.e., Kveraga, Boshyan, & Bar, 2009). Gibson also argued, however, that affordances are processed via direct perception, and thereby do not require abstract or symbolic representation. Early visual perception is thus conceptualized fundamentally as action oriented, bypassing intermediate processes that can impact adaptive responding.

Affordances are also influenced by an organism's attunements to an environment. Gibson defined attunements as the perceiver's sensitivity to stimulus features associated with affordances. Thus, attunements amplify the already existing affordances—for example, when one first sees food or water after starving or thirsting for days, the food and water now may seem to *scream*, "eat me!" and "drink me!" Although certain perceiver affordances are thought to be innately prepared, they can vary within and across individuals in meaningful ways, underscoring just how tightly bound bottom-up and top-down processes can be, particularly in vision (Kveraga, Boshyan, & Bar, 2007, 2009; Kveraga, Ghuman, & Bar, 2007; Kveraga et al., 2011).

Leslie Zebrowitz and colleagues (Zebrowitz, 1997; Zebrowitz & Collins, 1997; Zebrowitz & Montepare, 2008) extended the ecological model to person perception through what they refer to as *overgeneralization effects*. At the most basic level, overgeneralization effects assume a biologically endowed response to specific cues that indicate certain adaptive traits such as affiliation or health. Because these traits are so advantageous to the organism's survival, they are generalized to persons whose appearance incidentally resembles such cues. Behavioral work and computational modeling suggest that there are at least four separate overgeneralization effects that influence person perception: (1) health/attractiveness, (2) baby-facedness, (3) specific emotion, and (4) familiarity (Zebrowitz & Montepare, 2008).

In terms of emotion overgeneralization, neutral faces that incidentally resemble expressions presumably trigger similar impressions as the expressions themselves (Adams, Nelson, Soto, Hess, & Kleck, 2012; Montepare & Dobish, 2003). Thus, emotion overgeneralization seemingly reflects modularized responses that are so entrained in our perception that they color impressions even when not adaptively relevant. A face with downward-turned brows and thin lips on an otherwise neutral face will be perceived as less approachable and more aggressive due to its resemblance to anger. The logic is that it is so important to our survival that we respond to certain configurations of facial cues in a particular way, that the occasional false alarm is considered less detrimental to survival than not responding during accurate detection. This application of the ecological approach to vision remains limited in much the same way as some face processing models and discrete emotion theories, however, by not adequately addressing combined influences of various cues on emotion perception.

We build on the seminal work of Gibson, Zebrowitz, Dunbar, and others by extending similar principles to human facial expression perception. Our work, among a host of others, suggests that the human brain, specifically the visual system, evolved to meet the demands of our social world. Humans compete with each other for resources, necessitating the continued evolution of our socio-visual perceptive abilities. Because of this competition, it makes adaptive sense that our visual system is able to integrate multiple social cues in a highly efficient manner. In turn, it stands to reason that the social stimuli being perceived (e.g., faces) likewise evolved to exploit these integration processes. Indeed, we see evidence for both of these processes, which we detail in this chapter.

THE COMBINATORIAL NATURE OF EXPRESSION PERCEPTION

Notably, in one review Zebrowitz (2006) states: "A perceived identity, social category, emotion, or psychological trait may each specify the same behavioral affordance" (p. 668). This notion is consistent with Adams and colleagues' shared-signal approach to examining compound social cues (see also Adams & Kleck, 2003, 2005; Adams, Ambady, Macrae, & Kleck, 2006). In their work, core dimensions of social perception are emphasized (approach/avoidance, dominance/affiliation). If various social cues share, or together create, a shared fundamental meaning (i.e., *shared signal value*), then the social affordances they confer on an observer will likewise share fundamental functions. Some of this integrative processing may well involve a sort of "direct perception," in that it may occur reflexively in a feedforward manner. However, as we will discuss in detail later, much of the time this process may require top-down guidance, implicating cognitive intervention even at low levels of visual processing.

Stimulus-Driven Integration

Recent work has lent theoretical and empirical support to the idea that facial expressions may have evolved to mimic stable facial appearance cues to take advantage of their social affordances (Adams et al., 2010; Becker et al., 2007; Marsh, Adams, & Kleck, 2005). These findings resonate with Darwin's early observation of piloerection in animals, which makes them appear larger and thus more threatening to ward off attack (see, for example, 1872/1965; p. 95 and p.104). This account suggests too that compound cue integration may also begin at the level of the stimulus itself.

In his ecological model of vision, Gibson (1979) proposed that examining the stimulus itself can provide insight into the mechanisms mediating the perception/action link. Gender-modulated facial appearance, emotion, and facial maturity are examples of convergent facial cues that not only convey a similar dominance and/or affiliation signal value (Adams & Kveraga, 2015), but do so in part through confounded facial cues. Anger cues are signaled by a low, prominent brow ridge and small, narrowed eyes, resembling a mature, dominant face. Conversely, fear is characterized by a raised and arched brow ridge and widened eyes, which resembles a submissive "baby-face." Gender appearance is similarly associated with facial features that perceptually overlap with facial maturity (see Zebrowitz, 1997), in that "babyish" features (e.g., large, round eyes, high eyebrows, full lips) are more typical in women, and "mature" features (e.g., square jaw, pronounced and lower brow ridge) are more typical in men. These facial gender cues perceptually overlap with expression as well, with masculine face configurations more closely resembling anger, and feminine faces resembling aspects of both fear and happiness (Hess, Adams, Grammer, & Kleck, 2009). Insofar as form follows function, the overlap of gender, emotion, and facial maturity as social cues to dominance and affiliation suggests that our perceptual system is also functionally organized to integrate compound cues that, in concert, reinforce shared social affordances.

"Feedforward" Integration

Tamietto and de Gelder (2010) reviewed evidence for the existence of very early social vision, in which combining information from different social cues begins in subcortical structures. To this point, they highlight work showing that body language, visual scenes, and vocal cues all influence the processing of facial displays of threat (Meeren, van Heijnsbergen, & de Gelder, 2005), even at the earliest stages of face processing and across conscious and nonconscious processing routes (de Gelder, Morris, & Dolan, 2005). They argue that these findings suggest that compound cue integration is at least partly the result of early bottom-up integration, driven by the shared functional value of these cues.

If this proposition is validated by further research, it would mean that the visual system is wired to respond to shared social affordances of different social cues at the very earliest stages of processing, beginning even in evolutionarily older subcortical structures. Indeed, it is difficult to think of a reason it would be otherwise—what evolutionary advantage would be conferred upon organisms that do not efficiently combine various threat cues? Presumably it is not only humans, with their highly developed cortex and conscious perception, but other organisms too, who have to solve the problem of rapidly identifying compound threat cues. Perhaps not surprisingly then, much of what happens neurally during threat detection takes place in evolutionarily older midbrain, brainstem, and deep subcortical structures, such as the periacqueductal gray, locus coeruleus, substantia nigra, the superior colliculus/optic tectum, pulvinar, hypothalamus, and the amygdala (Mobbs et al., 2007; Vuilleumier, Armony, Driver, & Dolan, 2003).

Integration of face cues that seems to occur in subliminally presented stimuli offers preliminary evidence for such nonconscious integration. For example, cues relevant to threat that share a congruent underlying signal value facilitate the processing efficiency of an emotion. One study revealed functional interactions in processing various pairings of eye gaze direction (direct versus averted) and threat displays (anger versus fear). Using speeded reaction time tasks and self-reported perception of emotional intensity, Adams and Kleck (2003, 2005) found that direct gaze facilitated processing efficiency, accuracy, and increased the perceived intensity of facially communicated approach-oriented emotions (e.g., anger and joy), whereas averted gaze facilitated processing efficiency, accuracy, and perceived intensity of facially communicated avoidance-oriented emotions (e.g., fear and sadness). As such, these findings are in line with the *shared signal hypothesis* (Adams, Ambady, Macrae, & Kleck, 2006; Adams & Kleck, 2003, 2005). Adams et al. (2011), using functional magnetic resonance imaging (fMRI), went on to find evidence for interactivity in amygdalar responses to these same threat-gaze pairings, even when subliminally presented. Similarly, Milders and colleagues (2011) found that direct gaze anger and averted gaze fear were detected more readily in an attentional blink paradigm compared to averted gaze anger and direct gaze fear, suggesting that congruent pairings (i.e., shared signals) of gaze and emotion demand more preconscious attentional awareness.

Using a similar logic, Tamietto and De Gelder (2010) describe a series of studies in which patients with visual blindsight (i.e., with striate cortex damage that impairs conscious visual perception in either the left or right visual field) were asked to respond to a facial expression presented in their unimpaired visual field. They found faster recognition of expressions in the unimpaired visual field if an identical expression was presented in the "blind" visual field (de Gelder et al., 2001, 2005), presumably via subcortical projections to extrastriate visual areas bypassing V1. Even more compelling were faster responses to facial expressions presented in the unimpaired visual field when the same emotion was expressed by a body in the "blind" visual field (Tamietto, Weiskrantz, Geminiani, & de Gelder, 2007). This latter finding suggests that the bodily expressions of emotion, even though nonconsciously perceived, were integrated in the response to the facial display of emotion. This is remarkable because faces and bodies represent highly divergent visual characteristics, meaning visual integration must be due to shared social affordances.

The notion that certain social visual cues may already be combined in early subcortical structures may seem provocative. However, consider that even animals lacking a highly developed cortex have to respond efficiently to aversive and appetitive cues, and this ability must be present in rather primitive structures. Evidence is accumulating that this may indeed be the case.

Evolutionarily old subcortical structures, such as the superior colliculus (SC), for instance, do appear to be sensitive to threat cues (Maior et al., 2011). The SC (known as the optic tectum in nonmammals) is a laminar structure that has visual and motor maps overlaid and in register, whose role is to produce gaze shifts to salient features of the animal's environment as quickly and efficiently as possible. The SC has connections with the evolutionarily older pathways, receiving projections from the magnocellular (M) layers of the lateral geniculate nucleus, and retinal projections from the koniocellular ganglion neurons (K), which also projects to the pulvinar and mediodorsal nuclei of the thalamus. The latter thalamic nuclei project to many cortical and subcortical regions involved in social and threat perception, such as the amygdala. This putative pathway has been proposed to be responsible for right amygdala responses to subliminally presented threat stimuli, presumably out of participants' conscious visual experiences (Morris, Öhman, & Dolan, 1998; see also Öhman, 2005).

Although it is not yet clear whether these pathways are entirely subcortical or feedforward (see Pessoa & Adolphs, 2010), what is clear is that some pathways bypass the primary visual cortex (and thus, conscious awareness) and are particularly responsive to low spatial frequencies, thereby implicating magnocellular system involvement (Vuilleumier et al., 2003), and perhaps the even more evolutionarily ancient koniocellular pathway (Hendry & Reid, 2000; Xu et al., 2001). These pathways feed heavily into the dorsal visual stream via projections to the middle temporal area (i.e., area MT), a major way station to action-related vision. The dorsal visual stream, among whose major functions are perceiving, predicting, and modeling action, provides the neural underpinnings necessary to support Gibson's notion of affordance-based vision (see also Nakayama, 2011). Gibson's original notion of direct perception implies that this system does not require cognitive intervention. In the next section, however, we discuss top-down modulated, but presumably still reflexive, action-oriented visual integration, which is guided by associative influences.

Top-Down Modulation of Visual Experience

Although the term "top-down modulation" evokes notions of consciously generated states guiding perception (e.g., focusing attention on particular features of the face), it does not need to be a conscious process. Unconsciously perceived visual threat cues, such as angry or fearful faces, can trigger subconsciously generated top-down control processes that activate the sympathetic ("fight-or-flight") and parasympathetic ("rest-and-digest") systems. Massive top-down projections, which vastly outnumber the corresponding bottom-up projections, exist in lower animals, including lower primates whose brains presumably are not invoking conscious top-down goals and expectations (Salin & Bullier, 1995). Under real-world viewing conditions, visual stimuli are often ambiguous because of occlusion, poor lighting, blending into the background, and the like. It is highly adaptive for the brain to reduce this ambiguity rapidly and arrive at the correct interpretation of, and action toward, a stimulus. In many cases, the action in response to a stimulus occurs before its conscious recognition; for example, we freeze mid step or jump away from a snake-like shape in the grass before consciously recognizing why we are doing it, or whether it is a snake at all.

In object recognition, it has been proposed that when a coarsely analyzed form of a visual stimulus matches a stored template (Bar, 2003), a top-down facilitation process is triggered in the orbitofrontal cortex (OFC) that then reduces the set of possible objects to those roughly matching the current, partially processed stimulus via feedback to the ventral occipito-temporal object recognition regions. This feedback may not only reduce the set size of possible stimuli but also bias the competition between the possibilities, based on contextual influences and internal state (Trapp & Bar, 2015). For example, whether a coiled shape in the grass is more likely to be perceived as a snake or a garden hose can depend on whether you are seeing it in a freshly mowed lawn or wild grass in an area known for venomous snakes, and whether you have been reading recently about gardening, or reptiles.

It has been shown that the magnocellular (M) pathway, which conveys coarse, luminance-based information quickly to the dorsal stream action-oriented regions and the prefrontal cortex, plays a critical role in this process (Kveraga et al., 2007). In this study, M-biased line drawings of objects evoked activity in OFC, whose amplitude negatively correlated with recognition reaction times (RT), while parvocellular (P)-biased stimuli did not evoke much OFC activity and their recognition RT positively correlated with fusiform cortex activity. Dynamic causal modeling revealed that the best model for the observed activity was a model positing feedforward M projections to the OFC, feedback projection from OFC to fusiform cortex, but only a feedforward projection to fusiform cortex for P-biased stimuli. Another recent study showed that OFC is activated by low spatial frequency stimuli, but only if they resemble known objects (Chaumon, Kveraga, Barrett, & Bar, 2014). The confidence with which these neutral objects could be identified predicted the amplitude of activity in the medial OFC and the amygdala. It also mediated the connectivity of lateral OFC with ventral temporal object recognition regions. As such, these findings strongly implicate a top-down associative influence in simple object recognition.

Although research extending these findings to compound threat cue processing is scant, there is some initial evidence that shows that a similar M-based facilitation process also underlies perception of threat scenes (Kveraga, 2014). Indeed, given their importance to the organism, we should expect such top-down contributions to social vision to be even more powerful than for neutral object recognition, and to involve early unconscious top-down triggering of preparatory states by subcortical regions. One recent study, for instance, examining gender perception in the face, found that although responses in the fusiform cortex tracked closely with the objective linear gradations in face gender between male and female faces (manipulated using a morphing algorithm to average the texture and structural maps of male and female faces), OFC activity reflected categorical (and thus nonlinear) decision boundaries of face gender (Freeman, Rule, Adams, & Ambady, 2009). This study reflects the important role of OFC in generating associative predictions about the nature of a social visual stimulus presented, and as such strongly underscores this as a fruitful, and necessary, direction for future social visual inquiry.

Recent work examining eye gaze and emotion interactions also reveals different adaptive attunements across the temporal stream that likely implicate different visual pathways. For instance, greater amygdala responses have been found to clear-threat cues when *rapidly* presented (33 ms and 300 ms), and to ambiguous-threat cues when presented for a more *sustained* period (1 s, 1.5 s, 2 s; Adams et al., 2011, 2012). These findings support an adaptive dual-process framework that favors quick and efficient attentional orienting toward threat-congruent information, perhaps driven by an M-based facilitation process ("action" vision), and a later attentional maintenance system necessary for processing ambiguous threat information ("analysis vision"). In this framework, compound threat cues that are congruent, and thus clearly signal threat, activate highly overlearned or even innate templates, which trigger an "action decision" very early in the process, in one or two processing cycles. Conversely, ambiguous threat cues engage a neural competition, requiring further top-down guidance to be resolved. There is some evidence that stimulus ambiguity may be reduced in successive cycles during which higher and lower regions exchange and refine information about the stimulus, shrinking the space of possible interpretations with each cycle (Garrett et al., 2000).

FUNCTIONAL ATTUNEMENTS

Gibson's affordances are relative to the organism. For example, a relatively dense, horizontal, and long surface affords an organism, such as humans, a place to walk. Water, however, only affords organisms such as water bugs potential for ambulation. This relativity extends to objects in the environment as well. Some may call a stone a weapon, while others call it a paperweight, "this does not mean you cannot *learn* how to use things and perceive their uses. You do not have to classify and label things in order to perceive what they afford" (Gibson, 1979/2015, p. 134). Gibson contends that the meaning of something is extracted from it before basic qualities such as its substance, color, and form. These affordances are invariant properties of the thing that signal adaptive value to the perceiver. Notably, although Gibson focused on physical objects in an organism's environment, he states "behavior affords behavior" (p. 127), implying that perception of things outside of physical reality adheres to these same general principles.

We have already mentioned that an organism is tuned to invariant properties of affordances, but we have not discussed how these attunements appear and interact with affordances. Affordances, as well as their invariant properties, are stable, as the name suggests, but may evolve over time or with circumstances. A wooden chair, for example, offers the affordance of sitting, but with decay or need, it could be used as wood for burning. On the other hand, attunements develop over a period of the organism's evolution, or learned in the process of navigating the social world. In this next section, we review possible evolutionary, learned, and individually varying functional attunements.

We start by describing attunements from an evolutionary perspective. Organisms should be biologically predisposed to be aptly tuned to their environment, and as such behaviors that afford basic evolutionary needs (i.e., mating and survival) should be evident. Next, we describe examples of both learned social identities that cue affordances and some of the attunements that affect these affordances. Lastly, we examine individual differences that can impact functional attunements.

Evolutionary Domains

Kenrick et al. (2002) suggested that social life is defined by six core behaviors that revolve around passing on one's genetics: (1) self-protection, (2) coalition formation, (3) status seeking, (4) mate choice, (5) relationship maintenance, and (6) offspring care. Although an in-depth analysis of how all these fundamental domains align with ecological theory is beyond the scope of this chapter, we briefly examine examples pertinent to two core behaviors, mating and survival.

A necessary precursor to mating is survival, which affords the opportunity for an increased likelihood to pass on one's genes to future generations. Ample evidence has shown that threat detection is quick and automatic, as would be expected for survival-relevant functions. This facilitation of responses to threats can be acquired during evolution (e.g., snakes for primates; Isbell, 2006) or learning (e.g., images of hand guns elicit a greater threat response than images of hair dryers). However, the context in which a gun is seen modulates the threat response (Kveraga et al., 2015). These responses also appear "tunable." For instance, Maner and colleagues showed that when perceived threat is high, individuals observed greater anger to out-group faces (Maner et al., 2005), and they were more likely to categorize unfamiliar faces as belonging to an out-group (Miller, Maner, & Becker, 2010; see also Maner & Miller, 2013).

Mate selection is also necessary for humans to optimize passing of their genes to their progeny. Similar to threat, when mate selection goals were activated, men perceived more sexual arousal in opposite-sex faces (Maner et al., 2005). If this is a biologically tuned response, then combining congruent pairings should provide greater affordances. Indeed, combining attractive faces with direct gaze and smiling expressions appears to enhance perceptions of attractiveness, cues that on their own signal a variety of social meanings (Jones, DeBruine, Little, Conway, & Feinberg, 2006; Kampe, Frith, Dolan, & Frith, 2001).

Socially Learned Domains

Although Gibson's ecological approach to vision is logically evolutionarily based, he did leave room for learned responses to influence affordances in an organism's environment. These learned responses also affect attunement to affordances, just like how evolution has tuned organisms to be particularly adept at picking up cues such as threat and attraction. Here we provide a few examples of social stereotypes to illuminate the intersection of socially learned stereotypes and stimuli affordances. For example, Caucasian participants higher in prejudice toward African Americans recognized anger expressions on African American faces more quickly than on other race faces (Hugenberg, 2005; Hugenberg & Bodenhausen, 2003). Hugenberg and Bodenhausen (2004) showed that those high in prejudice had a tendency to categorize racially ambiguous faces expressing anger as African American, while the same faces expressing happy expressions showed no such bias (Hugenberg & Bodenhausen, 2004). Even cross-culturally, stereotypic configurations of emotion expression are recognized faster than nonstereotypic configurations (Bijlstra, Holland, Dotsch, Hugenberg, & Wigboldus, 2014).

Individual Differences

Individual differences can also influence perceptual attunements to facial expression. For example, progesterone levels during menstrual cycles have been associated with increased detection of potential threat and contagion on faces (Conway et al., 2007). Specifically, women with high progesterone levels viewed fearful faces with averted gaze (threat) and disgusted faces with averted gaze (contagion) as more intense than displays with direct gaze. Critically, this did not occur for happy expressions (Conway et al., 2007). Presumably, this attunement to threat and contagion is linked to avoiding likely sources in the environment that may disrupt normal fetus development. Furthermore, Fox et al. (2007) found that anxiety levels influence the extent to which fear expressions coupled with averted gaze yielded greater gaze-cued attentional shifts compared to neutral or anger expressions, and to which anger expressions coupled with direct gaze yielded greater attention capture than did neutral or fear expressions.

Just like individual differences, personal history should also affect expression perception from an ecological approach. To our knowledge, no research has examined this relationship directly. However, we can extrapolate from work done outside of an ecological approach. For instance, research with abused and maltreated children has shown that these children direct attention away from threatening faces (Pine et al., 2005) and have quicker reaction times to labeling fearful faces (Masten et al., 2008) than children who have not been abused or maltreated.

CONCLUSIONS

We have drawn on recent behavioral, neuroscience, and vision research to provide a framework that is fundamentally ecological in nature, while incorporating known empirical evidence for both top-down and bottom-up neural influences in visual perception. Unlike some face processing models that focus on differentiating the "source" of information (e.g., expression versus appearance), central to the functional approach put forth here is the unified meaning conveyed by various social cues and their combined ecological relevance to the observer. We have argued that assuming encapsulated, noninteracting processes misses a full understanding of how various social cues meaningfully interact in emotion perception to yield the kind of unified perceptions that guide our adaptive behavioral responses to one another within an inherently social world.

Visual processing of even simple objects is guided by associative influences ("predictive brain"; Kveraga et al., 2007). Emotional expressions conveyed by social agents are particularly rich associative stimuli, and thus should be expected to engage similar mechanisms of influence, perhaps to an even greater extent, to organize visual processing in a functionally meaningful way. Examining emotion expression processing in this way draws on the fields of emotion expression, vision cognition, and neuroscience. Through a conceptual merger of these fields, the ecological approach allows us to link perceptual mechanics with functional affordances in a way that elucidates the compound nature of emotion expression processing beginning at its earliest stages of visual perception.

ACKNOWLEDGMENTS

The work on this chapter was supported by NIH grant R01MH101194 to KK and RBA Jr.

REFERENCES

Adams, R. B., & Kleck, R. (2003). Perceived gaze direction and the processing of facial displays of emotion. *Psychological Science, 14*, 644–647.

Adams, R. B., & Kleck, R. (2005). Effects of direct and averted gaze on the perception of facially communicated emotion. *Emotion, 5*, 3–11.

Adams, R. B., Ambady, N., Macrae, C., & Kleck, R. (2006). Emotional expressions forecast approach-avoidance behavior. *Motivation and Emotion, 30*, 177–186.

Adams, R. B., Franklin, R. G., Nelson, A. J., Gordon, H. L., Kleck, R., Whalen, P. J., & Ambady, N. (2011). Differentially tuned responses to restricted versus prolonged awareness of threat: A preliminary fMRI investigation. *Brain and Cognition, 77*, 113–119.

Adams, R. B., Jr., Nelson, A. J., & Soto, J. A., Hess, U., & Kleck, R. E. (2012). Emotion in the neutral face: A mechanism for impression formation? *Cognition and Emotion, 26*, 131–141.

Adams R. B., & Kveraga K. (2015). Social vision: Functional forecasting and the integration of compound threat cues. *Review of Philosophy and Psychology*, 1–20.

Bar, M. (2003). A cortical mechanism for triggering top-down facilitation in visual object recognition. *Journal of Cognitive Neuroscience, 15*, 600–609.

Barlow, H. B. (1961). Possible principles underlying the transformation of sensory messages. In W. R. Rosenblith's (Ed.), *Sensory communication* (pp. 217–234). Cambridge, MA: MIT Press.

Becker, D. V., Kenrick, D. T., Neuberg, S. L., Blackwell, K. C., & Smith, D. M. (2007). The confounded nature of angry men and happy women. *Journal of Personality and Social Psychology, 92*, 179–190.

Bijlstra, G., Holland, R. W., Dotsch, R., Hugenberg, K., & Wigboldus, D. H. J. (2014). Stereotype associations and emotion recognition. *Personality and Social Psychology Bulletin, 40*, 567–577.

Bruce, V., & Young, A. (1986). Understanding face recognition. *British Journal of Psychology, 77*(3), 305–327.

Chaumon, M., Kveraga, K., Barrett, L. F., & Bar, M. (2014). Visual predictions in the orbitofrontal cortex rely on associative content. *Cerebral Cortex, 24*, 2899–2907.

Clark, A. (2013). Whatever next? Predictive brains, situated agents, and the future of cognitive science. *Behavioral and Brain Sciences, 36*(3), 1–24.

Conway, C. A., Jones, B. C., DeBruine, L. M., Welling, L. L. M., Law Smith, M. J., Perrett, D. I., Sharp, M. A., & Al-Dujaili, E. A. S. (2007). Salience of emotional displays of danger and contagion in faces is enhanced when progesterone levels are raised. *Hormones and Behavior, 51*, 202–206.

Darwin, C. (1872). *The expression of emotion in man and animals*. London, UK: John Murray.

de Gelder, B., Pourtois, G., van Raamsdonk, M., Vroomen, J., & Weiskrantz, L. (2001). Unseen stimuli modulate conscious visual experience: Evidence from inter-hemispheric summation. *Neuroreport, 12*, 385–391.

de Gelder, B., Morris, J. S., & Dolan, R. J. (2005). Unconscious fear influences emotional awareness of faces and voices. *Proceedings of the National Academy of Sciences of the United States of America, 102*, 18682–18687.

Dunbar, R. I. M. (1998). The social brain hypothesis. *Evolutionary Anthropology: Issues, News, and Reviews, 6*, 178–190.

Ekman, P. (1972). Universals and cultural differences in facial expressions of emotions. In J. Cole (Ed.), *Nebraska Symposium on Motivation* (pp. 207–282). Lincoln, NB: University of Nebraska Press.

Ekman, P. (1973). Universal facial expressions in emotion. *Studia Psychologica, 15*, 140–147.

Ekman, P. (1997). Expression or communication about emotion? In G. E. Segal & C. C. Weisfeld. (Eds.), *Uniting psychology and biology: Integrative perspectives on human development* (pp. 315–338). Washington, DC: American Psychological Association.

Fox, E., Mathews, A., Calder, A. J., & Yiend, J. (2007). Anxiety and sensitivity to gaze direction in emotionally expressive faces. *Emotion, 7*, 478–486.

Freeman, J. B., Rule, N. O., Adams Jr, R. B., & Ambady, N. (2009). Culture shapes a mesolimbic response to signals of dominance and subordination that associates with behavior. *Neuroimage, 47*, 353–359.

Fridlund, A. J. (1994). *Human facial expression: An evolutionary perspective*. London, UK: Academic Press.

Frijda, N. H. (1995). Expression, emotion, neither, or both? *Cognition and Emotion, 9*, 617–635.

Frijda, N. H., & Tcherkassof, A. (1997). Facial expressions as modes of action readiness. In J. A. Russell & J. M. Fernandez-Dols (Eds.), *The psychology of facial expression* (pp. 78–102). Cambridge, UK: Cambridge University Press.

Garrett, A. S., Flowers, D. L., Absher, J. R., Fahey, F. H., Gage, H. D., Keyes, J. W., . . . & Wood, F. B. (2000). Cortical activity related to accuracy of letter recognition. *Neuroimage, 11*, 111–123.

Gibson, J. J. (1979/2015). *The ecological approach to visual perception: Classic edition*. New York, NY: Psychology Press.

Haxby, J. V., Hoffman, E., & Gobbini, M. (2000). The distributed human neural system for face perception. *Trends in Cognitive Sciences, 4*, 223–233.

Hendry, S. H., & Reid, R. C. (2000). The koniocellular pathway in primate vision. *Annual Review of Neuroscience, 23*, 127–153.

Hess, U., Adams, R. B., Grammer, K., & Kleck, R. (2009). Face gender and emotion expression: Are angry women more like men? *Journal of Vision, 9*, 1–8.

Hugenberg, K. (2005). Social categorization and the perception of facial affect: Target race moderates the response latency advantage for happy faces. *Emotion, 5*, 267–276.

Hugenberg, K., & Bodenhausen, G. V. (2003). Facing prejudice: Implicit prejudice and the perception of facial threat. *Psychological Science, 14*, 640–643.

Hugenberg, K., & Bodenhausen, G. V. (2004). Ambiguity in social categorization: The role of prejudice and facial affect in race categorization. *Psychological Science, 15*, 342–345.

Humphrey, N. (1976). The social function of intellect. In P. P. G. Bateson & R. A. Hindes (Eds.), *Growing points in ethology* (pp. 303–317). Cambridge, UK: Cambridge University Press.

Izard, C. E. (1971). *The face of emotion*. New York, NY: Appleton Century Crofts.

Jones, B. C., DeBruine, L. M., Little, A. C., Conway, C. A., & Feinberg, D. R. (2006). Integrating gaze direction and expression in preferences for attractive faces. *Psychological Science, 17*, 588–591.

Kampe, K. K., Frith, C. D., Dolan, R. J., & Frith, U. (2001). Psychology: Reward value of attractiveness and gaze. *Nature, 413*(6856), 589-589.

Keltner, D., Ekman, P., Gonzaga, G. C., & Beer, J. (2003). Facial expression of emotion. In K.R. Scherer & H.H. Goldsmith (Eds), Handbook of affective sciences (pp. 415-432). New York, NY, US: Oxford University Press

Kenrick, D. T., Maner, J. K., Butner, J., Li, N. P., Becker, D. V., & Schaller, M. (2002). Dynamical evolutionary psychology: Mapping the domains of the new interactionist paradigm. *Personality and Social Psychology Review, 6*, 347–356.

Kveraga, K. (2014). Threat perception in visual scenes: Dimensions, action and neural dynamics. In K. Kveraga & M. Bar (Eds.), *Scene vision: Making sense of what we see* (pp. 291–304). Cambridge, MA: MIT Press.

Kveraga, K., Boshyan, J., Adams, R. B., Mote, J., Betz, N., Ward, N., Hadjikhani, N., Bar, M., & Barrett, L. F. (2015). If it bleeds, it leads: Separating threat from negativity. *Social Cognitive and Affective Neuroscience, 10*, 28–35.

Kveraga, K., Boshyan, J., & Bar, M. (2009). The proactive brain: Using memory-based predictions in visual recognition. In S. Dickinson, M. Tarr, A. Leonardis, & B. Schiele (Eds.), *Object categorization: Computer and human vision perspectives* (pp. 384–400). New York, NY: Cambridge University Press.

Kveraga, K., Ghuman, A. S., & Bar, M. (2007). Top-down predictions in the cognitive brain. *Brain and Cognition, 65*, 145–68.

Kveraga, K., Ghuman Singh, A., Kassam, K. S., Aminoff, E. A., Hamalainen, M. S., Chaumon, M., & Bar, M. (2011). Early onset of neural synchronization in the contextual associations network. *Proceedings of the Natation Academy of Sciences, 108*, 3389–3394.

Lazarus, R. S. (1991). Progress on a cognitive-motivational-relational theory of emotion. *American Psychologist, 46*, 819–834.

Le Gal, P. M., & Bruce, V. (2002). Evaluating the independence of sex and expression in judgments of faces. *Perception & Psychophysics, 64*, 230–243.

Maior, R. S., Hori, E., Barros, M., Teixeira, D. S., Tavares, M. C. H., Ono, T., . . . & Tomaz, C. (2011). Superior colliculus lesions impair threat responsiveness in infant capuchin monkeys. *Neuroscience Letters, 504*, 257–260.

Maner, J. K., & Miller, S. L. (2013). Adaptive attentional attunement: Perceptions of danger and attention to outgroup men. *Social Cognition, 31*, 733–744.

Maner, J. K., Kenrick, D. T., Becker, D. V., Robertson, T. E., Hofer, B., Neuberg, S. L., . . . & Schaller, M. (2005). Functional projection: How fundamental social motives can bias interpersonal perception. *Journal of Personality and Social Psychology, 88*, 63–78.

Marsh, A. A., Adams, R. B., & Kleck, R. (2005). Why do fear and anger look the way they do? Form and social function in facial expressions. *Personality and Social Psychology Bulletin, 31*, 73–86.

Masten, C. L., Guyer, A. E., Hodgdon, H. B., McClure, E. B., Charney, D. S., Ernst, M., Monk, C. S. (2008). Recognition of facial emotions among maltreated children with high rates of post-traumatic stress disorder. *Child Abuse & Neglect, 32*, 139–153.

Matsumoto, D. (1992). American-Japanese cultural differences in the recognition of universal facial expressions. *Journal of cross-cultural psychology, 23*(1), 72-84.

Meeren, H. K., van Heijnsbergen, C. C., & de Gelder, B. (2005). Rapid perceptual integration of facial expression and emotional body language. *Proceedings of the National Academy of Sciences of the United States of America, 102*, 16518–16523.

Milders, M., Hietanen, J. K., Leppänen, J. M., & Braun, M. (2011). Detection of emotional faces is modulated by the direction of eye gaze. *Emotion, 11*, 1456.

Miller, S. L., Maner, J. K., & Becker, D. V. (2010). Self-protective biases in group categorization: Threat cues shape the psychological boundary between "us" and "them." *Journal of Personality and Social Psychology, 99*, 62–77.

Mobbs, D., Petrovic, P., Marchant, J., Hassabis, D., Seymour, B., Weiskopf, N., Dolan, R. J., & Frith, C. D. (2007). When fear is near: Threat imminence elicits prefrontal—periaqueductal grey shifts in humans. *Science, 317*, 1079–1083.

Montepare, J. M., & Dobish, H. (2003). The contribution of emotion perceptions and their overgeneralizations to trait impressions. *Journal of Nonverbal Behavior, 27*, 237–254.

Morris, J. S., Öhman, A., & Dolan, R. J. (1998). Conscious and unconscious emotional learning in the human amygdala. *Nature, 393*, 467–470.

Öhman, A. (2005). The role of the amygdala in human fear: Automatic detection of threat. *Psychoneuroendocrinology, 30*, 953–958.

Pessoa, L., & Adolphs, R. (2010). Emotion processing and the amygdala: from a 'low road' to 'many roads' of evaluating biological significance. *Nature reviews neuroscience, 11*(11), 773-783.

Pine, D. S., Mogg, K., Bradley, B. P., Montgomery, L., Monk, C. S., McClure, E., et al. (2005). Attention bias to threat in maltreated children: Implications for vulnerability to stress-related psychopathology. *American Journal of Psychiatry, 162*, 291–296.

Redican, W. K. (1982). An evolutionary perspective on human facial displays. In P. Ekman (Ed.), *Emotion in the human face* (2nd ed., pp. 212–280). New York, NY: Cambridge University Press.

Russell, J. A. (1997). Reading emotion from and into faces: Resurrecting a dimensional-contextrual perspective. In J. A. Russell & J. M. Fernandez-Dol's (Eds.), *The psychology of facial expression* (pp. xx–xx). Cambridge, UK: Cambridge University Press.

Salin, P. A., & Bullier, J. (1995). Corticocortical connections in the visual system: Structure and function. *Physiological Reviews, 75*, 107–154.

Tamietto, M., & De Gelder, B. (2010). Neural bases of the non-conscious perception of emotional signals. *Nature Reviews Neuroscience, 11*, 697–709.

Tamietto, M., Weiskrantz, L., Geminiani, G., & de Gelder, B. (2007). The medium and the message: Non-conscious processing of emotions from facial expressions and body language in blindsight. Paper presented at Cognitive Neuroscience Society Annual Meeting, New York, NY.

Trapp, S., & Bar, M. (2015). Prediction, context, and competition in visual recognition. *Annals of the New York Academy of Sciences, 1339*, 190–198.

Vuilleumier, P., Armony, J. L., Driver, J., & Dolan, R. J. (2003). Distinct spatial frequency sensitivities for processing faces and emotional expressions. *Nature Neuroscience, 6*, 624–631.

Xu, X., Ichida, J. M., Allison, J. D., Boyd, J. D., & Bonds, A. B. (2001). A comparison of koniocellular, magnocellular and parvocellular receptive field properties in the lateral geniculate nucleus of the owl monkey (Aotus trivirgatus). *Journal of Physiology, 531*, 203–218.

Zebrowitz, L. A. (1997). *Reading faces: Window to the soul?* Boulder, CO: Westview Press.

Zebrowitz, L. A. (2006). Finally, faces find favor. *Social Cognition, 24*, 657–701.

Zebrowitz, L. A., & Collins, M. A. (1997). Accurate social perception at zero acquaintance: The affordances of a Gibsonian approach. *Personality and Social Psychology Review, 1*, 204–223.

Zebrowitz, L. A., & Montepare, J. M. (2008). Social psychological face perception: Why appearance matters. *Social and Personality Psychology Compass, 2*, 1497–1517.

18

Inherently Ambiguous

An Argument for Contextualized Emotion Perception

HILLEL AVIEZER AND RAN R. HASSIN

Perhaps the most central distinction in emotion experience is that between positive and negative valence (Bradley & Lang, 1994; Mehrabian & Russell, 1974; Osgood, 1952). We approach ice cream stands and avoid dirty toilets, savor kisses from a loved one and suffer in agony when stubbing our toe. Knowing good from bad involves distinct brain networks (Barrett & Bliss-Moreau, 2009) and is automatic (Chen & Bargh, 1999; Fazio, Sanbonmatsu, Powell, & Kardes, 1986). Adults universally refer to valence as a central aspect of their affective experience (Barrett, 2006b), and newborns show clear behavioral preferences for positive versus negative tasting stimuli (Steiner, 1979). In short, in the world of emotional experience, the difference between positive and negative seems to be fundamental, robust, and omnipresent, the cornerstone of affective life.

As most psychological models posit that facial expressions faithfully convey affective states, telling apart positive from negative emotions in others should be a fairly easy task. In fact, it seems undeniable that we constantly read out affective states from faces—from the scowls of a grouchy boss to the wide smiles of children receiving their Christmas gifts. All we seemingly need to do is look at their facial expressions and presto! Their true emotions are revealed.

It is against this strongly ingrained and intuitive experience that we contest in this chapter (see also, Hassin, Aviezer, & Bentin, 2013). Although many people believe that facial expressions are highly informative and reliable sources of affective information, we argue that, in fact, facial expressions are often quite baffling. Indeed, the phenomenological experience of reading emotions and affective states from faces is often but a compelling illusion. As we will argue, it is often the contextual information, not the face itself, which is critical for recognizing emotion. Ironically, though, the role of context in emotion perception is often underappreciated or even unnoticed.

VALENCE AMBIGUITY IN REAL-LIFE INTENSE FACIAL EXPRESSIONS

Jack loses his life savings in a stock market crash while Jill wins the national lottery. Imagine we were there, taking their photograph at the moment they heard the life-changing news. Taking a close look at their pictures, leading psychological models (as well as common intuition) would predict very distinct facial expressions of agony and ecstasy, respectively.

According to *basic* emotion models, positive (e.g., happiness) and negative (e.g., fear) emotions arise from distinct affect programs, each equipped with dedicated hardwired neurological systems and distinct universally recognized facial movements (Ekman, 1993; Ekman & Cordaro, 2011; Tracy & Matsumoto, 2008). According to this line of thought, positive and negative emotions are expressed with very different facial muscular activity (i.e., different Action Units of facial muscles) and thus rarely confused.

According to *dimensional* emotion models, there is no need to postulate discrete affect programs for separate emotions. Rather, this view holds that a small number of bipolar dimensions serve as the basic buildings blocks of affective experience and affect recognition (Fontaine, Scherer, Roesch, & Ellsworth, 2007; Russell, 1980). Specifically, the dimension of valence, ranging from pleasant to unpleasant, is crucial in defining emotional experience and expression. According to dimensional theorists, positive and negative affective states are located on opposite sites in affective space and consequently they are conveyed in a highly distinct manner (Carroll & Russell, 1996; Russell, 1997; Russell & Bullock, 1985). In fact, valence has been considered to be part of the "normative preeminence" of the face which is read out rapidly, effortlessly, and universally (Carroll & Russell, 1996).

Furthermore, both basic and dimensional models agree that positive and negative expressions should grow more distinct and recognizable as they become more intense. For example, basic emotion models predict that intense emotions activate maximally distinct facial muscles which increase discrimination (Calder et al., 2000; Hess, Blairy, & Kleck, 1997; Tracy, 2014). Similarly, dimensional emotion models predict that intense emotions are located on more extreme and distant positions on the pleasure-displeasure axis, and thus their positivity or negativity should be easier to decipher (Carroll & Russell, 1996; Russell, 1997).

Notwithstanding these predictions, the models just described have mostly been based on research with lab-created stimuli. In an attempt to move beyond the popular but artificial sets of posed facial expressions (e.g., Ekman & Friesen, 1976; Matsumoto & Ekman, 1988), recent work has examined real-life affective displays of tennis players during professional matches (Aviezer, Trope, & Todorov, 2012a). In that study, Aviezer et al. (2012a) presented different groups of participants with images of tennis players winning or losing a critical point in a tennis match. Critically, the images were presented in one of three formats: face alone (with no body), body alone (with no face), or face with body (the original image). Participants were requested to rate the valence of the image on a scale ranging from very negative to very positive with a neutral midpoint. This type of judgment should be easy and straightforward according to both basic (Ekman, 1993) and dimensional (Russell, 1997) models of emotion.

Not surprisingly, participants successfully differentiated the valence of the winners and losers when they rated the full image with the face and body. However, a striking difference was revealed when comparing the ratings of the face versus the body (see Fig. 18.1a-b). Faceless bodies were almost as informative as the full pictures, with participants easily differentiating the valence of winners from losers. In contrast, when rating the face alone, participants utterly failed in differentiating the winners from losers. Specifically, the decontextualized faces resulted in similarly negative ratings irrespective of the actual situational valence of the faces (see Fig. 18.1c).

These findings are surprising because they clearly illustrate that intense facial expressions are actually uninformative to viewers when rating valence. Differentiating positive from negative valence is perhaps the most basic and simple task in emotion perception (also known as "mapping"; Aviezer, Hassin, Bentin, & Trope, 2008), yet viewers simply cannot do it based on the face alone. These results also pose a puzzle: If intense faces are so poorly recognized in isolation, why aren't viewers aware of this when they encounter such faces in real life?

We propose that objectively nondiagnostic facial expressions appear to viewers as informative due to a contextual illusion. For example, in the aforementioned tennis study, when participants rated the valence of faces together with bodies, roughly half of them reported that they based their judgment on specific idiosyncratic facial movements while giving little credit to the body. As the isolated faces were in fact not diagnostic—our previous experiments with faces in isolation show that people cannot identify the valence they express—this phenomenological report qualifies as illusory in nature.

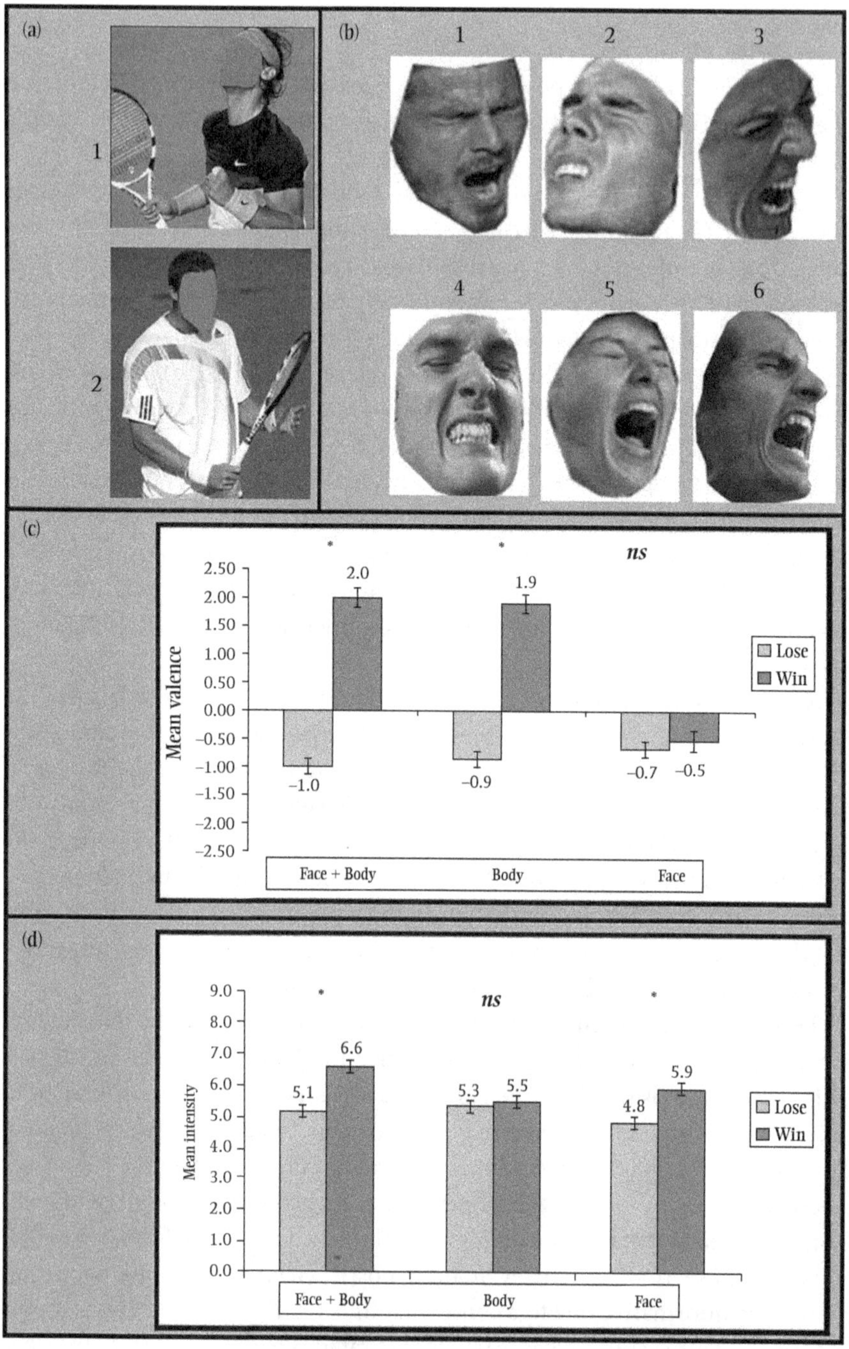

Figure 18.1 (*A*) Examples of reactions to (1) winning and (2) losing a point. (*B*) Examples of isolated faces (1, 4, 6 = losing point; 2, 3, 5 = winning point). (*C*) Mean valence ratings for face + body, body, and face. Results are converted from the original scale which ranged from 1 (most negative) to 9 (most positive), with 5 serving as a neutral midpoint. (*D*) Mean intensity ratings for face + body, body, and face. (Adapted with permission from Aviezer et al., 2012)

We hypothesized that the illusion arose because the valence from the body was accurately registered and then read into the highly intense faces, tainting their perceived valence. This was further demonstrated by seamlessly crossing the faces and bodies of winners and losers using Photoshop and asking participants to rate the facial valence (Fig. 18.2a). As predicted, the valence

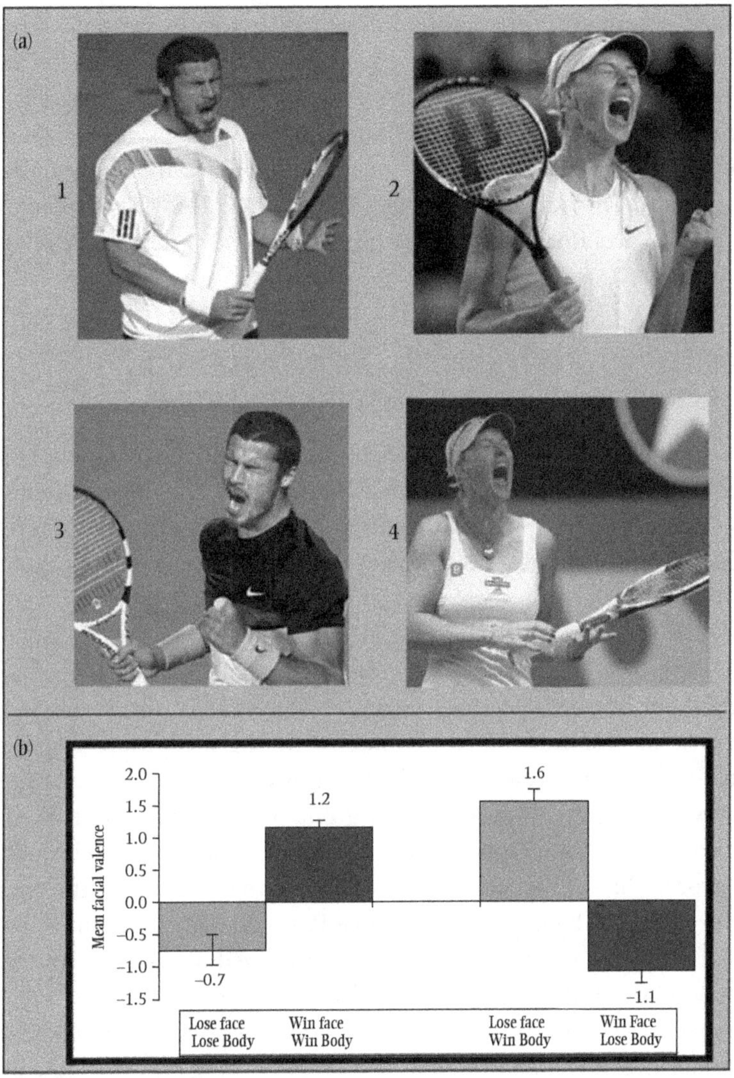

Figure 18.2 (*A*) Examples of original images of players (1) losing or (2) winning a point. The same faces combined with incongruent-valence bodies such as (3) a losing face on a winning body and (4) a winning face on a losing body. (*B*) Mean valence ratings of the facial expressions. (Adapted with permission from Aviezer et al., 2012)

of the contextual body had a strong influence such that identical faces were rated as conveying opposite valence as a function of their accompanying bodies (Fig. 18.2b; Aviezer et al., 2012a).

Importantly, these findings are not limited to the domain of victory and defeat in sports events. For example, facial expressions of extreme pain (e.g., nipple piercing) and extreme pleasure (e.g., experiencing an orgasm) are also poorly differentiated. Similarly, expressions of intense joy (e.g., during surprise soldier reunions) are poorly differentiated from expressions of intense anguish and fear (e.g., during funerals or while witnessing terror attacks) (Aviezer et al., 2012a; Wenzler, Levine, Dick, Oertel-Knöchel, & Aviezer, 2016). These examples demonstrate that contrary to common psychological dogma and human intuition, real-life intense facial expressions are highly ambiguous when perceived in isolation. Although viewers may think about and experience them as an informative source for valence, they are actually relying on contextual cues.

AMBIGUITY IN SPONTANEOUS AND INTENSE FACIAL EXPRESSIONS: A SELECTIVE HISTORICAL REVIEW

Our discussion so far focused on recent research covering a special class of face reactions that occur during intense emotional situations. Although the studies we reviewed expose novel findings, a review of the literature reveals an established line of studies showing that real-life intense facial expressions are highly ambiguous.

Consider, for example, the influential (and ethically dubious) work of Landis (1924, 1929), who photographed the facial expressions of participants while putting them through a series of emotionally evocative situations (reacting to surprise firecrackers exploding under their chair, exposure to pornography, being forced to decapitate a rat, to name a few). He then presented the decontextualized face images to a new group of participants and asked them to describe the photographed person's emotion. Landis's conclusions were unequivocal: "it is practically impossible to name accurately the 'emotion' being experienced by a subject when one has only a photograph of the face" (p. 69). In fact, the valence of the emotions assigned to the faces was often in contradiction with the actual valence of the situation.

Sherman (1927) examined the facial reactions of newborn infants undergoing various negative manipulations (e.g., experiencing hunger, being pricked by a needle, being dropped, etc.) and demonstrated that viewers greatly disagreed on the classification of the isolated faces. Furthermore, when facial reactions were contextualized by matching and mismatching them with the eliciting situations, participants relied on the situations, but not on the faces, when judging the emotion of the infants.

More than a decade later, Munn (1940) used a different approach: He presented participants with candid pictures of intense emotional situations from magazines such as *Life*. In one condition the faces were presented in isolation (e.g., a fearful face), and in another they were embedded in a full visual scene (e.g., a fearful face displayed by a woman fleeing an attacker). His results, too, indicated significant influence of context on emotion perception, suggesting much ambiguity in the facial signal.

These and other studies were integrated in two highly influential reviews by Bruner and Tagiuri (1954), and Tagiuri (1969), who concluded that "All in all, one wonders about the significance of studies of the recognition of 'facial expressions of emotions', in isolation of context" (1954, p. 638).

Later studies examined intense expressions out of interest in the influence of social audience effects. Taking an ethological approach, Kraut and Johnston (1979) conducted a series of seminal studies comparing the facial reactions of individuals during various positive versus negative events. The most intense of these studies likely involved the reactions of hockey fans to various game events. Although fans were more likely to smile following positive than negative events, this effect was strongly modulated by whether a social interaction was taking place between the fans or not. In fact, social interactivity was a better predictor of smiling than the positivity or negativity of the situation.

One limitation of the hockey study was that the emotion of the fans was not known, but rather inferred from the situation. More recently, this study was replicated with soccer fans who also rated their affective experience while watching important matches (Ruiz-Belda, Fernández-Dols, Carrera, & Barchard, 2003). When situations did not involve direct social interaction between the fans, the correlation between reported emotion and facial behavior was weak. For example, self-reportedly happy fans displayed few smiles as well as facial expressions of surprise, sadness, and fear (Fernandez-Dols & Ruiz-Belda, 1997).

Surprisingly weak links between positive affective states and expressive behavior were also found for Gold medal winners whose smiles strongly depended on social interactions with others (Fernández-Dols & Ruiz-Belda, 1995). In a recent review of spontaneous facial behavior, Fernández-Dols and Crivelli (2013) concluded that the link between emotion and facial expressions is "weak, nonexistent, or unpredicted."

To summarize, a long line of research on intense real-life facial expressions suggests that they are far less informative than one would have thought.

AMBIGUITY IN STEREOTYPICAL BASIC FACIAL EXPRESSIONS

The fact that facial expressions may be highly ambiguous and prone to contextual influences stands in contrast to a long tradition of research stressing their importance as a diagnostic signal (Smith, Cottrell, Gosselin, & Schyns, 2005). Nevertheless, one may argue that perhaps the ambiguity of such facial reactions simply reflects the ambiguity of the affective episodes which are often poorly controlled.

By contrast, emotional expressions during pure prototypical basic emotions (e.g., disgust, fear, sadness, etc.) should be unambiguous and well recognized. While a set of spontaneous basic emotions has yet to be constructed, sets of posed basic facial expressions are available. In such sets, theoretically proposed muscular movements are modeled for each emotion (e.g., Ekman & Friesen, 1976; Langner et al., 2010; Matsumoto & Ekman, 1988; Van Der Schalk, Hawk, Fischer, & Doosje, 2011). The images in these sets are often selected based on their high recognition and classification to a specific emotional category. Thus, such faces would surely demonstrate a high diagnostic value.

We have shown, however, that this is not the case, and that significant ambiguity can be found even in the lab-made basic facial expressions that are carefully selected to convey specific emotions. Although basic facial expressions in standardized research sets are, by definition, well recognized in isolation, they are highly ambiguous in context.

THE BODIES OF FACES

In our own work we examined the effects of bodies and contextual paraphernalia on facial expression perception. We focused on bodies because we had an intuition that faces are usually accompanied by bodies, and that bodies, like faces, are expressive (see also Meeren, van Heijnsbergen, & de Gelder, 2005). We were also encouraged by the fact that face and body processing share many cognitive and brain characteristics (de Gelder, 2006; Peelen & Downing, 2007; Yovel, Pelc, & Lubetzky, 2010) and by the finding that affective face-body Stroop-like interferences occur very early (by 100 ms) during visual processing (Meeren et al., 2005).

We proposed two simple hypotheses. First, based on the arguments briefly presented earlier, we predicted that bodies would serve as powerful contexts. Second, we hypothesized that perceptual similarity—that is, the perceived similarity between facial expressions—is an important determinant of context effects. To take an example, the categorization of a smiling face is unlikely to be strongly affected by a context displaying disgust, because the two facial expressions (happiness, disgust) are very dissimilar. An angry face, however, is more likely to be affected by disgust context because the facial expressions of anger and disgust are relatively similar (Susskind, Littlewort, Bartlett, Movellan, & Anderson, 2007).

In our first set of studies we seamlessly planted faces that in isolation are consensually categorized as conveying disgust on bodily postures that in isolation are consensually categorized as conveying other emotions (Aviezer, Hassin, Bentin, et al., 2008; Aviezer, Hassin, Ryan, et al., 2008) (see Fig. 18.3). This resulted in a design with four levels of perceptual similarity between the presented face and the body-expected face: low, medium, high, and an identity (disgust face on a disgust body). Participants in all experiments were asked to choose, among six options, which emotion is conveyed by *the face*.

Three experiments documented powerful effects of context on facial expression recognition and showed that the impact of context in the high-similarity condition was robust. For example, the categorization of "disgust facial expressions" as disgust-expressing dropped from 91% in the identity condition to a mere 11% in the high-similarity condition. Similarly, the categorization of "sadness expressions" dropped from 72% in the identity condition to a mere 17% in the high-similarity condition (Aviezer, Hassin, Bentin, et al., 2008; Aviezer, Hassin, Ryan, et al., 2008). Supporting our second hypothesis, these

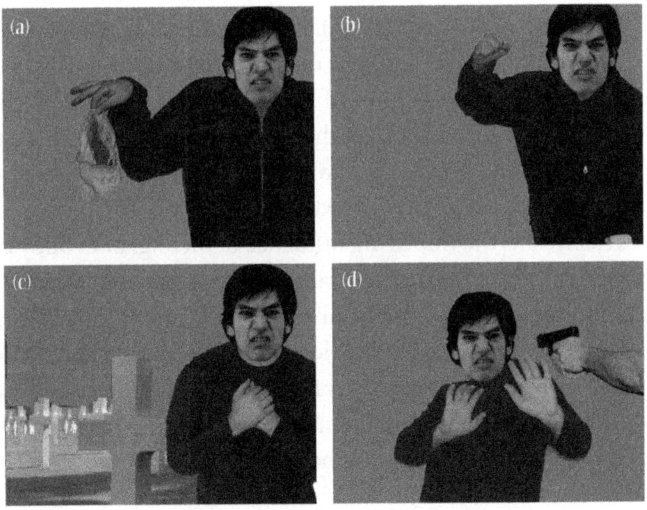

Figure 18.3 Stereotypical facial expression of disgust in context. (*A*) Disgust face on disgusted body (identity condition); (*B*) disgust face on angry body (high similarity condition); (*C*) disgust face on sad body (medium similarity condition); (*D*) disgust face on fear body (low similarity condition). (The facial expression in the figure has been adapted from Van Der Schalk et al., 2011)

experiments revealed that the magnitude of contextual influence was strongly correlated with the degree of perceptual similarity: The more similar the facial expressions, the stronger the influence of context. We refer to this finding as the *confusability effect*.

The categorization data do not tell us much about the underlying process: Does context affect late and relatively controlled stages of processing (e.g., the judgment) or relatively early and automatic ones? Support for the latter view emerged from an eye-tracking experiment, which demonstrated that initial fixations in the face space are systematically affected by the context (Aviezer, Hassin, Ryan, et al., 2008). Specifically, context shifts the scanning pattern of emotional expressions in context-congruent ways. To further examine this issue, we conducted a series of experiments in which we examined three markers of automaticity: intentionality, stoppability, and effortlessness (Bargh, 1994). In one of these experiments participants viewed the stimuli described earlier and were instructed in various ways, and motivated by means of a monetary prize, to avoid using the bodies. Neither motivation nor instructions made a difference. The results of another experiment showed that the effects of bodily context do not diminish under cognitive load (Aviezer, Bentin, Dudarev, & Hassin, 2011).

Additional research supports the notion that the face and body are perceived as an integrated, gestalt-like unit. One line of experiments used a face-body variant of the composite face effect, a measure of holistic processing (Aviezer, Trope, & Todorov, 2012b). Participants judged facial expressions combined with emotionally congruent or incongruent bodies which have been shown to influence the recognition of emotion from the face. Critically, the faces were either aligned with the body in a natural position or slightly misaligned in a manner that breaks the ecological person form. As predicted, spatially breaking the person form reduced the facilitating influence of congruent body context as well as the impeding influence of incongruent body context on the recognition of emotion from the face. Interestingly, such composite face-body effects emerge early and can be observed in 6- to 8-year-old participants (Mondloch, 2012), but not in 4-year-olds (Mondloch, Horner, & Mian, 2013). Taken together, the results suggest that faces and bodies are strongly and automatically integrated early on, a phenomenon that helps explain how the recognition of basic facial expressions can be influenced, at times dramatically so, by incongruent body context.

FACES IN NONBODY CONTEXT

Although the influence of the body on the face may be compelling, one may argue that the strength of the effects results from the body being a special class of contextual information. After all, the body and face are both parts of the same individual. In such cases the context includes "within sender features" (Wieser & Brosch, 2012), and therefore its impact may be strengthened. However, contextual effects on prototypical facial expressions are not limited to body context. As next briefly reviewed, a large corpus of data suggests that also context that is external to the expresser has a robust influence on the recognition of basic facial expressions (for a more comprehensive review, see Wieser & Brosch, 2012).

Using an emotional visual context paradigm, participants were required to categorize facial expressions presented against backgrounds of natural scenes such as a garbage dump versus a field of flowers (Righart & de Gelder, 2008). The results showed a significant effect of context on facial expression perception. In a related set of experiments, Masuda et al. (2008) examined how the categorization of a target's facial expression is affected by the presence of surrounding individuals' faces. Participants viewed a cartoon image of a central figure displaying, for example, an angry face, while in the background a group of other individuals displayed happiness. The results indicated that Japanese were influenced by the surrounding context, whereas Westerners were not, thereby demonstrating two types of context effects: visual and cultural.

Additional work demonstrating the influence of social context on emotion perception can be seen in the work of Mumenthaler and Sander (2012). These authors showed how the functional relation between emotions serves as context influencing emotion perception. For example, the recognition of prototypical fear in a target is strongly facilitated when a contextual angry face is gazing at a fearful individual—presumably because the perceiver infers that the fearful response results from angry expression. Strikingly, this integration of social information occurs automatically, even when the contextual face appears below the threshold of conscious perception (Mumenthaler & Sander, 2015).

Barrett (2006a) proposed the *conceptual act model* in which facial muscles convey basic affective information (e.g., approach vs. avoid; positive vs. negative), and more specific emotions are inferred using accessible conceptual context (i.e., words). In one set of studies the role of accessibility was examined using a semantic satiation procedure. The results showed that participants' performance depended on conceptual satiation (Barrett, Lindquist, & Gendron, 2007; Lindquist, Barrett, Bliss-Moreau, & Russell, 2006). The importance of conceptual knowledge on emotion perception can also be seen in earlier work showing that short emotional vignettes strongly alter the recognition of emotion from basic facial expressions (Carroll & Russell, 1996).

FACIAL EXPRESSIONS REVISITED

In this chapter we challenged the modal views of emotion perception (see Hassin, Aviezer, & Bentin, 2013). We presented evidence from multiple projects in multiple labs, across dozens of years, which clearly shows that contexts in general—and bodily contexts more specifically—play a crucial role in face-based expression perception. In fact, what seems to us to be face-based expression perception is often just an illusion: We gather the information from other sources, but we misattribute it to the face.

Although, as the modal views suggest, some faces are unequivocal signals of emotion even in isolation, many others are either ambiguous, in that they strongly express more than one emotion, or rather vague, weakly expressing various emotions (Trope, 1986). In both types of faces, contexts automatically and generally without awareness imbue the face with emotional meaning. The basic expressions view does not easily allow for the documented effects (note that some of these findings were obtained using faces that were pretested using the toolbox of the basic expressions view). The dimensional views are more flexible in nature, but the findings reported here do not easily sit with them either.

The field's view of the importance of context has waxed and waned in the history of emotion perception, and we hope that what we see in recent years, and review here and elsewhere, is the beginning of a new and serious swing of the pendulum.

Although one conclusion to be drawn from this chapter is that emotion perception is contextual in nature, as we have done herein, we think that an even more extreme conclusion might be warranted. In fact, it is us scientists who devise experiments in which "context" and "text" are so clearly defined and easy to separate. Based on the data and arguments we developed earlier, we believe that emotion perception is a quintessential example of a set of processes in which this separation might be artificial and may hamper scientific progress. At least in the case of bodies and faces—two social stimuli that usually go places together, and if they don't, then one is in serious trouble—it seems that the whole is different from its constituents in important and meaningful ways.

Although parsimony favors simpler theories, we think that the data gathered so far are enough to seriously challenge the modal views and push us toward new theories (for an early attempt, see Aviezer et al., 2008). Developing these new theories will not only allow us to better account for existing data, it will also allow us to refrain from paying the price of sticking with the modal view. Consider, for example, the wide-scale attempts to link specific emotions to well-defined brain structures. In recent decades we experienced a few "highs" during which it seemed that research successfully identified brain regions that specialize in basic emotions (Adolphs, 2002; Adolphs et al., 2005; Phillips et al., 1998; Sprengelmeyer et al., 1996, 1997). Yet it seems fair to say that the news about (some of) these identifications was premature, and that currently the picture seems more complex than it had appeared (Barrett, 2006a; Johnson et al., 2007; Lindquist, Wager, Kober, Bliss-Moreau, & Barrett, 2012; Pessoa & Adolphs, 2010; Touroutoglou, Lindquist, Dickerson, & Barrett, 2015). Given the centrality of this endeavor to social and affective neurosciences, and given the time and resources devoted to it, this state of affairs might be informative. It may suggest, for example, that our current techniques of probing the brain are not sufficiently developed, or that we use the wrong level of analyses. More relevant to our discussion, however, these difficulties may partly stem from assuming the basic expressions view, which leads us to look for brain areas (or neural patterns) specialized in the perception of basic facial expressions. But if the task of categorizing faces is not as simple as is suggested by this view, then performing it may require more complex processes, and maybe even (explicit) strategies. Hence, facial expression recognition may rely on more general mechanisms of inference and categorization, and prediction making, thereby rendering the difficulties in locating brain areas devoted to the processing of "basic expressions" less surprising (Barrett et al., 2007; Lindquist & Gendron, 2013).

CONCLUSIONS

Facial expressions of emotions are inherently ambiguous, so much so that many contexts easily shift how they seem to us. So although it seems to us that in "real life" we see *faces* as angry, fearful, and so on—it is often not the faces that we see, it is face-context combinations. We think that the right thing to do is to stop using terms such as "disgusted face" or "fearful face." These faces are disgusted or fearful in very specific contexts, most of which are unnatural and unlikely to capture many of the essences of emotion perception. The expression "disgusted face," for example, should be taken as a shorthand for *a face that, in isolation, and when one uses one of the frequently used categorization methods, is likely to be categorized as disgusted.* Alas, we are too old to be really hopeful. People, present company included, are unlikely to stop using these terms. They are way too natural for us, at this point in history and culture. But we should try. The reviewed evidence provides a strong incentive to expand the cognitive, social, and neuroscientific inquiry of the nature of emotion perception.

REFERENCES

Adolphs, R. (2002). Neural systems for recognizing emotion. *Current Opinion in Neurobiology, 12*(2), 169–177. doi: 10.1016/s0959-4388(02)00301-x

Adolphs, R., Gosselin, F., Buchanan, T. W., Tranel, D., Schyns, P., & Damasio, A. R. (2005). A mechanism for impaired fear recognition after amygdala damage. *Nature, 433*(7021), 68–72.

Aviezer, H., Bentin, S., Dudarev, V., & Hassin, R. R. (2011). The automaticity of emotional face-context integration. *Emotion, 11*(6), 1406–1414.

Aviezer, H., Hassin, R. R., Bentin, S., & Trope, Y. (2008). Putting facial expressions into context. In N. Ambady & J. Skowronski (Eds.), *First impressions* (pp. 255–286). New York, NY: Guilford Press.

Aviezer, H., Hassin, R. R., Ryan, J., Grady, C., Susskind, J., Anderson, A., . . . Bentin, S. (2008). Angry, disgusted, or afraid? Studies on the malleability of emotion perception. *Psychological Science, 19*(7), 724–732.

Aviezer, H., Trope, Y., & Todorov, A. (2012a). Body cues, not facial expressions, discriminate between intense positive and negative emotions. *Science, 338* (6111), 1225–1229. doi: 10.1126/science.1224313

Aviezer, H., Trope, Y., & Todorov, A. (2012b). Holistic person processing: Faces with bodies tell the whole story. *Journal of Personality and Social Psychology, 103*(1), 20.

Barrett, L. F. (2006a). Solving the emotion paradox: Categorization and the experience of emotion. *Personality and Social Psychology Review, 10*(1), 20–46.

Barrett, L. F. (2006b). Valence is a basic building block of emotional life. *Journal of Research in Personality, 40*(1), 35–55. doi: 10.1016/j.jrp.2005.08.006

Barrett, L. F., & Bliss-Moreau, E. (2009). Affect as a psychological primitive. *Advances in Experimental Social Psychology, 41*, 167–218.

Barrett, L. F., Lindquist, K. A., & Gendron, M. (2007). Language as context for the perception of emotion. *Trends in Cognitive Sciences, 11*(8), 327–332.

Bradley, M. M., & Lang, P. J. (1994). Measuring emotion: The self-assessment manikin and the semantic differential. *Journal of Behavior Therapy and Experimental Psychiatry, 25*(1), 49–59.

Bruner, J. S., & Tagiuri, R. (1954). The perception of people. In G. Lindzey (Ed.), *Handbook of social psychology* (Vol. 2, pp. 634–654). Reading, MA: Addison-Wesley.

Calder, A. J., Rowland, D., Young, A. W., Nimmo-Smith, I., Keane, J., & Perrett, D. I. (2000). Caricaturing facial expressions. *Cognition, 76*(2), 105–146. doi: 10.1016/S0010-0277(00)00074-3

Carroll, J. M., & Russell, J. A. (1996). Do facial expressions signal specific emotions? Judging emotion from the face in context. *Journal of Personality and Social Psychology, 70*(2), 205–218. doi: 10.1037/0022-3514.70.2.205

Chen, M., & Bargh, J. A. (1999). Consequences of automatic evaluation: Immediate behavioral predispositions to approach or avoid the stimulus. *Personality and Social Psychology Bulletin, 25*(2), 215–224.

de Gelder, B. (2006). Towards the neurobiology of emotional body language. *Nature Reviews Neuroscience, 7*(3), 242–249.

Ekman, P. (1993). Facial expression and emotion. *American Psychologist, 48*(4), 384–392.

Ekman, P., & Cordaro, D. (2011). What is meant by calling emotions basic. *Emotion Review, 3*(4), 364–370. doi: 10.1177/1754073911410740

Ekman, P., & Friesen, W. V. (1976). *Pictures of facial affect*. Palo Alto, CA: Consulting Psychologists Press.

Fazio, R. H., Sanbonmatsu, D. M., Powell, M. C., & Kardes, F. R. (1986). On the automatic activation of attitudes. *Journal of Personality and Social Psychology, 50*(2), 229–238. doi: 10.1037/0022-3514.50.2.229

Fernández-Dols, J.-M., & Crivelli, C. (2013). Emotion and expression: Naturalistic studies. *Emotion Review, 5*(1), 24–29.

Fernández-Dols, J.-M., & Ruiz-Belda, M.-A. (1995). Are smiles a sign of happiness? Gold medal winners at the Olympic Games. *Journal of Personality and Social Psychology, 69*(6), 1113.

Fernandez-Dols, J. M., & Ruiz-Belda, M. A. (1997). Spontaneous facial behavior during intense emotional episodes: Artistic truth and optical truth. In J. A. Russell & J. M. Fernandez-Dols (Eds.), *The psychology of facial expression* (pp. 255–274). New York, NY: Cambridge University Press.

Fontaine, J. R., Scherer, K. R., Roesch, E. B., & Ellsworth, P. C. (2007). The world of emotions is not two-dimensional. *Psychological Science, 18*(12), 1050–1057. doi: 10.1111/j.1467-9280.2007.02024.x

Hassin, R. R., Aviezer, H., & Bentin, S. (2013). Inherently ambiguous: Facial expressions of emotions, in context. *Emotion Review, 5*(1), 60–65.

Hess, U., Blairy, S., & Kleck, R. E. (1997). The intensity of emotional facial expressions and decoding accuracy. *Journal of Nonverbal Behavior, 21*(4), 241–257. doi: 10.1023/a:1024952730333

Johnson, S. A., Stout, J. C., Solomon, A. C., Langbehn, D. R., Aylward, E. H., Cruce, C. B., . . . Julian-Baros, E. (2007). Beyond disgust: Impaired recognition of negative emotions prior to diagnosis in Huntington's disease. *Brain, 130*(7), 1732–1744.

Kraut, R. E., & Johnston, R. E. (1979). Social and emotional messages of smiling: An ethological approach. *Journal of Personality and Social Psychology, 37*(9), 1539.

Landis, C. (1924). Studies of emotional reactions. II. General behavior and facial expression. *Journal of Comparative Psychology, 4*(5), 447.

Landis, C. (1929). The interpretation of facial expression in emotion. *Journal of General Psychology, 2*, 59–72.

Langner, O., Dotsch, R., Bijlstra, G., Wigboldus, D. H. J., Hawk, S. T., & van Knippenberg, A. (2010). Presentation and validation of the Radboud Faces Database. *Cognition & Emotion, 24*(8), 1377–1388.

Lindquist, K. A., Barrett, L. F., Bliss-Moreau, E., & Russell, J. A. (2006). Language and the perception of emotion. *Emotion, 6*(1), 125–138.

Lindquist, K. A., & Gendron, M. (2013). What's in a word? Language constructs emotion perception. *Emotion Review, 5*(1), 66–71. doi: 10.1177/1754073912451351

Lindquist, K. A., Wager, T. D., Kober, H., Bliss-Moreau, E., & Barrett, L. F. (2012). The brain basis of emotion: A meta-analytic review. *Behavioral and Brain Sciences, 35*(03), 121–143.

Masuda, T., Ellsworth, P. C., Mesquita, B., Leu, J., Tanida, S., & Van de Veerdonk, E. (2008). Placing the face in context: Cultural differences in the perception of facial emotion. *Journal of Personality and Social Psychology, 94*(3), 365–381.

Matsumoto, D., & Ekman, P. (1988). Japanese and Caucasian facial expressions of emotion (IACFEE). San Francisco, CA: Intercultural and Emotion Research Laboratory, Department of Psychology, San Francisco State University.

Meeren, H. K. M., van Heijnsbergen, C. C. R. J., & de Gelder, B. (2005). Rapid perceptual integration of facial expression and emotional body language. *Proceedings of the National Academy of Sciences, 102*(45), 16518–16523. doi: 10.1073/pnas.0507650102

Mehrabian, A., & Russell, J. A. (1974). *An approach to environmental psychology.* Cambridge, MA: MIT Press.

Mondloch, C. (2012). Sad or fearful? The influence of body posture on adults' and children's perception of facial displays of emotion. *Journal of Experimental Child Psychology, 111*(2), 180–196.

Mondloch, C. J., Horner, M., & Mian, J. (2013). Wide eyes and drooping arms: Adult-like congruency effects emerge early in the development of sensitivity to emotional faces and body postures. *Journal of Experimental Child Psychology, 114*(2), 203–216.

Mumenthaler, C., & Sander, D. (2012). Social appraisal influences recognition of emotions. *Journal of Personality and Social Psychology, 102*(6), 1118.

Mumenthaler, C., & Sander, D. (2015). Automatic integration of social information in emotion recognition. *Journal of Experimental Psychology: General, 144*(2), 392.

Munn, N. L. (1940). The effect of knowledge of the situation upon judgment of emotion from facial expressions. *The Journal of Abnormal and Social Psychology, 35*(3), 324–338. doi: 10.1037/h0063680

Osgood, C. E. (1952). The nature and measurement of meaning. *Psychological Bulletin, 49*(3), 197.

Peelen, M. V., & Downing, P. E. (2007). The neural basis of visual body perception. *Nature Reviews Neuroscience, 8*(8), 636–648.

Pessoa, L., & Adolphs, R. (2010). Emotion processing and the amygdala: From a "low road" to "many roads" of evaluating biological significance. *Nature Reviews Neuroscience, 11*(11), 773–783.

Phillips, M., Young, A., Scott, S. K., Calder, A., Andrew, C., Giampietro, V., . . . Gray, J. (1998). Neural responses to facial and vocal expressions of fear and disgust. *Proceedings of the Royal Society of London. Series B: Biological Sciences, 265*(1408), 1809.

Righart, R., & de Gelder, B. (2008). Recognition of facial expressions is influenced by emotional scene gist. *Cognitive, Affective, & Behavioral Neuroscience, 8*(3), 264–272.

Ruiz-Belda, M. A., Fernández-Dols, J. M., Carrera, P., & Barchard, K. (2003). Spontaneous facial expressions of happy bowlers and soccer fans. *Cognition & Emotion, 17*(2), 315–326.

Russell, J. A. (1980). A circumplex model of affect. *Journal of Personality and Social Psychology, 39*(6), 1161–1178. doi: 10.1037/H0077714

Russell, J. A. (1997). Reading emotions from and into faces: Resurrecting a dimensional contextual perspective. In J. A. Russell & J. M. Fernandez-Dols (Eds.), *The psychology of facial expressions* (pp. 295–320). New York, NY: Cambridge University Press.

Russell, J. A., & Bullock, M. (1985). Multidimensional scaling of emotional facial expressions: similarity from preschoolers to adults. *Journal of Personality and Social Psychology, 48*(5), 1290.

Sherman, M. (1927). The differentiation of emotional responses in infants. I. Judgments of emotional responses from motion picture views and from actual observation. *Journal of Comparative Psychology, 7*(3), 265.

Smith, M. L., Cottrell, G. W., Gosselin, F., & Schyns, P. G. (2005). Transmitting and decoding facial expressions. *Psychological Science, 16*(3), 184–189. doi: 10.1111/j.0956-7976.2005.00801.x

Sprengelmeyer, R., Young, A. W., Calder, A. J., Karnat, A., Lange, H., Hömberg, V., . . . Rowland, D. (1996). Loss of disgust. *Brain, 119*(5), 1647.

Sprengelmeyer, R., Young, A. W., Sprengelmeyer, A., Calder, A. J., Rowland, D., Perrett, D., . . . Lange, H. (1997). Recognition of facial expressions: Selective impairment of specific emotions in Huntington's disease. *Cognitive Neuropsychology, 14*(6), 839–879.

Steiner, J. E. (1979). Human facial expressions in response to taste and smell stimulation. *Advances in Child Development and Behavior, 13*, 257–295.

Susskind, J. M., Littlewort, G., Bartlett, M. S., Movellan, J., & Anderson, A. K. (2007). Human and computer recognition of facial expressions of emotion. *Neuropsychologia, 45*(1), 152–162. doi: 10.1016/j.neuropsychologia.2006.05.001

Tagiuri, R. (1969). Person perception. In G. Lindzey & E. Aronson. (Eds.), *Handbook of social psychology* (Vol. 3, pp. 395–449). Reading, MA: Addison-Wesley.

Touroutoglou, A., Lindquist, K. A., Dickerson, B. C., & Barrett, L. F. (2015). Intrinsic connectivity in the human brain does not reveal networks for "basic" emotions. *Social Cognitive and Affective Neuroscience, 10*(9):1257–65. doi: 10.1093/scan/nsv013

Tracy, J. L. (2014). An evolutionary approach to understanding distinct emotions. *Emotion Review, 6*(4), 308–312. doi: 10.1177/1754073914534478

Tracy, J. L., & Matsumoto, D. (2008). The spontaneous expression of pride and shame: Evidence for biologically innate nonverbal displays. *Proceedings of the National Academy of Sciences, 105*(33), 11655–11660. doi: 10.1073/pnas.0802686105

Trope, Y. (1986). Identification and inferential processes in dispositional attribution. *Psychological Review, 93*(3), 239–257. doi: 10.1037/0033-295x.93.3.239

Van Der Schalk, J., Hawk, S. T., Fischer, A. H., & Doosje, B. (2011). Moving faces, looking places: Validation of the Amsterdam Dynamic Facial Expression Set (ADFES). *Emotion, 11*(4), 907.

Wenzler, S., Levine, S., van Dick, R., Oertel-Knöchel, V., & Aviezer, H. (2016). Beyond pleasure and pain: Facial expression ambiguity in adults and children during intense situations.*Emotion, 16*(6), 807

Wieser, M. J., & Brosch, T. (2012). Faces in context: A review and systematization of contextual influences on affective face processing. *Frontiers in Psychology*, 3, 471. doi: 10.3389/fpsyg.2012.00471

Yovel, G., Pelc, T., & Lubetzky, I. (2010). It's all in your head: Why is the body inversion effect abolished for headless bodies? *Journal of Experimental Psychology: Human Perception and Performance, 36*(3), 759–767.

PART VIII

Appraisal

19

Facial Expression Is Driven by Appraisal and Generates Appraisal Inference

KLAUS R. SCHERER, MARCELLO MORTILLARO, AND MARC MEHU

Emotions are defined as brief, episodic processes when several of an organism's subsystems temporarily work together in synchrony, driven by the appraisal of events that are highly relevant for an individual. These appraisals generate motivational effects accompanied by changes in expression, autonomic physiology, and feeling. As emotions are phylogenetically functional, changes in facial and vocal expression allow observers to infer appraisal results and the emotions generated in consequence. This is the basic assumption of the component process model of emotion (CPM; for more detailed descriptions of the model, see Scherer, 1986, 2001, 2009). Specifically it is suggested that the results of individual appraisal checks drive the dynamics and configuration of the facial expression of emotion and that emotion recognition is based on appraisal inference (Scherer, 1992; Scherer & Ellgring, 2007; Scherer, Mortillaro, & Mehu, 2013). Here we systematically review the empirical evidence from different research domains that strongly supports the appraisal-based model of facial expression production and emotion recognition. As shown elsewhere in this volume, many different conceptualizations of the nature and function of the facial expression of emotion have been proposed in the literature. The theoretical model suggested here is largely compatible with many of these as the proposed mechanisms encompass most of the claims of alternative models. What sets our *appraisal patterning* model apart is that it is an integral part of the complex mechanisms postulated by a more general theory of emotion, the CPM, rather than a conceptualization specifically generated to explain facial expression. Our approach therefore renders the link between the elicitation of emotion and the response patterning, especially facial and vocal expression, more explicit.

Furthermore, the CPM makes specific predictions about the effects of the results of certain appraisal checks on the autonomic and somatic nervous systems, indicating exactly which physiological changes and which motor expression features are expected. These predictions are based on specific motivational and behavioral tendencies that are expected to be activated to enable the adaptive response demanded by a particular SEC result. In species that live in social groups, adaptive responses are required for not only the internal physical regulation and motor action but also for interaction and communication with others.

THEORY: APPRAISAL-DRIVEN FACIAL EXPRESSION

The specific predictions for facial expression (see Scherer, 1984; Scherer & Ellgring, 2007) have been elaborated on the basis of several classes of determinants: (a) the effects of typical physiological changes, (b) the preparation of specific instrumental motor actions such as searching for information or approach/avoidance behaviors, and (c) the production of signals that communicate to the social group. The first two determinants can be subsumed under what the first author has called "push effects," that is, internal changes that affect the expressive motor system. In contrast, the social signaling function is served by "pull effects," that is, particular configurations of external visual or auditory signals that are part of a socially shared communication code. These two push and pull classes of determinants closely interact (Scherer & Ellgring, 2007). Push effects can be subdivided into three major instrumental functions of the face (lips, nose, ears) and the vocal tract (mouth, pharynx, larynx): (a) passing matter (light, air, liquids, solids) to and from internal organs, for example in breathing, metabolizing, and gland secretion; (b) positioning sensory organs to optimally perceive stimuli (e.g., raising eyebrows, flaring nostrils, pupil dilation; see Lee, Susskind, & Anderson, 2013); and (c) acting directly on objects and other organisms (biting, licking, kissing).

Given the different functions served by the muscles in the face and the vocal tract, and the fact that different demands upon the system may be more or less prevalent in particular situations, only approximate predictions can be made. Table 19.1 shows the CPM predictions for the facial movement results of individual appraisal checks. The model suggests that the cumulative results of a sequential series of checks which meet the central appraisal

Table 19.1 COMPARISON OF ORIGINAL COMPONENT PROCESS MODEL OF EMOTION ACTION UNIT PREDICTIONS FOR DIFFERENT APPRAISALS WITH EMPIRICALLY OBTAINED PROPORTION OF ACTORS USING SPECIFIC ACTION UNITS TO PORTRAY MAJOR EMOTIONS AND EKMAN'S EMFACS PREDICTIONS

		EMOTIONS	Pleasure	Joy/Happiness	Pride	Sadness/Despair	Fear	Disgust	Anger
		Ekman Emfacs predictions for basic emotions	—	6+12	—	1 + 4 + 15	1 + 2 + 4+ 5 + 7 + 20 + 26	9+15+16	4+5+7+23
		Empirical findings for major emotions	6, 7, 10, 12, 17, 18, 25, 26, 43	6, 12, 25, 53 (1, 2, 26)	6, 7, 10, 12, 18, 25 (1, 2, 17)	45, 53 (1, 4, 15, 17)	1, 4, 5, 25, 26, 53 (2, 16)	10 (4, 6, 17)	4, 21, 30, 53, 57 (1, 2, 16)
Sequence	*APPRAISAL CHECKS*	*CPM predictions for appraisal results*							
1	**Novelty**								
	Suddenness (orientation, widen visual field)	1, 2, 5, 26, 38	#	*1, 2, 26	—1, 2	#	**1, 2, 26	—	*1, 2
	Unpredictability (focusing, improve sharpness)	4, 7	#	—	—	#4	*4	#	—4

(continued)

Table 19.1 CONTINUED

		EMOTIONS	Pleasure	Joy/Happiness	Pride	Sadness/Despair	Fear	Disgust	Anger
2	**Intrinsic Pleasantness**								
	Pleasant (approach, capture, savor)	5, 26, 38 or 12, 25	** 12, 25, 26	* 12, 25, 26	* 12, 25	#	#	#	#
	Unpleasant (avoidance, defense)	4, 7, 9, 10, 15, 17, 24, 39; or 16, 19, 25, 26	#	#	#	*4, 15, 16, 17	— 4, 25, 26	*4, 10, 17	*4
3	**Goal/Need Significance**								
	Conduciveness (relaxation, enjoying)	12, 25	— 12, 25	* 12, 25	* 12, 25	#	#	#	#
	Obstructiveness (effort mobilization, tension, action preparation)	4, 7, 23, 17	#	#	#	*4, 17	*4	— 4, 17	*4
4	**Coping Potential**								
	High power/control (loss of tension)	4, 5 (or 7), 23, 25 (or 23, 24)	— 7, 25	— 25	**25	##	##	—	*
	Low power/control (threat, attack)	15, 25, 26, 41, 43 (or 1, 2, 5, 26, 20)	— 25, 26,43	— 25, 26	#25	*15	#25, 26	—	—

Note: Empirical findings—details and list of studies in Supplementary Material, Table SM1 in Scherer et al., submitted; action units in parentheses were only rarely found; Appraisal check column—in parentheses functional basis for description; Cells—symbols refer to the component process model of emotion predictions on appraisal results that are constitutive for certain emotions, ** presence essential, * important, ## absence essential, # important,—no prediction; numbers represent the intersection between predicted and empirically found action units.

Source: Adapted from Scherer, Sergi, and Trznadel (submitted).

objectives (Novelty, Intrinsic pleasantness, Goal attainment, Power/control, Compatibility with external and internal standards) produce a wide variety of complexly patterned emotion episodes. Despite this variability, there are a number of modal emotions caused by predominant SEC outcomes such as anger, fear, or joy that can be identified and predicted (Scherer, 2001). The expression resulting from this sequential cumulative process can be predicted based on the patterns shown in Table 19.1. The specific facial configurations predicted as outcomes for a number of modal emotions are shown in Scherer and Ellgring (2007, Table 2).

It is useful to contrast this approach to the discrete or basic emotions view of facial expression of emotion. Although both approaches agree on the phylogenetic functionality of emotional expression, there is a major difference in the assumed architecture, involving a different conceptualization of the emotion system and yielding two divergent sets of predictions—concerning (a) the number and prototypicality of emotion-specific facial configurations, and (b) the nature of the underlying mechanism. Discrete emotion theories focus on a small set of basic emotions and predict that a prototypical affect program is triggered by appropriate conditions. Figure 19.1 illustrates this central difference in the assumed mechanisms. Part A of the figure, based on Ekman (2004), suggests that a basic emotion is selected by matching the eliciting event with stored schemata, triggering a prototypical facial expression pattern. Part B of the figure, based on the CPM, illustrates how the eliciting event is sequentially appraised on a series of checks. The result of each check produces a facial action that is adaptive for further stimulus processing or action preparation and signaling. These facial movements cumulatively combine in a dynamic fashion, producing a large variety of different patterns of expression corresponding to variants of modal emotions.

Given discrete emotion theorists' insistence on emotion-specific expression patterns, these should be found frequently in empirically observed facial expressions. In other words, there should be many instances of prototypical expressions of basic emotions and only relatively few that do not fit the prototype. Furthermore, these prototypical patterns should be maximally different for different emotions. In comparison, componential theories would predict a much larger variety of patterns. This is because of its assumption that there are many different appraisal outcome combinations and consequent expression patterns. In addition, the elements of the facial expression should be interpretable in terms of the particular appraisal results. As some appraisal checks play a similar role in the unfolding process for different emotions, often the same facial movements are expected to occur for different emotions.

In consequence, the divergent predictions of the two theories seem empirically testable. In what follows, we will briefly describe the evidence to date.

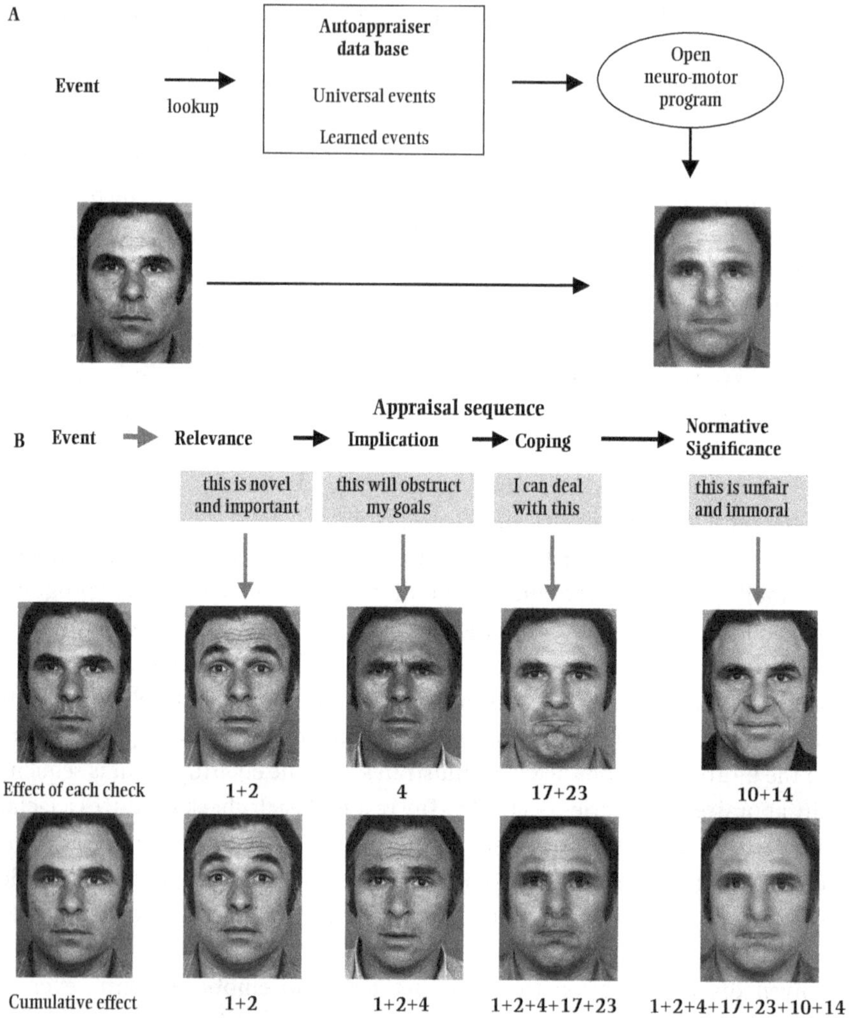

Figure 19.1 Contrasting Ekman's (2004) conceptualization of the mechanism of facial expression of emotion with the cumulative appraisal patterning model as part of the component process model of emotion (Scherer, 2001, 2009).

EVIDENCE FOR APPRAISAL-DRIVEN FACIAL EXPRESSION

In this section, we will describe the evidence for the appraisal patterning mechanism published to date. Research on this topic is rendered difficult by three major factors: (1) like most cognitive processes, appraisal cannot be assessed directly in an objective fashion, that is, self-report is required; (2) individuals are often not conscious of their own appraisals; and (3) appraisal results change extremely rapidly and are difficult to capture. In consequence, researchers have often used indirect methods to determine the relationship between appraisals and different types of facial expressions, by using ratings of self-perception or by obtaining ratings on the inferences drawn from specific facial actions. Despite these inherent difficulties, there is now an appreciable amount of empirical evidence for the theoretical proposals described earlier.

Two major paradigms have been used: production and perception/inference. Using the production paradigm entails manipulating a person's appraisals and measuring the resulting expression, whereas the perception/inference paradigm systematically manipulates expressions and measures to what extent observers infer the appraisals expected to underlie specific expressions. The justification for using perception to search for evidence for production mechanisms (appraisal-driven facial expression) is that one can assume that, in the interest of effective communication, the inference rules mirror the production rules. In what follows, we will briefly review the accumulated evidence from both production and perception/inference studies.

Appraisal Induction

The most direct evidence stems from the manipulation of different appraisals in participants through appropriate stimulation. This allows the direct observation of the nature of the facial actions units produced in response. Facial action units (AUs) are observable movements in the face, often corresponding to the contraction, or relaxation, of specific muscles (Ekman, Friesen, & Hager, 2002).

As the intensity of the effect of experimentally manipulated appraisals on facial expression can be expected to be quite low and difficult to detect by judges, electromyographic measurement (EMG) is often used as a variable that measures the degree of innervation of specific muscles. Although not directly oriented toward an appraisal framework, there is copious EMG research on the plausibility of expecting specific muscle responses to stimuli that are likely to elicit appraisals. Smith (1989, p. 342) reviewed some of this work: Contraction of the corrugator supercilii to produce the eyebrow frown has been clearly linked to the appraisal of unpleasant stimuli and contraction of the zygomatic major to produce the smile has been linked to pleasant stimuli and emotions. Several studies have suggested that something further, often interpreted as "concentration," is reflected in corrugator activity. In early work, Smith and Pope (Pope & Smith, 1994; Smith, 1989) described a positive relationship between the pleasantness of an imagined scenario and activity at the zygomaticus major site. Activity at the corrugator supercilii site, in contrast, was an indicator of goal obstacles (related to the CPM criterion of goal attainment).

Distinguishing between appraisals of relevance and goal conduciveness. Aue, Flykt, and Scherer (2007) presented participants, in the context of a memory task, with pictures displaying biological and cultural threat stimuli or neutral stimuli to manipulate the relevance appraisal. Symbols signaling monetary gains or losses were superimposed on these pictures to manipulate goal conduciveness appraisals. EMG results for the facial muscles showed differential effects for both stimulus relevance and goal conduciveness appraisals. Biological threat stimuli were associated with increased activity over the cheek region, which was explained by the participant's adoption of a response pattern that resembled the "fear grin" shown by nonhuman primates (Van Hooff, 1972). Consistent with the idea of a stronger need for effortful processing, because it is relatively "younger" in human evolutionary history than biological threat, the vision of cultural threat stimuli led to higher activity over the brow region. Furthermore, as expected, increased activity over the cheek region (zygomaticus, smiling) was observed in the winning condition and over the brow region (corrugator, frowning) in the losing condition (but the latter for neutral pictures only).

Aue and Scherer (2008) had participants view unpleasant and pleasant pictures to manipulate their intrinsic pleasantness appraisals. While viewing the pictures, participants were asked to perform either an arm extension or an arm flexion, leading to an increase or a decrease in picture size. Increasing the size of pleasant pictures and decreasing unpleasant pictures were considered goal conducive; decreasing pleasant picture size and increasing unpleasant picture size were considered goal obstructive. As predicted by the CPM, the two appraisals differentially affected zygomaticus and corrugator responses (measured by EMG), showing similar patterns of changes (i.e., pleasant events produced similar changes as conducive events; and unpleasant events produced similar changes as obstructive events). The zygomaticus and corrugator muscles in particular have proven to be reliable signatures for valence appraisals, both for intrinsic pleasantness and goal conduciveness (see Aue & Scherer, 2008).

Sequence of appraisals. Lanctôt and Hess (2007) empirically tested the CPM hypothesis that the evaluation of intrinsic pleasantness occurs before the evaluation of goal conduciveness. In two studies, intrinsically pleasant and unpleasant images were used to manipulate pleasantness, and a specific event in a Pac-Man-type video game was used to manipulate goal conduciveness. As predicted, the EMG results showed that facial reactions to the manipulation of intrinsic pleasantness occurred significantly faster than those to the goal conduciveness manipulation. The authors interpret these results as providing strong empirical support for the sequential nature of the appraisal process.

Considering another sensory channel, Delplanque et al. (2009) investigated the effects of odors on appraisal processes and consequent emotional responses. The main goal was to test whether an odor is detected as novel or familiar before it is evaluated as pleasant or unpleasant. Participants performed a recognition task in which they were presented with pairs of unpleasant or pleasant odors (sample and target odors). Within a pair, the sample and target were either identical or different to assess participants' novelty detection; unpleasant and pleasant target odors were contrasted to examine participants' appraisal of intrinsic pleasantness. The authors measured facial expressions using EMG in response to odors. The earliest effects on facial muscles occurred in response to novelty detection. Later effects on facial muscles were related to pleasantness evaluation, confirming the existence of a sequence of appraisal checks for odors eliciting an emotional reaction.

Gentsch, Grandjean, and Scherer (2015) examined, in two related experiments, facial muscle activity changes (via facial EMG recordings over the corrugator, cheek, and frontalis regions) in response to events in a gambling task. These events were experimentally manipulated with feedback stimuli that presented simultaneous information directly affecting goal conduciveness (gambling outcome: win, loss, or break-even) and power appraisals (Experiment 1 and 2), as well as control appraisal (Experiment 2). Repeatedly, main effects of goal conduciveness (starting ~600 ms) and power appraisals (starting ~800 ms after feedback onset) were found. Control appraisal main effects were inconclusive. Interaction effects of goal conduciveness and power appraisals were obtained in both experiments (Experiment 1: over the corrugator and cheek regions; Experiment 2: over the frontalis region), suggesting amplified goal conduciveness effects when power was high in contrast to invariant goal conduciveness effects when power was low. Furthermore, an interaction of goal conduciveness and control appraisals was found over the cheek region, showing differential goal conduciveness effects when control was high and invariant effects when control was low. These interaction effects suggest that the appraisal of having sufficient control or power affects facial responses toward gambling outcomes.

As a whole, the pattern of results suggests that corrugator and frontalis regions are primarily related to cognitive processes associated with motivation, whereas the cheek region would be more influenced by coping implications. These studies provide first evidence demonstrating that cognitive-evaluative mechanisms related to goal conduciveness, control, and power appraisals affect facial expressions dynamically over time, immediately after an event is perceived. In addition, the results provide further indications for the chronography of appraisal-driven facial movements and the underlying cognitive processes (see Figure 11 in Gentsch, Grandjean, & Scherer, 2013).

Van Peer et al. (unpublished data) examined facial muscle activity over the corrugator, cheek, and frontalis regions in an emotional oddball paradigm. Intrinsically pleasant, unpleasant, and neutral images were used to manipulate pleasantness, and the repetition of stimuli (no repetition versus many repetitions) was used to manipulate novelty (see also Van Peer, Grandjean, & Scherer, 2014). The results showed significant effects of both manipulations over the frontalis and brow regions, but not the cheek region. The frontalis region first showed an increase in activity for novel compared to familiar stimuli (starting ~300 ms), whereas this pattern was reversed in later stages (starting ~ 600 ms). Furthermore, activity in this region was overall (starting from ~100 ms) significantly increased for unpleasant and neutral compared to pleasant stimuli. The activity over the brow region also showed a significant effect of pleasantness, reflecting increased activity in response to unpleasant compared to neutral and pleasant pictures. Moreover, a significant interaction between novelty and pleasantness showed that this effect was stronger (i.e., differences were larger, started earlier. and lasted longer) for novel compared to familiar stimuli, suggesting that the appraisal of novelty amplifies the effects of the pleasantness appraisal.

Emotion Recall and Induction Studies

Smith (1989) reported an early pilot study in which participants rated their appraisals during recalled experiences of 15 different emotions and subsequently posed the facial expression they "would wear to show another person how [they] felt" during each experience. These data allow a direct examination of the relations between appraisal and expressive facial components. The videotaped poses were scored using the Facial Action Coding System (FACS; Ekman, Friesen, & Hager, 2002). Six appraisal dimensions (pleasantness, human agency, certainty, attentional activity, anticipated effort, and situational control) were used to predict the occurrence of different facial AUs. Consistent with previous findings, they found that the eyebrow frown reflects unpleasantness and that smiling indicates pleasantness.

Another indirect approach to study the effects of appraisal on facial expression is to obtain realistic enactments of emotional reactions from professional actors, using Stanislavski or method acting techniques. The resulting combinations of AUs can then be interpreted with respect to the appraisal patterns that are expected to generate the respective emotions. This approach was adopted by Scherer and Ellgring (2007), who analyzed the apex points of videotaped expressions of 12 German professional actors enacting emotion scenarios. Looking at the frequency with which the actors used major facial muscle actions individually and in combination to express 14 major emotions, the study showed little evidence for emotion-specific prototypical affect programs. Rather, the authors concluded that the results suggest the need for further empirical investigation of CPM predictions for dynamic configurations of appraisal-driven adaptive facial actions. Here are some of the leads that the authors put forward for such work based on a summary of the results of their study (Scherer & Ellgring, 2007, pp. 125–126):

- It was predicted that AUs 1 and 2 (inner and outer brow raiser) would occur mostly in response to novelty and lack of control. Their incidence is indeed significantly higher for emotions such as panic fear, anxiety, and despair in which appraisals of novelty, low control, and low power are particularly salient.
- AU 4 (brow lowerer) is predicted to result from appraisals of unexpectedness, discrepancy, and goal obstruction. It does indeed occur in all negative emotions and is particularly frequent in despair, panic, fear, sadness, anxiety, and disgust.
- AU 5 (upper lid raiser) is also predicted to occur as a result of appraisals of novelty and lack of control, presumably in the service of focusing the vision. It is not surprising that it also occurs frequently in portrayals of interest.
- As one expects based on the copious literature on smiling, AUs 6 (cheek raiser) and 12 (lip corner puller) are frequently used to portray positive emotions, notably pride. However, AU 6 also shows up in despair and disgust.
- AU 7 (lid tightener) is exclusively used in cold anger and contempt, possibly also indicating an element of intense staring.
- AU 9 (nose wrinkler) appears only rarely, as part of disgust and hot anger expressions.
- AU 10 (upper lip raiser) is prominent in disgust and contempt but also makes a minor showing in the portrayals of some other negative emotions.

Dimensions of emotions in facial expressions. A disadvantage of this type of emotion induction approach is that actors are generally asked to enact discrete, categorical emotions. However, the CPM fits more closely with a dimensional perspective that describes emotions in terms of various continuous qualities such as evaluation/valence, potency/power, and activity/arousal (Osgood, Suci, & Tannenbaum, 1957; Russell, 1980). In fact, there is a direct correspondence between these empirically found dimensions and the major appraisal checks (see Scherer, 1984, p. 38). The dimension of valence or strength corresponds directly to the intrinsic un/pleasantness, and the goal congruence dimension and the dominance or power dimension corresponds to the coping potential (control/power) appraisal check. The arousal dimension is probably related to degree of concern relevance and urgency of action.

This problem can be alleviated by placing the categorical emotions in a three-dimensional space formed by the three classic dimensions of affect: valence, arousal, and power. In creating a new corpus of emotion enactment by professional actors (the Geneva Multimodal Emotion Portrayal corpus [GEMEP]; Bänziger & Scherer, 2010), we systematically collected emotion enactments corresponding to the eight octants of the affect space described in the literature (see chapter 2 in Fontaine, Scherer, & Soriano, 2013; Russell, 1980), allowing to associate a basic appraisal structure to the enacted emotions.

Mehu and Scherer (2015) used the core set of the GEMEP corpus (Bänziger, Mortillaro, & Scherer, 2012) to investigate the production of facial behavior from both dimensional and categorical perspectives. First, we examined the relationship between the three emotional dimensions and the expressivity of the 22 facial AUs most commonly observed in the GEMEP-CS dataset. We then computed, for each AU, an expressivity index that reflects both the duration and intensity of the AU for a given emotional portrayal. Although facial expressivity was strongly influenced by emotional dimensions and by emotion categories, no clear pattern emerged that reflected specific links between discrete emotions and facial AUs on the one hand, nor specific associations between emotional dimensions and facial AUs on the other hand. Instead, most facial AUs were related to several emotions and several dimensions.

A discriminant analysis showed that differences between emotions could be accounted for by linear combinations of facial AUs. Two significant functions of intercorrelated AUs differentiate emotions into discrete groups characterized by positive/negative valence and high/low arousal (Mehu & Scherer, 2015). The pattern of associations between emotional dimensions and facial AUs indicated that most AUs surveyed were positively related to emotional arousal (with the exception of AU 7—lids tight and AU 43—eye closure). Positively valenced emotions (e.g., joy, pride) were characterized by increased activation of the cheek raiser (AU 6), lids tight (AU 7), lip corner puller (AU 12), and lip part (AU 25); whereas negative emotions involved the activation of the brow lowerer (AU 4), the upper lid raiser (AU 5), the lower lip depressor (AU 16), lip stretch (AU 20), and lip funneler (AU 22). Finally, high-power emotions (e.g., anger) showed increased activation of the lip corner puller (AU 12) as well as lip presser (AU 24), while portrayals of low-power emotions (e.g., sadness) included higher activity of the brow lowerer (AU 4).

At the production level, this study showed that facial behavior is neither specific to emotion categories nor dimensions but that facial activity reflects combinations of the general dimensions that underlie discrete emotion categories. The finding that facial expression reflects both dimensions and categories of emotion supports an appraisal model since the CPM proposes that emotions are in essence dimensional, but it also uses the concept of modal emotions (see Scherer, 2009) to explain discrete emotional categories such as joy, anger, and sadness.

To explore further the connection between facial behavior and emotion categories and dimensions, Mehu and Scherer (2015) combined this production paradigm where actors produced facial expressions based on appraisals, with a perception/inference paradigm, where judges rated videos of actor expressions. Ratings were performed for the general dimensions that reflect important appraisal criteria—valence, arousal, power, and novelty/predictability. These four dimensions of affect are also consistently found for emotion words in many different languages (Fontaine et al., 2013). The results showed that, at the perceptual level, emotion recognition could be significantly predicted by facial expressivity. Judges also appeared to use the facial expressivity to make ratings on the four general dimensions. Indeed, several AUs were significantly correlated with perceived valence, arousal, power/dominance, and predictability. More than half of the AUs surveyed correlated with either perceived valence or arousal. Perceived power/dominance showed a smaller number of significant correlations with facial AUs. More specifically, and in line with a previous study (Mortillaro, Mehu, & Scherer, 2011), perceived unpredictability was negatively associated with eye closure (AU43) but positively correlated with upper lid raise (AU5), suggesting that the predictability of an event is inversely related to the degree of eye opening.

An analysis of the correspondence between the production and perception of facial AUs revealed a good fit for most AUs, in that the facial movements that are associated with a particular dimension at the production level also show an association with the same dimension at the perceptual level (Mehu & Scherer, 2015). This provides further support for the CPM, suggesting that both production and perception of facial expressions rely on appraisal of the dimensions investigated in the research.

Distinguishing positive (valence) emotions. Further support for the adoption of an appraisal perspective on facial expressions comes from the recent study by Mortillaro et al. (2011) investigating the facial expressions of four positive emotions: elated joy, sensory pleasure, interest, and pride. They used perceptual ratings and dynamic FACS coding of portrayals also taken from the GEMEP coreset database (Bänziger et al., 2012). The results showed that different positive emotions can be distinguished solely from their facial expressions, particularly if an appraisal perspective as opposed to a discrete categorical perspective is adopted. This is because these four emotions share several appraisals that are reflected in common patterns in their facial expressions, whereas emotion-specific features are hard if not impossible to find. Indeed, differentiation between these emotions is greatly facilitated by taking into account the dynamic unfolding of the expression: It is not only the nature of facial movement that sets apart these emotions but also the *duration* of the AUs and their dynamic properties. For example, emotions that involve appraisals of unpredictability (suddenness) are characterized by a longer presence and higher frequency of AU 1 and AU 2 (eyebrow raise) when compared to emotions that do not involve this appraisal. Similarly, emotions characterized by high intrinsic pleasantness show a longer duration of AU 6 (cheek raiser) than other positive emotions that are not generally marked by the same level of this appraisal (e.g., interest). With regard to this time-based analysis of movements, it is worth mentioning that the concept of a dynamic unfolding of facial expressions is a central assumption of appraisal theory, which assumes that different facial actions are produced sequentially, following the appraisal sequence that leads the whole emotion experience process.

Perception/Inference Ratings

Rather than using ratings of "expressive meaning" or self ratings, it is possible to explicitly ask raters about the kind of inferences they make about underlying appraisal processes on the basis of specific facial features or feature combinations. The underlying assumption is that inference rules used consistently by many different judges may indicate the existence of specific production mechanisms. In a pioneering study, Frijda and Philipszoon (1963) related the viewers' judgments of expressive meaning of facial expression photographs to specific facial components (rather than the global expressions). They identified four factors of expressive meaning: pleasant-unpleasant, derisive-submissive, controlled-uncontrolled, and active-passive. Correlating these factors with measures of the facial features suggested that smiles and eyebrow frowns are associated with pleasantness and unpleasantness, respectively, and that widened eyes and narrowed or closed eyes are respectively associated with high and low levels of attention. Obviously, this evidence is indirect because it relies on observers' judgments of expressions rather than on information about what the posers intended to convey.

In recent work using this paradigm, specific facial movements have been manipulated by animation in synthetic faces of avatars. The latter paradigm is particularly promising because modern animation technology provides an extraordinary degree of control of the facial expression configurations and their dynamic unfolding. In an early study by Wehrle, Kaiser, Schmidt, and Scherer (2000), synthetic images of facial expression were used to assess whether judges can correctly recognize emotions exclusively based on configurations of facial muscle movements. A first study showed that static, synthetic images modeled on a series of photographs widely used in facial expression research yielded recognition rates comparable to posed photos. In a second study, animated synthetic images were used to examine whether schematic facial expressions consisting entirely of theoretically postulated facial muscle configurations can be correctly recognized. Recognition rates for the synthetic expressions were far above chance, and the confusion patterns were comparable to those obtained with posed photos. In addition, dynamic presentation increased overall recognition accuracy and reduced confusions between unrelated emotions. Recent advances in facial synthesis techniques have made it possible to produce realistic facial expressions that are fully controlled by the experimenter. Thus, de Melo, Carnevale, Read, and Gratch (2014) manipulated prototypical emotion displays in avatars in a gaming context that beliefs about others' appraisals mediate the effects of emotion displays on expectations about others' intentions.

One of the most noticeable systems is *FACSgen*, a new animation tool for creating realistic 3D facial expressions in avatar faces based on FACS, developed at the Swiss Center for Affective Sciences at the University of Geneva (Krumhuber, Tamarit, Roesch, & Scherer, 2012; Roesch et al., 2011). FACSgen provides researchers with full control over facial AUs' movements (the user can specify onset, duration, and intensity of each AU independently), and this allows direct testing of the predictions of appraisal theory with respect to the inferences made based on single or multiple facial movements.

The FACSGen technology was used in several studies in our laboratory to investigate the type of appraisal and emotional inferences that naïve raters usually make based on specific facial AUs and prototypical emotion configurations. FACSgen permits to create videos showing the activation of single AUs or combinations of different AUs as well as emotion prototypical configurations (as defined by Ekman et al., 2002) at different intensities and speeds. In one study, participants were assigned to one of two conditions: (a) an appraisal condition requiring participants to use a continuous scale to rate each video on six appraisal dimensions (Unpredictability, Pleasantness, Unpleasantness, Power, Agency, and Normative significance), and (b) an emotion condition requiring participants to rate the same videos by using six discrete emotion scales (anger, disgust, fear, surprise, sadness, and happiness). Results showed that participants could reliably and consistently use appraisal scales to rate the videos, confirming the hypothesis that appraisal inferences can be used to describe emotional expressions. More interestingly, a cluster analysis showed that AUs were rated in ways that were consistent with CPM predictions, allowing to identify AUs that are related to each appraisal dimension with the exception of agency. For example, (a) AU 1 (inner eyebrow raise), AU 2 (outer brow raise), AU 4 (brow lowerer), AU 5 (upper lid raise), AU 26 (jaw drop), and AU 27 (mouth stretch) were perceived as signs of unpredictability; (b) AU 4 (brow lowerer), AU 9 (nose wrinkle), AU 10 (upper lip raiser), and AU 15 (lip corner depressor) as signs of unpleasantness; and (c) AU 4 was both rated as a sign of unpleasantness and unpredictability, giving indirect support to the hypothesis that facial movements can have multiple emotion-related meanings. When considering the ratings of prototypical configurations, multiple-regression analyses showed that emotion and appraisal ratings were used in different ways. Appraisal ratings of prototypical configurations showed a cumulative effect; in other words, appraisal ratings of full facial configurations could, in most cases, be predicted based on the appraisal ratings of the individual AUs that make up the configurations. Conversely, emotion ratings of prototypical emotions have a more holistic quality that was reflected by the fact that emotion labeling of configurations cannot be reduced to the sum of the appraisal ratings of the individual AUs (Mortillaro & Rotondi, unpublished data).

Another study in our laboratory (Sergi, Fiorentini, & Scherer, submitted) used the same paradigm to test the appraisal inferences judges make based on systematically manipulated AU *combinations* in animated avatars. Based on specific CPM predictions, 42 AU combinations expected as probable outcomes of appraisal results on eight dimensions: Novelty, Unpredictability, Pleasantness/Unpleasantness, and Congruency with expectations, Goal conduciveness, Self- and Other-norm compatibility were specified. Dynamic facial expressions displaying each combination at three levels of intensity were created with FACSgen. Fifteen judges rated each of the resulting 126 videos on all eight dimensions. The study yielded three main results: (1) excellent agreement between participants' appraisal judgments, (2) appraisal ratings varied systematically between AU combinations, and (3) most of the predicted AU-appraisal associations were confirmed by significant results, although only a few AU combinations uniquely discriminated the predicted appraisals (suggesting that complex interactions between AUs disambiguate meaning).

More recently, Scherer, Sergi, and Trznadel (submitted) reported two studies using new generation avatars including different identities with varying hairstyles and backgrounds, in which the AUs and AU combinations manipulated were systematically selected to test specific hypotheses. In study 1, AU combinations that are frequently mentioned as simultaneous displays (e.g., 6+12, 4+7, 9+10) for certain appraisals were presented in a 2x2 present-absent design, asking judges to rate the degree to which the expression indicated a certain appraisal result on a continuous scale. The results showed that there is generally one dominant AU (e.g., 12, 9, and 4), which explains most of the variance in the appraisal judgments, the cumulative effect of the second AU being negligible. In addition, avatar identity had only a minor effect on the appraisal judgments. In study 2, the answer format was changed to forced choice between eight appraisal alternatives (two each for four appraisal checks). The AU combinations synthesized in the avatar faces were carefully selected on the basis of earlier predictions, empirical evidence to date, and typical photographs explicitly representing appraisal consistent mental content. The results showed a very high degree of accuracy of the judgments, clearly demonstrating the ability to recognize very specific appraisals on the basis of AU configurations.

This series of studies, for the first time directly manipulating the appearance, intensity, and complexity of facial actions, show that observers reliably infer different appraisals from specific facial expressions, in line with theoretical predictions.

CONCLUSIONS

This brief overview has shown the plausibility of a component process approach to understand the mechanisms underlying facial expression. To support the claims made by the model, we presented a wealth of empirical evidence. Admittedly, some of this evidence is indirect and circumstantial, but it seems difficult to deny the pertinence of the studies showing that a manipulation of specific appraisals leads to the expected increase in the activity of the predicted muscle combinations. In addition, it has been shown in several studies that corresponding patterns of brain activity (as measured by EEG; e.g., Gentsch, Grandjean, & Scherer, 2014), marking the occurrence of specific appraisal processes, occur a few milliseconds before the observed muscle innervations. Although more research is needed to deepen our understanding of the underlying processes, the general assumption that appraisal results generate specific behavioral adaptations and action tendencies that, in turn, give rise to the movement of specific facial muscle groups is strongly supported by the accumulated evidence.

Our review has also shown the utility of examining the relationship between the production and perception of facial AUs and emotional categories and dimensions, and the promise of investigating the possibility that emotion recognition from facial expression is mediated by perceived emotional dimensions reflecting appraisal processes. The analyses conducted by Mehu and Scherer (2015) indeed revealed that the relationships between three sets of intercorrelated AUs and emotion recognition accuracy were significantly mediated by the dimensions of perceived valence and arousal. This suggests that the correct labeling of emotional expressions using discrete emotion categories may require the perception of more general dimensions such as valence and arousal. In the same study, weaker associations were observed between facial activity and power/dominance, which could be an indication that the dimension of potency may be better expressed and perceived via another nonverbal channel than the face, for example the voice (Fontaine et al., 2013, chapter 10; Scherer, 1986). This emphasizes the importance of using dynamic material in which a wide variety of facial movements can be investigated in relation with multiple components of emotional experience as well as studying a large number of different emotional states that adequately represent a wide range of areas within the affective space.

To what extent does the evidence provided in this chapter affect the evaluation of the different theories of facial emotion expression proposed in this volume? We hold that the component process approach generally encompasses all of the other theoretical propositions. To the extent that modal emotions as described herein are based on relatively invariant patterns of appraisal, one would expect an almost program-like unfolding of these expressions, as postulated by discrete or basic emotion theories. Indeed, basic emotion theorists have increasingly tended to highlight the inherent variability of these processes due to individual and situational differences and have even embraced an appraisal framework (e.g., Ekman, 2004). The CPM model also encompasses Frijda's proposal that facial expressions mark states of action readiness (Frijda & Tscherkassof, 1997) as the CPM assumes that appraisal drives facial expression as mediated by different action tendencies such as information search, resignation, or confrontation. The CPM approach is equally compatible with dimensional approaches (e.g., Russell, 1997) as appraisals and action tendencies (as well as other components) can be reliably mapped into a four-dimensional space (Fontaine et al., 2013). Finally, the Tripartite Emotion Expression and Perception (TEEP) model of emotional communication (Scherer, 2013), associated with the CPM, holds that expressions serve functions as symptoms, appeals, and symbols, which encompasses Fridlund's claim (1994) that facial expressions serve as social signals (see Scherer & Grandjean, 2008; Shuman, Clark-Polner, Meuleman, Sander, & Scherer, 2015).

Given this large degree of convergence, it might be time to design more integrative research that attempts to generate and test a theoretical framework that is compatible with the different approaches in the literature and to further our understanding of the actual mechanisms underlying facial expression and recognition of emotion.

REFERENCES

Aue, T., Flykt, A., & Scherer, K. R. (2007). First evidence for differential and sequential efferent effects of goal relevance and goal conduciveness appraisal. *Biological Psychology, 74*, 347–357.

Aue, T., & Scherer, K. R. (2008). Appraisal-driven somatovisceral response patterning: Effects of intrinsic pleasantness and goal conduciveness. *Biological Psychology, 79*, 158–164.

Bänziger, T., Mortillaro, M., & Scherer, K. R. (2012). Introducing the Geneva Multimodal Expression Corpus for Experimental Research on Emotion Perception. *Emotion, 12*(5), 1161–1179. doi: 10.1037/a0025827

Bänziger, T., & Scherer, K. R. (2010). Introducing the Geneva Multimodal Emotion Portrayal (GEMEP) corpus. In Scherer, K. R., Bänziger, T., & Roesch, E. B. (Eds.), *Blueprint for affective computing: A sourcebook* (pp. 271–294). Oxford, UK: Oxford University Press.

Delplanque, S., Grandjean, D., Chrea, C., Aymard, L., Cayeux, I., Margot, C., Velazco, M. I., Sander, D., & Scherer, K. R. (2009). Sequential unfolding of novelty and pleasantness appraisals of odors: Evidence from facial electromyography and autonomic reactions. *Emotion, 9(3)*, 316–328.

de Melo, C. M., Carnevale, P. J., Read, S. J., & Gratch, J. (2014). Reading people's minds from emotion expressions in interdependent decision making. *Journal of Personality and Social Psychology, 106*(1), 73–88.

Ekman, P. (2004). What we become emotional about. In A. S. R. Manstead, N. H. Frijda, & A. H. Fischer (Eds.), *Feelings and emotions: The Amsterdam Symposium* (pp. 119–135). Cambridge, England: Cambridge University Press.

Ekman, P., Friesen, W. V., & Hager, J. C. (2002). *The Facial Action Coding System* (2nd ed.). Salt Lake City, UT: Research Nexus eBook.

Fontaine, J. R. J., Scherer, K. R., & Soriano, C. (Eds.). (2013). *Components of emotional meaning: A sourcebook.* Oxford, UK: Oxford University Press.

Fridlund, A. (1994). *Human facial expression: An evolutionary view.* San Diego, CA: Academic Press.

Frijda, N. H., & Philipszoon, E. (1963). Dimensions of recognition of emotion. *Journal of Abnormal and Social Psychology, 66*, 45–51.

Frijda, N. H., & Tcherkassof, A. (1997). Facial expressions as modes of action readiness. In J. A. Russell & J. M. Fernández-Dols (Eds.), *The psychology of facial expression* (pp. 78–102). Cambridge, UK: Cambridge University Press.

Gentsch, K., Grandjean, D., & Scherer, K. R. (2013). Temporal dynamics and potential neural sources of goal conduciveness, control, and power appraisal. *Psychophysiology, 50*(10), 1010–1022.

Gentsch, K., Grandjean, D., & Scherer, K. R. (2014). Coherence explored between emotion components: Evidence from event-related potentials and facial electromyography. *Biological Psychology, 98*, 70–81.

Gentsch, K., Grandjean, D., & Scherer, K. R. (2015). Appraisals generate specific configurations of facial muscle movements in a gambling task: Evidence for the component process model of emotion. *Plos One, 10*(8), e0135837. doi: 10.1371/journal.pone.0135837

Krumhuber, E. G., Tamarit, L., Roesch, E. B., & Scherer, K. R. (2012). FACSGen 2.0 animation software: Generating three-dimensional FACS-valid facial expressions for emotion research. *Emotion, 12*(2), 351–363.

Lanctôt, N., & Hess, U. (2007). The timing of appraisals. *Emotion, 7*, 207–212.

Lee, D. H., Susskind, J. M., & Anderson, A. K. (2013). Social transmission of the sensory benefits of eye widening in fear expressions. *Psychological Science, 24*, 957–965. doi:10.1177/0956797612464500

Mehu, M., & Scherer, K. R. (2015). Emotion categories and dimensions in the facial communication of affect: An integrated approach. *Emotion, 15*(6), 798–811.

Mortillaro, M., Mehu, M., & Scherer, K. R. (2011). Subtly different positive emotions can be distinguished by their facial expressions. *Social Psychological and Personality Science, 2*, 262–271.

Osgood, C. E., Suci, G. J., & Tannenbaum, P. H. (1957). *The measurement of meaning*. Urbana: University of Illinois Press.

Pope, L. K., & Smith, C. A. (1994). On the distinct meanings of smiles and frowns. *Cognition and Emotion*, *8*, 65–72.

Roesch, E.B., Tamarit, L., Reveret, L., Grandjean, D., Sander, D., & Scherer, K.R. (2011). FACSGen: A tool to synthesize emotional facial expressions through systematic manipulation of facial action units. *Journal of Nonverbal Behavior*, *35*, 1–16.

Russell, J. A. (1980). A circumplex model of affect. *Journal of Personality and Social Psychology*, *39*, 1161–1178.

Russell, J. A. (1997). Reading emotions from and into faces: Resurrecting a dimensional-contextual perspective. In J. A. Russell & J. M. Fernández-Dols (Eds.), *The psychology of facial expression* (pp. 295–320). New York, NY: Cambridge University Press.

Scherer, K. R. (1984). Emotion as a multicomponent process: A model and some cross-cultural data. In P. Shaver (Ed.), *Review of personality and social psychology: Vol. 5. Emotions, relationships and health* (pp. 37–63). Beverly Hills, CA: Sage.

Scherer, K. R. (1986). Vocal affect expression: A review and a model for future research. *Psychological Bulletin*, *99*, 143–165.

Scherer, K. R. (1992). What does facial expression express? In K. Strongman (Ed.), *International review of studies on emotion* (Vol. 2, pp. 139–165). Chichester, England: Wiley.

Scherer, K. R. (2001). Appraisal considered as a process of multilevel sequential checking. In K. R. Scherer, A. Schorr, & T. Johnstone (Eds.), *Appraisal processes in emotion: Theory, methods, research* (pp. 92–120). New York, NY: Oxford University Press.

Scherer, K. R. (2009). The dynamic architecture of emotion: Evidence for the component process model. *Cognition and Emotion*, *23*(7), 1307–1351.

Scherer K. R. (2013). Emotion in action, interaction, music, and speech. In M. A. Arbib (Ed.), *Language, music, and the brain: A mysterious relationship* (pp. 107–139). Cambridge, MA: MIT Press.

Scherer, K. R., & Ellgring, H. (2007). Are facial expressions of emotion produced by categorical affect programs or dynamically driven by appraisal? *Emotion*, *7*, 113-130.

Scherer, K. R., & Grandjean, D. (2008). Facial expressions allow inference of both emotions and their components. *Cognition and Emotion*, *22*, 789–801. doi:10.1080/02699930701516791

Scherer, K. R., Mortillaro M., & Mehu M. (2013). Understanding the mechanisms underlying the production of facial expression of emotion: A componential perspective. *Emotion Review*, *5*(1), 47–53.

Scherer, K. R., Sergi, I., & Trznadel, S. (submitted). Appraisal-driven motor responses as building blocks for facial emotion expression and recognition.

Sergi, I., Fiorentini, C., Trznadel, S., & Scherer, K. R. (submitted). Cognitive appraisals can be inferred from facial expressions: Evidence from computer-manipulated animated facial actions.

Shuman, V., Clark-Polner, E., Meuleman, B., Sander, D., & Scherer, K. R. (2015). Emotion perception from a componential perspective. *Cognition and Emotion*, doi: 10.1080/02699931.2015.1075964.

Smith, C. A. (1989). Dimensions of appraisal and physiological response in emotion. *Journal of Personality and Social Psychology*, *56*, 339–353.

Van Hooff, J. A. R. A. M. (1972). A comparative approach to the phylogeny of laughter and smiling. In R. A. Hinde, Ed., *Non-verbal communication* (pp. 209–241). Cambridge, UK: Cambridge University Press.

van Peer, J. M., Grandjean, D., & Scherer, K. R. (2014). Sequential unfolding of appraisals: EEG evidence for the interaction of novelty and pleasantness. *Emotion*, *14*(1), 51–63. doi: 10.1037/a0034566.

Wehrle, T., Kaiser, S., Schmidt, S., & Scherer, K. R (2000). Studying dynamic models of facial expression of emotion using synthetic animated faces. *Journal of Personality and Social Psychology*, *78*(1), 105–119.

20

The Social Signal Value of Emotions

The Role of Contextual Factors in Social Inferences Drawn From Emotion Displays

URSULA HESS AND SHLOMO HARELI

Human interactions are full of emotions. In fact, even though emotions are often experienced when alone, most of the time emotions are experienced within a social context. Even emotions that are experienced when alone can have an implicit social context in that we imagine an interaction partner or think back to an emotional event involving others (Fridlund, 1991). Importantly, emotion expressions serve as social signals that provide information about the expresser but also about the situation (Hess, Kappas, & Banse, 1995) and that help to coordinate and facilitate interpersonal interaction and communication (Niedenthal & Brauer, 2012; Parkinson, Fischer, & Manstead, 2005). In the present chapter, we are presenting a model of emotional facial expressions in context (MEEC; Hess & Hareli, 2016), which proposes a pertinent but not exclusive role for context information in emotion perception by postulating the social appraisal of the expression as the limiting frame for reinterpretation. The model, just as do social constructivist accounts, considers perceivers as active agents in the processes of decoding emotions and of drawing inferences from them, but as ones who are limited with regard to their constructive freedom.

In the history of the study of emotion expressions, the question of what in particular emotion expressions express has loomed large, and arguments for and against the notion that emotion expressions express an internal state—the experienced emotion—have been raised and defended (see Hess & Thibault, 2009). However, in some ways the question of what emotions actually express is less important when considering how they are interpreted—that is, when focusing on the decoding process. Specifically, as is amply demonstrated by the use of facial expressions in the arts, film, and literature, people understand emotional facial expressions to express emotions, and they react in function of this understanding (cf. Niedenthal & Brauer, 2012). This is also relevant to the conclusions they draw from facial expressions, that is, the inferences about a person's character and his or her goals and intentions, which can be drawn from observing or learning about an individual's emotional reaction to an event. That is, people treat emotion expressions as if they express emotions and act in accordance. Thus, for the purpose of this discussion, we will treat emotion expressions as signals of emotions.

As mentioned earlier, emotion expressions typically occur in a social context. In fact, it is impossible to present an emotion expression completely without context because the very medium that conveys the expression—the face, the voice, the body—already conveys context information. Thus, faces but also voices and bodies signal the social group membership of the person, including such obvious aspects as gender, age, and ethnicity but also social dominance (Mueller & Mazur, 1997) and even sexual orientation (Rule, Ambady, & Hallett, 2009). And all of these factors impact on our understanding of the emotion expressed and its larger meaning.

In what follows, we will discuss why context plays an integral role for emotion decoding. The discussion focuses on facial expressions. However, much of what we discuss can be applied to emotion decoding processes in general, both those based on nonverbal cues such as postures, tone of voice, and gestures and those based on second-hand information such as verbal descriptions of the expresser's behavior. We will then turn to the factors that limit the role of context for emotion understanding.

TYPES OF CONTEXT

In emotion research, the importance of context for both the production and the understanding of emotion expressions has long been recognized. Thus, the modified Brunswick lens model for person perception, which has then been applied to emotion communication by Scherer (1978), includes cultural context, social relationships, and situational context. For any type of context, two sources of information are relevant: information that is related to the situation in which the emotion occurs, and additional information that perceivers have and apply to the situation, for example stereotype knowledge about specific social groups. In this sense already, the perceiver can be said to be an active agent in the perception process (Kirouac & Hess, 1999).

Situational Context

First, there are all those elements of the situation that are informative about the emotion elicitor. This includes factual information but also the real-world knowledge that people have and that allows them to deduce further information. For example, information that a person just competed in a game is factual information; information that players in a competition have negative interdependence such that what is good for the one must be bad for the other is real-world knowledge.

These effects should be distinguished from the effect that the valence of the situation may have through priming or other perceptual effects. For example, when a face is shown together with a scene without there being a logical link between the two, the valence of the situation can activate affective response categories (a funny scene can activate response categories linked to positive affect) and hence influence emotion decoding. Thus, Righart and deGelder (2008) found that when participants were asked to categorize facial expressions that were shown against the backdrop of an emotional scene while ignoring the scene, the categorizations were biased by the emotional content of the scenes. Somewhat similar effects occur when faces are shown within a group of other individuals, especially when the presence of the others is not explained; these effects tend to be stronger for people high in interdependence (Hess, Blaison, & Kafetsios, 2016; Masuda et al., 2008).

The Perceiver as Context

Another important element of context is the perceiver. The two-path model of emotion perception (see later discussion) considers the perceiver not as a passive readout module but as taking an active part in the perception process. As such, not only the real-world knowledge mentioned earlier but the stereotypes the perceiver holds, the norms the perceiver is aware of, and the perceiver's own goals and motives are all relevant for this process. We will discuss these in turn.

STEREOTYPES EXPECTATIONS AND SOCIAL NORMS

Stereotypes are not the same as social norms. However, in this context we consider mostly prescriptive stereotypes that imply a behavioral norm. Thus, if someone holds the stereotype of women as more irrationally emotional and men as more controlled, they should expect men to act with more emotional restraint (Hess, David, & Hareli, 2016; Shields, 2005).

Clearly stereotype and norm knowledge require some level of situational knowledge, which anchors the relevant norm. However, insofar as the norm relates to specific social groups, which can be identified based on their face alone (e.g., racial groups, the elderly, men and women), this situational knowledge may be activated by the very expression that is to be decoded (Hess, Adams, & Kleck, 2009). Thus, when the perceiver knows that a person whose car was vandalized is a woman, norms of behavior relevant to women and anger will become more accessible. These norms may then influence the identification of an emotional cue associated with the target person. Specifically, women are expected to show sadness rather than anger in such a situation unless they were explicitly described as very dominant (Hess, Adams, & Kleck, 2005).

CULTURAL DISPLAY RULES

A specific case of norms are cultural display rules, that is, the sociocultural rules that guide the appropriate display of emotion expressions (Ekman & Friesen, 1971). These differences can in part be related to differences in cultural values such as individualism and collectivism (Koopmann-Holm & Matsumoto, 2011) but also openness to change (Sarid, 2015) or masculinity (Matsumoto, Seung Hee, & Fontaine, 2008) among others. Mostly, however, we can assume that cultural display rules are not linked to one specific cultural value but are the result of more complex processes involving more than one cultural attribute. Importantly, display rules have a converse side in social decoding rules, such that perceivers tend to be less accurate when decoding expressions that are proscribed in a given culture (Buck, 1984; Hess, 2001), and as such they impact not only on the expression but also on the perception of emotions.

THE PERCEIVERS' GOALS, NEEDS, AND OWN EMOTIONAL STATE

A second perceiver-related context factor are the perceivers' goals and needs and even their own emotional state (cf. Showers & Cantor, 1985). These factors specifically affect what is extracted from the available bottom-up information, for example, by determining the degree of effort that the perceiver invests in understanding the situation. Thus, being highly motivated and having the ability to do so, a perceiver may pay more attention to the available cues. By contrast, if motivation and/or ability are low, less attention may be paid. Thus, Thibault et al. (2006) found that perceivers who strongly identified with members of a group were better at labeling emotion expressions from members of that group. This finding fits well with the more general idea that people often invest relatively little effort in learning about the characteristics of outgroup others (Park & Rothbart, 1982). In a similar vein, research on gender differences in emotion recognition shows that motivational factors may have a substantial impact on recognition accuracy and may explain why in some studies women outperform men in this task (Ickes & Simpson, 2004).

Not only attention to cues but also their processing can be influenced by perceiver characteristics. A good example would be the way the emotional state of the observer affects decoding. An individual's emotional state influences how social information is processed. Specifically, according to Forgas's (1995) "affect infusion model" perceivers' information processing strategies differ in the extent to which a full search of information occurs and how open or closed this search is and hence in the use of perceiver knowledge. At one extreme of this process, the perceiver may directly and automatically retrieve a preexisting label when encountering a stimulus. At the other extreme, the perceiver may engage in an extensive and open search of information. This latter strategy involves substantive processing using preexisting knowledge in a relatively unbiased manner (Bower & Forgas, 2000). Thus, the degree to which subtle cues and situational information are integrated, when, for example, trying to label a smile, depends also on the emotions felt by the perceiver.

Obviously, both processes mentioned herein may operate at the same time such that low motivation and/or ability will both result in partial attention to cues and in the limited processing of these cues, such that more easily accessible stereotype knowledge may serve as readymade templates for recognition based on a superficially observed feature.

TWO WAYS TO RECOGNIZE EMOTIONS

There are two ways to identify emotions from nonverbal cues. Most research on emotion recognition implicitly assumes a pattern-matching process, where specific features of the expression are associated with specific emotions (Buck, 1984). For example, upturned corners of the mouth or lowered brows are recognized as smiles or frowns, respectively, and a perceiver can thus conclude that the individual is happy or angry. In this process the perceiver is a passive decoder, who could and in fact can be replaced by an automated system (e.g., Dailey, Cottrell, Padgett, & Adolphs, 2002) and context information may play no or only a minimal role. However, this process works best for very clear—prototypical—emotion signals. It tends to break down in many everyday situations where the nonverbal signal is often weak and ambiguous (Motley & Camden, 1988). In this case, a second process is more useful (Kirouac & Hess, 1999).

Specifically, when the perceiver knows the expresser or is aware of the situation in which the emotion is shown, she or he can adopt an active role in the emotion identification process. Knowing about the event allows people to use their naïve emotion theories about the emotions that are typically elicited by certain events to predict the most likely emotion. For example, knowing that someone's car was vandalized typically leads to the expectation that the person will be angry (Hess et al., 2005). Thus, even if the person is not very expressive, we can still assume that she is angry. Knowing the goals and values of others allows the perceiver to take their perspective and to infer their likely emotional state. Knowing about the temperament and emotional dispositions of the expresser further allows us to refine predictions. Thus, in the earlier case, we may expect more intense anger from a choleric person than from an easy-going one and more anger if the car was cherished than if it was not.

But what happens if the expresser does not know the other person well or at all? In this case, any social category that the perceiver is aware of and for which expectations regarding emotional reactions exist can affect emotion identification in that the perceiver is more likely to attribute the more expected emotion evidenced in the ambiguous expression. For example, knowing that a (male) expresser is Black or of high status leads observers to more readily label the expression as angry (Hugenberg & Bodenhausen, 2003; Ratcliff, Franklin, Nelson Jr., & Vescio, 2012). In the same vein, when a person is identified as a surgeon, participants rate the facial expressions of the person as less intensely emotional than the same person and expression when associated with a different identity, following the stereotype expectation that surgeons control and restrain their emotions (Hareli, David, & Hess, 2013).

In sum, the identification of emotions can be accomplished via either a passive pattern-matching process or an active process where the perceiver generates a label for the likely emotional state of the sender based on both the expression and her or his knowledge of the context. This knowledge can take either the form of individualized knowledge about the expresser or be based on the expresser's social group and the stereotypes, expectations, and beliefs associated with members of this group.

INFERENCES FROM EMOTION PERCEPTION

Appraisal theories of emotion (for an overview, see Moors, Ellsworth, Scherer, & Frijda, 2013) posit that emotions are elicited by the spontaneous and intuitive appraisal of (internal or external) relevant stimulus events according to the perceived nature of the event. Importantly, appraisals relate to the subjective perception of the stimulus characteristics and not its objective characteristics.

Even though appraisals are typically not the product of reasoning processes, people can and do reconstruct appraisal processes consciously after the fact (Robinson & Clore, 2002). And they can do so for other people's emotions as well (e.g., Parkinson et al., 2005; Roseman, 1991; Scherer & Grandjean, 2008). As such, emotion expressions can be seen as encapsulated or compacted signals that tell a story. Part of this story relates to the person. Thus, a person who reacts with anger to an injustice can be expected to be someone who cares about justice. Another part of the story relates to the situation. Thus, that a person reacts with anger to a situation implies that the situation likely involved an injustice. That is, reverse-engineered appraisals (Hareli & Hess, 2010), describe the perception of appraisals of a situation by the emoter as reflected in the emoter's emotion expression. This implies that emotional facial expressions that occur in response to an event are not only a consequence of the event but also provide social information about the emoter's view of the event and thereby, indirectly, about the event.

This process is quite similar to the social referencing (Klinnert, Campos, Sorce, Emde, & Svejda, 1983) observed in infants. This process is also related to social appraisal (Manstead & Fischer, 2001). However, there are two differences; first, social appraisal describes the direct appraisal of the expression of another person, not the reverse-engineered appraisal of the situation that elicited the expression (however, in many cases the results of these processes are likely to converge). Second, social appraisals are presumed to be most relevant to secondary appraisals associated with efforts at coping (see, Lazarus, 1991), whereas reverse-engineered appraisals are presumed to relate to primary appraisals as well.

When people are confronted with complex or ambiguous situations, the reverse-engineered information garnered from the expresser's reaction can then be used as an input to one's own emotional reaction to, and appreciation of, the event (cf., Parkinson, Phiri, & Simons, 2012). For example, in a recent study by Landmann, David, Hareli, and Hess (2015), participants were asked to evaluate stories describing behaviors that varied in impoliteness or immorality. Participants also saw a picture showing another person who had supposedly reacted to these events with either anger, disgust, or neutrality. The same event was rated as more immoral when the participant saw someone reacting to it with anger or disgust rather than with neutrality. These effects were mediated via reverse-engineered appraisals of the perceived expressions, specifically with the appraisal that the expresser considered the event to violate a moral standard. That is, participants reverse-engineered the appraisals from the expressions and used these to inform their own reactions to the event.

In sum, context can be defined in a variety of ways and includes both the situation and the perceiver. The perceiver's knowledge, naïve emotion theories, motivations, goals, and emotions all enter into the active process described in the two-path model of emotion recognition. However, this raises the question regarding the limits of this influence.

LIMITS TO THE MALLEABILITY OF EMOTION PERCEPTION

The pervasive influence of context on emotion perception can give the impression that early critics of Darwin (1872/1965) were right in saying that facial expressions per se are meaningless. That at best they can—as claimed by Bruner and Tagiuri (1954)—be culturally learned signals, which are not meaningfully linked to an underlying state or are to be considered as constructed within the moment either at the interface between individual and environment (Mesquita & Boiger, 2014), or in the head of the individual (Barrett, 2009, 2013). That is, in the vein of strong psychological constructivism (Faucher, 2013); emotional measing is created in a "simulator," which constructs "on-the-fly" emotion concepts adapted to particular instances of a category.

We think that this impression is false. It is important to note that even though context frames the way people interpret cues and the attention that is paid to the cues as well as the level of processing that is applied to this endeavor, context is also confronted and limited by the stories that emotion expressions tell. More specifically, context is limited by a framework based on the core appraisals that distinguish one emotion from another and that create the emotion's story. With core appraisals we mean those appraisals that characterize the emotion expression or the event that gave rise to it. When considering tables of emotion predictions based on appraisals, for example by Scherer (1986) or Roseman (1991), we find that for each emotion some appraisal dimensions are defined, whereas others are not. Thus, events that elicit fear are goal obstructive and those that elicit happiness are goal conducive. However, events that elicit disgust may well be either, as many helpful home remedies demonstrate, which for all that they help are still disgusting in taste. With core appraisals we therefore refer to those appraisals that are defined for the specific emotion under consideration. We assume that it will be easier to misidentify between emotions that share core appraisals.

That is, only within the frame provided by that story and only within the limits of these appraisals can context change our perception of emotions. In fact, this notion can be supported by research originally designed to underline the power of context. Thus, Aviezer et al. (2008) in an attempt to show the malleability of emotion perception, created stimuli that combined an emotion expression with a body stance. In Study 1, a disgust face was combined with stances communicating disgust, anger, sadness, and fear. There are two types of disgust: physical disgust in reaction to noxious stimuli, and moral disgust in reaction to morally inappropriate behavior (Rozin, Lowery, Imada, & Haidt, 1999), and appraisals for this latter disgust resemble appraisal for anger in that it is associated with goal obstruction and high coping potential combined with an appraisal of norm violation. By contrast, fear and sadness are both emotions that are characterized by low coping potential, and norm appraisal is not very relevant. The findings show that the disgust face combined with an aggressive body posture was indeed overwhelmingly miscategorized as anger (87%). However, when the disgust face was combined with fear (13%) and sadness postures (29%), which are much less compatible with the appraisal pattern for moral disgust, it was miscategorized to a substantially smaller degree. In sum, context plays a very important role in emotion perception and for the inferences drawn from emotions; however, it plays this role within the—admittedly large—framework of the core appraisals characterizing this emotion.

A MODEL OF SOCIAL SIGNALS IN CONTEXT

Based on the notions discussed earlier, we formulated a model of the meaning of emotion expressions in context (MEEC, see Fig. 20.1, Hess & Hareli, 2016). In this model, expressions are perceived within a situational context (the real world) and then interpreted within an interpreted context (the perceived world). The information from the real world will determine the encapsulated meaning of the expression (the story that the emotion tells), and this process will be influenced by the perceiver-as-context processes outlined earlier. If the information provided by the context and the interpretation of the expression falls within the frame of the core appraisals associated with the emotion, the process can go on to allow for inferences to be drawn from the expression. In case of a mismatch the perceiver has to reevaluate the match explicitly. One outcome of this process can be to discount the expresser as "deviant" (Szczurek, Monin, & Gross, 2012). In this case no further effort to "reconcile" expression and emotion elicitor is made. Another similar outcome could be to reevaluate the situation. For example, most people react positively to kittens. If a person shows fear in response to the kitten, one might consider

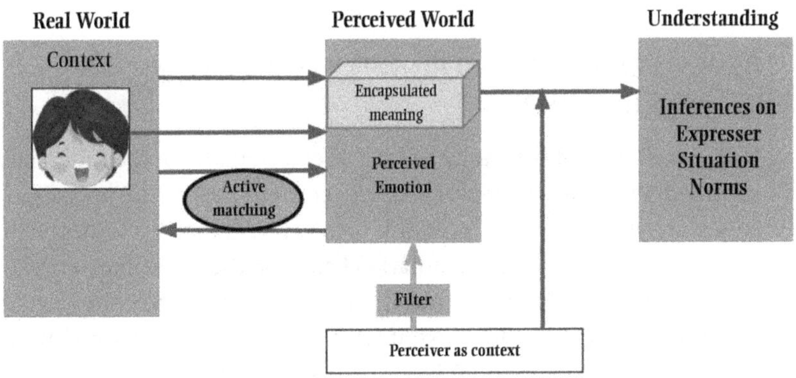

Figure 20.1 A model of the meaning of emotion expressions.

the possibility that the person suffers from an extreme form of ailurophobia (fear of cats). However, as in horror movies, it might be that just behind the kitten a large aggressive drooling, likely rabid, dog can be seen, which changes the situation completely. That is, another way to reconcile the expression and the emotion elicitor is by either postulating a specific significance of the situation for the expresser (i.e., the expresser is ailurophobic) or by changing the meaning of the situation (i.e., there is in fact something dangerous to be seen). That is, congruence can be recreated by reinterpreting either the situation, the significance of the situation to the specific expresser, or the facial expression. This process differs from such proposals as those, for example, by Aviezer et al. (2008) or Righart and DeGelder (2008) who presume that the meaning of the context that is contrasted with the facial expressions remains stable. This also raises the question as to which of these processes will be used by the observer. We propose that observers will reinterpret the aspect of the expression-situation combination for which appraisals are more pliable. Thus, the same object (chocolate) may be motive congruent or incongruent depending on whether I am on a diet or not. By contrast, valence is a fundamental characteristic of objects. Thus, it is easy to change a situation into one that is more or less motive congruent, but it requires very specific assumptions, such as the additional presence of a dangerous dog, to turn a kitten into a threat object. Also, a person high in coping potential may on occasion show weakness, but it is much more difficult if not impossible for a weak person to suddenly show high coping potential. Thus, as shown by Aviezer et al. (2008), it is easily possible to misidentify (moral) disgust as anger if the context suggests an anger reaction, as both are negative emotions denoting high coping potential; by contrast it is much less likely (but still possible) to identify disgust as fear or sadness, since the latter imply low coping potential. Yet, we would posit that a fear expression would only rarely be misidentified as anger or disgust; in this case it would be more likely for the situation to be reinterpreted.

ON THE MALLEABILITY AND RIGIDITY OF EMOTION EXPRESSIONS IN CONTEXT

The MEEC predicts that for the decoding of emotions the impact of context will be limited within a "conceptual corset" created by the core appraisals of the emotion shown. However, the MEEC also predicts that to the degree that the reengineered appraisals of the situation based on the facial expression and the appraisal of the context do not match, these two have to be reconciled.

A study was conducted to demonstrate this process. A total of 191 (101 men) participants with a mean age of 37.5 (SD = 11.5) years, who were recruited via Amazon MTurk, completed the survey. They first saw for 2 seconds a picture taken from the International Affective Picture Set (IAPS; Bradley & Lang, 2007) showing either a disgust, anger, or fear context, or one of two pictures of kittens taken from the Internet.[1] This was followed by a picture showing a facial expression. For the latter, expressions of happiness, disgust, anger, or fear were taken from the Amsterdam Dynamic Facial Expression Set (ADFES, Van Der Schalk, Hawk, Fischer, & Doosje, 2011) for two men and two women. Participants then saw both images together and were asked in an open question to explain why the person showed the expression he or she did show. They then were asked in a forced-choice format to indicate which of seven emotions (anger, fear, sadness, disgust, surprise, contempt, or happiness) the person had shown. Finally, they answered a series of 15 questions based on a short version of the appraisal section of the GRID questionnaire (Fontaine, Scherer, & Soriano, 2013).

The appraisals that can be considered as core appraisals for the emotions happiness, anger, disgust, and fear are pleasantness and control potential (Scherer, 1986). That is, the reengineered appraisals of the situation by the expressers should vary foremost with regard to these appraisals. Intrinsic pleasantness mainly distinguishes between happiness on one hand and the three negative emotions on the other. The appraisal of control potential determines the extent to which the situation that elicited the emotion can be handled by the expresser. Thus, whereas surprise, sadness, and fear are elicited in situations that are low in control potential, anger, moral disgust, and contempt are associated with high control potential. This means that anger may be misinterpreted as (moral) disgust or contempt, but also to some degree as fear or sadness, as it is easier for a person high in control potential to show weakness at some point than the reverse (that is, it is easier for participants to come up with a story which makes this possible). This implies also that fear expressions should be misidentified as surprise but not as anger. They may, however, also be misidentified as physical disgust. Disgust is in fact a somewhat interesting emotion in this regard because, as mentioned earlier, there are two types of disgust, moral and physical disgust. Whereas moral disgust would suggest high control potential, physical disgust is basically undefined for most appraisals except intrinsic pleasantness (Scherer, 1986). That is, it should be quite easy to create a story by adapting either the person's motive or the situation to match a disgust expression with just about any situation except a pleasant one. The reverse, however, should not be the case, as for the other emotion expressions additional appraisals are defined.

Table 20.1 shows the choices for the expression ratings. As can be seen, there are considerable differences in the degree to which facial expressions were misidentified as a function of context. In fact, as predicted, expressions of happiness were essentially never misidentified because all other choice

Table 20.1 CLASSIFICATION OF EMOTION EXPRESSIONS AS A FUNCTION OF CONTEXT

Expressions	Anger		Disgust		Fear		Happiness	
	Mean	SD	Mean	SD	Mean	SD	Mean	SD
Ratings	Anger Context							
Anger	**0.44**	**0.51**	0.00	0.00	0.00	0.00	0.00	0.00
Contempt	0.06	0.25	0.00	0.00	0.00	0.00	0.00	0.00
Disgust	0.19	0.40	**0.91**	**0.30**	0.08	0.29	0.00	0.00
Fear	0.00	0.00	0.00	0.00	**0.67**	**0.49**	0.00	0.00
Happiness	0.00	0.00	0.00	0.00	0.00	0.00	**1.00**	**0.00**
Sadness	0.25	0.44	0.00	0.00	0.00	0.00	0.00	0.00
Surprise	0.06	0.25	0.09	0.30	0.25	0.45	0.00	0.00
			Disgust Context					
Anger	**0.10**	**0.32**	0.00	0.00	0.00	0.00	0.00	0.00
Contempt	0.00	0.00	0.00	0.00	0.00	0.00	0.00	0.00
Disgust	0.90	0.32	**1.00**	**0.00**	0.50	0.53	0.00	0.00
Fear	0.00	0.00	0.00	0.00	**0.40**	**0.52**	0.00	0.00
Happiness	0.00	0.00	0.00	0.00	0.00	0.00	**1.00**	**0.00**
Sadness	0.00	0.00	0.00	0.00	0.00	0.00	0.00	0.00
Surprise	0.00	0.00	0.00	0.00	0.10	0.32	0.00	0.00
			Fear Context					
Anger	**0.60**	**0.52**	0.00	0.00	0.00	0.00	0.00	0.00
Contempt	0.20	0.42	0.00	0.00	0.00	0.00	0.09	0.30
Disgust	0.00	0.00	**0.73**	**0.47**	0.00	0.00	0.00	0.00
Fear	0.20	0.42	0.18	0.42	**0.82**	**0.40**	0.00	0.00
Happiness	0.00	0.00	0.00	0.00	0.00	0.00	**0.91**	**0.30**
Sadness	0.00	0.00	0.00	0.00	0.00	0.00	0.00	0.00
Surprise	0.00	0.00	0.00	0.00	0.18	0.40	0.00	0.00
			Happy Context					
Anger	**0.42**	**0.51**	0.13	0.35	0.00	0.00	0.00	0.00
Contempt	0.08	0.29	0.07	0.26	0.00	0.00	0.00	0.00
Disgust	0.25	0.45	**0.80**	**0.41**	0.06	0.24	0.00	0.00
Fear	0.08	0.29	0.00	0.00	**0.65**	**0.49**	0.00	0.00
Happiness	0.00	0.00	0.00	0.00	0.00	0.00	**1.00**	**0.00**
Sadness	0.08	0.29	0.00	0.00	0.00	0.00	0.00	0.00
Surprise	0.08	0.29	0.00	0.00	0.29	0.47	0.00	0.00

Note: Numbers in bold refer to the target ratings for the expressions.

options were unpleasant. This matches the prediction that pleasantness cannot be reversed.

Expressions such as fear, which signal low coping potential, can only be misinterpreted as other expressions that also signal low coping potential such as surprise or disgust, which is open with regard to this appraisal. Correspondingly, fear was sometimes misinterpreted as surprise or as disgust—the latter especially in a disgust context. Disgust expressions, by contrast, were rarely misidentified and there was no clear trend with regard to which other emotion label would be chosen. This was predicted—because disgust expressions are "open" with regard to most appraisals and hence it is easy to adapt a given context to the disgust expression, but the reverse does not work as well, because these contexts are associated with specific appraisals, which are not part of the social appraisal of disgust.

Interestingly, the most malleable expression was anger. In fact, when anger expressions were shown in a disgust context, they were overwhelmingly rated as disgust. In all other contexts, anger was the modal choice for anger expressions, but other labels were also used. Interestingly, these were not necessarily the labels indicated by the context. Thus, in anger contexts, anger was the modal choice, but disgust and surprise were also chosen. In the fear context, anger was also the modal choice (and more often chosen than in the anger context), and the expressions were sometimes misidentified as fear but also as contempt. In a happy context, anger expressions were most often miscategorized as disgust, but otherwise no clear pattern emerged. This matches the prediction that anger matches most of the situation appraisals that were available or can be adapted by "weakening" the coping potential appraisal.

In all, only the miscategorization of anger expressions as disgust in a disgust context was a case of a clear tendency to reinterpret the meaning of an expression as a function of context. In all other cases, the emotion expressed in the face remained the modal choice and a clear pattern of choices along core appraisals was found.

This raises the question of what people did when they encountered a scene-expression mismatch. To answer this question, we coded the open questions for two aspects—adding information about the person that was not provided by the stimulus (such as attributing a motivation or preference) or adding information to the scene that was not shown (such as making reference to something that happened before or is out of sight). As can be seen in Table 20.2, participants generally tended to add information about the person that was not part of the stimulus for all contexts and expressions. However, this tendency was notably stronger for expressions for which social appraisals did not match the situational appraisal. Thus, when participants saw a cute kitten and a person showing a negative facial expression, they added person information

Table 20.2 PERCENT OF PARTICIPANTS WHO ADDED PERSON INFORMATION TO EXPLAIN THE EMOTIONS SHOWN BY THE EXPRESSER AS A FUNCTION OF EMOTION EXPRESSION AND CONTEXT

Expressions	Anger		Disgust		Fear		Happiness	
Context	Mean	SD	Mean	SD	Mean	SD	Mean	SD
Happy	0.58	0.51	0.80	0.41	0.53	0.51	**0.00**	**0.00**
Anger	**0.13**	**0.34**	0.00	0.00	0.08	0.29	0.80	0.42
Disgust	0.30	0.48	**0.18**	**0.40**	0.20	0.42	0.79	0.43
Fear	0.40	0.52	0.36	0.50	**0.27**	**0.47**	0.82	0.40

Note: Numbers in bold refer to the target ratings for the expressions.

that allowed to reconcile the expression and the situation. When the kitten was accompanied by a fear face, fear of cats was invoked; in the case of anger or disgust expressions, a general dislike of cats was invoked. More rarely, participants also reinterpreted the situation by adding that the kitten may have misbehaved or scratched the person. Some of the stories were quite inventive such as this attempt to reconcile the kitten with a fear expression: "While the kitten was on its back, looking for attention and play, the woman's large dog came up behind the cat, seemingly intent on attacking it. The woman saw this playing out and wasn't close enough to stop it, so she was horrified at the idea that her dog was going to kill her kitten." In all, the data suggest that even though people misidentify most expressions at least sometimes, the misinterpretation is not necessarily congruent with the situation. Rather, participants' misinterpretation of the expressions is limited by the associated appraisals. For expressions that signal pleasantness, situational context does not change the meaning of expressions and participants can only reconcile the appraisals by either assuming that this specific person has a more uncommon motive (thus turning the situation into an unpleasant or at least motive-incongruent one) or by adding additional unpleasant elements to the situation (such as a dangerous dog). However, for anger expressions a wider choice of "matching" social appraisals was possible and, indeed, we found that anger expressions were particularly strongly affected by context—and even in a congruent context, a wider range of labels was chosen.

CONCLUSIONS

We proposed, based on the MEEC and demonstrated in a small study, that context has a strong influence on the perception of emotions but that this influence is limited. Situations do not typically determine the meaning of an expression and, if they do, then only in specific circumstances. In particular, we proposed that expressions "tell stories" because observers will reverse-engineer the appraisal of the situation by the expresser based on the expressions. Only when these reverse-engineered appraisals and the appraisal of the situation match in the eyes of the observer can the expression be misidentified. For example, in our study an anger expression in a disgust context may well be misidentified as disgust because of the similarities in the social appraisals of these expressions. If the appraisals do not match, the observer will attempt to reconcile the appraisals by adding plausible information based on her or his naïve emotion theories. Expressions and situations vary in the degree to which such plausible additional information can be found. For example, the well-known fear of cats is readily available plausible information why a person would show fear in response to a cute kitten. Notably, the expression is still identified as fear and the kitten as cute—that is, neither observation is changed—but the two now make sense to the observer. That is, emotional meaning can be reconstructed on the fly, but this will be achieved while conserving the meaning of both the expression and the situation. Thus, in this study, what was most often reconstructed was the link between both. This makes evolutionary sense. Darwin (1872/1965) already emphasized the evolutionary importance of emotion expressions as communicative signals. This notion remains relevant (Hess & Thibault, 2009; Niedenthal & Brauer, 2012). It would be strange if a communicative signal that has evolutionary roots would suddenly be discounted at the slightest provocation. Rather, observers tend to take the social appraisals transmitted by the facial expressions at "face value." In some instances these appraisals can fit more than one emotion expression, including one suggested by the appraisal of the situation. In this case the misidentification in terms of the use of a different emotion label occurs. Yet, notably, this is not a misinterpretation of the appraisal information. If this is not an option, observers try to find a plausible explanation for the information conveyed by the face that maintains both this information and the gist of the emotion-eliciting situation as they understand it.

The MEEC as described here only focuses on context information that is relevant to the emotion elicitor. However, as noted earlier, there are other types of context that have been shown to influence emotion perception (Hess & Hareli, 2015; Matsumoto & Hwang, 2010). Thus, body posture has been considered a context for facial expressions (Aviezer et al., 2008), but from a multimodel emotion decoding perspective (Bänziger, Grandjean, & Scherer, 2009), facial expressions and body postures are both emotion signals and not a context for each other. Also, when an unattached head is floating above an image without an obvious link between the two, it is not clear that the scene in the image is a context for the face, even though it certainly influences the perception of the face (Righart & De Gelder, 2008). It may do so because, as noted earlier, a scene that is depicted together with a face can—through affective priming—activate response categories, which in turn facilitate or hinder the categorization of the expression.

Discussions about the role of context for the construction of emotional meaning, therefore, require a clearer definition of both what is considered to be signal and what is considered to be ancillary information, as not everything that is perceived at the same time as an expression has the same epistemological standing with regard to the meaning of this expression.

Future research and theorizing need to pay more attention to the specific processes engaged in the construction of the meaning of emotion expressions and in the limits of this process. In this vein, it would be important to not only show when a specific context influences perception but also when it does not.

NOTE

1. 1525, 1930, 6212, 9810, 3250, 9301.

REFERENCES

Aviezer, H., Hassin, R., Ryan, J., Grady, C., Susskind, J., Anderson, A., . . . Bentin, S. (2008). Angry, disgusted, or afraid? Studies on the malleability of emotion perception. *Psychological Science, 19*, 724–732.

Bänziger, T., Grandjean, D., & Scherer, K. R. (2009). Emotion recognition from expressions in face, voice, and body: The Multimodal Emotion Recognition Test (MERT). *Emotion, 9*, 691-704.

Barrett, L. F. (2009). Variety is the spice of life: A psychological construction approach to understanding variability in emotion. *Cognition and Emotion, 23*(7), 1284–1306.

Barrett, L. F. (2013). Psychological construction: The Darwinian approach to the science of emotion. *Emotion Review, 5*(4), 379–389.

Bower, G. H., & Forgas, J. P. (2000). Affect, memory, and social cognition. In E. Eich, J. F. Kihlstrom, G. H. Bower, J. P. Forgas, & P. M. Niedenthal (Eds.), *Cognition and emotion* (pp. 87–168). New York, NY: Oxford University Press.

Bradley, M. M., & Lang, P. J. (2007). The International Affective Picture System (IAPS) in the study of emotion and attention. In J. A. C. J. J. B. Allen (Ed.), *Handbook of emotion elicitation and assessment* (pp. 29–46). New York, NY: Oxford University Press.

Bruner, J. S., & Tagiuri, R. (1954). The perception of people. In G. Lindzey (Ed.), *Handbook of Social Psychology* (Vol. 2, pp. 634-655). Cambridge, MA: Addison-Wesley Publishing.

Buck, R. (1984). *The communication of emotion*. New York, NY: Guilford Press.

Dailey, M. N., Cottrell, G. W., Padgett, C., & Adolphs, R. (2002). EMPATH: A neural network that categorizes facial expressions. *Journal of Cognitive Neuroscience, 14*, 1158–1173.

Darwin, C. (1872/1965). *The expression of the emotions in man and animals.* Chicago, IL: The University of Chicago Press. (Originally published, 1872).

Ekman, P., & Friesen, W. V. (1971). Constants across cultures in the face and emotion. *Journal of Personality and Social Psychology, 17,* 124–129.

Faucher, L. (2013). Comment: Constructionisms? *Emotion Review, 5*(4), 374–378.

Fontaine, J. R. J., Scherer, K. R., & Soriano, C. (2013). *Components of emotional meaning: A sourcebook*. Oxford, UK: Oxford University Press.

Forgas, J. P. (1995). Mood and judgment: The Affect Infusion Model (AIM). *Psychological Bulletin, 117,* 39–66.

Fridlund, A. J. (1991). The sociality of solitary smiling: Potentiation by an implicit audience. *Journal of Personality and Social Psychology, 60,* 229–240.

Hareli, S., David, S., & Hess, U. (2013). Competent and warm but unemotional: The influence of occupational stereotypes on the attribution of emotions. *Journal of Nonverbal Behavior, 37,* 307–317. doi:10.1007/s10919-013-0157-x

Hareli, S., & Hess, U. (2010). What emotional reactions can tell us about the nature of others: An appraisal perspective on person perception. *Cognition and Emotion, 24,* 128–140.

Hess, U. (2001). The communication of emotion. In A. Kaszniak (Ed.), *Emotions, qualia, and consciousness* (pp. 397–409). Singapore: World Scientific Publishing.

Hess, U., Adams, R. B., Jr., & Kleck, R. E. (2005). Who may frown and who should smile? Dominance, affiliation, and the display of happiness and anger. *Cognition and Emotion, 19,* 515–536.

Hess, U., Adams, R. B., Jr., & Kleck, R. E. (2009). The face is not an empty canvas: How facial expressions interact with facial appearance. *Philosophical Transactions of the Royal Society London B, 364,* 3497–3504.

Hess, U., Blaison, C., & Kafetsios, K. (2016). Judging facial emotion expressions in context: The influence of culture and self-construal orientation. *Journal of Nonverbal Behavior, 40,* 55–64.

Hess, U., David, S., & Hareli, S. (2016). Emotional restrant is good for men only: The influence of emotional retraint on the perception of competence. *Emotion, 16,* 208–213.

Hess, U., & Hareli, S. (2015). *The influence of context on emotion recognition in humans.* Paper presented at the Proceedings of the 11th IEEE International Conference on Automatic Face and Gesture Recognition, Ljubljana, Slovenia, May 4–7.

Hess, U., & Hareli, S. (2016). The impact of context on the perception of emotions. In: Abell, C. and Smith, J. (Ed.). *The Expression of Emotion: Philosophical, Psychological, and Legal Perspectives* (pp. 199–218). Cambridge University Press.

Hess, U., Kappas, A., & Banse, R. (1995). The intensity of facial expressions is determined by underlying affective state and social situation. *Journal of Personality and Social Psychology, 69,* 280–288.

Hess, U., & Thibault, P. (2009). Darwin and emotion expression. *American Psychologist, 64,* 120–128.

Hugenberg, K., & Bodenhausen, G. V. (2003). Facing prejudice: Implicit prejudice and the perception of facial threat. *Psychological Science, 14,* 640–643.

Ickes, W., & Simpson, J. A. (2004). Motivational aspects of empathic accuracy. In M. B. Brewer & M. Hewstone (Eds.), *Emotion and motivation: Perspectives on social psychology* (pp. 225–246). Malden, MA: Blackwell.

Kirouac, G., & Hess, U. (1999). Group membership and the decoding of nonverbal behavior. In P. Philippot, R. Feldman, & E. Coats (Eds.), *The social context of nonverbal behavior* (pp. 182–210). Cambridge, UK: Cambridge University Press.

Klinnert, M. D., Campos, J. J., Sorce, J. F., Emde, R. N., & Svejda, M. (1983). Emotions as behavior regulators: Social referencing in infancy. In R. Plutchik & H. Kellerman (Eds.), *Emotion: Theory, research and experience* (Vol. 2, pp. 57–86). New York, NY: Academic Press.

Landmann, H., David, S., Hareli, S., & Hess, U. (2016). How I see you depends on what you see and vice versa: The bidirectional relation of emotion perception and morality. Manuscript submitted for publication.

Lazarus, R. S. (1991). *Emotion and adaptation*. New York, NY: Oxford University Press.

Manstead, A. S. R., & Fischer, A. H. (2001). Social appraisal: The social world as object of and influence on appraisal processes. In K. R. Scherer, A. Schorr, & T. Johnstone (Eds.), *Appraisal processes in emotion: Theory, methods, research* (pp. 221–232). New York, NY: Oxford University Press.

Masuda, T., Ellsworth, P. C., Mesquita, B., Leu, J., Tanida, S., & Van de Veerdonk, E. (2008). Placing the face in context: Cultural differences in the perception of facial emotion. *Journal of Personality and Social Psychology, 94*, 365–381

Matsumoto, D., & Hwang, H. S. (2010). Judging faces in context. *Social and Personality Psychology Compass, 4*(6), 393–402.

Matsumoto, D., Seung Hee, Y., & Fontaine, J. (2008). Mapping expressive differences around the world: The relationship between emotional display rules and individualism versus collectivism. *Journal of Cross-Cultural Psychology, 39*(1), 55–74.

Mesquita, B., & Boiger, M. (2014). Emotions in context: A sociodynamic model of emotions. *Emotion Review, 6*(4), 298–302.

Moors, A., Ellsworth, P. C., Scherer, K. R., & Frijda, N. H. (2013). Appraisal theories of emotion: State of the art and future development. *Emotion Review, 5*(2), 119–124. Retrieved from http://emr.sagepub.com/content/5/2/119.short

Motley, M. T., & Camden, C. T. (1988). Facial expression of emotion: A comparison of posed expressions versus spontaneous expressions in an interpersonal communications setting. *Western Journal of Speech Communication, 52*, 1–22.

Mueller, U., & Mazur, A. (1997). Facial dominance in Homo sapiens as honest signaling of male quality. *Behavioral Ecology, 8*, 569–579.

Niedenthal, P. M., & Brauer, M. (2012). Social functionality of human emotion. *Annual Review of Psychology, 63*(1), 259–285. doi:10.1146/annurev.psych.121208.131605

Park, B., & Rothbart, M. (1982). Perception of out-group homogeneity and levels of social categorization: Memory for the subordinate attributes of in-group and out-group members. *Journal of Personality and Social Psychology., 42*, 1051–1068. doi:10.1037/0022-3514.42.6.1051

Parkinson, B., Fischer, A. H., & Manstead, A. S. R. (2005). *Emotion in social relations: Cultural, group, and interpersonal processes*. New York, NY: Psychology Press.

Parkinson, B., Phiri, N., & Simons, G. (2012). Bursting with anxiety: Adult social referencing in an interpersonal Balloon Analogue Risk Task (BART). *Emotion, 12*(4), 817–826. doi:10.1037/a0026434

Ratcliff, N. J., Franklin, R. G., Nelson Jr., A. J., & Vescio, T. K. (2012). The scorn of status: A bias toward perceiving anger on high-status faces. *30*, 631–642. doi:10.1521/soco.2012.30.5.631

Righart, R., & De Gelder, B. (2008). Recognition of facial expressions is influenced by emotional scene gist. *Cognitive, Affective, & Behavioral Neuroscience*, *8*(3), 264–272.

Robinson, M., & Clore, G. (2002). Belief and feeling: Evidence for an accessibility model of emotional self-report. *Psychological Bulletin*, *128*, 934–960.

Roseman, I. J. (1991). Appraisal determinants of discrete emotions. *Cognition & Emotion*, *5*, 161–200.

Rozin, P., Lowery, L., Imada, S., & Haidt, J. (1999). The CAD triad hypothesis: A mapping between three moral emotions (contempt, anger, disgust) and three moral codes (community, autonomy, divinity). *Journal of Personality and Social Psychology*, *76*, 574–586.

Rule, N. O., Ambady, N., & Hallett, K. C. (2009). Female sexual orientation is perceived accurately, rapidly, and automatically from the face and its features. *Journal of Experimental Social Psychology*, *45*, 1245–1251.

Sarid, O. (2015). Assessment of Anger Terms in Hebrew: A Gender Comparison. *The Journal of Psychology*, *149*, 303-324.

Scherer, K. R. (1978). Personality inference from voice quality: The loud voice of extraversion. *European Journal of Social Psychology*, *8*, 467–487.

Scherer, K. R. (1986). Vocal affect expression: A review and a model for future research. *Psychological Bulletin*, *99*(2), 143–165.

Scherer, K. R., & Grandjean, D. (2008). Facial expressions allow inference of both emotions and their components. *Cognition & Emotion*, *22*, 789–801.

Shields, S. A. (2005). The politics of emotion in everyday life: "Appropriate" emotion and claims on identity. *Review of General Psychology*, *9*, 3–15.

Showers, C., & Cantor, N. (1985). Social cognition: A look at motivated strategies. *Annual Review of Psychology*, *36*(1), 275–305.

Szczurek, L., Monin, B., & Gross, J. J. (2012). The stranger effect: The rejection of affective deviants. *Psychological Science*, *23*(10), 1105–1111. doi:10.1177/0956797612445314

Thibault, P., Bourgeois, P., & Hess, U. (2006). The effect of group-identification on emotion recognition: The case of cats and basketball players. *Journal of Experimental Social Psychology*, *42*, 676–683.

Van Der Schalk, J., Hawk, S. T., Fischer, A. H., & Doosje, B. (2011). Moving faces, looking places: Validation of the Amsterdam Dynamic Facial Expression Set (ADFES). *Emotion*, *11*(4), 907.

PART IX

Concepts

21

Embodied Simulation in Decoding Facial Expression

PAULA M. NIEDENTHAL, ADRIENNE WOOD, MAGDALENA RYCHLOWSKA, AND SEBASTIAN KORB

Theories of embodied simulation hold that mental processes are determined by the specific form of the human nervous system and body, and their interaction with the external, physical environment (Niedenthal & Barsalou, 2009). In this view, the processing of information about, for instance, furniture, odors, sports, a favorite comfort food, and even abstract ideas, is influenced by, and sometimes dependent upon, perceptual, somatosensory, and motor resources. Emotional experiences are specifically linked to the nervous system and body, as noted long ago by William James (1896). So, embodied simulation theories should be particularly powerful for modeling the processing of emotional information (Niedenthal, 2007; Winkielman, Niedenthal, & Oberman, 2008). For example, when we listen to someone recounting a story of a moment of deep personal shame, we may re-experience some part of the subjective experience of shame in ourselves. What is the purpose of this re-experience? Theory and research in this tradition suggest that the re-experience grounds comprehension of emotional meaning (Niedenthal, Winkielman, Mondillon, & Vermeulen, 2009). Of course, while we hear emotional stories often, we encounter at least as many, perhaps many more, facial expressions of emotion in our daily lives. How do we perform the complex task of decoding the meaning of the innumerable facial expressions we perceive?

The present chapter explores evidence for the role of embodied simulation in the decoding of facial expression of emotion. When we use the term "embodied simulation," we refer to the idea that the perception of a facial expression has triggered in the observer a simulation of the corresponding state in the motor, somatosensory, affective, and reward systems that is used to comprehend the expression's meaning (Wood, Lupyan, Sherrin, & Niedenthal, 2015). Facial mimicry, or imitation of the perceived expression, should be an important part of this process. This is suggested by theories that hold that the activity of one's own facial expressions feeds back into the brain and causes or delimits emotional responses, and guides emotional judgments (Adelmann & Zajonc, 1989; Buck, 1980; McIntosh, 1996). Research demonstrates, consistent with popular songs and expressions, that producing emotional facial expressions results in distinct physiological activity (Ekman, Levenson, & Friesen, 1983) and produces corresponding subjective feelings. Facilitating or inhibiting smiling, by holding a pen between the teeth or the lips, respectively, may thus affect emotional responding to humorous stimuli (Soussignan, 2002). And results of clinical research suggest that depression may be lifted by procedures involving the paralysis of the corrugator muscle (involved in frowning), because feedback from this facial muscle contributes to the maintenance of sad and hopeless feelings (Finzi & Rosenthal, 2014; Wollmer et al., 2012). The facial feedback theory already suggested, several decades ago, that facial mimicry may participates in the decoding of facial expression (Zajonc, Adelmann, Murphy, & Niedenthal, 1987).

We begin the chapter by reviewing evidence in favor of the hypothesis that mimicking a perceived facial expression helps the perceiver achieve greater decoding accuracy. We report experimental and correlational evidence in favor of the general effect, and we also examine the assertion that facial mimicry influences perceptual processing of facial expression. Finally, after examining the behavioral evidence, we look into the brain to explore the roles of neural circuitry and chemistry in embodied simulation of facial expressions.

Although we cite findings from laboratories other than our own, we highlight recent research that we have conducted, with a particular focus on the human smile. Because of its great complexity—the ability to convey so many different emotions by combining the activation of the zygomaticus (smile) muscle with the contraction of other muscles—we have argued elsewhere that the smile is the ideal case for testing principles of theories of embodied simulation (Niedenthal, Korb, Wood, & Rychlowska, 2016; Niedenthal et al., 2010).

BEHAVIORAL EVIDENCE OF A ROLE FOR MIMICRY IN DECODING EXPRESSION

Although people can voluntarily decide to imitate another person, low-intensity facial mimicry is thought to occur spontaneously and unconsciously. It unfolds rapidly within 200 ms from the onset of a picture of a face, and it is difficult to suppress (Korb, Grandjean, & Scherer, 2010). Substantial evidence now exists to suggest that disrupting or altering feedback from facial muscles and neural processes involved in facial mimicry reduces the speed and accuracy with which people process the emotion expressions of others. This may be particularly true for subtle, ambiguous displays, since recognition of more prototypical expressions can be achieved using less costly pattern-matching perceptual strategies (Hess & Fischer, 2013; Smith, Cottrell, Gosselin, & Schyns, 2005).

To demonstrate the role of facial feedback in expression recognition, researchers first typically disrupt participants' natural facial movements and then ask them to complete a challenging emotion recognition task. The task may involve selecting the best emotion label for the expression (Neal & Chartrand, 2011), evaluating the expression's meaning (Rychlowska et al., 2014), or explicitly identifying the onset or offset of an emotional expression (Niedenthal, Brauer, Halberstadt, & Innes-Ker, 2001). As an example, in our laboratory, Maringer and colleagues (2011) presented participants with videos of "true" and "false" dynamic smiles that had been created and validated in prior work (Krumhuber et al., 2007). All participants rated the genuineness of the smiles. However, mimicry of half of the participants was disrupted because they were instructed to hold a pen between their teeth and lips. The remaining participants held no pen in their mouths and could freely mimic the smiles. Findings revealed that participants who could mimic the smiles rated true smiles as significantly more genuine than false smiles. That is, they appeared to distinguish between the two types of smiles. This difference was not observed for the participants whose mimicry was inhibited. Those participants rated both types of smile as equally genuine, suggesting that they distinguished far less well between the two.

In subsequent research in our laboratory, Rychlowska and colleagues (2014) employed a rugby mouthguard as an alternative method for altering mimicry of facial expressions involving the lower mouth. To validate the effectiveness of the mouthguard for disrupting facial activity, we first showed videos of true and false smiles to participants with and without mouthguards and measured the contraction of their zygomaticus muscles with electromyographic (EMG) recording. We then compared the activation of all participants' zygomaticus activity to the dynamics of the activation of zygomaticus in the video smile stimuli. These dynamics were estimated using the Computer Expression Recognition Toolbox (CERT; Littlewort et al., 2011).

As expected, the zygomaticus activation of participants wearing mouth-guards was not correlated with the facial action of the stimuli as quantified by CERT. In contrast, a positive correlation between the two was observed for participants without mouth guards. In two main studies, mouthguards were then used to block facial mimicry in some of the participants while they rated the genuineness of true and false smiles. Results of both studies showed that individuals who could mimic freely rated true smiles as significantly more genuine than false smiles. This difference was smaller for the participants whose facial mimicry was blocked by the mouthguard. For these individuals, the true and false smiles seemed similar, further supporting the idea that facial mimicry is indeed involved in accurate decoding of smiles (see also Manera et al., 2013).

Finally, in a correlational study aimed at assessing the role of more facial muscles in the simulation of smiles, Korb and colleagues (2014) also found that spontaneous facial mimicry predicts subsequent ratings of the genuineness of smiles. In particular, we presented 2-second-long video clips of 19 different types of dynamic smiles to 31 participants. Participants rated smile genuineness on a 100-point Likert scale. True smiles were defined as "the type of smile a person makes spontaneously when she is happy, joyful, or amused." The definition of a false smile was "the type of smile a person makes voluntarily when she wants to be polite, but does not actually feel very happy, joyful, or amused." Activity of the zygomaticus, orbicularis oculi, and corrugator supercilii muscles was recorded throughout the task with EMG. Results showed that participants mimicked the perceived smiles such that the activations of zygomaticus and orbicularis were strongest, and activations of the corrugator lowest, in response to the videos with the strongest smiles. In addition, the overall intensity of participants' smile mimicry predicted their ratings of smile genuineness.

Together, such studies establish a causal link between mimicry and the decoding of facial expression of emotion. Facial mimicry occurs spontaneously and helps us decide whether somebody is smiling at us with genuine happiness or with faked joy.

Social Inhibition of Facial Mimicry

Although the studies described earlier demonstrate the consequences of blocking spontaneous mimicry by *mechanical* means, it is important to note that embodied simulation can also be inhibited by rules or other pressures present in *social* situations. Indeed, facial mimicry varies as a function of social context (e.g. Penner, 1971; van der Schalk et al., 2011), and Niedenthal and colleagues (2010) have suggested that this may be due in part to the social regulation of eye contact. Eye contact is a strong, attention-capturing signal that elicits neural activations in the areas involved in inference of others' mental states (Cavallo et al., 2015). A growing body of research links this behavior with triggering others' automatic responses to our actions (Sato & Itakura, 2013), as well as with the mimicry of gestures (Wang, Newport, & Hamilton, 2011) and smiles (Marschner, Pannasch, Schulz, & Graupner, 2015; Neufeld, Ioannou, Korb, Schilbach, & Chakrabarti, 2015; Rychlowska, Zinner, Musca, & Niedenthal, 2012; Soussignan et al., 2012).

Initial evidence for the role of eye contact in mimicry demonstrated that mimicry of facial expressions of physical pain increases the more the perceiver can see the eyes of the individual experiencing pain (Bavelas, Black, Lemery, & Mullett, 1986). Similarly, (Schrammel, Pannasch, Graupner, Mojzisch, & Velichkovsky, 2009) showed that participants' zygomaticus muscles were activated more while observing happy versus angry or neutral faces and, importantly, that this effect was stronger when eye contact with the faces could be achieved. In addition, angry faces elicited more negative affect and happy faces elicited more positive affect in an eye-contact, relative to a no-eye-contact, condition.

In our laboratory, Rychlowska and colleagues (2012) showed that portraiture paintings achieving eye contact with the viewer elicit higher emotional impact than paintings displaying models with gaze averted to the left or to the right. In two follow-up studies, photographs displaying smiles accompanied by direct eye gaze were judged as more positive and genuine, and elicited higher EMG activity in participants' smile muscles, than photographs whose models gazed to the left or to the right. Soussignan and colleagues (2012) provided a similar demonstration. Those researchers used dynamic facial expressions of virtual agents and also found that the effects of eye contact may vary depending on the nature of emotion displayed. Together, these research findings support the claim that ongoing social engagement, indexed by eye contact, promotes facial mimicry and embodied simulation of facial expressions of emotion.

Perceptual Effects of Facial Mimicry

Most demonstrations of sensorimotor influence on visual processing of facial expressions, such as those reviewed thus far, involve the measurement of verbally mediated conceptual judgments, such as ratings of genuineness of smiles. The precise level of emotion recognition that is affected by disrupting facial feedback therefore remains unclear. Does embodied simulation of perceived facial expressions facilitate the ease with which people can process the conceptual *meaning* of the expression, or does it go even deeper and contribute to their ability to perceive and represent the visual stimulus itself?

According to one possible account of how facial feedback influences performance on emotion recognition tasks, the perception of a facial expression elicits automatic facial mimicry (Carr, Iacoboni, Dubeau, Mazziotta, & Lenzi, 2003), but such mimicry reflects a process of emotion contagion—a corresponding change in feelings—that causes the perceiver to experience the emotion expressed by the actor (e.g., McIntosh, 2006). The emotion experience activates affectively relevant categories (Niedenthal, Halberstadt, & Setterlund, 1997), which facilitates the perceiver's ability to apply such category labels (e.g., "happy") to the stimulus.

According to an alternative account, and the one that we endorse (Wood et al., 2016), sensorimotor activity is cross-modally involved in building the visual percept of the facial expression. In this case, the perceiver "offloads" some of the perceptual representation onto facial regions of the somatosensory and motor cortices during visual processing of another person's facial expression. In so doing, he or she can perceive and remember the percept more accurately.

We tested the latter account using a visual discrimination task that did not require semantic processing (Wood, Lupyan, Sherrin, & Niedenthal, 2015). Participants applied to their faces either a gel that dried to become a constrictive peel-off mask, thus altering their somatosensory feedback, or a plain moisturizing lotion in the control condition. Then, they completed a perceptual discrimination task where they saw an image that disappeared and then reappeared next to a highly similar distractor, at which point they indicated the image that matched the original. The images were morphed facial expressions and nonface control images.

Participants wearing the gel facemask were significantly less accurate than control participants on the facial expression trials, but not on the nonface trials. Disrupting facial feedback even affected performance on trials that involved *within-category* comparisons (such as two highly similar expressions of sadness), suggesting the gel facemask was not simply changing the nature or accessibility of participants' emotion categories (see Roberson, Damjanovic, & Pilling, 2007). The facemask did not affect responses on a subsequent emotion labeling task, further suggesting the effects were occurring at the perceptual level.

This study not only clarifies when embodied simulation enters the emotion recognition process, but also contributes to evidence that different perceptual modalities, such as sensorimotor, visual, and auditory, interact with each other at early stages (for a review, see Driver & Noesselt, 2008). Much more research on this question is ongoing in our laboratory, and questions of cross-modality influences (for instance, influences of auditory emotion information on visual perception) also remain.

NEURAL BASES OF FACIAL MIMICRY

The neural basis of facial mimicry is slowly being mapped out. A tentative account of how this works goes as follows: First, a subcortical circuitry involving the amygdala allows for fast, coarse, and unconscious visual perception of another person's facial expression. This assumption is based on a series of physiological (LeDoux, 2000), patient (Adolphs, Tranel, Damasio, & Damasio, 1994; de Gelder, Vroomen, Pourtois, & Weiskrantz, 1999), and neuroimaging studies (Morris, Ohman, & Dolan, 1999; for a review, see Vuilleumier & Pourtois, 2007), which have suggested that unconscious perception of emotional faces can bypass sensory cortices (but see Pessoa & Adolphs, 2010). The amygdala, a structure in the medial temporal lobe, is also involved in the detection of eye gaze and eye contact (Kawashima et al., 1999), and it may guide attention toward the eyes of perceived faces (Adolphs et al., 2005; Kennedy & Adolphs, 2010). This is relevant because the eye region carries important emotional cues (Baron-Cohen, Wheelwright, Hill, Raste, & Plumb, 2001), and because as we proposed earlier, eye contact appears to automatically trigger facial mimicry (Niedenthal et al., 2010; Schrammel et al., 2009).

Second, spontaneous facial mimicry of the perceived facial expression is generated both subcortically, for example, in the basal ganglia, as well as cortically, for example, in cingulate motor areas, the supplementary motor area (SMA), and in somatomotor cortices that are part of the mirror neuron system (MNS; di Pellegrino, Fadiga, Fogassi, Gallese, & Rizzolatti, 1992; Gazzola & Keysers, 2009; Molenberghs, Cunnington, & Mattingley, 2012; Mukamel, Ekstrom, Kaplan, Iacoboni, & Fried, 2010). This hypothesis is based on several lines of evidence. Patient studies indicate that lesions of the thalamus, the striatocapsular area, the frontal subcortical white matter, the insula, the medial frontal lobe including the supplementary motor area (SMA), or the dorsolateral pontine tegmentum area can lead to emotional facial paresis (EFP), that is, total or partial loss of the capacity to show emotional facial expressions with, at the same time, intact voluntary control of the facial musculature (Hopf, Muller-Forell, & Hopf, 1992). Tracing studies of the cortical innervation of the facial nuclei in nonhuman primates point in the same direction (Morecraft, Louie, Herrick, & Stilwell-Morecraft, 2001). If facial mimicry is a spontaneous facial reaction, then it is likely to originate, at least partly, in these mostly subcortical areas. However, recent neuroimaging studies in humans have led to partially different results, pointing to the involvement of cortical motor and somatosensory areas in facial mimicry (van der Gaag, Minderaa, & Keysers, 2007). For example, Schilbach, Eickhoff, Mojzisch, and Vogeley (2008) reported increased brain activity in the face area of the left primary motor cortex (M1) and in the bilateral posterior cingulate gyrus during a time window in which facial mimicry was expected to occur. Likowski et al. (2012) reported significant correlations between the amplitude of facial mimicry and brain activity in various areas that belong, or are functionally connected, to the MNS, including the inferior frontal gyrus (IFG), the SMA, the insula, the medial temporal gyrus (MTG), and the superior temporal sulcus (STS). In summary, motor and premotor areas of the MNS (M1, IFG, medial premotor cortices), in addition to subcortical motor areas, might constitute the "output" centers of facial mimicry. As we will discuss later, the role of the primary motor cortex in the production of facial mimicry has been supported by a recent study of our laboratory, in which repetitive transcranial magnetic stimulation (rTMS) was used to inhibit cortical activity in M1 (Korb, Malsert, Rochas, et al., 2015).

Third, the facial feedback resulting from facial mimicry is fed back to the brain and processed by (right) somatosensory cortices. This has been suggested based on the observation, that, in over 100 patients, lesions of these areas led to impaired recognition of emotional facial expressions (Adolphs, Damasio, Tranel, Cooper, & Damasio, 2000). In healthy controls, inhibition of the right SI and neighboring somatosensory cortices through TMS resulted in slower responses and reduced accuracy in emotion-matching tasks (Pitcher, Garrido, Walsh, & Duchaine, 2008; Pourtois et al., 2004). Taken together, these findings suggest that somatosensory cortices are an efferent target of tactile and proprioceptive facial feedback, which accompanies facial mimicry (Niedenthal et al., 2010). As such, (right) somatosensory cortices constitute the "input" centers of facial mimicry.

Fourth, simultaneously to the aforementioned steps occurring in the amygdala and motor and somatosensory areas, a more precise analysis of the facial expression takes place in visual and associative cortices through feedforward and feed-back loops (Lamme, Supèr, & Spekreijse, 1998). Finally, an integration of the visual percept, one's facial feedback, and contextual knowledge may take place in higher associative cortices. In addition, visual perception of the face itself might be influenced at its earliest stages by the co-occurring facial feedback, acting as an additional and congruent sensory input. In line with this, multisensory integration has been shown to occur at basically all levels of the brain, down to "unisensory" cortices and the superior colliculus (Alais, Newell, & Mamassian, 2010; Ghazanfar & Schroeder, 2006).

In a recent study, we examined the roles of output and input centers of facial mimicry, and their differences across male and female genders, using rTMS (Korb, Malsert, Rochas, et al., 2015). In a within-subjects design, 30 healthy participants (17 females) were first scanned with structural and functional magnetic resonance imaging (MRI), in order to determine the areas of primary motor (M1) and somatosensory (S1) cortices activated during, respectively, smiling and being touched on the cheek. Then, over three separate sessions, 33.3 seconds of rTMS were delivered, with a neuronavigation system at an intensity of 80% of the motor threshold (MT), to inhibit the activity of the cheek region of the right M1 or S1. Delivery of rTMS over the vertex (VTX, midline midpoint between inion and nasion) served as an active control condition. Following each rTMS procedure, participants completed two tasks that involved rating the intensity of dynamically unfolding expressions of happiness, and detecting the change between angry and happy facial expressions gradually morphing into each other. These tasks were chosen to reliably elicit facial mimicry based on previous research (Achaibou, Pourtois, Schwartz, & Vuilleumier, 2008; Niedenthal et al., 2001). Figure 21.1 illustrates the procedure.

Participants' facial mimicry was measured with surface EMG over the zygomaticus and corrugator muscles. Results showed that in female participants

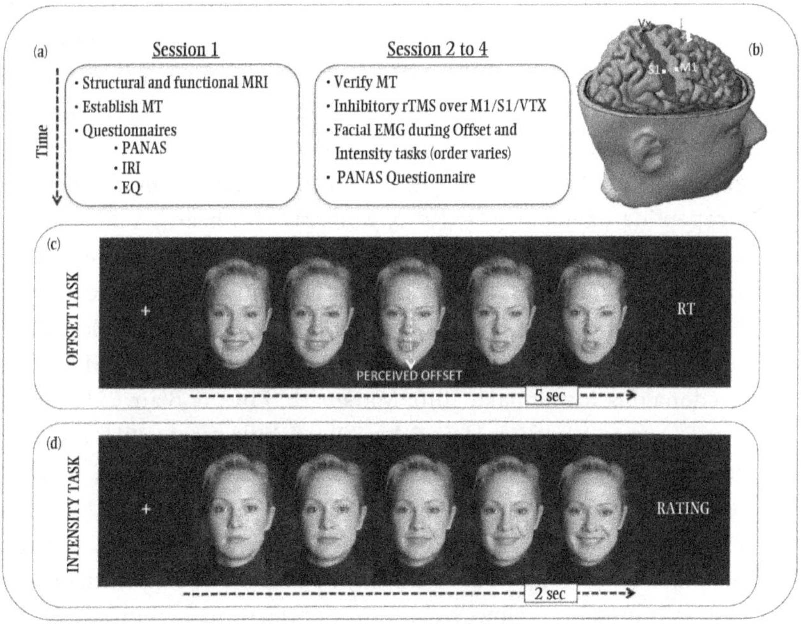

Figure 21.1 (*A*) Description of the experimental design; (*B*) average locations of M1, S1, and VTX where rTMS was applied (indicates pre- and post-central gyrus); (*C*) example of an Angry-To-Happy trial in the Offset task; (*D*) example of a Happy trial in the Intensity task.

rTMS over M1 and S1 compared to VTX led to reduced mimicry and, in the case of M1, delayed detection of smiles. However, there was no effect of rTMS in males. These findings support the hypothesis that the M1 and S1 are involved in facial mimicry, and they point to important differences between males and females in the neural circuitry underlying emotion simulation. Another lesson learned from this study is that a strict separation of "input" and "output" regions of facial mimicry, as suggested earlier, may not be possible to achieve with this experimental design because, although not a motor output area per se, S1 receives expected sensory representations before and during movement execution (Gazzola & Keysers, 2009). Possibly, watching dynamic facial expressions on the computer screen automatically changes the activity in somatosensory areas, as suggested by the finding that somatosensory processing in S1 is modulated by visual information relevant for movement (Staines, Popovich, Legon, & Adams, 2014).

Oxytocin Facilitates Mimicry

The latency and amplitude of facial mimicry can be modulated by a series of factors (in addition to eye contact, as described earlier). Increased facial mimicry has been reported in people high in self-reported empathy (Dimberg, Andréasson, & Thunberg, 2011; Sonnby-Borgstrom, 2002), and hormonal levels can also modulate the mimicry response. For example, a single dose of testosterone administration was shown to reduce facial mimicry in healthy female participants (Hermans, Putman, & van Honk, 2006).

We explored whether facial mimicry is also modulated by the hormone and neuropeptide oxytocin (OT; Korb, Malsert, Strathearn, Vuilleumier, & Niedenthal, 2015). Previous research had shown that OT modulates the perception of social stimuli and, of relevance for facial mimicry, has been associated with increased accuracy in the decoding of facial expression (Bartz, Zaki, Bolger, & Ochsner, 2011; Fischer-Shofty, Shamay-Tsoory, Harari, & Levkovitz, 2010; Macdonald & Macdonald, 2010; Marsh, Yu, Pine, & Blair, 2010; Meyer-Lindenberg, Domes, Kirsch, & Heinrichs, 2011; Schulze et al., 2011) and, relatedly, increased empathic responding (Domes, Heinrichs, Michel, Berger, & Herpertz, 2007; Hurlemann et al., 2010). In addition, OT was found to increase visual processing of the eye region of the face (Guastella, Mitchell, & Dadds, 2008), a behavior that might partly explain its positive effects on the perception of facial expressions. However, the straightforward hypothesis that OT improves the recognition of facial expressions by increasing facial mimicry had not been tested so far.

In a double-blind, placebo-controlled, between-subjects design, 60 healthy male participants received as nasal spray 24 IUs of either OXT or a placebo. Their voluntary facial movements, as well as spontaneous facial mimicry, were measured with facial EMG across two tasks in which dynamic facial expressions of happiness and anger, or gradual changes between the two, were shown in infant and adult faces. Results showed that mimicry of angry, but not happy, facial expressions increased after the administration of intranasal OXT compared to placebo, and that these effects were more pronounced in response to infant compared to adult faces. Voluntary frowning, which was measured in a separate task, was not modulated by intranasal OXT. These findings suggest that facial mimicry can be increased through administration of intranasal OXT, and that this increase in mimicry could be the mechanism underlying previously reported increased accuracy in the perception of facial expressions. Future studies will have to elucidate precisely why OT led to increased mimicry of anger, but not happiness.

CONCLUSIONS

The recognition of facial expression can be accomplished in a number of ways. One way involves the use of low-level perceptual features, such as the contraction of certain muscles, and comparison of those features to perceptual templates for prototypic expressions stored in memory. This process may be most efficient for performing lower demand tasks, such as the classification of prototypical expressions into basic categories (Buck, 1984).

While a perceptual pattern-matching operation may be an efficient way to distinguish between basic categories of emotion expressions, different processes may be required to recognize less prototypic, perhaps more realistic, emotion expressions or to represent their subtle meanings. In such cases, perceivers may recruit nonvisual information, such as conceptual emotion knowledge about the expresser and the social situation (Kirouac & Hess, 1999; Niedenthal, 2008). Conceptual knowledge about emotion has been shown to exert effects early in the processing of ambiguous facial expressions, and it can be represented by embodied simulation (Barrett, 2011; Halberstadt et al., 2009; Hess et al., 2009a).

The importance of embodied simulation that accompanies or is generated by facial mimicry was the topic of the current chapter. We cited new and existing evidence that facial mimicry plays a role in supporting the accurate interpretation of facial expression and that eye contact is involved in automatically triggering this process. Finally, we provided evidence that motor and somatosensory cortices play expected roles in shaping responses to facial expressions and that oxytocin can facilitate facial mimicry, especially for infant faces.

REFERENCES

Achaibou, A., Pourtois, G., Schwartz, S., & Vuilleumier, P. (2008). Simultaneous recording of EEG and facial muscle reactions during spontaneous emotional mimicry. *Neuropsychologia, 46*(4), 1104–1113. http://doi.org/10.1016/j.neuropsychologia.2007.10.019

Adelmann, P. K., & Zajonc, R. B. (1989). Facial efference and the experience of emotion. *Annual Review of Psychology, 40*(1), 249–280.

Adolphs, R., Damasio, H., Tranel, D., Cooper, G., & Damasio, A. R. (2000). A role for somatosensory cortices in the visual recognition of emotion as revealed by three-dimensional lesion mapping. *Journal of Neuroscience, 20*(7), 2683–90.

Adolphs, R., Gosselin, F., Buchanan, T. W., Tranel, D., Schyns, P., & Damasio, A. R. (2005). A mechanism for impaired fear recognition after amygdala damage. *Nature, 433*(7021), 68–72.

Adolphs, R., Tranel, D., Damasio, H., & Damasio, A. (1994). Impaired recognition of emotion in facial expressions following bilateral damage to the human amygdala. *Nature, 372*(6507), 669–672.

Alais, D., Newell, F. N., & Mamassian, P. (2010). Multisensory processing in review: From physiology to behaviour. *Seeing and Perceiving, 23*(1), 3–38. http://doi.org/10.1163/187847510X488603

Baron-Cohen, S., Wheelwright, S., Hill, J., Raste, Y., & Plumb, I. (2001). The "Reading the Mind in the Eyes" Test revised version: A study with normal adults, and adults with Asperger syndrome or high-functioning autism. *Journal of Child Psychology and Psychiatry, and Allied Disciplines, 42*(2), 241–251.

Bartz, J. A., Zaki, J., Bolger, N., & Ochsner, K. N. (2011). Social effects of oxytocin in humans: Context and person matter. *Trends in Cognitive Sciences, 15*(7), 301–309. http://doi.org/16/j.tics.2011.05.002

Bavelas, J. B., Black, A., Lemery, C. R., & Mullett, J. (1986). " I show how you feel": Motor mimicry as a communicative act. *Journal of Personality and Social Psychology, 50*(2), 322.

Buck (1980). http://psycnet.apa.org/psycinfo/1981-12788-001

Buck, R. (1984). *The communication of emotion.* Guilford Press.

Carr, L., Iacoboni, M., Dubeau, M. C., Mazziotta, J. C., & Lenzi, G. L. (2003). Neural mechanisms of empathy in humans: A relay from neural systems for imitation to limbic areas. *Proceedings of the National Academy of Sciences, 100*(9), 5497–5502. doi: 10.1016/j.actpsy.2014.11.012

Cavallo, A., Lungu, O., Becchio, C., Ansuini, C., Rustichini, A., & Fadiga, L. (2015). When gaze opens the channel for communication: Integrative role of IFG and MPFC, *NeuroImage*, doi: 10.1016/j.neuroimage.2015.06.025

de Gelder, B., Vroomen, J., Pourtois, G., & Weiskrantz, L. (1999). Non-conscious recognition of affect in the absence of striate cortex. *Neuroreport, 10*(18), 3759–3763.

di Pellegrino, G., Fadiga, L., Fogassi, L., Gallese, V., & Rizzolatti, G. (1992). Understanding motor events: A neurophysiological study. *Experimental Brain Research, 91*(1), 176–180.

Dimberg, U., Andréasson, P., & Thunberg, M. (2011). Emotional empathy and facial reactions to facial expressions. *Journal of Psychophysiology, 25*(1), 26–31. http://doi.org/10.1027/0269-8803/a000029

Domes, G., Heinrichs, M., Michel, A., Berger, C., & Herpertz, S. C. (2007). Oxytocin improves "mind-reading" in humans. *Biological Psychiatry, 61*(6), 731–733. http://doi.org/10.1016/j.biopsych.2006.07.015

Driver, J., & Noesselt, T. (2008). Multisensory interplay reveals crossmodal influences on "sensory-specific" brain regions, neural responses, and judgments. *Neuron, 57*(1), 11–23. doi: 10.1016/j.neuron.2007.12.013

Ekman, Levenson, & Friesen (1983). https://www.ncbi.nlm.nih.gov/pubmed/6612338?dopt=Citation

Finzi, E. & Rosenthal, N. (2014). Treatment of depression with onabotulinumtoxinA: A randomized, double-blind, placebo controlled trial. *Journal Of Psychiatric Research, 52*, 1–6. doi: 10.1016/j.jpsychires.2013.11.006.

Fischer-Shofty, M., Shamay-Tsoory, S. G., Harari, H., & Levkovitz, Y. (2010). The effect of intranasal administration of oxytocin on fear recognition. *Neuropsychologia, 48*(1), 179–184. http://doi.org/10.1016/j.neuropsychologia.2009.09.003

Gazzola, V., & Keysers, C. (2009). The observation and execution of actions share motor and somatosensory voxels in all tested subjects: Single-subject analyses of unsmoothed fMRI data. *Cerebral Cortex, 19*(6), 1239–1255.

Ghazanfar, A. A., & Schroeder, C. E. (2006). Is neocortex essentially multisensory? *Trends in Cognitive Sciences, 10*(6), 278–285. http://doi.org/10.1016/j.tics.2006.04.008

Guastella, A. J., Mitchell, P. B., & Dadds, M. R. (2008). Oxytocin increases gaze to the eye region of human faces. *Biological Psychiatry, 63*(1), 3–5. http://doi.org/10.1016/j.biopsych.2007.06.026

Hermans, E. J., Putman, P., & van Honk, J. (2006). Testosterone administration reduces empathetic behavior: A facial mimicry study. *Psychoneuroendocrinology, 31*(7), 859–866.

Hess, U., & Fischer, A. H. (2013). Emotional mimicry as social regulation. *Personality and Social Psychology Review, 17*, 142–157, doi: 10.1177/1088868312472607

Hopf, H. C., Muller-Forell, W., & Hopf, N. J. (1992). Localization of emotional and volitional facial paresis. *Neurology, 42*(10), 1918–1923. http://doi.org/10.1146/annurev.ps.40.020189.001341

Hurlemann, R., Patin, A., Onur, O. A., Cohen, M. X., Baumgartner, T., Metzler, S., . . . Kendrick, K. M. (2010). Oxytocin enhances amygdala-dependent, socially reinforced learning and emotional empathy in humans. *The Journal of Neuroscience: The Official Journal of the Society for Neuroscience, 30*(14), 4999–5007. http://doi.org/10.1523/JNEUROSCI.5538-09.2010

Kawashima, R., Sugiura, M., Kato, T., Nakamura, A., Hatano, K., Ito, K., . . . Nakamura, K. (1999). The human amygdala plays an important role in gaze monitoring. A PET study. *Brain: A Journal of Neurology, 122*(Pt 4), 779–783.

Kennedy, D. P., & Adolphs, R. (2010). Impaired fixation to eyes following amygdala damage arises from abnormal bottom-up attention. *Neuropsychologia, 48*(12), 3392–3398. http://doi.org/10.1016/j.neuropsychologia.2010.06.025

Kirouac, G., & Hess, U. (1999). Group membership and the decoding of nonverbal behavior. In: *The social context of nonverbal behavior* (pp. 182–210). Cambridge University Press.

Korb, S., Grandjean, D., & Scherer, K. R. (2010). Timing and voluntary suppression of facial mimicry to smiling faces in a Go/NoGo task—An EMG study. *Biological Psychology, 85*(2), 347–349. http://doi.org/10.1016/j.biopsycho.2010.07.012

Korb, S., Malsert, J., Rochas, V., Rihs, T., Rieger, S., Schwab, S., . . . Grandjean, D. (2015). Gender differences in the neural network of facial mimicry of smiles—an rTMS study. *Cortex, 70*, 101–114. doi:10.1016/j.cortex.2015.06.025

Korb, S., Malsert, J., Strathearn, L., Vuilleumier, P., & Niedenthal, P. M. (2016). Sniff and mimic—Intranasal oxytocin increases facial mimicry. DOI: 10.1016/j.yhbeh.2016.06.003.

Korb, S., With, S., Niedenthal, P. M., Kaiser, S., & Grandjean, D. (2014). The perception and mimicry of facial movements predict judgments of smile authenticity. *PLoS ONE, 9*(6), e99194. doi: http://doi.org/10.1371/journal.pone.0099194

Krumhuber, E., Manstead, A. S., Cosker, D., Marshall, D., Rosin, P. L., & Kappas, A. (2007). Facial dynamics as indicators of trustworthiness and cooperative behavior. *Emotion, 7*(4), 730.

Lamme, V. A., Supèr, H., & Spekreijse, H. (1998). Feedforward, horizontal, and feedback processing in the visual cortex. *Current Opinion in Neurobiology, 8*(4), 529–535.

LeDoux, J. E. (2000). Emotion circuits in the brain. *Annual Review of Neuroscience, 23*, 155– 184. http://doi.org/10.1146/annurev.neuro.23.1.155

Likowski, K. U., Mühlberger, A., Gerdes, A. B. M., Wieser, M. J., Pauli, P., & Weyers, P. (2012). Facial mimicry and the mirror neuron system: Simultaneous acquisition of facial electromyography and functional magnetic resonance imaging. *Frontiers in Human Neuroscience, 6*, 214. http://doi.org/10.3389/fnhum.2012.00214

Littlewort, G., Whitehill, J., Wu, T., Fasel, I., Frank, M., Movellan, J., & Bartlett, M. (2011, March). The computer expression recognition toolbox (CERT). In *Automatic Face & Gesture Recognition and Workshops (FG 2011), 2011 IEEE International Conference* (pp. 298–305). IEEE.

Macdonald, K., & Macdonald, T. M. (2010). The peptide that binds: A systematic review of oxytocin and its prosocial effects in humans. *Harvard Review of Psychiatry, 18*(1), 1–21. http://doi.org/10.3109/10673220903523615

Manera, V., Grandi, E., & Colle, L. (2013). Susceptibility to emotional contagion for negative emotions improves detection of smile authenticity. *Frontiers in Human Neuroscience, 7.*

Maringer, M., Krumhuber, E. G., Fischer, A. H., & Niedenthal, P. M. (2011). Beyond smile dynamics: Mimicry and beliefs in judgments of smiles. *Emotion, 11*(1), 181–187. http://doi.org/10.1037/a0022596

Marschner, L., Pannasch, S., Schulz, J., & Graupner S.T. (2015). Social communication with virtual agents: The effects of body and gaze direction on attention and emotional responding in human observers. *International Journal of Psychophysiology, 97*, 85–92. doi: 10.1016/j.ijpsycho.2015.05.007

Marsh, A. A., Yu, H. H., Pine, D. S., & Blair, R. J. R. (2010). Oxytocin improves specific recognition of positive facial expressions. *Psychopharmacology, 209*(3), 225–232. http://doi.org/10.1007/s00213-010-1780-4

McIntosh, D. N. (1996). Facial feedback hypotheses: Evidence, implications, and directions. *Motivation and Emotion, 20*(2), 121–147. http://doi.org/10.1007/BF02253868

McIntosh, D. N. (2006). Spontaneous facial mimicry, liking and emotional contagion. *Polish Psychological Bulletin, 37*(1), 31.

Meyer-Lindenberg, A., Domes, G., Kirsch, P., & Heinrichs, M. (2011). Oxytocin and vasopressin in the human brain: Social neuropeptides for translational medicine. *Nature Reviews Neuroscience, 12*(9), 524–538. http://doi.org/10.1038/nrn3044

Molenberghs, P., Cunnington, R., & Mattingley, J. B. (2012). Brain regions with mirror properties: A meta-analysis of 125 human fMRI studies. *Neuroscience and Biobehavioral Reviews*, *36*(1), 341–349. http://doi.org/10.1016/j.neubiorev.2011.07.004

Morecraft, R. J., Louie, J. L., Herrick, J. L., & Stilwell-Morecraft, K. S. (2001). Cortical innervation of the facial nucleus in the non-human primate: A new interpretation of the effects of stroke and related subtotal brain trauma on the muscles of facial expression. *Brain*, *124*, 176–208.

Morris, J. S., Ohman, A., & Dolan, R. J. (1999). A subcortical pathway to the right amygdala mediating "unseen" fear. *Proceedings of the National Academy of Sciences of the United States of America*, *96*(4), 1680–1685.

Mukamel, R., Ekstrom, A. D., Kaplan, J., Iacoboni, M., & Fried, I. (2010). Single-neuron responses in humans during execution and observation of actions. *Current Biology*, *20*(8), 750–756. http://doi.org/10.1016/j.cub.2010.02.045

Neal, D. T., & Chartrand, T. L. (2011). Embodied emotion perception amplifying and dampening facial feedback modulates emotion perception accuracy. *Social Psychological and Personality Science*, *2*(6), 673–678. doi: 10.1177/1948550611406138

Neufeld, J., Ioannou, C., Korb, S., Schilbach, L., & Chakrabarti, B. (2015). Spontaneous facial mimicry is modulated by joint attention and autistic traits. *Autism Research*. http://doi.org/10.1002/aur.1573

Niedenthal, P. M. (2007). Embodying emotion. *Science*, *316*(5827), 1002–1005.

Niedenthal, P. M. (2008). Emotion concepts. In M. Lewis, J. M. Haviland-Jones & L. F. Barrett (Eds.), *Handbook of emotion*. Guilford Press.

Niedenthal, P. M., & Barsalou, L. W. (2009). Embodiment. In D. Sander and K. S. Scherer (Eds.), *Oxford companion to emotion and the affective sciences* (p. 140). London, UK: Oxford University Press.

Niedenthal, P. M., Brauer, M., Halberstadt, J. B., & Innes-Ker, Å. H. (2001). When did her smile drop? Facial mimicry and the influences of emotional state on the detection of change in emotional expression. *Cognition and Emotion*, *15*(6), 853–864. http://doi.org/10.1080/02699930143000194

Niedenthal, P. M., Halberstadt, J. B., & Setterlund, M. (1997). Being happy and seeing "happy'": Emotional state mediates visual word recognition. *Cognition & Emotion*, *11*(4), 403–432.

Niedenthal, P.M., Korb, S., Wood, A., Rychlowska, M. (2016). Revisiting the Simulation of Smiles Model: The what, when, and why of mimicking smiles. In Ursula Hess & Agneta Fisher (Eds.), *Emotional mimicry in social context* (pp. 44–71). Cambridge: Cambridge University Press

Niedenthal, P. M., Mermillod, M., Maringer, M., & Hess, U. (2010). The simulation of smiles (SIMS) model: Embodied simulation and the meaning of facial expression. *Behavioral and Brain Sciences*, *33*, 417–433. doi: 10.1017/S0140525X10000865

Niedenthal, P. M., Winkielman, P., Mondillon, L., & Vermeulen, N. (2009). Embodiment of emotion concepts. *Journal of Personality and Social Psychology*, *96*(6), 1120.

Penner, L. A. (1971). Interpersonal attraction toward a Black person as a function of value importance. *Personality: An International Journal*, *2*, 175–187.

Pessoa, L., & Adolphs, R. (2010). Emotion processing and the amygdala: From a "low road" to "many roads" of evaluating biological significance. *Nature Reviews. Neuroscience*, *11*(11), 773–783. http://doi.org/10.1038/nrn2920

Pitcher, D., Garrido, L., Walsh, V., & Duchaine, B. C. (2008). Transcranial magnetic stimulation disrupts the perception and embodiment of facial expressions. *Journal of Neuroscience, 28*(36), 8929–8933.

Pourtois, G., Sander, D., Andres, M., Grandjean, D., Reveret, L., Olivier, E., & Vuilleumier, P. (2004). Dissociable roles of the human somatosensory and superior temporal cortices for processing social face signals. *European Journal of Neuroscience, 20*(12), 3507–3515.

Roberson, D., Damjanovic, L., & Pilling, M. (2007). Categorical perception of facial expressions: Evidence for a "category adjustment" model. *Memory & Cognition, 35*(7), 1814–1829. doi:10.3758/bf03193512

Rychlowska, M., Cañadas, E., Wood, A., Krumhuber, E. G., Fischer, A., & Niedenthal, P. M. (2014). Blocking mimicry makes true and false smiles look the same. *PloS ONE, 9*(3), e90876. doi:10.1371/journal.pone.0090876

Rychlowska, M., Zinner, L., Musca, S. C., & Niedenthal, P. M. (2012, October). From the eye to the heart: Eye contact triggers emotion simulation. *Proceedings of the 4th Workshop on Eye Gaze in Intelligent Human Machine Interaction* (p. 5). ACM Digital Library.

Sato, A., & Itakura, S. (2013). Intersubjective action-effect binding: Eye contact modulates acquisition of bidirectional association between our and others' actions. *Cognition, 127*, 383–390. doi: 10.1016/j.cognition.2013.02.010

Schilbach, L., Eickhoff, S. B., Mojzisch, A., & Vogeley, K. (2008). What's in a smile? Neural correlates of facial embodiment during social interaction. *Social Neuroscience, 3*(1), 37– 50.

Schrammel, F., Pannasch, S., Graupner, S.-T., Mojzisch, A., & Velichkovsky, B. M. (2009). Virtual friend or threat? The effects of facial expression and gaze interaction on psychophysiological responses and emotional experience. *Psychophysiology, 46*, 922– 931. http://doi.org/10.1111/j.1469-8986.2009.00831.x

Schulze, L., Lischke, A., Greif, J., Herpertz, S. C., Heinrichs, M., & Domes, G. (2011). Oxytocin increases recognition of masked emotional faces. *Psychoneuroendocrinology, 36*(9), 1378–1382. http://doi.org/10.1016/j.psyneuen.2011.03.011

Smith, M. L., Cottrell, G., Gosselin, F., & Schyns, P. G. (2005) Transmitting and decoding facial expressions of emotions. *Psychological Science, 16*, 184–189. doi: 10.1111/j.0956- 7976.2005.00801.x

Sonnby-Borgstrom, M. (2002). Automatic mimicry reactions as related to differences in emotional empathy. *Scandinavian Journal of Psychology, 43*(5), 433–443.

Soussignan, R. (2002). Duchenne smile, emotional experience, and autonomic reactivity: A test of the facial feedback hypothesis. *Emotion, 2*, 52-74. doi: 10.1037/1528-3542.2.1.52

Soussignan, R., Chadwick, M., Philip, L., Conty, L., Dezecache, G., & Grèzes, J. (2012). Self- relevance appraisal of gaze direction and dynamic facial expressions: Effects on facial electromyographic and autonomic reactions. *Emotion*. doi:10.1037/a0029892

Staines, W. R., Popovich, C., Legon, J. K., & Adams, M. S. (2014). Early modality-specific somatosensory cortical regions are modulated by attended visual stimuli: Interaction of vision, touch and behavioral intent. *Frontiers in Psychology, 5*, 351. http://doi.org/10.3389/fpsyg.2014.00351

van der Gaag, C., Minderaa, R. B., & Keysers, C. (2007). Facial expressions: What the mirror neuron system can and cannot tell us. *Social Neuroscience, 2*(3–4), 179–222.

van der Schalk, J., Fischer, A. H., Doosje, B. J., Wigboldus, D., Hawk, S. T., Hess, U., & Rotteveel, M. (2011). Congruent and incongruent responses to emotional displays of ingroup and outgroup. *Emotion, 11*, 286–298.

Vuilleumier, P., & Pourtois, G. (2007). Distributed and interactive brain mechanisms during emotion face perception: Evidence from functional neuroimaging. *Neuropsychologia, 45*(1), 174–194.

Wang, Y., Newport, R., & Hamilton, A. F. D. C. (2011). Eye contact enhances mimicry of intransitive hand movements. *Biology Letters, 7*(1), 7–10. doi: 10.1098/rsbl.2010.0279

Wang, Y., Newport, R., & Hamilton, A. F. D. C. (2011). Eye contact enhances mimicry of intransitive hand movements. *Biology letters, 7*(1), 7-10. DOI: 10.1098/rsbl.2010.0279

Winkielman, P., Niedenthal, P. M., & Oberman, L. (2008). The embodied emotional mind. In G.R. Semin and E.M. Smith (Eds.) *Embodied grounding: Social, cognitive, affective, and neuroscientific approaches* (pp 263–288). New York, NY: Cambridge University Press.

Wollmer, M. A., de Boer, C., Kalak, N, Beck, J., Gotz, T., Schmidt, T., . . . Kruger, T. H. (2012). Facing depression with botulinum toxin: a randomized controlled trial. *Journal of Psychiatric Research, 46*, 574–581. doi: 10.1016/j.jpsychires.2012.01.027.

Wood, A., Lupyan, G., Sherrin, S., & Niedenthal, P. (2015). Altering sensorimotor feedback disrupts visual perceptual discrimination of facial expressions. *Psychonomic Bulletin and Review.* doi: 10.3758/s13423-015-0974-5.

Wood, A., Rychlowska, M., Korb, S., Niedenthal, P. (2016). Fashioning the face: Sensorimotor simulation contributes to facial expression recognition. *Trends in Cognitive Sciences, 20*, (3), 227–240. doi: 10.1016/j.tics.2015.12.010

Zajonc, R., Adelmann, P., Murphy, S., & Niedenthal, P. (1987). Convergence in the physical appearance of spouses. *Motivation And Emotion, 11*(4), 335–346. doi: 10.1007/bf00992848.

22

Language and Emotion

Hypotheses on the Constructed Nature of Emotion Perception

CAMERON M. DOYLE AND KRISTEN A. LINDQUIST

Throughout much of daily life, humans detect emotional "expressions" in the faces of our loved ones, friends, colleagues, babies, pets—even in certain machines (see Fig. 22.1). Traditionally, the science of emotion assumed that these "expressions" are broadcast on the faces of others for perceivers to automatically and reflexively "recognize." However, growing evidence suggests that facial "expressions" are not merely "recognized" during perception—they are instead *psychologically constructed* when processes in the mind of the perceiver, such as emotion concept knowledge, impact how visual sensations are made meaningful as instances of different emotions (as occurs when the features of both the car and the face in Fig. 22.1 are made meaningful as an instance of happiness). We begin by introducing two different approaches to understanding the perception of emotion on faces: the basic emotion model versus the psychological constructionist model. We then propose three key psychological constructionist hypotheses about facial emotion perception. Our first hypothesis is that on the "experiencer's" end, facial muscle movements do not automatically communicate emotion. Our second hypothesis is that on the "perceiver's" end, conceptual knowledge that is supported by language is used to make meaning of others' facial muscle movements to construct perceptions of emotion. Finally, our third hypothesis is that language enables perceivers to see emotion on faces by reactivating sensorimotor representations of prior

Figure 22.1 Many perceivers make meaning of the features of this car (citizen of the deep, 2009) as an instance of happiness, just as they do with this smiling face (Gendron, Lindquist, & Barrett, unpublished data).

experiences that shape perception of the present sensory array in a top-down manner. We discuss each of these hypotheses in turn and present growing evidence that supports them.

MODELS OF EMOTION PERCEPTION: BASIC EMOTION VERSUS PSYCHOLOGICAL CONSTRUCTIONIST THEORIES

The commonsense view of emotion perception is that facial "expressions" are broadcast on the faces of experiencers for perceivers to automatically and reflexively "recognize." This idea is consistent with the family of basic emotions approaches (Izard, 2009; Levenson, 2003; Panksepp, 2011; Shariff & Tracy, 2011). In the basic emotion view, all cultures share a set of emotion categories (e.g., anger, disgust, fear, happiness, sadness, etc.) that are biologically given responses to social and environmental stimuli that were once "adaptive in our evolutionary past" (Ekman & Cordaro, 2011, p. 368). It was originally assumed that a specific mechanism called a facial affect program "links each primary emotion to a distinctive patterned set of neural impulses to the facial muscles" (Ekman, 1972, p. 216). Today, the idea of facial affect programs is considered a "metaphor" as opposed to a specific biological mechanism (cf. Ekman & Cordaro, 2011). However, it is still largely assumed that emotions are linked to facial expressions in a 1:1 manner such that the face consistently and specifically produces clear and unambiguous signals during the experience of certain emotions (e.g., experiencing anger results in a scowl across almost all instances, barring times that facial expression is regulated). Correspondingly, specific facial muscle movements (e.g., a scowl) are thought to necessarily denote to perceivers that the experiencer is experiencing a specific emotion (e.g., anger) (Ekman & Friesen, 1971; Izard, 1971; Tracy & Matsumoto, 2008).

An alternate approach to understanding the nature of facial emotion is the psychological constructionist family of approaches, which proposes that specific emotions such as anger, disgust, fear, and so on are constructed in the minds of perceivers based on perceptions of general affective facial movements and concept knowledge about emotions (Barrett, 2006; James, 1890/1998; Lindquist & Barrett, 2008; Russell, 2003; Schachter & Singer, 1962). In psychological constructionist views, all cultures share the experience of basic affective feelings that can be described as having some degree of positive versus negative valence and high versus low arousal (Russell, 1980; Russell & Barrett, 1999). Individuals communicate valence and/or arousal to some extent in automatic facial muscle movements, but the specific emotion categories "recognized" on the faces of others are the result of categorization when a perceiver uses his or her knowledge about emotion categories to make meaning of another person's facial muscle movements. It has been long known that people play active roles in constructing perceptions of the world around them based on their motivations, expectations, and category knowledge (Bruner, 1957; for a more recent discussion, see Bar, 2009), and emotion perception is no exception (see Barrett et al., 2011; Hassin et al., 2013; Lindquist & Gendron, 2013; Lindquist, MacCormack, & Shablack, 2015; Lindquist, Satpute, & Gendron, 2015; Nelson & Russell, 2013). The psychological constructionist view predicts that a perceiver sees another person as emotional when he or she makes meaning of facial muscle movements as an instance of emotion using concept knowledge that differs across cultures (Gendron, Roberson, van der Vyver, & Barrett, 2014; Jack et al., 2012) and perhaps even within individuals of the same culture (see Nook et al., 2015, for a discussion).

According to our particular psychological constructionist model, the theory of constructed emotion (TCE) (Barrett, in press), formerly the conceptual act theory (Barrett, 2006), language is integral to emotion perception because it helps individuals acquire, organize, and use the concept knowledge that guides emotion perception (Barrett, Lindquist, & Gendron, 2007; Lindquist & Gendron, 2013; Lindquist, MacCormack, & Shablack, 2015; Lindquist, Satpute, & Gendron, 2015). Of course, not all research hypothesizing a role of language in emotion perception takes the TCE approach (for other reviews on the role of language in emotion perception, see Roberson, Damjanovic, & Kikutani, 2010; Russell, 1991; Widen, 2013). Nor does all research on the constructed nature of emotion perception focus on the role of language (for reviews on how other forms of context construct the perception of emotion on faces, see Barrett et al., 2011; Fernandez-Dols, 1999; Hassin, Aviezer, & Bentin,

2013). The TCE is thus unique in that it offers mechanistic predictions of how emotion concepts supported by words help construct perceptions of emotion. The TCE proposes that language scaffolds emotion concept knowledge because it enables perceivers to group perceptually dissimilar facial muscle movements together as instances of the same emotion category (Lindquist, MacCormack, & Shablack, 2015; see Barrett, Wilson-Mendenhall, & Barsalou, 2015, for a discussion). For example, the word "anger" might cohere together an individual's embodied knowledge about the causes and consequences of the emotion concept *anger*, as well as stored representations of what others' angry facial "expressions" have looked like across different contexts in the past. This knowledge, in turn, allows a person to see a face as angry when encountering strained smiles between colleagues in the boardroom or a person scowling at a puppy with a half-eaten shoe in its mouth. The word "anger" allows an individual to store both representations as instances of the same category and link them to representations of the context, even when the facial muscle movements associated with "anger" share no perceptual similarities (i.e., smiles are visually distinct from scowls). The role of language in emotion perception can be described by three key hypotheses. We introduce these hypotheses in turn and discuss evidence in support of each.

HYPOTHESES ON THE CONSTRUCTED NATURE OF EMOTION PERCEPTION

Hypothesis 1: The Face Automatically Communicates Affect and Moves During Adaptive Behaviors but Does Not Automatically and Specifically Express Discrete Emotions

To understand emotion perception, it is first necessary to know what the face does and does not do during experiences of emotion. We hypothesize that although the face moves in emotion (as well as in other mental phenomena, e.g., concentration), facial muscle movements do not correspond to specific discrete emotional experiences in a 1:1 manner. What is being perceived during emotion perception is thus not likely to be a clear and universal signal for emotion.

Evidence for this hypothesis comes from objective measurements of facial muscle movements such as facial electromyographical readings (facial EMG). There have been few studies using facial EMG to compare patterns of facial muscle movements across multiple specific discrete emotion categories, but a set of older meta-analyses (Cacioppo & Gardner, 1999; Cacioppo et al., 2000) failed to reveal configurations of specific facial muscle movements that correspond to specific emotional experiences. Instead, these findings suggest that the face at most expresses the valence (pleasantness vs. unpleasantness) of an experiencer's affective state (Tassinary, Cacioppo, & Vanman, 2007). Of course, it remains a possibility that EMG is methodologically limited in its ability to detect discrete emotion from facial actions. The face contains a considerable number of muscles (Tassinary et al., 2007), so activity from a given muscle might spread to others, impeding accurate detection of discrete emotion from electrical activity (cf. van Boxtel, 2010). In contrast to the findings of EMG, experts trained in facial emotion recognition can reliably code facial actions (e.g., FACS; Ekman & Friesen, 1978) that are hypothesized to be associated with specific discrete emotion categories; yet these findings cannot rule out the possibility that the human observer is actually adding something to the perception (i.e., using context or emotion concepts to disambiguate the meaning of otherwise ambiguous facial muscle configurations).

A second source of evidence for this hypothesis stems from observational studies of emotional facial expressions. Based on these studies, it is not clear that facial muscle movements occur in a consistent and specific pattern in relation to a specific emotion experience. Studies tend to find variability in which facial muscle configurations are present on a person's face during emotional experiences, and variability in whether the predicted facial muscle movements occur at all (see Lindquist & Gendron, 2013; Reisenzein, Studtmann, & Horstmann, 2013; Russell, Bachorowski, & Fernández-Dols, 2003, for discussions). A review of naturalistic studies of emotion and facial expressions revealed only weak correlations between emotion experience and the predicted corresponding facial muscle movements (Fernández-Dols & Crivelli, 2013). In some cases, the experience of specific emotions corresponds to facial muscle movements that are completely inconsistent with the stereotype for that emotion, such as frowns on the faces of Olympic gold medalists (Fernández-Dols & Ruiz-Belda, 1995) and grimaces during other sports wins (Aviezer, Trope, & Todorov, 2012). Naturalistic, as opposed to posed, facial expressions seem not to correspond to the predicted emotional facial configuration (Naab & Russell, 2007).

It is possible that we assume that the face consistently and specifically produces configurations associated with certain emotions due to stereotypes about the configurations that are associated with certain contexts and emotions. It is often claimed that facial muscle movements are adaptations that took on a communicative function (Allport, 1924; Ekman, 1972; Sharif & Tracy, 2011; Susskind et al., 2008), and so we often assume that emotional experiences correspond to specific adaptive facial muscle movements. Of course, it is clear that people move their faces in ways that may be adaptive—we open our mouths to scream, we scrunch up our eyes to cry, we open our mouths to gasp or growl, and we blink when objects approach our eyes. For instance, it has been shown that a by-product of widening the eyes during high attentional demand is an increase the receptive visual field (Susskind et al., 2008). Similarly, nasal passages may close to protect a person from inhaling noxious fumes (Susskind et al., 2008). However, it is far from clear that these facial muscle movements are linked to the experience of discrete emotions in a consistent and specific manner (e.g., the eyes do not always widen in fear and the nose does not always scrunch up in disgust). Rather, it may be that humans have constructed concepts about the stereotypical facial expressions that correspond to specific emotions *because* of these adaptive facial muscle movements. Emotion concepts may thus include facial muscle movements that are a by-product of other processes such as attention (widening eyes) or pathogen aversion (closing nasal passages), and those facial muscle movements may have become stereotypical of certain emotion categories, even if they occur in a small number of emotional instances, both within a given category or between categories. For instance, because we associate experiences of fear with startle and increased vigilance in Western cultures, our conceptual script for the category *fear* involves widened eyes and a screaming mouth. Of course, not all instances of *fear* involve wide eyes because not all instances of *fear* involve startle. By contrast, our concept for the category *sadness* involves scrunched-up eyes and a pouting, frowning mouth—two facial muscle movements that result from crying. However, crying occurs across multiple types of emotional experiences (joy, fear, awe, gratitude, etc.) and is not unique to sadness. The relevant ethnographic data have not been collected to demonstrate whether individuals consistently and specifically make the types of facial muscle movements associated with our English-language emotion stereotypes in daily life, but existing evidence suggests that consistency and specificity are not likely to be found. For instance, in the case of the *fear* stereotype, individuals report seeing facial expressions with widened eyes and mouths agape (stereotypical fearful expressions) at very low base rates in daily life (Whalen et al., 2001). More generally, when raters are asked to judge the meaning of naturalistic images of spontaneous, unposed facial muscle movements (which do not typically include stereotypical facial muscle movements), their "accuracy" at guessing the presumed emotion (see Ekman & Friesen, 1975) is quite low (Aviezer et al., 2012, 2015; Fernández-Dols, Carrera, & Crivelli, 2011; Motley & Camden, 1988; Naab & Russell, 2007). Moreover, the people most likely to associate stereotypical facial muscle movements with culture-specific emotion categories are the individuals who have received the most formal education (Russell, 1994). These findings suggest that the facial muscle movements associated with English emotion categories are learned via formal schooling rather than mere experience with other humans. Indeed, we mime exaggerated versions of these facial muscle movements when teaching our children about emotions, culture-specific stereotypes of facial expressions appear as cartoons in children's books (Tsai et al., 2007), are used as stimuli in studies at universities, and appear in textbooks throughout formal social science education. Stereotypes of facial muscle movements are now even displayed in the emoticons used in online communication.

A novel prediction of the constructionist view is thus that our English-language conceptual stereotypes of facial muscle movements may have been formed around facial muscle movements that we have linked conceptually to certain discrete emotions (even if they are not actually prototypical of those emotional experiences). In this view, adaptive facial muscle movements did not become linked to certain emotional feelings via evolution (e.g., Ekman & Cordaro, 2011; Sharif & Tracy, 2011) but became linked to those feelings via the powers of the human ability to create concepts (also a great evolutionary feat). A separate question, then, is why do humans "see" discrete emotions on others' faces if facial muscle movements are ambiguous and unreliably related to specific discrete emotions? This brings us to the next novel hypothesis of a psychological constructionist approach: that the emotion concepts people know as a result of their language and culture shape how they see the facial muscle movements of others as instances of specific emotions.

Hypothesis 2: Conceptual Knowledge That Is Supported by Language Is Used to Categorize Facial Muscle Movements Into Perceptions of Discrete Emotion

Our second hypothesis is that perceptions of specific emotions—for instance, seeing sadness on another person's face—are constructed in the minds of perceivers when linguistic concept knowledge about emotion categories is used to make meaning of facial muscle movements.

Concept knowledge about emotion refers to what someone "knows" about emotion categories. According to the TCE, such knowledge is stored as representations of prior experiences that become partially reactivated when used to make meaning of sensations in the present environment (Barrett & Lindquist, 2008; Wilson-Mendenhall et al., 2011). In the case of emotion concept knowledge, sensorimotor representations can include modality-specific information about the facial muscle movements, vocal sounds, and bodily actions associated with given emotion categories. Individuals might also possess conceptual knowledge related to who tends to experience and express which types of emotions (of course, this conceptual knowledge may be accurate or inaccurate, in the case of social stereotypes; see Hess, this volume). Critically, conceptual knowledge is always situated and is associated with the types of situational contexts that are related to certain sensorimotor representations (see Aviezer, this volume, for evidence of how knowledge of the context shapes emotion perception). It is possible to have multiple sensorimotor representations for a single emotion category, even if those perceptual representations share few perceptual similarities (cf. Lindquist, MacCormack, & Shablack, 2015). For instance, a person might possess a perceptual representation of fearful facial expressions on a roller coaster versus on a podium versus in a dark alley. When perceiving the world around them, perceivers are always automatically and nonconsciously relying on their conceptual knowledge to make predictions of the meaning of the present sensory array (Bar, 2009; Barrett & Simmons, 2015; Friston, 2012). In the case of emotion perception, perceivers are relying on their concept knowledge of emotion to make predictions about the meaning of experiencers' facial muscle movements as instances of specific emotion categories (e.g., a sensorimotor representation of a smile when someone was offended at the office).

Concepts shape emotion perception through an automatic and effortless process; the role of emotion categories on emotion perception is thus likely to go unnoticed in most contexts. In fact, the covert role of emotion concepts may have contributed to the appearance of strong universality in emotion perception because many studies that find evidence for universal emotion perception actually prime emotion concepts by including emotion word labels and/ or vignettes about emotional scenarios in their experiments (e.g., Ekman & Friesen, 1971). Evidence suggests that this conceptual influence in turn constrains how participants make meaning of the posed affective facial muscle movements they are viewing (see Lindquist & Gendron, 2013, for a discussion).

Indeed, recent studies formally investigated the hypothesis that including English-language concepts in studies produces evidence more consistent with so-called universal emotion perception (see Gendron, Roberson, & Barrett, 2015, for a discussion). The researchers asked a group of Himba participants from a remote village in Namibia, Africa, to sort posed facial emotion stimuli into piles anchored by emotion word labels that were translated from English (i.e., anger, disgust, fear, happiness, sadness, neutral). By contrast, a second group of Himba participants was asked to freely sort the faces, which required participants to rely on their own emotion category knowledge to guide sorting (Gendron et al., 2014). Himba participants in the word-anchored condition were more likely than Himba participants in the free-sorting condition to adhere to the so-called universal (Ekman & Friesen, 1971) pattern of emotion perception.

Perhaps most notably, in the absence of emotion words, there were even clearer cultural differences in emotion perception (Gendron et al., 2014). In particular, Himba participants consistently made piles consisting of multiple different emotion categories (e.g., included happy, neutral, disgusted, angry, and sad faces in one pile; included disgusted, angry, and sad faces in another pile). One interpretation of these findings is that Himba participants performed differently than Western participants because they possess different concept knowledge about which emotion categories are depicted on people's faces or which facial muscle movements are associated with which categories. Although this hypothesis has yet to be addressed with Himba participants, data from a separate study are suggestive.

Chinese and English speakers were presented with videos of computerized facial muscle movements that changed over time in random patterns. Participants were asked to indicate when the facial muscle movements were consistent with their representation of the categories *happy, surprised, fearful, disgusted, angry,* or *sad* (Jack et al., 2012). The authors then determined which facial muscle movements were on average most associated with each emotion category across cultures using a reverse correlation technique that identified the facial actions that were most associated with the emotion words participants chose across trials. Whereas English speakers represented each of the six so-called universal categories with a distinct configuration of facial muscle movements, Chinese speakers did not, showing considerable overlap in the facial muscle movements they considered to be indicative of *surprise, fear, disgust,* and *anger.* There was less agreement among Chinese participants about which facial muscle movements corresponded to each category, perhaps because the response options included in the task were translations of English emotion words, rather than the emotion category words used most frequently by Chinese speakers. Presumably, English-speaking participants would perform more poorly if the categories in the task were translations of the emotion categories deemed most important in Chinese culture.

Of course, concepts and language are linked but not necessarily identical constructs (see Lupyan, 2012, for a discussion). The TCE uniquely predicts that language shapes emotion perception because language helps individuals initially acquire and then use conceptual knowledge about emotion during online perceptions (for reviews, see Lindquist, MacCormack, & Shablack, 2015; Lindquist, Satpute, & Gendron, 2015; Lindquist, Gendron, & Satpute, 2016). We suggest that language is especially important to the domain of emotion because the phonological form of a word helps perceivers acquire concept knowledge about categories (Lupyan, Rakison, & McClelland, 2007) and, in particular, abstract categories that do not have strong statistical regularities within the visual, auditory, and interoceptive modalities (Barsalou, 1999). Because instances of facial muscle movements may share few perceptual regularities (e.g., people can smile, frown, scowl, and have a slack face during experiences of anger), emotion categories are particularly likely to be abstract categories (cf. Lindquist, MacCormack, & Shablack, 2015).

We predict that over time, using emotion words to label facial actions as depicting discrete emotions helps a person acquire and expand upon his or her emotion concept knowledge. For instance, it is thought that language helps children acquire the emotion categories specific to their culture over the early years of life. Before children learn from adults to reliably use emotion labels such as "anger," "fear," "sadness," and "disgust," they can only differentiate between different facial muscle movements based on valence (i.e., whether faces depict a positive or negative emotion; Widen & Russell, 2008; for a review, see Roberson et al., 2010). It is presently unknown to what extent language is instrumental in the acquisition of emotion concept knowledge, or to what extent directed instruction from adults is important in this process, but there are several reasons to suspect that words learned from adults help children develop the emotion concept knowledge that is important for perceiving emotions on faces. First, there is evidence that children whose parents speak to them more about emotions have greater understanding of emotion concepts (see Halberstadt & Lozada, 2011, for a discussion). Second, there is evidence that language guides acquisition of novel categories in adults (Lupyan et al., 2007) and induces "categorical perception" (Goldstone, 1994), the ability to perceive categories within a continuous dimension of sensory information.

The classic evidence for categorical perception is participants' superior ability to distinguish between pairs of stimuli that cross a perceptual category boundary (e.g., see an angry face as different from a fearful face) and inferior ability to distinguish between pairs of stimuli that do not cross a perceptual category boundary (e.g., see one fearful face as different from another fearful face) (Fugate, 2013; Harnad, 1987). Experimental evidence suggests that language helps adults achieve categorical perception within arrays of affective facial movements because linguistic categories help participants impose categories on perceptual stimuli (Fugate, Gouzoules, & Barrett, 2010). In the first phase of an experiment, adults simply viewed pictures of unfamiliar chimpanzee facial actions (e.g., a "bared teeth" or "scream" face) or viewed the faces while learning to associate them with nonsense words. Participants were later shown two images taken from a continuous morphed array of two facial expressions (e.g., an image of a face containing a percentage of both the bared teeth expression and scream expression) and were asked to indicate whether two faces from random points throughout the array were similar to one another or different. On some trials, participants compared faces that did not cross the learned category boundary (e.g., they compared an 86% bared teeth, 14% scream expression with a 71% bared teeth, 29% scream expression), whereas on others, they compared faces that *did* cross the learned category boundary (e.g., compared a 43% bared teeth, 57% scream expression with a

29% bared teeth, 71% scream expression). If participants demonstrated categorical perception, they would see the first set of faces as similar but the second set of faces as different. Yet, only participants who learned to associate the faces with words in the first phase of the experiment demonstrated such categorical perception. Participants who did not learn to associate faces with labels did not perceive a categorical distinction between the faces.

The TCE suggests that once conceptual knowledge is acquired via language, it helps a perceiver to make meaning of novel visual sensations. The human conceptual and linguistic systems become linked over the course of adulthood, such that the activation of concepts activates language and vice versa (Lupyan, 2012). Thus, when a perceiver is accessing concept knowledge to make meaning of visual sensations, the phonological form of the word may become active and cue the perceiver to use specific conceptual representations to make meaning of another person's facial muscle movements. Consistent with this argument, much research has amassed to suggest that access to linguistic concepts is necessary during online perception of emotion in faces.

For instance, temporarily impairing participants' access to the meaning of emotion words impairs categorical perception (see Roberson et al., 2010). A classic study demonstrated that verbal interference impaired participants' advantage at detecting differences between faces that crossed a category boundary (Roberson & Davidoff, 2000). On a given trial, participants saw a target face followed by interference that was either visual (i.e., participants looked at pictures of facial features) or verbal (i.e., participants repeated adjectives describing facial expressions aloud), or they received no interference. Participants then saw two faces, one of which matched the target face. Critically, the pairs of faces either belonged to the same or different emotion categories, and participants were asked to indicate which face matched the target face they initially saw. Verbal interference uniquely hindered participants' advantage at identifying the target face in pairs of faces that ostensibly conveyed different emotions (i.e., they crossed a category boundary; Roberson & Davidoff, 2000). This finding suggests that perceivers regularly access concept knowledge that is supported by language when making meaning of facial muscle movements as instances of emotion.

Semantic satiation of emotion words also impairs emotion perception. Semantic satiation renders concepts temporarily inaccessible through the repetition of a relevant word (Jakobovits, 1962). When participants are asked to repeat an emotion word (e.g., "anger") 30 times and are subsequently presented with a relevant emotional face (e.g., a scowl), they are temporarily unable to categorize the face as depicting that particular emotion, even when asked to merely judge whether two faces (e.g., two scowls) match in emotional content, a task that does not explicitly require access to emotion words (Lindquist, Barrett, Bliss-Moreau, & Russell, 2006). Semantic satiation has also been shown to disrupt simple perceptual priming of emotional faces, a process that should operate without access to language (Gendron, Lindquist, Barsalou, & Barrett, 2012). These studies demonstrate that access to conceptual information that is supported by language is necessary for perceivers to make meaning of the information provided by affective facial muscle movements. Consistent with these findings, patients with semantic dementia, who have permanently impaired access to the meaning of concepts due to a neurodegenerative disease, perceive emotional faces in terms of valence rather than discrete emotion categories (Lindquist et al., 2014).

Although growing evidence is consistent with the role of concept knowledge and language in emotion perception, questions remain about the specific mechanisms by which language influences the perception of visual sensations during emotion perception. This brings us to our final hypothesis, that the modality-specific concept knowledge supported by language might interact with external visual sensations from the present sensory array to allow perceivers to "see" emotions on others' faces.

Hypothesis 3: Language Allows Perceivers to See Emotion on Faces by Reactivating Sensorimotor Representations of Prior Experiences

Our third hypothesis is that language allows a person to access the concept knowledge associated with certain emotion categories during visual perception, which may in turn shape how visual sensations are attended to and encoded in the first place. We refer to the process by which reenactments of prior experience shape how meaning is made of the present sensory array as the "sensory inference hypothesis" (cf. Barrett et al., 2007).

The sensory inference hypothesis suggests that the role of language runs "deeper" in emotion perception than might be assumed by commonsense, because a concept word (e.g., "anger") reactivates the sensorimotor representations that became associated with that concept across prior experiences. Sensorimotor representations of prior experiences then serve as a source of prediction about the meaning of incoming visual information from faces. Evidence for the sensory inference hypothesis comes from studies of nonemotional visual perception. One study found that expectations created by the presence of a word facilitate the detection of objects in the visual field that would otherwise not be selected for conscious awareness (Lupyan & Ward, 2013). Participants were cued with either a verbal label (e.g., the word "pumpkin") or auditory noise, after which they were either shown an object (e.g., a pumpkin or a chair) masked by continuous flash suppression (CFS), or the mask in the absence of an object. CFS is a technique in which a static stimulus is presented to one eye, while a series of rapidly changing stimuli are simultaneously presented to the other eye. Under normal circumstances, the dynamic stimuli render the static stimulus "invisible" by suppressing the conscious representation of those visual sensations (Tsuchiya & Koch, 2005). However, despite the presence of CFS, participants were more likely to actually detect the stimulus on trials where participants heard a cue (e.g., "pumpkin") that matched the suppressed stimulus (e.g., an image of a pumpkin), compared to trials in which there was no cue, or when the cue did not match the stimulus (Lupyan & Ward, 2013). Language likely brings online concept knowledge about object categories, thereby making information about those categories more salient during visual perception and helping the brain select category-consistent visual sensations for conscious experience. In some cases, the brain might even be "filling in" sensations that were not present, as is observed in studies where participants are asked to detect emotional facial "expressions" in random visual noise (Gosselin & Schyns, 2003). Despite there being no emotional signal present in visual noise, participants use their conceptual knowledge to "fill in" the presence of specific emotional faces, and a reverse correlation technique reveals patterns resembling stereotypical facial movements (e.g., a smiling face across trials in which participants expected to see a facial expression of "happiness").

Similarly, emotion words may serve as a sort of prime to help individuals fill in missing details about the information presented on a face. For instance, Halberstadt and Niedenthal (2001) demonstrated that labeling faces with words actually shifted participants' perceptions of those faces toward more stereotypical portrayals of the emotion category. Specifically, labeling morphed happiness-anger faces as depicting *anger* led participants to remember the faces as more intensely angry (e.g., closer to anger on the happiness-anger continuum). This may be because emotion words activate representations of the most stereotypical facial muscle movements that are associated with a given emotion category (Roberson, Damjanovic, & Pilling, 2007). Consistent with this hypothesis, individuals were more sensitive to quickly pair a face with an emotion word compared to a same-category face in a sequential priming paradigm (Nook et al., 2015). Words likely helped individuals narrow in on category-prototypical features to guide their judgments, whereas other faces did not cue category-prototypical features as readily. More extremely, the presence of emotion words in studies can even lead to the false recognition of emotion on faces (e.g., Fernández-Dols, Carrera, Barchard, & Gacitua, 2008; see Lindquist & Gendron, 2013), perhaps because words cause participants to attend to facial features consistent with the named category and ignore other facial features.

CONCLUSIONS

In sum, this chapter outlines growing evidence that faces do not unambiguously signal specific emotions and that conceptual knowledge supported by language is necessary for perceiving categories of emotions (*anger, disgust, fear*, etc.) on others' faces. We also discussed a new hypothesis for the mechanism by which language influences emotion perception. In particular, we considered the sensory inference hypothesis, in which language reactivates sensorimotor representations of emotion from prior experiences, changing how affect is seen on the faces of others and enabling the perceiver to "fill in" visual details with information from his or her conceptual knowledge about emotion categories.

What is clear from these findings is that language has a much stronger role in emotion perception than predicted by commonsense or by other models of emotion. However, many questions still remain about how words interact with concepts and visual sensations to influence perception of emotions on faces. For instance, it is still unclear to what extent concepts can override information present on the face to shape perception, how the context might prime concept knowledge to shape perceptions of emotion, or how the activation of different concepts might compete to shape perception. We look forward to continued research examining the mechanisms by which language helps construct the perception of facial emotion in others.

REFERENCES

Allport, F. H. (1924). *Social psychology*. New York, NY: Houghton Mifflin.

Aviezer, H., Messinger, D. S., Zangvil, S., Mattson, W., Gangi, D. N., & Todorov, A. (2015). Thrill of victory or agony of defeat? Perceivers fail to utilize information in facial movements. *Emotion*, 1–7.

Aviezer, H., Trope, Y., & Todorov, A. (2012). Body cues, not facial expressions, discriminate between intense positive and negative emotions. *Science, 338*, 1225–1229.

Bar, M. (2009). The proactive brain: Memory for predictions. *Philosophical Transactions of the Royal Society B, 364*, 1235–1243.

Barrett, L. F. (2006). Solving the emotion paradox: Categorization and the experience of emotion. *Personality and Social Psychology Review, 10*, 20–46.

Barrett, L. F. (in press). The theory of constructed emotion: An active inference account of interoception and categorization. *Social Cognitive and Affective Neuroscience*.

Barrett, L. F., & Lindquist, K. A. (2008). The embodiment of emotion. In G. R. Semin & E. R. Smith (Eds.), *Embodied grounding: Social, cognitive, affective, and neuroscientific approaches*. New York, NY: Cambridge University Press.

Barrett, L. F., Lindquist, K. A., & Gendron, M. (2007). Language as context for the perception of emotion. *Trends in Cognitive Sciences, 11*, 327–332.

Barrett, L. F., Mesquita, B., & Gendron, M. (2011). Context in emotion perception. *Current Directions in Psychological Science, 20*, 286–290.

Barrett, L. F., & Simmons, W. K. (2015). Interoceptive predictions in the brain. *Nature Reviews Neuroscience*, 16, 1–11.

Barrett, L. F., Wilson-Mendenhall, C. D., & Barsalou, L. W. (2015). The conceptual act theory: A road map. In L. F. Barrett and J. A. Russell (Eds.), *The psychological construction of emotion* (pp. 83–110). New York, NY: Guilford.

Barsalou, L. W. (1999). Perceptual symbol systems. *Behavioral and Brain Sciences, 22*, 577–609.

Bruner, J. S. (1957). On perceptual readiness. *Psychological Review, 64*, 123–152.

Cacioppo, J. T., Berntson, G. G., Larsen, J. T., Poehlmann, K. M., & Ito, T. A. (2000). The psychophysiology of emotion. In R. Lewis & J. M. Haviland-Jones (Eds.), *The handbook of emotion* (2nd ed., pp. 173–191). New York, NY: Guilford.

Cacioppo, J. T., & Gardner, W. L. (1999). Emotion. *Annual Review of Psychology, 50*, 191–214.

Citizenofthedeep (artist). (2009), Mazda MX-5 NC Facelift at Chicago Auto Show (2009) [digital image]. Distributed under a CC-BY 2.0 license. Retrieved from Wikimedia Commons website: https://commons.wikimedia.org/wiki/File:Mazda_MX-5_NC_FL_-_Chicago_Auto_Show.jpg

Ekman, P. (1972). Universals and cultural differences in facial expressions of emotion. In J. Cole (Ed.), *Nebraska Symposium on Motivation* (Vol. 19, pp. 207–283). Lincoln, NE: University of Nebraska Press.

Ekman P., & Cordaro D. (2011). What is meant by calling emotions basic. *Emotion Review, 3*, 364–370.

Ekman, P., & Friesen, W. V. (1971). Constants across cultures in the face and emotion. *Journal of Personality and Social Psychology, 17*, 124–129.

Ekman, P., & Friesen, W. V. (1975). *Unmasking the face*. Englewood Cliffs, NJ: Prentice Hall.

Ekman, P., & Friesen, W. V. (1978). *Facial Action Coding System: A technique for the measurement of facial movement*. Palo Alto, CA: Consulting Psychologists Press.

Fernández-Dols, J. M. (1999). Facial expression and emotion: A situational view. In P. Philippot, R. S. Feldman, & E. J. Coats. (Eds.) *The social context of nonverbal behavior* (pp. 242–261). Cambridge, UK: Cambridge University Press.

Fernández-Dols, J. M., Carrera, P., & Crivelli, C. (2011). Facial behavior while experiencing sexual excitement. *Journal of Nonverbal Behavior, 35*, 63–71.

Fernández-Dols, J. M., Carrera, P., Barchard, K. A., & Gacitua, M. (2008). False recognition of facial expressions of emotion: Cause and implications. *Emotion*, 8, 530–539.

Fernández-Dols, J. M., & Crivelli, C. (2013). Emotion and expression: Naturalistic studies. *Emotion Review, 5*(1), 24–29.

Fernández-Dols, J. M., & Ruiz-Belda, M A. (1995). Are smiles a sign of happiness? Gold medal winners at the Olympic Games. *Journal of Personality and Social Psychology, 69*, 1113–1119.

Friston, K. (2012). Embodied inference and spatial cognition. *Cognitive Processing, 13*, S171-S177.

Fugate, J. M. B. (2013). Categorical perception for emotional faces. *Emotion Review, 5*, 84–89.

Fugate, J. M. B., Gouzoules, H., & Barrett, L. F. (2010). Reading chimpanzee faces: Evidence for the role of verbal labels in categorical perception of emotion. *Emotion, 10*, 544–554.

Gendron, M., Lindquist, K. A., & Barrett, L. F. (unpublished data). Ratings of IASLab facial expression stimuli. http://www.affective-science.org/

Gendron, M., Lindquist, K. A., Barsalou, L. W., & Barrett, L. F. (2012). Emotion words shape emotion percepts. *Emotion, 12*, 314–325.

Gendron, M., Roberson, D., & Barrett, L. F. (2015). Cultural variation in emotion perception is real: A response to Sauter et al. *Psychological Science, 26*, 357–359.

Gendron, M., Roberson, D., van der Vyver, J. M., & Barrett, L. F. (2014). Perceptions of emotion from facial expressions are not culturally universal: Evidence from a remote culture. *Emotion, 14*, 251–262.

Goldstone, R. (1994). Influences of categorization on perceptual discrimination. *Journal of Experimental Psychology: General, 123*, 178–200.

Gosselin, F., & Schyns, P. G. (2003). Superstitious perceptions reveal properties of internal representations. *Psychological Science, 14*, 505–509.

Halberstadt, A. G., & Lozada, F. T. (2011). Emotional development in infancy through the lens of culture. *Emotion Review, 3*, 158–168.

Halberstadt, J., & Niedenthal, P. M. (2001). Effects of emotion concepts on perceptual memory for emotional expressions. *Journal of Personality and Social Psychology, 81*, 587–598.

Harnad, S. (1987). Psychophysical and cognitive aspects of categorical perception: A critical overview. In S. Harnad (Ed.), *Categorical perception: The groundwork of cognition* (pp. 1–28). Cambridge, UK: Cambridge University Press.

Hassin, R. R., Aviezer, H., & Bentin, S. (2013). Inherently ambiguous: Facial expressions of emotions, in context. *Emotion Review, 5*, 60–65.

Izard, C. (1971). The face of emotion. New York, NY: Appleton-CenturyCrofts.

Izard, C. E. (2009). Emotion theory and research: Highlights, unanswered questions, and emerging issues. *Annual Review of Psychology, 60*, 1–25.

Jack, R. E., Garrod, O. G. B., Yu, H., Caldara, R., & Schyns, P. G. (2012). Facial expressions of emotion are not culturally universal. *Proceedings of the National Academy of Sciences of the United States of America, 109*(19), 7241–7244.

Jakobovits, L. A. (1962). *Effects of repeated stimulation on cognitive aspects of behavior: Some experiments on the phenomenon of semantic satiation* (Order No. 0261356). Available from ProQuest Dissertations & Theses Full Text. (302130233).

James, W. (1998) *The principles of psychology.* Bristol, UK: Thoemmes Press. (Original work published 1890).

Levenson, R. W. (2003). Autonomic specifity and emotion. In R. J. Davidson, K. R. Scherer, & H. H. Goldsmith (Eds.), *Handbook of affective sciences* (pp. 212–224). New York, NY: Oxford University Press.

Lindquist, K. A., & Barrett, L. F (2008). Constructing emotion: The experience of fear as a conceptual act. *Psychological Science, 19*, 898–903.

Lindquist, K. A., Barrett, L. F., Bliss-Moreau, E., & Russell, J. A. (2006). Language and the perception of emotion. *Emotion, 6*, 125–138.

Lindquist, K. A., & Gendron, M. (2013). What's in a word? Language constructs emotion perception. *Emotion Review, 5*, 66–71.

Lindquist, K. A., Gendron, M., Barrett, L. F., & Dickerson, B C. (2014). Emotion perception, but not affect perception, is impaired with semantic memory loss. *Emotion, 14*, 375–387.

Lindquist, K. A., MacCormack, J. K., & Shablack, H. (2015). The role of language in emotion: Predictions from psychological constructionism. *Frontiers in Language: Special Issue.*

Lindquist, K. A., Satpute, A. B., & Gendron, M. (2015). Does language do more than communicate emotion? *Current Directions in Psychological Science, 24*, 99–108.

Lindquist, K. A., Gendron, M., & Satpute, A. B. (2016). Language and emotion: Putting words into feelings and feelings into words. In L.F. Barrett, M. Lewis, & J. M. Haviland-Jones (Eds.), *Handbook of emotions* (4th ed.). New York, NY: Guilford.

Lupyan, G. (2012). Linguistically modulated perception and cognition: The label-feedback hypothesis. *Frontiers in Cognition, 3*, 1–13.

Lupyan, G., Rakison, D. H., & McClelland, J. L. (2007). Langugae is not just for talking: Labels facilitate learning of novel categories. *Psychological Science, 18*, 1077–1083.

Lupyan, G., & Ward, E. J. (2013). Language can boost otherwise unseen objects into visual awareness. *Proceedings of the National Academy of Sciences, 110*, 1419–1420.

Motley, M. T., & Camden, C. T. (1988). Facial expression of emotion: A comparison of posed expressions versus spontaneous expressions in an interpersonal communication setting. *Western Journal of Speech Communication, 52*, 1–22.

Naab, P. J., & Russell, J. A. (2007). Judgments of emotion from spontaneous facial expressions of New Guineans. *Emotion, 7*, 736–744.

Nelson, N., & Russell, J. A. (2013). Universality revisited. *Emotion Review, 5*, 8–15.

Nook, E. C., Lindquist, K. A., & Zaki, J. (2015). A new look at emotion perception. Concepts speed and shape facial emotion recognition. *Emotion, 15*, 569–578.

Panksepp, J. (2011). The basic emotional circuits of mammalian brains: Do animals have affective lives? *Neuroscience and Biobehavioral Reviews, 35*, 1791–1804.

Reisenzein, R., Studtmann, M., & Horstmann, G. (2013). Coherence between emotion and facial expression: Evidence from laboratory experiments. *Emotion Review, 5*, 16–23.

Roberson, D., Damjanovic, L., & Kikutani, M. (2010). Show and tell: The role of language in categorizing facial expression of emotion. *Emotion Review, 2*, 255–260.

Roberson, D., Damjanovic, L., & Pilling, M. (2007). Categorical perception of facial expressions: Evidence for a "category adjustment" model. *Memory & Cognition, 35*, 1814–1829.

Roberson, D., & Davidoff, J. (2000). The categorical perception of colors and facial expressions: The effect of verbal interference. *Memory & Cognition, 28*, 977–986.

Russell, J. A. (1980). A circumplex model of affect. *Journal of Personality and Social Psychology, 39*, 1161–1178.

Russell, J. A. (1991). In defense of a prototype approach to emotion concepts. *Journal of Personality and Social Psychology, 60*, 37–47.

Russell, J. A. (1994). Is there universal recognition of emotion from facial expression? A review of the cross-cultural studies. *Psychological Bulletin, 115*, 102–141.

Russell, J. A. (2003). Core affect and the psychological construction of emotion. *Psychological Review, 110*, 145–172.

Russell, J. A., Bachorowski, J. A., & Fernández-Dols, J. M. (2003). Facial and vocal expressions of emotion. *Annual Review of Psychology, 54*, 329–349.

Russell, J. A., & Barrett, L. F. (1999). Core affect, prototypical emotional episodes, and other things called emotion: Dissecting the elephant. *Journal of Personality and Social Psychology, 76*, 805–819.

Schachter, S., & Singer, J. E. (1962). Cognitive, social, and physiological determinants of an emotional state. *Psychological Review, 69*, 379–399.

Shariff, A. F., & Tracy, J. L. (2011). What are emotion expressions for? *Current Directions in Psychological Science, 20*, 395–399.

Susskind, J. M., Lee, D. H., Cusi, A., Feiman, R., Grabski, W., & Anderson, A. K. (2008). Expressing fear enhances sensory acquisition. *Nature Neuroscience, 11*, 843–850.

Tassinary, L. G., Cacioppo, J. T., & Vanman, E. J. (2007). The skeletomotor system: Surface electromyography. In J. T. Cacioppo, L. G. Tassinary, & G. G. Berntson (Eds.), *Handbook of psychophysiology* (3rd ed., pp. 267–302). New York, NY: Cambridge University Press.

Tracy, J. L., & Matsumoto, D. (2008). The spontaneous expression of pride and shame: Evidence for biologically innate nonverbal displays. *Proceedings of the National Academy of Sciences, 105*, 11655–11660.

Tsai, J. L., Louie, J., Chen, E. E., & Uchida, Y. (2007). Learning what feelings to desire: Socialization of ideal affect through children's storybooks. *Personality and Social Psychology Bulletin, 33*, 17–30.

Tsuchiya, N., & Koch, C. (2005). Continuous flash suppression reduces negative afterimages. Nature Neuroscience, 8, 1096–1101.

van Boxtel, A. (2010). Facial EMG as a tool for inferring affective states. In J. Spink, F. Grieco, O. Krips, L. Loijens, L. Noldus, & P. Zimmerman (Eds.), *Proceedings of measuring behavior* 2010 (pp. 104–108). Wageningen, the Netherlands: Noldus Information Technology.

Whalen, P. J., Shin, L. M., McInerney, S. C., Fischer, H., Wright, C. I., & Rauch, S. L. (2001). A functional MRI study of human amygdala responses to facial expressions of fear versus anger. *Emotion, 1*, 70–83.

Widen, S. C. (2013). Children's interpretation of facial expressions: The long path from valence-based to specific discrete categories. *Emotion Review, 5*, 72–77.

Widen, S. C., & Russell, J. A. (2008). Children acquire emotion categories gradually. *Cognitive Development, 23*, 291–312.

Wilson-Mendenhall, C. D., Barrett, L. F., Simmons, W. K., & Barsalou, L. W. (2011). Grounding emotion in situated conceptualization. *Neuropsychologia*, 49, *1105–1127.*

PART X

Social Interaction

23

Interpersonal Effects and Functions of Facial Activity

BRIAN PARKINSON

Faces contribute to a variety of human actions and reactions. They communicate motives (Fridlund, 1994), embody action tendencies (Frijda & Tcherkassof, 1997), and regulate conversations (Kendon, 1967). They look different when people yawn, sneeze, eat, talk, and think. People use their faces to ironize verbal statements, direct someone's attention, or indicate agreement. How do these different functions relate to the most intensively investigated function of facial activity, to express or communicate emotional information? Is this a separate function or does it depend on other things that faces do?

This chapter addresses this question by considering how facial activity operates in the social world, how it affects and is affected by other people and their reciprocal facial activity. Facial movements are often best understood as parts of more widely articulated processes involving bodies and brains in interaction with other bodies and brains situated in a shared environment. Faces can play a special role in these processes partly because they are often both the medium and target of people's attention when they interact with each other.

To date, psychologists have only scratched the surface of interpersonally directed facial activity partly because of the variety and complexity of the processes involved. For practical as well as theoretical reasons, researchers usually focus on particular facial configurations with established associations to emotional meanings. Studies assessing social effects of emotion communication use these same faces as stimuli, thereby sustaining the presupposition that interpersonal effects of facial activity are mediated by transmission of emotional information. In these studies, facial messages are decoded in emotional terms and their decoding leads to other psychological effects. Even implicit forms of interpersonal influence such as "primitive emotion contagion" (Hatfield, Cacioppo, & Rapson, 1994) imply a translation of facial configuration into emotional meaning, although in this case perceivers decode internal facial feedback rather than external signals.

The emphasis on emotion-communicating faces restricts our understanding of processes underlying face-to-face interaction. Faces communicate in ways that are not always reducible to the encoding and decoding of emotional meanings, and faces affect others in ways that do not always involve communication in the first place (e.g., gaze following; D'Entremont, Hains, & Muir, 1997). In this chapter I explore some of these other processes and consider how they might relate to emotion communication.

The chapter has three main sections. The first section distinguishes three general functions of facial activity that provide the basis for many of its interpersonal effects. First, facial movements are involved in lines of practical action directed at environmental objects and events (e.g., Dewey, 1895). Second, facial activity regulates direct face-to-face interpersonal interaction. Third, reciprocal facial activity helps to coordinate orientations toward objects, events, and people. The second section considers how these three functions and the communicative possibilities that they provide are implicated in psychological research into interpersonal effects of gaze. The third section moves beyond gaze to discuss interpersonal effects of facial configurations and movements more generally, focusing on mimicry and social appraisal.

FUNCTIONS OF FACIAL ACTIVITY

Is the central purpose of facial activity to express emotions? Darwin (1872) did not think so. One of his main aims was to show that facial movements served nonemotional functions that led to their subsequent association with emotions, partly as a way of dismissing claims that God had provided facial muscles precisely to permit emotion expression. However, Darwin's focus on faces with emotional connotations helped sustain some of the restrictive implications of earlier views. Instead of assuming divine origins for facial movements, subsequent researchers often concluded that natural selection had equipped humans with emotionally expressive faces.

This section considers three general functions served by facial activity that are not primarily emotion related but may help to explain and distinguish facial activity's many interpersonal effects, including other people's attributions of emotion to faces. First, faces play a role in practical action directed at physical objects and events (i.e., action oriented to nonsocial instrumental goals). Second, they operate directly on other people with whom we are interacting in a reciprocated process. Third, they can align or divert other people's orientations toward practical or social objects and events.

Practical Action

According to Darwin's principle of associated serviceable habits, facial movements can assist in the performance of certain practical actions, which in turn may be associated with emotions. For example, widened eyes facilitate vigilant intake of visual information and may therefore be useful in many fear-inducing situations (e.g., Susskind et al., 2008).

As Dewey (1894) pointed out, Darwin's principle already accounts for so-called facial expressions without the need for any additional invocation of emotion: "The reference to emotion in explaining the attitude is wholly irrelevant; the attitude of emotion is explained positively by reference to useful movements" (Dewey, 1894, p. 556). In other words, a central function of facial activity is to serve practical goals, some of which are associated with emotion, but emotion does not exert an independent influence on how the face moves.

Bull's (1951) attitude theory of emotion drew an explicit distinction between two kinds of expression that serve different practical functions. The first is a preparatory configuration where the body takes an appropriate stance in anticipation of the required action. For example, sprinters get ready for a quick getaway when positioned on the blocks waiting for the starting pistol. The second relates to the movements that are part of the action that is subsequently performed. For example, a sprinter's face shows movements associated with the frenetic breathing that provides the oxygen for extreme exertion as well as the characteristic forward gaze needed to track the course of the run (with occasional deflections to monitor other competitors).

Mead (1934) explained how preparatory attitudes come to acquire communicative and ultimately symbolic functions. The postural configuration not only readies the body for action but also indicates visibly to others what that body is about to do. For example, a dog's upright tense posture and bared teeth may serve as a cue to another dog that a fight is imminent. If the other dog consequently backs down, the first dog may ultimately learn that adopting the ready-to-fight posture provides a useful means of intimidation.

In human societies, the meanings that get attached to practically oriented facial activity partly depend on cultural norms, practices, and concepts.

For example, an intensely focused other-directed gaze, gritted teeth, and clenched fists provide practical preparation for physically punching someone, and probably acquire the pragmatic meaning of threatening aggression across a range of societies. In many English-speaking countries, a readiness to punch and the associated threat of aggression provide a prototype for the development of a hypercognized (Levy, 1973) concept of "anger." A stylized version of the facial configuration can thus be used as a convenient and easily detectable shorthand for conveying this emotion concept, thus explaining its conventionalization over the course of cultural history. In societies with different anger-related concepts and different norms about its appropriate expression, the communicative meaning and practical effect of the display (e.g., physical threat) may be less directly related to the emotion concept in question.

Preparatory attitudes (or "intention movements") may acquire communicative functions as a consequence of natural selection as well as ontogenetic learning. Ethologists argue that certain postures and muscular configurations (such as a dog's snarling jaw) become stylized signals over the course of natural selection because of their consistent effects on conspecifics who have coevolved sensitivity to their signal value. In this ritualization process (e.g., Andrews, 1963), the displays may become exaggerated versions of the originally functional postural attitudes in order to enhance the extent of their social influence.

Whether ritualization of facial activity occurs in humans as well as other primates is contested by those who believe that distinctively human socialization supplants the necessity for such a process (e.g., Tomasello & Call, 1997). However, some aspects of human facial morphology do seem to have evolved partly to facilitate signaling. For example, the highly visible contrast between the eye's sclera and iris allows easy tracking of someone else's gaze (Kobayashi & Kohshima, 1997). When eyes are widened to improve information sensory uptake, this further enhances the visibility of this contrast and permits signaling to others the location of something in the environment that needs urgent attention (Lee, Susskind, & Anderson, 2013).

In sum, some of facial activity's interpersonal effects depend on its grounding in practical activities oriented to objects in the environment. Over the course of natural selection and cultural history, practically oriented motor attitudes become attuned to their social consequences and start to function as signals as well. The communicative effects of these signals may sometimes depend on simultaneous detection by other people of the practical object at which the face's sensory organs are oriented. For example, the implications of someone's gaze may be clarified by being able to discern the object at which they are gazing.

Regulating Interpersonal Interaction

Some of the most important objects at which facial activity is directed are other people. Sometimes, interpersonally directed facial activity may be practically oriented and follow similar principles to those set out in the previous section. For example, facial activity may play similar roles in approach or avoidance in relation to both other people and practical objects. Indeed, I may stare at you intently to collect practically relevant information just as I might stare at a box of valuables when there is no obvious way of opening it.

However, interpersonally directed facial activity also serves person-directed regulatory goals that are not directly practical. From an early age, humans are equipped with resources that facilitate effective engagement with other humans, including the capacity for facial interaction. This capacity typically precedes the development of object-directed facial activity. Newborn infants orient gaze preferentially to faces and face-like stimuli (e.g., Farroni et al., 2007), and by the age of 4 months they are already playing a more active role in soliciting attention from caregivers (e.g., Reddy, 1999). Even at 2 months, infants are attuned to the dynamic responsivity of caregivers' facial activity, and they react with distress if direct interactivity is disrupted (e.g., Murray & Trevarthen, 1985). Soon after life begins, then, some of the main functions performed by faces are to establish, maintain, break, or otherwise regulate interpersonal contact.

Coordinating Orientations

Infants start to share their attention between people and objects during their first year (e.g., Gredebäck, Fikke, & Melinder, 2010). With the onset of secondary intersubjectivity (Trevarthen & Hubley, 1978), they become attuned not only to other people and objects but also to relations between other people and objects. Instead of simply adjusting to caregivers' dynamic relational stances, infants now begin to adjust their orientation to other people or things to match (or to modify) caregivers' orientations. For example, they may adopt a facial orientation toward an object as a way of bringing it to the caregiver's attention (Striano & Rochat, 1999), or correspondingly look to the caregiver in order to collect (or solicit) social referencing information that can disambiguate an unfamiliar situation (e.g., Sorce et al., 1985).

Many aspects of adult interpersonal interaction can be understood in terms of referential triads involving two people with interacting orientations toward objects (or other people) in the shared environment. Sometimes the interpersonal influence process in these triads is explicit and strategic. For example, caregivers may widen their eyes in a vigilant pose when looking at objects in order to convey their attitude for the benefit of young children. At other times, perceivers may pick up information about an object's evaluation or affordances from observing someone else's unregulated orientation to it. A third case involves two parties adjusting their respective orientations to an object and each other in a genuinely coregulatory manner (cf. Fogel, 1993).

Emotion Expression

Where does facial activity's emotion-expression function fit into the picture sketched out so far? Over the course of individual development, cultural evolution, and natural selection, the practical advantages of being able to influence others using facial displays may lead to their consolidation and exaggeration. Ritualized or conventionalized signals may develop to encapsulate certain communicative meanings. For example, scrunching of the nose extends the reflexive facial response to exposure to foul-smelling or vomit-inducing objects and can convey repulsion in a more direct and temporally attuned way than simply saying, "That is disgusting!"

Thus, practical facial activity can acquire communicative functions, including the function of expressing emotions. However, in all cases these functions derive from prior practical, interaction-regulating, or orientation-coordinating functions. Exaggeration only provides advantages when the signals that are exaggerated already have a functional basis. Furthermore, even communicative facial activity may continue to serve the functions on which it was originally based. For example, widened eyes may simultaneously increase visual sensitivity and indicate to others an object that potentially requires their attention, too (Lee, Susskind, & Anderson, 2013).

Socialized humans also use a more explicit kind of facial expression, when they pull faces specifically to convey certain meanings in conversation. The conceptual meanings attached to these faces again often reflect some aspect of their more primary practical or interaction-regulating functions but also depend on the norms, rules, and ideology of the particular society. For example, in cultures where a particular emotion is hypocognized (Levy, 1973), it is less likely that conventional facial positions become associated with the associated relational meaning. Although these facial movements originally depend on conversational intentions, they may ultimately acquire more direct associations with contexts in which they are habitually deployed, just as we may come to say "ouch" automatically when seeing someone getting hurt (cf. Bavelas et al., 1986).

INTERPERSONAL EFFECTS OF GAZE

How do other people's facial movements affect us? The three functions sketched out so far provide some general answers. Facial activity carries implications about orientation to practical objects and thereby directs other people's attention and orientation. Facial activity regulates relations with other people by signaling readiness to interact or desire to break from interaction. Facial activity coordinates actors' respective orientations to objects. In the present section, I illustrate each of these interpersonal effects on facial activity by focusing on the particular example of gaze. Gaze is interesting in the present context because its interpersonal effects clearly do not always depend on attribution of emotional meaning to the face doing the gazing.

Eyes are generally the first target of people's visual attention when scanning faces (Bindemann, Scheepers, & Burton, 2009). One reason is that gaze cues tell us directly whether the other person is looking at us, or away from us at something else. Looking at something permits us to identify it or track its movements (practical action) but also indicates to other people that there is something that may be worth looking at. Looking at someone conveys a readiness for social engagement (Cary, 1978), and the other person responds with signals that encourage or discourage this engagement (e.g., eye contact vs. averted gaze serving regulation of interaction). Combining these two functions, gaze can coordinate two people's attention toward an object perceived by both of them (joint attention serving coordination of orientations). Thus, gaze can fulfil all three of the primary functions of facial activity distinguished earlier and exert each of the corresponding interpersonal effects. Gaze can guide other people's orientation to practical objects, regulate direct contact with other people, and help coordinate people's orientations toward practical objects or other people. The following subsections consider these interpersonal effects of gaze in turn.

Object-Directed Gaze

Object-directed gaze performs the practical function of collecting information about the object to which it is directed. The corresponding interpersonal effect is to direct someone else's attention to the same object. Here, I focus on this interpersonal effect of object-directed gaze.

Even newborns can discriminate between direct and averted gaze and make faster saccades toward objects when the eyes on a stimulus face move in the direction of those objects (gaze cueing; Farroni et al., 2004). By the age of 4 months, infants are able to follow someone else's gaze to a specific object situated within their focal field of vision (e.g., d'Entremont et al., 1997).

Research into adult gaze cueing also shows that gaze can enhance another person's detection and processing of visual stimuli at which it is directed (Frischen, Bayliss, & Tipper, 2007). Many of the effects are automatic and not easily modulated by strategic intentions. For example, telling participants that eyes will point away from presented objects does not disrupt the early facilitative effects of gaze cueing on stimulus discrimination in the gazed-at region of the visual field (e.g., Driver et al., 1999). Clearly, not all interpersonal effects of object-directed gaze depend on top-down processing of its meaning.

Lee, Susskind, and Anderson (2013) provided specific evidence that interpersonal effects of object-directed gaze do not depend on attribution of emotion. They found that participants were better able to detect the direction of gaze from schematic pictures of "fearful" eyes (widened to show a larger proportion of the sclera) than from "neutral" or "disgusted" eyes (narrowed to decrease the sclera's visibility). Inversion of the schematic stimuli reduced participants' perceptions of their emotional aspects but did not reduce the effect on detection of gaze direction. In other words, widened "fearful" eyes better indicated gaze direction regardless of participants' perception of their fearfulness. Widened eyes also led to greater improvement in discrimination of peripheral stimuli in the region of the visual field at which they were directed. These results suggest that both eye widening and gaze direction have interpersonal effects on stimulus processing that do not depend on their emotional meaning.

The primary functions of object-directed gaze seem to be attention related rather than emotion related. The primary practical function is to direct attention at, or deflect attention from, a practical object or event. The primary signal function is to direct someone else's attention at or deflect someone else's attention from an object. This signal provides emotionally relevant information but cannot fully specify any particular emotion category without additional facial cues and/or contextual information (e.g., Adams & Kleck, 2005, as discussed later).

However, it is also true that the interpersonal effects of object-directed gaze interact with those of other emotion-relevant facial signals (Rigato & Farroni, 2013). For example, Bayliss and colleagues (2007) showed that pairing "disgust" faces with pictures of household objects led to less positive subsequent evaluations than did pairing smiling faces with the same objects, but only when the eyes on these faces directed their gaze at rather than away from these neutral stimuli. As in social referencing (e.g., Sorce et al., 1985), someone else's oriented facial activity changed the evaluation of the object at which it was directed.

Moving from evaluation to interpretation, Mumenthaler and Sander (2012, 2015) found comparable effects of facial stimuli on perceptions of emotion in

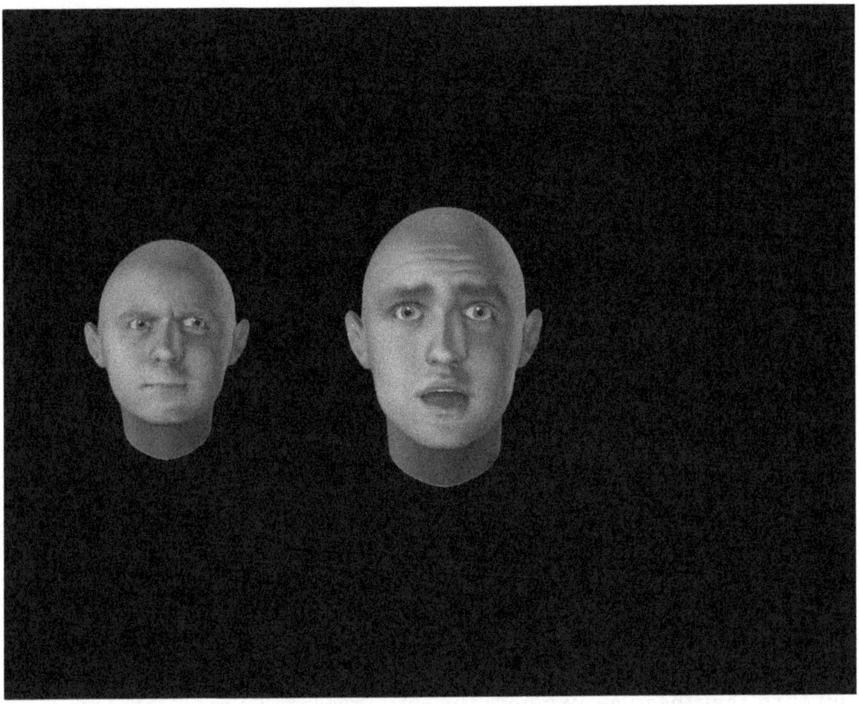

Figure 23.1 Perception of fear in referential context (Mumenthaler & Sander, 2015).

target faces (see Fig. 23.1). In their 2012 study, an animated peripheral face showed a dynamic "emotion expression" as its gaze turned toward or away from a centrally presented face also showing a variety of expressions. Perceptions of the target face's emotion were influenced more by the peripheral face's expression when its gaze turned toward the target face. For example, a peripheral "angry" face turning its gaze toward a centrally presented "fear" face increased perceptions of fear, probably because fear is a more likely reaction from someone at whom anger is directed. Comparable effects have also been found when a peripheral anger face was presented subliminally (Mumenthaler & Sander, 2015). Thus, effects of interpersonally oriented facial activity on observers' perceptions of target faces do not seem to depend on explicit inferential processes.

Person-Directed Gaze

Gaze directed at the self can have even more powerful effects than gaze directed at practical objects. Direct gaze not only signals attention to the self but also serves to regulate interpersonal contact. A returned gaze indicates a readiness to engage with someone else (Cary, 1978), whereas gaze aversion indicates interpersonal avoidance in response to someone else's engagement. Looking at someone looking back at you involves both you and the other person simultaneously perceiving each other performing a corresponding activity. Many theorists attach special status to this mutual state of primary intersubjectivity (Trevarthen, 1979).

Some of the resources that facilitate the development of social contact are already present at birth. Neonates show preferential looking toward faces showing direct gaze, but only when these faces are presented upright, suggesting that they have an innate sensitivity to this particular signal of potential social engagement (Farroni, Menon, & Johnson, 2006). Responsiveness to gaze as an engagement cue develops rapidly, leading 2-month-old infants to smile more when adults gaze at their eyes rather than their ears (Muir & Hains, 1999).

However, mutual gaze is not a steady state that can be maintained indefinitely, and infants behave in ways that regulate its cyclical time course from an early age. For example, Reddy (2000) video-recorded the facial activity of 2-month-old infants during naturalistic interactions with adults or their own reflection in a mirror. Her particular interest was in a recurrent sequence of infant facial movement where infants start to smile but turn their head away before the smile reaches its peak (see Fig. 23.2). Observers viewing the videotapes consistently perceived this patterned movement as reflecting coyness, bashfulness, or embarrassment (Draghi-Lorenz, Morris, & Reddy, 2005).

Although it is difficult to draw strong conclusions about the function of these "coy smiles," their dependence on prior exposure to the other person's prolonged gaze suggests that they partly reflect the infant's desire to escape this gaze, perhaps because of its impact on arousal levels. However, this does not explain the socially oriented smiling that consistently accompanied gaze withdrawal. One possible interpretation is that infants are signaling the desire to break contact but only for a temporary period. Indeed, infants often resumed attentional contact with the other person after a brief

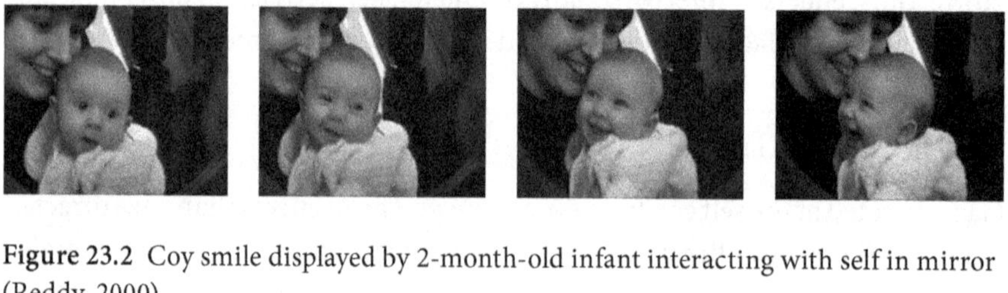

Figure 23.2 Coy smile displayed by 2-month-old infant interacting with self in mirror (Reddy, 2000).

respite. Thus, gaze diversion in these cases not only serves the practical function of removing an unwanted social stimulus from the visual field, but also presents a visible cue to the other person about the infant's orientation toward continued interpersonal engagement. The changing direction of the smile moving away from the other's face undermines its signal value as a specific invitation for social interaction, but still implies willingness for future affiliation. Such connotations need not be directly intended by the infant or explicitly perceived by the caregiver, but may instead reflect the moment-by-moment coregulation of mutual activity. Similarly, "coy smiles" do not encapsulate a prior emotion but form the basis for an emergent relational meaning.

Based on these and related findings, Reddy (2008) concludes that infants have an awareness of self-directed attention from others that precedes, and provides a basis for, the development of joint attention to external objects. Whether or not this is true, it seems clear that one of gaze's primary functions is to solicit, maintain, and regulate relationships with other people.

Person-directed gaze may or may not be related to emotion. According to Adams and Kleck's (2005) shared signal hypothesis, approach emotions such as happiness and anger are associated with direct gaze, whereas avoidance emotions such as fear are associated with averted gaze. Consistent with this account, Adams and Kleck (2005) showed that canonical "fear" expressions are categorized more readily when gaze is averted, and "anger" and "happiness" expressions are categorized more readily when gaze is directed at the person viewing the stimulus faces (see also Bindemann, Burton, & Langton, 2008; Graham & LaBar, 2012). Correspondingly, discrimination of averted gaze direction is enhanced when the gazing face has a "fearful" rather than "neutral" expression (Adams & Franklin, 2009).

These findings demonstrate that person-directed gaze can signal approach and that approach information is relevant to some emotion discriminations. However, it is clear that the information conveyed by gaze in this research is not directly or exclusively emotional. Indeed, Adams and Kleck's (2005) study 1 showed that direct gaze on a "neutral" face encouraged participants to attribute *either* an angry or a happy disposition to the target. In other words, gaze cues conveyed general approach-related information to perceivers rather than indicating either the valence or the specific quality of the associated emotion. Furthermore, associations of emotion with gaze direction can be reversed depending on the object at which the emotion is directed: If I am angry with someone else, then my gaze is often directed away from rather than at you. More generally, gaze's informational content depends not only on its orientation to the perceiver but also on other stimuli in the shared environment.

Gaze in Shared Attention

In addition to its attention-directing and relationship-regulatory functions, gaze can also help coordinate people's orientations toward objects at which it is directed. Research into gaze cueing typically uses methodologies that remove the possibilities for direct interaction between people (Pfeiffer, Vogeley, & Schilbach, 2013). Participants react to the gaze of a stimulus face but cannot exert mutual influence on that face. In more naturalistic social interactions, coordination of attention operates reciprocally. When two people calibrate their gaze toward an object that is visually available to both of them, a true state of shared attention emerges (Emery, 2000).

Interrelations between object- and person-directed gaze are apparent from an early age. For example, Farroni and colleagues (2003) showed that 4-month-old infants only respond to object-directed gaze if it is preceded by self-directed gaze. The initial self-directed gaze probably serves to engage the infant's attention before it can be directed toward the object. By the age of 12 months, infants are able to extrapolate an object's location in their visual field from the relative position and orientation of another person's eyes. In the next few months, this ability extends to objects that are not immediately available to their perception (Butterworth & Jarrett, 1991). Infants of this age not only have the capacity to alternate attention between other people and the objects to which they are oriented but can also orient to relations between people and objects (*secondary intersubjectivity*; Trevarthen & Hubley, 1978). In particular, the other person's object-directed gaze now itself becomes a focus of the infant's attention.

This development provides the basis for the coordination of orientations toward objects using gaze cues coupled with other signals. For example, in Sorce and colleagues' (1985) social referencing study, toddlers turn their gaze from an unfamiliar object to their mother's face as a way of soliciting information about her orientation to that object. In turn, the mother explicitly communicates her orientation with the help of gaze cues that also switch back and forth from the infant's face to the object. Her widened eyes signal that this object merits vigilance.

In this setting, the toddler's gaze mainly serves an information-collection function, and the mother's gaze mainly performs an information-communication function. In other circumstances, gaze simultaneously collects and communicates information about an object for both parties, providing a coregulated system for coordinating orientations, as discussed in more detail later in this chapter.

EXPLAINING INTERPERSONAL EFFECTS

What processes explain the interpersonal effects of facial activity? At the explicit end of the spectrum, we may try to work out what others are thinking, feeling, or intending by inspecting their faces for clues. At the implicit end of the spectrum we may flinch or start at sudden and dramatic changes in other people's facial configurations. Between these extremes lies a range of more or less controlled and controllable processes, where people use others' faces as information or respond more directly to the affordances those faces present. Research into facial activity other than gaze has usually focused on a limited subset of these processes, mostly treating facial configurations as stimuli that carry emotional meaning. In the following sections, I discuss two kinds of interpersonal effects that may be explicable by reference to implicit processes in addition to more explicit emotion inference processes. The first kind of effect involves matching someone else's facial activity (mimicry) when interacting directly with that person. This is usually explained by implicit processes, but these may also have more explicit counterparts. The second kind of effect involves changing one's evaluation of, or behavior toward, an object, in response to someone else's facial orientation to that object (a form of social appraisal, Manstead & Fischer, 2001). The most common explanations for these social appraisal effects invoke explicit emotion inferences, but as noted in the earlier discussion of attention-directing effects of gaze, more direct implicit processes may also be relevant.

Mimicry

Under appropriate conditions, infants not only respond to another person's direct gaze with returned gaze but also match other aspects of that person's facial activity (e.g., Meltzoff & Moore, 1977). Many theorists interpret this facial matching as mimicry, but there are other possible interpretations. In particular, one reason why infants often meet someone else's gaze is to look at something attention grabbing (i.e., a face gazing directly at them). Similarly, smiles in response to other people's smiles may constitute affiliative responses to someone else's affiliative gesture rather than mimicry per se.

Partly for this reason, researchers wishing to establish genuine mimicry often attempt to focus on movements with no intrinsic social meaning. For example, to establish the "chameleon effect," Chartrand and Bargh (1999) exposed adult participants to a model engaging in either face-rubbing or foot-shaking movements and assessed their differential production of both behaviors (thus also ruling out general effects on activity level). When researching infant imitation, researchers are constrained by the behavioral repertoire of their participants. Behaviors that infants commonly perform are often precisely those that serve practical or interpersonal functions, and these functions may provide an alternative explanation for apparent mimicry. Indeed, a common dependent measure in infant mimicry research is tongue protrusion, which has obvious roles in sensory exploration, especially during breast-feeding. Critics have therefore argued that apparent mimicry of this behavior is, in fact, a more direct response to arousal (Jones, 2009). However, Meltzoff and Moore (1989) convincingly demonstrate the proto-intentionality of mimicked tongue protrusion on the basis of its delayed occurrence when the response is initially blocked using a pacifier. Furthermore, infant mimicry has often been observed as a progressively more accurate sequence of approximations of the perceived action, rather than a reflexive uncontrolled response (Kugiumutzakis, 1988). The evidence strongly suggests that mimicry is part of the process whereby infants engage in and regulate interpersonal contact with caregivers (Reddy, 2008).

Adult mimicry may also depend on wanting to affiliate. For example, Bourgeois and Hess (2008) found that participants mimicked negative facial expressions when they were displayed by in-group members, but not when they were displayed by out-group members. The difference probably reflected the fact that negative in-group mimicry tends to communicate empathy and solidarity, whereas negative out-group mimicry might communicate motives that are far from affiliative.

These findings suggest that facial mimicry is socially oriented and can contribute to relationship regulation. Hess and Fischer (2013) further propose that it depends specifically on the communication of emotional meanings: "emotional mimicry involves the interpretation of signals as *emotions*, conveying emotional intentions" (p. 146). In other words, interactants need to extract an emotional meaning from a facial movement before mimicking it. However, such an account excludes mimicry of socially meaningful facial activity that is not directly emotional (e.g., gaze patterns), and it rules out mimicry of emotion-related facial activity in infants before they are able to decode emotional meaning. An infant's returned smile would not count as emotional mimicry until the infant knew that smiles represented the emotion of happiness (rather than simply being invitations to social engagement, for example).

Relatedly, Hess and Fischer's formulation involves the postulation of an apparently unnecessary emotion-detection step in the process of facial mimicry. An alternative is that perceivers (including infant perceivers) pick up the attentional and orientational aspects of facial activity more directly (e.g., Scherer, Mortillarro, & Mehu, 2013), for instance as a function of bottom-up rather than top-down processing. In this context, we have already seen how gaze and eye widening can have potentially congruent interpersonal effects that are independent of their emotional meaning. Similar principles might also apply to other aspects of facial activity. Although adults may certainly infer an underlying emotion from someone else's facial activity and respond by expressing a matching emotion (possibly using other means) under certain circumstances, it seems unlikely that emotion inference always accompanies the dynamic coordinated exchanges of corresponding facial movements in ongoing face-to-face interactions.

One reason for proposing that mimicry is mediated by the decoding of emotional meaning is that people do not always copy the precise physical movements made by others, but instead "fill in the gaps" of a more inclusive activity configuration. For example, Hess and colleagues (2007) found that exposure to the lower half of a stimulus facial expression induced changes to the upper half of the perceiver's face if the presented expression was decoded in the intended way. Even patients with blindsight who are unaware of seeing an emotion-connoting postural stimulus responded with facial movements associated with the same emotion (Tamietto et al., 2009). Furthermore, Halberstadt and colleagues (2009) paired morphed facial pictures containing equal proportions of expressions connoting "happiness" and "anger" with verbal labels indicating either of the corresponding emotion concepts. When the same facial stimuli were presented later, participants' facial responses tended to correspond to the emotion label that had been associated with the expression at the earlier stage.

However, all of these findings derive from studies in which emotion-category labels were attached to the presented stimuli (either by experimenters or participants). In other words, the methods of these studies directly invoke precisely the mediator that Hess and Fischer (2013) claim underlies "emotion mimicry" more generally. When emotion concepts are explicitly activated in association with expressive stimuli, participants show tendencies to respond with facial activity corresponding to the emotion concept. However, this does not rule out mimicry by an alternative route when the same stimuli are not associated with emotion concepts. As noted earlier, nonemotional facial movements such as tongue protrusion are mimicked even by infants who lack relevant emotion concepts in the first place. Similarly, it seems possible that mimicry in response to supposed emotion expressions can occur in the absence of emotion attributions. As in infants, adult mimicry may also play more basic roles in engaging other people's attention and establishing interpersonal contact.

Most adult mimicry research involves presenting participants with decontextualized facial stimuli. This removes the possibility of interacting directly with the people whose faces are presented or of engaging with objects to which their facial activity might be oriented. Furthermore, the gaze depicted on stimulus faces is usually directed forward, thereby implying that the display is self-directed rather than object-directed. These factors in combination may help to explain why many of the reported effects only show mimicry of the valence of the presented emotion rather than of its specific referential meaning as object-directed "anger," "fear," and so on. In the next section, I consider interpersonal effects of facial activity which is specifically oriented to objects or events in real-time social interactions.

Social Appraisal and Triadic Relation Alignment

Do the processes operating in early social referencing also apply to adult interactions concerning objects of mutual interest? Are they necessarily mediated by the transmission of emotional meaning? Hareli (2014) argued that people may work backward from someone else's perceived emotion to infer what kind of appraisal that other person must have been making in order to experience this emotion (reverse engineering). For example, if we read someone's face as indicating anger, we may conclude that that person must have directed blame externally in order to arrive at the angry response. When the object of the anger is also evident, then we can also draw conclusions about what the blame is about. Potentially, this can change our own appraisal of that object or event (a form of social appraisal; e.g. Manstead & Fischer, 2001).

For example, participants in a study by de Melo and colleagues (2014) played prisoner's dilemma games with virtual agents programmed to display smiles or facial expressions of regret when defecting or cooperating. In one condition, the agents smiled when cooperating and showed regret when defecting. In the other condition, this pattern was reversed. As predicted, cooperation with the former agent was higher. Participants inferred self-blame appraisals from the regret expression and goal conduciveness appraisals from the smile, and these inferred appraisals mediated the effects. In other words, when an agent smiled after cooperating, participants inferred that cooperation was conducive to that agent's goals and were therefore more likely to reciprocate.

Similar effects were found after substituting the agents' programmed facial movements with verbal communications specifying appraisals and the object at which they were directed (e.g., "I do not like this outcome and I blame you for it"). De Melo and colleagues concluded that the two kinds of manipulation work by a similar process of explicit transmission of appraisal information. Indeed, participants may have read appraisal information directly from the presented facial movements rather than inferring them indirectly from the emotions that those facial movements were intended to express. Like Hess and Fischer's explanation of emotional mimicry, the reverse-engineering account may overcomplicate the interpersonal process by introducing an unnecessary emotion-attribution step.

Several aspects of de Melo and colleagues' procedure probably maximized the role of explicit appraisal inferences. The mixed-motive game made the possibility of conflicting orientations self-evident. The other player was an unfamiliar virtual agent about whom participants knew little. The agent's facial activity was timed to coincide with periodic game outcomes rather than continually attuned to the participant's ongoing responsivity to what was happening. Changing these parameters may increase dynamic interpersonal coordination of facial orientations and reduce the impact of inferential processes.

Parkinson, Phiri, and Simons' (2012) adult social-referencing procedure permitted more direct real-time contact between human agents. In their study, pairs of friends engaged in continuous facial interaction across a live video link while one of the pair performed the Balloon Analogue Risk Task (BART; Lejuez et al., 2002). When the other participant (reference person) had been covertly instructed to express anxiety freely as the player inflated a simulated balloon, the player stopped pumping sooner. In other words, players' risk-taking behavior was influenced by observers' facial activity of observers.

This kind of real-time two-way facial communication depends less on event-linked appraisal messages and more on participants continually adjusting their orientation toward ongoing events and to each other's orientation to events. Discrete messages were not sent by one interactant and then received by the other. Perhaps for this reason, Parkinson and colleagues found that the interpersonal effect of facial activity on risk behavior remained statistically significant after controlling for effects of self-reported risk appraisals, suggesting that it was not mediated by explicit conclusions about the dangers associated with the task. More intensive analysis of the contingencies between interactants' object- and person-directed gaze and other facial behaviors could potentially clarify how interpersonal coordination was achieved, and whether processes characterizing adult–infant interactions also apply here (Fogel, 1993).

In the two studies just described, facial activity was able to serve referential functions mainly because of its temporal correspondence with unfolding events. In de Melo et al's (2014) study, the virtual agent's distinctive facial movements were timed to be differentially contingent with game outcomes, making their relevance to these outcomes apparent to participants. In Parkinson et al.'s (2012) study, referentiality was achieved mainly by the reference person's real-time responsivity to the player's balloon inflation.

Unlike the object-directed gaze cues that conveyed orientation in earlier social referencing studies, temporal contingency permits the coordination of object-directedness even when an event has no specific environmental location, including topic-based coordination in face-to-face conversations. In this context, gaze cues probably serve more relationship-regulatory functions, including that of signaling the temporary engagements and disengagements associated with taking or conceding the floor and turn taking more generally (e.g., Argyle & Cook, 1976).

CONCLUSIONS

Facial activity affects other people in a variety of ways. Psychologists have usually focused on a subset of these processes wherein faces communicate specific emotional meanings. This research focus sustains an assumption that the face's emotion-expression functions are primary. I have argued instead that facial activity's primary functions involve preparing for and implementing practical actions, regulating interactions with other people, and coordinating orientations to objects, events, and other people. Faces only come to signal and symbolize emotions because practical action, interaction regulation, and orientation coordination also relate to emotion in many circumstances.

Some of facial activity's interpersonal effects depend on its object-directedness, which may be specified by gaze direction or by temporal calibration with unfolding events, including other people's facial activity. Orientation coordination requires mutual attention (also communicated by gaze or calibration) and shared focus on a common object. The communication of emotional meaning under these circumstances depends on the nature of the object toward which facial activity is directed as well as on the nature of the facial activity itself. To enrich our understanding, we need to look at how facial movements unfold in dynamic social and practical environments, and how they relate to what else is happening, including how other faces relate to them. We need to think about how facial activity contributes to the other things that people do when acting and interacting with other people.

REFERENCES

Adams, R. B., Jr., & Franklin, R. G., Jr. (2009). Influence of emotional expression on the processing of gaze direction. *Motivation and Emotion*, *33*, 106–112.

Adams, R. B., & Kleck, R. E. (2005). Effects of direct and averted gaze on the perception of facially communicated emotion. *Emotion*, *5*, 3–11.

Argyle, M., & Cook, M. (1976). Gaze and mutual gaze. Cambridge, UK: Cambridge University Press.

Bavelas, J. B., Black, A., Lemery, C. R., & Mullett, J. (1986). "I show how you feel": Motor mimicry as a communicative act. *Journal of Personality and Social Psychology, 50*, 322–329.

Bayliss, A. P., Frischen, A., Fenske, M. J., & Tipper, S. P. (2007). Affective evaluations of objects are influenced by observed gaze direction and emotion expression. *Cognition, 104*, 644–653.

Bindemann, M., Burton, A. M., & Langton, S. R. H. (2008). How do eye-gaze and facial expression interact? *Visual Cognition, 16*, 708–733.

Bindemann, M., Scheepers, C., & Burton, A. M. (2009) Viewpoint and center of gravity affect eye movements to human faces. *Journal of Vision, 9*(2), 7.1–16.

Bourgeois, P., & Hess, U. (2008). The impact of social context on mimicry. *Biological Psychology, 77*, 343–352.

Bull, N. (1951). *The attitude theory of emotion*. New York, NY: Coolidge Foundation.

Butterworth, G., & Jarrett, N. (1991). What minds have in common is space: Spatial mechanisms serving joint visual attention in infancy. *British Journal of Developmental Psychology, 9*, 55–72.

Cary, M. S. (1978). The role of gaze in the initiation of conversation. *Social Psychology, 41*, 269.

Chartrand, T. L., & Bargh, J. A. (1999). The chameleon effect: The perception–behavior link and social interaction. *Journal of Personality and Social Psychology, 76*, 893–910.

Darwin, C. (1872/1998). *The expression of the emotions in man and animals* (3rd ed.). London, UK: HarperCollins.

De Melo, C., Carnevale, P. J., Read, S. C., & Gratch, J. (2014). Reading people's minds from emotion expressions in interdependent decision making. *Journal of Personality and Social Psychology, 106*, 73–88.

D'Entremont, B., Hains, S. M. J., & Muir, D. W. (1997). A demonstration of gaze following in 3 to 6 month olds. *Infant Behavior and Development, 20*, 569–572.

Dewey, J. (1894). The theory of emotion I: Emotional attitudes. *Psychological Review, 1*, 553–569.

Draghi-Lorenz, R., Reddy, V., & Morris, P. (2005). Young infants can be perceived as shy, coy, bashful, embarrassed. *Infant and Child Development, 14*, 63–83.

Driver, J., Davis, G., Ricciardelli, P., Kidd, P., Maxwell, E., & Baron-Cohen, S. (1999). Gaze perception triggers reflexive visuospatial orienting. *Visual Cognition, 6*, 509–540.

Emery, N. J. (2000). The eyes have it: The neuroethology, function and evolution of social gaze. *Neuroscience and Biobehavioral Reviews, 24*, 581–604.

Farroni, T., Mansfield, E. M., Lai, C., & Johnson, M. H. (2003). Infants perceiving and acting on the eyes: Tests of an evolutionary hypothesis. *Journal of Experimental Child Psychology, 85*, 199–212.

Farroni, T., Massaccesi, S., Pividori, D., & Johnson, M. H. (2004). Gaze following in newborns. *Infancy, 5*, 39–60.

Farroni, T., Menon, E., & Johnson, M. H. (2006). Factors influencing newborns' preference for faces with eye contact. *Journal of Experimental Child Psychology, 95*, 298–308.

Farroni, T., Menon, E., Rigato, S., & Johnson, M. H. (2007). The perception of facial expressions in newborns. *European Journal of Developmental Psychology, 4*, 2–13.

Fogel, A. (1993). *Developing through relationships*. New York, NY: Harvester Wheatsheaf.

Fridlund, A. J. (1994). *Human facial expression: An evolutionary view*. San Diego, CA: Academic Press.

Frijda, N. H., & Tcherkassof, A. (1997). Facial expressions as modes of action readiness. In J. A. Russell & J.-M. Fernández-Dols (Eds.), *The psychology of facial expression* (pp. 78–102). New York, NY: Cambridge University Press.

Graham, R., & LaBar, K. S. (2012). Neurocognitive mechanism of gaze-expression interactions in face processing and social attention. *Neurospychologia, 50*, 553–566.

Gredebäck, G., Fikke, L., & Melinder, A. (2010). The development of joint visual attention: A longitudinal study of gaze following during interactions with mothers and strangers. *Developmental Science, 13*, 839–848.

Halberstadt, J., Winkielmann, P., Niedenthal, P. M., & Dalle, N. (2009). Emotional conception: How embodied emotion concepts guide perception and facial action. *Psychological Science, 20*, 1254–1261.

Hareli, S. (2014). Making sense of the social world and influencing it by using a naïve attribution theory of emotions. *Emotion Review, 6*, 336–343.

Hatfield, E., Cacioppo, J. T., & Rapson, R. L. (1994). *Emotional contagion*. New York, NY: Cambridge University Press.

Hess, U., & Fischer, A. (2013). Emotional mimicry as social regulation. *Personality and Social Psychology Review, 17*, 142–157.

Jones S. S. (2009). The development of imitation in infancy. *Philosophical Transactions of the Royal Society of London B - Biological Sciences, 364*, 2325–2335

Kendon, A. (1967). Some functions of gaze direction in social interaction. *Acta Psychologica, 32*, 1–25.

Kobayashi, H., & Kohshima, S. (1997). Unique morphology of the human eye. *Nature, 387*, 767–768.

Kugiumutzakis, G. (1988). Neonatal imitation in the intersubjective companion space. In S. Braten (Ed.), *Intersubjective communication and emotion in early ontogeny* (pp. 63–88). Cambridge, UK: Cambridge University Press.

Lejuez, C. W., Read, J. P., Kahler, C. W., Richards, J. B., Ramsey, S. E., Stuart, G. L., et al. (2002). Evaluation of a behavioral measure of risk taking: The Balloon Analogue Risk Task (BART). *Journal of Experimental Psychology: Applied*, 8, 75–84.

Lee, D. H., Susskind, J. M., & Anderson, A. K. (2013). Social transmission of the sensory benefits of eye widening in fear expression. *Psychological Science, 24*, 957–965.

Levy, R. (1973). *Tahitians*. Chicago, IL: Chicago University Press.

Manstead, A. S. R., & Fischer, A. H. (2001). Social appraisal: The social world as object of and influence on appraisal processes. In K. R. Scherer, A. Schorr, & T. Johnstone (Eds.), *Appraisal processes in emotion: Theory, methods, research* (pp. 221–232). New York, NY: Oxford University Press.

Mead, G. H. (1934). *Mind, self, and society*. Chicago, IL: Chicago University Press.

Meltzoff, A. N., & Moore, M. K. (1977). Imitation of facial and manual gestures by human neonates. *Science, 198*, 75–78.

Meltzoff, A. N., & Moore, M. K. (1989). Imitation in newborn infants: exploring the range of gestures imitated and the underlying mechanisms. *Developmental Psychology, 25*, 954–962.

Muir, D., & Hains, S. (1999). Young infants' perception of adult intentionality. In P. Rochat et al. (Eds.), *Early social cognition* (pp. 155–187). Mahwah, NJ: Erlbaum.

Mumenthaler, C., & Sander, D. (2012). Social appraisal influences recognition of emotions. *Journal of Personality and Social Psychology, 102*, 1118–1135.

Mumenthaler, C., & Sander, D. (2015). Automatic integration of social information in emotion recognition. *Journal of Experimental Psychology: General, 144*, 392–399.

Murray, L., & Trevarthen, C. (1985). Emotional regulation of interactions between two-month-olds and their mothers. In T. M. Field & N. A. Fox (Eds.), *Social perception in infants* (pp. 177–197). Norwood, NJ: Ablex.

Parkinson, B., Phiri, N., & Simons, G. (2012). Bursting with anxiety: Adult social referencing in an interpersonal Balloon Analogue Risk Task (BART). *Emotion, 12*, 817–826.

Pfeiffer, U. J., Vogeley, K., & Schilbach, L. (2013). From gaze cueing to dual eye-tracking: Novel approaches to investigate the neural correlates of gaze in social interaction. *Neuroscience and Behavioral Reviews, 37*, 2516–2528.

Reddy, V. (1999). Pre-linguistic communication. In M. Barrett (Ed.), *Language development* (pp. 25–50). New York, NY: Psychology Press.

Reddy, V. (2000). Coyness in early infancy. *Developmental Science, 3*, 186–192.

Reddy, V. (2008). *How infants know minds.* Cambridge, MA: Harvard University Press.

Rigato, S., & Farroni, T. (2013). The role of gaze in the processing of emotional facial expressions. *Emotion Review, 5*, 36–40.

Scherer, K. R., Mortillaro, M., & Mehu, M. (2013). Understanding the mechanisms underlying the production of facial expression of emotion: A componential perspective. *Emotion Review, 5*, 47–53.

Sorce, J. F., Emde, R. N., Campos, J., & Klinnert, M. D. (1985). Maternal emotional signaling: Its effect on the visual cliff behavior of 1 year olds. *Developmental Psychology, 21*, 195–200.

Striano, T. & Rochat, P. (1999). Developmental link between dyadic and triadic social competence in infancy. *British Journal of Developmental Psychology, 17*, 551–562.

Susskind, J. M., & Anderson, A. K. (2008). Facial expression form and function. *Communicative & Integrative Biology, 1*, 148–149.

Susskind, J. M., Lee, D. H., Cusi, A., Feiman, R., Grabski, W., & Anderson, A. K. (2008). Expressing fear enhances sensory acquisition. *Nature Neuroscience, 11*, 843–850.

Tamietto, M., Castelli, L., Vighetti, S., Perozzo, P., Geminiani, G., Weiskrantz, L., & de Gelder, B. (2009). Unseen facial and bodily expressions trigger fast emotional reactions. *Proceedings of the National Academy of Sciences of the United States of America, 106*, 17661–17666.

Tomasello, M., & Call, J. (1997). *Primate cognition*. Oxford, UK: Oxford University Press.

Trevarthen, C. (1979). Communication and cooperation in early infancy: A description of primary intersubjectivity. In M. Bullowa (Ed.), *Before speech* (pp. 321–347). Cambridge, UK: Cambridge University Press.

Trevarthen, C., & Hubley, P. (1978). Secondary intersubjectivity: Confidence, confiding and acts of meaning in the first year. In A. Lock (Ed.), *Action, gesture and symbol: The emergence of language* (pp. 183–229). New York, NY: Academic Press.

24

Natural Facial Expression

A View From Psychological Constructionism and Pragmatics

JOSÉ-MIGUEL FERNÁNDEZ-DOLS

The notion that there are universal facial expressions of basic emotion remains a dominant idea in the study of emotion. Ekman (2016) found that 80% of emotion researchers endorsed the idea. Russell and Fernández-Dols (1997) summarized this mainstream approach under the rubric "Facial Expression Program" (FEP). Three of the most important assumptions of FEP are (a) that expressions of basic emotion consist of a coherent pattern of facial expression and conscious experience; (b) that the production and recognition of true (honest, spontaneous) facial expressions of basic emotion constitute a signaling system, which is an evolutionary adaptation to some of life's major challenges; and (c) that these facial signals are easily recognized by all human beings through universal mental categories of basic emotion.

In this chapter, I explore an alternative to FEP. First, I describe the empirical findings and theoretical developments that question the FEP assumptions. Then, I discuss the conceptual drift of FEP from evolutionary theory to semantics. Finally, I argue for an alternative account that combines a constructionist approach to emotion and a pragmatic approach to facial expression, and that could reconcile the value of facial expression as a signal and a social tool.

ARE THERE COHERENT EXPRESSIONS OF BASIC EMOTION?

Some Lessons From the Study of Natural Language

Some important theoretical contributions in linguistics are driving a thorough reconsideration of the classical approach to the grammatical structure of language, which was based on the study of written language. Some of the lessons of this revision are relevant for a critical reappraisal of the concept of expression of basic emotion. Cognitive-functional research on language raises a number of important questions about the evolution of language itself, because "natural" language—that is, the forms of linguistic communication inherited from our ancestors as a universal feature of the human species—is spoken language. Written language is a cultural product that, due to its recency (by evolutionary standards), is practically irrelevant as an explanation of the origins of human language.

This approach, as Tomasello (2014) has pointed out, has implied "some surprises for psychologists." The most relevant surprise, for the aims of this chapter, is about what is the most valid reference frame for studying language, its structure and its evolutionary origins. It is not written language; rather, spoken language is the most natural, evolutionarily relevant form of language. Spoken language, however, is only weakly related to the written sentences studied in traditional linguistics. For example, there are very few prescriptive grammatical sentences in spontaneous spoken language; speakers express themselves through incomplete, irregular sentences in which the speaker *does not* produce a true utterance which automatically expresses a thought, but stretches of speech that acquire their meaning from the interaction between their incomplete grammatical structure and the hearers' inferences from the context, that is, typically from the social relationship between speaker and hearer (e.g., Du Bois, 2014).

Natural Facial Expression in Emotional Episodes

We can extrapolate this view on language to the study of other allegedly communicative phenomena such as facial behavior. In the same way as people do not actually speak "written language," people do not actually display "expressions of basic emotion."

As speakers utter incomplete, skewed sentences in which context plays a central role for conveying meaning, natural facial expression (NFE) does not fit into the prescriptive expressions of basic emotion predicted by traditional recognition studies (Fernández-Dols & Crivelli, 2013; Reisenzein, Studtmann, & Horstmann, 2013). Naturalistic studies have vividly illustrated the gap between the repertory of expressions of basic emotion (EBEs) and the NFE observed in intense emotional situations.

Empirical evidence suggests that NFEs are "unspecific" (Fernández-Dols, 1999; Fernández-Dols & Ruiz-Belda, 1997) or "inherently ambiguous" (see Hassin & Aviezer, this volume). NFEs are diverse, not necessarily universal facial movements that are coextensive with extremely high or low levels of arousal and pleasure or displeasure. NFEs do not "mean" a category of emotion. We (Fernández-Dols, Crivelli, & Carrera, 2015; Fernández-Dols, & Ruiz-Belda, 1995; García-Higuera, Crivelli, & Fernández-Dols, 2015; Ruiz-Belda, Fernández-Dols, Carrera, & Barchard, 2003) have found that NFEs in highly intense emotional episodes are complex displays that do not fit the expected EBE and have, in some cases, a puzzling apparent similarity to unexpected EBEs.

Aviezer et al. (2015; see also Aviezer, Trope, & Todorov, 2012) have also described these idiosyncratic, unpredicted NFEs in highly aroused tennis players. As in the aforementioned studies, the observed spontaneous expressions of highly aroused tennis players had no apparent communicative function in terms of basic emotions; lay judges could not distinguish victorious from defeated tennis players' expressions.

Duran, Reisenzein, and Fernández-Dols (this volume; see also Fernández-Dols & Crivelli, 2013; Reisenzein, Studtmann, & Horstmann, 2013) carried out a meta-analysis of the published experimental studies on the coherence between reports of emotion and actual facial behavior; the average coherence effect across emotions and studies was .35 [.28, .42] for correlations and .23 [.15, .31] for proportions of reactive participants; this extremely low explained variance hints at the prevalence of NFEs in all these experiments.

DO EXPRESSIONS OF BASIC EMOTION CONSTITUTE A FEASIBLE SIGNALING SYSTEM?

The Evolutionary Dimension of Facial Behavior

Since Darwin, one of the basic assumptions about expressions of basic emotion has been that they are communicative signals. The salience and universality of some facial movements strongly suggest that facial behavior must have an important signal value. EBEs are characterized as signals of emotion that stand out from their context and from other potential sources of noise. What makes EBEs attractive to scientists and lay audiences is the commonsensical assumption that they "reveal" the sender's emotion because they are honest, accurate readouts.

But, as Fridlund (1994) pointed out, the concept of "honest" expressions of emotion assumes the existence of signals that do not have any evolutionary advantage for either sender or receiver. A feasible signal must, from an evolutionary point of view, help the human species to survive in its environment. Such adaptive advantage requires a balance between sender and receiver: The signal should have some advantage for the human sender, but it would not evolve if it did not provide some evolutionary advantage for the human receiver, too; otherwise the receivers would evolve to ignore the signal.

On the sender's side, "honest" signals of emotion would be extremely disadvantageous because it would allow hostile receivers to "read" the sender's mind in advance and anticipate his or her actions.

On the receiver's side, the relevant concern is not whether the signal is honest or not, but whether it will have real consequences (see Dezecache, Mercier, & Scott-Phillips, 2013). And honesty is not a necessary predictor of the consequences predicted by a signal: Contextual factors are a better predictor of the accuracy of the sender's signal than the "honesty" of the expression of emotion. An "unfelt," "false" signal of happiness, anger, or fear could prompt a real social invitation, a real attack or a real retreat, whereas the predictive value of an "honest" signal would mainly depend on biological, physical, or symbolic factors that facilitated or impeded the predicted action (e.g., a "true" but inapplicable threat from a beaten foe or from a young child, etc.). Receivers should be especially vigilant about the viability of the actions announced by a facial signal. Such viability heavily depends on contextual factors, whereas the honesty of the supposed emotional experience behind such a facial signal is irrelevant.

The existence of an evolved signaling system consisting in honest expressions of basic emotion is thus doubtful, and this conclusion raises a large number of questions about the evolutionary foundations of the concept of *expression of basic emotion*. Why should humans have evolved signals that have no adaptive value for either the sender or the receiver?

THE SEMANTIC INTERPRETATION OF FACIAL BEHAVIOR

Despite the aforementioned serious empirical and theoretical limitations of the EBE hypothesis, FEP assumptions are still enormously popular among scientists and lay audiences. The reason for such a success is mainly due to the apparent confirmation of the third of the aforementioned FEP basic assumptions: that EBEs are easily recognized by all human beings through universal mental categories of basic emotion. This semantic approach to facial behavior implies that the face displays not only biological signals (*expressions*) but also symbols with specific meanings (*categories of basic emotion*).

The Semantic Drift

The mainstream Darwinian approach to facial behavior as a biologically based, evolutionarily relevant signal consecrated the term *expression*. In psychology the concept behind *expression* has undergone a progressive simplification that sharply divorces the psychological approach to expression in human communication from the evolutionary approach to signals in animal communication. Whereas in ethology signals are messages whose meaning depends on the context in which they are produced (Smith, 1965), in contemporary psychology and neuroscience facial expressions of basic emotion are practically "words" with a literal meaning irrespective of their context of production. A smile is seen as equivalent to the assertion "I am happy."

Darwin was in part responsible for this drift. The assimilation of facial expression into a sort of facial language has been presupposed in the method of preference in the study of the universality of facial expressions: the recognition studies. In the bible of the study of facial expression—*The Expression of Emotions in Man and Animals*—Darwin (1872) proposed an empirical test of the existence of the same expressions of emotion "in all the races of mankind" that consisted in showing to 20 "educated persons" a series of plates displaying facial expressions, expecting a high degree of consensus about the meaning of those expressions. This test was the source of inspiration for many subsequent studies on recognition. In these studies participants are forced to translate images of facial displays into a specific word (e.g., *happiness*, *anger*, etc.).

Thus, the Darwinian concept of "expression" was progressively assimilated into a classical semantic view of communication in which speakers encode their thoughts into symbols (e.g., words) and listeners retrieve, through a shared code, these thoughts from the expressed symbol. Researchers and lay people assume that facial expressions are a sort of pictorial symbol that represent emotions. This approach assumes that specific regions of the brain literally "speak" by themselves, like inner homunculi, through facial displays aimed at turning emotions inside out. For the main advocate of the concept of facial expression of basic emotion (Tomkins, 1975), emotion was literally in the face. Later on, Tomkins's disciples, Ekman (1972) and Izard (1971), enlarged this semantic approach by including a sort of grammar that prescribes the truthfulness of facial expressions.

As in a classical semantic approach to language, in which an honest speaker produces a true symbol that expresses a thought, an honest sender produces a *true facial expression* that expresses a basic emotion. As listeners "recognize" the meaning of an utterance through a shared code, receivers would also recognize the meaning of an expression through a shared code. The main difference between words and facial expressions would be that the meaning of a word is based on a cultural code, whereas the meaning of expressions would be based on a universal code.

Expressions of Basic Emotion

As a consequence, the study of facial expression has been limited to a corpus of static, bidimensional expressions of basic emotion (EBEs), which constitute a closed set of pictorial symbols that represent Western concepts of emotion through a very widespread code. The study of EBEs has contributed to the understanding of the perception of pictorial representations of faces by normal and clinical populations. Nevertheless, its contribution to the understanding of the actual facial behavior displayed in episodes of emotion is minor. EBE*s* are commonsensical—rather than scientific—ideal representations of the huge repertory of movements produced on the human face in emotional episodes, but they are not typical instances of NFEs in emotional episodes (see Hortsmann, 2002).

Psychology and neuroscience have focused their efforts on the search for the universal code governing the communication of the EBE repertory. Researchers have found that most of these EBEs can be "recognized"—under controlled conditions and for some specific tasks—in literate societies. However, the recognition of these EBEs is of very limited relevance or nonexistent in those societies in which written language does not play a central role in the everyday life of their members (Nelson & Russell, 2013). The most recent studies on the recognition of EBEs in isolated societies (Crivelli, Jarillo, Russell, & Fernández-Dols, 2016; Crivelli, Russell, Jarillo, & Fernández-Dols, 2016; Gendron, Roberson, van der Vyver, & Barrett, 2014) show puzzling, skewed, and incomplete—by Western standards—patterns of recognition.

EBEs should not be confused with NFEs. Rather than accurate descriptions of the actual facial behavior in emotional episodes, the EBEs are a sort of arbitrary symbolic repertory with their own dialectal variations (e.g., Elbenbein, Beaupré, Lévesque, & Hess, 2007) and a heavy dependence on verbal language (Lindquist & Gendron, 2013). A definitive proof of the human capacity for developing arbitrary coding conventions for facial expressions is offered in Nelson and Russell's (2016) studies, in which they found that children confronted with a facial display with no conventional meaning (e.g., swollen cheeks) but embedded in a set of EBEs were soon capable of assigning an arbitrary verbal category to such an expression (e.g., *pax*), and of learning and applying such a category to future recognition tasks, as if it were an expression of a basic emotion called *pax*.

A reasonable but troubling conclusion is that for almost 50 years psychologists have gathered a large amount of data about the human ability to spontaneously code ("recognize") those pictorial symbols of emotion called *expressions of basic emotion*. These findings are potentially important for a better understanding of how humans, in the framework of literate cultures, can develop alternative nonverbal codes that share some key features (e.g., semantic processing) with verbal codes. However, such findings are not necessarily informative about humans' actual facial behavior in emotional episodes.

In the next sections I suggest an alternative approach to facial behavior that might help to overcome this stalemate.

WHAT DOES CAUSE NATURAL FACIAL EXPRESSIONS?

My alternative account of the causes of facial expressions draws on a relatively new perspective on emotion called psychological construction (Russell, 2003). In this account, an emotional episode is a loose, rapidly changing assemblage of components. Components are widely recognized subevents within an emotional episode such as sensory-perceptual-cognitive processing of the precipitating event and its context; facial, vocal, and other behavioral cues; changes in the peripheral nervous system; instrumental behavior; and conscious subjective events, including the feeling of having what, in the Western culture, we categorize as "emotion." A key assumption is that no one component is "emotion." Nor is emotion the causal entity behind these components.

Psychological constructionism sets facial behavior apart from the processes and behaviors that have traditionally called "emotion"; emotion is not a necessary or sufficient cause of facial expression. Although many will perceive the abandonment of the concept of *expression of basic emotion* as an impoverishment of the field, I believe that such a separation expands the field by freeing facial behavior from its ancillary role with respect to emotion. Facial behavior becomes an object of study in itself, with potential—but complex and indirect—connections with other components of an emotional episode, as well as with other psychological processes.

A conceptual framework that explicitly precludes the assumption that emotions are entities that cause the components of the emotional episode comes up against an immediate challenge: What does cause facial movements if not emotions? Facial movements often occur during emotional episodes (as they do during nonemotional episodes), and some specific facial configurations, even isolated from other components, are labeled (in Western societies) with terms of "emotion" (for example, in English, terms such as *anger*, *fear*, and so on). But, all the same, the facial movements should not be accounted for by the everyday concept of "emotion."

Empirical evidence suggests that NFE can play an important role in the conscious or unconscious regulation of some of the affective and cognitive processes involved in an emotional episode. For example, NFEs can be self-regulatory tools that can help the sender to maintain an optimal level of arousal, to enhance visual exposure and the processing of sensorial inputs (Lee, Susskind, & Anderson, 2013), to prompt or sustain cognitive effort in appraisals of goal obstruction (Scherer, & Ellgring, 2007), or to prompt physical effort in the consequent actions (Morree & Marcora, 2010).

WHAT DO NATURAL FACIAL EXPRESSIONS EXPRESS?

In some cases, NFEs can be significantly uniform for most individuals in some particular contexts. Fernández-Dols, Carrera, and Crivelli (2011) found a notably uniform facial configuration—with a striking apparent similarity to the expression of pain—in episodes of intense sexual enjoyment. Garcia-Higuera, Crivelli, and Fernández-Dols (2015) found that triumphant bullfighters displayed a surprisingly uniform set of expressions (e.g., a funnel mouth) while fighting with the bull.

These expressions might have an unknown psychological function (e.g., a sensorial or affective regulatory function), but from a evolutionary point of view, such uniformity suggests that they might also have communicative value in humans. Does such a hypothesis support the semantic view of the EBE approach? The answer is negative; in the coming paragraphs I will argue that the communicative relevance of some facial expressions does not mean that they have a semantic function, but instead a pragmatic one.

More Lessons From the Study of Natural Language

Linguistics' new emphasis on natural, spoken language rather than on written language emphasizes the importance of the study of pragmatics, which, in contrast with semantics, has been ignored by the main contemporary theories of facial expression. The primary reference through which the sender can share her thoughts with the receiver is not exclusively a code, but a context that prompts an inference about the sender's intention while she tries to communicate. Meaning is a secondary outcome of such a process of inference.

A graphic illustration of this point is Van Der Henst, Carles, and Sperber's (2002) field experiment in which participants were approached by a stranger who asked what time it was; even though the question was strictly factual and the answer could have a clear truth value, participants' answers varied depending on the circumstances and practical consequences of the answer. For example, the reported time was more precise, instead of rounded ("7 minutes to 3" vs. "10 minutes to 3") depending on the senders' inferences about the receiver's need: When the senders inferred that the receiver had a close appointment (e.g., at 2:30), their response was more precise (e.g., "2:26" vs. "half past 2") than if they inferred that the appointment was much later (e.g., at 4:00). What this example shows is not only that the sender is extremely sensitive to the context of his utterance, but that the utterance does not have absolute truth values; it is rather an estimate, on the sender's side, of a balance between the effort required to produce the message and the desired effect on the receiver.

From a pragmatic point of view, natural spoken language is made up of actions, and actions are not true or false. Rather than "true" or "false," they are, using Austin's terms, "felicitous" or "infelicitous": actions that satisfy or do not satisfy the sender's desires or intentions. An important consequence of such a view, which constitutes the foundations of pragmatics, is that the meaning of spoken language is completely dependent on the context, or, in other words, it lacks absolute truth or falsehood values. A spoken statement, even the simplest one, has an undetermined truth value. It requires a complex process of inference in which the listener has to look for contextual cues that provide the statement with relevance: "In real life, as opposed to the simple situations envisaged in logical theory, one cannot always answer in a simple way if [a statement] is true or false. Suppose that we confront 'France is hexagonal' with the facts (. . .) is it true or false? (. . .) it is true enough for certain intents and purposes (. . .) It is a rough description; it is not a true or false one" (Austin, 1975, p. 143).

If the meaning of natural spoken language, which can be interpreted through an explicit discrete code, depends on the context in which it is produced, the meaning of NFE, which lacks such an explicit code, must be even more dependent on contextual information. It might be countered that *expressions* depend on an implicit domain-specific code made of precise discrete categories, but such an assumption is not supported by empirical data (see earlier). Even research exclusively focused on canonical EBEs, rather than natural expressions, have found that they are dependent on the linguistic (Barrett, Lindquist, & Gendron, 2007) and affective context (Aviezer et al., 2008) in which they have to be decoded by the receiver.

A Pragmatic View of Natural Facial Expression

NFEs can have an important role as an evolved communicative tool with a pragmatic, rather than semantic function. NFEs do not have a specific meaning, *but they hint at potential outcomes of an interaction for either the sender or the receiver.*

All NFEs share an important common trait: their pragmatic rather than semantic relevance; that is, they "make" things rather than "say" things. From this perspective, studying NFEs as if they were *expressions of basic emotion* does not make sense. NFEs are starting points of emergent inferential strategies coextensive with cognitive, affective, and/or behavioral consequences.

NFEs are not nature-made signals of specific basic emotions, and senders' intentions when displaying spontaneous NFEs are not semantic (a conscious intent to send a message through a shared code), but NFEs can play an important role as actions in a communicative interaction. NFEs direct the receiver's attention to the sender's affective state, and they can trigger inferential processes about the senders that can have important consequences on either the senders themselves or the receivers. In other words, facial behavior is relevant rather than meaningful. The most basic feature of an NFE is its affective relevance to which we are sensitive early in life (Walker-Andrews, 1997).

Although in pragmatics relevance has been defined in terms of changes in the cognitive environment of sender and receiver (Sperber & Wilson, 1986), there are empirical and theoretical reasons to assume that affect also plays an important role in the detection of relevance. Facial movements trigger infants' attentional resources and lead to contextual inferences about the affective valence of the event that apparently caused the sender's facial behavior (Campos & Sternberg, 1981). Affective relevance "emanates" from the sender (for example, cues of nonspecific arousal) through social interaction, and it can be more salient in individual senders with no acquired self-monitoring skills, such as young children. For example, Zivin (1977) observed that a specific facial behavior (the "plus" face: raised eyebrows, stare, and raised chin) predicted triumph in a struggle but only for children younger than 10 years old.

In any case, the affective relevance of NFEs is extremely important because they prompt, on the receiver's side, important *inferences about the context, the sender*, and *the course of the interaction between sender and receiver.*

Inferences About the Affective Relevance of the Context

Let's emphasize again that NFEs are not "signs" of affect with a crisp, univocal truth value; that is, they are not a closed semantic repertory. Their communicative function is an emergent property of their pragmatic functions. A basic pragmatic outcome of NFEs' affective relevance is *pointing*. It is well known that hand pointing is an important tool in the development of language, but there are also voluntary or involuntary forms of facial pointing through gaze or just facial movements that make a particular event salient for the receiver (Clark, 2003). In many cases, facial pointing helps to focus attentional resources on some particular objects that have potential important consequences for the receiver, which leads the receiver to make inferences (e.g., danger; see Hadjikhani, Hoge, Snyder, & de Gelder, 2008) about those objects. The inference of affective relevance through some forms of facial pointing, particularly the detection of negative core affect (Vaish, Grossman, & Woodward, 2008), is a plausible early adaptive skill in human babies. Researchers have found that infants of between 6 and 12 months are sensitive to cues of negative affect and can change their behavior accordingly (e.g., Hornik, Risenhoover, & Gunnar, 1987). Later on, 14-month-old babies can use others' positive or negative affective reactions to an object (e.g., from someone who has apparently hurt herself with that object) to modify their own behavior with respect to that object; such early capacity is based on an associative learning process driven by attentional, rather than emotional cues (Chiarella, & Poullin-Dubois, 2013).

Inferences About the Sender's Affective State

Only at 18 months do toddlers take into account not only the affective valence of the consequences of dealing with an object but also the valence of the sender's inner affective state, carrying out some sort of mind-reading (Chiarella & Poullin-Dubois, 2013; cf. Barna & Legerstee, 2005). This new skill introduces a second pragmatic function of NFEs: placing the sender in the scope of the receiver's attention. Some NFEs, such as visual interaction, and some muscular movements place senders into the receiver's optimal attentional range and help the receiver to hypothesize the sender's intentions, facilitating next steps in a joint activity.

NFEs increase the receiver's cognitive vigilance with regard to the sender's intentions and launch empathic processes. The full-fledged human version of these two parallel processes appears in older children and is probably the product of complex biological and cultural coevolution, but young children and some primates can also make fast, implicit, primitive pragmatic inferences from NFEs. Tomasello and his collaborators detected children's and great apes' inferences about willingness, goodness or meanness, direction, potential coordination, and competition. For example, chimpanzees "read" cooperative or competitive nonverbal cues that characterized a human experimenter as a competitor or as a cooperator (Hare & Tomasello, 2004), and they established some degree of association between the placement of behavioral cues and an actor's behavior (Buttelmann et al., 2012). Most important, great apes inferred the directedness and valence of some human facial expressions, and they used this understanding to infer desires (Buttelmann, Call, &Tomasello, 2009). With respect to young children, 4- and 5-year-olds made rather complex social inferences (e.g., decisions about future social interaction, inferences about the feelings of a victim) through their "reading" of "displays of guilt" (appeasement) by a transgressor (Vaish, Carpenter, & Tomasello, 2011). These inferences might be a key component of the ability, apparently shared by young children and great apes, to form characterizations of others (Herrmann et al., 2013).

Inferences About the Sender–Receiver Interaction

NFEs can be "entrained" into predictable social interactions that, in some cases, include characteristic facial configurations. An important instance of how facial behavior leads to inferences about the sender is the social smile. Fernández-Dols and collaborators (Crivelli, Carrera, & Fernández-Dols, 2015; Fernández-Dols & Ruiz-Belda, 1995; Ruiz-Belda, Fernández-Dols, Carrera, & Barchard, 2003; see also Kraut & Johnson, 1979) found that smiles are not displayed by lone happy senders; they are displayed when senders interact with others. Their function is pragmatic rather than semantic. Smiles place senders in the optimal attentional range of their targets, and they help the sender to lead the receiver to infer a social invitation. Such social invitation opens the way to cooperative exchanges. Mehu, Grammer, and Dunbar (2007; see also Mehu & Dunbar, 2008) found that intense smiles not only help to place the sender in a cooperative disposition but also induce cooperative responses on the receiver's side. In the same vein, laughter is probably more related to the induction or accentuation of positive affect in others than to the communication of emotional states (Gervais & Wilson, 2005; Owren & Bachorowski, 2003). These findings strongly suggest that episodes of friendly social interaction are powerful predictors of smiles (and that smiles are not necessary or sufficient EBEs of happiness).

There are other documented examples of NFEs in predictable social interactions. Martín-Aranguren and Tonnelat (2014) found that undesired physical contact in a crowded subway car triggered, in the angered passenger, a variable set of facial movements such as, for example, a combination of brow movements and frowning. These NFEs were typically entrained into an interaction that consisted, on the side of the offended passenger, in an ostensible head turn and staring at the offender, in a sort of facial reproach rather than an anger *expression of basic emotion*.

Some NFEs can be idiosyncratic (for only some individuals in some particular contexts) antecedents of the particular course of an interaction. A common anecdotal remark is that we all develop specific ways of navigating through emotional episodes with our close relatives or friends thanks to an in-depth knowledge of their nonverbal tics. Camras (1992) scientifically substantiated this remark by observing her daughter's affective responses to some of Camras's actions (e.g., washing the baby) during the infant's first 9 weeks; rather than instances of *expressions of basic emotion*, she found unpredicted facial displays (e.g., widened eyes and gaping mouth elicited by familiar stimuli), or complex series of mixed *expressions of basic emotion* in situations of distress (e.g., "expressions of pain," "anger," and "sadness" while crying), which, eventually, become good predictors of the course of an interaction between mother and baby. Gaspar and Esteves (2012) recorded 3-year-old kindergarten children in playful and agonistic episodes of joy, surprise, fear, or anger. The occurrence of instances of EBE was very rare; what they observed were idiosyncratic displays of muscular movements loosely related to the expected joy, surprise, fear, or anger EBEs. These idiosyncratic patterns have been also reported in the interaction between humans and animals. Hebb (1946) reported that workers at a primatological center learned how to deal with their chimpanzees not by decoding their expressions but by learning predictive behavioral patterns idiosyncratic to that chimp. Longitudinal studies of clinical samples yielded similar conclusions (Ellgring, 1986).

The interactive role of NFEs has important similarities with Eibl-Eibesfledt's (1989) concept of ritualizations as indicators of the sender's readiness to act in a particular way. However, in contrast with rituals, NFEs are not complex interactive strategies from a "universal grammar of human social behavior." NFE is inherently ambiguous but salient information that prompts the receiver to make inferences about the context. In a "Copernican turn" the target of the inferences about the NFEs is not the sender's emotional state but the context (e.g., the ongoing interaction) in which sender and receiver are embedded, and its affective consequences.

Inferences in Verbal Interaction

Finally, and against the prevalent tradition in the study of facial expression, NFEs should be studied in conjunction with speech, as a way of shaping or facilitating verbal exchanges, giving pragmatic force to verbal utterances.

A fascinating example of the early consequences of NFE's affective relevance in verbal interaction is facial motherese. Chong, Werker, Russell, and Carroll (2003) found a potentially universal set of facial displays in Chinese-speaking and English-speaking mothers while interacting with their 4- to 7-month-old babies. Three apparently exaggerated, caricature versions of kisses, startle faces, and play faces helped mothers to focus their babies' attention not only on their linguistic but also on themselves and their affective messages.

From a more global perspective, Levinson (2016) has underlined the decisive importance of turn taking as "part of the universal infrastructure of language" and as having a major role in the cognitive development of linguistic competence. Turn taking in adult human verbal interaction demands an extremely short response lapse (about 200 ms) that requires the receiver to literally predict the sender's message before it is finished. According to Levinson, this demanding task is carried out not only through semantic decoding but also through pragmatic heuristics, that is, fast, subjective inferences about the sender's intentions.

A pragmatic heuristic that is particularly relevant in emotional episodes consists of uttering marked expressions that contrast with those that the speaker would use to describe a normal, prototypical situation; what is said in an abnormal way points out an abnormal situation (Levinson, 2000). Such a fast process of inference must be facilitated by nonverbal cues. Coming back to the aforementioned example, the use of pragmatic heuristics could be supported not only by abnormal verbal utterances but also by deviations from the sender's facial baseline. Thus, NFE can play a major pragmatic role in emotional episodes that are mediated by speech.

Some empirical findings help us to illustrate the relevance of facial expression for pragmatic inferences in emotional episodes mediated by speech. For example, Fernández-Dols, Carrera, and Russell (2002) found that Spanish and Canadian participants who were asked to pair facial expression of basic emotion with the sender's mental appraisal of an unusual situation, or alternatively with the sender's verbal interaction about her appraisal (e.g., "So we have won the prize!" vs. "John, we have won the prize") almost unanimously paired the facial expression with the sender's verbal interaction, rather than with the mental appraisal.

A second, most impressive, and still not sufficiently explored example is the widespread use of emoticons in computer-mediated colloquial messages; as Dresner and Herring have concluded (2010; see also Marcoccia, Atifi, & Gauducheau, 2008), emoticons do not have the semantic function of transmitting the emotional state of the sender while sending her message, but the pragmatic function of disambiguating the sender's colloquial message and influencing the receiver. Use of emoticons constitutes a sort of spontaneous open-ended recognition task in which users have assigned facial expressions to their natural function: as pragmatic devices that facilitate the receiver's interpretation of the sender's intentions in an emotional episode. Emoticons are not an iconic representation of the sender's expression of emotion but an interactive strategy in an emotional colloquial episode (for example, a smiley after a criticism, as an interactive appeasement tactic).

CONCLUSIONS: BACK TO NATURAL FACIAL BEHAVIOR

People—at least Western people—report emotions. What Western people call "emotional experience" is another emergent property of emotional episodes. Facial behavior can be coextensive to emotional experience, but there is no causal relationship between emotional experience and actual facial behavior.

I claim that the concept of "expression of basic emotion" (EBE) hinders an objective account of the extremely diverse facial movements actually displayed in emotional episodes.

The facial movements that constitute NFE can be related to any of the components of an emotional episode: affect regulation, attributional processes, appraisals, actions, and so on. And NFEs can be flexible pragmatic tools in the framework of different situations (Table 24.1).

This approach to facial behavior draws a parallel with some new approaches in linguistics. As Levinson (2002) has pointed out:

> current perspectives on the relation between universal human nature and cultural factors often seem to me to be inverted: for example, language is held to be essentially universal, whereas language use is thought to be more open to cultural influences. But the reverse may in fact be far more plausible: there is obvious cultural codification of many aspects of language from phoneme to syntactic construction, whereas the uncodified, unnoticed, low-level background of usage principles or strategies may be fundamentally culture-independent. (p. xiv)

This is precisely the philosophy of the approach described in this chapter, extrapolated to the study of facial expression. Empirical research is progressively identifying the strong cultural background of the *expressions of basic emotion.* Their supposed universal recognition is heavily influenced

Table 24.1 EXPRESSIONS OF BASIC EMOTION VERSUS NATURAL FACIAL EXPRESSION

	Expressions of Basic Emotion	Natural Facial Expression
Its distinctive feature is	meaning	relevance
A relevant message is	a category of basic emotion	multiple (affective qualities of the context, the sender, or the future interaction)
Repertories are	prescriptive (true expressions)	descriptive
A representative face	fits into an canonical, ideal pictorial symbol (an honest expression of basic emotion)	is just frequent in some emotional episodes
Occurrences are	uniform	variable
Context is	a secondary reference	a primary reference
From an evolutionary view	they are fixed adaptations	they are adaptive strategies

by language and cultural representations (Jack et al., 2009; Jack, Caldara, & Schyns, 2011).

On the other hand, the study of "the uncodified, unnoticed, low-level background of usage principles or strategies" of *natural facial expression* is compatible with a parsimonious evolutionary approach that depicts humans as flexible, extremely adaptable creatures, rather than preprogrammed beings whose behavior is determined by a few given basic emotions. As in chess, there are a practically infinite number of potential *facial moves* from a finite number of expressive resources. Babies' smiles and cries are *facial moves*, as are adults' seductive smiles or treacherous tears; they use the same resources but in very different moves.

REFERENCES

Aranguren, M., & Tonnelat, S. (2014). Emotional transactions in the Paris subway: Combining naturalistic videotaping, objective facial coding and sequential analysis in the study of nonverbal emotional behavior. *Journal of Nonverbal Behavior, 38*, 495–512.

Austin, J. L. (1975). *How to do things with words* (2nd ed.). Cambridge, MA: Harvard University Press.

Aviezer, H., Hassin, R. R., Ryan, J., Grady, C., Susskind, J., Anderson, A., Moscovitch, M., & Bentin, S. (2008). Angry, disgusted, or afraid? Studies on the malleability of emotion perception. *Psychological Science, 19*, 724–732.

Aviezer, H., Messinger, D. S., Zangvil, S., Mattson, W. I., Gangi, D. N., & Todorov, A. (2015). Thrill of victory or agony of defeat? Perceivers fail to utilize information in facial movements. *Emotion, 15*, 791–797.

Aviezer, H., Trope, Y., & Todorov, A. (2012). Body cues, not facial expressions, discriminate between intense positive and negative emotions. *Science, 338* (6111), 1225–1229.

Barna, J., & Legerstee, M. (2005). Nine- and twelve-month-old infants relate emotions to people's actions. *Cognition and Emotion, 19*, 53–67.

Barrett, L. F., Lindquist, K. A., & Gendron, M. (2007). Language as context for the perception of emotion. *Trends in Cognitive Science, 11*, 327–332.

Buttelmann, D., Call, J., & Tomasello, M. (2009). Do great apes use emotional expressions to infer desires? *Developmental Science, 12*, 688–698.

Buttelmann, D., Schütte, S., Carpenter, M., Call, J., & Tomasello, M. (2012). Great apes infer others' goals based on context. *Animal Cognition, 15*, 1037–1053.

Campos, J. J., & Sternberg, C. R. (1981). Perception, appraisal, and emotion: The onset of social referencing. In M. E. Lamb & L. R. Sherrod (Eds.), *Infant social cognition: Empirical and theoretical considerations* (pp. 273–314). Hillsdale, NJ: Lawrence Erlbaum.

Camras, L. A. (1992). Expressive development and basic emotions. *Cognition & Emotion, 6*, 269–283.

Chiarella, S. S., & Poulin-Dubois, D. (2013). Cry babies and pollyannas: Infants can detect unjustified emotional reactions. *Infancy, 18*(Suppl. 1), E81–E96.

Chong, S. C. F., Werker, J. F., Russell, J. A., & Carroll, J. M. (2003). Three facial expressions mothers direct to their infants. *Infant and Child Development, 12*, 211–232.

Clark, H. H. (2003). Pointing and placing. In S. Kita (Ed.), *Pointing: Where language, culture, and cognition meet* (pp. 243–268). Hillsdale, NJ: Erlbaum.

Crivelli, C., Carrera, P., & Fernández-Dols, J. M. (2015). Are smiles a sign of happiness? Spontaneous expressions of judo winners. *Evolution and Human Behavior, 36*, 52–58.

Crivelli, C., Jarillo, S., Russell, J. A., & Fernández-Dols, J. M. (2016). Reading emotions from faces in two indigenous societies. *Journal of Experimental Psychology: General, 145*, 830–843.

Crivelli, C., Russell, J. A., Jarillo, S., & Fernández-Dols, J. M. (2016). The fear gasping face as a threat display in a Melanesian society. *Proceedings of the National Academy of Sciences of the United States of America, 113*(44), 12403–12407.

Dezecache, G., Mercier, H., & Scott-Phillips, T. C. (2013). An evolutionary approach to emotional communication. *Journal of Pragmatics, 59*, 221–233.

Dresner, E., & Herring, S. C. (2010). Functions of the nonverbal in CMC: Emoticons and illocutionary force. *Communication Theory, 20*, 249–268.

Du Bois, J. W. (2014). Discourse and grammar. In M. Tomasello (Ed.), *The new psychology of language: Cognitive and functional approaches to language structure, classic edition* (Vol. II, pp. 47–87). New York, NY: Psychology Press.

Eibl-Eibesfeldt, I. (1989). *Human ethology.* New York, NY: Aldine de Gruyter.

Ekman, P. (1972). Universals and cultural differences in facial expressions of emotion. In J. Cole (Ed.), *Nebraska Symposium on Motivation, 19* (pp. 207–282). Lincoln, NE: University of Nebraska Press.

Ekman, P. (2016). What scientists who study emotion agree about. *Perspectives in Psychological Science, 11*, 31–34.

Elbenbein, H. A., Beaupré, M., Lévesque, M., & Hess, U. (2007). Toward a dialect theory: Cultural differences in the expression and recognition of posed facial expressions. *Emotion, 7*, 131–146.

Ellgring, H. (1986). Nonverbal expression of psychological states in psychiatric patients. *European Archives of Psychiatry and Clinical Neuroscience, 236*, 31–34.

Fernández-Dols, J.M. (1999). Facial expression and emotion: A situational view. In P. Philippot, R.S. Feldman and E.J. Coats, (Eds.) *The social context of nonverbal behavior* (pp. 242- 261). Cambridge UK: Cambridge University Press.

Fernández-Dols, J. M., Carrera, P., & Crivelli, C. (2011). Facial behavior while experiencing sexual excitement. *Journal of Nonverbal Behavior, 35*, 63–71.

Fernández-Dols, J. M., Carrera, P., & Russell, J. A. (2002). Are facial displays emotional? Situational influences in the attribution of emotion to facial expressions. *The Spanish Journal of Psychology, 5*, 119–124.

Fernández-Dols, J. M., & Crivelli, C. (2013). Emotion and expression: Naturalistic studies. *Emotion Review, 5*, 24–29.

Fernández-Dols, J. M., & Ruiz-Belda, M. A. (1995). Are smiles a sign of happiness? Gold medal winners at the Olympic Games. *Journal of Personality and Social Psychology, 69*, 1113–1119.

Fernández-Dols, J.M.; Ruiz-Belda, M.A. (1997). Spontaneous facial behavior during intense emotional episodes: Artistic truth and optical truth. In J.A. Russell and J.M.

Fernández-Dols (Eds.), *The psychology of facial expression* (pp. 255-274). Cambridge, UK: Cambridge University Press.

Fridlund, A. J. (1994). *Human facial expression: An evolutionary view.* New York, NY: Academic Press.

Garcia-Higuera, J. A., Crivelli, C., & Fernández-Dols, J. M. (2015). Facial expressions during an extremely intense emotional situation: Toreros' lip funnel. *Social Science Information, 54*, 439–454.

Gaspar, A., & Esteves, F. G. (2012). Preschooler's faces in spontaneous emotional contexts—how well do they match adult facial expression prototypes? *International Journal of Behavioral Development, 36*, 348–357.

Gendron, M., Roberson, D., van der Vyver, J. M., & Barrett, L. F. (2014). Perceptions of emotion from facial expressions are not culturally universal: Evidence from a remote culture. *Emotion, 14*, 251–262.

Gervais, M., & Wilson, D.S. (2005). The evolution and functions of laughter and humor: A synthetic approach. *The Quarterly Review of Biology, 80*, 395–430.

Hadjikhani, N., Hoge, R., Snyder, J., & de Gelder, B. (2008). Pointing with the eyes: The role of gaze in communicating danger. *Brain and Cognition, 68*, 1–8.

Hare, B., & Tomasello, M. (2004). Chimpanzees are more skillful in competitive than in cooperative cognitive tasks. *Animal Behavior, 68*, 571–581.

Hebb, D. O. (1946). Emotion in man and animal: An analysis of the intuitive processes of recognition. *Psychological Review 53*, 88–106.

Herrmann, E., Keupp, S., Hare, B., Vaish, A., & Tomasello, M. (2013). Direct and indirect reputation formation in nonhuman great apes (*Pan paniscus, Pan troglodytes, Gorilla gorilla, Pongo pygmaeus*) and human children (*Homo sapiens*). *Journal of Comparative Psychology, 127*, 63–75.

Hornik, R., Risenhoover, N., & Gunnar, M. (1987). The effects of maternal positive, neutral, and negative affective communications on infant responses to new toys. *Child Development, 58*, 937–944.

Horstmann, G. (2002). Facial expressions of emotion: Does the prototype represent central tendency, frequency of instantiation, or an ideal? *Emotion, 2*, 297-305.

Izard, C. (1971). *The face of emotion.* New York, NY: Appleton-Century-Crofts.

Jack, R. E., Blais, C., Scheepers, C., Schyns, P. G., & Caldara, R. (2009). Cultural confusions show that facial expressions are not universal. *Current Biology, 19*, 1543–1548.

Jack, R. E., Caldara, R., & Schyns, P. G. (2011). Internal representations reveal cultural diversity in expectations of facial expressions of emotion. *Journal of Experimental Psychology. General, 141*, 19–25.

Lee, D. H., Susskind, J. M., & Anderson, A. K. (2013). Social transmission of the sensory benefits of fear eye-widening. *Psychological Science, 24*, 957–965.

Levinson, S. C. (2000). *Presumptive meanings: The theory of generalized conversational implicature.* Cambridge, MA: The MIT Press.

Levinson, S. C. (2016). Turn-taking in human communication—Origins and implications for language processing. *Trends in Cognitive Sciences, 20*, 6–14.

Lindquist, K., & Gendron, M. (2013). What's in a word? Language constructs emotion perception. *Emotion Review, 5*, 66–71.

Marcoccia, M., Atifi, H., & Gauducheau, N. (2008). Text-centered versus multimodal analysis of instant messaging conversation. *Language@Internet, 5*, article 7. Retrieved from http://www.languageatinternet.de.

Mehu, M., & Dunbar, R. I. M. (2008). Naturalistic observations of smiling and laughter in human group interactions. *Behaviour, 145*, 1747–1780.
Mehu, M., Grammer, K., & Dunbar, R. I. M. (2007). Smiles when sharing. *Evolution and Human Behavior, 28*, 415–422.
Morree, H. M. de, & Marcora, S. M. (2010). The face of effort: Frowning muscle activity reflects effort during a physical task. *Biological Psychology, 85*, 377–382.
Nelson, N. L., & Russell, J. A. (2013). Universality revisited. *Emotion Review, 5*, 8–15.
Nelson, N. L., & Russell, J. A. (2016). A facial expression of Pax: Assessing children's "recognition" of emotion from faces. *Journal of Experimental Child Psychology, 141*, 49–64.
Owren, M. J., & Bachorowski, J. A. (2003). Reconsidering the evolution of nonlinguistic communication: The case of laughter. *Journal of Nonverbal Behavior, 27*, 183–200.
Reisenzein, R., Studtmann, M., & Horstmann, G. (2013). Coherence between emotion and facial expression: Evidence from laboratory experiments. *Emotion Review, 5*, 16–23.
Ruiz-Belda, M. A., Fernández-Dols, J. M., Carrera, P., & Barchard, K. (2003). Spontaneous facial expressions of happy bowlers and soccer fans. *Cognition & Emotion, 17*, 315–326.
Russell, J. A. (2003). Core affect and the psychological construction of emotion. *Psychological Review, 110*, 145–172.
Russell, J. A., & Fernández-Dols, J. M. (1997). What does a facial expression mean? In J. A. Russell & J. M. Fernández-Dols (Eds.), *The psychology of facial expression* (pp. 3–30). Cambridge, UK: Cambridge University Press.
Scherer, K. R., & Ellgring, H. (2007). Are facial expressions of emotion produced by categorical affect programs or dynamically driven by appraisal? *Emotion, 7*, 113–130.
Smith, W. J. (1965). Message, meaning and context in ethology. *The American Naturalist, 99*, 405–409.
Sperber, D., & Wilson, D. (1986). *Relevance: communication and cognition*. Oxford, UK: Basil Blackwell.
Tomasello, M. (2014). Introduction: Some surprises for psychologists. In M. Tomasello (Ed.), *The new psychology of language: Cognitive and functional approaches to language structure, classic edition* (Vol. II, pp. 1–15). New York, NY: Psychology Press.
Tomkins, S. (1975). The phantasy behind the face. *Journal of Personality Assessment, 39*, 551–560.
Vaish, A., Carpenter, M., & Tomasello, M. (2011). Young children's responses to guilt displays. *Developmental Psychology, 47*, 1248–1262.
Vaish, A., Grossmann, T., & Woodward, A. (2008). Not all emotions are created equal: The negativity bias in social-emotional development. *Psychological Bulletin, 134*, 383–403.
Van der Henst, J. B., Carles, L., & Sperber, D. (2002). Truthfulness and relevance in telling the time. *Mind & Language, 17*, 457–466.
Walker-Andrews, A.S. (1997). Infants' perception of expressive behaviors: Differentiation of multimodal information. *Psychological Bulletin, 121*, 437–456.

PART XI

Culture

25

Emotional Dialects in the Language of Emotion

HILLARY ANGER ELFENBEIN

Introductory psychology textbooks tell the story of Ekman (1972) and Izard (1971), who took photographs of American facial expressions around the world in order to demonstrate that emotions are universal. The data they collected have been analyzed and interpreted in several different ways, which are not necessarily mutually exclusive. The first interpretation, from the original researchers, was that participants were far more accurate than what would be predicted by chance—in other words, greater than 16.7% when selecting among six multiple choices. They argued that this finding demonstrates that basic emotions are universal across cultures—a conclusion that has been questioned in the years since then on multiple grounds (Nelson & Russell, 2013; Russell, 1994). The second interpretation, which is discussed later in this chapter in greater detail, was that some cultures were more accurate than others (Matsumoto, 1989). The third interpretation is that the cultural groups that performed the best were from the nation where the photographs originated, followed by those most culturally similar. This last observation was key to developing what has been called *dialect theory.*

In 1964, Tomkins and McCarter used a metaphor that cultural differences in emotional expression are like "dialects" of the "more universal grammar of emotion" (p. 127). Dialect theory takes seriously this linguistic metaphor for communicating emotion. Linguistic dialects of a language can differ subtly in accent, grammar, and vocabulary—for example, consider American versus British English. As in verbal language, it is more challenging to understand someone speaking a different dialect. Although linguistic dialects are mutually intelligible, it is often necessary to listen more carefully, and some of the meaning can get lost along the way.

There are two interconnected processes within dialect theory that need to be distinguished from each other. In the first process, members of different cultural groups have subtly but systematically different styles of generating nonverbal cues of emotion. This process is also called expression, although that term implies that emotion cues are generated intentionally, even though people can also generate cues without trying. In the second process, individuals tend to judge other people's cues based on their own cultural style. That is, people typically interpret cues based on what they would have meant if they had themselves used those kinds of cues. This judgment process is also called recognition, although likewise this term implies that the process of judging emotional cues is always intentional, when it can also be implicit. According to dialect theory, accuracy breaks down through cultural differences that are effectively the flip coins of each other, existing on both sides of the process. Communication accuracy is maximized to the extent that there is a match between expression style and the style expressed by the perceiver, and it suffers the extent to which there is a mismatch. Note that even the term *communication* can be preemptive in that it implies a conscious goal, and dialect theory is intended to describe both deliberate and spontaneous processes. That said, as discussed later, the vast majority of existing evidence tests posed expressions, and the relatively small body of research testing has used spontaneous expressions.

In keeping with the distinction between the emotion expression and recognition processes, dialect theory makes a distinction between *nonverbal accents* and dialects. Nonverbal accents are any difference across cultures in the appearance of an emotional expression. Nonverbal dialects are a subset of these accents—namely, dialects are the nonverbal accents that also impede accurate recognition. In the linguistic metaphor, typically one can notice another person's accent, but it is not that challenging to understand the actual content of what the person is saying. However, a dialect can create actual difficulty in understanding another person's speech. Furthermore, consistent with the linguistic metaphor, the distinction between dialect and accent might become fluid in the face of cultural contact. It is possible that large differences in cues could merely remain accents if individuals are familiar through cross-group contact, but among less acquainted groups there can be difficulty based on even small differences.

DISPLAY AND DECODING RULES

The most prominent accounts for cultural differences in emotional expression and recognition that have been presented as alternatives to dialect theory focus on deception. In describing the expression process, dialect theory argues that culturally specific cues can still appear even while trying to be as clear as possible. By contrast, Klineberg (1938) and Ekman's (1972) concept of *display rules* focuses on deliberately deceptive emotion regulation with the goal of improving social harmony, and further that individuals from more interdependent cultures make greater use of these display rules. Ekman (1972) defined display rules as conscious management techniques to deintensify, intensify, neutralize, and mask displays with qualitatively different displays. Taking a strong position on the topic, he argued that members of each culture would express their emotions in exactly the same way if some groups were not constantly monitoring themselves and adjusting their displays to fit social norms. Ekman grounded this discussion in a summary of W. Friesen's unpublished dissertation (described in Ekman, 1972), in which Japanese participants were said to have masked their facial displays in the presence of an observer while American participants did not. These findings have been controversial due to incomplete reporting, in that there was actually an additional experimental condition that Ekman did not mention in his summary, and which would have changed the interpretation of the results had it been considered (Fridlund, 1994). Even so, this notion of display rules decreasing the recognition of emotional expressions by members of interdependent cultures has been a powerful idea within cross-cultural research in emotion. In contrast, the dialect theory argues that individuals do not necessarily have to undertake any kind of deliberate deception to produce cultural differences in emotional expression style.

Likewise, in emotion recognition, which is the flip side of the communication process, individuals can face challenges in judging others' emotions even while trying to be as perceptive as possible. As an alternate view, Matsumoto (1989) extended the notion of display rules to detail a corresponding notion of *decoding rules*. Like display rules, decoding rules focus on deliberately deceptive regulation. In his attempt to explain the cultural differences in Ekman's (1972) and Izard's (1971) studies, Matsumoto (1989) argued that Americans are simply more effective at recognizing emotions. His reasoning was that Americans purportedly do not suppress their true understanding of emotional displays out of concern for group harmony. In contrast, dialect theory argues that cultural differences in recognition can still emerge when people are trying to be as accurate as possible in perceiving other people's emotions. It is not necessary to ignore other people's emotions deliberately to produce cultural differences in emotion recognition accuracy.

Instead, individuals can stumble over differences in the styles of expressions from cultural out-groups.

Although these explanations have been presented as alternatives, indeed differences in dialects can exist alongside the deliberate emotion regulation strategies represented by display and decoding rules. These explanations have often been considered in opposition due to the inaccurate claim that display and decoding rules alone can explain the body of findings on cultural differences in emotion recognition (Matsumoto, 2002). The following discussion explains why they cannot serve as complete explanations—if not dialect theory, something else is necessary to close the gap.

EMPIRICAL EVIDENCE

The initial evidence for dialect theory came from the observation *in-group advantage*—that is, individuals are more accurate when judging emotional expressions from their own cultural group versus foreign cultural groups. Nalini Ambady and I demonstrated this in a meta-analysis that included 182 independent samples from 87 academic articles, the majority of which examined facial expressions (Elfenbein & Ambady, 2002b). Many of these samples came from the very same original papers that were intended to demonstrate universality. Interestingly, many other samples were from unintentionally cross-cultural research, for which investigators borrowed research protocols from international colleagues without hypotheses that cultural differences could result. It is important to note that the magnitude of in-group advantage did not differ significantly across research teams, nor did it vary along methodological lines (which frequently coincided with research teams). This speaks against the possibility that in-group advantage was merely an artifact of poor-quality research. Issues of language could not explain away in-group advantage, because the effect was also found across cultural groups that shared the same native language. Racial bias could not explain away in-group advantage either, because it existed among all-Caucasian groups. It was noteworthy that the only significant moderator was cross-cultural exposure, such that the in-group advantage was smaller when judging more familiar cultural groups.

The earliest research that established evidence for accents used a design that was particularly stringent (Marsh, Elfenbein, & Ambady, 2003). During the process of conducting the meta-analysis, I noticed that the brochure for Matsumoto and Ekman's (1988) collection of Japanese and Caucasian facial expressions included a combination of Japanese and Japanese Americans. These stimuli were perfectly consistent in every other way—the same lighting, clothing, and so on. For the purpose of consistency, the developers instructed participants exactly how to move their facial muscles, which meant that the resulting expressions should have been the same in every way other than the apparent ethnicity of the face. Even so, collaborator Abby Marsh and I found that the two of us could tell the Japanese apart from the Japanese Americans. In the resulting experiment, participants could also make this distinction. They were no more accurate than chance when attempting to distinguish the nationality of neutral photographs that were taken of the same actors. This rules out nuisance explanations such as hairstyle or the possible effects on facial appearance of diet, climate, and so on. However, when these same people attempted to pose emotional expressions, their nationality became visible to participants. We interpreted this finding as strong support for nonverbal accents, because it showed that—even in a set of facial expressions for which researchers attempted to dampen every possible cultural difference in appearance—these cultural differences still leaked through. Note that these accents were not dialects, because emotion recognition accuracy was not impaired.

It has now been over a decade since the initial research was published that found evidence for an in-group advantage and began to outline the dialect theory. In the time since then, the body of evidence has been increasing and has become more direct in testing the specific propositions of dialect theory. In one study, my colleagues and I linked the in-group advantage directly to differences in the appearance of expressions using a novel methodology (Elfenbein, Mandal, Ambady, Harizuka, & Kumar, 2004). In this study, we used composite facial expressions based on the left and right hemispheres of a face—that is, one photograph was turned into two different pictures. One picture showed the left side of the face twice, and the other picture showed the right side of the face twice. Participants showed greater in-group advantage when judging the left hemisphere, which is more intense and mobile, compared with the right hemisphere, which is more prototypical. The only plausible explanation was subtle differences in expression style, because there was a fully within-subjects design for both the photograph posers and the facial hemispheres being judged. In a study that sampled Quebecois and Gabonese participants (Elfenbein, Beaupré, Lévesque, & Hess, 2007), we documented accents in a more direct manner. We were able to identify specific muscle movements—that is, action units (AUs)—that varied across the groups' posed facial expressions. Consistent with the hypotheses of dialect theory, there were greater cultural differences in judgment accuracy for the emotions that also had greater cultural differences in expression style. Taken together, these studies strongly support dialect theory.

There has also been increasing evidence from other researchers. This evidence includes work with facial expressions and also work with nonverbal channels such as the voice and body language, for which the propositions of dialect theory also apply. The more recent studies included a number that were balanced 2x2 designs, for example showing in-group advantage among Americans and Japanese viewing facial expressions (Dailey et al., 2010), and British and Chinese listeners of vocal tones (Paulmann & Uskul, 2014). In Kang and Lau (2013), European and Asian Americans viewed both full-channel videos of spontaneous emotions as well as still photographs of culturally erased stimuli. Consistent with the predictions of dialect theory, they found in-group advantage for the first but not second of these conditions. Looking at affective states beyond the basic emotions, in-group advantage appeared for judgments of sarcasm, sincerity, and humor in a 2x2 design among English-speaking Canadians and Cantonese Chinese (Cheang & Pell, 2011). Interestingly, in-group advantage appeared for more versus less intense facial expressions (Zhang et al., 2015). In a balanced 2x2 design that did not yield in-group advantage for Australian and mainland Chinese participants judging facial photographs of European and Chinese ancestry, it is worth noting the stimuli originated in the United States and Singapore versus in Australia and mainland China (Prado et al., 2013), and that past work suggests the in-group advantage appears due to culture rather than race (Elfenbein & Ambady, 2003).

Some studies have involved remote cultural groups. In a study that included participants from England as well as a preliterate tribal culture in Namibia called the Himba, judgments of nonlinguistic vocalizations showed in-group advantage (Sauter, Eisner, Ekman, & Scott, 2010). Gendron, Roberson, van der Vyver, and Barrett (2014a) showed that US participants were more accurate than the Himba when judging vocal stimuli from English speakers. This was the case whether accuracy was analyzed in terms of discrete emotional categories or in terms of affective dimensions, that is, positive versus negative valence or high versus low arousal. In a heated debate, this latter paper interpreted itself as a nonreplication of Sauter et al.'s (2010) finding that the Himba could recognize English emotional expressions at all, because their mean values of emotion recognition accuracy were very low, particularly when they were tested in terms of specific emotion categories. Gendron et al. (2014a) concluded that Himba participants were accurate only in judging positive versus negative valence. Sauter, Eisner, Ekman, and Scott (2015) responded by returning to their original data and analyzing responses in terms of the valence and intensity of distractor choices. Again, they found evidence that the Himba were more accurate than chance in judging the foreign emotional expressions. As with the debate on in-group advantage, this debate—which concerns overall accuracy levels rather than the differences in accuracy levels across groups—includes disagreements about issues that one side sees as methodological and the other as substantive. Notably, Sauter et al. (2015)

point out that Gendron et al. (2014a) did not include manipulation checks, whereas Gendron et al.'s (2015) response argued that manipulation checks for understanding the emotion category are a matter of imposing categorical learning.

Although it didn't measure accuracy per se, another study with remote cultural groups is worth mentioning, in which the Himba and US participants viewed African American stimuli (Gendron, Roberson, van der Vyer, & Barrett, 2014b). The authors used a free-sorting task, in which participants were asked to place the stimuli into piles that they later named. The US versus Namibian participants showed greater consistency in the clusters they produced around these US photographs of basic categorical emotions.

In addition to these balanced designs, there were one-way comparison studies in which members of multiple cultural groups judged a single set of stimuli. These studies showed in-group advantage for the following: British and Swedish participants judging British vocal tones (Sauter & Scott, 2007); African students in the United States judging facial expressions and vocal tones (Wickline, Bailey, & Nowicki, 2009); English, German, Arabic, and Spanish speakers judging nonsense syllables from Spain (Pell, Monetta, Paulmann, & Kotz, 2009); speakers of English, German, Chinese, Japanese, and Tagalog judging voices from the United States (Thompson & Balkwill, 2006); Japanese, Sri Lankans, and Americans judging Japanese postures (Kleinsmith, De Silva, & Bianchi-Berthouze, 2006); and Germans, Romanians, and Indonesians judging German vocal tones (Jürgens et al., 2013).

There were several papers that provided evidence for the basic propositions of dialect theory, namely that the lower recognition of out-groups' emotions results from subtle differences in expression style. Kleinsmith et al. (2006) found that perceivers who judged still images of body posture in Japan, Sri Lanka, and the United States used different cues. Dailey et al. (2010) used a neural network that imitated the receptive fields in the visual cortex that "learn" how to represent objects visually and modeled the conditions that reproduce in-group advantage. In their study, when neural networks were trained with sample stimuli that were culturally normative for the United States versus Japan, the neural network developed slightly different visual representations. Sauter (2013) found that in-group advantage existed for Dutch participants judging Namibian but not English vocalizations, even when these participants were unable to identify the cultural origin of the stimuli. Furthermore, she used a clever test of dialect theory: presenting a fully crossed 2x2 collection of in-group versus out-group stimuli that were labeled to participants as originating from an in-group versus an out-group. Participants showed in-group advantage based on the actual origin of stimuli, not the origin they were led to believe.

Most studies have examined cultural differences in emotion recognition vis-à-vis cultural differences in emotional expression. This is most likely due to methodological feasibility, as it is far easier to collect judgments of a standardized set of stimulus materials than it is to elicit emotional expressions, record them, and code them for differences in expression style. Our Elfenbein et al. (2007) study is among the few to have done this. In another study, Matsumoto, Olide, and Willingham (2009) photographed Olympic judo athletes at the moment that their matches ended and coded the still images for their facial muscle movements. The authors hand-selected as stimuli only those images that already fit their preconceived notion of what muscle movements constituted a facial expression of emotion. For this reason their finding that people across cultures produced expressions of basic emotion was tautological, and not logically usable as evidence for universality.

In terms of demonstrating the potential importance of these findings for society, some papers have made applied use of insights from dialect theory. There have been findings that African American versus Caucasian schizophrenics show greater emotional impairments, but this past finding no longer held when researchers used stimuli from both ethnic groups (Pinkham et al., 2008). This suggests that previous instruments used by clinicians to diagnose mental illness may have suffered from a subtle bias. The in-group advantage might also create communication challenges in the United States for White doctors working with ethnic minority patients (Levine & Ambady, 2013). In a marketing context, service providers were better able to understand the level of anger self-reported by culturally matched versus mismatched customers in simulation videos (Tombs, Russell-Bennett, & Ashkanasy, 2014).

As mentioned earlier, the majority of research on this topic uses posed expressions, which has led some critics to speculate that in-group advantage exists only for poses (Matsumoto, Olide, & Willingham, 2009). However, there are two notable exceptions to this potential gap. In-group advantage has been found for judging spontaneous full-channel videos (Kang & Lau, 2013) and for spontaneous anxiety during interracial interactions (Gray, Mendes, & Denny-Brown, 2008). As mentioned earlier, Elfenbein et al. (2004) found greater dialects in the more spontaneous versus posed side of the face. In one intriguing study, Naab and Russell (2007) collected judgment data in the United States using spontaneous photographs of individuals from a remote region of Papua New Guinea, which Ekman (1980) originally collected and discussed as valid representations of specific universal expressions. Although there was not a direct cross-cultural comparison in Naab and Russell (2007), the poor recognition rates they documented for their US participants—with a mean of 24.2%—are far lower than what US participants typically achieve in recognizing other stimulus sets, which suggests a likely in-group advantage in these data.

CRITICAL ACCOUNTS

The in-group advantage and dialect theory have sparked controversy due to their implications for dominant theories about cross-cultural differences in emotion, namely display and decoding rules. However, evidence for in-group advantage cannot be explained away by these factors alone—that is, for the sake of harmony, participants suppressing their displays using display rules and suppressing their perceptions using decoding rules. Among the sources of data that speak against this explanation, Japanese participants perform better than Americans when the tasks originate in Japan versus the United States (Elfenbein & Ambady, 2002).

Matsumoto (2002) wrote a commentary on this work, in which he asserted there was a set of three methodological requirements that he would require before he would believe the evidence. For two of these so-called requirements, we were in agreement about their content, but noted that they were indeed already included in the original analysis or controlled for, respectively (Elfenbein & Ambady, 2002a). The first of these was to have balanced designs, where each culture involved in the study was represented with both stimuli and participant judgments. This allows for the removal of potential main effects—such as stimulus quality or participant familiarity with experimental research—so that in-group advantage can be calculated as an expressor x perceiver interaction term. The second of these was that stimuli from the various cultural groups should be equally clear. This is also an important practice, and we follow it in our own empirical work, but point out that balanced designs already control for this potential nuisance as part of the main effect for expressor group.

Matsumoto's last purportedly methodological concern was actually a difference in perspective that gets to the heart of dialect theory. He argued that the in-group advantage would disappear if members of each culture expressed their emotions in precisely the same way. In the case of facial expressions, this involves moving precisely the same muscles in the same combinations. This is a matter of "violent agreement." According to dialect theory, without differences in the style of emotional expression, then there should be no in-group advantage. As an analogy: If British people spoke in exactly the same manner as Americans, using the same exact words, then there would be no room for linguistic dialects to cause confusion. For this reason, we referred to Matsumoto's recommendation as a "cultural eraser" (Elfenbein & Ambady, 2002a, p. 244). It is an oxymoron that all cross-cultural studies should first have to eliminate all cultural differences from their stimuli. Although Matsumoto referred to this as a methodological flaw, this is actually the central point where our theories differ.

Consistent with the dialect theory, in studies that force stimuli to have exactly the same appearance is a cultural eraser, numerous researchers have replicated a lack of in-group advantage (Beaupre & Hess, 2005, 2006; Kang & Lau, 2013; Lee, Chiu, & Chan, 2005; Matsumoto et al., 2009; Tracy & Robins, 2008). Elfenbein et al. (2007) conducted a direct test of comparing in-group advantage for stimuli with cultural dialects versus cultural erasers. In a between-subjects design, they used both culturally erased stimuli alongside dialect stimuli and found in-group advantage for the second but not for the first. Some researchers do find in-group accuracy using culturally erased stimuli—employing ethnic groups (van der Schalk, Hawk, Fischer, & Doosje, 2011), minimal groups (Young & Hugenberg, 2010), and false feedback about group membership (Thibault, Bourgeois, & Hess, 2006). In one dramatic example, European participants of Christian religious background saw identical still photographs of women's eyes either apparently embedded within a cap and scarf or within a Muslim burqa (Kret & Gelder, 2012). Participants were more accurate in judging fear expressed alongside a burqa, and with happiness and sadness alongside a cap and scarf. In these cases, the phenomenon appears to be a matter of out-group bias leading to lesser effort, motivation, or the application of stereotypes, rather than sincere failure of comprehension. It may also be a complex interaction among these factors.

A THEORETICAL ACCOUNT OF ORIGINS: TAKING THE LINGUISTIC METAPHOR SERIOUSLY

Whereas Kurt Lewin argued that "there is nothing so practical as a good theory (1951, p. 169), in the present case it can be argued that there is nothing so theoretical as hard data. It is concerning that the dominant models of cultural differences in emotion have been subjected to relatively minimal testing. By contrast, dialect theory arose primarily from an attempt to explain within a single framework the diverse body of evidence that the dominant theories couldn't explain. Beyond mere argumentation, it is important to distinguish theoretical perspectives from each other by making competing predictions and collecting the data to test them. Now that the empirical base is starting to fill in, it is time to develop a deeper theoretical account for the origin and meaning of accents and dialects.

It is important to wrestle with the question of origin: Why should cultures have accents and dialects in their nonverbal communication of emotion? Answers to this question benefit from taking the linguistic metaphor seriously. Drawing from the base of knowledge in linguistics, one can likewise ask: Why does verbal language have accents and dialects? Scholars in linguistics argue that spoken language continually evolves, and that it tends to diverge across groups of people who are separated by geographic or social boundaries (O'Grady et al., 2001). When separation between groups is smaller, these accents can be noticeable without impeding communication. However, with increasing separation—both physical separation and social stratification within a society—these dialects create challenges to comprehension. In linguistics, dialects are defined in terms of communication challenges that can largely be overcome. With enough separation, distinct languages emerge that cannot be mutually understood.

In this sense, in understanding nonverbal dialects, the concept of social stratification looms large. It is worthwhile to ponder the underlying psychological mechanisms that result from the sociological construct of stratification. Two distinct processes are likely to act separately and in tandem. First, over time there are changes in verbal—and presumably nonverbal— language merely through random drift. Particularly when there are no formal records, passing down language from one generation to the next has evolution through no deliberate effort. Over time, there is change due to constant mutations and even errors—such as "an apkin" becoming "a napkin," or "a napron" becoming "an apron" (Palmer, 1882). When there is linguistic drift, social stratification creates dialects indirectly, because these drifts become shared among some speakers but not others (O'Grady et al., 2001). By contrast, in the second psychological mechanism, changes in expression style can occur deliberately through the process of asserting a distinct social identity. Notably, jargon and slang can create a marker or even deliberate barrier that defines group membership.

The exact form of an accent does not necessarily need a functional goal. For example, there isn't necessarily a specific reason why Bostonians drop the retroflex *r* at the end of a word instead of the dental *t*. It is not clear to what extent this is or isn't the case for nonverbal accents. Research shows that perceivers from Eastern versus Western groups tend to focus more on the eyes than on the mouth, and this is perhaps because the eyes provide greater diagnostic cues to hidden meaning (Yuki, Maddux, & Masuda, 2007). Another study used "reverse-correlation" to map out internal representations of emotions by asking participants to attribute emotional judgments to random noise, and then used these judgments to generate visual images with the appearance of their inferred mental model (Jack, Blais, Scheeepers, Schyns, & Caldara, 2009). In this work, there was greater consensus in East Asian perceivers for eye-related cues versus Westerners for mouth and eyebrow-related cues (see also Jack, Garrod, Yu, Caldara, & Schyns, 2012).

WHAT DO WE GET FROM THE LINGUISTIC METAPHOR?

Taking the linguistic metaphor seriously helps theorists grapple with the role of culture in emotion for several reasons. First, it allows research to proceed without resolving the question of whether emotions are universal. The existence of dialects does not deny the possibility that there is a universal language to emotion. Indeed, if emotion is a universal language, then nonverbal dialects should be expected, given that every verbal language with geographic range has regional varieties (O'Grady et al., 2001). On the other hand, the existence of dialects does not necessarily speak in favor of universality. One could also see basic similarity in emotional expression style across cultures if it resulted from a biologically based affect program, as posited by Ekman's (1972) neurocultural theory. Alternately, it could result from convergent evolution, whereby similar concerns and selection pressures led to similar solutions. For example, the penguin and puffin birds came to look alike but are related only distantly. As a verbal example, most languages use *m* in the word for mother, presumably because labial sounds are the first consonants babies develop and mothers around the world enjoy being the subject of their babies' first words. As a nonverbal example, disgust may appear similarly because it adapted from crinkling one's nose as a response to strong smells by reducing the openness of nasal passages. Modern evolutionary accounts emphasize adaptation and the potential social functions of emotional expressions, and argue that emotional expressions are more sophisticated than mere leftover vestiges that automatically read out our internal states (Owren & Rendall, 2001).

The linguistic metaphor benefits theorists by encouraging them to borrow theories from the allied social science of linguistics. Furthermore, it emphasizes that cultural differences in the expression and perception of emotion are mirror-image processes, which suggests that unlocking one can also help to unlock the other. By contrast, the theories of display and decoding rules were developed separately and these two different rules do not necessarily correspond to each other. The linguistic metaphor also emphasizes that cultural differences in emotional expression and recognition can be automatic. As discussed earlier, display rules and decoding rules are a matter of conscious management techniques, whereas no such tactics are required by dialect theory. It is hard to imagine that Americans adjust their speech with each utterance to avoid sounding British.

Even so, the value of the linguistic metaphor is not to imply that it must become a new shackle. It needs to be acknowledged that there may be explanations for in-group advantage that do not necessarily follow linguistic principles. For example, an *appraisal view* of nonverbal dialects could preserve the notion that people across cultures have a universal mapping from their internal feeling states to their outward displays. The appraisal view observes that emotions exist within broader families—such as irritation, rage, and anger—and cultures may differ in their modal experience within these emotion families (Fontaine, Scherer, & Soriano, 2013). If there is a one-to-one mapping from experiences to the appearance of facial expressions, it is possible for this difference in modal experience to lead to dialects that are better recognized by in-group members (Hess & Thibault, 2009). There is promising preliminary evidence for this account (Hess, Thibault, Levesque, & Elfenbein, 2008), for which a great deal more empirical support would be necessary. However one accounts for the empirical regularity of in-group advantage, the account needs to be able to explaining the large body of existing findings. The accounts of display and decoding rules alone simply do not.

There is untapped room for additional theoretical development in reconciling the notion of in-group advantage with the three distinct functions for emotional expressions posited by Bühler's (1934/1990) Organon model (Scherer, 1988). The idea is that faces express internal feelings directly and automatically, and even Darwin himself argued that the term "expression" may be preemptive (Parkinson, 2005). This idea is merely the first of the three functions in Organon's model. This "push" function has received the most attention, and it is at least implicitly the focus of most research reviewed earlier. The second is the "pull" function, namely that expressions are used as signals to produce a reaction in others (see also Fridlund, 1994; Owren & Rendall, 2001; Parkinson, 2013). This function received relatively less empirical attention. The third is the "symbolic" function, namely that expressions represent objects or events, similar to linguistic expressions. This has been studied the least of all. These different functions are not mutually exclusive, as they can exist alongside each other. They can even reinforce each other over time, in that simple reflexes such as the startle or nose crinkle produce reliable signals that later are used deliberately (Russell, Bachorowski, & Fernandez-Dols, 2003). The in-group advantage could potentially be the greatest in magnitude for the second and third functions, which have been studied the least, because these correspond more naturally to the linguistic metaphor for interpersonal communication. Universals in emotion may be better preserved in expressions serving "push" functions. That said, the empirical evidence still suggests that there can be an in-group advantage in spontaneous or semispontaneous settings.

BRIDGING THE GAP

It can be a somewhat gloomy finding that there is a cross-cultural barrier in communicating emotions. However, there are also reassuring data this barrier can be overcome. Notably, in-group advantage is lower across cultural groups enjoying greater physical proximity or greater cross-group communication

(Elfenbein & Ambady, 2002b), which is consistent with the linguistic metaphor. Also like linguistic dialects, individuals experience cultural learning when they are exposed to a new host culture (Elfenbein & Ambady, 2003). In one study, the in-group advantage in recognizing facial expressions appeared to disappear in as little as 10 minutes of practicing while receiving feedback after each judgment (Elfenbein, 2006). In this sense, dialect theory and the linguistic metaphor can provide some guidance for how to overcome cross-cultural challenges. Because the in-group advantage results from familiarity with culturally specific elements of nonverbal expression, it is possible to increase familiarity through training and intervention programs that focus on these elements. This kind of training is already starting to take place, for example in work commissioned by the U.S. Army Research Institute for soldiers going overseas (Rosenthal et al., 2009). However, it would be harder to reduce the in-group advantage if it resulted solely from motivation or bias instead of knowledge and information. For this reason, empirical findings about dialect theory suggest optimism for our increasingly global and multicultural societies.

ACKNOWLEDGMENTS

This chapter is adapted, expanded, and updated from the brief-format article Elfenbein (2013) in *Emotion Review*. I thank James Russell, José-Miguel Fernández Dols, and longtime collaborators (alphabetically) Abby Marsh, Dana Carney, Manas Mandal, Martin Beaupré, Nalini Ambady, Petri Laukka, and Ursula Hess.

REFERENCES

Beaupre, M. G., & Hess, U. (2005). Cross-cultural emotion recognition among Canadian ethnic groups. *Journal of Cross-Cultural Psychology, 36*, 355–370.

Beaupre, M. G., & Hess, U. (2006). An ingroup advantage for confidence in emotion recognition judgments: The moderating effect of familiarity with the expressions of outgroup members. *Personality and Social Psychology Bulletin, 32*, 16–26.

Bühler, K. (1934/1990). *Theory of language. The representational function of language.* (D. F. Goodwin, Trans.). Amsterdam, the Netherlands: John Benjamins.

Cheang, H. S., & Pell, M. D. (2011). Recognizing sarcasm without language: A cross-linguistic study of English and Cantonese. *Pragmatics and Cognition, 19*, 203–223.

Dailey, M. N., Joyce, C., Lyons, M. J., Kamachi, M., Ishi, H., Gyoba, J., & Cottrell, G. W. (2010). Evidence and a computational explanation of cultural differences in facial expression recognition. *Emotion, 10*, 874–893.

Ekman, P. (1972). Universals and cultural differences in facial expressions of emotion. In J. Cole (Ed.), *Nebraska Symposium on Motivation*, 1971 (Vol. 19, pp. 207–282). Lincoln: University of Nebraska Press.

Ekman, P. (1980). *The face of man*. New York, NY: Garland.

Elfenbein, H. A. (2006). Learning in emotion judgments: Training and the cross-cultural understanding of facial expressions. *Journal of Nonverbal Behavior, 30*, 21–36.

Elfenbein, H. A., & Ambady, N. (2002a). Is there an in-group advantage in emotion recognition? *Psychological Bulletin, 128*, 243–249.

Elfenbein, H. A., & Ambady, N. (2002b). On the universality and cultural specificity of emotion recognition: A meta-analysis. *Psychological Bulletin, 128*, 203–235.

Elfenbein, H. A., & Ambady, N. (2003). When familiarity breeds accuracy: Cultural exposure and facial emotion recognition. *Journal of Personality and Social Psychology, 85*, 276–290.

Elfenbein, H. A., Beaupré, M. G., Lévesque, M., & Hess, U. (2007). Toward a dialect theory: Cultural differences in the expression and recognition of posed facial expressions. *Emotion, 7*, 131–146.

Elfenbein, H. A., Mandal, M. K., Ambady, N., Harizuka, S., & Kumar, S. (2004). Hemifacial differences in the in-group advantage in emotion recognition. *Cognition and Emotion, 18*, 613–629.

expressions of complaining customers. *European Journal of Marketing, 48*, 1354–1374.

Fontaine, J., Scherer, K. R., & Soriano, C. (Eds.) (2013). *Components of emotional meaning: A sourcebook*. Oxford, UK: Oxford University Press.

Fridlund, A. J. (1994). *Human facial expression: An evolutionary view*. San Diego, CA: Academic Press.

Gendron, M., Roberson, D., & Barrett, L. F. (2015). Cultural variation in emotion perception is real: A response to Sauter, Eisner, Ekman, and Scott (2015). *Psychological Science, 26*, 357–359.

Gendron, M., Roberson, D., van der Vyver, J. M., & Barrett, L. F. (2014a). Cultural relativity in perceiving emotion from vocalizations. *Psychological Science, 25*, 911–920.

Gendron, M., Roberson, D., van der Vyver, J. M., & Barrett, L. F (2014b). Perceptions of emotion from facial expressions are not culturally universal: Evidence from a remote culture. *Emotion, 14*, 251–262.

Gray, H. M., Mendes, W. B., & Denny-Brown, C. (2008). An in-group advantage in detecting intergroup anxiety. *Psychological Science, 19*, 1233–1237.

Hess, U., & Thibault, P. (2009). Darwin and emotion expression. *American Psychologist, 64*, 120–128.

Hess, U., Thibault, P., Levesque, M., & Elfenbein, H. A. (2008). Where do emotional dialects come from? A comparison of understanding emotion terms between Gabon and Quebec. Paper at the 29th International Congress of Psychology, Berlin.

Jack, R. E., Blais, C., Scheepers, C., Schyns, P. G., & Caldara, R. (2009). Cultural confusions show that facial expressions are not universal. *Current Biology*, 19, 1543–1548.

Jack, R. E., Garrod, O. G. B., Yu, H., Caldara, R., & Schyns, P. G. (2012). Facial expressions of emotion are not culturally universal. *Proceedings of the National Academy of Sciences, 109*, 7241–7244.

Jürgens, R., Drolet, M., Pirow, R., Scheiner, E., & Fischer, J. (2013). Encoding conditions affect recognition of vocally expressed emotions across cultures. *Frontiers in Psychology, 4*, 111. doi:10.3389/fpsyg.2013.00111.

Kang, S-M., & Lau, A. S. (2013). Revisiting the out-group advantage in emotion recognition in a multicultural society: Further evidence for the in-group advantage. *Emotion, 13*, 203–215.

Kleinsmith, A., De Silva, P. R., & Bianchi-Berthouze, N. (2006). Cross-cultural differences in recognizing affect from body posture. *Interacting with Computers, 18*, 1371–1389.

Klineberg, O. (1938). Emotional expression in Chinese literature. *Journal of Abnormal and Social Psychology, 33*, 517–520.

Kret, M. E., & de Gelder, B. (2012). Islamic headdress influences how emotion is recognized from the eyes. *Frontiers in Psychology, 3*, 110. doi: 10.3389/fpsyg.2012.00110.

Lee, S. L., Chiu, C. Y., & Chan, T. K. (2005). Some boundary conditions of the expressor culture effect in emotion recognition: Evidence from Hong Kong Chinese perceivers. *Asian Journal of Social Psychology, 8*, 224–243.

Levine, C. S., & Ambady, N. (2013). The role of non-verbal behaviour in racial disparities in health care: Implications and solutions. *Medical Education, 47*, 867–876.

Lewin, K., and Cartwright, D. (Eds.) (1951). *Field theory in social science; selected theoretical papers.* New York, NY: Harper & Row.

Marsh, A. A., Elfenbein, H. A., & Ambady, N. (2003). Nonverbal "accents": Cultural differences in facial expressions of emotion. *Psychological Science, 14*, 373–376.

Matsumoto, D. (1989). Cultural influences on the perception of emotion. *Journal of Cross-Cultural Psychology, 20*, 92–105.

Matsumoto, D. (2002). Methodological requirements to test a possible ingroup advantage in judging emotions across cultures: Comments on Elfenbein and Ambady and evidence. *Psychological Bulletin, 128*, 236–242.

Matsumoto, D., & Ekman, P. (1988). *Japanese and Caucasian facial expressions of emotion (JACFEE).* [Slides]. San Francisco, CA: Intercultural and Emotion Research Laboratory, Department of Psychology, San Francisco State University.

Matsumoto, D., Olide, A., & Willingham, B. (2009). Is there an ingroup advantage in recognizing spontaneously expressed emotions? *Journal of Nonverbal Behavior, 33*, 181–191.

Naab, P. J., & Russell, J. A. (2007). Judgments of emotion from spontaneous facial expressions of New Guineans. *Emotion, 7*, 736–744.

Nelson, N.L., & Russell, J.A. (2013). Universality revisited. *Emotion Review, 5*, 8–15.

O'Grady, W., Archibald, J., Aronoff, M., & Rees-Miller, J. (2001). *Contemporary Linguistics* (4th ed.). Boston, MA: Bedford/St. Martin's.

Owren, M. J., & Rendall, D. (2001). Sound on the rebound: Bringing form and function back to the forefront in understanding nonhuman primate vocal signaling. *Evolutionary Anthropology, 10*, 58–71.

Palmer, A. S. (1882). *Folk-etymology; a dictionary of verbal corruptions or words perverted in form or meaning, by false derivation or mistaken analogy.* London, UK: G. Bell and Sons.

Parkinson, B. (2005). Do facial movements express emotions or communicate motives? *Personality and Social Psychology Review, 9*, 278–311.

Parkinson, B. (2013). Contextualizing facial activity. *Emotion Review, 5*, 97–103.

Paulmann, S., & Uskul, A. K. (2014). Cross-cultural emotional prosody recognition: Evidence from Chinese and British listeners. *Cognition and Emotion, 28*, 230–244,

Pell, M. D., Monetta, L., Paulmann, S., & Kotz, S. A. (2009). Recognizing emotions in a foreign language. *Journal of Nonverbal Behavior, 33*, 107–120.

Pinkham, A. E., Sasson, N. J., Calkins, M. E., Richard, J., Hughett, P., Gur, R. E., & Gur, R. C. (2008). The other-race effect in face processing among African American and Caucasian individuals with schizophrenia. *American Journal of Psychiatry, 165*, 639–645.

Prado, C., Mellor, D., Byrne, L. K, Wilson, C., Xu, X., & Liu, H. (2013). Facial emotion recognition: a cross-cultural comparison of Chinese, Chinese living in Australian, and Anglo-Australians. *Motivation and Emotion, 38*, 420–428.

Rosenthal, D. B., Wadsworth, L. A., Russell, T. L., Mathew, J., Elfenbein, H. A., Sanchez-Burks, J., and Ruark, G. A. (2009). *Training soldiers to decode nonverbal cues in cross-cultural interactions* (ARI Research Note 2009–12). Arlington, VA: U.S. Army Research Institute for the Behavioral and Social Sciences

Russell, J. A. (1994). Is there universal recognition of emotion from facial expression? A review of the cross-cultural studies. *Psychological Bulletin, 115*, 102–141.

Russell, J. A., Bachorowski, J. A., Fernandez-Dols, J. -M. (2003). Facial and vocal expressions of emotion. *Annual Review of Psychology, 54*, 329–349.

Sauter, D. A., & Scott, S. K. (2007). More than one kind of happiness: Can we recognize vocal expressions of different positive states. *Motivation and Emotion, 31*, 192–199.

Sauter, D. A. (2013) The role of motivation and cultural dialects in the ingroup advantage for emotional vocalizations. *Frontiers in Psychology, 4*, 814. doi: 10.3389/fpsyg.2013.00814.

Sauter, D. A., Eisner, F., Ekman, P., & Scott, S. K. (2010). Cross-cultural recognition of basic emotions through nonverbal emotional vocalizations. *Proceedings of the National Academy of Sciences, 107*, 2408–2412.

Sauter, D. A., Eisner, F., Ekman, P., & Scott, S. K. (2015). Emotional vocalizations are recognized across cultures regardless of the valence of distractors. *Psychological Science, 26*, 354–356

Scherer, K. R. (1988). On the symbolic functions of vocal affect expression. *Journal of Language and Social Psychology, 7*, 79–100.

Thibault, P., Bourgeois, P., & Hess, U. (2006). The effect of group-identification on emotion recognition: The case of cats and basketball players. *Journal of Experimental Social Psychology, 42*, 676–683.

Thompson, W. F., & Balkwill, L. L. (2006). Decoding speech prosody in five languages. *Semiotica, 158*, 407–424.

Tombs, A. G., Russell-Bennett, R., & Ashkanasy, N. M. (2014). Recognising emotional

Tomkins, S. S., & McCarter, R. (1964). What and where are the primary affects: Some evidence for a theory. *Perceptual and Motor Skills, 18*, 119–158.

Tracy, J. L., & Robins, R. W. (2008). The nonverbal expression of pride: Evidence for cross-cultural recognition. *Journal of Personality and Social Psychology, 94*, 516–530.

van der Schalk, J., Hawk, S. T., Fischer, A. H., & Doosje, B. (2011). Moving faces, looking places: Validation of the Amsterdam Dynamic Facial Expression Set (ADFES). *Emotion, 11*, 907–920.

Wickline, V. B., Bailey, W., & Nowicki, S. (2009). Cultural in-group advantage: Emotion recognition in African American and European American faces and voices. *Journal of Genetic Psychology, 1*, 5–28.

Young, S.G., & Hugenberg, K. (2010). Mere social categorization modulates identification of facial expressions of emotion. *Journal of Personality and Social Psychology, 99*, 964–977.

Yuki, M., Maddux, W.W., & Masuda, T. (2007). Are the windows to the soul the same in the East and West? Cultural differences in using the eyes and mouth as cues to recognize emotions in Japan and the United States. *Journal of Experimental Social Psychology, 43*, 303–311.

26

Facial Expressions and Emotions in Indigenous Societies

CARLOS CRIVELLI AND MARIA GENDRON

In our chapter, we review and evaluate a key source of evidence for the universality thesis (UT): the claim that recognition of facial expressions of certain emotions is pancultural.[1] We refer to the studies conducted in indigenous societies, which can uniquely speak to consistency across cultures because their cultural contact with the West is minimized.[2] By "key," we mean that this evidence on facial expressions in indigenous societies has been a cornerstone of the view that certain emotions such as anger and fear are biologically hardwired mechanisms (i.e., basic emotion theory; Ekman, 1993, 2003; Keltner, Tracy, Sauter, Cordaro, & McNeil, 2016). Our review challenges the widespread belief that the studies with indigenous societies strongly support UT.

Still, Keltner and Cordaro (this volume) and Ekman (this volume) find the evidence gathered so far as highly supportive for the UT. Similarly, a survey of active researchers in the emotion field found that 80% also found the evidence highly supportive, but 20% did not (Ekman, 2016). On the other hand, recent tests of the UT show more diversity than uniformity (Crivelli, Jarillo, Russell, & Fernández-Dols, 2016; Crivelli, Russell, Jarillo, & Fernández-Dols, 2016, in press; Gendron, Roberson, van der Vyver, & Barrett, 2014).

We first underscore the need to conduct studies in indigenous societies. Second, we review the few such studies available. Third, we discuss several approaches used to summarize the results and to make inferences on universality. Fourth, we examine some major challenges that researchers face in the field by reviewing two main strategies—less centered on Western assumptions and methods—to overcome these barriers and to expose the extent and nature of human diversity.

WHY INDIGENOUS SOCIETIES?

Although psychologists are often interested in human nature, (a) they generally sample only a narrow part of the human population (Arnett, 2008; Henrich, Heine, & Norenzayan, 2010), and (b) they often underestimate changes over time in the constructs they measure (Schmittmann, Cramer, Waldorp, Epskamp, Kievit, & Borsboom, 2013).

First, research in indigenous societies allows us not only to test more diverse samples in order to generalize the results observed in Western industrialized societies but also to integrate diversity of practices, epistemologies, and peoples for a better understanding of scientific enquiries (Bender & Beller, 2016; Medin & Bang, 2014). In the study of emotion, Western theories often serve as the starting point for hypotheses that are then tested cross-culturally (Pike, 1967; Tomkins & McCarter, 1964). Much of the "cross-cultural" research consists of cross-national studies of groups with considerable contact with one another, either directly or via media exposure (Duran, Reisenzein, & Fernández-Dols, this volume; Elfenbein & Ambady, 2002; Nelson & Russell, 2013). The cross-national consistency observed in these studies is often invoked as evidence for universal psychological processes. However, cultural diffusion and assimilation can also explain consistency.[3]

Second, replication represents a general problem in psychology (Open Science Collaboration, 2015; Pashler & Wagenmakers, 2012), but it is especially critical for the cross-cultural study of emotion recognition because only a few studies have been conducted and even fewer directly published in peer-reviewed outlets. The UT is based on a handful of studies (Ekman, 1972; Ekman & Friesen, 1971; Ekman, Sorenson, & Friesen, 1969) conducted with the Fore indigenous group in the former Territory of Papua and New Guinea (Eastern Highlands, Papua New Guinea). This research is widely cited in introductory psychology textbooks and emotion handbooks as providing the definitive evidence in favor of the UT (Matsumoto, Keltner, Shiota, O'Sullivan, & Frank, 2008; Myers & DeWall, 2015). Moreover, this research was selected as one of just forty studies that changed psychology (Hock, 2012). Yet, until recently, no replications in indigenous societies were conducted. Instead, replications were conducted with Western and Eastern samples of college students (e.g., Matsumoto et al., 2002).[4]

STUDIES CONDUCTED IN INDIGENOUS SOCIETIES

We now turn to tests of UT in indigenous societies, which are surprisingly few in number and much less supportive of UT than commonly believed. Many of the results simply fail to support UT, and those results that appear to support it suffer from methodological problems that undermine any claim of support.

Foundational Studies of the Universality Thesis

In 1967, a multidisciplinary research team of two psychologists (Paul Ekman and Wallace Friesen) and one anthropologist (Richard Sorenson) tested the UT in a remote and indigenous society: the Fore of the former Territory of Papua and New Guinea (nowadays, Eastern Highlands Province of Papua New Guinea). This research team went to the field to test whether a set of facial displays—developed through research in the West—was recognized by the Fore (Ekman, 1972, 1980).

The design was within-subjects: Participants were asked to match an emotion label from a short list of terms to a picture of an actor posing one of the hypothesized facial expressions of emotion (Table 26.1). Three groups were studied: Fore members speaking a Pidgin, Fore members speaking only their vernacular, and an additional indigenous sample previously tested by Sorenson (the Sadong of Borneo, also known as Bidayuh). Ekman, Sorenson, and Friesen (1969) indicated that the vernacular-speaking Fore required specialized judgment procedures and additional experiments because of their unfamiliarity with the task, but details were not reported. All in all, Pidgin and Fore speakers' overall matching scores were very similar, with high values for recognizing "happiness" from a smiling face, but more moderate values for the other expressions (Table 26.2). Although some mislabeling was found (e.g., a majority of the vernacular-speaking Fore chose anger for the sad expression), Ekman et al. (1969) attributed the most modest matching scores obtained by the Fore and Bidayuh to language barriers and task unfamiliarity.

As noted by the authors, there were several barriers in this initial endeavor. The language and task unfamiliarity barriers may have been exacerbated by the fact that the multidisciplinary team did not adopt an ethnographic approach (e.g., exploratory and descriptive studies were not conducted prior to data collection). Consequently, we can think of several uncontrolled variables influencing Ekman et al.'s (1969) "universalist" outcomes (e.g., translators leaking the correct response; see Sorenson, 1976, pp. 139–140). Indeed, Sorenson did not speak the vernacular (the psychologists—Ekman and Friesen did not speak either Pidgin or Fore) (Sorenson, 1975, p. 365).

Table 26.1 METHOD AND DESIGN OF STUDIES CONDUCTED IN INDIGENOUS SOCIETIES

			Stimuli		Response		
Publication	Sample	*N*	Type	*n*	Type	Options	Procedure
Ekman, Sorenson, & Friesen (1969)	Sadong	15	Faces	23	Labels	6	Matching labels to faces
	Fore (Fore speakers)	14	Faces	24	Labels	6	Matching labels to faces
	Fore (Pidgin speakers)	18	Faces	24	Labels	6	Matching labels to faces
Ekman & Friesen (1971)	Fore (Children)	130	Stories	6	Faces	2	Matching faces to stories
	Fore (Adults)	189	Stories	6	Faces	3	Matching faces to stories
Tracy & Robins (2008)	Burkinabe	39	Faces	16	Labels	10	Matching labels to faces

Note. Faces = Sets of prototypical facial expressions of emotion. Gendron et al.'s (2014) study was aimed at testing whether language facilitated emotion perception among the pastorialist Himba of Namibia. Due to the nature of the design (a sorting task with two between-subject conditions) and data (multivaried correlated data), the results are not displayed here.

In 1968, Ekman and Friesen returned to the same field site with a new method, aimed at overcoming the problems of the first expedition. In the new method, participants were asked to match a face from an array of faces to an eliciting scenario (e.g., for happiness, "his friends have come, and he is happy") in a within-subjects design (Table 26.1). For Fore adults, the target face was presented with two distractor faces, whereas for Fore children, only one distractor face was presented. This new procedure was aimed at (a) minimizing the impact of translation between English language concepts into Fore by providing additional conceptual content (single-word translations were also included); (b) simplifying the response output (participants did not have to speak—just point at a picture); and (c) minimizing cognitive load (participants did not have to remember a list of emotion labels for the task) (Ekman & Friesen, 1971, p. 125).

Table 26.2 MATCHING SCORES' PERCENTAGES PRODUCED IN RECOGNITION STUDIES CONDUCTED IN INDIGENOUS SOCIETIES

			Matching scores						
Publication	Sample	*N*	Overall	Happiness	Sadness	Anger	Fear	Disgust	Surprise
Ekman, Sorenson, & Friesen (1969)	Sadong	15	46	92	52	64	40	23	36
	Fore (Fore speakers)	14	50	82	n/a	50	54	44	19
	Fore (Pidgin speakers)	18	50.5	99	55	56	46	29	38
Ekman & Friesen (1971)	Fore (Children)	130	91.38	92.75	81.5	90	93.33	86.5	98.33
	Fore (Adults)	189	81	92.25	79	85.33	64.29	83	68
Tracy & Robins (2008)	Burkinabe	39	47.5	84	51	33	30	44	58
Median			50.25	92.13	55	60	50	44	48

Note. Overall matching scores represent the median value resulting of averaging the different emotion categories' matching scores.

Ekman and Friesen (1971) tested a large sample of Fore children (N = 130) and adults (N = 189), reporting that their data provided strong empirical support for the UT (Table 26.2). Children performed better than adults on overall matching scores (91% vs. 81%). Indeed, Fore children's matching scores were higher than those of college-educated Americans (85%), Brazilians (82%), and Japanese (78%) reported in Ekman et al. (1969).

Part of the explanation for the high matching scores from Fore participants may have to do with the scenario descriptions. Scenarios provided contextual information helpful in choosing the facial expression (Barrett, Mesquita, & Gendron, 2011; Carroll & Russell, 1996). For example, if some participants had observed smiling in the context of greeting friends, they might select the smiling face for greeting even without recognizing happiness. We know from data gathered in the West, at least, that smiling is not limited to instances in which one feels happiness (Fernández-Dols & Crivelli, 2013). Smiles are mainly produced in cooperative settings (e.g., a mother–son interaction), suggesting that they are often used as displays aimed at signaling a potential nonagonistic interaction (Fridlund, 1994, this volume). From the UT perspective, individuals should not require additional context in order to judge the emotional state of the target—facial expressions are assumed to be self-sufficient cues to emotion (Ekman, Friesen, & Ellsworth, 1982). Yet this method modification allowed individuals to rely on the situation context, not emotional states, and still perform the experimental task.

Another possibility is that the within-subjects design and multiple-choice nature of the task allowed for a process-of-elimination strategy. By eliminating previously used matches, the participant might pair an unrecognized face to an unknown scenario (Russell, 1994; Yik, Widen, & Russell, 2013). Responses based on process of elimination and multiple-choice tasks might simply reflect the best fit based on what is available (Nelson & Russell, 2016).

Tracy and Robins (2008)

In 2008, Tracy and Robins reported research aimed at showing that a new display—a smiling face, the head tilted back, the expanded chest, and arms akimbo—was a universal signal for the emotion of pride. One of their studies was conducted in an indigenous society, "one of the poorest and most isolated countries in the world," Burkina Faso (Tracy & Robins, 2008, p. 519). The method was similar to that used in many studies conducted in industrialized Western and Eastern societies: Participants were asked to match an emotion label from a short list to a posed facial expression in a within-subjects design (Table 26.1).

Matching scores ranged from high (for happiness, 84%), to moderate (e.g., for surprise, 58%), to low (e.g., for anger, 33%; for fear, 30%; see Table 26.2). Tracy and Robins (2008) interpreted their data as providing strong support for the UT. Unlike the extensive modifications made by Ekman and colleagues for their studies with the Fore, Tracy and Robins did not report any changes made for the task and design in order to accommodate the study to this indigenous population. For example, although the procedure included 10 response options, the researchers did not report any problematic issue regarding participants' ability to remember all the labels. Furthermore, no issues were noted in the process of using educated locals to translate from English to French and then from French to the vernacular as well as using local collaborators to collect the data.

Testing an Alternative Hypothesis: Gendron et al. (2014)

Gendron, Roberson, van der Vyver, and Barrett (2014) conducted a conceptual replication of UT's foundational studies, testing the alternative framework of minimal universality (Russell, 1995). This research was aimed at addressing several of the limitations noted in previous UT studies, notably the use of forced-choice methods and invoking emotion concepts (via both words and situation knowledge) in the task (Russell, 1994). Specifically, Gendron and colleagues worried that prior evidence with indigenous people apparently supporting UT may have depended, in part, on the specific methods used.

Gendron et al. (2014) tested participants from the pastoralist Himba ethnic group dwelling in villages located in the remote Kunene region of Namibia. The research team included individuals with extensive experience with the Himba ethnic group: a psychologist (Roberson), who had previously conducted longitudinal research in Himba communities (e.g., Roberson, Davidoff, Davies, & Shapiro, 2005), and a local collaborator (Jakurama), who had worked in the Himba communities as a translator and guide for over a decade. In this research, participants completed a within-subjects free-sorting task on posed Western-style facial expressions of "emotion." The key factor was a between-subjects manipulation. Half of the Himba participants were provided with a list of six emotion terms (translated by Jakurama and confirmed by a language scholar) repeatedly over the course of the sorting task. The other half was not.

The authors used several analytical strategies to assess Himba's performance. First, they conducted a cluster analysis aimed at testing whether the perception of faces conformed to UT predictions (i.e., that items would cluster neatly by the emotion categories posed by the faces). Second, they computed multidimensional scaling coupled with empirically driven identification of the dimensions in order to capture the underlying properties that were structuring sorting.

A cluster analysis of the data yielded clear clusters for smiling ("happy"), neutral, and gasping ("fear") poses, but not for scowling ("angry"), nose-scrunching ("disgusted"), or pouting ("sad") poses. The clusters did not correspond to the hypothesized emotions even when emotion words were included in the task. Multidimensional scaling of the data suggested an alternative process underlying the sorting decisions. Dimensions suggested behaviors (e.g., looking, smiling, crying, smelling) rather than emotions as properties (e.g., fear, happiness, sadness, disgust). Consistent with this data-driven finding, Himba participants provided considerably more action descriptions than emotion descriptions in a free-labeling task, whereas an American control group demonstrated the reverse effect.

Gendron et al.'s (2014) data were interpreted as failing to support the UT. Instead, they interpreted their results within a constructionist account, in which more basic processes (e.g., affect, conceptualization, labeling) contribute to emotion perception (Barrett, Lindquist, & Gendron, 2007; Russell, 2003, this volume).

Crivelli, Jarillo, Russell, and Fernández-Dols (2016)

Crivelli, Jarillo, Russell, and Fernández-Dols (2016) conducted further tests of the UT in two indigenous societies of subsistence gardeners and fishermen: the Trobrianders of Papua New Guinea (Trobriand Islands, Milne Bay Province; see Malinowski, 1935/1965) and the Mwani of Mozambique (Matemo Island, Cabo Delgado Province; see Bonate, 2010). To do so, the authors assembled a multidisciplinary research group of psychologists and an anthropologist. Both epistemological traditions were a key element in the development of a global and long-term research project aimed at generating robust descriptions and hypothesis testing.

Jarillo—an experienced social anthropologist with 2 years of accumulated experience in the field—and Crivelli—a psychologist with expertise in research methods—performed data collection together in both field sites. In addition to Jarillo's experience in the field, Crivelli spent more than 9 months of fieldwork. Unlike previous tests of the UT, both experimenters developed a robust descriptive base of emotion concepts and local understanding of facial displays aided by speaking the vernacular, conducting participant observation, and building rapport with the host community (Crivelli, Jarillo, & Fridlund, 2016). Although the former approach has been previously used in other fields of cognitive science when studying indigenous populations (e.g., Medin & Atran, 2004), it is novel in the field of emotion and facial behavior.

In both indigenous societies and a Western control (Spaniards), Crivelli et al. (2016) used a multiple-choice format to test the UT on a sample of children and adolescents (N = 217, aged 6–16 years). Participants were shown an array of prototypical facial expressions taken from standardized sets developed in the West and were asked to point to the person feeling a specific emotion: happiness, sadness, anger, fear, or disgust. In Study 1, Trobrianders were randomly assigned to an emotion label (e.g., *ninamwau*, sadness) in order to match the label to a static facial expression in a between-subjects design. In contrast, in Study 2, Mwani participants were randomly assigned to match five different emotion labels (e.g., anger, disgust, and so on) to its corresponding dynamic or static facial expression.

In Study 1, Spaniards matched faces to emotions as predicted by UT (overall matching score, 93%): Matching was seen on 83% (disgust) to 100% (happiness) of trials. On the contrary, Trobrianders performed poorly (overall matching score, 32%), producing matching scores that ranged from moderate (e.g., for happiness, 58%), to low (e.g., for fear, 31%; for disgust, 25%), to extremely low (e.g., for anger, 7%).

In Study 2, Mwani showed a similar pattern as Trobrianders did (overall matching score, 38%), producing matching scores that ranged from moderate (e.g., for happiness, 58%) to low (e.g., for sadness and anger, 22%). In any case, matching dynamic over static faces to a given emotion label did not provide a significant increase on matching scores.

In both indigenous samples, disconfirming evidence of the UT was robust across differences in age, gender, and education. Interestingly, correspondence analyses of Trobrianders and Mwani's judgments suggested that they did not answer randomly. Crivelli et al. (2016) found evidence that Trobrianders and Mwani's associations of facial expressions and emotion labels could be explained by their interpretation of the facial expressions along a continuum of pleasure and displeasure, and, to a lesser extent, to low and high activation (Russell, 1980, 2003).

EVALUATING THE EVIDENCE ON THE UNIVERSALITY THESIS

Available studies on UT in indigenous societies raise a question: What should be taken as support for UT and what should not? We discuss several considerations.

Ruling Out Chance, Ruling In the Universality Thesis

Some researchers claimed support for UT when the proportion of responses matching prediction significantly exceeded the proportion expected by chance (e.g., with 10 options, then a proportion significantly greater than 0.10 would be taken as supporting UT). This approach is an example of null hypothesis significance testing (NHST), the limits of which are increasingly being noted (Cumming, 2014; Dienes, 2011). Thus, although UT supporters have made strong universality claims, their interpretation of the results has not relied on measures of effect size, just the rejection of the null (for a recent meta-analysis see, Duran, Reisenzein, & Fernández-Dols, this volume). The rejection of the null without providing a measure of its effect size is uninformative of the theoretical relevance of the finding and it is not acceptable even for NSTH standards (Kirk, 1996). For example, 3 out of 10 participants in Tracy and Robins's (2008) Burkina Faso sample assigned the label "fear" to the hypothesized fear face, significantly exceeding chance-level set at 0.10. All the same, computing the effect size of the fear label-face matching is sobering. The odds of the Burkinabe *not* "recognizing" the fear face as fear is 5.44 times higher than the odds of a "correct" recognition. In sum, ruling out chance does not rule in a theory (Nelson & Russell, 2013).

An Arbitrary Cutoff Point

Perhaps recognizing problems in the "above chance" criterion, Haidt and Keltner (1999, p. 238) proposed that a specific range must be reached to support UT. On their proposal, UT predicts that responses in the 70%–90% range are highly likely to be universal. This arbitrary cutoff approach is strikingly similar to other statistical rules of thumb, such as the different thresholds established for many indicators of model fitting (e.g., RMSEA, CFI) in structural equation modeling (Hu & Bentler, 1999). In any case, Haidt and Keltner's (1999) criterion has not been used by other UT supporters. This may be because this rule of thumb would have called into question the appropriateness of strong UT conclusions based on Ekman et al. (1969) and Tracy et al.'s (2008) data (see Table 26.2). Moreover, this criterion would likely put at risk even the universalistic claims made on literate non-Western societies (e.g., anger, fear, and disgust; see Nelson & Russell, 2013, p. 9).

Further Considerations in Evaluating Findings

Findings from a study in an indigenous society must be interpreted in light of a background of understanding of such societies and how performance on the given task might be achieved.

First, performance on the task presented can occur for a variety of reasons. When a participant chooses the label *fear* for the hypothesized facial expression of "fear," universal recognition of fear is only one of many possible explanations for that choice. Several possibilities have already been mentioned: reliance on the scenario accompanying the emotion word in one task, help from an indigenous translator, and process of elimination. Above-chance performance can be achieved by recognizing broad affective dimensions (pleasure-displeasure and degree of arousal) from the face and then guessing within the reduced set of relevant emotion words (Russell, 1980, 1994). Recognizing that a face shows displeasure and high arousal reduces the set of plausible emotions to fear, anger, and disgust; random choice among these three would produce 33% "recognition," which is above chance when chance is calculated as if all emotion labels were equally likely. An account of the cross-cultural data based on this line of thinking was called minimal universality (Russell, 1995).

Second, contact between cultures is not either-or. Describing an indigenous population as "untouched," "primitive," "stone age," or "isolated" can be misleading. Rather, cultural contact is on a continuum. For example, the Fore—described by Ekman (1980, 2003) as a "stone-age" and isolated society—reside in a region that had been a protectorate of British, Germans, and Australians since 1888 until their independence in 1975. The Fore interacted with Christian missionaries and Western settlers for more than a century. Their wooden and stony tools (e.g., axes) had been replaced with metal counterparts from the West. A documentary, *First Contact*, shows footage of interactions between Australian mining extractors and the local populations of seemingly isolated areas of the Highlands of Papua New Guinea back in the 1930s (Connelly & Anderson, 1983). Moreover, Tracy and Robins's (2008) "isolated" sample lived within 10 to 30 km of the second (Bobo-Dioulasso) and fifth (Banfora) most populated cities of Burkina Faso. The people they studied were able to travel by foot to a regional town.

Finally, the coauthors of this chapter have had firsthand experience conducting studies in different areas of Africa and Papua New Guinea. We found that poverty does not entail cultural isolation, even in "remote" populations (who frequently travel to provincial urban centers to trade their goods). Thus, despite the real value in studying relatively isolated indigenous societies, we cannot rule out cultural transmission as a factor in the explanation of similarity across cultural groups. Pushing our argument a bit further, Fridlund (1994) noted more than two decades ago:

> The importance attributed to the study of preliterate cultures relies on the hidden and unsupportable assumption that whereas various languages are transmitted culturally, facial displays are not. The interpretations of preliterate studies also tend to regard cultures like those populating

regions of Papua New Guinea as though they arose *de novo*, rather than via general eastern migration. (p. 282)

CHALLENGES AND OPPORTUNITIES IN THE FIELD

Unfortunately, the scarcity of studies conducted in the field, the diversity of methods used, and the limited knowledge of the societies that researchers tested render it difficult to perform meta-analysis for comparison purposes or even to extract strong conclusions on the assumption that all human beings "recognize" basic emotions from a set of theory-driven facial expressions. This lack of consensus points to the need for more evidence, but huge difficulties in gathering such evidence in indigenous societies persist (Astuti & Bloch, 2010; Crivelli, Jarillo, & Fridlund, 2016; Levinson, 2012). Here we discuss two paths to doing so in the hope of encouraging researchers studying emotions and facial behavior to take up the challenge.

The Collaborative Approach

One obvious approach is the formation of a team of researchers from different disciplines as collaborators. Within cognitive science, anthropologists have proved to be good travel companions for psychologists. Anthropologists can serve as gatekeepers by consulting during preliminary stages in the lab and anchoring the research (in terms of community interactions, research implementation, interpretation, etc.) once in the field.[5] For example, social anthropologists can provide background knowledge of the customs and vernacular and, once in the field, serve as gatekeepers to a network of informants. That psychology and anthropology are separate disciplines with little contact is a most unfortunate historical accident (Bender, Hutchins, & Medin, 2010).

A second collaborative approach is to seek out and rely on locals with experience in the field. On the one hand, native psychology has been gradually developing in communities with access to national universities and funding to promote emic approaches in certain areas of research (Cheung, van der Vijver, & Leong, 2011; Medin & Bang, 2014). Local collaborators can provide a critical source of expertise by sharing knowledge of their own culture and circumstances (in what have been termed "experience near" concepts; Geertz, 1983). But the benefits of this approach will only be seen in the long run due to the difficulties of training—formally and informally—indigenous members into Western scientific practices. Of course, there can be inherent limitations in some "collaborative approaches," including the potential overreliance on gatekeepers and the necessity of integrating knowledge gleaned from local informants into one's own scientific vernacular. Furthermore, at least one collaborator on the research team should gain the experience in the field first, through what we have termed "the embedded approach."

The Embedded Approach

In the embedded approach, rather than rely on a collaborator to anchor one's work in a given society, the researcher will do the work to gain experience in a society prior to undertaking psychological theory testing. Although access to the host community will depend upon gatekeepers initially, researchers following the embedded approach should gradually become independent of gatekeepers, building their own network of informants. This is critical since gatekeepers can have undue influence over research practices (e.g., the selection of participants based on friendships and enmities; coaching participants to accommodate researcher expectations) that can call into question the validity of results. For example, Sorensen expressed concerns regarding the influence of gatekeepers on participants' performance in Ekman's foundational UT studies (Sorenson, 1975, pp. 367–368).

Researchers in the field should generate a descriptive-exploratory base prior to data collection if they want to stop relying on gatekeepers—especially if they act as interpreters (Rai & Fiske, 2010). To build a robust descriptive base, the researcher will have to build rapport with the host community, to engage in participant observation, and, ideally, to learn the vernacular (Crivelli, Jarillo, & Fridlund, 2016). Speaking the vernacular can help the researcher in the descriptive task of mapping emotion concepts to its local referents, the discovery of indigenous emotion terms, and the constitutive features of emotional episodes related to the indigenous emotion lexicon.

The ability to speak the vernacular is extremely useful in building rapport and engaging in daily life activities in order to gather meaningful data via participant observation. For example, Ekman interacted with Fore members without operating from a descriptive-exploratory base. In his book *The Face of Man* (1980), Ekman published photographs he took of Fore community members' "spontaneous expressions" along with his inferences about their emotional states. The emotion inferences were based on Ekman's own (Western) frame of reference on daily life events within the indigenous culture (Fernández-Dols & Crivelli, 2014), rendering his approach deeply ethnocentric. Two recent cross-cultural studies tested whether perceivers would match those "spontaneous expressions" with Ekman's inferences, finding extremely poor recognition. On the one hand, Kayyal and Russell (2013) reported matching scores lower than 30% in three industrialized samples: English-speaking Americans, English-speaking Palestinians, and Arabic-speaking Palestinians. On the other hand,

Crivelli, Russell, Jarillo, and Fernández-Dols (in press) found that members of another indigenous society of Papua New Guinea rarely produced—in a free-labeling task—UT's expected labels (0% for the lowest and 16% for the highest scores), whereas matching Fore faces to Ekman's predicted labels increased recognition slightly (matching scores ranged from 13% to 38%).

THE FUTURE AGENDA

Some writers debate two extreme views: absolutism and relativism. Absolutism denies variation, whereas relativism denies any commonalities across societies and individuals. Both are unacceptable.

"Universalism makes the assumption that basic psychological processes [such as memory or emotion] are common to all members of the species and that culture influences the development and display of psychological characteristics" (Berry, Poortinga, Segall, & Dasen, 2002, p. 5; for a similar point see, Matsumoto, 2001). For example, D'Andrade (1981) advocated a division of labor between psychologists and anthropologists. Psychologists were to be experts in the study of processes (i.e., *how* people think), whereas anthropologists in the study of the content of those processes (i.e., *what* people think). In this view, psychological processes were invariant across individuals and cultures, whereas the content was variable (Beller, Bender, & Medin, 2012; Bender, Hutchins, & Medin, 2010).

Views of psychological processes that are universal and culture-free are increasingly met with inconsistent data (Kitayama & Uskul, 2011; Nisbett & Miyamoto, 2005; Park & Huang, 2010). Indeed, emerging findings from neuroscience and genetics reveal just how deeply our biology is shaped by culture both phylogenetically and ontogenetically (Kim & Sasaki, 2014). Culture affects both content and processes, a fact that makes a reified view of "culture," used as a mere nominal variable in prior etic-approach cross-cultural studies, inadequate (Ojalehto & Medin, 2015).

We argue here that multidisciplinary collaboration is precisely what the study of facial expressions requires, particularly when psychologists are unable to make the investment in an embedded approach. For example, multidisciplinary research teams with anthropologists should be sought after due to (a) the amount of evidence they have gathered on content variation, (b) their expertise on overcoming the challenges of the home-field disadvantage, and (c) the importance of integrating different, but complementary, methodological approaches within science (Bender & Beller, 2011). Indeed, this approach is gradually providing relevant insights into human diversity, challenging commonsense assumptions rooted in Western theories, and breaking new ground in the study of facial expressions and emotions (e.g., Crivelli, Russell, Jarillo, & Fernández-Dols, 2016).

Thus, the scientific endeavor should not be aimed at verifying "basic" cognitive processes as invariant across cultures (a premise already falsified in cognitive science), but to understand and map diversity in as many domains and societies as possible, providing a better understanding of human nature. The study of facial expressions and emotion should be no exception.

ACKNOWLEDGMENTS

This paper was supported by Universidad Autónoma de Madrid's PG scholarship FPI-UAM (2012-2016) awarded to C. C., and by a NIMH F32 Fellowship (MH105052) awarded to M. G. The authors would like to thank James A. Russell, José-Miguel Fernández-Dols, and Alan J. Fridlund for their helpful comments on previous versions of this chapter.

NOTES

1. Throughout the chapter we will use the term "recognition" to refer to experimental tasks in which participants are asked to match a facial expression to a predicted emotional component (e.g., emotion label), with the underlying assumption that participants are decoding the affective information transmitted from the stimuli's structural and/or dynamic properties. Researchers from the field of categorical perception have proposed to substitute "recognition" with "emotion perception."
2. To overcome the ethnocentric and outdated categorizations of cultures in terms of "primitive" or "stone-age" versus "civilized," many alternatives have been proposed. We have decided to use the term "indigenous," even though it could be currently interpreted as too broad for being extended beyond its former reference to precolonial populations. Other alternatives at hand are problematic as well because, on the basis of their categorizations, they overemphasize either sociopolitical (e.g., small-scale societies) or historical (e.g., preliterate) features, or they make multiple categorizations based on subsistence patterns (e.g., foragers, pastoralists, horticulturalists).
3. Since the world is becoming increasingly more global, due to shifting technological, economic, and social forces (Gewald, 2010), ruling out these sources of consistency is becoming increasingly more difficult. In any case, data collected in indigenous societies are much needed in the science of emotion and facial expression.
4. Although we refer to "Western" or "the West" as a uniform category of people, we recognize that the societies so grouped have diverse values, practices, norms, artifacts, political systems, and so on.
5. A gatekeeper is a person mediating between the researcher and the host community. Gatekeepers are often local individuals or anthropologists who are fluent in the experimenter's language. Gatekeepers can also be political or religious leaders or simply charismatic individuals who will speak for host community members and will often provide community consent. Gatekeepers are typically rewarded for

their help and are responsible for distributing payments (often termed "rewards" in this context) among the members of the host community.

REFERENCES

Arnett, J. J. (2008). The neglected 95%: Why American psychology needs to become less American. *American Psychologist, 63*, 602–614.

Astuti, R., & Bloch, M. (2010). Why a theory of human nature cannot be based on the distinction between universality and variability: Lessons from anthropology. *Behavioral and Brain Sciences, 33*, 83–84.

Barrett, L. F., Lindquist, K. A., & Gendron, M. (2007). Language as context for the perception of emotion. *Trends in Cognitive Sciences, 11*, 327–332.

Barrett, L. F., Mesquita, B., & Gendron, M. (2011). Context in emotion perception. *Current Directions in Psychological Science, 20*, 286–290.

Beller, S., Bender, A., and Medin, D. L. (2012). Should anthropology be a part of cognitive science? *Topics in Cognitive Science, 4*, 342–353.

Bender, A., & Beller, S. (2011). The cultural constitution of cognition: Taking the anthropological perspective. *Frontiers in Psychology, 2*(67), 1–6.

Bender, A., & Beller, S. (2016). Current perspectives on cognitive diversity. *Topics in Cognitive Science, 7*:509.

Bender, A., Hutchins, E., & Medin, D. L. (2010). Anthropology in cognitive science. *Topics in Cognitive Science, 2*, 374–385.

Berry, J. W., Poortinga, Y. H., Segall, M. H., & Dasen, P. R. (2002). *Cross-cultural psychology: Research and applications* (2nd ed.). New York, NY: Cambridge University Press.

Bonate, L. (2010). Islam in Northern Mozambique: A historical overview. *History Compass, 8*(7), 573–593.

Carroll, J. M., & Russell, J. A. (1996). Do facial expressions signal specific emotions? Judging emotion from the face in context. *Journal of Personality and Social Psychology, 70*, 205–218.

Cheung, F. M., van de Vijver, F. J. R., & Leong, F. T. L. (2011). Toward a new approach to the study of personality and culture. *American Psychologist, 66*, 593–603.

Connelly, B., & Anderson, R. (Producers & Directors) (1983). *First contact* [Motion picture]. Australia: Filmakers Library.

Crivelli, C., Jarillo, S., & Fridlund, A. J. (2016). A multidisciplinary approach to research in small-scale societies: Studying emotions and facial expressions in the field. *Frontiers in Psychology, 7*:1073.

Crivelli, C., Jarillo, S., Russell, J. A., & Fernández-Dols, J. M. (2016). Reading emotions from faces in two indigenous societies. *Journal of Experimental Psychology: General, 145*, 830–843.

Crivelli, C., Russell, J. A., Jarillo, S., & Fernández-Dols, J. M. (2016). The fear gasping face as a threat display in a Melanesian society. *Proceedings of the National Academy of Sciences of the United States of America, 113*(44), 12403–12407.

Crivelli, C., Russell, J. A., Jarillo, S., & Fernández-Dols, J. M. (in press). Recognizing spontaneous facial expressions of emotion in a small-scale society of Papua New Guinea. *Emotion*.

Cumming, G. (2014). The new statistics: Why and how. *Psychological Science, 25*, 7–29.

D'Andrade, R. G. (1981). The cultural part of cognition. *Cognitive Science, 5*, 179–195.

Dienes, Z. (2011). Bayesian versus orthodox statistics: Which side are you on? *Perspectives on Psychological Science, 6*, 274–290.

Ekman, P. (1972). Universal and cultural differences in facial expressions of emotion. In J. R. Cole (Ed.), *Nebraska Symposium on Motivation*, 1971 (Vol. 19, pp. 207–283). Lincoln, NE: Nebraska University Press.

Ekman, P. (1980). *The face of man.* New York, NY: Garland.

Ekman, P. (1993). Facial expression and emotion. *American Psychologist, 48*, 384–392.

Ekman, P. (2003). *Emotions revealed.* New York, NY: Times Books.

Ekman, P. (2016). What scientists who study emotions agree about. *Perspectives in Psychological Science, 11*, 31–34.

Ekman, P., & Friesen, W. V. (1971). Constants across cultures in the face and emotion. *Journal of Personality and Social Psychology, 17*, 124–129.

Ekman, P., Friesen, W. V., & Ellsworth, P. (1982). What are the relative contributions of facial behavior and contextual information to the judgment of emotion? In P. Ekman (Ed.), *Emotion in the human face* (2nd ed., pp. 111–127). New York, NY: Cambridge University Press.

Ekman, P., Sorenson, E. R., & Friesen, W. V. (1969). Pan-cultural elements in facial displays of emotions. *Science, 164*, 86–88.

Elfenbein, H. A., & Ambady, N. (2002). On the universality and cultural specificity of emotion recognition: A meta-analysis. *Psychological Bulletin, 128*, 203–235.

Fernández-Dols, J. M., & Crivelli, C. (2013). Emotion and expression: Naturalistic studies. *Emotion Review, 5*, 24–29.

Fernández-Dols, J. M., & Crivelli, C. (2014). Recognition of facial expressions: Past, present, and future challenges. In M. Mandal & A. Awasthi (Eds.), *Understanding facial expressions in communication: Cross-cultural and multidisciplinary perspectives* (pp. 19–40). New Delhi, India: Springer.

Fridlund, A. J. (1994). *Human facial expression: An evolutionary view.* New York, NY: Academic Press.

Geertz, C. (1983). *Local knowledge: Further essays in interpretive anthropology.* New York, NY: Basic Books.

Gendron, M., Roberson, D., van der Vyver, J. M., & Barrett, L. F. (2014). Perceptions of emotion from facial expressions are not culturally universal: Evidence from a remote culture. *Emotion, 14*, 251–262.

Gewald, J-B. (2010). Remote but in contact with history and the world. *Proceedings of the National Academy of Sciences, USA, 107*, E75.

Haidt, J., & Keltner, D. (1999). Culture and facial expression: Open-ended methods find more faces and a gradient of recognition. *Cognition and Emotion, 13*, 225–266.

Henrich, J., Heine, S. J., & Norenzayan, A. (2010). The weirdest people in the world? *Behavioral and Brain Sciences, 38*, 61–83.

Hock, R. R. (2012). *Forty studies that changed psychology* (7th ed.). Upper Saddle River, NJ: Pearson.

Hu, L., & Bentler, P. M. (1999). Cutoff criteria for fit indexes in covariance structure analysis: Conventional criteria versus new alternatives. *Structural Equation Modeling, 6*, 1–55.

Kayyal, M. H., & Russell, J. A. (2013). Americans and Palestinians judge spontaneous facial expressions of emotion. *Emotion, 13*, 891–904.

Keltner, D., Tracy, J. L., Sauter, D. A., Cordaro, D. C., & McNeil, G. (2016). Expression of emotion. In L. F. Barrett, M. Lewis, & J. M. Haviland-Jones (Eds.), *The handbook of emotions* (4th ed., 467–482). New York, NY: Guilford.

Kim, H. S., & Sasaki, J. Y. (2014). Cultural neuroscience: Biology of the mind in cultural contexts. *Annual review of psychology, 65*, 487–514.

Kirk, R. E. (1996). Practical significance: A concept whose time has come. *Educational and Psychological Measurement, 56*, 746–759.

Kitayama, S., & Uskul, S. (2011). Culture, mind, and the brain: Current evidence and future directions. *Annual Review of Psychology, 62*, 419–449.

Levinson, S. C. (2012). The original sin of cognitive science. *Topics in Cognitive Science, 4*, 396–403.

Malinowski, B. (1965). *Coral gardens and their magic: A study of the methods of tilling the soil and agricultural rites in the Trobriand Islands, vol. 1 and vol. 2.* New York, NY: American Books. (Original work published 1935)

Matsumoto, D. (2001). Culture and emotion. In D. Matsumoto (Ed.), *The handbook of culture and psychology* (pp. 171–194). New York, NY: Oxford University Press.

Matsumoto, D., Consolacion, T., Yamada, H., Suzuki, R., Franklin, B., Paul, S., . . . & Uchida, H. (2002). American-Japanese cultural differences in judgments of emotional expressions of different intensities. *Cognition and Emotion, 16*, 721–747.

Matsumoto, D., Keltner, D., Shiota, M. N., O'Sullivan, M., & Frank, M. (2008). Facial expressions of emotion. In M. Lewis, J. M. Haviland-Jones, & L. F. Barrett (Eds.), *Handbook of emotions* (3rd ed., pp. 211–234). New York, NY: Guilford Press.

Medin, D. L., & Atran, S. (2004). The native mind: Biological categorization and reasoning in development and across cultures. *Psychological Review, 111*, 960–983.

Medin, D. L., & Bang, M. (2014). *Who's asking? Native science, Western science, and science education.* Cambridge, MA: MIT Press.

Myers, D. G., & DeWall, C. N. (2015). *Psychology* (11th ed.). New York, NY: Worth.

Nelson, N. L., & Russell, J. A. (2013). Universality revisited. *Emotion Review, 5*, 8–15.

Nelson, N. L., & Russell, J. A. (2016). Building emotion categories: Children use a process of elimination when they encounter novel expressions. *Journal of Experimentl Child Psychology, 151*, 120–130.

Nisbett, R. E., & Miyamoto, Y. (2005). The influence of culture holistic vs. analytic perception. *Trends in Cognitive Science, 9*, 467–473.

Ojalehto, B. L., & Medin D. L. (2015). Perspectives on culture and concepts. *Annual Review of Psychology, 66*, 249–275.

Open Science Collaboration. (2015). Estimating the reproducibility of psychological science. *Science, 349*(6251), aac4716.

Park, D. C., & Huang, C-M. (2010). Culture wires the brain: A cognitive neuroscience perspective. *Perspectives in Psychological Science, 5*, 391–400.

Pashler, H., & Wagenmakers, E. J. (2012). Editors' introduction to the special section on replicability in psychological science: A crisis of confidence? *Perspectives on Psychological Science, 7,* 528–530.

Pike, K. L. (1967). *Language in relation to a unified theory of structure of human behavior* (2nd ed.). The Hague, Netherlands: Mouton.

Rai, T. S., & Fiske, A. (2010). ODD (observation-and description-deprived) psychological research. *Behavioral and Brain Sciences, 33,* 106–107.

Roberson, D., Davidoff, J., Davies, I. R. L., & Shapiro, L. R. (2005). Color categories: Evidence for the cultural relativity hypothesis. *Cognitive Psychology, 50,* 378–411.

Russell, J. A. (1980). A circumplex model of affect. *Journal of Personality and Social Psychology, 39,* 1161–1178.

Russell, J. A. (1994). Is there universal recognition of emotion from facial expression? A review of the cross-cultural studies. *Psychological Bulletin, 115,* 102–141.

Russell, J. A. (1995). Facial expressions of emotion: What lies beyond minimal universality? *Psychological Bulletin, 118,* 379–391.

Russell, J. A. (2003). Core affect and the psychological construction of emotion. *Psychological Review, 110,* 145–172.

Schmittmann, V. D., Cramer, A. O. J., Waldorp, L. J., Epskamp, S., Kievit, R. A., & Borsboom, D. (2013). Deconstructing the construct: A network perspective on psychological phenomena. *New Ideas in Psychology, 31,* 43–53.

Sorenson, E. R. (1975). Culture and the expression of emotion. In T. R. Williams (Ed.), *Psychological anthropology* (pp. 361–372). Chicago, IL: Aldine.

Sorenson, E. R. (1976). *The edge of the forest: Land, childhood, and change in New Guinea protoagricultural society.* Washington, DC: Smithsonian Institution Press.

Tomkins, S. S., & McCarter, R. (1964). What and where are the primary affects? Some evidence for a theory. *Perceptual and Motor Skills, 18,* 119–158.

Tracy, J. L., & Robbins, R. W. (2008). The nonverbal expression of pride: Evidence for cross-cultural recognition. *Journal of Personality and Social Psychology, 94,* 516–530.

Yik, M., Widen, S. C., & Russell, J. A. (2013). The within-subjects design in the study of facial expressions. *Cognition and Emotion, 27,* 1062–1072.

INDEX